In the Age of Jackson, private enterprise set up shop in the American penal system. Working hand in glove with state government, by 1900 contractors in both the North and the South would go on to put more than half a million imprisoned men, women, and youth to hard, sweated toil for private gain. Held captive, stripped of their rights, and subjected to lash and paddle, these convict laborers churned out vast quantities of goods and revenue, in some years generating the equivalent of more than $30 billion worth of work. By the 1880s, however, a growing cross-section of American society came to regard the prison labor system as morally corrupt and unbefitting of a free republic: it fostered torture and other abuses, degraded free citizen-workers, corrupted the government and the legal system, and defeated the supposedly moral purpose of punishment. *The Crisis of Imprisonment* tells the remarkable story of this controversial system of penal servitude – how it came into being, how it worked, how the popular campaigns for its abolition were ultimately victorious, and how it shaped and continues to haunt America's modern penal system. The author takes the reader into the vital, robust world of nineteenth-century artisans, industrial workers, farmers, clergy, convicts, machine politicians, and labor leaders and shows how prisons became a lightning rod in a determined defense of republican values against the encroachments of an unbridled market capitalism. She explores the vexing moral questions that prisons posed then and that are still exigent today: What are the limits of state power over the minds, bodies, and souls of citizens – is torture permissible under certain circumstances? What, if anything, makes the state morally fit to deprive a person of life or liberty? Are prisoners slaves and, if so, by what right? Should prisoners work? Is the prison a morally defensible institution? The eventual abolition of prison labor contracting plunged the prisons into deep fiscal and ideological crisis. The second half of the book offers a sweeping reinterpretation of Progressive Era prison reform as above all a response to this crisis. It concludes with an exploration of the long-range impact on the modern American penal system of both penal servitude and the movement for its abolition.

Rebecca M. McLennan is Associate Professor of History at The University of California, Berkeley. In 1999, she received Columbia University's Bancroft Award for her doctoral dissertation on the rise of the American penal state.

CAMBRIDGE HISTORICAL STUDIES IN AMERICAN LAW AND SOCIETY

Series Editor
Christopher Tomlins, *American Bar Foundation*

Previously published in the series:
Tony A. Freyer, *Antitrust and Global Capitalism, 1930–2004*
Davison Douglas, *Jim Crow Moves North*
Andrew Wender Cohen, *The Racketeer's Progress*
Michael Willrich, *City of Courts, Socializing Justice in Progressive Era Chicago*
Barbara Young Welke, *Recasting American Liberty: Gender, Law and the Railroad Revolution, 1865–1920*
Michael Vorenberg, *Final Freedom: The Civil War, the Abolition of Slavery, and the Thirteenth Amendment*
Robert J. Steinfeld, *Coercion, Contract, and Free Labor in Nineteenth Century America*
David M. Rabban, *Free Speech in Its Forgotten Years*
Jenny Wahl, *The Bondsman's Burden: An Economic Analysis of the Common Law of Southern Slavery*
Michael Grossberg, *A Judgment for Solomon: The d'Hauteville Case and Legal Experience in the Antebellum South*

The Old System—and

The New

Anon., "The Old System – and the New," ca. 1916. By permission, Osborne Family Papers, Syracuse University Library, Special Collections Research Center.

The Crisis of Imprisonment

PROTEST, POLITICS, AND THE MAKING OF THE
AMERICAN PENAL STATE, 1776–1941

Rebecca M. McLennan

The University of California, Berkeley

CAMBRIDGE
UNIVERSITY PRESS

CAMBRIDGE UNIVERSITY PRESS
Cambridge, New York, Melbourne, Madrid, Cape Town, Singapore, São Paulo, Delhi

Cambridge University Press
32 Avenue of the Americas, New York, NY 10013-2473, USA

www.cambridge.org
Information on this title: www.cambridge.org/9780521830966

First published 2008

Printed in the United States of America

A catalog record for this publication is available from the British Library.

1006448327

Library of Congress Cataloging in Publication Data

McLennan, Rebecca M., 1967–
The crisis of imprisonment : protest, politics, and the making of the American penal
state, 1776–1941 / Rebecca M. McLennan.
p.   cm. – (Cambridge historical studies in American law and society)
Includes bibliographical references and index.
ISBN 978-0-521-83096-6 (hardback) – ISBN 978-0-521-53783-4 (pbk.)
1. Protest movements – United States – History.   2. Convict labor – United States –
History.   3. Imprisonment – United States – History.   4. Punishment – United States –
History.   5. Criminal law – United States – History.   6. Labor movement – United
States – History.   7. United States – Politics and government.   I. Title.
HN59.M222   2008
365'.97309034–dc22   2007018519

ISBN   978-0-521-83096-6 hardback
ISBN   978-0-521-53783-4 paperback

For Ásta, Felicity, and Roy

Contents

Acknowledgments   *page* xi

Introduction: The Grounds of Legal Punishment   1

1   Strains of Servitude: Legal Punishment in the Early Republic   14

2   Due Convictions: Contractual Penal Servitude and Its
    Discontents, 1818–1865   53

3   Commerce upon the Throne: The Business of Imprisonment
    in Gilded Age America   87

4   Disciplining the State, Civilizing the Market: The Campaign
    to Abolish Contract Prison Labor   137

5   A Model Servitude: Prison Reform in the Early Progressive Era   193

6   Uses of the State: The Dialectics of Penal Reform in Early
    Progressive New York   239

7   American Bastille: Sing Sing and the Political Crisis of
    Imprisonment   280

8   Changing the Subject: The Metamorphosis of Prison Reform
    in the High Progressive Era   319

9   Laboratory of Social Justice: The New Penologists at Sing
    Sing, 1915–1917   376

10 Punishment without Labor: Toward the Modern Penal State   417

Conclusion: On the Crises of Imprisonment   469

Select Bibliography   473

Index   485

Acknowledgments

This book originated, more years ago than I care to admit, as a doctoral dissertation in Columbia University's Department of History. It matured as a book manuscript at Harvard University and was finally put to rest at the University of California, Berkeley. Each of these institutions generously funded its research and writing. Columbia's Richard Hofstadter and Whiting fellowships provided funding and release from teaching for the first phase of the work. Subsequently, faculty research grants from the History Department at Harvard University, the Charles Warren Center for Studies in American History, the Committee on Degrees in Social Studies, and Harvard's Cooke-Clark and Dunwalke funds enabled me to undertake the fresh research needed to turn a doctoral dissertation into a book manuscript. A sabbatical and research funding from the UC Berkeley History Department made it possible for me to write up the new material and to completely overhaul, polish, and, finally, dispatch the manuscript.

Colleagues, staff, and students at these universities and others played an instrumental role in the book's fruition. Sven Beckert, Elizabeth Blackmar, Lizabeth Cohen, Nancy Cott, Elizabeth Dale, Timothy J. Gilfoyle, Jon Gjerde, David Hollinger, Akira Iriye, Pratap Mehta, Michael Meranze, Ira Katz Nelson, Anders Stephanson, Chris Sturr, Charles Tilly, and Michael Willrich all generously read and commented upon one or other version or section of the manuscript. Eric Foner repeatedly turned around dissertation chapters with lightning speed and impressed upon me time and again the importance of relating my story of penal crisis and conflict to the broader sweep of American political and social history. I am particularly indebted to my doctoral advisor, Barbara J. Fields, for her years of deep and patient engagement, close reading, criticism, guidance, and mentorship. It is no exaggeration to say that neither the dissertation nor the book would have been possible without her. Fellow graduate students Michael Berkowitz, Eliza Byard, Sam Haselby, Mae Ngai, Adam Rothman, Mike Sappol, Nathalie Silvestre, Jeffrey Sklansky, David Suisman and members of the Americanist dissertation reading group at Columbia engaged early drafts with the dedication and ruthless honesty that are the graduate student's prerogative.

Their insights proved indispensable to the task of strengthening and sharpening the book's central arguments. Colleen Lye's critical acumen, unflagging friendship, and good humor carried me through more than one crisis of *The Crisis of Imprisonment.* Thanks also to Michael Berkowitz, Hillary Kunins, Despina Kakoudaki, and Linda Voris for their true friendship and for being such generous sources of intellectual and culinary sustenance. In a different, but equally vital, vein, Molly Sullivan and Margaret Hornick played no small role in the book's fruition.

Sometimes, the simplest of questions and the shortest of dialogues can expose the weakest point in a book manuscript's argument or structure and bring to light alternative, perhaps more fruitful, paths of inquiry. Over the years, a number of people generously wreaked this type of creative havoc on the project. Conversations with David Blackburn, Daniel Botsman, Joseph Cleary, James Currie, Robin Einhorn, Paula Fass, Kathleen Frydl, David Henkin, Carla Hesse, Martin Jay, Kevin Kenny, Thomas Laqueur, Lisa McGirr, Marla Reed, Lisa Rivera, Julie Saville, Margo Schlanger, Daniel Shearer, Susanna Siegel, Jonathan Simon, Nikhil Pal Singh, Jacqueline Stevens, James Vernon, and Peter Zinoman prompted me to rethink and refine some parts of the book, and to significantly extend others. Likewise, discussions with a number of gifted graduate and undergraduate students, including Nina Billone, at UC Berkeley, and Zachary Ramirez, Ria Tabacco, Ezra Tessler, and other members of my "Rule of Law" seminar at Harvard, helped me discover what was – and wasn't – working in the argument. In a similar vein, faculty forums at the American Bar Foundation; the University of Texas, Austin; the University of Chicago; New York University; Columbia University; York University; and Harvard Law School significantly influenced my thinking and the book. I have tried my best to incorporate or otherwise engage the critiques and insights that these various and ongoing encounters afforded. I should add that, while my interlocutors undoubtedly helped me improve the book, I take sole responsibility for any errors of fact or interpretation that may remain.

A special thanks is due Christopher Tomlins, the legal historian and series editor at Cambridge University Press, who challenged me to write the best book I could, and who later – much later – graciously accepted a far longer, far more ambitious manuscript than the one for which he had bargained. Thanks also to Frank Smith and his Cambridge staff, most especially Simina Calin and Jessica Schwarz, and to the project manager, Mary Cadette, and my indexer, Teri Grimwood, for expertly ushering the text through to publication. James Zimmerman, David Pickell, and Nancy Shaw of the Provincetown Art Association and Museum deserve special mention for their assistance with the cover artwork. At the opposite end of the process, the task of research was significantly eased by the expert help and guidance of the staff of the Special Collections Research Center at Syracuse University Library; Teresa Capone and her colleagues at the Lloyd Sealy Library, John Jay College of Criminal Justice; the archivists at the New York State Archives; and my dedicated research assistants, Ari Waldman and Judy Collins. Many thanks, also, to the many dedicated administrators, including Janet Hatch and Corey Paulson at Harvard and Linda Finch Hicks, Deborah Kerlegon, and fellow staff of the UC Berkeley History Department, for providing essential infrastructural support over the years.

Although conceived in New York, a great deal of encouragement and preparation for the writing of this book originated a continent and an ocean away. In New Zealand, my father, the late Roy McLennan, engaged the dissertation critically and thoughtfully in its earlier stages. My mother, Felicity McLennan, was a vital source of support and encouragement throughout. Thanks also to Claudia Geiringer, Jackie Hay, Kate O'Keeffe, Barbara Middleton, Peter Middleton, and Peter McLennan for their moral and material support in connection with the project. Recognition is also due the late John Omer-Cooper, and his colleagues, Barbara Brookes, Tom Brooking, Erik Olsson, the late Hugh McLeod, Dorothy Page, Roberto Rabel, and Ann Trotter, of the History Department at the University of Otago for giving me an unusually good berth from which to embark on advanced studies in the field of modern history. Finally, I owe a profound debt of gratitude to Ásta Kristjana Sveinsdóttir. Her careful reading of multiple early drafts, philosopher's insistence upon analytic precision, and *ást og umhyggja* made all the difference.

The Grounds of Legal Punishment

In 1913, amid the oppressive humidity of a mid-summer's evening in the lower Hudson Valley, a crowd of men, women, and children from the village of Ossining joined a bevy of reporters and photographers on a hill overlooking Sing Sing Prison. Roused by rumors that a large-scale prison break was imminent, they watched as 1,500-odd convicts shuffled quietly across the prison yard and into the old stone cellhouse, each clasping his nightly ration of a half-loaf of bread in hand. The keepers, townspeople, and reporters may well have heaved a sigh of relief as the last few prisoners filed into the cellhouse and the heavy iron door swung closed behind them. With its thick granite walls, double-shelled construction, and centralized locking system, this "bastille on the Hudson" was all but immune to escape; once entombed within its gloomy masonry, even the most ingenious of prisoners stood little chance of emancipation.[1]

But a prison-break is only one kind of trouble convicts can concoct; and, on that tense July evening, as the last few stragglers were secured in the cellhouse, the guards and the free citizens of New York were about to be rudely reminded that, even under the condition of lockdown, prisoners are capable of turning the tables on their keepers and throwing the state into crisis. As reporters from the *New York Times* would recount the evening's events, the trouble began as hundreds of convicts simultaneously hurled their heels of bread through the cellhouse's outer window panes, causing a great shower of bread and glass to crash into the yard and street below. A cacophony of whistling and howling swiftly followed, and then a volley of raucous denunciations of the warden, the food, and the general conditions of incarceration. The convicts' point, rudely punctuated by bread so stale it could shatter thick glass, was unambiguous: "They are starving us!" the prisoners yelled at the reporters on the hill beyond; "give it a good write up in your paper!"[2]

The following morning, and for several days following, headlines, photographs, and detailed stories about the defenestration of one of America's most infamous prisons emblazoned the front pages of local, regional, and

[1] One of the first recorded uses of the term "bastille" in connection with Sing Sing can be found in ex-prisoner Levi S. Burr's 1833 publication, *A Voice From Sing Sing, Giving a General Description of the State Prison ... A Synopsis of the Horrid Treatment of the Convicts in that Prison* (Albany, n.p., 1833).
[2] Unidentified prisoners, quoted in *New York Times*, Jul. 24, 1913, 1.

national newspapers. Even the editors of the usually sedate *New York Times* splashed photographs and sensationalist headlines across their paper's front page through most of the following week. Back at Sing Sing, the bread throwing and cat-calling subsided after a few hours; but trouble continued to erupt sporadically over the following three days. Only after a series of tense negotiations between the warden and the prisoners, carried out under the forceful gaze of the National Guard and the critical scrutiny of the press corps, did the prisoners' unruliness come to an end. Sing Sing's troubles, however, would not end with the formal restoration of rule; they merely changed form. In the wake of the spectacle of the bread riot, a crowd of senators, prison commissioners, Grand Jurors, newspaper reporters, and social reformers from New York and beyond swept through the prison in search of explanations and culprits. As the investigations spurred accusations of mismanagement and corruption, from the office of Governor William Sulzer on down to the kitchens of prison cook Louis Beaulieu, the prisoners and keepers of Sing Sing found themselves embroiled in one of the fiercest political battles ever to have been fought in the Empire State.

Sing Sing, like most American prisons, had seen a number of strikes and riots in the course of its eighty-year history, and most of these had sparked political debate over the causes of the trouble, living conditions, and the general administration of the prisons. However, none had precipitated as divisive and embittered a crisis as that which unfolded in the summer of 1913. A deceptively simple act, the prisoners' bread riot had combined drama, protest, and a rather blunt demonstration of the convicts' grievances, to great – and eminently newsworthy – effect. In a few short minutes, and wielding nothing more than their paltry rations, the prisoners had managed to take possession of the very edifice that was supposed to guarantee the good order of both the state's prison and the state of New York. More than simply breaking the rules and disrupting the normal routine (which more commonplace acts of defiance, such as refusing to eat or resisting a lock-down, could have achieved just as well), the convicts had succeeded in turning their prison into a stage upon which to dramatize their grievances and publicly indict their captors. However fleetingly, the convicts had substituted a voice of their own for that of the state, and, with the aid of the press, they had made their voice heard well beyond the high walls of New York's stone "bastille."

Although, in the American imagination, Sing Sing has long stood apart from other prisons as an institution at once famous and infamous, the protest and ensuing political crisis of 1913 were neither unprecedented nor, in the context of the day, markedly exceptional. As I shall argue in the pages to follow, a long continuum of episodic instability, conflict, and political crisis has characterized prison-based punishment in the United States, from the early republican period, down through the nineteenth century, and deep into the twentieth. Far from being the exception to the norm, Sing Sing stood squarely within a long, broad, American tradition of debate, riot, and political and moral crisis over the rights and wrongs of legal punishment, the proper exercise of state power, and the just deserts of convicted offenders. This book traces the lineage, meaning, and consequences of popular conflicts over legal punishment, from the early republican penitentiary-house, through the great prison factories of the Gilded Age and the penal-social laboratories of the Progressive Era, to the ambitious, penal state-building programs of the New Deal era.

That the American prison has historically been an unstable and highly contested institution ought not to surprise us. Historically, it has been at once a highly visible apparatus of state coercion, a concentrated mass of human energies and desires, an official symbol of justice, security, and the state's presumed right over life and death, and the outstanding example of an unfree institution in a putatively free society. As such, this powerful and symbolically-laden institution has inevitably been both an object of debate and contestation in and of itself and a critical battleground and potent instrument in the larger social conflicts that have episodically shaken and recreated American government and society since the Revolution. While prisoners and their keepers were often at the forefront of these various struggles to remake and control the prison and the penal arm of the state, they were by no means alone in the fray. In the two centuries or more following independence from Great Britain, a remarkably diverse array of communities, classes, and sections of American society, animated by a variety of religious convictions, moral beliefs, and political affiliations, actively contested and struggled to determine the proper means and ends of legal punishment. As I argue in the pages to follow, many of these struggles had important and lasting consequences, not only for the practice and ideology of legal punishment and the penal arm of government, but for the structure and legitimating fictions of American social order more generally.

American lawmakers grappled with the twin questions of by what means and to what ends the state ought to punish convicted offenders almost as soon as the republic began the transition to peacetime, in the mid-1780s. In the wake of independence from Britain and her "royal" mode of punishment, strict Calvinists, liberal Quakers, common laborers, artisans, merchants, farmers, and jurists earnestly debated the meaning of a truly Christian and republican penal practice. Early republican efforts to establish such a practice eventually resulted in the founding of the house of repentance, and the penitential system of legal punishment. Although, initially, merchants, jurists, physicians, and lawmakers proclaimed the house of repentance (and the penitential mode of punishment more generally) an enlightened and humane alternative to the discredited penal practices of the old world monarchies, other Americans – including strict Calvinist clergy, laboring republicans, and the penitentiary's captive subjects – openly challenged its moral legitimacy. By the late 1810s, these strains of dissent and subversion had prompted such widespread public disillusionment with the penitentiary system that the penal arm of state government was plunged into a protracted crisis of legitimacy. In state after state, that crisis proved fatal; in the early

1820s, lawmakers began to cast around, once again, for a new approach to legal punishment.

The mode of punishment that lawmakers, jurists, and keepers eventually substituted in the troubled penitentiary's stead was that of contractual penal servitude. Improvised earliest at Auburn prison in New York (in the 1820s), contractual penal servitude went on to become the dominant mode of legal punishment in almost all Northern (and, eventually, all Southern) states down through the turn of the nineteenth century. Combining cellular technology with hard, productive labor, the formal deprivation of political and civil rights, and liberal doses of the lash and paddle, it resolved many of the disciplinary, fiscal, and political crises that had beset the early republican house of repentance. By 1835, this system of contractual penal servitude had all but eclipsed the rival "Pennsylvania system" of perpetual isolation to become the dominant mode of legal punishment across the several states. Both at home and in Europe, lawmakers and penal reformers hailed it as the most enlightened and economic penal system of its day. The apparent stability of the new mode of legal punishment, however, proved short-lived. At the same time that Alexis de Tocqueville and his fellow European investigators were touting its peculiar advantages, that system had been quietly sowing the seeds of its own set of controversies and crises. As we shall see, the source of contractual penal servitude's instability was the practice upon which that system of punishment was founded and the interests of which it had increasingly come to serve: that is, the sale of prisoners' labor power to private business interests. In the course of the nineteenth century, prison labor contracting would provoke, first, a series of small-scale, local protests among free workingmen and, eventually, a large-scale, popular campaign for its abolition. As that campaign gathered momentum in the late Gilded Age, state after state would ultimately be compelled to abolish or otherwise severely retrench the offending practice. Like a prisonhouse of cards, the larger edifice of contractual penal servitude would first list and then collapse in the wake of the destruction of the labor contracting practice that had been its fiscal, disciplinary, and ideological foundation.

Although, with the notable exception of historians of the American South,[3] few scholars have commented upon the abolition of prison labor contracting, that event proved a watershed in American penal history. Abolition defused the mounting popular outrage at the remarkably profitable, and often gruesomely exploitative use of sweated prison labor in industry,

---

[3] See, for example, David M. Oshinsky, *Worse Than Slavery: Parchman Farm and the Ordeal of Jim Crow Justice* (New York: Free Press, 1996); Alex Lichtenstein, *Twice the Work of Labor: The Political Economy of Convict Labor in the New South* (London: Verso, 1996); C. Vann Woodward, *Origins of the New South, 1877–1913* (Baton Rouge: Louisiana State University Press, 1951); and Edward Ayers, *Vengeance and Justice: Crime and Punishment in the Nineteenth Century American South* (New York: Oxford University Press, 1984). See also, Blake McKelvey, "Penal Slavery and Southern Reconstruction," *Journal of Negro History* 20:2 (Apr. 1935), 153–79; Karin Shapiro, *A New South Rebellion: The Battle Against Convict Labor in the Tennessee Coalfields, 1871–1896* (Chapel Hill: University of North Carolina Press, 1998).

and it carved a wide moat between the sphere of the market and that of legal punishment. (It also reined in and partially "civilized" the market, as we will see). But, at the same time, abolition opened up a remarkably intractable set of disciplinary, fiscal, and ideological problems within the penal arm of the state and spurred an outpouring of discourse around the social question that contemporaries referred to as "the prison labor problem." Most critically, abolition activated and deeply conditioned the progressive prison reform movement and the penal state-building initiatives of the late-nineteenth and early-twentieth centuries.

Far from being an exceptional and isolated event, the Sing Sing protest of 1913 was a particularly acute instantiation, both of the crises into which the penal arms of most Northern states were propelled following the abolition (or, in some states, severe scaling back) of prison labor contracting, and of the power struggles that progressives' efforts to solve the prison labor problem set in motion. When, in the late Gilded Age, Massachusetts, Ohio, California, New York, and other Northern legislatures moved to abolish or significantly scale back contractual penal labor, they, in effect, destroyed the linchpin of everyday prison discipline, the foundation of nineteenth-century penal ideology, and a critical source of funding for the penal arm of government. Despite the strenuous efforts of prison administrators in the first two decades of the twentieth century to erect a state-use system of penal labor upon the grave of the old contractual system, the vacuum of discipline and ideology, and the uncertain basis of prison funding, persisted well into the twentieth century. What unfolded, first within the penal arm of state government itself, and, eventually, in courtrooms, voting booths, union halls, the popular Northern press, and the U.S. Congress, was a complex and, at times, bitter series of struggles to determine the content of the new, postcontractual prison order. In New York's case, the first wave of these struggles would climax at Sing Sing, in riot and scandal. Eventually, those conflicts would engender the formation of a new penal state – a process that would be greatly accelerated by new federal legislation and court rulings in the New Deal era.

The history I narrate in the following pages builds upon, and is indebted to, the expansive and richly varied field of crime and punishment history. But it also seeks to inject into that field greater awareness of certain key, neglected or undeveloped themes within American penal history; I hope, in addition, to offer up a fresh and illuminating way of conceptualizing legal punishment as an object of historical inquiry (chiefly by extending the scope of the inquiry beyond the institution of the prison proper to the legal, political, economic, and cultural dimensions of legal punishment), and to cast new light upon legal punishment's place in the broader sweep of American history. The ten chapters that follow touch upon many themes, but the most important of these are: first, the centrality of productive labor, both as an activity and as an element of penal ideology, to the nineteenth-century American penal system; second, the practical and formal reinvention, in the nineteenth century, of legal punishment as a species of involuntary servitude; third, the workings of power within and around the penal systems

of the nineteenth and early twentieth centuries; and, finally, the critical role
that the abolition of contractual prison labor played in the making of the
modern American penal state.

Although, as I illustrate in the pages to follow, the activity and ideology
of forced productive labor, and the legal condition of penal servitude with
which that labor was tightly entwined, hung, like a heavy iron chain, across
a century-and-a-half of American legal punishment, most scholars of penal
history have either glossed over it, treated it as a peculiar affliction of the New
South (made symptomatic in chain gangs, convict leasing, and penal farms),
or denied it played any significant role in prison life, administration, or politics north of the Mason-Dixon Line. We have several excellent accounts of
the place of hard labor in early republican penal practice and ideology,[4] and,
at the other end of the nineteenth century, a number of deeply researched
studies of the New South's penal labor camps and prisons.[5] However, we
still know relatively little about the expansive, industrial prison contracting
systems that flourished in almost all the Northern states between 1820 and
1890, and that gave concrete substance to the ubiquitous legal sentence
of confinement to hard labor. There are but two systematic histories of
prison labor contracting in the North: Larry Goldsmith's nuanced history
of life, labor, and resistance in the Massachusetts State Prison at Charlestown,
and Glen A. Gildemeister's doctoral dissertation on competition between
free workers and prison labor in industrializing America.[6] These impressive

---

[4] Michael Meranze, *Laboratories of Virtue: Punishment, Revolution, and Authority in Philadelphia,
1760–1835* (Chapel Hill: The University of North Carolina Press, 1996); Adam Jay Hirsch,
The Rise of the Penitentiary: Prisons and Punishment in Early America (New Haven: Yale University
Press, 1992); Louis P. Masur, *Rites of Execution: Capital Punishment and the Transformation of
American Culture, 1776–1865* (New York: Oxford University Press, 1989); Michael S. Hindus,
*Prison and Plantation: Crime, Justice and Authority in Massachusetts and South Carolina, 1767–
1878* (Chapel Hill: The University of North Carolina Press, 1980).

[5] Supra, n. 3. See also, Mary Ellen Curtin, *Black Prisoners and Their World, Alabama, 1865–
1900* (Charlottesville and London: University Press of Virginia, 2000); Matthew Mancini,
One Dies, Get Another: Convict Leasing in the American South, 1866–1928 (Columbia: University
of South Carolina Press, 1996); Robert Perkinson, "The Birth of the Texas Prison Empire,
1865–1915" (Ph.D. diss., Yale University, 2001); and Donald R. Walker, *Penology for Profit: A
History of the Texas Prison System, 1867–1912* (College Station, Texas: Texas A & M University
Press, 1988).

[6] Larry Goldsmith, "Penal Reform, Convict Labor, and Prison Culture in Massachusetts, 1800–
1880" (Ph.D. diss., University of Pennsylvania, 1987); Glen A. Gildemeister, "Prison Labor
and Convict Competition with Free Workers in Industrializing America, 1840–1890" (Ph.D
diss., Northern Illinois Press, 1977/New York: Garland, 1987). See also, Larry Goldsmith,
"'To Profit by His Skill and Traffic in His Crime': Prison Labor in Early Massachusetts," *Labor
History* 40 (Nov. 1999): 439. A few texts include a chapter on prison industries: See, for
example, W. David Lewis, *From Newgate to Dannemora: The Rise of the Penitentiary in New York,
1796–1848* (Ithaca, NY: Cornell University Press, 1965), 178–200, and Anne Butler, *Gendered Justice in the American West: Women Prisoners in Men's Penitentiaries* (Urbana: University
of Illinois Press, 1997), 174–98. See also John A. Conley, "Prisons, Production, and Profit:
Reconsidering the Importance of Prison Industries," *Journal of Social History* 14:2 (Winter
1980), 257–275. Interestingly, sociologists and criminologists have been more attuned than
historians to the question of the social and political significance of convict labor and its

works of scholarship suggest that the practice of selling the labor power of imprisoned men and women very probably played a critical role not only in the everyday life of American prisons, as a whole, but in the larger political field in which the prisons, as public institutions, were firmly anchored. As yet, however, these important insights have not been expanded upon and have had little appreciable impact on the master narrative of American penal history.

That master narrative was first penned, thirty-five years ago, by David J. Rothman, in his groundbreaking study of the origins of the ante-bellum prison; it has since been retold, largely without amendment, in the leading synthetic treatments of American crime and punishment history.[7] In *The Discovery of the Asylum: Social Order and Disorder in the New Republic*, Rothman provided what remains an unrivaled account of the élite reformers who guided the establishment of the first state prison systems proper (in the 1820s and 1830s) and of the social anxieties and moral ideals they brought to their work. Rothman's book tells us a great deal about the *weltanschauung* of Jacksonian elites, and the content of official prison rules and doctrines. However, framed chiefly as a study of norms and ideas, and drawing mainly on official reports and reform literature, his work discloses much less about the quotidian experience and rhythms of prison life, the push-and-tug of power relations among keepers, prisoners, and reformers, and the larger political force-field in which the state prisons, in the "Age of Democracy," were firmly grounded. As something that was practiced, more than written about by reformers, the hard labor of convicts is also rendered all but invisible in Rothman's account. Although noting that the idea and doctrine of labor were central to reformers' and officials' efforts to organize prison life, and conceding (in a typically pithy paragraph) that the contracting-out of prison labor "became increasingly popular" in the 1850s and 1860s, his book as a whole conveys the impression that prison labor was of negligible importance, both to prison life and to the legal and ideological structures of antebellum

discontents in the North: See for example, Christopher Adamson, "Toward a Marxist Penology: Captive Criminal Populations as Economic Threats and Resources," *Social Problems* 31:4 (Apr. 1984), 435–58; Henry Calvin Mohler, "Convict Labor Policies" (MA thes., University of Wisconsin, 1923), published in the *Journal of the American Institute of Criminal Law and Criminology* 15:4 (Feb. 1925), 530–97; and Rosalind P. Petchesky, "At Hard Labor: Penal Confinement and Production in Nineteenth-Century America," in *Crime and Capitalism: Readings in Marxist Criminology*, ed. David F. Greenberg (Palo Alto: Mayfield Pub. Co., 1981). Curiously, in their transnational history of legal punishment and its relation of "correspondence" with changing modes of production, Georg Rusche and Otto Kirchheimer make little mention of the great contract labor prisons of the American North. Rusche and Kirchheimer, *Punishment and Social Structure* (New York: Columbia University Press, 1939).

7 Rothman's book played a key role in establishing penal history as a legitimate field of inquiry within the American historical profession. David J. Rothman, *Discovery of the Asylum: Social Order and Disorder in the New Republic* (Boston and Toronto: Little, Brown and Co, 1971). For a leading synthetic treatment of American crime and punishment history, see Lawrence M. Friedman, *Crime and Punishment in American History* (New York: Basic, 1993), espec. 77–82.

punishment.[8] A central objective of my work has been to trace the rise of contracting to "popularity;" another has been to assess the influence of prison labor contracting on what Alexis de Tocqueville and Gustave de Beaumont made famous at home and abroad as the so-called "American system"[9] of legal punishment.

As part of the field's general neglect of prison labor, the most influential of penal historians have also significantly underestimated the profitability of the contracting systems under which productive convict labor was generally organized between 1830 and 1890. Although David J. Rothman's approach is fundamentally different from that of Michel Foucault,[10] both claim that nineteenth-century prisons were generally unprofitable, and that the profit imperative was a negligible force within the life of the institution. Although it is certainly the case that élite prison reformers of the nineteenth century did not usually place much emphasis on making the prisons profitable, and that in both the American North and Western Europe, the *state* did not generally make significant profits from its prison industries, in America the private contractors who purchased convict labor power well below free-market rates and set up machinery in the prisons almost always profited handsomely from the traffic. Moreover, the profit imperative these businessmen quite logically took into the prison workshops with them was far more influential on prison life and administration than were either the well-heeled, well-intentioned reformers of the Boston Prison Discipline Society or the enlightened doctrines of convict rehabituation and spiritual reform. (As we shall see in Chapters Two and Three, Northern prison labor was not quite as unprofitable or as irrelevant to state government as Foucault and Rothman infer, either; in the mid-1880s, for example, it was contributing almost two dollars for every three dollars the states spent on maintaining their prisons).[11] In exploring the rise of prison labor contracting, then, I also flesh out the impact of the profit imperative on various aspects of the nineteenth-century prison system, and the nature of the relation between the market and the penal arm of the state.

The second theme I foreground in the pages to follow is the reinvention of American legal punishment, after the Revolution and, particularly, after 1830, as a distinctive species of involuntary servitude. In almost every Northern state, by the middle of the nineteenth century, legal punishment had not only been "institutionalized" (in the form of the prison), but had

---

[8] Rothman offers a paragraph on free labor's protests against prison competition, but does not explore the upshot of that protest and its impact on the politics of legal punishment.

[9] Gustave de Beaumont and Alexis de Tocqueville referred to the Philadelphia (or Pennsylvania) system of perpetual isolation and the Auburn (or New York) system of congregate labor and nightly isolation as two variants of a single "American system," and recommended that France adopt the latter rather than the former (on the grounds that the Auburn plan was "much cheaper in its execution"). Gustave de Beaumont and Alexis de Tocqueville, *On the Penitentiary System in the United States and Its Application in France* (Carbondale and Edwardsville: Southern Illinois University Press, 1964), 119, 134.

[10] Michel Foucault, *Discipline and Punish: The Birth of the Prison* (New York: Pantheon, 1977).

[11] See subsequent discussion, 90.

assumed legal, symbolic, and practical status as a distinctive species of involuntary servitude. That system of penal servitude would go on to receive official recognition and implicit approval in the Thirteenth Amendment to the U.S. Constitution and all but four of the state constitutions. The justices of the U.S. Supreme Court would also repeatedly recognize it as constitutional.[12] (As late as 1914 the Court reiterated, with a discernible tone of exasperation: "There can be no doubt that the State has authority to impose involuntary servitude as a punishment for crime. This fact is recognized in the Thirteenth Amendment, and such punishment expressly excepted from its terms").[13]

In tracing the fruition of this distinctive, American system of penal servitude, I engage and elaborate upon the insights of two legal historians, both of whom have grappled with the question of punishment's reinvention, after the Revolution, as a system of bondage. In his original and conceptually dense study, *The Rise of the Penitentiary: Prisons and Punishment in Early America*, Adam Jay Hirsch argues both that the early republican penitentiary strongly resembled chattel slavery and that some early republican penal reformers believed the penitentiary imposed a "justifiable" form of slavery on convicted offenders.[14] In a similar vein, James Q. Whitman writes that "the status of [American] prisoners came, by the time of the Thirteenth Amendment, to be explicitly assimilated to slaves" and that prisoners were "treated as slaves."[15] Although I take seriously these scholars' basic insight that American penitentiaries and state prisons were institutions of bondage, and prisoners, the involuntary bondsmen of the state, my research suggests that the penal systems of the nineteenth century constituted a separate and distinct species of involuntary servitude, and not one that is usefully confounded with that of chattel slavery. Penal involuntary servitude drew, particularly in some Southern states after the Civil War, on the law and ideology of American chattel slavery, but it also drew, far more directly, on other variants of servitude (both voluntary and involuntary). Moreover, it generated its own legal form and its own particular fictions concerning the master–servant relationship. In the pages to follow, I track the reinvention of legal punishment as a form of involuntary servitude and tease out its

---

[12] Thirteenth Amendment, §1; Slaughter-House Cases, 83 U.S. 36, 69 (1873); *United States v. Reynolds* 235 U.S. 133, 149 (1914).

[13] *United States v. Reynolds* 235 U.S. 133, 149 (1914).

[14] Hirsch, op cit., 71–92.

[15] James Q. Whitman, *Harsh Justice: Criminal Punishment and the Widening Divide between America and Europe* (New York: Oxford University Press, 2003), 173, 176. In his wide-ranging study of the impact of slavery on the evolution of penal practices from flogging in ancient Greece to the chain gangs, lease camps, and prison farms of the American South, sociologist J. Thorsten Sellin makes no mention of the Northern states' forced labor prisons, while devoting three of twelve chapters to the American South. He thereby reinforces the orthodox (and, as I argue here, false) assumption that slavery and involuntary servitude left their imprint exclusively on Southern penal practice. J. Thorsten Sellin, *Slavery and the Penal System* (New York: Elsevier, 1976).

relation to the practice of selling the labor power of convicts to private, typically industrial, manufacturing concerns.

Both involuntary servitude and contract prison labor are intimately related to the third theme of this book: the workings of power within and around the prison. The path by which legal punishment was reinvented as a system of involuntary servitude was neither smooth nor straight. In the early republican period, the very effort to cast free men and women into a condition of penal servitude or otherwise subject them to one or more of its badges precipitated diverse forms of protest, subterfuge, resistance, and evasion of authority, both among prisoners and their families and communities, and among the men who were supposed to be their "keepers." Once the back of their defiance was broken (as it eventually was, by a variety of means, in the 1820s and 1830s), convict laborers nonetheless remained a mass of people who, under certain conditions, could – and did – strike tools or turn them into weapons to be wielded against masters. Although the contracting system was deeply entrenched in the prisons and highly profitable for the contractor, it was also prone to crisis and periods of instability. Paradoxically, the relations of dependency (however unequal) that developed among and between the contractors, the keepers, the prison authorities, and convict laborers, had the effect of empowering, in certain subtle but clearly discernible ways, the prisoners relative to the contractors. The same relations also enfeebled and involuted the state.

Outside the prison, meanwhile, the forced, sweated nature of productive prison labor provoked free workingmen to discourse, strike, petition, boycott, and vote in protest of the contract prison labor system, on grounds that were at once moral and economic. Although these protests had somewhat limited impact on the state penal systems before the Civil War, in the Gilded Age they attracted considerable support among the citizenry at large, and in every region of the country. They ultimately precipitated a far-reaching crisis of legitimacy for the penal arm of state government. The book fleshes out the ways in which organized labor's popular movement against the private use of convict labor transformed the moral, political, and legal ground upon which legal punishment stood; as we shall see, the campaign to abolish the private sale of convicts' labor power changed, in enduring ways, what was possible in the field of legal punishment, and what was not. State after state would resolve the crisis of legitimacy engulfing the penal arm of government by abolishing or severely scaling back the offending contract systems of prison labor and closing the open market to prisonmade goods.

It is at this juncture in the narrative, that the fourth, major theme of the book comes into view: that is, the making of the modern penal state. The abolition of contracting thrust forth old questions about how to organize, govern, and fund the penal arm of the state (now, in the absence of private capital and walled off from the open market). It also reinvigorated the country's intermittent moral debates about the sources of crime, the just deserts of offenders, and the duties of the state toward its free citizens and imprisoned wards. At first, in the ten years either side of 1900, progressives attempted to solve the prison labor problem by salvaging and reinventing prison labor in ways that would be politically and legally acceptable: Still caught on the ideological terrain of what they referred to as the "old system" of contractual penal servitude, they could not imagine, let alone countenance, a penal (or any kind of social) order that was founded on anything other than the activity of productive labor. However, as the project of productive labor for all prisoners became ever less tenable, progressives slowly began to innovate their ideas about discipline, the value of labor, the sources of moral reform, and the state's role within its own penal system. Around 1913, a second wave of progressive reformers, newly conscious of the limited scope afforded hard, productive labor in the prisons, emerged to grapple afresh with the prison labor problem. Their efforts to find a solution – and the resistance they encountered along the way – would generate new, postindustrial forms of discipline and novel conceptions of human subjectivity, and they would lay the foundations of the modern penal state.

Like the history it relates, the narrative of this book unfolds in three parts. The first four chapters trace the origins and rise of the American system of penal servitude; the role of contractors, markets, and productive labor in the making of that system; and the rolling series of crises that eventually unmade it, in the Gilded Age. I begin with a discussion of the strains of servitude present in early republican efforts to reinvent legal punishment as a properly republican and Christian institution, and the various forms of critique and resistance those efforts encountered. Chapter Two relates these conflicts over punishment to the making of the state prison system in the 1820s and 1830s, the rise to dominance of the practice of selling convicts' labor power to private interests, and the foundational role this practice came to play in the new, prison-based regime of penal servitude. After a brief discussion of the nationwide effort, during Reconstruction, to roll back contract prison labor, revive certain early republican ideas about punishment, and reinvent imprisonment as a specifically *moral* practice, I trace out the fruition of large-scale, monopolistic prison labor contracting in the Gilded Age and explore the ways in which contractors and the profit imperative left their assigned place in the workshops to shape other spheres of prison life, law, and administration (including disciplinary techniques). The succeeding chapter narrates the response of prisoners, farmers, workers, lawmakers, the courts, and, eventually, voters to large-scale contracting, and organized labor's rolling series of victories over contracting in a number of Northern and Southern states in the decades either side of 1900.

The middle third of the book (Chapters Five through Seven) treat the early Progressive Era (c. 1895–1913), the aftermath of the abolition or severe-scaling back of prison labor contracting, and the efforts of the first wave of progressive reformers to define and solve the so-called prison labor problem in Massachusetts, Pennsylvania, and, especially, New York. These states offered other industrial states three separate solutions to the problem, all of which aimed to salvage productive labor as the disciplinary, fiscal, and ideological foundation of legal punishment. Chapter Five explores these solutions and explains how New York's effort to remodel penal servitude was the most influential. Chapter Six returns to the political and moral grounds of legal punishment and the peculiar set of power struggles that early progressive prison reform set in motion, both within the polity and the prison; the last chapter in this section (Seven) traces the climax of those struggles in and around the "bastille" of Sing Sing.

The last third of the book tells the story of "high" or late progressive reform, in the years 1913–19, and its legacies. Here I explore progressives' recasting of the prison labor problem in light of the disciplinary and political crises that unfolded around and through the first phase of the reform effort. Chapter Eight addresses the metamorphosis of the methods and objectives of progressive reform in and after 1913. It was at this point that progressives began to grapple in a serious way with the political reality that productive labor most probably could not be salvaged in the prisons, and began to cast around for an alternative mode of discipline. An aggressive new reform organization, the National Committee on Prisons and Prison Labor, now moved to generalize New York's state-use system to the rest of the country; this endeavor and the Committee's transformation (via Thomas Mott Osborne) of Sing Sing prison into a laboratory of social justice are treated in Chapter Nine. The final chapter of the book assesses the legacy of progressive reform, both in New York and more broadly, in the interwar years. It traces the route by which the basic legal and political grounds of punishment that had obtained in New York since the 1890s became, in the course of the early New Deal, the general condition of all penal systems throughout the country, and the ways in which New York, with its several decades' worth of crisis and innovation around the prison labor problem, proved an important resource for other states. The book concludes with a brief analysis of the crisis-prone character of American legal punishment, and contemplates some of the questions that this history poses our understanding of American power, politics, and the state more generally.

As the foregoing summary suggests, New York plays a prominent role in the narrative that follows. A note on the book's New York orientation thus seems in order. Sing Sing Prison, the "Bastille on the Hudson," figures prominently in three of the ten chapters in the book, and New York state has an important presence throughout. Although, in every chapter, I relate the history of Sing Sing and New York to the national context, overall, these two sites receive considerably more attention than other prisons and states. As I hope will become clear in the course of the narrative, there are sound reasons for this. The birthplace of the state prison system (the Auburn plan) that would serve as the explicit model for almost every other Northern penal system after 1830, and home to the largest prison system in the country throughout the period in question, New York remained on the vanguard of virtually every important development in the field of legal punishment in the industrial states between 1820 and 1940. Organized labor's succession of victories against contract prison labor in New York in the 1880s and 1890s, and its later success in constricting the scope of the progressives' state-use system of labor, galvanized and provided a model for the American labor movement's national campaign against convict labor. The late progressives' subsequent effort in New York to work with the unions for a systematic solution to the prison labor problem later served as a model upon which the framing of critical federal legislation regarding convict labor would proceed. New York – and, especially, Sing Sing – also operated as a laboratory and staging ground for a disciplinary system, and mode of penal governance, that would only grow in national relevance as the country's remaining prison industries were all but legislated out of existence between 1900 and 1935. As a large industrial state that was forced, earlier than most, to separate legal punishment from the marketplace, New York tested, refined, and pioneered many of the alternative disciplinary techniques that other states would eventually turn to when they, too, were compelled to take prisons, prisoners, and their product out of the market.

Finally, New York bore a direct, organic connection to the federal arena in which the fate of penal servitude would finally be sealed: Many of the lawmakers, jurists, penologists, and reformers who led the way in New York's progressive prison reform movement of the 1910s would join former New York Governor and close personal ally of New York's leading prison reformers, Franklin D. Roosevelt, in Washington DC, in 1933. From their seat in the nation's capital, these progressives would proceed to shape the penal legislation and policy of the New Deal.

1

Strains of Servitude: Legal Punishment in the Early Republic

Neither slavery nor involuntary servitude, except as a punishment for crime whereof the party shall have been duly convicted, shall exist within the United States, or any place subject to their jurisdiction.

Thirteenth Amendment, §1, United States Constitution (1865)

In historical scholarship and American collective memory alike, the Thirteenth Amendment is celebrated as the constitutional death notice of Southern chattel slavery. Ratified in 1865, as the Confederacy crumbled and four million slaves walked off the plantations, the Amendment recognized in law the practical destruction of slavery. That the Amendment proscribed chattel slavery of the sort that had flourished in the South for almost two centuries is incontrovertible; but that it was "an absolute declaration that slavery or involuntary servitude shall not exist in any part of the United States," in Justice Joseph P. Bradley's oft-quoted phrase,[1] is much less certain, for as well as pronouncing dead one kind of involuntary bondage, the Amendment breathed symbolic life into another. Slavery and involuntary servitude were prohibited, "except as a punishment for crime whereof the party shall have been duly convicted." On its face, the Amendment declared penal varieties of slavery and involuntary servitude permissible; It made conviction for crime the sole grounds for the imposition of involuntary servitude on American soil, and exempted those "duly convicted" of crime from the otherwise universal prohibition on slavery and involuntary servitude.

---

[1] "By its own unaided force and effect [the Thirteenth Amendment] abolished slavery, and established universal freedom.... [T]he amendment is not a mere prohibition of state laws establishing or upholding slavery, but an absolute declaration that slavery or involuntary servitude shall not exist in any part of the United States," Civil Rights Cases, 109 U.S. 3, 20 (1883). Through the turn of the nineteenth century, the Supreme Court considered penal involuntary servitude neither controversial nor a logical contradiction of the accepted claim that the Thirteenth Amendment universally and absolutely proscribed slavery and involuntary servitude. Justice Field, in his dissent in the Slaughter-House Cases, for example, wrote that the "amendment prohibits slavery and involuntary servitude, except as a punishment for crime . . . " and, in the same paragraph: "the language of the amendment is not used in a restrictive sense. It is not confined to African slavery alone. It is general and universal in its application. Slavery of white men as well as of black men is prohibited, and not merely slavery in the strict sense of the term, but involuntary servitude in every form." Slaughter-House Cases, 83 U.S. (16 Wall.) 36, 69 , 71–72 (1873).

This would not be the only occasion, in the revolutionary days of the late Civil War and early Reconstruction, that Congressional lawmakers would author legislation chiefly intended to establish and guarantee the rights of former slaves and their descendants, but which also exempted (whether implicitly or explicitly) convicts and the operations of legal punishment from a general rule of freedom. Indeed, the subject matter of convicts, due conviction, and legal punishment surfaced in two other groundbreaking laws of the Reconstruction period. The Civil Rights Act of 1866 defined "citizens" as all persons born in the United States who were neither "untaxed Indians" nor persons subject to a foreign power, and provided that all citizens were to enjoy a range of legal rights (including the right to make and enforce contracts, to sue, to give evidence, and to own property), without regard for previous condition of involuntary servitude – except where that servitude had been imposed "as punishment for crime whereof the party shall have been duly convicted."[2] The following year, the framers of the Fourteenth Amendment prohibited racial disfranchisement while implicitly authorizing the disfranchisement (at the state level) of any adult man convicted of "rebellion or other crime": The level of a state's political representation in the House of Representatives was to be diminished in proportion to the number of men twenty-one years and older that the state barred from voting – less those disfranchised for "rebellion or other crime."[3] Where a state disfranchised male adult voters on racial grounds, it would be penalized; but where a state disfranchised convicted rebels and "other" lawbreakers, it would suffer no penalty. Once more, Congress demarcated the extent and limit of a fundamental freedom through reference to crime, convicts, and the penalties for crime.

Despite the recent proliferation of historical scholarship on the emancipation amendments, Reconstruction, and antebellum crime and punishment, the questions of why, and with what historical upshot, convicts, criminal conviction, and legal punishment figured so prominently in the language of the emancipation amendments, are not easily answered. Eric Foner and other historians of Reconstruction have traced out the contested and changing meanings of freedom in that era, but make no mention of the ways in which legal punishment delimited the freedoms and rights enumerated and guaranteed by the amendments.[4] Likewise, legal historians have said comparatively little about either the penal exemptions of the Civil

---

[2] Civil Rights Act (1866), § 1. That act also implicitly licensed state and federal government to suspend the citizen's right to "full and equal protection of the laws and proceedings for the security of persons and property, . . . like punishments, pains, and penalties and, to none other" if that citizen had been previously held in involuntary servitude as punishment for crime.

[3] Fourteenth Amendment, United States Constitution, §2.

[4] Leading studies of various and conflicting conceptions of freedom in nineteenth-century America include Eric Foner, *Reconstruction: America's Unfinished Revolution, 1863–1877* (New York: Harper Row, 1988) and *The Story of American Freedom* (New York: Norton, 1998), especially 95–137; Leon F. Litwack, *Been in the Storm So Long: The Aftermath of Slavery* (New York: Vintage, 1980), especially 167–335; and Michael Vorenberg, *Final Freedom: The Civil*

Rights Act of 1866 or the Fourteenth Amendment's implicit authorization
of criminal disfranchisement.[5] Although there are now a number of comprehensive histories of the Thirteenth Amendment (some of which explore
permutations in the legal and popular meanings of "involuntary servitude"
since 1865),[6] no commentator has explained why it was that the framers
wrote legal punishment into the amendment in the first place, or how conviction for crime came to be seen as legitimate grounds for abridging rights
and liberties otherwise held to be "universal." Nor have scholars working
in the emerging field of crime and punishment history cast much light on
the matter: They have explored the great prison reform initiatives of the
Jacksonian era, and traced out the institutional history of each of some
dozen nineteenth-century prisons.[7] However, we still lack both a comprehensive, synthetic account of what Alexis de Tocqueville and Gustave de
Beaumont called the "American System"[8] of prison-based punishment in
the antebellum period, and a sustained treatment of the changing legal, ideological, political, and fiscal fields in which that mode of legal punishment

War, the Abolition of Slavery, and the Thirteenth Amendment (New York: Cambridge University
    Press, 2001).

[5] Alexander Keyssar briefly chronicles the enactment of state criminal disfranchisement as
    part of his sweeping study, *The Right to Vote: The Contested History of Democracy in the United
    States* (New York: Basic, 2000), 302–6. Regarding discussions of the Fourteenth Amendment
    in which criminal disfranchisement is not noted, see the otherwise incisive work of David
    Montgomery, *Citizen Worker, The Experience of Workers in the United States with Democracy and
    the Free Market During the Nineteenth Century* (New York: Cambridge University Press, 1993),
    37; Vorenberg, *Final Freedom*; Rogers M. Smith, *Civic Ideals: Conflicting Vision of Citizenship in
    U.S. History* (New Haven, Connecticut: Yale University Press, 1997).

[6] For a detailed discussion of the origins of the Thirteenth Amendment and a survey of evolv-
    ing legal and popular interpretations of the meaning of "involuntary servitude" (although
    one that does not discuss the penal exemptions), see Michael Vorenburg, *Final Freedom*,
    especially 211–50. James Q. Whitman asserts that "the status of [American] prisoners came,
    by the time of the Thirteenth Amendment, to be explicitly assimilated to slaves." However,
    he does not furnish a sustained analysis of the precise meaning, causes, and historical tra-
    jectory of this supposed "assimilation" of the prisoner's status to that of the slave. James Q.
    Whitman, *Harsh Justice: Criminal Justice and the Widening Divide Between America and Europe*
    (New York: Oxford University Press, 2003). (See especially, Chapter 5, "Low Status in the
    Anglo-American World.")

[7] Leading works include: Edward Ayers, *Vengeance and Justice: Crime and Punishment in the 19th-
    Century American South* (Oxford: Oxford University Press, 1984); Larry Goldsmith, "Penal
    Reform, Convict Labor, and Prison Culture in Massachusetts, 1800–1880" (Ph.D. diss., U.
    Pennsylvania, 1987); W. David Lewis, *From Newgate to Dannemora: The Rise of the Penitentiary
    in New York, 1796–1848*, (Ithaca, NY: Cornell University Press, 1965); Louis P. Masur, *Rites
    of Execution: Capital Punishment and the Transformation of American Culture, 1776–1865* (New
    York: Oxford University Press), 1989; Michael Meranze, *Laboratories of Virtue: Punishment,
    Revolution, and Authority in Philadelphia, 1760–1835* (Chapel Hill: The University of North
    Carolina Press, 1996), 217–328; David J. Rothman, *Discovery of the Asylum: Social Order and
    Disorder in the New Republic* (Boston and Toronto: Little, Brown and Co, 1971), 79–109, 237–
    64; and Wallace Shugg, *A Monument to Good Intentions: The Story of the Maryland Penitentiary,
    1804–1995* (Baltimore: Maryland Historical Society, 2000), 29–71.

[8] Gustave de Beaumont and Alexis de Tocqueville, *On the Penitentiary System in the United States
    and Its Application in France*, trans. Frances Lieber (Carbondale: Southern Illinois University
    Press, 1964).

was grounded. In sum, the historiography affords neither a systematic account of the conceptual lineage of the amendments' penal exemptions nor an explanation of the various laws, practices, and institutions of punishment that those exemptions recognized.

The current chapter is the first of two that flesh out the origins and rise to dominance of the distinctive mode of legal punishment – contractual penal servitude – that eventually impressed its mark on the Constitution of the United States. Synthesizing the rich historiography of punishment in the late colonial and early republican periods, and incorporating new research in newspaper, reform, labor, and legal archives, it begins with a brief study of Revolutionary era critiques of "tyrannical" modes of punishment and the states' subsequent efforts to formulate a properly republican, and Christian, penal practice. As we shall see, the search for such a practice gave rise to three successive, and distinct, experiments in the field of legal punishment. The first of these, undertaken in Pennsylvania in 1786 and subsequently replicated in most other states, consisted of the formal abolition of most capital crimes and other sanguinary punishments and the enactment of laws mandating that all convicted offenders other than murderers be put to hard, public labor (as "wheelbarrow men") on roads, canals, and other public works. After 1789, for reasons I will explain, Pennsylvania was the first of several states to abolish that system and embark on a second experiment: the confinement of convicted offenders to labor in a "house of repentance" (or "penitentiary-house"). Under this penitential mode of punishment, the majority of inmates ate, slept, and worked together in one large household and, theoretically, submitted to the hard, Christian labor of repenting their sins and repairing their souls.

The subsequent chapter narrates the history of the third, and most enduring, post-Revolutionary penal system: that of contractual penal servitude, which New York's lawmakers, jurists, and penitentiary-keepers first forged at Auburn Prison, in the 1820s, and which most other Northern states eventually replicated. Under this system, the state committed convicted offenders to fortress-like prisons, typically located some distance from towns and cities; sold the convicts' labor power to private manufacturers, who set up shop in the prison and put their prison laborers to productive, "congregate labor" by day; and locked their prisoner-workers down in great stone cellhouses by night. Over time, these arrangements were reinforced, on the outside, by statutes and court rulings that stripped convicts of most of their common and positive rights, and, on the inside, by the liberal infliction of corporal punishments of the sort that, just a generation earlier, republican legislators had condemned and outlawed as "tyrannical" and decidedly unrepublican in nature. Despite stiff competition from Pennsylvania's "separate plan" of imprisonment, New York's system of contractual penal servitude went on to become the dominant mode of punishment in most Northern states after 1830.

As we shall see, the history of this succession of penal systems – from hard, public labor, to the house of repentance, to the contractual prison labor system – was neither linear nor seamless. None of these distinctive penal systems was merely a technical refinement of the mode it succeeded and none left the formal objectives of the prior system intact: Both the means and ends of legal punishment changed significantly from one system to the next. Most importantly, all were subject, at varying points in their history, to vigorous and ultimately transformative moral and political contestation, both at the hands of those undergoing punishment and by diverse sections of the wider community. More than mere chatter or isolated, easily contained acts of dissent, these strains of protest bore down upon the offending penal laws and practices, undermining them to the point of collapse, and redrawing the political and moral grounds of possibility in the arena of punishment. As well as tracing the succession of penal experiments that took place after 1776, this chapter and the next explore these conflicts, the political and moral crises to which they gave rise, and the impact of those crises on the practice and politics of post-Revolutionary legal punishment.

*   *   *   *   *

In the arena of criminal law and legal punishment, as in other fields of law and government, the American Revolution set in motion diverse and frequently conflicting quests for a properly Christian and "republican" set of principles and practices.[9] Although sanguinary punishments of the sort enumerated in England's "Bloody Code"[10] had been the object of sustained

---

[9] Louis Masur formulates the question as that of "how to make punishment consistent with the objects of Christian, republican institutions"; Masur, *Rites of Execution*, 54.

[10] The "Bloody Code" of 1688 – 1815 raised the number of capital crimes from fifty, in 1688, to one hundred and sixty-five by 1765, and two hundred and twenty-five by 1815. In these years, Parliament widened the noose to accommodate a remarkable range of thitherto petty offenses, most of which were property crimes: At the beginning of the period, only those convicted of a crime of treason, rape, murder, or arson were liable to execution; by 1765, stealing gathered fruit or a single sheep, pick-pocketing, breaking a pane of glass at 5 P.M. on a winter's night with intent to steal, and dozens of other petty acts were all capital crimes. Although the rate of actual execution in England was generally in decline during this period (largely because of rising rates of pardon, reprieve, and commutation of the sentence of death to that of transportation to the colonies), English authorities executed felons at a much higher rate than did the Northern colonies in the same years. McLynn observes that the Code was pocked with anomalies: For example, many injurious acts were not capital crimes, and the penalty for a crime often turned on the time and place in which it was committed. McLynn explains the high rates of pardon in terms of the interests and ideology of the English ruling elite: They were not committed to the principle of certainty in law (wherein conviction for a particular crime always results in the same punishment) because they approached criminal law less as an instrument of deterrence than as an instrument of social control. Aiming for "an ordered hierarchy of authority, deference, and obedience," elites were concerned that too many hangings could, in fact, delegitimize their rule, whereas pardons and judicial mercy were legitimating, theatrical displays of the 'justice' of the system. *Blackstone's Commentaries: with Notes of Reference, to the Constitution and Laws of the Federal Government of the United States; and of the Commonwealth of Virginia*, Vol. IV, (Oxford: Clarendon Press, 1765–9), Ch. 1; Frank McLynn, *Crime and Punishment in Eighteenth Century England* (Oxford: Oxford University Press, 1989), xi, 258. See also J. M. Beattie, *Crime and Courts in England, 1600–1800* (Princeton, NJ: Princeton

criticism on both sides of the North Atlantic since at least 1764 (when Cesare Beccaría published his celebrated critique of capital punishment),[11] the experience of war itself proved an important catalyst in the articulation, first, of a coherent American critique of what the revolutionaries argued were "monarchical" penal laws and practices, and, eventually, of a positive republican theory of crime, penal law, and penal practice. Drawing variously on the works of Beccaría and Montesquieu, Quaker theology, classical republicanism, English country ideology, and the former colonies' own penal practices, the revolutionaries launched a wave of impassioned critiques of the death penalty and other sanguinary punishments in which the British government had commonly engaged, both in times of peace and in times of war. A diverse group of American patriots frequently and passionately condemned the British power's liberal use of the gallows, and what they decried as the monarchy's "cruel," "savage," and lawless treatment of American civilians and soldiers. Connections were drawn between British "savagery" on the battlefield and the frequency with which the courts in England reputedly condemned Englishmen, found guilty of crimes grand and petty, to swing from the "hanging tree."[12]

Although there was some variation of emphasis among these early revolutionary critiques, as early as 1777, two basic and closely related themes united them: Critics argued that capital and related sanguinary punishments were inherently despotic and immoral in nature, and that such punishments were also irrational and even detrimental to the society they were allegedly intended to protect. Bloody and "excessive" spectacles of punishment, reasoned Thomas Jefferson, Benjamin Rush, John Adams, and Benjamin Franklin, among others, were the native weapons of kings and despots. Capital punishment, in particular, was emblematic of the monarchical mode of government; while some revolutionary critics countenanced the punishment of death by hanging for the most serious of crimes, others sought the outright abolition of all forms of the death penalty. One such absolute opponent of capital punishment, Benjamin Rush, argued that the punishment of death for murder not only "propagated" murder itself but,

---

University Press, 1986), 451–5,530–8; and Lawrence M. Friedman, *Crime and Punishment in American History* (New York: Basic Books, 1993), 41–2.

[11] Cesare Beccaría (trans. Henry Paolucci), *On Crimes and Punishments* (Indianapolis: Bobbs Merrill, 1963).

[12] Masur, *Rites of Execution*, 54–60. In 1782, for example, Thomas Paine wrote an outraged, open letter to Sir Guy Carleton in which he protested the summary hanging, from a tree, of a patriot taken captive by the British at New York: The patriot (a Captain Huddy) "was taken out of the provost down to the water-side, put into a boat, and brought again upon the Jersey shore, and there, contrary to the practice of all nations but savages, was hung up on a tree, and left hanging till found by our people who took him down and buried him." "What sort of men must Englishmen be . . . ?" Paine implored: "The history of the most savage Indians does not produce instances exactly of this kind. They, at least, have a formality in their punishments. With them it is the horridness of revenge, but with your army it is a still greater crime, the horridness of diversion." "A Supernumerary Crisis, To Sir Guy Carleton," *Crisis Papers*, Philadelphia, May 31, 1782.

in his words, was "unchristian": "Power over human life," he wrote, "is the solitary prerogative of HIM who gave it."[13]

The idea that execution and dismemberment ought not to be the dominant forms of punishment had particular appeal in a part of the world in which there was both a real and perceived shortage of settlers and laborers. Such punishments deprived society of a valuable resource: As Jefferson put it, sanguinary penal practices "weaken the State by cutting off so many, who, if reformed, might be restored sound members to society...."[14] But Jefferson and other critics of "royal" penal law also argued that harsh punishments injured society in other, more subtle ways: The penal laws themselves (as distinct from the act of punishment) paradoxically undermined both the machinery of law and the interests of justice. Before the war, juries had repeatedly proven themselves disinclined to return a "guilty" verdict in less serious cases of crime, where the punishment was "infamous" and effectively rendered the punished *civiliter mortuus*, or dead in the eyes of the law.[15] Even more so, republican critics argued, sanguinary punishments tended to undermine justice because the specter of imminent pain and suffering led prosecutors, juries, and judges to empathize with the accused to such a degree that they lost the will and ability to duly apply the law: "[T]he experience of all ages and countries hath shewn that cruel and sanguinary laws defeat their own purpose," Jefferson wrote, "by engaging the benevolence of mankind to withhold prosecutions, to smother testimony, or to listen to it with bias."[16] Harsh penal laws, on this view, tended to disrupt the rational process of criminal law and subvert justice by engendering excessive leniency in the courtroom and allowing criminal acts to go unpunished.

By 1778, lawmakers in a number of states had translated critiques of the "royal" mode of punishment into constitutional provisions that provided for the abolition or severe restriction of the offending practices. The most radical of the early state constitutions (those of Vermont and Pennsylvania) directed the legislature to scale back sanguinary and capital punishments; South Carolina's first constitution also provided that sanguinary punishments be restricted, whereas in Virginia, Jefferson drafted a constitution that provided that "(t)he General assembly shall have no power to pass any law inflicting death for any crime, excepting murder, [and] those offences in the military service for which they shall think punishment by death

---

[13] Benjamin Rush, "An Enquiry into the Effects of Public Punishments upon Criminals, and Upon Society, Read in the Society for Promoting Political Enquiries," Convened at the House of His Excellency Benjamin Franklin, Esquire ... in Philadelphia, March 9th 1787 (Philadelphia, 1787), 16.

[14] Thomas Jefferson, "A Bill for Proportioning Crimes and Punishments" (1778), in *Thomas Jefferson, Public Papers, 1775–1825* (Oxford Text Archive: 1993), §1.

[15] W. David Lewis, *From Newgate to Dannemora*, 14–15.

[16] Jefferson, "A Bill for Proportioning Crimes and Punishments," §1. See also, Thomas Jefferson, "Autobiography," in *The Life and Selected Writings of Thomas Jefferson*, ed. Adrienne Koch and William Peden (New York: Modern Library, 1998), 44–5.

absolutely necessary;...all capital punishments in other cases are hereby abolished."[17] Just two of the state constitutions – Pennsylvania's and Vermont's – prescribed an alternative punishment: Both mandated the construction of "houses" in which convicts would be put to "hard labour," either on public projects or "for reparation of injuries done to private persons." In Pennsylvania's case, these houses were to be open to the public, on the view that the sight of offenders being held and put to hard labor would deter the citizenry from committing crimes. Beyond these basic provisions, however, the framers of the state constitutions provided only a cursory description of these alternative punishments: Entirely absorbed into the battle for independence from the world's mightiest empire, no state fleshed out, in any systematic way, an alternative theory and practice of punishment.[18]

Just as the revolutionaries' rejection of the colonial power did not automatically produce a new system of laws and government, constitutional directives to abolish or scale-back the old, sanguinary system of punishments did not, in and of themselves, constitute a positive and substantive theory of republican punishment: Such a theory still had to be worked out. A number of the early constitutions did incorporate a relatively novel principle that would eventually assume critical importance in each of the three penal systems with which the states experimented – the principle of proportionality, as it had been most fully articulated by Cesare Beccaría in his 1764 treatise, *On Crimes and Punishments* (for the English translation of which John Adams had written an introduction in 1775, and which had enjoyed wide circulation among revolutionary élites).[19] This principle held that the intensity and duration of punishment meted out to a convicted offender ought to be determined by the gravity of his or her crime. Jefferson and most other early republican lawmakers explicitly endorsed proportionality: In his draft penal code for Virginia, for example, Jefferson argued that making punishments proportionate to the crime would ensure that juries and judges no longer hesitated, out of empathy, to carry out the law.[20] Several of the state constitutions provided that punishments be made proportionate to the crime: In

---

[17] Draft Constitution for Virginia, June 1776. Unless otherwise noted, all state constitutions cited or quoted herein are taken from: "Eighteenth Century Documents," The Avalon Project at Yale Law School (Electronic Texts), (New Haven, Connecticut: Yale University).

[18] Constitution of the State of Pennsylvania (1776), Art. 39. For a discussion of the constitution's penal content see Meranze, *Laboratories of Virtue*, 61–2.

[19] Cesare Beccaría, *An Essay On Crimes and Punishments* (Brookline, Massachusetts: Branden Press, 1983 [1775 trans.]).

[20] Offenders ought not, by their crimes, permanently forfeit the protection from pain they had enjoyed as members of society: Although government owed society a duty to "restrain...criminal acts by inflicting due punishments" on the perpetrators, wrote Jefferson, "a member [of society], committing an inferior injury, does not wholly forfeit the protection of his fellow citizens." Instead, "after suffering a punishment in proportion to his offence" the offender "is entitled to [the citizens'] protection from all greater pain...it becomes a duty in the Legislature to arrange in a proper scale the crimes which it may be necessary for them to repress, and to adjust thereto a corresponding gradation of punishments." Jefferson, "A Bill for Proportioning Crimes and Punishments," §1.

the words of South Carolina's original constitution, for example, "the penal laws, as heretofore used, shall be reformed, and punishments made in some cases less sanguinary, and in general more proportionate to the crime."[21]

However, as foundational as the principle of proportionality would be in republican penal law, it was nonetheless an abstract principle, rather than a substantive prescription for a new set of punishments. Although Beccaria and other advocates of classical penology were highly critical of sanguinary punishments, there was nothing in the principle of proportionality *per se* to indicate how, exactly, convicted offenders should be punished – whether under a republican or any other kind of legal system. Proportionality calibrated the severity of punishments; it was not a principle according to which the content of the punishments themselves could be determined. Even sanguinary punishments could, in theory, be organized with an eye to Beccarian "intensity and duration" – as the penal bill that Jefferson co-authored with two other lawmakers for Virginia in 1779 aptly demonstrated. That bill, which substituted hard labor in the public works for some previously capital offenses, nonetheless fused the principle of proportionality with the ancient principle of *lex talionis*, prescribing a series of bloody punishments for crimes against the person. Among these were castration for a convicted rapist, ducking and whipping for witchcraft, and the boring of a hole at least one-half inch in diameter through the cartilage of the nose of any woman convicted of sodomy. (The Assembly deferred the bill for the duration of the war years; it was finally debated and defeated in the Virginia Assembly in 1785–86. According to James Madison, who attempted to shepherd the bill through the Assembly while Jefferson was in France, local outrage over roving bands of "horse stealers" dissuaded enough legislators from supporting a bill that, in the case of horse theft, substituted a mere three years' "hard labor" and restitution of property for the traditional penalty of death).[22]

Although many of the states embraced the principle of proportionality, in the early years of independence, few elaborated on the nature of the

[21] The Pennsylvania state constitution of 1776 directed the state legislature to reform the penal laws in such a way that the severity of the punishment became proportionate to the gravity of the crime; Vermont provided that "sanguinary" punishments be made "less necessary." Constitution of the State of Pennsylvania (1776), Art. 38 (see also, Masur, *Rites of Execution*, 61); Constitution of the State of South Carolina (1778), Art. XL. Vermont's 1777 state constitution also provided that "sanguinary" punishments were to be made "less necessary" (Constitution of the State of Vermont [1777], Art. XXXV).

[22] Virginia would not undertake systematic penal reform until 1796. Madison to Jefferson, Feb. 15th. [11th?] 1787(1), in *Letters of Delegates to Congress*, Vol. 24, Nov 26, 1786 – Feb. 27, 1788, 92. For a detailed discussion of Jefferson's work on penal reform, see Kathryn Preyer, "Crime, the Criminal Law, and Reform in Post-Revolutionary Virginia," *Law and History Review* 1:1 (Spring 1983), 53–85, especially 56–61. Preyer notes that as Governor of Virginia, Jefferson assumed executive prerogative and pardoned felons convicted of capital crimes on condition that they work for a term of years on public works. Succeeding governors continued this practice until 1785, at which time the Virginia Court of Appeals ruled the arrangement unconstitutional. Preyer, "Crime, the Criminal Law, and Reform in Post-Revolutionary Virginia," 68–9, and fn.56, 68.

punishments to be proportioned. Indeed, as much as a decade after independence from Britain was declared, it was by no means obvious what, exactly, would replace the old system of punishment. Through these years, and for some time afterwards, no legislature undertook systematic reform of the penal codes. (Although historians still know strikingly little about the practical workings of the penal and legal systems during the war, it appears that pre-Revolutionary practices tended to prevail, and that the imperatives of war making delayed systematic penal reform).[23] What is clear is that once the war ended and the states began to transition to peacetime governance (in 1783), legislators and the citizenry began to debate in earnest the question of what a properly republican system of legal punishment might look like.

In this endeavor, the states entered new and relatively uncharted territory. American lawmakers did not have a working model of a republican, or any other postmonarchical, penal system upon which to draw. Although colonial practice offered clear guidance in the arena of criminal procedure (the right to trial by jury and so on), the colonies' penal codes had more or less hewed to the discredited English system: With but one important exception (penal servitude), much the same sets of punishments were to be found on either side of the Atlantic in the colonial period. Differences between the penal practices of the colonies and the mother country had tended to be more those of intensity and frequency than of kind. Although there were variations among the colonies, punishment had generally consisted of some form of ignominious public and corporal chastisement – such as being locked in the stocks, whipped, branded, or ear-cropped – in the town square, or admonishment before the townspeople. Fines and other monetary penalties had also been very common, both on their own and in combination with corporal punishment. As in England, persons convicted of infamous crimes were liable to be publicly hanged. With the important exception of chattel slaves, however, corporal and capital penalties in the eighteenth-century colonies had tended to be far milder, both in law and in practice, than in England;[24] the colonial law listed far fewer capital crimes than England's "Bloody Code," and colonial execution rates were also significantly lower than those of the mother country. As in the mother country, incarceration *per se* had not been unknown in the colonies: Most had operated a workhouse, a house of correction, or both. But these institutions almost exclusively operated as a means of concentrating and disciplining itinerants, and enforcing the payment of debts, rather than as instruments of criminal punishment.[25] Massachusetts had briefly experimented with detention in the workhouse as an alternative form of criminal

---

[23] As far as legal punishment is concerned, the Revolutionary War years are among the least understood periods of American penal history: Most historians begin their accounts in 1785, with the founding of a public penal labor system in Pennsylvania. Fragmentary accounts of penal practice during the war years suggest that despite constitutional restrictions on sanguinary punishments, punishment was swift, bloody, and not infrequently summary.

[24] Friedman, *Crime and Punishment*, 41–4.   [25] Rothman, *Discovery of the Asylum*, 25–9.

punishment (typically, for the crimes of counterfeiting and forgery), and Pennsylvania's "Great Law" of 1682 had prescribed the workhouse not only for the usual "Vagrans and Loose abusive and Idle persons" but also for all "fellons and thieves" (original spellings).[26] However, neither the Pennsylvanian nor the Massachusetts experiment in the confinement of convicts had endured.[27]

If colonial penal practice offered republican lawmakers little obvious guidance in the arena of legal punishment, colonial theology and legal thought were even less helpful. The colonies produced no sustained body of penological theory upon which republican reformers of the 1780s could draw. The Reverend Cotton Mather had once counseled his congregation that a "*Workhouse* would be a juster (sic) or wiser Punishment than the gallows, for some *Felonies*, which yet in several Nations are Capitally Prosecuted,"[28] and William Penn had made workhouse labor the punishment for many of the crimes enumerated in the "Great Law" of 1682. But neither man spilled very much ink on the matter.[29] Across the Atlantic, the *philosophes* had discoursed at length on the nature of crimes and on the immorality and inefficacy of capital and sanguinary punishments, but had devoted little attention to the less abstract question of what, exactly, an alternative system of punishment should consist. Beccaría had commended, in passing, the punishment of "life-long servitude" as an alternative to the death penalty.[30] But he had not elaborated upon the form or content of that

---

[26] Linda Kealey, "Patterns of Punishment: Massachusetts in the Eighteenth Century," *The American Journal of Legal History* 30:2 (Apr., 1986), 163–86; Hirsch, *The Rise of the Penitentiary*, 27–8; The Great Law Or the Body of Laws of the Province of Pennsilvania and territorys thereunto Belonging past at an Assemble at Chester alias Upland the 7th day of the 10th Month December 1682, Ch. 64 [fair copy], in Gail McKnight Beckman, *The Statutes at Large of Pennsylvania in the Time of William Penn*, Vol. I, 1680–1700 (New York: Vantage Press, 1976). Massachusetts never systematically practiced criminal incarceration, and Pennsylvania's Great Law was repealed in 1718.

[27] Linda Kealey, "Patterns of Punishment," 27–8.

[28] Cotton Mather, "Flying Roll," 6, quoted in Adam Jay Hirsch, *The Rise of the Penitentiary: Prisons and Punishment in Early America* (New Haven, Connecticut: Yale University Press, 1992), 153.

[29] Masur notes that, although William Penn's Great Act (1682) prescribed hard labor in the workhouse as the punishment for most crimes, "(t)he statutory record was silent on the ideological underpinnings of this code." Masur, *Rites of Execution*, 28, 152. See also, Thomas Dumm, "Friendly Persuasion: Quakers, Liberal Toleration, and the Birth of the Prison," *Political Theory* 13:3 (Aug., 1985), 399. Notably, in distinction to the prison codes of the nineteenth century, Pennsylvania's workhouse was not cellular and the Great Law directed that prisoners "shall have liberty to provide themselves bedding, food, and other necessaries during their imprisonment." Dumm, "Friendly Persuasion," 399. See also, Harry Elmer Barnes, *The Evolution of Penology in Pennsylvania: A Study in American Social History* (Indianapolis: Bobbs Merrill, 1929).

[30] Arguing that the deprivation of liberty might be more efficacious as a deterrent, and less politically damaging, than execution, Beccaría wrote: "It is not the terrible yet momentary spectacle of the death of a wretch, but the long and painful example of a man deprived of liberty, who, having become a beast of burden, recompenses with his labors the society he has offended, which is the strongest curb against crime. That efficacious idea – efficacious because very often repeated to ourselves – 'I myself shall be reduced to so long and

servitude, or advanced any positive and substantive theory of penal *practice*. Montesquieu had indicted as "despotic" those governments that used "severe" punishments, and called for punishments that, as well as being proportionate to the crime, shamed the offender: "Let us follow nature, who has given shame to man for his scourge;" he wrote, "and let the heaviest part of the punishment be the infamy attending it."[31] But, like Beccaría, he offered no substantive account of the content of those punishments or of how, exactly, the offender might be shamed. Nor, before the American War of Independence, had any of distinguished jurists of Europe and Britain, including Joseph Servan, William Blackstone, and William Eden, systematically theorized an enlightened alternative to the various punishments they catalogued as cruel and bloody.[32] With the loss of the American colonies and the suspension of the convict transportation system (by which thieves and other felons, many of whom would have otherwise been hanged, were banished from Britain for a period of years), Eden, Blackstone, and Jeremy Bentham had begun to theorize a carceral system of punishment. But, thanks in part to the resumption of convict transportation (this time, to New South Wales and Van Diemen's Land), Eden and Blackstone's hastily drafted Penitentiary Act of 1779 was not implemented.[33] Meanwhile, Parliament

miserable a condition that if I commit a similar misdeed' is far more potent than the idea of death, which men envision always at an obscure distance." Cesare Beccaría, *On Crimes and Punishments* (New York: Bobbs-Merrill, 1963 [1764]), 46–9.

[31] Charles de Secondat, Baron de Montesquieu, *The Spirit of the Laws, 1752* (trans. Thomas Nugent, 1752) (London: G. Bell & Sons, Ltd., 1914), Book VI, Ch. 9 ("Of the Severity of Punishments in Different Governments"). Jean-Jacques Rousseau also pondered questions of criminal law and punishment, but offered a much less sanguine view of than that of either Montesquieu or Beccaría. Developing the contractarian principles of government found in Hobbes (*Leviathan*) and Locke (*Two Treatises on Government*), Rousseau posited that a person who breaks the laws of his homeland is nothing less than a rebel and a traitor who has waged war upon his homeland. Such a person is "less a citizen than . . . an enemy," he opined, and should be treated according to the right of the war – that is, killed or exiled. On the Social Contract, in Rousseau, *Selections* (Indianapolis: Hackett,1983), 159.

[32] McLynn, *Crime and Punishment*, 297; Foucault, "The Punitive Society," Ethics, Subjectivity, and Truth (*Essential Works of Foucault, 1954–1984*, Vol. I) (New York: The New Press, 1997), 23–37; Simon Devereaux, "The Making of the Penitentiary Act, 1775–1779," *The Historical Journal*, 42:2 (Jun., 1999), 405–33. William Eden, the most renowned of the late eighteenth-century commentators on English penal law, included a chapter on imprisonment in his *Principles of Penal Law* (1771), but even here, Eden did not consider the uses to which imprisonment might be put as a form of legal punishment. In his *Commentaries*, Blackstone listed perpetual confinement, slavery, and exile as three means to the end of "depriving the party . . . to do future mischief" and warned that such penalties ought to be imposed only in "incorrigible" cases. In a lengthy catalogue of various forms of punishment, he notes the punishment of "loss of liberty by perpetual or temporary imprisonment," and, for the indigent offender, the ignominious punishment of hard labor in a house of correction. Nowhere, however, does he elaborate upon prison-based forms of punishment. William Blackstone, *Commentaries on the Laws of England*, Book IV, Ch. 1, 12; Book IV, Ch. 29, 370 (Oxford: Clarendon Press, 1765–69), The Avalon Project at Yale Law School, (Electronic Texts), (New Haven, Connecticut: Yale University).

[33] Beattie, *Crime and Courts*, 574–7.

and politics stymied Bentham's efforts to build his panoptical penitentiary.[34] His utilitarian theory of punishment, and the Panopticon, would remain little known on the American side of the Atlantic until the early nineteenth century, when the dispirited, half-maddened Bentham began peddling his scheme to the States of Vermont and New Hampshire, and to the United States government.[35]

In the 1780s, then, early republicans had little in the way of either a working penal system or a well-worked-up body of thought to which they could turn in the search for an appropriately postmonarchical mode of punishment. Yet it was not the case that, upon winning their independence from England, the states were somehow entirely freed of the influence of past practice and ideology, or that there had not been fragments of discourse, circulating in the Atlantic world, that afforded brief glimpses at a different way of doing things. In England in the 1750s, the magistrate, Henry Fielding, and the economist, Joseph Massie, had both advanced the argument that petty offenders – and the working and nonworking poor more generally – might be "corrected" and habituated to honest work through internment in a house of correction; Fielding and Massie did not offer a systematic theory for a new kind of penal system, but they nonetheless raised new questions about the purpose of punishment, and linked the performance of labor with punishment for crime.[36] In the same decade, amidst mounting fears that the country was in the grips of a great crime wave, Parliament had debated and voted down a bill designed to substitute "Confinement, and Hard Labour, in His Majesty's Dock Yards" (1752) for convict transportation (to the American colonies): Under the bill, certain classes of felons, who thitherto had

---

[34] For Jeremy Bentham's early work on the subject, see Bentham, *A View of the Hard-Labour Bill* (London: 1778). His later work (on the famous Panopticon) was based on his brother's adaptation of monastic architecture for a manufactory commissioned by the Russian statesman, Grigori Aleksandrovich Potemkin. See Jeremy Bentham, *Panopticon: or, the Inspection-House*: Containing the idea of a new principle of construction applicable to penitentiary-houses, prisons, houses of industry, work-houses, poor-houses, manufactories, mad-houses, hospitals, and schools. With a plan of management adapted to the principle. In a series of letters, written . . . 1787, from Crecheff to a friend in England (Dublin: Thomas Byrne, 1791); Jeremy Bentham, *Panopticon Writings*, ed. Miran Bozovic (London: Verso, 1995). Robert Alan Cooper discusses Bentham's torment over Parliament's failure to follow through on his scheme. "Jeremy Bentham, Elizabeth Fry, and English Prison Reform," *Journal of the History of Ideas* 42:4 (Oct–Dec. 1981), 675–90, 681.

[35] For Bentham's unsuccessful efforts in the United States and the debates his ideas prompted, see: "Intelligencer, Bellows Falls," *Vermont Intelligencer and Bellows' Falls Advertiser*, Aug. 6, 1808; "To Jeremy Bentham, Esq., London," *Weekly Messenger*, May 28, 1818; "Panopticon, and Codification," May 28, 1818, *Weekly Messenger*; "Concord," *Concord Gazette*, June 2, 1818; "Legislative," *Portsmouth Oracle*, June 8, 1818; "Miscellany from the Federal Republican," *Salem Gazette*, June 19, 1818; "Legislative," *Farmer's Cabinet*, June 13, 1818; "Codification & Panopticon," *Salem Gazette*, June 16, 1818; "Legislative," *Weekly Messenger*, June 18, 1818; "(Copy.) to Jeremy Bentham Esq. London. New Hampshire, (U. States) Epping, Oct. 2, 1817," *Repertory*, May 21, 1818; "Intelligencer, Bellows Falls, June 22, 1818," *Vermont Intelligencer*, June 23, 1818; "Codification and Panopticon," *Massachusetts Spy*, June 24, 1818; "Legislative," *Newburyport Herald*, July 3, 1818; "Panopticon and Codification," *Farmer's Cabinet*, July 4, 1818; "Panopticon Once More," *New Hampshire Sentinel*, Nov. 25, 1820.

[36] Beattie, *Crime and Courts*, 552–53.

been banished over the seas, were to remain in England and be chained, dressed in distinctive clothes, put to hard labor, and made "visible and lasting Examples to others."[37] As J. M. Beattie observes, however, the Dock Yards bill was not intended "to signal an attack on the fundamental bases of punishment as they had been well understood for generations." Rather, its sponsors aimed to shore up "a penal system that few people thought could work without frequent public displays of the consequences of breaking the law."[38] The bill was strictly motivated by the well-established penology of deterrence and it in no way aimed to establish a system of punishment that would reform or rehabilitate the offender. Nonetheless, it innovated deterrence theory, in that the means of making an example of an offender was expanded beyond that of the gallows (and related acts of corporal chastisement) to include public forced labor and loss of liberty of the person. Although the bill failed in the House of Lords (partly on the grounds that the existence of such a system of forced, hard public labor on English soil was "incompatible with the status and dignity of a free people,"[39] the idea would surface again in the American states' first round of debates about the need for a properly republican penal code in the 1780s.

An even more important influence upon republican thinking on the subject of legal punishment was the colonial practice of penal involuntary servitude, and the particular ideology of labor that reinforced that practice. The early republicans knew the legal condition of penal servitude, both as an indirect result of Britain's convict transportation system and the colonies' own laws concerning the fate of convicted offenders who were unable to pay their court-ordered fines. The principal form of penal servitude found in the colonies was that which attended transportation of British convicts to American (and Caribbean) shores. Upon a court-ordered penalty of transportation, upwards of 55,000 British convicts had been carried across the seas to the West Indian and American colonies between 1609 and 1775; a full 50,000 of these had been transported after 1718.[40] They were borne

---

[37] A Bill to change the Punishment of Felony in certain Cases . . . to Confinement and hard Labour, in his Majesty's Dock Yards, *Journal of the House of Commons*, 26 (1750–54), 400, quoted in Beattie, *Crime and Courts*, 522.

[38] Beattie, *Crime and Courts*, 522–4, 523.

[39] Leon Radzinowicz, *A History of English Criminal Law and Its Administration from 1750*, Vol. 5 (London: Stevens, 1948–).

[40] Transportation to the American colonies had been practiced since 1606, though not as systematically as after 1718 and the enactment of the Transportation Act (4 Geo. I, c. 11). Transportation commenced after the enactment of the 1597 Vagrancy Act; vagrants made up most of the initial transports; later, under an Order in Council (1617) the courts commenced the practice of reprieving and transporting those condemned robbers and felons who "for strength of bodie or other abilities shall be thought fitt to be ymploid in forraine discoveries or other services beyond the seas" (original spellings). In these years, before 1718, transportation was ordered as part of a conditional pardon from the death penalty: Healthy convicted robbers and felons were given the option of death or transportation: Some six thousand convicts "chose" transportation. After 1718, the courts could also impose the penalty directly for certain kinds of theft, and regardless of the health and fitness of the convict: The conditional and direct penalties co-existed through the remainder of the eighteenth century. In extending the penalty of transportation to property crimes, the

by merchant–entrepreneurs, who charged the British authorities between three and five pounds per head, and, upon laying anchor in the colonies, auctioned or otherwise sold their human cargo into involuntary servitude under private masters.[41] Most such "transports" were sold in the labor-hungry colonies of Virginia and Maryland, but a significant number were also sold in Pennsylvania.[42]

Notably, under British law, the penalty of transportation was not, in and of itself, a sentence to servitude. Despite the steady traffic in convicts between British jails and colonial masters, English jurists insisted that Englishmen were "immune from transportation *under any form of bondage*"[43] (emphasis added). Transportation was solely an act of banishment, wrote William Eden in 1771, by which "the criminal . . . is merely transferred to a new country."[44] On this arguably sophistic reading of penal law, the criminal sentence of transportation may have enabled the sale of convicts into involuntary bondage, but it in no way mandated or endorsed that course of action: The involuntary servitude into which penal transports were invariably sold upon arriving in the colonies was imposed not by British law but by those entrepreneurial merchants and factors who performed the "public service" of carrying the convicts out of Britain. And colonial law countenanced that servitude. Although, in the 1730s and 1740s, a number of colonial assemblies had unsuccessfully attempted to prohibit the transportation of the British convicts into the colonies, they nonetheless permitted the sale of these men and women into bondage. Indeed, by the moral standards of a society characterized by various relations of servitude (both involuntary and

1718 Act made the marginal punishment of transportation the cornerstone of English legal punishment. As Kenneth Morgan has shown, even in 1776, a year after the official end of convict transportation to the thirteen American colonies, convict servants were still being regularly imported and sold in the Chesapeake. Kenneth Morgan, "The Organization of the Convict Trade to Maryland: Stevenson, Randolph and Cheston, 1768–1775," *The William and Mary Quarterly*, 3rd Ser., 42:2 (Apr., 1985), 218–19. On convict transportation, see A. Robert Ekirch, *Bound for America: The Transportation of British Convicts to the Colonies, 1718–1775* (Oxford: Oxford University Press, 1987); McLynn, *Crime and Punishment*, 285–7; Rusche and Kirchheimer, *Punishment and Social Structure* (New York: Columbia University Press, 1939), 59–60; Smith, *Colonists in Bondage: White Servitude and Convict Labor in America, 1607–1776* (Chapel Hill: University of North Carolina Press, 1947), 91–3, 119; and Alan Atkinson, "The Free-born Englishman Transported," *Past and Present* 144 (Aug. 1994), 88–115.

[41] Merchants sold their transports typically at a rate of between ten and fourteen pounds per male convict, and around five pounds per woman. Kenneth Morgan, "The Organization of the Convict Trade to Maryland," 218–19.

[42] Kenneth Morgan, "The Organization of the Convict Trade to Maryland," 218–19.

[43] Alan Atkinson, "The Free-born Englishman Transported," 91.

[44] William Eden, *The Principles of Penal Law* (London 1771), quoted in Atkinson, "The Free-born Englishman Transported," 92. Most jurists also considered the formal penalty of "mere" banishment to be noncoercive, and even consensual, despite the fact that, after 1718, courts directly sentenced most transports to banishment (rather than offering the convict the "choice" of consenting to banishment as a reprieve from the gallows). Atkinson, "The Free-born Englishman Transported," 94.

voluntary), bonding these men and women in some way or other appeared the natural thing to do.[45] In the early phase of this system of penal servitude, the legal and moral standing of penal involuntary servants (in colonial law) had not differed significantly from that of ordinary indentured servants. According to Alan Atkinson, before 1748, "transport" servants in Virginia enjoyed much the same set of liberties as indentured servants. Convict servants collected freedom dues upon completion of service, and despite the fact that some convicts had been banished for a term of fourteen years, the duration of servitude was much closer to that of ordinary, indentured servants and rarely longer than seven years. In Virginia, if a former convict servant met the property and other franchise requirements, he could vote and, also, testify in court. Although, in Maryland, colonial lawmakers tried (and failed) to establish a system of registration, by which they hoped to keep track of the transports, many observers viewed the convicts not as intrinsically debased or morally corrupt criminals, but as men and women who had been given a chance to work off their otherwise capital offense. Upon completion of their term of servitude, many were absorbed into colonial society, in much the same way as other former servants.[46]

In the middle of the eighteenth century, however, the legal and moral status of transported servants began to change. Although the evidence is incomplete, it appears that in the two colonies to which most of these transports were consigned (Maryland and Virginia), penal transports began to be distinguished, both in political discourse and in law, from other servants and, specifically, as "*convict* servants."[47] A succession of laws enacted in the mid-eighteenth century carved a deep line between convict and other servants, and moved the legal status of convict servants closer to that of chattel slaves. In the words of one Virginia lawmaker, "putting Volunteers and Convicts on the same Footing as to Rewards and Punishments, is discouraging the Good and Encouraging the Bad."[48] Especially after 1748, "convict servants" lost a number of liberties: The Virginia assembly denied convict servants trial by a jury drawn from their vicinage and barred them from testifying in court (except against another convict). In 1749, recusants (people who refused to attend Church of England services), convicts, and transports joined free

45 For discussions of the complex array of unfree and less-than-free relations that characterized North American society from earliest colonial times until the Jacksonian Era, see Edmund S. Morgan, *American Slavery, American Freedom* (New York: Norton, 1975); Mark A. Peterson, "The Selling of Joseph: Bostonians, Antislavery, and the Protestant International, 1689–1733," *Massachusetts Historical Review* 4 (2002), 1–22; Eric Foner, *The Story of American Freedom* (New York: Norton, 1998), 3–28; Richard B. Morris, "The Measure of Bondage in the Slave States," *The Mississippi Valley Historical Review* 41:2 (Sep., 1954), 219–40, 220, and A. Robert Ekirch, *Bound for America*, 133–93.

46 Atkinson, "The Free-born Englishman Transported," 100–01, 105.

47 Alan Atkinson, "The Free-born Englishman Transported," 101–04, 106–07.

48 *Legislative Journals of the Council of Colonial Virginia*, ed. H. R. McIlwaine, 3 vols. (Richmond, 1918–19), ii, 1034–5 (11 Apr. 1749) quoted in Atkinson, "The Free-born Englishman Transported," 101.

negroes, mulattos, and Indians, as classes of people barred from voting: None of these groups could vote, regardless of whether they met property and other criteria of enfranchisement.[49] In both colonies, convict servants lost their customary right to freedom dues. In Maryland, where the assembly had periodically tried to limit the entry of penal transports since the 1720s, convict servants were now sometimes included in laws aimed at regulating slave movements off the plantations: In some laws, slaves and convict servants were made subject to the same, generally bloody, kinds of punishments.[50]

Most of these new laws applied to a second kind of convict servant found in the colonies. Several of the colonies provided that, under certain conditions, persons convicted of property crimes could be sold into servitude.[51] In most colonies, the adoption of this species of penal servitude followed upon the colonial assemblies' scaling back of the death penalty for property crimes, and was justified on the grounds that automatically laying waste to a thief's life (by executing him) made little sense in colonies that were labor starved and "meanly and Thinly Inhabited."[52] The Maryland assembly, for example, abolished the penalty of execution for most property crimes and substituted fines and corporal chastisements in 1681; when, subsequent to this reform, the courts discovered that offenders did not always have the means with which to pay their fines, magistrates began ordering such offenders sold into servitude, as a means of executing the fine. The Maryland assembly gave this practice statutory force in 1718;[53] it survived the Revolution and, as late as 1786 and 1787, at least fifteen percent of all offenders convicted in Maryland's busiest court (Frederick county) were sold into servitude.[54] The sale of convicted offenders into servitude was not unknown in the Northern colonies (where there were also chronic labor shortages and high labor costs), either. In the 1630s, for example, Massachusetts provided that convicted property offenders and convicts who failed to pay the fines levied as

---

[49] Virginia's 1723 slave code had barred free negroes, mulattoes, and Indians – but not convicts or convict servants – from voting. See, An act directing the trial of slaves committing capital crimes; and for the more effectual punishing conspiracies and insurrections of them; and for the better government of Negros, Mulattos, and Indians, bond or free, XXIII Laws of Virginia, 1723, *Hening's Statutes at Large* (1820), Vol. 4.

[50] Atkinson, "The Free-born Englishman Transported," 106–7.

[51] This was one of the few instances in which colonial penal law diverged significantly from English legal norms (which permitted "hard labour" for petty offenders but forbade involuntary servitude on English soil).

[52] Jim Rice, "'This Province, so Meanly and Thinly Inhabited': Punishing Maryland's Criminals, 1681–1850," *Journal of the Early Republic* 19:1 (Spring, 1999), 20–1.

[53] An ACT for the Speedy trial of Criminals, and ascertaining their Punishment in the County Courts when prosecuted there; and for Payment of Fees due from Criminal Persona. Lib. LL. N° 4. fol. 164, 3 Jun., 1715, §1–2 (reprinted in Bacon's *Laws of Maryland, 1765*, Vol. 75, Ch. 26, 220). A person convicted of a crime of larceny involving goods worth under one thousand dollars was ordered to repay the "Party grieved" to the four-fold value of goods stolen: If unable to do so, that "Person or Persons shall receive the corporal Punishment . . . and satisfy the Four-fold, and Fees of Conviction, by Servitude," either to the aggrieved party or to a third party who effectively purchased the convict's service by paying the restitution and conviction fees on the spot.

[54] Rice, "This Province," 24.

punishment for their crimes could be sold as servants to masters for a term of some years, or even for life. Although it is unclear how many offenders were in practice sold in this manner, court records show that it was not an uncommon occurrence and that offenders, both black and white, were "sould for a slave" (original spelling).[55] As in Maryland, the Massachusetts law was still both on the books and in force as late as 1786.[56]

There are no reliable sources indicating how many convict servants were living and working in the various states in the mid-1780s, when the states set about enacting new penal codes. However, there were enough that in 1787, the framers of the Continental Congress's most significant piece of legislation, the Northwest Ordinance, were compelled to exempt persons undergoing servitude as punishment for crime from their otherwise universal prohibition upon slavery and involuntary servitude in the newly acquired Northwestern territories. The Ordinance provided: "(t)here shall be neither slavery nor involuntary servitude in the said territory, otherwise than in the punishment of crimes whereof the party shall have been duly convicted."[57] Unlike masters of slaves, masters of convicts could take their involuntary servants with them into the territories. Despite the well-known outrage of Benjamin Franklin and other patriots over the mother country's dumping of convicts on American shores, and despite the colonies' forcible closure of the trans-Atlantic trade in 1776, the mechanism that the colonies used to manage that segment of their population – penal servitude – survived the Revolution.[58] Indeed, more than that, it received official recognition in the Continental Congress's most important law.

[55] The term of servitude could be for a fixed number of years, for life, or until such time as restitution to the wronged party was complete. Court records typically used the word "slavery" (and not "servitude") to describe the punishment. A. Leon Higginbotham, Jr. shows that both black convicts and white convicts were subject to this punishment, as well as Native Americans captured in war. Apart from the work of Rice, Kealey, and Higginbotham, very little is known about the legal punishment of "penal slavery" in colonial and early republican North America. A. Leon Higginbotham, Jr., *In the Matter of Color: Race and the American Legal Process: The Colonial Period* (New York: Oxford University Press, 1978), 66–8.

[56] In 1786, the Massachusetts Supreme Judicial Court was still directing some (though not all) convicted offenders who could not pay their fines to be sold into servitude. Proceedings of the Supreme Judicial Court, reported in *The Pennsylvania Packet, and Daily Advertiser*, Sept. 30, 1786, Iss. 2389, 2.

[57] Northwest Ordinance: An Ordinance for the government of the Territory of the United States northwest of the River Ohio, July 13, 1787, Art. 6, The Avalon Project at Yale Law School (Electronic Texts), (New Haven, Connecticut: Yale University).

[58] In a oft-quoted missive, written shortly after one of the colonies convicted a transport-servant of manslaughter and sentenced him to death, Franklin wrote: "These are some of thy favours, BRITAIN.... Thou art called our MOTHER COUNTRY; but what good Mother ever sent Thieves and Villains to accompany her children; to corrupt some with their infectious Vices, and murder the rest? What Father ever endeavour'd to spread the Plague in his own family? We do not ask Fish, but thou gavest us Serpents, and more than Serpents!" Franklin went on to suggest that the colonies send Britain a rattlesnake for every convict unloaded on American shores: "Rattle-Snakes seem the most suitable Returns for the Human Serpents sent by our Mother Country." *New-York Gazette* (Revived in the *Weekly Post-Boy*, Apr. 15, 1751, 2), and *The Pennsylvania Gazette*, May 9, 1751.

As the state legislatures set about the transition to peacetime in the mid-1780s, the revision of state penal codes got underway in earnest. Initially, most state legislatures moved slowly and in a piecemeal manner. Massachusetts appointed a committee to review the penal code and, at its prompting, the legislature enacted a law authorizing the confinement of "thieves and other convicts to hard labor" on Castle Island in Boston harbor. The scope of the law, however, was relatively narrow, for it was aimed specifically at petty larsonists; the legislature retained the older, sanguinary chastisements of cropping, branding, and whipping for lesser crimes as well as the death penalty for higher crimes (including murder, treason, rape, sodomy, burglary, and arson). The century-old supplemental penalty for convicted thieves who could not pay their fines – sale into servitude – remained in force. There is some evidence to suggest that, by the 1780s, it was becoming more difficult to find buyers for these involuntary penal servants; indeed, in at least one session of the Massachusetts Supreme Judicial Court, the justices sentenced several offenders to the usual whipping, fines, and supplemental sale with the caveat that in the event the offenders were not sold, they should be sent to Castle Island.[59] The authors of the Massachusetts hard labor law did not, at this point, envision the punishment as either the foundation for an alternative system of punishment or as an instrument with which to reform offenders. As the state Attorney-General, James A. Sullivan, put it, "no reformation is to be expected from the mode of punishment;" rather, the "good effect" of the Castle Island scheme was its deterrent effect on the free citizenry and its incapacitation of offenders.[60] Nonetheless, the substitution of hard labor on Castle Island marked an important departure from previous practice. New York and Connecticut also adopted hard public labor at this time, putting some classes of convicts to work for periods of anything from one year to life, but neither state advanced a substantive plan for an alternative penal order.

The first state to undertake systematic reform of its penal system was Pennsylvania. Pennsylvania's distinction of having the largest city and busiest port in the country was an important factor in the legislature's comparatively early commitment to overhauling the state's penal system. As Michael Meranze writes, in the mid-1780s, legislators were prompted to undertake this task against a backdrop of the ruling élite's "growing fear of criminality and immorality" within Philadelphia's population at large.[61] Wartime inflation, heightening economic inequality, an influx of displaced persons, and rising concerns among merchants, lawyers, and landholders that vice and crime were on the incline all served to bring tremendous pressure to bear

59 William Coloim was to be "whipped fifteen stripes, pay costs, &c. and if not sold to pay the damages, to be confined to hard labour on Castle-Island"; David Norris was to be punished similarly (but with thirty stripes). Proceedings of the Supreme Judicial Court, reported in *The Pennsylvania Packet, and Daily Advertiser*, Sep. 30, 1786, 2.
60 J. A. Sullivan to the Philadelphia Gazette, *Philadelphia Gazette and Universal Daily Advertiser*, Jan. 21, 1795.
61 Meranze, *Laboratories of Virtue*, 67.

on lawmakers. In 1785 and 1786, legislators were deluged with petitions and requests for systematic penal reform. A succession of reports by the justices and jurists of the Court of Oyer and Terminer, and a Philadelphia grand jury's finding that the city was succumbing to "vice and immorality," all underscored the idea that the city was undergoing a crisis of disorder and that immediate penal reform was required. Building on this theme, the justices of the Pennsylvania Supreme Court and members of the Grand Jury explained in a petition of support to the state legislature that it was vital that lawmakers act on the constitution and institute a system of hard, public labor for convicted offenders. Such a system would not only reform the culprits and preserve their lives, the justices and jurors petitioned, but would make an example of them for the wider (and supposedly increasingly unruly) citizenry: Public hard labor would "lessen the number of offenders, by proving a reasonable warning, and a durable example to others, and thereby perpetually reminding them of the dangerous consequences of an aberation (sic) from virtue, and a breach of the laws."[62]

In 1786, the legislature finally acted. Legislators enacted a penal code that provided that all convicts other than those sentenced to hang be put to "servitude" as "wheelbarrowmen" on the state's roads, highways, forts, and mines. In echoes of Beccaría and the English parliament's failed Dock Yards bill, Pennsylvania lawmakers reasoned that the sight of convicts, shorn of their hair and beards, working silently and obediently, in distinctive garb whose markings identified the convict's particular crime, would both impress upon free passers-by the idea that ignominious punishment awaited anyone who committed a crime and allow the elimination of bloody chastisements from the state's penal system. However, moving beyond the familiar logic of deterrence theory, its authors theorized that the penalty would make good citizens of the offenders and render up to the public useful labor along the way.[63]

As provided by law, Pennsylvania's wheelbarrow men went to work in the summer of 1786. Lawmakers congratulated themselves on their enlightened new system of punishment and anticipated the return of order to the city. What unfolded on various streets and public works, however, was far from the orderly, rational, instructive scene of punishment they had envisioned. Rather than striking respect for the law into the hearts of convicts and passers-by, public labor quite often became the occasion for raucous, violent, and drunken behavior, on the part of both the convict wheelbarrow men and ordinary Philadelphians. Even when the wheelbarrow men labored in more or less orderly fashion, some free citizens invariably took the opportunity to consort – and engage in various forms of illicit commerce – with

---

[62] *The Pennsylvania Mercury and Universal Advertiser*, Sep. 16, 1785, 3.

[63] In Rhode Island, an act of 1787 prescribed "hard labour" for up to two years on wheelbarrows and boats for anyone convicted of theft or larceny. Subsequently, lawmakers in other states, including New York, Massachusetts, Maryland, and Virginia legislated similar wheelbarrow schemes. *The Providence Gazette and Country Journal*, Nov. 10, 1787, 2; Rice, "This Province," 24; Meranze, *Laboratories of Virtue*, 68.

the convicts.[64] Nor was the system secure: Large numbers of convict laborers in Philadelphia absconded (and on at least one occasion, ran away to New York, allegedly committing a string of robberies along the way and exchanging their distinctive wheelbarrow garb for their victims' clothing).[65] In one particularly startling incident, which took place in Philadelphia during the federal constitutional convention, a group of escapee wheelbarrow men descended upon the carriage of Alexander Hamilton and his wife, blunderbusses and pistols blazing, with the apparent intent of robbing the couple. The Hamiltons, who were returning from the convention to their Bush Hill home in New York, narrowly avoided being robbed, or worse (thanks to their driver, who was said to have outrun the assailants). Nonetheless, the audacity of this attack, and the fact that the alleged assailants were the very "foot-pads" the wheelbarrow law was designed to contain, was reported with great alarm throughout the states.[66]

In the wake of repeated and widely publicized incidents such as these, jurists, lawmakers, and concerned citizens began questioning the efficacy of the first significant experiment in republican punishment.[67] Some argued that the wheelbarrow scheme not only failed to hold the wheelbarrow men securely, but failed to mark them out, in the eyes of the citizenry, as persons undergoing punishment: One such critic pointed out that, contrary to law, some wheelbarrow men routinely enjoyed liberties such as running errands and fetching rum and water; indeed, he argued, free citizens became so accustomed to seeing them at liberty on the streets of Philadelphia that, on at least one occasion, members of the public had witnessed an escape without knowing it.[68] Other critics noted that when wheelbarrow men finished their sentences or absconded (which they did with some regularity) they showed few signs of being "reformed," but promptly resumed their former occupations as pickpockets, plunderers, and thieves.[69] By 1788, wheelbarrow men were immediately suspected of being responsible in the event of a property crime, regardless of whether or not there was any direct evidence of their

---

[64] Meranze, *Laboratories of Virtue*, 91–2; Masur, *Rites of Execution*, 80.

[65] Another group of wheelbarrow men broke out of the jail in March 1787, and, according to reports in the press, gave "new specimens of their abilities in the lines of their profession," committing "several robberies within these few nights past." *The Columbia Magazine*, Mar. 1787, 349. Other escapes of wheelbarrow men were reported in *The Carlisle Gazette*, and the *Western Repository of Knowledge*, II:99 (June, 27, 1787), 3; *Essex Journal*, IV:157 (July 4, 1787), 2 (also reported in *State Gazette of South-Carolina*, XLVI:3531 [July 30, 1787], 2); *The American Museum: or, Repository of Ancient and Modern Fugitive Pieces*, 4 (Oct. 1788), 391; and *The New-York Packet*, 1099 (Aug. 5, 1790), 2.

[66] *The Pennsylvania Herald, and General Advertiser*, VI:44 (June 23, 1787), 3, and *The Independent Gazetteer*, VI:479 (June 25, 1787), 2.

[67] See, for example, *The Daily Advertiser*, IV:904 (Jan. 16, 1788), 2; *The Pennsylvania Mercury and Universal Advertiser*, Iss. 290 (Sep. 20, 1788), 4; *The Independent Gazetteer*, III:887 (Oct. 15, 1788), 3; *The Federal Gazette, and Philadelphia Evening Post*, Oct. 23, 1788, 3.

[68] *The Pennsylvania Mercury and Universal Advertiser*, 290 (Sep. 9, 1788), 4.

[69] See for example, *The Independent Gazetteer*, VIII:887, (Oct. 15, 1788), 3; *The Pennsylvania Mercury and Universal Advertiser*, 301 (Oct. 16, 1788), 3; and *The Daily Advertiser*, IV:1145 (Oct. 22, 1788), 2.

involvement. Philadelphia had become, in the words of one critic, a place in which a "lawless and wandering banditti of wheelbarrowmen" endangered people's lives "every hour of the night and day"; the state assembly should not be permitted to adjourn for the year, he concluded, without enacting some relief.[70] Following the mass escape of some thirty-three wheelbarrow men in 1788, the local press warned: "Such citizens as are obliged to go abroad in the evening, would do well to arm themselves."[71] "Is there a man in the state who does not see the absurdity of the present wheelbarrow law?" implored an exasperated "Despiser of Demagogues, Would-be-ats, and Wheelbarrow-men."[72]

Far from embodying the rational, humane, deterrent workings of the law, the wheelbarrow men quickly came to signify a weak and failing criminal legal system, and all that was unrepublican, lawless, and ugly. Traces of the contempt in which many citizens held the scheme could be found even in articles on subjects wholly unrelated to the penal system. One "Lutius," an aspiring grammarian of a properly republican English, argued that the word, "inculcate," ought to be committed "to the care of the wheelbarrowmen . . . and it should never appear above ground again."[73] As the federal constitution went to the states to be ratified in 1788, wheelbarrow men figured once again as the embodiment of lawlessness and unreason: Only thirty-seven Philadelphians opposed ratification of the federal constitution, one Federalist mocked, and a full fifteen of those were wheelbarrow men.[74]

Whether they were the butt of public humor or the alleged origin of lawlessness and disorder, the wheelbarrow men and the system to which they were subject demonstrably failed both to make obedient laborers of convicts and to strike respect and awe for the law into the hearts of free citizens. The Pennsylvania press printed numerous complaints about the convicts and the new penal system through 1787 and 1788, but not a single defense of either the wheelbarrow men or the public penal labor system. One critic's claim that the "merciful tenderness of the [wheelbarrow] law serves only to encourage [the men's] bloody depradations," appeared widely accepted.[75] Within a year of its inception, the first great republican experiment in legal punishment was embroiled in a crisis of legitimacy.

Chastened by the apparent failure of their penal system and repeatedly petitioned for relief, lawmakers in Pennsylvania began to cast around for an alternative. As the disorders of the wheelbarrow system began to mount in the fall of 1787, Benjamin Rush, the prolific Philadelphian essayist, physician, and signatory to the Declaration of Independence, issued a stinging

[70] *The Federal Gazette and Philadelphia Evening Post*, Nov. 3, 1788, 3.

[71] *The Daily Advertiser*, IV:1145 (Oct. 22, 1788), 2. This event was also reported in other states: for example, *The American Herald and the Worcester Recorder*, VIII:379 (Nov. 6. 1788), 2.

[72] *The Pennsylvania Mercury and Universal Advertiser*, 290 (Sep. 20, 1788), 4.

[73] *The Independent Gazetteer*, VI:454 (May 26, 1787), 3.

[74] *The Pennsylvania Mercury and Universal Advertiser*, 183 (Jan. 15, 1788), 4.

[75] *Essex Journal*, 275 (Oct. 7, 1789), 3.

attack on the practice, and all forms of public punishment, in his *Enquiry into the Effects of Public Punishments Upon Criminals, and Upon Society* (which he originally presented at a gathering of Benjamin Franklin's Society for Political Enquiries).[76] Rush argued that public punishments, including the wheelbarrow variety, both failed to reform the "criminal" and adversely affected the sensibilities of the very citizen-spectators whom the punishment was also designed to discipline: The infamy attached to public punishment crushed, rather than restored, the criminal's sense of shame. Where the punishment was a whipping or other bodily chastisement, he continued, it was not of long enough duration to change the criminal's mind and body; and where punishment took the form of public labor it was of such a long duration that the destructive effects of infamy were magnified.[77] In citizen-spectators, meanwhile, public punishments produced either undue sympathy for criminals or unholy contempt for them. Sympathy for those undergoing legal punishment, Rush cautioned, bred contempt for the law in its harshness, while contempt for the criminal would eventually extinguish the sensibility of sympathy that supposedly bonded a good republican society.[78] Public punishments produced the very opposite of the desired effect, Rush argued, and they did so because they contravened the laws of human nature. The punishment of public labor, in addition, tainted the act of labor itself, through the natural law of association: "(E)mploying criminals in public labour will render labour of every kind disreputable," he warned, "more especially that species of it which has for its objects the convenience or improvement of the state." Just as "white men decline labour" in slave-holding states, because they associate it with "Negro slaves," free citizens who witnessed the hard public toil of criminals would come to consider labor *per se* degraded and degrading.[79]

Rush's answer to the question of what legal punishment ought to be was to retain hard labor but to coerce convicts far from the gaze of the public: He recommended that convicted offenders be sequestered in a "house of repentance." Within this house, the convict would be compelled to confront his or her guilty conscience by being subjected to the strict routines of "BODILY PAIN, LABOUR, WATCHFULNESS, SOLITUDE AND SILENCE...joined with CLEANLINESS and a SIMPLE DIET" (capitals in original). By sequestering the convict and carefully managing his or her every waking moment, Rush argued, government would perform a "surgery" on the convict's soul, causing sinful lawbreakers to reflect upon and repent the sins of their past. The labor of the convicts was to be "profitable to the state," Rush recommended, and involve "useful manufactures." Criminals would also be compelled to raise their own food on a farm attached to the

[76] Benjamin Rush, "An Enquiry into the Effects of Public Punishments upon Criminals, and Upon Society," read in the Society for Promoting Political Enquiries, Convened at the House of His Excellency Benjamin Franklin, Esquire...in Philadelphia, March 9th 1787 (Philadelphia, 1787).

[77] Rush, "An Enquiry," 4–5.   [78] Rush, "An Enquiry," 6–8.

[79] Rush, "An Enquiry," 9. See also Hirsch, *The Rise of the Penitentiary*, 85.

house.[80] Modifying Beccarían ideas concerning the disciplinary effects of terror, Rush also theorized that the complete seclusion of convicts from free citizens would deter the latter from crime: Uncertain of what, exactly, went on behind penitential walls, citizens would be left to imagine the "horrors" of imprisonment, and, in time, their children would "press upon the evening fire in listening to tales that will be spread from this abode of misery."[81] At the same time, the convict would be spared the loss of shame that a public display of his humbled condition inflicted.

As criticism of the wheelbarrow scheme intensified, Rush's ideas began to find traction in the Pennsylvania legislature. Following intensive lobbying by Rush and the Philadelphia Society for Alleviating the Miseries of Public Prisons, the legislature directed, in 1790, that all people convicted of crimes (other than murder and a handful of similarly grave offenses) or misdemeanors be committed to the Walnut Street Jail for a term of hard labor; shortly thereafter, renovations began on the old Walnut Street Jail: Several workshops were built, as well as a series of large rooms in which the prisoners were to sleep.[82] Essentially an extension of the older institution, the house of correction, rather than a precursor to the cellular prison, the new Walnut Street penitentiary followed the design of the larger frame houses of the period: Convicts would eat, sleep, and work communally in this "penitentiary house."[83] (A few years later, the legislature added some isolation cells, but these were used strictly as a supplemental form of punishment. Convicts were put in solitary confinement not as a matter of routine but as punishment for transgressing the household rules).[84] In stark contrast to later practice, upon release from the penitentiary-house, the prisoners were to receive the full value of their labor, less the cost of maintenance and work-related expenses.[85]

Quite quickly, similar houses of repentance sprang up in other states: In 1796, the New York legislature abolished corporal punishment, reduced capital crimes to just three in number (treason, murder, and theft from a church), and directed the construction in lower Manhattan of what was to become Newgate penitentiary. Thomas Eddy, its architect and first "agent," modeled the institution on Walnut Street.[86] New Jersey opened its penitentiary the following year, hanging over its entrance a sign that distilled Rush's penological principles: "LABOR – SILENCE – PENITENCE" (caps in original).[87] A few years later, the U.S. Congress also began substituting the carceral punishment of imprisonment at hard labor (beginning

---

[80] Rush, "An Enquiry," 12–13.
[81] Rush, "An Enquiry," 11–13.
[82] Meranze, *Laboratories of Virtue*, 167.
[83] Rothman, *Discovery of the Asylum*, 61–2.
[84] Rothman, *Discovery of the Asylum*, 90–3.
[85] William Blackstone, *Commentaries*, Vol. IV, Ch. 1.
[86] W. David Lewis, *From Newgate to Dannemora*, 30. Lewis notes that Newgate differed from Walnut Street in that only felons were confined in the former, whereas the latter held felons, vagrants, debtors, and people awaiting trial; unlike Walnut Street, Newgate also had a chapel.
[87] *The Albany Centinel*, II:25, Sep. 25, 1798, 3.

with the counterfeit coin law of 1806) for corporal and public chastisements.[88] By 1810, eight Northern states, and Maryland and Virginia (whose
penitentiary was designed by Thomas Jefferson)[89] had opened penitentiary
houses; for the first time, the great majority of the country's duly convicted
offenders were undergoing their punishment within the walls of a carceral
institution.

In principle, the penitentiary house offered an alternative to the various "monarchical" forms of punishment of which early republican lawmakers were so critical, and solved the disciplinary problems associated
with the states' first wave of penal experimentation (with the wheelbarrow
scheme). Theoretically, the penitentiary would perform the double duty
of cutting the communicative bonds that had existed between the free citizenry and the wheelbarrow men, and concentrating offenders in such a
way that the state's agents could easily subject them to discipline; penitential discipline would, in turn, effect a spiritual transformation in offenders
such that they became orderly, law-abiding, citizens. In practice, however,
the penitentiary mode of punishment operated quite differently. Much as
the inventors of the wheelbarrow schemes had discovered just a few years
earlier, theorizing and legislating a properly "republican" penal system was a
much easier task than actually building and governing one. At Walnut Street,
Newgate, and elsewhere, the task of establishing and successfully governing
the new penitentiary system presented not only a narrowly *technical* set of
problems (for example, the challenge of designing an unscaleable wall or
of devising the most time-efficient labor schedule), but, also, a complex
set of theological, political-economic, and popular ethical and customary
problems.

The degree to which Rush's model of repentance-based punishment presented a radical innovation both of English common law and penal practice
is suggested by Blackstone's matter-of-fact claim (in his 1763 *Commentaries*)
that in English law legal punishment appropriately had only the (technico-
legal) end of "a precaution against future offences of the same kind" and
that questions of "atonement or expiation for the crime committed . . . must

---

[88] Because the federal government did not itself build any prisons (until after the Civil War),
in 1825, Congress provided that any convict sentenced in a federal court to imprisonment at hard labor serve the sentence in a state prison or penitentiary. Finally, in 1839,
Congress abolished the punishments of whipping and the pillory, substituting imprisonment at hard labor as the punishment for almost all ignominious federal crimes. U.S. Laws
of 1806 (Ch. 49); 1825 (Ch. 65). After the punishments of whipping and of standing in
the pillory were abolished by the act of February 28, (U.S. Laws of 1839, [Ch. 36, § 5])
imprisonment at hard labor was substituted for nearly all other ignominious punishments
other than capital. Noted in *Ex Parte Wilson*, U.S. Sup. Ct., 114 U.S. 417 (1885) U.S. LEXIS
1776.

[89] Thomas Jefferson discusses the Virginia penitentiary in his "Autobiography" (47). Penn-
sylvania, New York, New Jersey, Connecticut, Tennessee, Virginia, Kentucky, Massachusetts,
Vermont, New Hampshire, and Maryland had all opened penitentiaries by 1810. Rothman,
Discovery of the Asylum, 61.

be left to the just determination of the supreme being."[90] Indeed, Rush's concept of a house of repentance became the subject of intense controversy almost as soon as the ink dried on his 1787 *Enquiry*. As the Society lobbied to have the penitential house adopted by the state legislature, small but vocal minorities of clergy, jurists, and lawmakers condemned Rush's idea of a penitential mode of punishment. They did so on various religious and political-economic grounds.[91] Most strikingly, the principles of the penitentiary mode of punishment offended the deepest precepts of a strict Christian constructivism or fundamentalism, according to which the sole source of authority, including the authority of mortal man to determine the kind and amount of punishment to be meted out to offenders, was divine in nature. In a way that, paradoxically, amplified Blackstone's implicit critique of penitential aims in legal punishment yet rejected the secularism of the legal system he endorsed, members of the Calvinist clergy assailed Rush's plan as a "blasphemy against God" (itself a sin punishable by death).

One such protestant, the Reverend Robert Annan (a Calvinist minister who sometimes wrote under the pen name of "Philochorus," the ancient Greek historian of religion) charged that incarceration offended morality because it presumed to operate upon the souls of mortals. The spiritual work of curing and cleansing souls was – and ought to be – strictly reserved

---

[90] Blackstone asserted that there were properly just three means to the end of deterring crime, and that each means suggested its own set of penal techniques: "either by the amendment of the offender himself; for which purpose all corporal punishments, fines, and temporary exile or imprisonment are inflicted: or, by deterring others by the dread of his example from offending in the like way . . . which gives rise to all ignominious punishments, and to such executions of justice as are open and public; or, lastly, by depriving the party injuring of the power to do future mischief; which is effected by either putting him to death, or condemning him to perpetual confinement, slavery, or exile. The same one end, of preventing future crimes, is endeavoured to be answered by each of these three species of punishment." *Commentaries*, Book I, Ch. 4, p. 12.

[91] Historians of the early republican and Jacksonian penitentiaries have overwhelmingly focused upon reformers and reform ideology, conceiving of prison history as, first and foremost, a chapter in the intellectual history of social reform. Two historians who have broken with the prison historiography's exclusive emphasis upon the ideas and aspirations of élite social reformers and administrators are Meranze, *Laboratories of Virtue*, and Larry Goldsmith, "Penal Reform, Convict Labor, and Prison Culture in Massachusetts, 1800–1880" (Ph.D. diss., University of Pennsylvania, 1994). Historians have yet to discover any sustained body of written critiques authored by the early protestants of the penitentiary (and we still know very little about the experience of imprisonment in general). James McGrath Morris's study of "jailhouse journalism" includes some useful discussions of several late nineteenth-century prison newspapers, and the one known prison newspaper of the early republican era, *Forlorn Hope*, written and published by William Keteltas, of the New York debtors' jail. Established in 1800, Keteltas's weekly paper contained articles criticizing debt laws that directed the imprisonment and impressment into labor of impoverished debtors; Keteltas also occasionally criticized the degrading conditions of the debtors' jail. James McGrath Morris, *Jailhouse Journalism: The Fourth Estate Behind Bars* (Jefferson, North Carolina: McFarland and Co., 1998), especially 19–29.

to the Lord God, "Philochorus" argued. Moreover, on this view, the only righteous punishments were those enumerated in Leviticus, Isaiah, Paul, and other books of the Holy Bible. Secluding the offender from the view of the citizenry and subjecting him or her to a process of spiritual habituation, as Rush directed, was a far cry both from Paul's instruction that sinners be rebuked before the community and from the Old Testament's prescription of banishment and execution as the proper punishments for crime. Indeed, on a strict reading of scripture, the moral grounds for imprisoning convicted lawbreakers were nowhere to be found in the Bible.[92] (Annan also accused Rush and other critics of capital punishment of "'(l)iberality, in religious sentiments,'" warning that sparing murderers from execution, as critics proposed, would render "injustice . . . more powerful than justice" and "Satan stronger than the Almighty").[93] Farther North, in Boston, the Reverend Stephen West condemned the scaling back of capital punishment on similar grounds: Citing Mosaic law, he exclaimed: "God has appointed civil rulers to bear his sword, to avenge the wrongs of society, and to execute wrath upon evil-doers. . . . The good of society, here in this world, forbids that atonement should be made for certain crimes, even be the criminal ever humble and penitent; but absolutely requires, if on no other account, yet for a terror and a warning to others, the utter excision – the death of the perpetrator."[94]

Other critics of the penitentiary idea voiced objections of a different stripe, and from a perspective that drew on both the liberal political philosophy of John Locke and Adam Smith, and on classical republicanism. As one such critic (writing under the penname of "Cato") asserted, the punishment of confinement to penitent labor had no basis in the "social contract" upon which civil society was supposedly founded. Specifically, argued Cato, the taxes that would have to be raised in order to maintain a penitentiary – or any other governmental institution for the "support (of) the vicious" – compromised the property rights of the citizenry and breached the social contract.[95] Furthermore, Cato argued, such an arrangement threatened to

---

[92] Meranze, *Laboratories of Virtue*, 146–8. For another rich discussion of key doctrinal differences between Rush and other "liberal" interpreters of Christian doctrine, on the one hand, and stricter, Calvinist and Mosaic interpretations, on the other, see Masur, *Rites of Execution*, 66–70.

[93] Philochorus [Robert Annan], "Observations on Capital Punishment: Being a Reply to an Essay on the Same Subject," *American Museum* 4 (Nov. and Dec. 1788), 553, 558. See also Masur, *Rites of Execution*, 69; Philip E. Mackey, *Hanging in the Balance: The Anti-Capitalist Punishment Movement in New York, 1776 – 1865* (New York: Taylor and Francis, 1982), 155; Friedman, *Crime and Punishment*, 73.

[94] Stephen West, "A sermon, preached in Lenox in the county of Berkshire, and Commonwealth of Massachusetts, December 6, 1787; at the execution of John Bly and Charles Rose, for crimes of burglary" (Hudson [N.Y.]: Printed by Ashbel Stoddard, M,DCC,LXXXVIII [1788]). Also cited in Kealey, "Patterns of Punishment," 183.

[95] "Cato," *Pennsylvania Mercury*, Apr 1, Sept. 6., 1788, in Meranze, *Laboratories of Virtue*, 148.

undermine free citizens' virtuous love of labor; for, when they found "the produce of [their labors] perverted from the purposes for which society was established," they would no longer be motivated to labor. The penitentiary simply preserved "dishonest men" and reproduced the "criminal codes" by which they lived, and, as such was, "destructive of the first principles of civil society." A true republican government, Cato concluded, would not "attempt to reclaim [offenders] at the expense of their fellow citizens"; rather its "duty" was to "remove dishonest men by death, or banishment," and to punish offenders by those means alone.[96]

These arguments about divine authority and the social contract were supplemented by a third set of fundamental objections, emanating from yet another section of the community – the journeymen and laborers from among whose ranks the majority of convicted offenders tended to be drawn. Unlike Cato and Philochorus, these antagonists of the penitentiary made themselves heard – and sometimes, viscerally felt – not from the pulpit or in the press, but in and around the penitentiary itself. As laboring republicans understood very well, the new, penitential mode of legal punishment prescribed by the law of 1790 signaled an important departure not only from established religious and political-economic conventions, but from certain established principles of customary and natural rights: The novelty of the penitential system of punishment lay also in its prescription of a set of practices that, on their face, appeared to constitute a new form of involuntary bondage – and a new kind of bondsman. Under the letter of the law, any person duly convicted of a crime was to be forcibly removed from home and community, held and confined, put to hard labor, and subjected to the general discipline of keepers, whether for a set number of years or for life. Moreover, on Rush's plan, the length of the sentence to be served in the house of repentance would not be fixed by any court of law, but, in each case, decided at the discretion of a nonjudicial body whose task it was to assess the inmate's progress: As Rush himself predicted, "freemen" turned out not to be in favor of "entrusting power to a discretionary court."[97] Although, in 1790, the full extent and workings of this system had still to be elaborated, it was clear that in fusing forced, confined labor with legal punishment, the penal code provided for the creation of a new type of master (the imprisoning state), a new kind of involuntary servant (the duly convicted prisoner), and a new mode of forced servitude (involuntary penitential servitude).

Critically, Rush and other theorists of the penitentiary mode of punishment conceived of the house of repentance precisely at a time in which the various forms of bonded labor in which propertyless white men typically

---

[96] "Cato," *Pennsylvania Mercury*, Sept. 6, 1788.

[97] Rush, "An Enquiry," 12. Rush noted but failed to engage this objection; at this point in the *Enquiry*, he simply amplifies his view that "crime should be punished" in private. As he baldly asserts: "There is no alternative."

engaged, such as indentured servitude and the apprentice system, were in decline. (Indeed, in the 1790s, widespread anxiety among the governing classes about a small but growing mass of "masterless" men very likely accounts for the receptiveness of many merchants, lawyers, and landholders to the idea of confining convicted offenders and subjecting them to masterly discipline). At the same time, laboring men and women also increasingly viewed *forced* servitude as an institution that had no place in a republic of "free" men, and even various forms of *voluntary* servitude, as demeaning. In the course of a Revolution that many had waged in the name of the radical principle of legal and moral equality, laboring republicans had come to see themselves as the free-born bearers of certain rights, both of the "natural and unalienable" kind, to which the Declaration of Independence gave voice, and the common law, customary sort. In this distinctive, deeply rooted, moral universe, the most fundamental of all such rights was the right of free-born men never to be reduced to a condition of slavery – or, indeed, any species of *involuntary* servitude.

An *idée-force*, more than simply an abstract principle, this perceived right to immunity from forced servitude lay at the core of laboring republicans' self-conception in the 1790s, and broadly informed and shaped not only their political and moral outlook but their everyday conduct in the streets and workshops, on farms, and in town squares. Their equally robust conception of customary rights reinforced and elaborated the practical consequences of this basic self-conception: Originating in the collective, historical efforts of the English laboring classes to craft basic protections and reciprocal duties in relation to their masters, and hard-fired in the crucible of the American Revolution, these customary rights pertained to the conditions and relations of their labor, including the intensity and kind of punishment a master might mete out to his journeyman or servant, the hours of work a master might expect his journeyman to work, and the rules of ownership regarding the fruits of their labor.[98] As laboring republicans appear to have understood very well, the legislation of the legal punishment of "confinement to labour" opened up the dual possibility that they – and other free men – might yet be forcibly reduced to a condition of servitude, and that the state, however revolutionary in origin, might engage in precisely the kinds of

[98] By 1800, indentured servitude, artisanal apprenticeship, and the other "halfway houses" between slavery and freedom" in which white men had been engaged through the seventeenth and eighteenth centuries had all but disappeared (See Foner, *The Story of American Freedom*, 19). In the North, women, "free" African Americans, paupers, vagrants, and soldiers and seamen would occupy "half-way houses" of various kinds through the Jacksonian era; free African Americans, in particular, would experience formal restrictions of their rights (most notably, disfranchisement) in the 1820s and 1830s. Meanwhile, in the antebellum South, as Richard B. Morris has observed, "a portion of the laboring population of both races... dwelt in a shadowland, enjoying a status neither fully slave nor entirely free." White debtors and tenants would join seamen, prisoners, free African Americans, and women in the juridical "shadowland." Morris, "The Measure of Bondage," 220; Keyssar, *The Right to Vote*, 53–64.

tyrannical practices against which the Revolution itself had supposedly been fought.[99]

Laboring republicans wasted no time in registering their alarm at this strange new system – within the penitentiary as well as outside it. Inside the penitentiary, the laborers and apprentices who made up the bulk of the prisoners engaged in everyday acts of real and symbolic sabotage, rebellion, and disobedience – and the occasional lawsuit. Prisoners made it clear, through a series of riots, arsons, and multiple, small acts of defiance, that they intended to carry many of the rights of the free-born republican into jail with them. On the first night of the Walnut Street Jail's reopening as a penitentiary (in 1790), the convicts very nearly succeeded in perpetrating a mass escape. Historians of the early republican penitentiary report multiple other instances in which America's first convict-prisoners proper attempted to subject their keepers to the same body of customary rules and formal laws by which master artisans in the free world were bound to abide in their dealings with their journeymen and apprentices. As Larry Smith writes of Charlestown, Massachusetts in the 1810s, "(d)espite reformers' visions of rigid control and lockstep discipline, prisoners took advantage of the imperfect seams in the disciplinary fabric of the institution – and they often relied on official complicity to do so. Like slaves and wage workers, prisoners occasionally resorted to outright rebellion, but they frequently found subtler and more durable means of easing their working conditions, acquiring various

---

[99] Foner notes that after 1776, "there could be no such thing as 'partial liberty.'" Early republicans even came to view indentured servitude (into which servants were supposed to have freely entered), as "contrary to...the idea of liberty this country has so happily established." As Joyce Appleby has observed, even after the Revolution, Americans retained a robust connection to common law, whose "commanding presence" was in tension with the U.S. Constitution. Foner, *The Story of American Freedom*, 19; Joyce Appleby, "The American Heritage: The Heirs and the Disinherited," *Journal of American History* 74:3 (Dec. 1987), 809; Leon Radzinowicz, *A History of English Criminal Law and Its Administration from 1750*, Vol. 5 (London: Stevens, 1948). See Radzinowicz for a rich discussion of popular and parliamentary conflicts over plans to establish the legal punishment of imprisonment in England in the eighteenth century. For an account of English Jacobins' attack on their country's first penitentiaries (in the 1790s), which they claimed were cruel and unconstitutional "Bastilles," see Michael Ignatieff, *A Just Measure of Pain: The Penitentiary in the Industrial Revolution, 1750–1850* (New York: Pantheon, 1978), 114–42, especially 123, 141. The fact that the penitential law effectively projected the creation of a new form of involuntary servitude tended not to trouble the conscience of the governing classes; even people like Rush, who condemned the most extreme species of involuntary servitude (chattel slavery), suffered no moral qualms about forced servitude for convicted offenders. Indeed, according to Adam Jay Hirsch, outspoken abolitionists were often vocal supporters of the penitentiary, and, later, the modern prison, and saw no contradiction in their position. Other supporters of the penitentiary idea denied it imposed a form of servitude on the imprisoned (Hirsch, *The Rise of the Penitentiary*, 75–8). Notably, critics such as Cato and Philochorus did not object to the penitentiary on the grounds that it would inevitably cast freeborn men into a state of involuntary servitude. However, it was precisely the penitentiary system's apparent imposition of a form of servitude that exercised the apprentices, workingmen, and laboring poor, from among whose number the majority of convicted offenders were drawn.

perquisites, and otherwise softening their circumstances."[100] Similarly, at Walnut Street, convicts routinely succeeded in enforcing the customary working man's "rights," including that of "Blue Monday," laying down tools and ceasing work in flagrant violation of the penitentiary's rules. In 1798, the prisoners of Walnut Street set fires, razing some of the workshops to the ground. At Newgate (the New York penitentiary), convicts were equally jealous of their common rights: In 1799, sixty-odd prisoners took their keepers hostage; a year later, they staged another rebellion, and this time, the prison authorities were able to restore some semblance of order only once the military arrived. Although outright rebellions declined at Walnut Street between 1800 and 1815, four large-scale prison riots broke out again between 1817 and 1821. The 1820 rebellion, in which between 400 and 500 prisoners attempted a mass break-out, was quelled only when the authorities brought in the militia, armed citizens, and, in the days after the rebellion, the U.S. Army.[101]

Everywhere, in the early republican period, the prisoners made a habit of "mutiny" (as the early republican press put it), and local authorities found themselves having to repeatedly call out the militia to restore order. Prisoners at Newgate staged serious insurrections in 1818, 1819, 1821, and 1822. Massachusetts' prisoners staged a massive uprising at Charlestown in 1816, and the dormitory wing at the Maryland penitentiary was burnt to the ground, allegedly by inmate arsonists, the following year. The convicts at the new state penitentiary in Auburn, New York, burnt a wing of their institution to the ground in 1820; Virginia's prisoners followed suit in 1823. Far from being matters purely of local or statewide concern, these rebellions were typically reported well afield of the states in which they occurred; and, just as, in the antebellum South, a slave uprising on one plantation had the potential to ignite slave rebellions elsewhere, one penitentiary riot sometimes triggered demonstrations at other institutions: On one such occasion in 1823, Newgate convicts rose up in rebellion upon receiving news of the prisoners' arson of the Virginia penitentiary. The possibility that free citizens would join the prisoners in rebellion was also an ever present danger: Administrators, fully conscious of the penitentiary's proximity to the free citizenry, constantly worried that rebellious prisoners would receive aid from their friends and family on the outside.[102]

---

[100] Larry Goldsmith, "'To Profit by His Skill and Traffic in His Crime': Prison Labor in Early Massachusetts," *Labor History 40* (Nov. 1999), 439.

[101] "Mutiny in the State Prison of Philadelphia," *New – York Commercial Advertiser*, XXIII:60 (Mar. 29, 1820), 2; Meranze, *Laboratories of Virtue*, 217–19.

[102] Such concerns were not misplaced: In the North, since the pre-Revolutionary era, rioting had taken various forms and had been a semi-legitimate form of protest and expression; it continued to enjoy much the same status in the early republican period. Gary Nash notes that in the late nineteenth century, crowds were the "watchdogs" of urban politics; they "voted with their fists" and acted to counterbalance wealthy office-holders. Unlike the ruling élites of the nineteenth century, those of the eighteenth considered their actions to have a certain kind of legitimacy. Gary Nash, *The Urban Crucible: Social Change, Political Consciousness, and the Origins of the American Revolution* (Cambridge, Massachusetts: Harvard

When early republican prisoners were not rioting, escaping, or committing arson, they were pressing their claims in other ways. At Walnut Street, as Meranze notes, the prisoners simply "maintained the practices of the laboring poor." Prisoners intentionally worked slowly and poorly, apparently impervious of the inspectors' attempts to raise quality and production levels.[103] During the workweek at Newgate, convicts quite regularly sabotaged machinery and materials, refused to labor, staged slow-downs, and, upon occasion, napped at their worktables. So too did various aspects of laboring culture flourish inside the penitentiary, despite the existence of formal rules to the contrary. On Sundays, rather than reflecting upon and repenting their sinful pasts, convicts sang bawdy songs, gambled, and wrestled with one another around the penitentiary yard. Some prisoners also put workshop tools and materials to various nefarious uses, including the production of counterfeit coins and bank bills, and duplicates of keys. In one, particularly sensational case (which was reported by the Boston Prison Discipline Society in 1826), a convicted master counterfeiter incarcerated in an unnamed penitentiary was happily plying his illegal trade with the outside world: Assigned to the penitentiary's whitesmith shop, he was soon printing counterfeit bills, which he delivered to customers via the workshop window (quite conveniently, the window opened directly onto the street below).[104]

Far from imposing silence, solitude, and labor on prisoners, then, the republican penitentiary gestated unruliness, petty vice, crime, and, not uncommonly, outright rebellion. Attempts on the part of the prison authorities to crack down on these and other practices frequently met with acts of open defiance, or were gradually neutralized by more clandestine forms of refusal.[105] Prisoners insisted on shaping the way all manner of things were done in the penitentiary. At Newgate (where a prisoner was ten times more

University Press, 1979), 36, 133–5. Acquiescence was replaced by suppression in the course of the nineteenth century. See also Iver Bernstein's nuanced discussion of the changes in the social meaning and practical policing of popular action in New York City between 1820 and the 1863 draft riot. Iver Bernstein, *The New York City Draft Riots: Their Significance for American Society and Politics in the Age of the Civil War* (New York: Oxford University Press, 1990). On the rebellions, see "Mutiny at the State Prison," *The Centinel of Freedom*, XXII: 39 (June 9, 1818), 3; Meranze, *Laboratories of Virtue*, 211, 218–19, 247; Lewis, *From Newgate to Dannemora*, 33–7, 50; Lewis Edward Lawes, *Twenty Thousand Years in Sing Sing* (New York: Ray Long and Richard R. Smith, 1932), 71; Negley K. Teeters, *The Cradle of the Penitentiary: Walnut Street Jail at Philadelphia, 1773–1835* (Philadelphia: Temple University Press, 1955), 86, 100; Mark Colvin, *Penitentiaries, Reformatories, and Chain Gangs: Social Theory and the History of Punishment in Nineteenth-Century America* (New York: St. Martin's Press, 1997), 61, 68. Meranze notes that when reformers announced plans to remake Walnut Street as a penitentiary in 1790, the jail keeper, some state justices, and the prisoners actively attempted to defeat the reforms: "(d)espite their legal authority, the actual power of the inspectors was always contested." Meranze, *Laboratories of Virtue*, 189.

[103] Meranze, *Laboratories of Virtue*, 190, 227, 247.

[104] Boston Prison Discipline Society, First Annual Report (1826), 46.

[105] Lewis, *From Newgate to Dannemora*, 40, 42, 49; Myra Glenn, *Campaigns Against Corporal Punishment: Prisoners, Sailors, Children, and Women in Antebellum America* (Albany, NY: State University of New York Press, 1984), 46. Rothman notes that penitentiary laborers, on the

likely to be released from the penitentiary by a Governor's pardon than by expiration of sentence), for example, the "semiannual pardoning season" engendered in the convicts a strong sense of entitlement and the belief that they possessed certain enforceable rights *viz.* the imprisoning authorities.[106] Although the pardoning season had no force of law and the granting of pardon resembled a privilege more than a right, convicts nonetheless came to see regular pardoning as a customary right. As New York's prison commissioners lamented, not only were "state-prison solicitors and pardon-brokers" an important presence in life at Newgate, but it had become "a kind of common understanding that every prisoner on serving out half his time is, in some certain sense, entitled to a pardon."[107] Convicts committed sabotage and rioted whenever they felt that the customary schedule of pardons had been disrupted. Likewise, when guards and civilian foremen attempted to flog them, in the early 1820s, prisoners often fiercely resisted. Indeed, by all accounts, prisoners actively repelled authorities' sporadic attempts to dish out certain kinds of corporal punishment – particularly the form that everywhere symbolized slavery: the lash. In 1823, at Charlestown, Massachusetts, a mass of tool-wielding convicts prevented guards from flogging three of their fellow prisoners; similar incidents were recorded at Auburn penitentiary in New York.[108] Insisting that they possessed certain rights that the state was bound to recognize, prisoners in some institutions also succeeded in establishing punishment "courts," in which convicts and guards confronted one another in a parajudicial setting and argued their cases before prison inspectors who played the role of judge.[109]

By all accounts, three decades into the penitential experiment, prisoners were as defiant and insistent about their rights as when inmates of the

whole, "worked slowly and sloppily, shirking whatever tasks they could." Rothman, *Discovery of the Asylum*, 93.

[106] New York, Massachusetts, and Pennsylvania all made extensive use of the pardon in the 1790s and 1800s. At Walnut Street, seventy-three percent of prisoners were released by pardon between 1791 and 1809; forty-three between 1810 and 1819; and forty percent between 1820 and 1830. Pardons declined dramatically after 1830 (Teeters, *The Cradle of the Penitentiary*, 135). New York followed a similar pattern through to 1825, with more than ninety percent of prisoners released on pardon between 1820 and 1825. Pardoning was, however, in decline in the mid-1820s, and was radically reduced after 1830. Lewis, *From Newgate to Dannemora*, 41–5. See also, Roger Panetta, "Up the River: A History of Sing Sing in the Nineteenth Century," (Ph.D. diss., City University of New York, 1999), 108–9.

[107] Report of the New York State Prison Commissioners, excerpted in "Penitentiary System," *The Watch-Tower*, XI:569 (Feb. 21, 1825). Eugene Genovese notes a similar dynamic at work on the antebellum slave plantation: A particular custom or privilege, lacking the force of law, often became, in the eyes of the slaves, a customary right: "woe to the master or overseer who summarily withdrew the 'privilege.'" Genovese, *Roll Jordan, Roll: The World the Slaves Made* (New York: Vintage, 1976), 30–1.

[108] Glenn, *Campaigns Against Corporal Punishment*, 46; Lewis, *From Newgate to Dannemora*, 40, 42, 49; Rothman, *Discovery of the Asylum*, 93.

[109] Lewis, *From Newgate to Dannemora*, 93. Convicts at both Newgate and Auburn penitentiaries were authorized to leave the prison if accompanied by a guard. Lewis, *From Newgate to Dannemora*, 59.

renovated Walnut Streeet penitentiary house had rioted in 1790. Certain sections of the free citizenry, for their part, were no less assertive in regard to their contact with prisoners. Just as portions of the free citizenry had shown little interest in observing the wheelbarrow law's prohibition upon interaction with the convict laborers, many of the families and friends of America's first penitentiary inmates were ill-disposed toward the strange new laws that provided for the sequestration of their loved ones for a period of several years or more. Like many of the convicts, prisoners' families and friends developed and acted upon certain expectations about how the penitentiary authorities ought to treat both the prisoners and themselves. Above all, family and friends asserted a right of access to the prisoners, which ran directly contrary to the penitentiary's foundational principle of segregating convicted offenders away from the community. Their efforts made the penitentiary a notoriously porous institution, and a far cry from the secluded "house of horror" that Rush had imagined. A voluminous traffic in goods, people, money, and news flowed through the penitentiary's gates on a daily basis. For anything from a few pennies to one shilling, just about anybody could purchase a concession pass and wander about the penitentiary at will; contractors, legal hucksters, friends, and family congregated around the prisons, quite openly conveying letters, snuff, food, tools, money, knives, and rum to prisoners. The illegal practice of open visitation soon became a semi-legitimate custom and, by the 1810s, convicts and their families and friends were prepared to enforce in a court of law what they took to be their common right of access to the prison and to prisoners. The new agent (warden) at Newgate learned this lesson first-hand when he naïvely announced the end of public visitation at the penitentiary: When visitors threatened lawsuits, the agent was compelled to abandon his efforts.[110] Some years later, New York's penitentiary commissioners complained that visiting Newgate penitentiary "on the payment of a shilling has been treated as a right, and submitted to as such by the inspectors, under the threat of a suit."[111]

Free laborers also brought a variety of pressures to bear on the penitentiary authorities between 1799 and 1825. Occasionally, free laborers worked alongside or in close proximity to prisoners; in New York, in the early 1820s, for example, convicts and free laborers worked on the construction site of the new wing of the state penitentiary at Auburn, the Great Western Canal, and the Rochester aqueduct.[112] These encounters sometimes engendered the forging of a bond of solidarity between free and penal labor and occasionally pitched both against the prison authorities. At Auburn, in 1821, for

---

[110] Lewis, *From Newgate to Dannemora*, 49–50.

[111] Report of the New York State Prison Commissioners, excerpted in "Penitentiary System," *The Watch-Tower*, XI:569 (Feb. 21, 1825).

[112] William Brittin, former agent of Auburn prison, was widely reported to have purchased the labor of 150 prisoners from Auburn and New York penitentiaries, and put them to work on the canal in 1821. *The Evening Post*, 5950 (July 19, 1821), 2; *Independent Chronicle and Boston Patriot*, LIV:4203 (Aug. 4, 1821), 1; *The Evening Post*, 5982 (Aug. 25, 1821), 2.

example, free laborers undertook to protect a handful of convict laborers from a punitive whipping; when a free artisan attempted to do the guards' job for them and flog the prisoners in question, a small army of free laborers deployed a much older kind of punishment against the whip-happy artisan: They tarred and feathered him, before, quite literally, riding him through town on a rail. Notably, New York and most other states subsequently abandoned the practice of putting free workers and penal laborers to work together: In the late 1820s, the new prison at Ossining (Sing Sing) would be built entirely by convict laborers. (As we shall see in Chapter III, the practice of putting convict and free labor to work side-by-side would resurface in New York and elsewhere after the Civil War, under the contract prison labor system; by that time, however, whatever solidarity may have existed between incarcerated laborers and free workers in the 1810s and 1820s would have long-since collapsed).[113]

The task of translating the word of law into actual disciplinary practice, then, was by no means an easy one. Legislatures and penal reformers could not simply conjure into existence the orderly penitentiaries they desired, nor wave a legislative wand and turn unruly inmates into well-disciplined subjects. As the disorders of the penitentiary wore on, in the 1810s, it became increasingly clear that for the penitentiary to work as its founders had prescribed, state authorities would have to actively confront, struggle with, and somehow overcome the deeply rooted practices and moral culture of convicts and convicts' friends, families, and workmates. Nor was that all: They would also have to create and discipline the new class of overseers, keepers, and turnkeys, whose legislated task it was to enforce the rules of penitential life. These supposed agents of discipline had quickly proven to be, if not as openly rebellious as the convicts, certainly as stubbornly resistant to some of the very rules they were supposed to be enforcing. Through much of the early republican era, turnkeys and keepers (and sometimes even the principal keeper) bucked or simply ignored the rules and laws of the penitentiary. In the early 1790s, when Rush and other reformers attempted to reinvent the Walnut Street Jail as a house of repentance, they met with stiff resistance from the jail's old principal keeper, who considered the penitential concept simply unworkable – and then proceeded to make it so.[114] Twenty years later, the inspectors of Walnut Street still complained of keepers who brazenly traded all manner of contraband with the prisoners. In 1820, Walnut Street's Board of Inspectors criticized guards for "laxity of discipline" and their "considerable collusion" with convicts; a similar situation was to be found at the Auburn penitentiary in New York in the early 1820s.[115] That the keepers wielded less than perfect power at the Newgate penitentiary was confirmed by the prison inspector's creation of

---

[113] Lewis, *From Newgate to Dannemora*, 60–1. However, free workers in New York and elsewhere would once again labor alongside prisoners, after the Civil War and through the 1870s. See later in this book, Chapter IV.

[114] Meranze, *Laboratories of Virtue*, 189.

[115] Teeters, *The Cradle of the Penitentiary*, 119; Meranze, *Laboratories of Virtue*, 222.

an impromptu prison "court," in which keepers and prisoners confronted one another and argued the case for and against the meting out of punishment for an alleged infraction of the rules. (These "trials" proceeded "much like the proceedings in a small legal case," the state prison commissioners lamented).[116]

As the trouble-torn history of the country's first penitentiaries suggests, a deep fissure divided the workaday reality of the penitentiary and the abstract theory of penitential penology. Efforts to carry the principles of Rush's penitentiary house into practice were constantly frustrated not only by convicts and their communities, but the guards, keepers, and, in some instances, the wardens. The state failed to establish more than a modicum of mastery over either its wards or its own agents of discipline. For the duration of its existence, the penitentiary house remained an unstable, crisis-prone institution – one that resembled the orderly repentance house of Benjamin Rush's fertile imagination in name more than in fact. In part, the state's lack of mastery was attributable to the impoverished organizational and technical means available to it. But to say that the unruly penitentiary was solely the result of inadequate resources or "ineffective administration" (as most historians have argued) is to describe more than explain the penitentiary's disorders;[117] what is critical to grasp is that the administration of the penitentiary was, in large part, "ineffective" because convicts, families, friends, workmates, the keepers, and even some of the higher ranking administrators to whom lawmakers entrusted the running of the penitential system were able to, and did in fact, render it so. In the early republic, the novel fantasy of penitential servitude projected by the new penal laws proved no match for laboring republicans' still robust and deeply rooted sense of themselves as freemen – nor for their individual and collective willingness to defend that hard-won freedom, whenever and wherever they sensed it was under attack.

As convicts rioted and the disorders of the penitentiary proliferated, in the late 1810s, the penitential mode of legal punishment entered a full-scale crisis of legitimacy. The growing perception that the penitentiaries were ruining rather than reforming men, and exacerbating rather than alleviating social disorder, was reinforced by the widespread view that crimes (particularly larceny and robbery) were on the increase. Between 1816 and 1820, lawmakers and the press became convinced that a great wave of murder, forgery, rape, and theft was breaking across the country, and that this wave was of a magnitude thitherto found only in the corrupt and corrupting

---

[116] Report of the New York State Prison Commissioners, excerpted in "Penitentiary System," *The Watch-Tower* XI:569 (Feb. 21, 1825). See also, Lewis, *From Newgate to Dannemora*, 93.

[117] W. David Lewis argues that "Newgate's disciplinary short-comings" were the result of "ineffective administration." Lewis, *From Newgate to Dannemora*, 48. However, he skirts the question of why it was that prison administration was so "ineffective." As Lewis's own evidence strongly suggests, the regime of imprisonment for which administrators and reformers hoped ran up against well-grounded opposition from convicts, convicts' families and friends, guards, and laborers, and appears not to have enjoyed a critical minimum of popular legitimacy.

cities of Europe.[118] Although it is difficult to know with any degree of accuracy whether these crimes were, in fact, on the rise in these years, it is clear that newspapers, legislators, merchants, and others of the governing classes were all but convinced that the country as whole was in the grips of a thorough-going breakdown of public order: In the words of one commentator, "(t)he increase of crimes of every description . . . extends throughout our land."[119] Newspapers in a number of Northeastern and Mid-Atlantic states began printing regular columns (typically under the title, "Increase in Crimes") in which various crimes against persons and property were reported in extended detail.[120]

Crucially, these reports often traced the supposed increase in robberies and murders to the disorderly, overcrowded penitentiaries, frequently ascribing crimes to former prisoners, even when there was no evidence that ex-prisoners were involved.[121] Commentators repeatedly argued that the penitentiary was gestating rather than extinguishing criminal conduct. Throughout the states, the complaint was heard that the penitentiary was simply congregating thieves and other villains together in order to better instruct them in the "science of robbery": These students of crime were then released back into the community, far more skilled in their craft than before they entered the penitentiary.[122] This view was reinforced by reports from grand juries and the increasingly besieged prison authorities. In New York, in 1816, the state penitentiary inspectors declared that pardons had become routine and "indispensable" to the government of the penitentiary, and that this practice was defeating the point of incarcerating convicted offenders. Pardoning rates of between forty and fifty percent meant that many convicts were not finishing their sentences but being let loose on the streets, where, according to the inspectors, they returned to their former criminal practices.[123] In Philadelphia, grand juries reported that the state's penitentiary system was an important factor in a recent public health crisis (as a source of disease) and that it had played a role in priming a large crowd of citizens to run riot at a balloon ascent in the Vauxhall Gardens in

---

[118] See, for example, "Increase of Crimes," *The Yankee*, V:47 (Nov. 15, 1816); "Increase of Crimes," *Columbian Centinel*, 3407 (Nov. 30, 1816), 2.

[119] These typically reported recent criminal trials; some also noted legislative action concerning matters of crime and punishment. See for example, "Increase of Crimes," *The Yankee*, V:47 (Nov. 15, 1816); "Increase of Crimes," *Columbian Centinel*, 3407 (Nov. 30, 1816), 2; "Increase of Crimes," *Columbian Centinel*, 3379 (Aug. 24, 1816), 2; *The New-York Columbian*, VIII:2340 (Sep. 12, 1817), 2; "Increase of Crimes," *Columbian Centinel*, 3502 (Oct. 29, 1817), 2; "Increase of Crimes," *Rhode-Island American, and General Advertiser*, X: 7 (Oct. 31, 1817), 1; "From the Cooperstown Federalist of Jun. 20" *Connecticut Journal*, L:2540 (July 2, 1816), 3; "Increase of Crimes," *Columbian Centinel*, 3379 (Aug. 24, 1816), 2.

[120] "Increase of Crimes," *The Yankee*, V:47 (Nov. 15, 1816); "Increase of Crimes," *Columbian Centinel*, 3407 (Nov. 30, 1816), 2; "Increase of Crimes," *Columbian Centinel*, 3379 (Aug. 24, 1816), 2.

[121] *New England Palladium & Commercial Advertiser*, XLV:41 (Nov. 21, 1817), 2; "Increase of Crimes," *The Farmers' Cabinet*, XVI:36 (May 30, 1818), 2.

[122] "Increase of Crimes," *The Providence Gazette*, LIII:2793, (Jul. 5, 1817).

[123] "Increase of Crimes," *The Farmers' Cabinet*, XV:12 (Dec. 14, 1816), 2.

1819:[124] as the "receptacle for the crimes and vices of the whole state," one grand jury reported, the state penitentiary was responsible for gathering together and then releasing onto the streets of the city the most "dangerous persons" from across the state. Such persons, the jury strongly implied, bore considerable responsibility for the Vauxhall riot.[125]

As criticism of the penitentiary escalated in the late 1810s, longstanding critics of the house of repentance once again called for the abolition of that institution, arguing that it was not only a failed experiment, but an actively destructive and vicious one, as well. Old arguments against the penitentiary system of punishment resurfaced in the press and the legislative assemblies. "Cato"'s original objection that penitential punishment necessitated a tax to which the citizenry had not consented was now fortified with concrete examples of ill-spent tax revenue and the increasingly heavy fiscal burden that these disorderly institutions were placing on the imprisoning state. Once again, strict Calvinist critics called for a return to the old Biblical punishments of banishment, execution, and public chastisement. The legislatures of New York, Pennsylvania, New Hampshire, and several other states with penitentiaries revisited old debates about the efficacy and fairness of the penitential mode of punishment.[126] By the end of 1816, governors and lawmakers were stressing the urgent need for legislative relief: The Governor of New York (Daniel D. Tompkins) called on the state legislature to take action regarding what most legislators had come to see as the mutually imbricated problems of "the rapid increase in crimes, and the crowded condition of the State prison."[127]

By 1818, it was palpably evident that, throughout the states, the penitential mode of punishment was caught up in a crisis of legitimacy, equal in magnitude to that which had engulfed the wheelbarrow and other public labor schemes in the 1780s. Penitentiary inspectors and legislators in many states now debated abolishing the penitential mode of punishment altogether. A special legislative committee in Maryland recommended abandoning the penitentiary, on the grounds that it was both a fiscal and a disciplinary failure.[128] In New York, the state penitentiary inspectors recommended the

---

[124] According to the Philadelphia press, violence broke out at a balloon ascent in the gardens, after a guard struck a boy who was climbing the garden's fence (so as to avoid having to pay the $1 entry fee): As rumors spread that the boy had been killed, members of the thirty-thousand-strong crowd smashed street lamps and houses, tore down the garden fence, and set the temple alight. The riot persuaded Philadelphia's merchants, lawmakers, and jurists that the city was in the grips of a full-scale crisis of public morality. Meranze, *Laboratories of Virtue*, 230–3.

[125] Meranze, *Laboratories of Virtue*, 244.

[126] Not only did Walnut Street's chronic disciplinary problems spill into the political sphere, but the penitentiary became a central referent in struggles between state authorities and county officials over matters of fiscal and administrative responsibility. Teeters, *The Cradle of the Penitentiary*, 86–100, especially 90; Colvin, *Penitentiaries, Reformatories, and Chain Gangs*, 69.

[127] "Increase of Crimes," *The Yankee*, V:47 (Nov. 15, 1816).

[128] Shugg, *A Monument to Good Intentions*, 43, fn 2.

establishment of either a federally administered penal colony in the Pacific Northwest or a state penal colony in an area of western New York populated mostly by Native Americans.[129] Other proposals included demolishing the penitentiaries outright and putting convicts back to hard public labor – this time building roads to and beyond the western frontier. In 1818, following yet another riot at Newgate, a New York legislative committee recommended that ex-prisoners simply be taken to the state line and banished.[130] Finally, the new governor of that state, DeWitt Clinton, implored the legislature to act: Communing in large rooms, resistant to all forms of discipline, Clinton exclaimed, prisoners were not only "exempt from [the] grievous privation and severe labor" that was their legal and moral due, but had enrolled in a "school of turpitude" that graduated them back into society "with corrupt principles, . . . depraved feelings, . . . and every disposition to renew their crimes."[131] The ambitious republican experiment of the penitential incarceration of convicts was a "failure," he concluded: A new system of legal punishment was urgently required.

[129] "Increase of Crimes," *The Farmers' Cabinet* XV:12 (Dec. 14, 1816), 2.
[130] Lewis, *From Newgate to Dannemora*, 61–4.
[131] De Witt Clinton, address to the legislature, 1818, in *Niles' Weekly Register*, Vol. 15, 1818, 59.

2

Due Convictions: Contractual Penal Servitude and Its Discontents, 1818–1865

You laggards there on guard! look to your arms!
In at the conquer'd doors they crowd! I am possess'd!
Embody all presences outlaw'd or suffering,
See myself in prison shaped like another man,
And feel the dull unintermitted pain.
For me the keepers of convicts shoulder their carbines and keep watch,
It is I let out in the morning and barr'd at night.

Walt Whitman, "Song of Myself," Leaves of Grass (1855)[1]

New York, with its growing and infamously ungovernable convict population, was the first state to confront the escalating crisis of the penitential system of punishment. In the course of the 1820s, New York lawmakers, jurists, and keepers would lay the foundation both of a novel kind of penal institution and a new mode of legal punishment: that of contractual penal servitude. By a process of trial and improvisation, they would gradually weave together four distinctive lines of force – separation and concentration; hard productive labor; harsh corporeal chastisements; and the abridgement of the convicted offender's natural rights, freedoms, and common law liberties – to produce a powerful new mode of legal punishment. After 1830, almost every Northern (and some Southern) states would adopt this system, and it would go on, in the 1860s, to impress its mark upon the Constitution of the United States. Born out of the rolling series of crises that had broken over the penitentiary system in the 1810s, contractual penal servitude was at once a response to the sources of instability within and around the penitential system, a refutation of certain foundational principles of early republican penology, and the means by which the formal, republican, penalty of "confinement to hard labor" would be realized in practice.

In the pages to follow, I argue that, contrary to the conventional scholarly view that the activity of labor was of negligible significance to the nineteenth-century "American System" of imprisonment,[2] forced, hard, productive labor was of foundational importance to the penal order that the states erected on the ruins of the old penitential mode of punishment. The contract prison labor system, under which the state sold the labor power

[1] Walt Whitman, "Song of Myself," verse 37, lines 1–7, Leaves of Grass (East Rutherford, N.J.: Penguin Classics, 1986 [1855]).
[2] "Introduction: The Grounds of Legal Punishment" p. 8, earlier.

53

of convicts to private interests, quickly became the fiscal and disciplinary foundation of the new system at Auburn; it subsequently proved decisive in the decision of most Northern (and some Southern) states to replace their old penitentiary systems, not with the "isolation" prison system that Pennsylvania was refining at the Eastern Penitentiary, but with New York's "Auburn plan." Although the genteel theorists and reformers associated with the leading prison reform society of the day (the Boston Prison Discipline Society [BPDS]) initially tended to disapprove of prison labor contracting; in the age of Jackson, it, rather than they, proved far more influential over the everyday life, administrative structures, and official doctrines of the state penal systems. Moreover, as state after state adopted the Auburn system, the practice of selling the labor of convicts to private enterprise gradually became widely and deeply entrenched in penal ideology; even the once reluctant leadership of the BPDS came to view it as an essential part of the new penal order. The present chapter fleshes out the making of the new mode of punishment and explains the foundational role that the activity of hard, productive labor came to play in it. As we shall see, the contract labor system would help deliver the penal arm of state government from the turbulence of the previous decades. But as it did so, it would quietly incubate a fresh series of crises within and about the sphere of legal punishment.

* * * * *

In the late 1810s, lawmakers from Virginia and Maryland to Massachusetts and Vermont earnestly debated banishment and penal colonization as possible alternatives to the penitential mode of punishment. However, they eventually rejected these on the grounds that such schemes were impractical and potentially injurious of interstate relations and that state government lacked the necessary capacity to effectively administer them. Instead, beginning in 1818, New York legislators prescribed a series of reforms that, while retaining the general principle of detention and sequestration upon which the penitential system had been based, also eliminated the penitentiary's avowedly moral objectives (that is, to compel convicts to repent their sins) in favor of more technical, administrative sets of objectives: Most important among these were the enforcement of order within the penitentiaries, making the penitentiaries financially self-sufficient, and ensuring, in the words of De Witt Clinton, that the "dangerous spirit" of the prisoners would be "crushed."[3]

Beginning in 1819, the legislature embarked on an intensive three-year period of penal reform. Lawmakers proceeded on many fronts at once. In 1819, the legislature repealed early republican laws that banned the use of stocks, flogging, and irons in the penitentiary, and directed that the principal keeper could whip male convicts or throw them into the stocks or irons, provided that the penitentiary inspectors were present (the law

---

[3] De Witt Clinton, *Speech of Governor Clinton to the Legislature of the State of New York on the Sixth Day of January, 1819* (New York: Register Office, 1819), 15.

prohibited the whipping of female convicts).[4] Meanwhile, largely in an effort to break prisoners' capacity for rebellion, the legislature mandated the classification and separation of particularly rebellious and "hardened" prisoners from the rest of the prison population.[5] Seeking to relieve the congestion of the penitentiaries (which, as we have seen, many observers considered to be an important cause of both intramural and civil disorder), the legislature provided in 1820 that a suitable location for a new state prison be found in Westchester county. That law also included provisions aimed at reining in the spiraling costs of maintaining the penitentiaries: The inspectors were instructed to find a site in or near a marble quarry in which the prisoners might be profitably put to work; in a similar vein, the law provided that the Auburn prison be leased out to private manufacturing interests.[6] The 1819 flogging law was extended in 1821, when the legislature granted every keeper and turnkey (not just the principal keeper) the authority to mete out a summary whipping of any convict.[7] Finally, in 1821, representatives at the state constitutional convention laid the groundwork for banishing felonious convicts from the body politic (while, at the same time, eliminating the property requirement for white men): The constitution now gave permission to the legislature to exclude "from the right of suffrage persons . . . convicted of infamous crimes."[8]

These legislative reforms sparked a series of radical innovations within the penitentiaries themselves. As W. David Lewis has noted, although the construction of Auburn's famous cellhouse was not explicitly mandated by law, its origins nonetheless lay "at least in part" in the 1819 classification and segregation law that mandated the separation of "dangerous" convicts from the rest of the prison population.[9] Following the passage of that law, the agent at Auburn (a former British military officer, by the name of William Brittin), set his prisoners to work building a cellhouse in which he could securely separate "hardened" prisoners from other prisoners, as provided by the 1819 law.[10] Built out of stone, the new cellhouse consisted of an

---

[4] W. David Lewis, *From Newgate to Dannemora: The Rise of the Penitentiary in New York, 1796–1848* (Ithaca, NY: Cornell University Press, 1965), 63; Laws of the State of New York, 42nd Session (1819), 87. In *Lewis, From Newgate to Dannemora,* 95.

[5] Lewis, *From Newgate to Dannemora,* 67.

[6] Glen A. Gildemeister, "Prison Labor and Convict Competition with Free Workers in Industrializing America, 1840–1890" (Ph.D. diss., Northern Illinois Press, 1977/New York: Garland, 1987), 10.

[7] *Journal of the Assembly of the State of New York,* 44th Session (1820–1821), 904, in Lewis, *From Newgate to Dannemora,* 93.

[8] "New York State Constitution, 1821," in Alexander Keyssar, *The Right to Vote: The Contested History of Democracy in the United States* (New York: Basic, 2000), Appendix, Table A7 (no page number).

[9] Lewis, *From Newgate to Dannemora,* 67.

[10] Lewis, *From Newgate to Dannemora,* 66–70. Lewis notes that there is no evidence that Brittin, or any of the other agents, keepers, and inspectors responsible for developing Auburn's cell-based mode of punishment in the 1820s, drew on European models or sought out the advice of European penologists. Brittin, Cray, Lynds, and Hopkins were critical of penal theorizing and championed what they took to be a practical, "common-sense" approach to

inner building containing five tiers of some six hundred cells (each cell measuring seven feet long, three and one-half feet wide, and seven feet high) placed back to back, and an outer "shell" building that was, itself, contained within the high walls of the prison compound. A "prison within a prison," as Lewis has aptly described it, this new architectural form promised to solve many problems at once: In theory, the thick walls separating the cells would frustrate prisoner communication, hold the convicts securely, and substitute the inanimate, incorruptible heft of stone and iron for the all too human, and demonstrably corruptible, keepers and guards.[11]

When the cellhouse was completed in 1821 (following a setback caused by an arson attack by some of the convicts), the authorities undertook two widely publicized experiments in cellular incarceration: The first consisted of the perpetual isolation of each of the penitentiary's eighty-odd oldest and most "hardened" convicts in a cell for the duration of his sentence. In a reversal of the early republican insistence on putting convicts to penitential "hard labor," these prisoners were to be neither given nor *allowed* any work whatsoever, and were also to be prevented from sleeping, lying down, or doing anything besides sitting or standing in their cells during the day: The prisoner would be forced to be idle.[12] The rationale for this treatment was that the cell's fusion of enforced idleness and isolation would conduce the prisoner to the hard, spiritual labor of reflection, repentance, and reform. As one theorist of this perpetual isolation method would later explain: "There is no punishment which affects the mind so powerfully, as solitary confinement; none so much dreaded even by the most hardened. The offender is compelled to think"; isolation and enforced inactivity would overcome the efforts of the "guilty mind . . . to escape from reflection," bring prisoners "to a proper sense of their guilt," and, by so doing, lead the prisoner "to seek relief, where alone it can be found, in the consolations of religion."[13]

The second experiment undertaken at Auburn, upon completion of the cellhouse, consisted of cellular incarceration of the remainder of the convicts by night and their impressment into silent, congregate labor in the penitentiary's workshops by day. Consistent with the 1819 classification law, these convicts were to be divided into two classes, according to their "dangerousness"; the least dangerous class was to be put to congregate labor on a daily basis, while the agent would determine how much time members of the intermediary class would have out of the cells. Drawing directly on a proposal developed by the Governor of New York, De Witt Clinton, in 1818, the congregate labor experiment aimed not only to put a halt to prisoner communication (and hence, it was hoped, prison conspiracies), but

legal punishment, in which the principal aim was to render prison populations governable, and the principal means was physical coercion.
[11] Lewis, *From Newgate to Dannemora*, 67.   [12] Lewis, *From Newgate to Dannemora*, 68.
[13] "Report of the Commissioners to Superintend the Erection of the Eastern Penitentiary, Philadelphia, on the Penal Code (1828)," 3 (reprinted in *The Register of Pennsylvania* [1828–1831] 1:17 [Apr. 26, 1828], 260).

also to relieve the state treasury of the spiraling costs both of maintaining the penitentiary and suppressing rebellions. With convicts put to hard, silent labor by day and secured in cellular isolation by night, Clinton had reasoned, "punishment would be appalling, . . . cleanliness, order and regularity would predominate, . . . no conspiracies could be formed, no riots or insurrections would occur, and no military guard would be required."[14]

By its own lights, and certainly by any measure of common humanity, the perpetual isolation experiment was an abject failure: Within one year, many of the men in continuous solitary confinement had fallen desperately ill (often, with consumption) or lost their sanity; several died and at least three inflicted serious injuries upon themselves in apparent attempts at suicide. Few exhibited signs of the spiritual transformation that isolation in the cells was supposed to have induced.[15] The prisoners' condition was so dismal and public outrage so palpable, that in 1823, the newly elected Governor, Robert Yates, pardoned almost all the survivors.[16] The second experiment, conversely, was widely adjudicated as having "worked": the convicts who were isolated by night and put to congregate labor by day neither became as ill as their unlucky counterparts in the perpetual isolation wing, nor behaved as willfully as before the beginning of the experiment.[17] Moreover, those who labored under lease in the tool manufacturing business also demonstrated that, unlike either its penitential predecessor or the perpetual isolation plan, the new system could, potentially, significantly defray the operating expenses of the prison. Persuaded that this "congregate" experiment had been a great success, New York prison authorities now set about putting the entire prison system on what would come to be known, around the United States and in Europe, as the "Auburn plan" or "congregate system" of imprisonment. Beginning in 1825, the state pursued the construction of a second such prison (this time in one of the marble quarries the prison commissioners had located in Westchester county), and strengthened the legislation that directed prison agents to put the prisoners to productive labor. The new statute called upon prison agents, both at Auburn and in the future prison in Westchester, "to cause all the expense . . . of any kind, to be supported wholly, or as nearly as shall be practicable, by the labor of the prisoners." Shortly thereafter, Auburn's agent (Elam Lynds) and the state prison inspectors began looking for private contractors interested in paying the state for the labor of the prisoners and setting up shop in the state prison.[18]

---

[14] De Witt Clinton, *Speech of Governor Clinton* (1819), 15. Clinton reiterated the theme of saving the militia from costly prison duty in 1820. *Niles' Weekly Register*, 19:12 (Nov. 18, 1820), 182.

[15] Lewis, *From Newgate to Dannemora*, 69. Similar isolation experiments undertaken around the same time in Maine, New Jersey, and Virginia, on a smaller scale, met with much the same outcome. See, Anon., "The Penal Code," *The Register of Pennsylvania*, 1:17 (Apr. 26, 1828), 260.

[16] Lewis, *From Newgate to Dannemora*, 69.   [17] Lewis, *From Newgate to Dannemora*, 81–85.

[18] Journal of the Assembly of the State of New York , 48th session (1825), Appendix C, 30. Quoted in W. David Lewis, *From Newgate to Dannemora*, 99.

Contrary to the commonplace view that labor was an insignificant element of the "Auburn system" of imprisonment,[19] this activity and the revenues it generated quite rapidly became indispensable to the financial and disciplinary order of Auburn prison and the dozens of other prisons that would eventually adopt the plan. As early as the mid-1830s, it had also accrued critical ideological importance, even among many of the well-heeled prison reformers who had initially objected to the practice (on the grounds that contractors' "private interests" were not necessarily the same as those of the state and that the presence of private persons in the prison punctured the line of authority between state agents and state prisoners). The efforts of Elam Lynds and the prison inspectors to comply with the law requiring the prison to be self-supporting, in 1825, set in motion the creation and refinement of an elaborate contract prison labor system which, in its turn, would become the foundation of a distinctive new mode of legal punishment: that of contractual penal servitude.

America's nineteenth-century system of legal punishment (of period 1830–1890) cannot be fully understood apart from the history of the origins and development of the contract prison labor system. The tremendous impact that the practice of prison labor was to have on American penal practice was glimpsed as early as 1825. When Lynds and the prison inspectors set about recruiting local manufacturers to set up shop in Auburn prison, they immediately encountered a formidable obstacle: Local manufacturers were reluctant to take on convict laborers. As the agent noted, manufacturers feared that convicts would destroy their materials and tools (this was not surprising, given that just a few years earlier Auburn convicts had wrecked tools and materials, rioted and struck in the workshops, and allegedly set the prison alight), and that the public would not buy goods made by convict labor.[20] It quickly became clear that if the Auburn system was to work at all, the authorities would have to make the prison safe and profitable for the contractors. That primarily meant subjecting the convicts to rigorous discipline and selling prison labor at low rates.[21] Although getting contractors into the prison was not the sole motivation for innovating new disciplinary techniques (as we have seen, simply securing the prison so as to avoid having to call out the militia every year was also a key concern), in all likelihood it added considerably to the inspectors' sense of urgency that a new and effective disciplinary regime be established at Auburn.

The inspectors requested that Auburn's principal keeper initiate a thorough overhaul of prison discipline. Over the following year, the keeper and his successor innovated an entirely new array of tactics by which they might subjugate their unruly charges. The guiding principle informing these new tactics was the suppression of any and all communication, verbal and otherwise, between and among convicts: By vigorously and swiftly punishing

[19] Supra, p. 8.   [20] Lewis, *From Newgate to Dannemora*, 180.
[21] Lewis notes the lower rates, but does not draw a link between the development of industrial discipline and recruitment of contractors. W. David Lewis, *From Newgate to Dannemora*, 180.

efforts at communication, and thereby isolating each prisoner from his fellows, the keepers would destroy the ability of convicts to collude or take collective action. Here, military models of discipline proved a useful arsenal. Like many of the new generation of keepers that came to the fore in the 1820s and 1830s, both the men who undertook this work at Auburn (John D. Cray and his successor, Lynds) had served as officers in the War of 1812;[22] the tactics they subsequently developed in service of this large countercommunicative strategy owed much to military models of governance. Cray was very probably responsible for inventing the ubiquitous lockstep march for prisoners (whereby prisoners marched in cramped, single file, each prisoner placing his hand on the shoulder of the man in front, and his head turned toward the keeper), and for imposing a strict, military-style timetable on prison life; Lynds continued and refined that system, both at Auburn, and later, at Sing Sing.[23]

When he assumed the principal keepership at Auburn in 1825, Captain Lynds (as he was known) instructed the keepers that any and all instances of convict communication were to be instantly punished. He strictly prohibited talking, grimacing, signaling by hand, singing, and even attempting to make eye contact with anyone other than the guards. Communicative acts such as these were to be rewarded with a swift application of the lash (which had been legalized in 1819).[24] Lynds also forced the convicts to wear identical striped suits; to submit to having their hair cropped; and to march between cellhouse and workshop in Cray's lockstep, all under threat of summary lashing.[25] In an apparent effort to destroy the power relations of the old penitentiary (in which, as we have seen, prisoners had exercised quite some

[22] It was alleged in 1852 that Cray had been a petty officer in – and deserter from – the British army during the War of 1812. *Documents of the the Assembly of the State of New York*, 75th Session (1852), I:20, 77, cited in W. David Lewis, *From Newgate to Dannemora*, 84. Both Lynds and William Brittin (Auburn's first agent and keeper) had served at the rank of captain in the U.S. military. Gildemeister, "Prison Labor," 9; Mark Colvin, *Penitentiaries, Reformatories, and Chain Gangs: Social Theory and the History of Punishment in Nineteenth-Century America* (New York: St. Martin's Press, 1997), 82. Here it is important to underscore the distinction between, on one hand, the keepers (such as Lynds) who innovated the disciplinary techniques that would become the hallmark of the "Auburn plan" and the legislators and penal reformers who later justified and championed the "plan" (most of whom were associated with the Boston Prison Discipline Society, which was established chiefly for the purpose of promoting the Auburn system). Auburn's distinctive disciplinary techniques were improvised on the spot and via an adaptation of its practitioners' military experience; they were not spun from the imaginations of well-meaning reformers. Chief among the Auburn system's boosters were New York State legislators George Tibbits and Stephen Allen (both merchants) and legislator Samuel M. Hopkins (a Connecticut-born farmer and lawyer); Auburn's agent, Gerhsom Powers (who wrote two well-known pamphlets on the Auburn system); and the Reverend Louis Dwight of the Boston Prison Discipline Society.

[23] Lewis, *From Newgate to Dannemora*, 93.

[24] For a detailed discussion of the disciplinary system of Cray and Lynds, see Lewis, *From Newgate to Dannemora*, 81, 85, 87–93.

[25] Lewis, *From Newgate to Dannemora*, 92–93. See Beaumont and Tocqueville for Lynds's sustained defense of his practice of flogging prisoners. "Conversation With Mr. Elam Lynds," Gustave de Beaumont and Alexis de Tocqueville, *On the Penitentiary System in the United States*

leverage), he did away with the paralegal prison "courts" that had implicitly recognized prisoners as the bearers of certain customary rights, who, as such, were entitled to certain procedures of justice,[26] and abolished the informal system of privileges and incentives that had evolved under the old system, including the custom of doling out tobacco to the prisoners. So, too, did Lynds crack down on the insubordinate keepers, whose well-known fraternization with convicts and generally relaxed approach to the formal duties of their office had frustrated penitentiary reformers since the 1790s. As Lynds would explain to Alexis de Tocqueville and Gustave de Beaumont at Sing Sing in 1831: In order to subjugate the convicts, he needed to "watch incessantly the keepers," and not just the prisoners.[27]

As Lynds, a shrewd tactician of power, was also keenly aware, the task of instilling discipline at Auburn presented something of a paradox: Although, in an effort to make the prison safe for contractors, his superiors had ordered a new disciplinary regime, the contractors and their foremen were private citizens who, as such, were not directly subject to Lynds' authority. As a "foreign" presence in the prison, Lynds worried, contractors could easily subvert, whether knowingly or otherwise, the very regime that was designed to support them. For this reason, Lynds was highly critical of the very contract labor system his disciplinary system helped establish; likewise other penal disciplinarians such as Gershom Powers and General Moses Pilsbury of Connecticut, as well as the genteel reformers of the BPDS, were initially strongly opposed to selling the labor power of prisoners. Despite Lynds' antagonism to the contract system, however, it quite quickly took root at Auburn. As Lynds strove to turn unruly laboring men into "silent and insulated working machines" (in his words), manufacturers began to show interest in setting up shop in the prison. A handful of private manufacturers brought machinery and materials into the prison, paid a fixed, daily rate for the labor of prisoners (or, sometimes, a piece rate), and began production.[28] Before long, Auburn was a humming factory producing thousands of tools, rifles, shoes, clothing, combs, furniture, and barrels.[29]

By 1830, and in a few short years, the foundations of the Auburn system had been laid: Convicts were isolated in cells by night; put to congregate labor for a private contractor by day; subject to a strict disciplinary regime that drew on military models and older forms of corporal punishments; and, in the juridical sphere, stripped of their political rights. The more serious forms of prison disorder declined precipitously in the years after 1825: Most conspicuously, both the incidence of full-scale riot and the rate of escape fell. Although convicts and their supporters initially challenged the legality of the new practice of summary whippings at Auburn in 1825 and

and Its Application in France, trans. Frances Lieber (Carbondale: Southern Illinois University Press, 1964), 161–65.

[26] Lewis, *From Newgate to Dannemora*, 123.

[27] Elam Lynds, in "Conversation With Mr. Elam Lynds," in Beaumont and Tocqueville, *On the Penitentiary System*, 161–65.

[28] Lewis, *From Newgate to Dannemora*, 179.   [29] Lewis, *From Newgate to Dannemora*, 180.

1826, they were defeated when a local judge ruled that summary whipping, despite the existence of a statute to the contrary, was the "common law right" of the master.[30] After 1825, and for some years to come, Auburn's prisoners launched nothing as ambitious or as well-orchestrated as their previous actions against whipping. Nor did they press "Blue Monday" or other cherished common rights of early republican apprentices. Indeed, in a few short years, the system seemed to have met the challenge put forward by Governor De Witt Clinton in 1818: Prisoners' "dangerous spirit" appeared to have been convincingly crushed. The Reverend Louis Dwight, secretary of the BPDS and a great champion of the Auburn system, triumphantly exclaimed: "The whole establishment, from the gate to the sewer, is a specimen of neatness. The unremitted (sic) industry, the entire subordination, and subdued feeling of the convicts have probably no parralles (sic) among an equal number of criminals. In their solitary cells, they spend the night, with no other book but the Bible; and at sun-rise, they proceed to military order, under the eye of the turnkeys, in solid columns, with the lock march, to their workshops."[31]

New York, of course, was not the only state to produce a distinctive penal system in response to the crises of the old penitentiary. As Lynds fleshed out the new system in the mid 1820s, lawmakers in Pennsylvania resolved that they, too, would seek to reinvent, rather than abandon, the penitential mode of punishment. Like New York's lawmakers, they recognized in cellular technology an efficient and effective means by which they could break up and subjugate a disorderly mass of convicts. However, their design and use of the cellhouse, and some of their overarching objectives, differed in certain key respects from the Auburn system: The task of breaking the communicative relations of prisoners was to be achieved principally through the application of a modified cellular technology. Whereas Auburn prisoners were to be isolated at night and put to silent, congregate labor by day, Eastern isolated the prisoner in an individual cell, every hour of the day and every day of the week, for the duration of the sentence. Upon commitment to prison, convicts were to be whisked away to the cells under cover of hoods, so that they would be made thoroughly disoriented. Isolated entirely from the "society" of fellow human beings, the prisoner would receive no visitors for the duration of the sentence, and would eat, sleep, toil, worship, and exercise exclusively in his cell. He would be allowed to read nothing but the Bible. "In the solitary cell," one reformer explained the theory, "the unhappy victim of crime is not only saved from further contamination arising from corrupt society, but is constrained to reflect."[32]

---

[30] Lewis, *From Newgate to Dannemora*, 94–96.
[31] Louis Dwight, Boston Prison Discipline Society, First Annual Report (1826), quoted in *Middlesex Gazette*, XLI:3019 (July 5, 1826), 3.
[32] Report of the Commissioners to Superintend the Erection of the Eastern Penitentiary, Philadelphia, on the Penal Code (1828), 3, reprinted in *The Register of Pennsylvania*, I:17 (Apr. 26, 1828), 260.

In effect, Eastern administrators adopted the perpetual isolation plan that Auburn had tried and abandoned, and sought to improve upon it.[33] Eastern's cells were half again as big as Auburn's, and each opened out onto a small, enclosed garden, in which the prisoner could exercise and take fresh air, in solitude. Rather than deprive convicts of labor by day, as Auburn's administrators had done in their 1821 isolation experiment, or force them to labor, as the new Auburn system prescribed, every Eastern prisoner was to be given the opportunity to do handicrafts in their cell. Labor was not to be directly coerced; rather the tedium of perpetual isolation would lead the prisoner both to take up labor of his or her own accord, and to recognize its spiritual and material virtues. Whereas Auburn aimed primarily to habituate the prisoner to "honest industry" and orderly conduct, Eastern, in a reworking of Benjamin Rush's original penitential concept, aimed to conduce the prisoner to perform, for himself, a "surgery" on his soul. Rather than an abandonment of the penitential principle, Eastern represented an effort to refine and strengthen it. Not coincidentally, the Reverend Dwight and other vociferous critics of Eastern's "isolation" or "separate" system of incarceration marked this fact by pointedly referring to their beloved Auburn as the leading example of the "*state prison system*" and to Eastern as a "penitentiary system."[34]

By the early 1830s, the "separate" or "Eastern system" was as well-established, and well-publicized, as the Auburn system. Penal reformers were waging what David J. Rothman describes as an often bitterly fought "pamphlet war" over the virtues and vices of the respective systems.[35] The stakes were high: Many of the older states, and also a number of European governments, were poised to build replacements for their discredited and riotous penitentiaries; lawmakers in the newer American states were also keenly following developments in the hope of learning from the example – and mistakes – of the older states. As news of the rival systems reached Europe, many governments dispatched investigators to report on the respective systems' efficacy and their suitability for adoption in Europe. Alexis de Tocqueville, Gustave de Beaumont, and a slew of other European social investigators almost invariably came down on the side of the Eastern isolation model. (One famous exception to the rule was Charles Dickens, who liked neither. In an oft-quoted line from his famously curmudgeonly travelogue, *American Notes*, Dickens adjudged Eastern to inflict mental tortures of a "depth of

---

[33] Eastern was not, however, a perfect "panopticon": Its observation tower did not afford an unimpeded view into all cells at once. For a detailed discussion of the circumstance of Eastern's genesis, see Michael Meranze, *Laboratories of Virtue: Punishment, Revolution, and Authority in Philadelphia, 1760–1835* (Chapel Hill: The University of North Carolina Press, 1996), 247–64.

[34] Boston Prison Discipline Society, Annual Reports, 1826–40.

[35] David J. Rothman, *Discovery of the Asylum: Social Order and Disorder in the New Republic* (Boston and Toronto: Little, Brown and Co, 1971), 82–88, 97,102; Beaumont and Tocqueville, *On the Penitentiary System*, 54–60; 82–3; Meranze, *Laboratories of Virtue*, 293–328; Negley K. Teeters and John Shearer, *The Prison at Philadelphia: Cherry Hill* (New York: Columbia University Press for Temple University Publications, 1957), especially 55–76.

terrible endurance . . . immeasurably worse than any torture of the body"; in a less well-known passage, he lamented that Auburn's congregate factory system appeared to entirely disconnect the experience of imprisonment from its punitive objective).[36] In contrast to the Auburn system, Tocqueville and Beaumont wrote approvingly, Eastern's "perfect isolation secures the prisoners from all fatal contamination."[37] Perhaps persuaded by reports such as these, and possessing considerable fiscal and administrative capacity, a number of European states began to construct prisons along Pennslyvanian principles.

In the United States, where state governments generally lacked the administrative and fiscal wherewithal, and the political mandate, to build and operate the Pennsylvanian penal system, it was the Auburn system that became the standard form of incarceration after 1825: Between 1825 and 1850, state prisons of the Auburn type were built in Maine, Maryland, New Hampshire, Vermont, Massachusetts, Connecticut, New York, the District of Columbia, Virginia, Tennessee, Louisiana, Missouri, Illinois, and Ohio. (Rhode Island and New Jersey initially built Pennsylvania-style prisons, but soon abandoned or deeply modified the Pennslyvania system; Maine also briefly experimented with a solitary system. Georgia and Kentucky fused contract penal labor with the noncellular prison design of Walnut Street).[38] Of critical importance in lawmakers' deliberations on the merits of either system was the fact that Auburn's congregate prison was cheaper to build and to administrate, and that at a time in which handicraft was giving way to industrial forms of production, its congregate labor system was much better adapted to the task of getting convicts to pay for as much of the cost of their incarceration as possible.[39] On one estimate, the cost of building a Pennslyvania-style cellblock was eight times that of an Auburn block ($1,200 to $150 per cell); on another, the disparity was even greater: $1624 to

---

[36] Dickens, *American Notes*, [1842], 146, 148.

[37] Beaumont and Tocqueville, *On the Penitentiary System*, 75. See also Rothman, *Discovery of the Asylum*, 97.

[38] Rhode Island abandoned the Pennsylvania system in 1843, and New Jersey made extensive modifications of it within five years of its adoption, due to the high incidence of insanity among the perpetually isolated prisoners. See Francis C. Gray, *Prison Discipline in America* (Boston: Little and Brown, 1847). A prison modeled on the Auburn system was also established in Canada. W. David Lewis, *From Newgate to Dannemora*, 110; Adam Jay Hirsch, *The Rise of the Penitentiary* (New Haven: Yale University Press, 1992), 137; Colvin, *Penitentiaries, Reformatories, and Chain Gangs*, 95.

[39] Beaumont and Tocqueville noted that the system was more profitable, and therefore more appealing to American lawmakers, 67. Likewise, Francis Gray, in his widely read 1847 study of the Pennsylvania and Auburn systems, presented considerable evidence of the latter's relative inexpensiveness. Over the previous nineteen years, he argued, Pennsylvania's Eastern penitentiary cost the state treasury an average of $20,000 a year; in the same period of time, the Massachusetts state prison at Charlestown, which was run on the Auburn plan, generated a surplus (over operating costs) of about $500 a year. In the late 1840s, Ohio's prison (also run on the Auburn plan) was generating in excess of $10,000 a year in income after operating costs. Gray, *Prison Discipline in America*.

$80).⁴⁰ The straightforward reasoning of the Michigan penitentiary commissioners, who recommended their state follow the Auburn model, was typical: "The expense of building a Prison on this [Auburn] plan will be much less than it would be, were the Philadelphia system adopted. After the Prison is completed, the earnings of the convicts will be at least equal to the expenses of the Prison."⁴¹ Some states went so far as to see in the Auburn plan a means of shifting the cost, not only of holding prisoners on a day-to-day basis, but also of constructing the prison in the first place. In Maryland, for example, the prison inspectors borrowed $50,000 from the state treasury for the purpose of building an Auburn-style prison, complete with congregate workshops: Once the workshops were operational, they were pleased to report, the prison would gradually repay the loan ["by installments, with interest"] through the earnings of its laboring convicts.⁴²

In almost all the new state prisons, the convicts went to work for private manufacturers under one or other variant of the contract system of the sort in operation at Auburn. Indeed, in the 1830s, a sentence to "confinement at hard labor" increasingly became an experience of forced, productive labor for private contractors and lessees. Once convicts dispatched from Auburn had finished building a new state prison at Sing Sing, for example, they went to work in many of the same kinds of contract industries found at Auburn, as well as in a state-operated quarry, which furnished cut marble and stone for the construction of Manhattan's Grace Church, the United States Subtreasury, New York University, the state capitol, and multiple Westchester county homes. (Indeed, the private boarding house in which Alexis de Tocqueville and Gustave de Beaumont briefly stayed during their investigation of the American penal system was built of Sing Sing marble).⁴³ Sing Sing's agent,

---

⁴⁰ Beaumont and Tocqueville, *On the Penitentiary System*, 103–04; *North American Review* (July 1839), 39, cited in Wallace Shugg, *A Monument to Good Intentions: The Story of the Maryland Penitentiary* (Baltimore: Maryland Historical Society, 2000), 22. Shugg notes that Auburn's congregate labor system also made it a desirable system. He concludes, "Mainly for economic reasons, Maryland . . . adopted the Auburn system."

⁴¹ Boston Prison Discipline Society, Thirteenth Annual Report (1838), 63; See also, John R. Adan, Boston Prison Discipline Society, Twelfth Annual Report (1837), 86–87. Many Southern legislators and justices found the Auburn system appealing on the same grounds. Justices of the Alabama Supreme Court, for example, recommended in 1840 that their state adopt the Auburn system because it was less expensive to construct; the convicts' earnings would meet expenditures; its mode of discipline was "better suited" (than the Pennsylvania system) to the "nature of man"; and it had not been shown to be less effective (than the Pennsylvania system) as a method of reformation. Quoted in the Boston Prison Discipline Society, Fifteenth Annual Report (1840), 44.

⁴² The prison had already built one wing using this method: In 1828 it had borrowed 30,000 with which to pay for the construction of a new wing; by 1838, convicts' earnings had repaid half the principal. Boston Prison Discipline Society, 1838, 58.

⁴³ Tocqueville and Beaumont stayed in a boarding house made of convict-hewn limestone, at 24 State St., in Ossining. *In the Footsteps of Tocqueville: Traveling Tocqueville's America* (Baltimore: The Johns Hopkins University Press 1998). Marble cut and hewn by Sing Sing convicts was used in the construction of New York University's east Washington Square building.

Robert Wiltse, built a new complex of workshops that followed much the same geometric design of many of the free factories that were springing up in Massachusetts and other Northeastern states.[44] By 1841, the great majority of Sing Sing's 821 prisoners were working for one or another of nine contractors, making harnesses and saddlery, shoes, locks, carpets, and barrels.[45] Similarly, shortly after Connecticut opened the state prison at Wethersfield in 1827, prison administrators phased in the contract system. Wethersfield's agent, like most Northern prison agents, gradually decreased the number of industries at the prison and increased the scale of production: By the 1860s, just three large industries operated at Wethersfield.[46] New Hampshire and Vermont followed similar trajectories, as did most of the Western states in the 1840s: Michigan, for example, put its state prisoners to work for contractors;[47] in Illinois, after 1839, private contractors ran the state prison at Alton; after 1845, one contractor leased the entire prison for eight years (at a cost of $5,000), putting the prisoners to work manufacturing ropes, wagons, barrels, and other items.[48]

In the South, too, a similar pattern prevailed, albeit on a much smaller scale. Although the antebellum Southern prison population was as little as one-tenth the size of the North's and the penal arm of state government was considerably weaker, many Southern states (where the overwhelming majority of convicts were both freeborn and white)[49] followed the Auburn

[44] Roger Panetta, "Up the River: A History of Sing Sing in the Nineteenth Century," (Ph.D. diss., City University of New York, 1999), 278.

[45] "State Prison Contracts," *The New York State Mechanic, A Journal of the Manual Arts, Trades, and Manufactures* (Nov. 20, 1841), 1, 7. Sing Sing prisoners also cut marble and stone for use on New York building sites. Once the construction of Sing Sing was completed in 1831, that prison's force of 600-odd penal laborers were put to work as stone cutters in the prison's sizable marble and granite quarries. Much of the Sing Sing stone was shipped south to Manhattan, where it was used in the construction of Grace Church, the United States Subtreasury, New York University, and a number of other prominent buildings. Some of the stone found its way to Albany and the capitol construction site, while New York's railroad builders scattered tons of convict-made rubble between miles of freshly-laid railroad tracks.

[46] Report of the Directors of Connecticut State Prison, 1844, 7. For a brief history of prison labor (and its antagonists) in Connecticut, see Alba M. Edwards, "The Labor Legislation of Connecticut," *Publications of the American Economic Association* (3rd Series), 8:3 (Aug. 1907), 217–42.

[47] Boston Prison Discipline Society, Thirteenth, Fourteenth, Fifteenth, and Twenty-Fifth Annual Reports (1838, 1839, 1840, 1849).

[48] Likewise, Indiana leased out all its state prisoners for a two-year period, in 1849, and Ohio put hundreds of its state prisoners to work for just four private manufacturers. Boston Prison Discipline Society, Twenty-Fifth Annual Report (1849); "Convict Labor in Ohio," *Mechanic's Advocate* (Feb. 11, 1847), 85; David L. Lightner, *Asylum, Prison, and Poorhouse: The Writings of Dorothea Dix in Illinois* (Carbondale and Edwardsville: Southern Illinois University Press, 1999), 36. See also Dorothea Dix, "Memorial" (address to the General Assembly of the State of Illinois, February 1847), in Lightner, *Asylum, Prison, and Poorhouse*, 37–66.

[49] A leading historian of Southern criminal justice, Edward Ayers, notes that penitentiaries of the antebellum lower South contained almost no free black people. Four percent of Tennessee's prisoners and eight percent of Kentucky's prisoners were black. In the upper South, free black convicts made up half and one-third the prison populations of Maryland

model, complete with its contract labor system: In the 1830s, the Kentucky legislature turned the state prison at Frankfort over to a keeper who was directed to put the prisoners to hard labor, retain half the profit for himself, and pay the other half to the state. Kentucky prisoners proceeded to cut stone; make wagons, plows, furniture, barrels, brushes, and sleighs; weave cloth, carpeting, and flannel; and cobble shoes. Beginning in the 1840s, keeper-lessees ran the Missouri state prison, with the majority of the 180-odd prisoners working in coopering, blacksmithing, and carpentry, and the rest laboring away on local construction sites. After a brief experiment with a state-run textile industry (which aimed to undercut Northern imports of clothing destined for chattel slaves) the Louisiana legislature handed over the state prison and all its laborers – *gratis* – to private manufacturers in 1844, and twice again in the 1850s. The Alabama legislature leased the entire state prison to a private manufacturer of wagons, buckets, barrels, kegs, and other goods; Texas also leased its Huntsville prisoners to private contractors. Two states, Mississippi and Georgia, put their prisoners to work for state-owned enterprises, including Georgia's railroad company (Western and Atlantic Railroad) and Mississippi's cotton textiles factory, under an arrangement that would later be known as "public account."[50]

In the 1840s, the vast majority of American prisons so closely resembled the great textile manufactories for which free American industry was becoming internationally renowned that upon visiting one of these prisons Charles Dickens found it "difficult at first to persuade myself that I was really in a jail: a place of ignominious punishment and endurance."[51] In most states of the union, a free man convicted of felony crime could expect to spend several years imprisoned and at productive labor for the benefit of private contractors or, in some instances, a state-owned business. The great majority of men undergoing legal punishment found themselves sequestered in great cellular fortresses, "let out in the morning and barr'd at night," in the words of Walt Whitman. (In the 1840s, Whitman ministered to prisoners at Sing Sing and was appalled by the conditions under which they lived and

and Virginia respectively. Edward Ayers, *Vengeance and Justice: Crime and Punishment in the 19th-Century American South* (Oxford: Oxford University Press, 1984), 61. For a meticulous and highly original study of criminal law's relationship to slavery in the American South, see Thomas Morris, *Southern Slavery and the Law, 1619–1860* (Chapel Hill: University of North Carolina Press, 1996), 161–332. On the prison and slave plantation as mechanisms of social control, see Michael Stephen Hindus, *Prison and Plantation: Crime, Justice, and Authority in Massachusetts and South Carolina, 1768–1878* (Chapel Hill: University of North Carolina Press, 1980).

[50] Mississippi legislators, like Louisiana's, hoped the prison industry would lessen dependence on Northern manufactures. Ayers, *Vengeance and Justice*, 66–67. See also, Jerena East Giffen and Thomas E. Gage, "The Prison Against the Town: Jefferson City and the Penitentiary in the 19th Century," *Missouri Historical Review* 75 (July 1980), 414–432.

[51] Dickens exempted the Pennsylvanian system from this judgment. He believed he had found at Eastern penitentiary a form of punishment far more cruel and punitive than any he had seen in England. Dickens, *American Notes* (New York: Modern Library, 1996), 252.

worked).[52] In the North, Pennsylvania alone continued to reject outright both the congregate labor system and the contracting out of prisoners as laborers. Below the Mason Dixon line, only the South Carolinians and the Floridians failed to adopt the "Yankee invention" of imprisonment at hard labor – preferring instead older, biblically sanctioned punishments such as public flogging and executions.[53]

Wherever it was adopted, the Auburn system appeared to have ended the crises of discipline, finance, and legitimacy that had plagued the early republican penitentiary since the 1790s. The Reverend Louis Dwight and other members of the BPDS were largely correct when they boasted, in the 1830s, of Auburn's defeat of prisoners' capacity to act collectively or to enforce what they took to be their common and natural rights. As one member of the Society wrote (in connection with the Auburn plan, Massachusetts State Prison at Charlestown, in 1840): "the Arts of Mischief known in the institution fifteen years ago," had been "in a great degree done away with by constant supervision, silent hard labor during the day, and solitary confinement at night – the delightful results of wisdom and goodness!"[54]

Much as lawmakers had hoped, the Auburn system had also quickly set the economics of imprisonment on a far firmer footing than had previously been the case. Although it was rarely very profitable for the state, lawmakers and prison inspectors continued to view the contracting out of prison labor as a vital source of revenue. That confidence was not misplaced: In almost every Auburn-plan prison, revenue generated by convicts working under one variant or other of the contract prison labor system significantly defrayed and sometimes exceeded the annual cost incurred in running the prisons. In 1840, the earnings (for the states) of nine Auburn-plan prisons exceeded operating costs, and the annual earnings of a tenth, fell shy of annual expenses by a mere $179.[55] Conversely, two state prisons built on the Pennsylvania model (Eastern and the New Jersey State Prison), and the prison in Georgia did not break even.[56] Contrary to what some historians have argued, the Auburn-plan prisons often sustained their savings over the long-term. At Wethersfield, Connecticut, for example, over a seventeen-year period, convict laborers helped generate $93,000 in revenue – or approximately seventy-five percent of the running costs of the prison in the same period;[57] a number of other Auburn-plan prisons reported similar returns. Although it is difficult to ascertain exactly how profitable the system was for

---

[52] Whitman, "Song of Myself," verse 37, from *Leaves of Grass* (1855).

[53] J. Thorsten Sellin, *Slavery and the Penal System*, (New York: Elsevier, 1976), 141–2; Ayers, *Vengeance and Justice*, 59–72; Orlando F. Lewis, *The Development of American Prisons and Prison Customs, 1776–1845* (New York: New York Prison Association, 1925), chapters 17 and 20; Donald R. Walker, *Penology for Profit: A History of the Texas Prison System* (College Station: Texas A & M University Press, c1988).

[54] Boston Prison Discipline Society, Fifteenth Annual Report (1840), 34.

[55] Boston Prison Discipline Society, Sixteenth Annual Report (1841), 53.

[56] Boston Prison Discipline Society, Sixteenth Annual Report (1841), 53.

[57] Report of the Directors of Connecticut State Prison, 1844, 7.

contractors, anecdotal evidence suggests it was often remarkably lucrative: Some reportedly reaped profits as high as 150% over three years. Manufacturers in possession of long-term (ten- and twenty-year) contracts, such as Illinois' Samuel A. Buckmaster, accumulated vast fortunes through their prison industries.[58] Gideon Haynes, the warden of the Massachusetts State Prison in Charlestown, remarked in 1867 that "(o)ur contractors have always become wealthy, if they have retained their contracts for any length of time."[59]

So too did the contract prison labor system gradually accrue the support of many of the disciplinarian keepers and penal reformers who had initially been so strongly opposed to it. Once the revenue from selling prisoners' labor power began to routinely offset (or, in some cases, exceed) the prison's operating costs, reformers tempered their criticism of the system. By 1840, most accepted the principle of the contract system, if somewhat grudgingly, and acknowledged that the contractors were a necessary part of the Auburn system of imprisonment. Reformers at the BPDS now routinely opened their defense of the Auburn-plan prisons with a discussion of the greater cost savings of that system (relative to the Pennsylvania system). Although stopping short of explicitly endorsing the contract practice, or even fully acknowledging the degree to which Auburn-plan prisons had come to depend upon it, members of the Society unabashedly touted the revenues that contracting produced as positive proof of the Auburn plan's superiority.

The Auburn-plan prisons, then, were considerably more orderly, better financed, and more politically secure than their penitential predecessors. By the same token, however, these prisons were not quite as orderly as their prolific supporters (and, subsequently, most historians) reported them to be. Nor were they as politically stable.[60] Indeed, there is a growing body

---

[58] Enoch C. Wines and Theodore W. Dwight, *Report on the Prisons and Reformatories of the United States and Canada* (Albany, NY: Van Benthuysen, 1867), 259–60. Buckmaster was also a prominent Illinois Democrat and the twenty-third speaker of the Illinois House of Representatives (from 1863 to 1865). *Illinois Blue Book*, 2002–03, 473.

[59] Gideon Haynes, quoted in Wines and Dwight, *Report on the Prisons and Reformatories*, 257–8. Wines and Dwight noted that in general, the contractors' profits "are very large."

[60] For the most part, penal historians have tended to take at face value the supposedly objective reports of the Auburn system's officers and supporters (including the Boston Prison Discipline Society). However, these contemporaries frequently compounded the descriptive and prescriptive voices, and tended to overlook or underreport conflicts and difficulties within the system. For example, Rothman writes of the prisons of the Jacksonian period: "(l)ittle distance separated the ideas and the reality of the new penitentiaries; construction and organization to a considerable degree followed reformers' blueprints," and maintains that the Auburn and Eastern separation of ideas and reality was apparent only after 1850 (Rothman, *Discovery of the Asylum*, 94). In many of the historical accounts that are more attentive to life in the prisons themselves, there is also an unresolved tension between the supposedly well-ordered prison depicted in the official and promotional literature, and the riotous or otherwise disorderly prisons that occasionally burst into print in the popular press. Lewis, for example, carefully documents the prisoners' ongoing subversion of prison discipline, but nonetheless asserts that at Auburn, "the inmate became a living machine." Despite his own unearthing of rich evidence to the contrary, Lewis nonetheless writes that

of evidence to suggest that, while a new penal order was most certainly taking shape in the 1820s and 1830s, and the crises of the earlier years were abating, the Auburn system delivered neither the perfect regime of administrative domination of which Elam Lynds boasted, nor an entirely stable, or popularly legitimate, system of legal punishment. Within the high walls of the state prisons, new "arts of mischief" were materializing – not among the prisoners, but among the contractors and the keepers. Beyond the prison walls, moreover, new and more organized forces of opposition to the system were amassing. Indeed, in the same moment that the innovative, new Auburn system buried one set of disorders, it conceived another.

Although the Auburn system of discipline severely circumscribed the possibilities for collective action on the part of convicts, prisoners' practical ability to commune with one another was by no means destroyed. As the punishment ledgers and inspectors' reports suggest, almost from the very first day on which the new system was operant, the prisoners found many ways around the proscription of communication.[61] They talked and whispered under the cacophony of heavy machinery and the din of the weekly scrubbings of cells. Within a few years, convicts were also engaging with one another via intricate sign languages and communicating between cells by tapping on the hollow pipes that connected them. Neither did the new silent rule put an end to illicit communication between keepers and convicts. As Auburn's concerned inspectors noted, the recessed entrances to the cells enabled guards to converse and "collude" with prisoners. At Sing Sing, where the cells were explicitly designed to render such instances of convict–guard collusion impossible, the *absence* of recessed entrances enabled prisoners to converse with each other between cells on a routine basis. (By all indications, a similar state of affairs prevailed in other state prisons in the 1830s: William Crawford, the British prison investigator, noted that convicts at Baltimore talked in the yard and workshops and between cells.[62] Even under the perpetual isolation model in place at Pennsylvania's Eastern Penitentiary, prisoners reportedly discovered various ways of communicating with each other).[63]

Nor was the prison the perfect, hermetic fortress that Louis Dwight and others claimed it to be: Assistant keepers, contractors, and foremen in many state prisons kept a steady flow of liquor, cards, and tobacco coming into

the prison did, in fact, break the prisoner's will, much as Elam Lynds boasted, and that the prisoner became a "robot and a slave" (Lewis, *From Newgate to Dannemora*, 181). Only Meranze and Goldsmith have broken decisively with previous historians' tendency to treat official reports and early reform rhetoric as transparent representations of the reality of prison life and institutional order. Meranze, *Laboratories of Virtue*, 305–328; Larry Goldsmith, "Penal Reform, Convict labor, and Prison Culture in Massachusetts, 1800–1880" (Ph.D. diss., University of Pennsylvania, 1987).

[61] Lewis reports 173 whippings for talking in an eleven-month period in 1845. W. David Lewis, *From Newgate to Dannemora*, 130–35, 173–75, 181.

[62] William Crawford, "Penitentiaries in the United States," 95, quoted in Shugg, *A Monument to Good Intentions*, 25–26.

[63] Meranze, *Laboratories of Virtue*, 305–18.

the prison.[64] In the early 1840s, ex-prisoners were known to break *into* the Sing Sing yard to deliver tobacco and other contraband to the deprived prisoners.[65] New York's forty-odd women prisoners, who were housed in several large rooms in a separate Greek-revival building at Sing Sing after 1837, commonly flouted the rule of silence, singing bawdy songs and talking among themselves and with the many male convicts who passed by the house on the way to the marble quarry (and who, occasionally, fixed machinery inside the women's prison). And just as male prisoners had done at Newgate, Auburn, and Walnut St. in the 1810s and 20s, the women acted upon occasion to protect one of their sorority from punishments they considered unfair or excessive: In 1843, for example, twelve women prisoners intervened when a keeper attempted to punish an unruly workmate, throwing furniture and striking the guards.[66] In the Western regions of the country, many of the characteristics of the early republican penitentiaries prevailed in the face of prison authorities' attempts to apply the new disciplinary techniques. In Ohio in the 1840s, for example, a prison investigator reported that Ohio convicts seemed to be running their Auburn-plan prison, "communicating at will and controlling much of the routine." In language that recalls the feisty, rights-conscious prisoners of the early republic, the warden complained, "nearly all convicts were clamorous for what *they* claimed were their rights."[67] Once released from prison, convicts persisted in their efforts to join the polity, despite the profusion of criminal disfranchisement laws. The New York legislature considered the problem significant enough that in 1842, it added penal sanctions to the state's criminal disfranchisement law, making it a misdemeanor offense for any person convicted of an infamous crime to vote at State or local elections.[68]

Paradoxically, the fact that prisoners (and their associates) were able to assert themselves against prison authorities stemmed in large part from the very activity that was supposed to instill a respect for order in the convicts. When Charles Dickens reflected that the Auburn-style labor system "greatly favors those opportunities of intercourse – hurried and brief no doubt, but opportunities still . . . by rendering it necessary for them to be employed very near to each other, side by side, without any barrier or partition between them, in their very nature present,"[69] he struck upon the dynamic contradiction of that system. The very system of hard labor that the state's keepers were forcing convicts to serve, and which, in turn, was the financial linchpin of the prison system, was fostering many of the conditions under which convicts were able to commune with one another and evade the full force of their keepers' attempts at domination. Indeed, the organization of

[64] Incidents are reported in Boston Prison Discipline Society, Second Annual Report (1827), 85.
[65] Panetta, "Up the River," 282.
[66] W. David Lewis, *From Newgate to Dannemora*, 173–75.
[67] Annual Report of the Ohio Penitentiary for 1852, 25. Quoted in Rothman, *Discovery of the Asylum*, 100.
[68] Laws N.Y. 1842, chap. 130, title 4, §23.   [69] Dickens, *American Notes*, 252.

prisoners into industrial production often necessitated that the supreme rule of the prison – prisoners' perpetual silence – be broken so that the business of production could proceed. Foremen often needed to communicate with prison laborers, and prison laborers needed to communicate with each other.[70]

At labor in the shops, prisoners discovered various tangible and intangible resources useful to the act of resistance. Workshop materials provided makeshift writing implements and surfaces and convicts put these to use in passing notes between cells (using the pulley method that would be made famous in prison movies a century later).[71] As well as facilitating communication, the prison labor system fostered a brisk prison commerce, in which tobacco was the principal medium of exchange, and an incentive, among guards, contractors, and prisoners.[72] Upon finding themselves with a workforce of laborers to whom they were prohibited from offering wages or incentives, contractors at Auburn soon began smuggling in fruit, alcohol, tobacco, and other contraband and covertly rewarding the more productive laborers. In the 1840s, in New York and Massachusetts, administrators keen on motivating penal laborers introduced a system of conduct marks (modeled on the British system as it was developed in Irish prisons and Australian penal colonies) and reading and writing privileges, effectively making a dead letter of Lynds's principles of separation, silence, and enforced anonymity. In Massachusetts, keepers also systematically engaged in the well-established practice of smuggling contraband such as tobacco, money, newspapers, and letters into – and out of – the penitentiary.[73] In the Southern penitentiaries, convicts were even more assertive than their Northern counterparts, going so far as to burn several state prisons to the ground.[74]

The overall impact of prisoners' various organized and spontaneous efforts to alter the conditions of their imprisoned lives ought not to be overstated: In the 1830s and 1840s, prisoners had much less opportunity and far fewer resources with which to resist and subvert prison discipline than had been the case in the penitentiaries of the 1800s and 1810s. Although they tried on occasion, prisoners could not tear down, or even severely weaken, the increasingly solid structures of their imprisonment. It seems likely, in light of the decline of *attempted* escapes and mutinies, that convicts grasped that, between the stone cells, the lash, and civil death statutes, the power relations of the prison were overwhelming tipped in favor of its keepers. Yet, if prisoners increasingly recognized themselves as persons bearing few, if any, rights that the state was bound to observe, and if they understood that, by themselves, they were incapable of overthrowing or structurally altering the system of which they were captives, they also developed an incipient sense of themselves as useful, valuable, and even indispensable

[70] W. David Lewis, *From Newgate to Dannemora*, 178–200.

[71] Lewis, *From Newgate to Dannemora*, 139–41.

[72] W. David Lewis, *From Newgate to Dannemora*, 139–41; Panetta, "Up the River," 282–84.

[73] Boston Prison Discipline Society, Thirteenth Annual report (1838), 34–35.

[74] Ayers, *Vengeance and Justice*, 60.

to the very contractors who sought to exploit their energies (and also, in some degree, to the higher level administrators who sought fiscal stability for the prisons). In an irony familiar to scholars of slavery, a relationship of dependency evolved between master and servant. The contractor and, to some extent, the keepers, became in some irreducible degree dependent upon the convict whose labor and cooperation they sought to harness. Over time, as we shall see, the very system of discipline that engendered this dependency would, in turn, be transformed by it.

On the outside, too, the Auburn-plan prison was subjected to considerable pressure. The source of this pressure was the nascent workingmen's movement, whose members and leaders saw in the new prison labor system an imminent threat not only to their own employment as artisans but, on a larger scale, to the moral order of the republic. As prisoners were put to work in a systematic way in the late 1820s and early 1830s, and prisons became the great mechanized manufactories of which Charles Dickens wrote, free journeymen, such as those on New York's Committee of Mechanics, argued that putting prisoners to productive labor would bring "corruption and immorality . . . and . . . utter ruin" to free mechanics and the republic alike.[75] Over the next two decades, free mechanics in New York and elsewhere strenuously petitioned and lobbied, and occasionally struck tools, for an end to the practice of putting convicts to skilled, productive labor.

Their opposition to the system stemmed, in part, from the deleterious impact that the use of convict labor in the trades could have on free mechanics in the same trade. At a time in which many journeymen were experiencing the fracturing of the (ideally) mutual bonds of the artisanal apprenticeship system and a crushing pressure to become waged laborers, the intrusion of involuntary, bonded penal laborers into the sphere of production came as one more blow to their livelihoods and their dignity as craftsmen. In their petitions to state legislatures, mechanics repeatedly pointed out that the cost to the manufacturer of using prison labor was lower than the cost of the materials and tools that a manufacturer ordinarily supplied his free journeymen, and that, as a result, many free employers had failed or withdrawn from the business and "thousands" of journeymen had been driven out of the trade for which they had apprenticed.[76] As New York City stonecutters protested in the pages of the *Workingman's Advocate*: "By such competition [with convict labor] . . . many workmen will soon be thrown out of employment or compelled to work for low wages, and unless they can by other means obtain a livelihood, be reduced to a state of want and misery."[77] By making relatively large groups of prisoners available to manufacturers at a

75 Mechanics meeting, 1 Feb 1834, New York State Assembly Documents, #288 (1835), 36–37, quoted in Panetta, "Up the River," 265.

76 See for example, "Proceedings of the Meeting of Mechanics of Buffalo, Jan. 13, 1834," in *Literary Inquirer* (Jan. 15, 1834), 2.

77 *Workingman's Advocate* (Jan. 30, 1830), quoted in Philip S. Foner, *History of the Labor Movement in the United States: From Colonial Times to the Founding of the American Federation of Labor* (New York: International Publishers, 1982 [1947]), 125.

relatively low cost, they argued, the contract prison labor system made it impossible for the free manufacturer to compete and, consequently, workshops closed. That such a system fused the capital of the state with what the Buffalo mechanics described as the "depreciated energies" of convicts and opposed these to the "honest and industrious mechanics," made the injury even more egregious.[78]

Although free mechanics placed considerable emphasis upon what they took to be the direct and deleterious economic impact of convict labor on their livelihoods, this was not their only, or even most pressing, concern. The journeymen's opposition to productive convict labor issued not only from an understanding of what they took to be their own economic self-interest, but from a much deeper, heartfelt, moral sense of what a just and fair republic was – and of what it was not. Journeymen and apprentices, who were undergoing tremendous pressure in a number of crafts as production industrialized and many masters moved from the traditional apprenticeship system to waged labor, argued that, against all principles of justice, the prevailing convict labor system threatened to put honorable, free mechanics on the same moral level as that of a class of unfree, dishonored, disfranchised men (who were forced to live on "*six cents a day*," as *The Man's* editor put it). As many journeymen saw it, allowing mechanical labor to be undertaken in the prisons threatened to associate productive labor with the dishonorable, disfranchised, unfree convict – to "brand" work itself as punishment, as one mechanic put it[79] – in the public eye. In so branding work, convict labor demeaned and devalued the "honest" journeyman and apprentice. By putting convicts to work in the trades, they argued, the state fostered an association, in the minds of the public, between the otherwise honorable trade of the workingman, and the dishonored and "depreciated" convict. That association would be cemented when, upon release, prisoners entered the trades they had served in prison. As the mechanics of Buffalo protested in a citywide meeting in 1834, under the prevailing system, "we must be subjected to the moral taint of having added to our number the annual graduates of these state seminaries, who as a *punishment* have been qualified to compete with us, and whose crimes are thus opposed to our honest and laborious apprenticeships" (emphasis in original).[80]

As these various objections suggest, many workingmen critics of the prevailing system of convict labor determined that state government was taking

[78] "Proceedings of the Mechanics' Meeting, Buffalo, New York, January 13, 1834," *Literary Inquirer* (Jan 15, 1834), 2.
[79] "Change of the Prison System," *The New York State Mechanic, A Journal of the Manual Arts, Trades, and Manufactures* (Apr. 8, 1843), 2, 20.
[80] "Proceedings of the Mechanics' Meeting, Buffalo, New York, January 13, 1834," *Literary Inquirer* (Jan. 15, 1834), 2. The Silver Platters conceived of the problem of associative devaluation in a related vein: Upon release, newly skilled convicts would work side-by-side with young apprentices, thereby corrupting the young men, and with them, the dignity and good name of the trade. Panetta, "Up the River," 280. In a similar vein, the mechanics of Elmira denounced productive penal labor on the grounds that, contrary to all morality, the state "rewarded" felons by equipping them with labor skills. Panetta, "Up the River," 265.

a wrong-headed approach, not merely to matters of crime and punishment, but to the administration of justice and political economy more generally. Indeed, the new prison system quickly became a lightning rod for some of the most profound political-economic and moral questions of the day. In the 1830s, the convict labor system was one, particularly dramatic, emblem of a new political economic order that workingmen feared was materializing around them. As one critic wrote in *The Man*, poverty and ignorance arose because of the "monopolization" by government and well-to-do private citizens of large tracts of land that might otherwise be broken up into small farms for workingmen; poorer freemen who were unable (due to the unavailability of affordable parcels of land) to find means of subsistence and were reduced to committing crime in order to subsist. On this view, freemen of little means were being injured on three fronts: the state and private land "monopolists" who blocked freemen's access to land, closed down their chances at independence or even made them vulnerable to starvation; when some of those men turned to theft to survive they were arrested, tried, and sentenced to "confinement to hard labor";[81] and the state, by absorbing those men into the prison labor system, in turn, displaced freemen who had been lucky enough to find employment or an apprenticeship – or otherwise avoid having to expropriate the property of others.

In a related vein, *The Man* and many workingmen's advocates repeatedly argued in the 1830s that the system of putting convicts to labor in the same fields as free mechanics effectively made the latter bear most of the costs of imprisonment, while exempting large property holders from contributing substantial financial support to the system. Mechanics repeatedly asserted that the use of convicts in the trades placed almost the entire burden of financial support for the system on the shoulders of free tradesmen; as one mechanic argued, under a system in which convicts performed skilled labor for private manufacturers at a fraction of the cost of retaining a free mechanic, "the poor are the supporters of the prison convicts, and not the rich."[82] Many protested that such an arrangement was a betrayal of the most fundamental principles of the American revolution: "Is this the republic that declared to the world that all men are equal and had (sic) certain unalienable rights, such as life, liberty, and the pursuit of happiness?" J. Haskell implored New York legislators: "I look in vain, sir, for the fruit of that declaration in the State Prison monopoly."[83]

As well as undergoing the strains of industrialization in the 1830s, the journeymen protested convict labor against a backdrop in which chattel slavery had, on the one hand, come to define the very opposite of American freedom, and, on the other hand, revived and expanded in the American

---

[81] "The State Prison Monopoly," *The Man*, 2:19 (June 7, 1834), 74. A decade later, Boston's mechanics also demanded that government free up public lands and abolish the prevailing convict labor system. See, "Mechanics, Read This," *Workingman's Advocate* (Mar. 22, 1845), 1.

[82] "Convict Labor," *Mechanic's Advocate* (Feb. 11, 1847), 83.

[83] Remarks of J. Haskell, *Workingman's Advocate* (May 9, 1835), 6.

South. In the 1830s, small producers, for whom freedom turned on an artisanal conception of economic independence, explicitly conceived of the emergence of waged labor, and the dependence of the wage earner upon the employer, in terms of slavery. As Eric Foner has persuasively argued, Southern chattel slavery "was an immediate reality, not a distant symbol" in small producers' attempts to make sense of and oppose an insurgent free market capitalism.[84] The system of servitude that was taking shape in the prisons of the North, although clearly of a different order and magnitude than chattel slavery, nonetheless shared many of its hallmarks. Indeed, the rightsless prisoner, whom whip-wielding keepers drove to mechanical work for private manufacturers, embodied exactly the condition to which journeymen and some master craftsmen believed the modern wage relation would eventually reduce them: That is, to the condition of *industrial* slave, subject to a vicious servitude, in which the dependence, rightslessness, and allegedly debased morality of the chattel slave would be fused with the productive labor of the skilled journeyman. If left unchecked, J. Haskell warned, the new prison labor system one day "shall have amalgamated the convict with the citizen," and abolished the rights of citizenship altogether.[85] Not only was the prison labor system an unrepublican institution, then, it was plainly anti-democratic, as well.

The embattled mechanics floated a number of ideas for the construction of a democratic, republican penal system. Notably, they did not call for the outright abolition of imprisonment; rather, they advocated for government policies that partly obviated much of the need for prisons by relieving the social conditions that they believed gave rise to crimes such as larceny; they also argued that prisons should be put on a broader, more equitable funding basis, such that all sections of the community would share the expenses of maintaining the prison system equally. The editor of *The Man* wrote, "The most proper way to get rid of the evil of convict labor in competition with that of honest mechanics would be to remove the causes which produce convicts; to prevent *poverty* and *ignorance*"(italics in original).[86] The state and federal governments should adopt the "just and practicable measure of allowing every necessitous individual to cultivate (without charge) a portion of the uncultivated land, under such restrictions as would prevent any further monopoly of it." Until that time, the editor concluded (and other workingmen's leaders concurred), convicts should be put to publicly useful work such as hewing stone for the construction of a substitute for the decrepit wooden wharves of New York City; in the same spirit, other mechanics suggested that any proceeds from prison labor be invested in the establishment of a decent public education system.[87] In addition, some

---

[84] Eric Foner, *The Story of American Freedom* (New York: Norton, 1999), 59.
[85] Remarks of J. Haskell, *Workingman's Advocate* (May 9, 1835), 6.
[86] "The State Prison Monopoly," *The Man*, 2:19 (June 7, 1834), 74.
[87] "The State Prison Monopoly," *The Man*, 2:19 (June 7, 1834), 74; see also, "Substitute for Mechanical Labor in State Prisons," *The New York State Mechanic, A Journal of the Manual Arts, Trades, and Manufactures* (Nov. 20, 1841), 1.

mechanics argued, the entire citizenry, and not just two sections of it (prison laborers and free mechanics), should be made to bear the costs of running a prison-based system of legal punishment.[88] J. Haskell argued forcefully before the New York State Select Committee on State Prisons, in 1835, "[if] (i)t is a self-evident fact, . . . that when men commit crimes sufficient to forfeit their liberty, they should be imprisoned to protect the lives and property of every citizen of the state. Then, sir, by the rule of justice and equal rights, it necessarily follows that *every citizen* and *all property* ought to contribute to their support" (emphasis added).[89]

Persuaded that the new prison system presented a grave threat, in 1830, free mechanics embarked on a series of strikes, petitions, and organizing efforts aimed at halting the practice of putting convicts to work in the trades.[90] The stonecutters of New York City led the way, with a strike against the Sing Sing-cut granite and marble that had begun to flood the New York construction industry. When their strike failed to halt the practice, the stonecutters descended onto a building site in which Sing Sing granite was in use and attempted to force the masons to lay down their tools. The following year, the use of convict-cut marble (this time, in the construction of New York University) prompted free marble cutters, journeymen, and marble manufacturers to petition against the use of Sing Sing marble on the grounds that the arrangement gave the state a monopoly, which, by definition, they held to be unfair.[91] Shortly afterwards, a crowd of 150 men attacked the office of a contractor known to use convict-made goods. The mayor of the city responded by calling out the twenty-seventh regiment, whose soldiers soon restored order in the area.

The stone masons failed in their immediate objectives. But their strike – and the calling out of the militia to put it down – captured the attention of mechanics throughout the city and very likely helped galvanize them to organize. In the wake of this campaign, New York's mechanics (who, in the previous decade, had just been enfranchised, thanks to the elimination of the property qualification) turned their attention to the political sphere: New York's Committee of Mechanics petitioned the state legislature against the "evils" of using convicts in competition with mechanical labor, prompting the Committee of Manufacturing to call for the disbanding of the new

---

[88] "Convict Labor," *Mechanic's Advocate* (Feb. 11, 1847), 83.

[89] Remarks of J. Haskell, *Workingman's Advocate* (May 9, 1835), 6.

[90] Many mechanics' societies also prohibited their members from working for employers who used convict labor, directly or indirectly, and resolved to close down businesses whose owners used convict laborers. In 1834, for example, the Journeymen Marble Cutters Society of New York resolved that they would not work with convict-cut marble, nor work for masters who had used convicts in the cutting of marble, and pledged to "use all honorable means and efficient measures" to prevent any person who had used convict marble from obtaining employment in New York's marble trade. "To the Public" (Resolutions of the meeting of the Journeymen Marble Cutters Society, New York, February 11, 1834), *The Man* 2:19 (June 7, 1834), 75. The Marble Polishers Society passed similar resolutions. *The Man* 2:32, (June 23, 1834), 127.

[91] Panetta, "Up the River," 255–73; Lewis, *From Newgate to Dannemora*, 187–93.

system of prison labor. As the mechanics intensified their campaign against the use of prison labor in their trades, in 1833 and 1834, the newly formed General Trades Union also took up the issue in the political sphere,[92] as did a number of small artisans' associations around the state. The coopers petitioned the state legislature that the Sing Sing "labor saving machine" gave the state an unfair economic advantage over free workmen. The New York Legislature was subsequently besieged by petitions and letters demanding an end to the prison industrial system: The significance of this statewide mobilization is indicated by the fact that the Legislature received more petitions against convict labor in 1833–34 than it had received any other kind of petition at any point in its history.[93]

As a result of the actions of 1833–34, legislators took limited action, chiefly by seeking to put the letting of convict contracts on a competitive bidding basis. But, as the pages of the workingmen's papers attest, the 1834 reforms failed to meet the mechanics' basic objection, that "the labor of the convicts [be] placed in competition with their own in *any* manner" (italics in original).[94] Indeed, in New York, the state Prison Commissioners insisted that it was only in some trades that free workingmen were injured by competition from convict labor and, even then, only to "some extent"; moreover, the commissioners insisted, the workingmen's objection that the use of convicts in the mechanical arts degraded them in the public's eye was "unfounded and illusory."[95] Incredulous, the editor of *The Man* wrote, in early 1834, "Is it possible that our [legislative] Representatives can be so ignorant as to believe that freemen will submit to have the produce of their labor placed side by side, in the market, with that of men, who, having forfeited their liberty, are compelled to live on *six cents a day?*" (italics in original).[96]

Enraged but undeterred, New York's mechanics resumed their organizing efforts in 1834. Haskell warned state legislators that, if they failed to act, a "rolling column" of New York's 125,000 mechanics would "crush their oppressors at the ballot box." Candidates for gubernatorial office began to take notice: A number loudly pledged themselves opposed to any system that, in the words of one candidate, W. H. Seward, "substitutes the labor of felons, the outcasts of society, for the industry of honest and enterprising citizens."[97] Meanwhile, state lawmakers scrambled to appease the mechanics. Following extensive public hearings on the matter, the New York legislature

[92] Sean Wilentz, *Chants Democratic: New York City and the Rise of the American Working Class, 1788–1850* (New York: Oxford University Press, 1986); Daniel Walkowitz, "Artisans and Builders of 19th Century New York: The Case of the 1834 Stone-cutters," *Greenwich Village: Culture and Counterculture* (New Brunswick, NJ: Published for the Museum of the City of New York by Rutgers University Press, 1993), 89.

[93] Lewis, *From Newgate to Dannemora*, 191–93.   [94] *The Man*, 1:16 (Mar. 10, 1834), 63.

[95] Report of the New York State Prison Commissioners, January 29, 1835, re-published in *Workingman's Advocate* (Feb. 14, 1835).

[96] *The Man*, 1:16 (Mar. 10, 1834), 63.

[97] W. H. Seward, in "State Prison Labor," *Mechanics' Magazine, and Journal of the Mechanics' Institute* (Nov. 13, 1834), 4–5.

provided in 1835 that all contracts be open to public bidding and advertised in advance and that only those mechanical trades that supplied goods of the sort that were not produced in the state could be taught in the prison. The law also directed that only convicts with proof of prior training in a trade could be put to work in prison trades, and that where new trades were to be taught, only foreign teachers could be employed to teach them. In an effort to avert the introduction of heavy machinery into the prisons (which took time and money to move and set up), the law also directed that con-tracts would normally be no more than six months in duration and could be extended only with the permission of the state's prison inspectors.[98]

This legislation registered the objections of the mechanics. However, it offered them little practical relief. Some immediately condemned the law as deceptive and feeble: As one critic pointed out, the statute expressly provided that nothing should prevent the teaching of mechanical business in the state prisons, wherever such instruction was necessary to the state's obligation to comply with the terms of any existing contracts.[99] Given that many prison labor contracts still had several years to run, relief from the evils of convict labor would be deferred for some time: "It is all a farce," he informed the readers of *Workingmen's Advocate*, "a mere manoeuver to deceive the oppressed mechanic." New York's prison agents and the labor contractors found other ways around the new law, too: Some bribed local judges to falsify the credentials of prison laborers as pre-trained;[100] others shrewdly defeated the spirit, if not the letter, of the law by discovering ways of retaining the same contractors for long periods of time. Despite the law's provision that new contracts could not award convict labor for periods of longer than six months, several of the manufacturers working convicts at Sing Sing in 1835 managed to renew their contracts for periods of between three and five years; five of these contractors were still using Sing Sing labor in 1840.[101] Indeed, in 1841, when the Superintendent of Prisons was asked why it was that the contract system and its "evils" had changed very little, if at all, since 1835, he testified that he had never received any direction to implement the law.[102] Referring to the reforms as nothing more than a "legislative farce," the *New York State Mechanic* charged that the hard-won

[98] Laws of the State of New York, Passed at the Fifty-eighth Session of the Legislature ... 1835 (Albany, 1835), 341–44. Discussed in Lewis, *From Newgate to Dannemora*, 193; Panetta, "Up the River," 273.

[99] "§10 Nothing in this act contained shall prevent the TEACHING of mechanical business in the state prisons of this state, as far as may be necessary to fulfil (sic) the obligations of the state in the existing contracts for convict labor." Laws of the State of New York, Passed at the Fifty-eighth Session of the Legislature ... 1835 (Albany, 1835), quoted in "A Review of the New York State Prison Law," *Workingman's Advocate* (June 20, 1835), 6, 45.

[100] Lewis, *From Newgate to Dannemora*, 193–94.

[101] "State Prison Contracts," *The New York State Mechanic, A Journal of the Manual Arts, Trades, and Manufactures* (Nov. 20, 1841), 1, 7.

[102] "State Prison Monopoly," *The New York State Mechanic, A Journal of the Manual Arts, Trades, and Manufactures* (Oct. 29, 1842), 1. 49.

prison legislation had never been implemented and that, furthermore, the legislators had never intended it would.

By this time, mechanics in other parts of the country were joining the New York workingmen's struggle against the prevailing convict labor system. Boston's mechanics demanded the outright abolition of Massachusetts' Auburn-plan system of convict labor in 1845[103] and Ohio's deluged their state legislature with petitions for relief from competition from convict labor in the saddlery, carpeting, tailoring, and carpentry trades.[104] Similar action took place in Connecticut in 1842[105] and following protests by free labor and artisans in Kentucky in the early 1840s.[106] Also in the South, Baltimore's weavers and other mechanics petitioned the Maryland House of Delegates in 1836 and 1837, demanding an end to the "injurious competition" from the state prison industries,[107] while workers in the towns and cities of Tennessee, Georgia, and Alabama protested against the practice of putting penal labor to work in competition with free tradesmen.[108]

These efforts prompted a number of state legislatures to conduct investigations into prison industries; many subsequently attempted, in a more sustained way, to restrict the contract system.[109] In 1842, New York legislators forbade the prisons from putting convicts to work in any trade other "than that which the convict had learned and practiced previous to his conviction," and authorized the attorney general to annul contracts that he considered breached the law of 1835.[110] This time, state officials actively sought to enforce the law: The attorney general found ten contracts to be null and void and, at Sing Sing, the agent brought in contractors who put prisoners to work producing goods that would compete only with foreign manufactures (such as cutlery, rugs, and, for a short time, silk).[111] Prisoners were also put to unskilled labor, such as railroad building and fur-cutting, of the sort that was unlikely to provoke the ire of skilled, organized workingmen. The prison inspectors resolved to open a third state prison and dedicate its entire penal labor force to iron smelting (an industry in which few organized workers in New York were engaged).[112] After a decisive show

---

[103] "Mechanics, Read This," *Workingman's Advocate* (Mar. 22, 1845), 1.

[104] "Convict Labor in Ohio," *Mechanic's Advocate* (Feb. 11, 1847), 85–86.

[105] Edwards, "The Labor Legislation of Connecticut," 241–2.

[106] Sellin, *Slavery and the Penal System*, 142.

[107] Shugg, *A Monument to Good Intentions*, 29–30.

[108] Ayers, *Vengeance and Justice*, 65.

[109] Edwards, "The Labor Legislation of Connecticut," 241–2; Sellin, *Slavery and the Penal System*, 142; Shugg, *A Monument to Good Intentions*, 29.

[110] Laws of New York, 1842, quoted in Lewis, *From Newgate to Dannemora*, 197.

[111] Lewis writes that Auburn prison briefly ran a successful silk business after the passage of the 1835 law: Prisoners planted mulberry trees, reared silkworms, harvested the larvae, and, by 1843, operated some ten steam-driven mills. However, by 1842, the industry had fallen victim to a glut. Sing Sing's silk industry was even less successful, generating only $24.02 a full one year – and some $3,000 worth of investment – into the project. Lewis, *From Newgate to Dannemora*, 195–97.

[112] Lewis, *From Newgate to Dannemora*, 199.

of support from New York City workers, the workingmen's societies, and politicians from both the Whig and the Democratic parties, the legislature directed that an iron-smelting prison be built near large deposits of the metal located near Dannemora, in New York's far-flung Adirondack Mountains. In celebration of this development, mechanics from around the state, and their legislative allies, staged a great procession in the streets of New York in the summer of 1844.[113] Work on the new prison began in 1845: The prison would be named Clinton in honor of the governor who, a generation earlier, had been instrumental in setting the Auburn penitentiary on the path to becoming an industrial state prison.

With the enactment and enforcement of restrictions on trades in the prisons and the construction of Clinton, the long-standing struggle between free workingmen and the state prisons abated. An uneasy truce prevailed through most of the 1850s. One of the standard bearers in the New York mechanics' movement against the use of convict labor in the trades conceded in 1847, "(t)his cancerous evil is not so great as it used to be. Much that was wrong has been reformed away." By the same token, he warned, prison wardens and agents still occasionally published advertisements for multi-year contracts for the labor of "Convict Coopers" and other prison tradesmen: Such notices constituted "proof of the existence and operation of the most unwise, wicked and accursed monopoly that any government ever suffered itself to stand responsible for."[114] The manufacturers who retained prison labor and the prison agents who were required by law to put their convicts to profitable labor of some sort or other tested the boundaries of the law; in 1850, for example, the agent of Sing Sing signed a convict labor contract with a local saw manufacturer, even though saws were not imported to the state but crafted locally, and prisons were thereby prohibited from putting convict labor to sawmaking. A lone journeyman saw maker, by the name of Smith, unsuccessfully went to court to obtain a perpetual injunction against the signing of that or any prison labor contract for the manufacture of saws: Judge John W. Edmonds (who happened to be a former inspector at Sing Sing, a leading prison ameliorationist, and founder of the New York Prison Association [hereafter, NYPA]), ruled Smith had not shown how his business, or anyone else's, would be injured by convict saw makers and, consequently, denied the request for an injunction.[115]

Whereas many mechanics had shown some empathy for convicts in the early 1830s, many hardened their attitudes toward convicts in the years after 1834. Some critics of prison labor still took care not to denigrate the moral

---

[113] "Nation Affairs," *Niles' National Register* (June 1, 1844), 66, 14.

[114] "Convict Labor," *Mechanic's Advocate* (Feb. 11, 1847), 83.

[115] John W. Edmonds was the presiding judge; Edmonds had served as a Sing Sing prison inspector in the 1840s; in 1844 he had also led the campaign to establish the New York Prison Association. "Smith against Lockwood, Agent, &c., and Wood," *The New-York Legal Observer, Containing Reports of Cases Decided in the Courts of Equity and Common Law, and Important Decisions in the English Courts; also, Articles on Legal Subjects, with a Table of Cases, a General Index, and a Digest of the Reports*, 10 (Jan. 1852), 12.

character of convicts, preferring to make strictly political and economic arguments against the use of convict labor in the trades. But many more began to engage rhetoric that strongly implied that a deep and unbridgeable moral divide separated free workingmen from imprisoned men. J. Haskell's rhetoric prefigured and exemplified this apparent hardening of sentiment: "(A)re not the most abandoned villains, thieves, and robbers sent to the state prisons, and when they are discharged, are they not thrown, with all their infamy and vices upon their heads, into the ranks of mechanics? Yes, sir, all the dregs and sediment of society of every occupation in the state, after passing and taking a degree at state prison, are made by your laws the associates of the mechanics."[116] Particularly once the genteel reformers of the BPDS began insisting on the reformative virtues of putting convicts to productive labor and, at the same time, set about ameliorating prison conditions, many mechanics called for the outright abandonment of the Auburn system in favor of a strict system of deterrence. By 1842, the editors of *The New York State Mechanic* openly disparaged those "short-sighted philanthropists who would convert our prisons into seminaries of reformation." Punishment ought simply to deter criminals and to do so by inflicting "a terror" upon convicts, they opined; contrary to the positions espoused by the two leading prison reform societies (the BPDS and NYPA), Pennsylvania's isolation system of punishment was "one of the wisest that has yet been framed," and New York ought to adopt it.[117] The deep-seated solidarity that many laboring republicans had demonstrably felt with their imprisoned fellows in the 1810s and 1820s (and even as late as the mid-1830s) had all but disintegrated. In the first volume of *Democracy in America*, published in 1835, Alexis de Tocqueville had observed: "In Europe a criminal is a luckless man fighting to save his head from the authorities; in a sense the population are mere spectators of the struggle. In America he is an enemy of the human race and every human being is against him."[118] While, in 1835, this was something of an overstatement (at least in regard to America), by 1845 Tocqueville's words were proving prophetic.

By 1850, almost all Northern and most Southern states had carved out a distinctive new system of involuntary servitude. The new servitude was enforced, physically, in the great cellular prisons and congregate workshops that sprang up around the union after 1820. It was reinforced, fiscally, by the forced labor of its captives, and legally and symbolically, by penal codes

---

[116] Remarks of J. Haskell, *Workingman's Advocate* (May 9, 1835), 6. In the mid-1830s, mechanics' resolutions sometimes referred to convicts as "worthless outcasts." See, for example, "Proceedings of the Mechanics' Meeting, Buffalo, New York, January 13, 1834," *Literary Inquirer* (Jan. 15, 1834), 2. However, this did not become commonplace until the 1840s.

[117] "The Penal Code of America," *The New York State Mechanic, A Journal of the Manual Arts, Trades, and Manufactures* (Dec. 3, 1842), 2.

[118] Alexis de Tocqueville, *Democracy in America*, trans. George Lawrence (New York: Harper Perennial: 1988), 96. For comparative discussions of the "American System" in relation to European practice, see James Q Whitman, *Harsh Justice: Criminal Justice and the Widening Divide Between America and Europe* (New York: Oxford University Press, 2003).

and civil death and disability statutes. By the standards of early republican penal practice, this ensemble of penal practices was relatively stable. It was not, however, immune to subversion or even the occasional crisis: Inside the prison, for the reasons noted earlier, the very prison labor system upon which the Auburn plan depended ensured that neither Lyndsian fantasies of perfect penal discipline, nor polite reformers' aspirations for the reform of convicts' souls, were realized in practice. Outside the prison, concerted campaigns by skilled mechanics episodically embroiled the prisons in political conflict and resulted in the legislative restriction of the labor contracting practices upon which the prison system depended. Indeed, the antebellum prison was caught in a vice – one that had the potential to rupture the penal arm of the state: When the prison's contract labor system was running more or less smoothly, with most able-bodied convicts at productive labor for a private manufacturer and the state reaping a decent revenue from the sale of convict labor, mechanics and workingmen invariably campaigned against the convict labor system; when the contract system was subsequently restricted, as it was in many states after 1844, both the finances and good discipline of the prison fell into disrepair.

In New York, where restrictive legislation directed that convicts were to labor only in industries in which free labor was not employed, the legitimate industries were often precisely those that had little chance of succeeding in the marketplace. There were good reasons why the silk-raising industry had not prospered for any sustained period of time in New York, for example (including the bountiful supply of cheap foreign silk flowing into the state through the ports). Iron smelting, in which few free laborers were involved, also proved a losing proposition. After the first burst of enthusiasm over the new Clinton prison, by 1852, the prison's iron industry went into severe failure. The inspectors began transferring the idled convicts out of Clinton, and back to Sing Sing or Auburn. Subsequent overcrowding at the two older prisons, and the inability of prison contractors to absorb fully the swollen labor force, had the effect of locking the transferees out of the illicit prison economy of incentives and privileges and thereby ripened the conditions for a fresh round of prisoner rebellions. In 1855, for the first time since the 1820s, male prisoners staged an extremely noisy demonstration over prison conditions (this time, at Sing Sing); two years later, Sing Sing prisoners staged a mass break out. Prisoners tried on numerous occasions to escape (mostly to no avail), and at Auburn, sixty prisoners armed themselves with tools and pikes from the workshops, dispatched a delegation to the administration, and successfully negotiated the release of one of their workmates from the punishment cells.[119] W. David Lewis notes that a number of assassination attempts against the warden also occurred in the 1850s and that prisoners staged an uprising in the hame (that is, harness) shop in 1859.[120] Meanwhile, at the struggling iron-smelting prison, seven prisoners staged a breakout in 1867, killing a guard in the process. As went convict labor industries, so went the good order of the prison.

[119] Panetta, "Up the River," 283.   [120] Lewis, *From Newgate to Dannemora*, 273–75.

On the eve of the Civil War, the penal system was once again teetering on the edge of a full-scale disciplinary crisis of the kind that had destroyed the early penitentiaries. Outside the prisons, too, the uneasy détente between prison administrators and organized labor was threatening to fracture. In New York, the uneasy truce of the 1850s was broken when an iron-molding contractor by the name of I. G. Johnson locked Local 11 of the Union of Iron Molders out of his Spuyten Duyvil factory and moved his operation *in toto* to Sing Sing prison. That a Sing Sing laborer cost forty cents a day, against a free iron molder's $3 daily wage, no doubt attracted the industrialist; but equally attractive to Johnson was the possibility that he could use convict labor to break the union – which is what he proceeded to do, in 1862– 63.[121] In the months that followed the Johnson action, the iron molders urgently petitioned the legislature for relief.[122] Johnson's actions, which were reported in the general and workingmen's press, cemented organized labor's view of contract prison labor as both the embodiment of an industrial slavery to which free workingmen might be reduced, and the tool by which employers might achieve that: The leading workingmen's paper of the time noted in 1864 that "the 'lesson' of prison labor was the 'mercy we might expect should we fail to guard our rights with those potent weapons, co-operation and combination.'"[123] Confrontation appeared imminent.

No confrontation was forthcoming – at least, not immediately. While American prisons had seemed to be hurtling headlong toward a full-scale crisis, the Southern states had seceded from the Union and the country had erupted in civil war. Mobilization for war averted the mounting disciplinary and political crises of the prisons. It also committed the prisons ever more deeply to contract prison labor. After an initial collapse of prison indus-tries,[124] prison authorities – on both sides of the Mason Dixon line – put

---

[121] Panetta, "Up the River," 289.   [122] Ibid.

[123] *Fincher's Trades Review* (8 Oct., 1864); Brian Greenberg, "Free and Unfree Labor: The Strug-gle Against Prison Contract Labor in Albany, New York, 1830–85," *Business and Economic History*, 1980.

[124] At first, many labor contractors' businesses failed. Some lost the markets for their prison-made goods: Many Northern prison contractors who, before the war, had sold most of their boots, shoes, tents, harnesses, and other wares to Southern customers (including slave-holding planters), soon found it impossible to continue their operations. Production in other prisons, where convicts labored under the public-account system, also ground to a halt. At the Massachusetts State Prison, for example, warden Gideon Haynes lost a valu-able contract with a New Orleans wholesaler for hammered stone. Also, after the Union imposed the military draft, in 1863, the states' incarceration rates declined precipitously, with some prisons losing up to fifty percent of their fittest laborers. Judges were known to offer convicted offenders the choice of serving the Union or serving time. As one sheriff lamented in 1865, when asked why incarceration rates had declined so precipitously, during the war, "the penalty of crime . . . was to enlist in the army, and get a large bounty" (Wines and Dwight, *Report on the Prisons and Reformatories*, 312). It is unclear how widespread this practice was. Notably, incarceration rates for women increased somewhat, particularly in institutions in which women convicted of minor institutions were confined. For example, in 1854, women made up twenty percent of the prisoners of the various Massachusetts houses of correction; in 1864, they accounted for almost fifty percent. (Wines and Dwight, *Report on the Prisons and Reformatories*, 313, 319); Gildemeister, "Prison Labor," 63–64.

convicts to work for the war effort, manufacturing war materials and soldiers' kits, raising crops and tending stock, and building fortifications.
Some prison administrations signed lucrative contracts with the federal government and put prisoners to work manufacturing various war-time supplies. (At Massachusetts State Prison, for example, warden Gideon Haynes
replaced a large Louisana contract for hammered stone with a federal government contract for Union army field kits).[125] Just as the Civil War proved
a massive force for industrialization more generally in the North, war mobilization had the long-term effect of committing prisons – and prisoners –
ever more deeply to productive labor and profit-seeking enterprise. The
tendency, already evident before the war, to concentrate large numbers of
prisoners in just a handful of industries accelerated. As economies of scale
emerged in prison workshops, prisons became attractive sources of labor
for contractors whose operations were highly industrialized and required
mostly unskilled labor.[126]

By the end of the Civil War, almost all Northern and Western state prisons were once again contracting or leasing out the labor of the majority of
their prisoners to private interests, and prison contractors were commonly
enjoying annual profit margins of upwards of twice their costs.[127] Those few
state prisons that had briefly experimented with the "public-account" system,
under which the state owned and controlled prison labor and sold the product of their labor either on the open market or to government, soon converted to the contract system or introduced it alongside public-account.[128]
In the summer of 1865, as Congress drafted the Thirteenth Amendment
to the United States Constitution, Enoch O. Wines and Theodore Dwight
(son of the BPDS's Louis Dwight) conducted a systematic study of the various prison systems of the United States and Canada. Traveling through
some eighteen states, including four in the South, Wines and Dwight uncov-
ered a vast patchwork of prisons, jails, and reformatories whose prisoners
toiled away at hard productive labor, typically for a private contractor. To a
degree only glimpsed before the war, contractors and the imperatives of their

[125] Many of the Northern prison contractors who, before the war, had sold most of their
boots, shoes, tents, harnesses, and other wares to Southern customers (including large
slave-holding planters), soon found it impossible to continue their operations. Gildemeister,
"Prison Labor," 63–4.
[126] Gildemeister, "Prison Labor," 63–4.
[127] For a detailed discussion of the profitabiity (for contractors) of the contract prison labor
system in the 1860s, see Wines and Dwight, *Report on the Prisons and Reformatories*, 258–62.
[128] In 1865, the New York state prison at Clinton and the state prisons of Maine and Wisconsin
were all working prisoners on a public-account basis; Wines and Dwight also note public-
account was in "partial use" in New Hampshire. The Illinois state prison at Joliet experimented with the system in 1867–71. However, by 1880, Clinton's entire productive labor
force, almost seventy-five percent (1,271) of Illinois', twenty-five percent (78) of Maine's,
and more than thirty percent (231) of Wisconsin's productive labor force were working for
contractors. Wines and Dwight, *Report on the Prisons and Reformatories*, 253; National Prison
Association, *Transactions*, 1874, 291; Carroll Wright, op cit., 1880, 39; Gildemeister, "Prison
Labor," 39–40.

profit-seeking activities appeared to be exerting considerable influence over the means and ends of prison administration: "(O)ne thing is harped upon, *ad nauseum*," Wines and Dwight wrote of the prison keepers they encountered in the course of their investigation, " – money, money, money.... The directors of a bank or a railroad could hardly be more anxious for large dividends than these gentlemen are for good round incomes from the labor of their prisoners."[129] "'The main object... has [been] to make *nails*, and not *men*,'" one disillusioned prison chaplain lamented in an interview with the investigators (emphasis in the original).[130] No longer a mere means by which the state sought to finance and organize a new, prison-based mode of punishment, the contract system had elevated pecuniary objectives over all others. The contractor was "a power which coaxes, bribes, or threatens, according to the exigency of the case, in pursuit of its selfish ends," Wines and Dwight wrote; indeed, they concluded, he was "'a power behind the throne greater than the throne.'"[131]

*   *   *   *   *

Such were the roots and development of the practical system of penal servitude that the framers of the Thirteenth Amendment implicitly exempted from the otherwise universal prohibition upon slavery, involuntary servitude, and the badges of slavery. Much more than an incidental feature of the state prison system, the performance of forced productive labor for private interests was both an integral, constitutive practice of that system and the source of tremendous profits for the contractor. By 1850, almost all Northern, and some Southern, states had built Auburn-style prisons and put their convicts to hard labor under one or other of the contract arrangements. Like the state of New York, they had also legislated severe civil disabilities (and, in some instances "civil death") for their convicts; almost all had made *permanent* disfranchisement the automatic consequence of conviction for crime. Such laws gave both legal expression and force of law to the imprisoned convict's practical status (forced laborer, involuntarily separated from the community) and implicitly authorized the practice of selling the prisoners' labor power to private interests. They completed the relatively novel complex of practices found in the new state prison systems and made of them a distinctive, *penal* species of involuntary servitude. As the framers of the Thirteenth and Fourteenth amendments were apparently well aware, *an unqualified, truly universal, proscription of slavery and involuntary servitude would have effectively rendered most Northern penal systems illegal.* Hence, the framers explicitly exempted penal varieties of involuntary servitude from the scope of the Thirteenth Amendment. Reaching back to an early republican law – the Northwest Ordinance – they drew directly on that law's exemption clause

---

[129] Wines and Dwight, *Report on the Prisons and Reformatories*, 289.

[130] Chaplain Canfield to Wines, 1866, reported in Wines, National Prison Association, *Transactions*, 1874, 295.

[131] Wines and Dwight, *Report on the Prisons and Reformatories*, 261, 262.

to frame the Thirteenth Amendment. By 1865, the particular strains of servitude that the Continental Congress had written into the Ordinance (i.e, the convict-servant varieties under which an offender either worked off his or her court-ordered fine or had been a "transport" sold into servitude by the merchant carrier) had long since passed away; but a new and industrial variety of penal servitude had taken their place. Likewise, when they came to frame the Fourteenth Amendment, legislators were careful not to interfere with another constitutive characteristic of the prevailing systems of penal involuntary servitude: state laws that stripped prisoners of voting and various civil rights. Much as the Thirteenth implicitly affirmed the existing practices of criminal imprisonment, the Fourteenth implicitly legitimated the states' disfranchisement of ordinary convicts. Although the courts still had to interpret and apply the legal meaning of the Amendments, their symbolic content and their reference to prevailing penal practices needed no clarification: Despite its troubled origins and episodic crises, America's distinctive system of penal servitude had been implicitly recognized, affirmed, and *legitimated* by the highest law in the land.

3

Commerce Upon the Throne: The Business of Imprisonment in Gilded Age America

Business Chances

A manufacturer, who has a very favorable contract for prison labor, only a short distance from the city, fine workshops warmed by steam and fitted with engine and machinery, is desirous of getting some staple article to manufacture, or would sub-let part of the labor.

Classified advertisement, *New York Times*, 1870.[1]

In the 1870s, large-scale industrial interests set up shop in the American penal system. As Reconstruction was defeated in state after state in the South, and the great burst of post-bellum social reform in the North fell victim to economic depression and fiscal retrenchment, state and county governments consolidated their prison labor contracts, and conveyed the labor power of entire prison populations to just one or a few enterprises. In the course of the Gilded Age, the administration, discipline, routines, rituals, objectives, and human subjects of legal punishment became subject, in both direct and indirect ways, to the imperatives of profit-making. Those imperatives were given freest – and bloodiest – reign in the infamous convict lease camps of the "redeemed" American South. Taking full possession of their prison laborers, the great majority of whom were former slaves or the sons and daughters of slaves, large-scale private enterprise put prisoners to the dangerous, hard labor of draining malarial swamps, mining and heaving coal, tapping trees for turpentine, and laying mile upon mile of railroad track. By any measure, these convicts lived, toiled, and died under much harsher conditions than did their counterparts to the North and West. Driven longer and harder, and generally subjected to more and crueler forms of violence and deprivation, leased Southern convicts died at up to eight times the rate of convicts in other parts of the country. "(I)n no part of the modern world," an appalled W. E. B. DuBois would write of the convict lease system in 1935, "has there been so open and conscious a traffic in crime for deliberate social degradation and private profit" as in the "New" American South.[2]

---

[1] *New York Times*, classified advertisements, Dec. 22, 1870, 6.

[2] W. E. B. DuBois, *Black Reconstruction in America, 1860–1880* (New York: Free Press, 1998 [1935]), 698.

Although prison conditions in the rest of the country rarely approached the levels of brutality and degradation inflicted upon convict laborers in the Southern lease camps, in the Gilded Age, most prison systems outside the South nevertheless operated according to much the same organizing principle; that is, the principle that prisoners should be put to productive labor for large-scale, highly organized, profit-seeking enterprises. For the duration of the Gilded Age, consolidated and profitable contract prison labor systems, under which private business enterprise paid the state for the privilege of putting most or all the state's prisoners to work, flourished in the Northeast, the Midwest, and the Far West. In almost every state, the routines and structures of prison life became subject to the imperatives of large-scale profit-making. As Zebulon R. Brockway, the reform warden of the Elmira Reformatory for Boys, put it in 1883, "(r)egard for revenue is the prop of the southern and southwestern lease system, supposed to be bad, and of the prison contract system generally in vogue throughout the country."[3] Even in the handful of prisons around the country where convicts were not hired out to private enterprise, the imperative of profit-making ruled supreme: Under the "public account" system of prison labor, legislators and prison administrators reinvented penitentiaries along business lines, setting up state-administered prison factories, putting convicts to the same kind of hard, profit-making labor to which privately contracted convicts were pressed, and selling convict-made goods on the open market, at the highest price the market could bear.

The full extent of the American system of putting convicts to profit-making labor was systematically documented in 1887, with the publication of the first federal report on the country's prison labor practices. This exhaustive 604-page study (which was commissioned by Congress and conducted by the first U. S. Commissioner of Labor, Carroll Wright)[4] revealed that, on any one day, upwards of 45,000 prisoners – fully seventy percent of the

---

[3] Zebulon R. Brockway, "Debate on Convict Labor" (from the Proceedings of the General Meeting of the American Social Science Association, 1883), *Journal of Social Science* 18 (May 1884),316.

[4] Report of the Secretary of the Interior, Vol. 5, U.S. Commissioner of Labor, *Convict Labor in the United States* (Washington: Government Printing Office, 1887). This study (undertaken by Carroll D. Wright) was the most systematic of all prison labor studies undertaken in the Gilded Age. However, it is probable that it understates the full extent of prison industries and revenues, and underestimates the numbers of prisoners put to productive labor. Although Wright's study indicates that the prison system, on any day, held approximately 65,000 prisoner, in 1885/86, according to the U.S. Census Bureau, the reported total prison, reformatory, and jail population for the United States was 69,288 in 1880 and 95,480 in 1890. This suggests that Wright may have significantly undercounted the number of prisoners present in American prisons, jails, and reformatories in 1885/86, and, by extension, the number of prisoners put to productive labor. Moreover, several states did not submit full reports on their industries to Wright. (It is also the case that the census takers for 1880 undercounted the prison population, as no data were available for prisons in ten states and territories [mostly Southern], including Georgia, one of the largest Southern states). Margaret Werner Cahalan, *Historical Corrections Statistics in the United States, 1850–1984* (Washington: U.S. Government Printing Office, 1986), 29, 192.

nation's total population of incarcerated men, women, and youths – were being put to hard, productive labor in the service of profit-making enter-prises of one sort or another. Notably, while one in five of these convict laborers toiled within the Southern lease system, most of the rest labored in the great prison factories and convict work camps of the Northeast, the Mid-west, and the Far West. Contrary to what most historians have assumed, the labor to which convicts outside the South were put in these years was not sim-ply make-work in character, as was the oakum-picking, ditch-digging, and treadmilling of the system of "penal servitude" that flourished in Britain in the 1870s and 1880s;[5] nor were the prison goods of states such as

[5] James Q. Whitman is correct that the British government introduced the disciplinary sys-tem known as "penal servitude" into (domestic) British prisons in the 1850s and 1860s (Whitman, *Harsh Justice: Criminal Justice and the Widening Divide Between America and Europe* [New York: Oxford University Press, 2003], 177–8). However, he overstates its congruence with the American penal system of the same period: Unlike the American system, British penal servitude was generally not profit-oriented, and the hard labor to which British pris-oners were put was largely nonproductive (in the economic sense). Hard labor in the domestic British system was first and foremost a means of punishment; as punishing as the experience of hard labor could be in American prisons, it was primarily an economic activity (and, after 1876, a large-scale economic activity) aimed at generating profit. The British practice that does resonate more closely with the American experience (but which Whitman does not discuss) was that of putting colonial subjects, convicted of crime or rebellion, to hard productive labor. Outside the British Isles, the Empire directly and indi-rectly operated profit-oriented or otherwise productive prison labor systems in a number of its overseas possessions, including those in South and Southeast Asia, Africa, and New Zealand. The exploitative nature of this labor approached, and upon occasions, surpassed that found in the United States in the 1870s and 1880s. Maori prisoners from the Taranaki region of New Zealand, for example, were put to the hard, dangerous, and forced labor of road building in the South Island, at considerable loss of life, limb, and mana, in the 1880s (Jane Reeves, "Maori Prisoners in Dunedin, 1869–1872 and 1879–1881: Exiled for a Cause," [BA (Hons) thesis in history, University of Otago, 1989]). On British penal policy in Africa, see David Killingray, "Punishment to fit the crime? Penal Policy and Practice in British Colonial Africa," and Odile Goerg, "Colonial Urbanism and Prisons in Africa: Reflec-tions on Conakry and Freetown, 1903–1960," in Florence Bernault and Janet L. Roitman, *A History of Prisons and Confinement in Africa* (Portsmouth, NH: Heinemann, 2003). On the British Empire's South and Southeast Asian convict labor systems, see Satadru Sen, *Disci-plining Punishment: Colonialism and Convict Society in the Andaman Islands* (Oxford, 2000) and Anand A. Yang, "Indian Convict Workers in Southeast Asia in the Late Eighteenth and Early Nineteenth Centuries," *Journal of World History* 24:2 (2003), 179–208. On domestic British prisons of the nineteenth century, see Sean McConville, *History of English Prison Adminis-tration (London:* Routledge, 1981), and David Garland, *Punishment and Welfare: A History of Penal Strategies* (London: Ashgate, 1987). Likewise, productive prison labor in mainland France was never as extensive, profitable, or as consolidated as it was in the United States; it was also frequently carried out by the state itself (under a public-account system). See Patricia O'Brien, *The Promise of Punishment: Prisons in Nineteenth-Century France* (Princeton, NJ: Princeton University Press, 1982). The existence of a strong and well-organized labor movement in France may well account for the difference. As one contemporary critic of the American system of contract prison labor put it in the 1880s, any effort in Europe to impose an American-style system of large-scale contracting was likely to cause a "revolu-tion." The industrial workers' movement was much stronger in Europe than in the United States, and the workers had consistently and successfully mobilized against the expansion of prison labor contracting (*Proceedings of the National Conference of Charities and Correction*, 1884,

New York, Illinois, and Ohio lacking in market value. Unlike the well-known automobile license-plate workshops that pass for "prison industries" in our own time, the prison factories of New York, Illinois, and other non-Southern states tended to be highly productive and profitable enterprises. For example, in the fiscal year 1885–86, according to Wright's labor study, American prisoners made goods or performed work worth almost $29 million – a sum equivalent, as a relative share of Gross Domestic Product, to over $30 *billion* in 2005 dollars.[6] Notably, prisoners put to labor under the Southern form of convict lease produced under fifteen percent of the total value of goods made by American convict labor that year: Prisoners laboring under the contract, piece-price, and public-account systems (mostly outside the South) generated a full eighty-five percent of the value of all goods made, mined, or extracted by the country's prison labor force.[7]

The present chapter narrates the rise to prominence of the highly rationalized and remarkably profitable systems of contract prison labor that came to dominate most state penal systems in the 1870s and 1880s. I begin with a brief discussion of law-makers' short-lived efforts, in the immediate post-Civil War years, to rein in the power of the contractors, and the rapid collapse of these reforms as the "long depression" of 1873–76 set in, and as "Redeemer" Democrats set about dismantling radical Reconstruction in the South. I then explicate the highly rationalized system of contract prison labor that almost all American states would come to favor by 1880. The last section of the chapter fleshes out the ways in which the ubiquitous "regard for revenue" (in Brockway's delicate locution) increasingly bore down, not only on the bodies and souls of the imprisoned, but also on the fiscal, disciplinary, legal, and ideological structures of the penal arm of the state. As we shall see, regardless of legislators' intentions, their enactment, after 1873, of laws designed to rationalize and stabilize the contract prison labor system would have far-reaching consequences – not only for the internal workings of the penal system proper, but for the political and symbolic force field of American legal punishment, as well.

*   *   *   *   *

For a few short years, roughly corresponding to those of radical Reconstruction (1867–c. 1872), many states attempted to rein in the contract prison labor system that had come to play such a central role in most American

---

326–7). The workers' congresses of Gotha (1875), Lyon (1876), and Marseilles (1879) all voted for the suppression of prison labor.

[6] According to the five commonly used historical inflation indexes, $29 million in 1886 is "worth" (in 2005 dollars): $599,504,424.78 using the Consumer Price Index; $589,351,449.28 using the Gross Domestic Product (GDP) deflator; $3,533,953,488.37 using the unskilled wage; $5,877,189,026.69 using the nominal GDP per capita; and $30,101,903,574.40 using the relative share of GDP. Source: Economic History Services, Wake Forest and Miami University, EHNet, http//eh.net/hmit/compare/.

[7] Report of the Secretary of the Interior, Vol. 5, U.S. Commissioner of Labor, Convict Labor in the United States (Washington: U.S. Government Printing Office, 1887), 171.

prisons by the time of the Civil War. In every region of the country, legislators enacted laws aimed at limiting the influence of contractors and the profit motive on prison administration, and supplementing the forced, hard labor to which convicts were sentenced with other, supposedly "reformatory," activities, such as elementary education and craft instruction. These efforts were part of a general sweep of social reforms that lawmakers in many states pursued in the years following the Civil War. Much as the American Revolution had been an engine of sweeping social transformation, the world-altering events of civil war and slavery's destruction had engendered deep, structural change in American (and especially, Southern) society, and fostered the articulation of new conceptions of freedom and the meaning of citizenship. No sooner had the Union declared victory, than great bursts of organizing and reform activity broke out around the nation. In the South, despite the best efforts of many Confederate-era legislators to keep them in their place, four million freedpeople immediately set about realizing, in practice, the promise of freedom. In the North, in 1866, workingmen in more than a dozen states revived their unions and assemblies, commenced their historic drive to build a national (and, in some quarters, international) labor movement, mobilized upwards of three million workers in the cause, and vigorously lobbied the legislatures to recognize what they took to be the fundamental rights of the workingman. The suffrage movement, in the meantime, put women's political rights back on the legislative agenda, both in Congress and in the state legislatures, while Union war veterans and soldiers' widows spearheaded a series of campaigns for the establishment of a federal pension scheme.[8]

In the late 1860s, as different sections of the citizenry endeavored to turn swords into ploughshares, they also began to rethink the means and ends of government (local, state, and federal) and many of the foundational institutions of the antebellum world. Once again, government's exercise of the police power – particularly in the arena of legal punishment, where the state's capacity to exercise force and its regulation of life and death were so acutely and directly revealed – came under rigorous scrutiny.[9] In the North and West, a revived and rapidly growing labor

---

[8] Eric Foner's book on Reconstruction remains the definitive treatment of the period. Foner, *Reconstruction: America's Unfinished Revolution, 1863–1877* (New York: Harper Row, 1988) and *The Story of American Freedom* (New York: Norton, 1998), especially 95–137. See also *The Story of American Freedom*, same pages, on the contested meanings of freedom in that period. For a useful discussion of an important but generally neglected dimension of Reconstruction history – Northern society and politics – see Heath Cox Richardson, *The Death of Reconstruction: Race, Labor, and Politics in the Post-Civil War North, 1865–1901* (Cambridge, Massachusetts: Harvard University Press, 2001).

[9] Prison populations boomed in the years immediately following the end of the war, buoyed largely by an influx of thousands of Civil War veterans, many of whom had been unable to find employment after being mustered out of the services in 1866. Civil War veterans made up as many as ninety percent of prisoners in some Northern institutions in 1866 and, typically, over two-thirds of a prison's total population. As Richard Severo and Lewis Milford have persuasively argued, the mustering out flooded the labor market; many veterans were

movement pressed the state legislatures to abolish or severely restrict the contract prison labor system. The sixty workingmen's representatives who, in 1866, traveled from Georgia, New York, Michigan, Maine, Illinois, Iowa, and several other states to the first national labor congress (held in Baltimore, Maryland), reportedly discussed convict labor with "much excitement" and resolved that if the system could not be abolished altogether, convict labor be compensated at the same rate as civilian workingmen (which, by taking the competitive advantage out of convict labor, would have the effect of destroying it anyway); the National Labor Union that emerged from the Baltimore conference launched a nationwide campaign against the contract system, relentlessly petitioning Congress and the state legislatures (and directly lobbying President Andrew Johnson) for relief.[10]

As this new workingmen's movement mobilized, a new and vital coalition of clergy, reformist prison wardens, and moral reformers also took aim at the contractors' influence over prison life, and at the profit-oriented mode of imprisonment more generally. Galvanized by the publication of Enoch Wines and Theodore Dwight's *Report on the Prisons and Reformatories of the United States and Canada*,[11] in 1867, and animated by the general spirit of progressive reform that suffused American public life during the era of Reconstruction, these middle class prison reformers eventually convened the first national congress of prisons in 1870 (in Cincinnati, Ohio) and established the country's first national prison reform organization – the National Prison Association. The Association's "Declaration of Principles" (which emerged out of the Cincinnati congress, and were heavily influenced by Enoch Wines), endorsed and explained the so-called "reformatory" approach to legal punishment: The objective of prison discipline was the "moral regeneration" of the "criminal," through "reformation . . . not the infliction of vindictive suffering," the reformers wrote. Prison discipline should aim to activate in the prisoner his own "regulated self-interest," less through confinement to hard labor for the interests of profit than through

either unable to find work, or else were refused work on the grounds that military service had had a "demoralizing" effect on them and that they were therefore undesirable as employees. (Although the archives offer few clues as to whether or not imprisoned veterans had been unable to find work, that was certainly the impression of many contemporary commentators.) The presence in Northern prisons of so many citizen-soldiers – who had just risked their lives fighting for the Union – appears to have helped stimulate support for the prison reform movement of the late 1860s. The editors of the *North American Review* wrote in January, 1866: "Now that our prisons are filling up at an enormous rate . . . and drawing into their fatal contamination of returning soldiers and neglected children, it is the duty of every community to take serious thought for the welfare of these persons, remembering how and by whom it was said, 'Inasmuch as ye did it not to one of the least of these, ye did it not to me.'" Richard Severo and Lewis Milford, *Wages of War: When America's Soldiers Came Home: From Valley Forge to Vietnam* (New York: Simon and Schuster, 1989).

[10] *New York Times*, Aug. 21, 1866, 1, 2; Aug. 22, 1866, 5. For a general discussion of the Congress, see Philip S. Foner, *History of the Labor Movement in the United States*, Vol. 1 (New York: International, 1972), 371–3.

[11] Enoch C. Wines and Theodore W. Dwight, *Report on the Prisons and Reformatories of the United States and Canada* (Albany, NY: Van Benthuysen, 1867).

religious instruction, education, a merit mark system, a conduct-based system of probation, and, in general, the proper application of what the authors vaguely referred to as "prison science." Notably, the authors of the Declaration accorded productive labor, which had, up until then,served as the foundation of the American prison order, only marginal significance: Although they stated that "steady, active, honorable labor is the basis of all reformatory discipline," they nonetheless placed that principle well down their list of priorities. Indeed, the Declaration all but demoted the activity of productive labor to the lowest priority and promoted, in its stead, spiritual, psychotherapeutic, and pedagogical approaches to legal punishment.[12]

By the end of 1870, the diverse efforts of workingmen's unions and middle-class prison reformers to reform prison administration began to bear fruit. In the North and West, legislators sympathetic to the working-men or the prison reformers (or both) introduced bills designed to curtail or abolish the contract system; many state governors and lawmakers also established commissions to investigate prison labor. (In 1870, for example, New York's Governor Hoffman appointed a committee of two to investigate the question: Fittingly, in light of the origins of the political pressure for prison reform, the commissioners were Enoch Wines and Thomas Fencer, of the Workingmen's Union). Prison wardens and inspectors in many states also took steps to limit the power of the prison contractor: Specifically, they multiplied and diversified contracts and industries so that a number of small- and middle-sized contractors, instead of just two or three large-scale inter-ests, shared the prison workforce. In theory, this would have the twin effects of decreasing the state's dependency on any one contractor and limiting the impact of prison labor on free workers. As they attempted to dilute the influ-ence of the contractors, wardens in many states also introduced some rudi-mentary versions of the reformatory programs promoted by Enoch Wines and his fellow reformers at the National Prison Association. Oregon, in 1873, established what Governor Grover described as a "progressive sys-tem of improved discipline" at the state prison. Prisoners were given time to exercise in the yard and were allowed to converse, after meeting their task in the workshops. Local citizens established a library, a Sunday school, and guest lectures by local professors; the superintendent opened evening literacy classes. State officials undertook similar reforms in the prisons of California, Massachusetts, Ohio, and New York, as well.[13]

Likewise, in the South, lawmakers took steps to regulate and limit the con-tract and lease systems. After 1866, most Southern governments, including the Republican governments of the Radical Reconstruction period, leased or contracted out their prisoners as laborers. However, many did so reluc-tantly, and largely as an expedient, stop-gap solution to the enormous fiscal,

---

[12] "Declaration of Principles," Enoch C. Wines, *Transactions of the National Congress on Peniten-tiary and Reformatory Discipline*, 1870, 541–7.
[13] Superintendent Watkins remarked to Enoch Wines that this had been conducive to "a more cheerful obedience to rules and a prompt performance of labor." National Prison Association, *Transactions* (1874), 251–2.

administrative, and political challenges they faced in the devastated, post-war South. With few resources at their disposal and most prisons either bombed to ruins or otherwise incapable of properly sheltering and securing the convicts, many lawmakers turned to private enterprise in the hope that prison contractors would find a way of housing, feeding, and establishing discipline over the prisoners until such time as the state could afford to rebuild and run the prisons. The reasoning of the commissioners of North Carolina's first Board of Charities was commonplace: Charged by statute with the construction of a state penitentiary, the commissioners reported the difficult position in which they found themselves: "(T)he Board had no means appropriated for the prosecution of their work and did not feel at liberty to ask any in the present condition of the State finances, although the benefits of a wise use of a limited amount of means would be of great service to the State," they wrote in 1870; "There will be needed the prompt and liberal appropriation of large sums of money. . . . It is important that all the convicts be assigned to profitable labor as speedily as possible, thus reducing the annual expenses to the people."[14]

Few lawmakers envisioned that such an arrangement would later become the highly rationalized and deeply entrenched "*convict lease system*" of the Redeemed South.[15] Although Southern lawmakers and reformers increasingly turned to contracting and leasing in the late 1860s, many also strenuously pursued the regulation of these practices – and all the more so, once it became clear that Southern contractors, no less than their counterparts to the North, tended to drive their prison laborers brutally hard. As in the North, wardens and concerned lawmakers warned of the contract system's

[14] North Carolina Board of Public Charities, First Annual Report (Raleigh: Printed by Order of the Board, 1870), 6, 23.

[15] For Southern Republican governments (of the period of radical [or Congressional] Reconstruction), the effort to restrict leasing and forge a new penology was part of a general move away from the criminal justice system that had developed within, and in service of, a society built on chattel slavery. In Texas, for example, the radical Republicans who held power in 1872 sought to construct what Robert Perkinson has called "a re-oriented criminal justice system designed to protect a new, interracial, modernizing society." (To this end, the Republican government also established a racially integrated State police force). Like other Republican lawmakers in the era of Reconstruction, many Texan legislators saw in the leasing out of convicts a short-term, humanitarian solution to the diseased and overcrowded conditions at the state prison at Huntsville. They did not envision the practice becoming the foundation of the Texas prison system. Robert Perkinson, "The Birth of the Texas Prison Empire, 1865–1915" (Ph.D. diss, Yale University, 2001), espec. 83, and "Penology for Profit: A History of the Texas Prison System, 1867–1912" (Ph.D. diss, Texas Tech University, 1983). In Alabama, the state leased out prisoners to a private railroad building company and mining concerns at this time; prisoners were also put to farm work. Mortality rates were abysmally high throughout the period, and highest in 1869, when almost one of every three prisoners died. Mary Ellen Curtin, *Black Prisoners and Their World, Alabama, 1865–1900* (Charlottesville and London: University Press of Virginia, 2000), 63–4. For a general discussion of leasing during the Reconstruction period, see Edward Ayers, *Vengeance and Justice: Crime and Punishment in the 19th-Century American South* (Oxford: Oxford University Press, 1984), 186–92.

tendency to reduce the prisoner to little more than a money-making machine: One such Southern critic, C. W. Loomis (the warden of Missouri's state prison), reflected that although the lessees of prison labor might be "actuated by just and humane motives," when they paid money for the labor of convicts, "they will tax the convict to his utmost capacity"; the legislature should abolish the system, he concluded.[16] A number of Southern states took steps to restrict and regulate the practice of selling the labor of prisoners: In Georgia and Alabama, for example, Republican legislatures successfully restricted penal leasing; they abolished it altogether in South Carolina in 1871 and in Louisiana in 1873. Others, including North Carolina, took measures designed to check the power of the contractors: North Carolina's *Rules and Bylaws* for the government of the state penitentiary directed the state's superintendent of prison construction to "insist that contractors for work will fill all the conditions of their contract" and granted the superintendent, rather than the contractor, the authority to determine whether or not the prisoners' work met the conditions of the contract; the authority to order punishments was strictly reserved to the Deputy Warden.[17] Lawmakers in several Southern states (whose Republican governments were attempting to diversify their state economies, more generally), also experimented briefly with diversifying prison labor and contracts: Without offering many details, Tennessee's state prisons superintendent reported on efforts to "diversify" prison labor in 1873.[18] Texan state prisoners were put to a variety of handicrafts, as well as textile manufacturing, rather than concentrated in one or two industries.[19]

Like many of the Northern prisons, some Southern prisons during Reconstruction also adopted a range of reformatory programs, of the sort advocated by Enoch Wines and Theodore Dwight. In Texas, in the early 1870s, for example, prisoners enjoyed letter-writing privileges and they appear to have been paid for their labor (about $2 per month; they were free to spend this money on necessities for themselves or send it out to their families).[20] Under Republican rule, some Southern states also introduced "reformatory" programs designed to equip convicts with work skills. At first lacking appropriations from the state legislature, with which they might reduce the

---

[16] Loomis argued that such punishments as were taking place under the lease had not been contemplated in law; he continued: "The sentence of the court condemns the convict to hard labor; but such sentence does not import or imply that the prisoner is to be exposed to the burning rays of the sun, the drenching rains, or the piercing winds of winter." National Prison Association, *Transactions*, 1874, 350.

[17] *Rules and By-Laws for the Government and Discipline of the North Carolina Penitentiary During Its Management By the Commission*, (Raleigh, NC: M. S. Littlefield, 1869), 6–7.

[18] National Prison Association, *Transactions*, 1874, 367–70.

[19] Ibid.

[20] According to the annual reports for 1871–72, the prisoners worked in carpentry, smithery, tailoring, boot and shoemaking, milling, manufacture of rail cars, carriage making, agricultural implements, cabinet work, chair making, and mattress making. National Prison Association, *Transactions*, 1874, 367–8.

number of hours convicts spent in contract labor and establish educational
and trade programs, North Carolina's commissioners nonetheless provided
in the 1869 *Rules and Bylaws* that the Warden, physician, and all guards and
overseers take a reformatory approach to their duties: "The intercourse of
the prison officers must be respectful and kind – no improper language
should be used among themselves or before the convicts. . . . A deep respect
for morals and religion should mark their conduct before the prisoners.
Also great and unaffected interest in their welfare and concern for their
reformation, so that harmony may mark the official conduct of the prison –
that its moral tone and influence may benefit the convicts and the great
end of penal confinement shall be more successfully realized *in the reformation and restoration to society and the State of many valuable citizens.*"[21] Likewise,
the Deputy Warden "shalt instruct the under officers in their duties and
see that such treatment is awarded the prisoners as will tend to their reformation. He shall cause the prisoners to see that he is concerned for their
welfare, point out to them their prison duties, assure them of the solic-
itude for their restoration to society."[22] Four years later, the state prison
directors elaborated upon the reformatory approach, arguing that "(T)he
general assembly . . . is properly the *guardian* of all the criminal as well as
unfortunate classes of the state" (emphasis added), and the prison, a trade
school for the reformation of convicts. Prisoners should be "sentenced to
learn a trade," they concluded, and the state legislature ought to actively
help re-integrate prisoners into the community upon release from their
trade education.[23] Such thinking was a far cry from the official prison doctrines that would come to dominate Southern penology after the defeat of
Reconstruction.

The era of Reconstruction, then, saw widespread efforts to abolish or
severely restrict the contract prison labor system, and to demote the activity
of productive labor – long the foundation of the American prison system –
to just one of several fixtures in the prison regime. The reforms varied from
state to state (and even within states, as in New York) and were applied with
varying degrees of rigor. But their authors nonetheless shared a general commitment to substituting reformatory techniques of discipline for the profit-
oriented systems of contract labor. Reformers such as Missouri's Warden
Loomis and New York's Enoch Wines envisioned penal systems quite different from the contractual penal servitude of the antebellum and Civil War
years. They endeavored to build a penal system that did not depend upon
private contractors and in which the prison was more an instructional, repar-
ative agency, than a site of unbridled economic exploitation, penance, and
suffering. To the extent that the activity of labor retained some significance
in reformatory penology, it was as a pedagogical, more than a profit-making

[21] *Rules and By-Laws for the Government and Discipline of the North Carolina Penitentiary During Its
Management By the Commission* (Raleigh, NC: M. S. Littlefield, 1869), 23.
[22] *Rules and By-Laws for the Government and Discipline of the North Carolina Penitentiary During Its
Management By the Commission* (Raleigh, NC: M. S. Littlefield, 1869), 6.
[23] National Prison Association, *Transactions*, 1874, 350.

or punitive, activity: Labor was to be one of several activities that would impart to prisoners the skill and the will necessary to becoming self-reliant, self-disciplined republican citizens. Not since the 1790s had there been such a radical, widespread, and ambitious effort to rework the means and ends of legal punishment. Much as in the early years of the republic, Reconstruction-era reformers sought the overthrow of a "tyrannical" system of punishment and the creation of a properly "republican" penal institution.

Efforts to revolutionize penal justice during the era of Reconstruction may have been widespread, but they were far from enduring. Like so many of the remarkable social reforms of the period, reformatory prison programs had been all but retrenched by 1877 (and even earlier in some states; the most notable exception to the rule of retrenchment was the New York State Reformatory for Boys at Elmira). In most Northeastern and Midwestern states, the financial panic of 1873 and subsequent "long depression" first dampened and then extinguished the states' reform efforts. Reform in these states fell victim, in the first instance, to the widespread failure, in the early part of the long depression, of many of the small and middling businesses that tended to hold prison labor contracts. Although, during the Reconstruction era, many state prisons had restricted the hours of labor, diversified their contracts, and introduced reformatory programs, the contract system had remained vitally important to prison discipline, finances, and administration: The activity (and discipline) of productive labor still absorbed much more of the prisoners' time than any other activity, and revenue from the sale of prison labor continued to be an important source of funding for clothing, housing, feeding, and guarding prisoners. As the depression hit, and as the markets in laundry services, furniture, tools, brassware, and other goods and services in which prison contractors often specialized collapsed in 1873 and 1874, contractors suspended production or even cancelled their contracts altogether. Many declared bankruptcy. In New York, several businesses cancelled their prison labor contracts outright in 1874; two years later, well over half the convicts at Sing Sing and at Auburn prisons still had no work at all, while most of the remainder were being put to the nonproductive (and often make-work) labor of maintaining the institutions' kitchens, yards, and laundries.[24]

The collapse unleashed new forces of resistance and rebellion in the prisons. With whole prison populations left without productive labor of any kind, the daily routines, disciplinary structure, and financial arrangements of prison life were severely disrupted. For almost as long as the cellular prison had existed, productive labor had been the object around which institutional discipline in general was organized, and the activity of labor had, in turn, propped up institutional discipline. In the absence of productive labor, prison discipline lost not only its point of reference but one of its key supports. During the slump, as prison workshops ground to a halt, discipline

---

[24] *New York Times*, Feb. 16, 1876, 4. See Inspector Ezra Graves to *Utica Herald*, reproduced in *New York Times*, July 3, 1874, 2.

deteriorated rapidly, escape attempts escalated, and prisoners grew defiant. In many states, prisons showed signs of becoming completely ungovernable. Massachusetts, New York, New Jersey, Wisconsin, and Indiana were among the many industrial states that reported mass "idleness," widespread insubordination, a sudden loss of income, and dwindling food supplies in the early depression years. Prisoners at Auburn penitentiary were reportedly quarrelling and knife-fighting in idle workshops,[25] while Sing Sing prisoners executed a series of bold protests and attempted some especially daring escapes – all of which the New York press reported in increasingly alarmed tones. So dire was the situation, from the staff's point of view, that, years later, Northern prison administrators still blanched at the mere mention of the time "before '76." As the minutes of the annual meetings of the National Prison Association attest, such an oblique reference was enough to evoke the triple specter of mass insubordination among prisoners, financial collapse, and an enraged citizenry.[26]

Unsurprisingly, tales of disorder and immorality in the prisons, and the states' loss of revenue (which, as noted earlier, usually defrayed much of the cost of housing, guarding, and feeding the prisoners),[27] quickly became a political problem in many states. A number of legislatures commenced investigations into the condition of the prisons; their findings underscored and elaborated upon the financial and disciplinary breakdown of which the press had been apprising the citizenry. In New York, in 1876, for example, the Assembly Committee on State Prisons reported that, since 1869, New York's prisons had cost the state treasury more than $6 million.[28] As the depression deepened, prison authorities and successive legislative investigators came to share more or less the same analysis of the origins and nature of the crisis: The contract system had tethered the activity of prison labor, and hence the governance and finances of the prisons, to a market that was deeply unstable and unpredictable; the small- and medium-scale contractors that the diversification of prison industries (in the Reconstruction period) had invited into the prisons had been unable to weather the storms of the depression. New

---

[25] *New York Times*, Feb. 16, 1876, 4.

[26] Following a guard's beating of an unruly prisoner in 1874, sixty-five Sing Sing prisoners en route to Auburn slipped their handcuffs with the help of keys made in one of the prison workshops and proceeded to riot in protest. The following year, five prisoners, armed with revolvers, jumped onto a Hudson railroad driver's car, ordered the engineer and fireman to jump off, disconnected the cars, and headed toward New York City at break-neck speed. (Eventually flooding the steam engine's boiler, the convicts took to ground; three were shortly apprehended by armed civilians.) *New York Times*, Aug. 31, 1874, 1; May 15, 1875, 1.

[27] Supra, Chapter II, p. *

[28] *New York Times*, Mar. 10, 1876, 5. These numbers may have been overstated: Louis Pilsbury, the warden of Albany penitentiary, who was already a champion of large-scale contracting and went on in late 1876 to spearhead the drive to expand contracting in New York, served on the committee. (Other members were Sinclair Tousey, George R. Babcock, and A. C. Nevin). See also Glen A. Gildemeister, "Prison Labor and Convict Competition with Free Workers in Industrializing America, 1840–1890" (Ph.D. diss., DeKalb: Northern Illinois Press, 1977; New York: Garland, 1987), 62.

York State prison inspector, Ezra Graves, noted that the contract system, as it was then constituted, had made convict labor – and prison life and administration more generally – dependent upon the fate of the market, with dire consequences for prisons in times of economic depression. "The convicts should have steady and uniform employment," he opined, "and this should not depend upon an active or a dull market. . . . "[29] Graves, like other prison administrators, concluded that the good order of the prison could only be restored and maintained by insulating the prisons from the worst excesses of the unregulated, and demonstrably turbulent, market.

One way of reducing the destructive impact of market forces on the prisons would have been to abolish or radically scale back prison industries, remove prison laborers and prisonmade goods from the open markets, and raise taxes or find some alternative source of revenue with which to pay the costs of feeding and housing tens of thousands of prisoners; certainly, the British and many European governments conducted their domestic (although, not all their colonial) prisons along these lines. However, in 1870s America, such a solution was barely conceivable, let alone politically viable. Most state governments lacked the fiscal and administrative capacity that a wholesale transition to a British-style system would necessitate. Nor was there the political will to expand state capacity. The dominant political ideology, according to which government was inherently prone to despotism and ought, therefore, to be strictly limited in its scope and function, ruled out the construction of the kind of well-funded, expansive state bureaucracy that such a system would require. In a related vein, the early republican doctrine that public agencies of all kinds, and not just prisons, ought to pay for themselves was finding as much traction among the citizenry in the 1870s as it had in 1800. (Indeed, the principle of self-support had enjoyed considerable currency even within the radical prison reform circles of the Reconstruction era.) The general political commitment to keeping government relatively weak was reinforced by the popular moral sentiment that convicts ought to "live by the sweat of their brow" and not by the taxed income of the "honest" workingmen whose laws they had transgressed. This political and moral "commonsense" made abolishing prison industries and restructuring prison finances all but unthinkable.

The path most states took, as the long depression of the 1870s wore on, led in the opposite direction from abolition. Legislators and prison administrators resolved to strengthen, consolidate, and rationalize the contract prison labor system; they did so in the belief that replacing multiple small-scale businesses (which had shown themselves vulnerable to bankruptcy in times of recession) with just one or two large-scale enterprises would enable prison industries to better absorb the shocks and bumps of the demonstrably volatile markets of the American economy. One by one, after 1876, states and counties that had been distributing their prison laborers across a diversity of small and middle-scale business enterprises began contracting

[29] Ezra Graves to Utica Herald, republished in *New York Times*, July 3, 1874, 2.

out the labor of large portions of their prisoners to just one or a few, large-scale enterprises.[30] In New York, the birthplace of the prototypical "Auburn plan" of congregate, contract prison labor, the State Assembly's investigative committee recommended in 1876 that the state adopt the "Pilsbury system" of convict labor. Originally developed by a second-generation prison warden, Amos Pilsbury (Moses Pilsbury's son) at the Albany county penitentiary after the Civil War and championed by his son and third-generation warden, Louis Pilsbury, this system combined rigid industrial discipline with a single, consolidated contract for the labor of all able-bodied prisoners.[31] Invited to serve on the State Assembly Committee on Prisons, Louis Pilsbury quickly persuaded his fellow investigators that the Albany penitentiary was a "model institution of discipline and economy,"[32] and its model should be adopted in the state's troubled prisons. Shortly thereafter, the Governor of New York appointed Louis superintendent of prisons for the state and charged him with the reorganization of the state's entire prison system.

Pilsbury immediately set about putting New York's state prisons on his father's system, contracting most of each prison's labor force to just one or two large-scale enterprises, and cracking down, with considerable force, on rebellious and disaffected prisoners. In 1877, the State of New York contracted out 200, and by the following year, 900, of its Sing Sing's prisoners to just one oven-molding manufacturer, John Sherwood Perry.[33] The award of this enormous contract gave Perry control of ten percent of New York State's entire (free and imprisoned) workforce of oven-molders and reportedly made his operation the largest oven-manufacturing business in the world. Over the next few years, Perry's Sing Sing workforce grew to include more than 1,300 prisoners.[34] Likewise, at far-flung Clinton state prison in Eastern New York, 500 prisoners were put to work for a single hat manufacturer after 1878.[35] Prisoners in New York's six county penitentiaries now also went to work for just one or two contractors.[36]

---

[30] 796 of Sing Sing's 1,480 convicts, and well over half of the Auburn convicts, had no work; many of the remainder had only institutional labor.

[31] Amos Pilsbury developed the system and Louis took over when Amos retired in 1873. *New York Times*, Feb. 16, 1876, 4. There is some irony in the fact that the grandson (Louis) championed a prison labor system that the grandfather (Moses) had bitterly opposed as an inherently demoralizing practice.

[32] *New York Times*, June 7, 1876, 2.

[33] Perry was a respectable and well-known New York businessman; among other things, he was the president of the U.S. Patent Association and, in the 1870s, an ardent advocate of extending patent law. See, "Our Patent System," *Scientific American*, 33:1, (July 3, 1875), 9; "Why Not?" *Scientific American*, 35:12 (Sep. 16, 1876), 178.

[34] Roger Panetta, "Up the River: A History of Sing Sing in the Nineteenth Century," (Ph.D. diss., City University of New York, 1998), 293.

[35] Gildemeister, "Prison Labor," 50.

[36] At Kings County Penitentiary in Brooklyn, for example, 350 male and 50 female "able-bodied" convicts went to work for a women's shoe manufacturer (C. D. Bigelow and Co) in the early 1870s (*New York Times*, Apr. 2, 1874); later that decade, 500 of the convicts were sent to work for the Bay State Shoe and Leather Company. Albany penitentiary's full complement of 500-odd prisoners also worked under a single contract.

Other states followed a similar trajectory, as the long depression wore on. Across the Hudson River from New York city, 400 of the 516 prisoners at the state prison at Trenton, New Jersey were contracted out to one boot and shoe manufacturer;[37] likewise, in Connecticut, all state prisoners went to work for just one shoe manufacturer.[38] In the Midwest, a shoe manufacturer won a contract for the labor power of all Wisconsin's state prisoners.[39] Even the State of Pennsylvania, the legislature and leading penal reformers of which had traditionally rejected the contract system (on the grounds that its principle motive was pecuniary in nature, and, thereby, a corruption of the penitentiary's supreme, *moral* mission of spiritual reform) put the convicts at Western penitentiary to contract labor and more than half their brethren at Eastern penitentiary to industrial piece-price labor, for a hosiery manufacturer.[40] (The rest of its prisoners went to work on the state-owned and operated "public account" system). By 1886, thirteen state and territorial prisons in the Northeast and Midwest had put the great majority of their prisoners to work for three or fewer contractors;[41] numerous county penitentiaries had also adopted a rationalized, Pilsbury-like system of contract prison labor.

Much the same process of rationalization got underway in the South in these years. As Louis Pilsbury sang the praises of his father's prison factory system in New York, the new, Democratic "Redeemer" governments of the South quietly entrenched, rationalized, and extended their own prison labor contracts. Unlike many Republican lawmakers, the Democrats who wrested the reins of power from the party of Lincoln in state after state in the 1870s suffered no obvious ambivalence about selling the labor of convicts to private enterprise. To the contrary, the Redeemers set about

---

[37] In 1871, 400 of 516 Connecticut state prisoners worked for one shoe manufacturer. *New York Times*, Mar. 15, 1873; in 1879, the New Jersey prison labor commission reported that 368 of 600 able-bodied Trenton prisoners worked on the shoe contract. Cited in Report of the Secretary of the Interior, Vol. 5, U.S. Commissioner of Labor, "Convict Labor in the United States" (Washington: U.S. Government Printing Office, 1887), 341.

[38] Alba M. Edwards, "The Labor Legislation of Connecticut," *Publications of the American Economic Association*, 3rd Series 8:3 (Aug. 1907), 216–251.

[39] The Wisconsin contract was for 300 prisoners (M. D. Wells, 1878), Gildemeister, "Prison Labor," 52.

[40] (In 1869 and 1886, respectively).

[41] Sing Sing, Connecticut, Iowa, Massachusetts, Michigan, Minnesota, New Hampshire, New Jersey, Ohio, Rhode Island, Illinois (Chester), Vermont, and Wisconsin state prisons contracted out either all or the vast majority of their productive labor workforce to three or fewer contractors. The Indiana state prisons (at Michigan City and Jeffersonville) contracted out upward of ninety percent of their prisoners to just four contractors. Two small territorial prisons, in New Mexico and Washington, also leased out all of their convicts. The Illinois State Prison at Joliet was the exception to the norm: That prison's productive labor force was contracted out to seven different interests. Even at Joliet, however, there were signs a process of consolidation was underway: More than one-third of the prison's 1,215 contracted laborers were contracted out to a single boot and shoe manufacturer. Report of the Secretary of the Interior, Vol. 5, United States Commissioner of Labor, "Convict Labor in the United States" (Washington: U.S. Government Printing Office, 1887), 9–30.

strengthening, rationalizing, and consolidating their prison labor contracts almost immediately upon taking office. In 1874, Missouri's Redeemer government abandoned the reformatory programs of the defeated Republican government and undertook to put the state prison in Jefferson on an entirely independent fiscal basis: The state built a series of factories within the prison walls and awarded a long-term contract for the labor of its prisoners to shoe manufacturer, August Priesmeyer.[42] Two years later, Mississippi's Redeemer government leased all its state prisoners to just one contractor – J. S. Hamilton and Associates – who in turn subleased the prisoners out to "'planters, speculators, and railroad and levee contractors.'"[43] Tennessee let hundreds of convicts to just one company – the Tennessee Coal, Iron, and Railroad Company – which put some convicts to work on its own operation and ran a lucrative business subletting the rest of the convicts to other enterprises.[44] In Alabama, in 1882, John Pratt's Coal and Coke Company found a loophole in the state law prohibiting the letting-out of groups of more than 200 prisoners to any one contractor by subletting additional prisoners from a supposedly independent lessee. As Mary Ellen Curtin has shown in her insightful study of the Alabama prison system,[45] subletting effectively conveyed control over the majority of Alabama's state and county prisoners to the Pratt company (and, later, the Tennessee Coal and Iron Company). By the mid-1880s, eight of the twelve Southern state prisons operating the convict lease system were leasing out all their fit and able state prisoners to just one lessee; only one Southern state (Alabama) leased state prisoners out to more than three lessees. (Even in Alabama, the practice of subletting enabled a *de facto*, if not *de jure*, monopoly of prison labor).[46]

By the time the United States finally emerged from the long depression of the 1870s, large-scale prison labor contracting was well on its way to becoming the norm around the country. A majority of the states were now selling the labor of most or all of their state prison populations to private contractors; in most states, three or fewer large-scale contractors exercised an oligopoly over prison labor. The states' previous policy of maintaining diversified prison contracts had been all but reversed. Indeed, as the states moved their convicts to larger operations, contracting increasingly became an interprison and, even, an interstate affair. As well as controlling all or a large portion of the prison labor of a particular state or county, several prison

---

[42] Gary R. Kremer, "The City of Jefferson: The Permanent Seat of Government, 1826–2001," in the State of Missouri, Official Manual, 2001–2002; Jerena East Giffen and Thomas E. Gage, "The Prison Against the Town: Jefferson City and the Penitentiary in the 19th Century," *Missouri Historical Review* 75 (July 1980), 414–32.

[43] J. Thorsten Sellin, *Slavery and the Penal System* (New York: Elsevier, 1976) 147.

[44] Karin A. Shapiro, *A New South Rebellion: The Battle Against Convict Labor in the Tennessee Coalfields, 1871–1896* (Chapel Hill: University of North Carolina Press, 1998), 215.

[45] Curtin, *Black Prisoners and Their World*, 77–8. Alabama's 525 productive state prison laborers worked for five lessees. The penal labor practices of the post-bellum South, unlike those of the North, are the subject of a rich body of scholarship. See supra, "Introduction: The Grounds of Legal Punishment," 4, fn. 3.

[46] Curtin, *Black Prisoners and Their World*, 77–8.

labor contractors acquired contracts for prison labor in multiple states in these years. Peter Hayden's harness and saddle company, for example, grew by 1877 to include prison workshops in New York, Ohio, and California.[47] The Bay State Shoe and Leather Company also employed over 1,000 convicts spread across a number of states.[48] After 1876, some lessees of Southern convict labor (most notably the Tennessee Coal, Iron, and Railroad Company) commanded the labor of prisoners across several states, and a Boston shoe manufacturer by the name of Joseph Davis held contracts for large numbers of prison laborers in Virginia, Maryland, and several other states.[49] By the 1890s, another private interest established itself as a large-scale subletter of prison labor in both Florida and Georgia.[50]

As state governments in every section of the union consolidated their prison labor contracts, and large-scale contractors moved into the prisons, they also rationalized the systems of labor under which the convicts worked and the terms and conditions of the contracts themselves. By 1880, three distinct and more or less uniform systems of contractual prison labor, and a fourth, public system of labor had replaced the hodge-podge of local variations that had characterized prison industries in previous years. The largest and most productive of the three was the prison factory system,[51] under which the state sold the labor power of a set number of prisoners to a contractor, who set-up shop on prison premises. This contract factory system operated mostly within the great industrial belt that stretched between New England and the mid-Atlantic states, in the East, to the prison factories of Illinois and Michigan, in the Midwest. Under the prison factory contract, the manufacturer paid the state for a certain number of convict laborers, on a *per capita, per diem* basis, and for a period of anywhere between one and twenty years.[52] The manufacturer generally supplied work materials, civilian foremen, and (often, though not always) power and machinery; the state furnished a disciplinary force of state's guards, suitable workshops, food, medical care, and the prisoners' clothing.

The second standardized system to emerge in the Gilded Age was that of piece-price. Closely related to the prison factory system, although never

[47] Gildemeister, "Prison Labor," 55.
[48] The Bay State Shoe and Leather Company held contracts at the Auburn State, Kings County, New Jersey State, and Rhode Island State prisons.
[49] "Death of Joseph Davis," *New York Times*, Jan. 26, 1897, 2.
[50] According to Collis Lovely, who undertook a study of convict labor for the Missouri Department of Labor, Dr. W. B. Hamby and his partner possessed a lease for 585 Georgia convicts and acquired a four-year lease for Florida's entire convict population 1,100–1,200 (in 1903). They then sublet the prisoners in large lots to other contractors. Lovely, "The Abuses of Prison Labor" (Unknown; republished in *The Shoeworkers' Journal*, 1906).
[51] Contemporary commentators often referred to this system as "the contract system," which is confusing, given that all three labor systems were contractual in nature. For clarity's sake, I shall refer to it as the prison factory variant of the contract prison labor system.
[52] Gildemeister notes that contracts not uncommonly ran for ten and even twenty years in this period, and many ran for five (such as those at the Kings County penitentiary in Brooklyn, New York, and New York's State Prison at Auburn).

as widespread or as profitable, the piece-price contract typically provided that the private manufacturer requisition goods from the prison, supply the prison with all necessary work materials, and pay for the finished goods (by "piece").[53] Like prisoners laboring under the factory system, piece-price prison laborers were to be found almost exclusively in the industrial belt that ran through the Northeast, upper South, and Midwest. (California also briefly experimented with it at San Quentin).

The most infamous of the prison labor systems, the convict lease, was found mostly in the deep South but also in Washington, Nebraska, and New Mexico; under this variant of contractual prison labor, the lessee took full possession of the convicts, supplied his own guard force, and was generally responsible for the care, feeding, labor discipline, housing, clothing, and guarding of the convicts. Typically, although not always, under the convict lease system, prisoners lived in camps, stockades, or rolling prison cars, and worked in mines, fields, and the occasional factory owned and operated by the lessee, rather than the state's own prison. The lessee paid for convicts either on a *per diem, per capita* basis, or in a lump sum, for a set number of years (as in the industrial contract).

A fourth prison labor system – public account – was also in use, on a limited scale, in a number of states at this time. As noted earlier, under public account, prisoners worked for and under the state, and their product was sold on the open market. Public account had its birth in Pennsylvania's "isolation" model of imprisonment, which proscribed the presence of contractors – and other potentially corrupting "foreign" influences – in its penitentiaries. Despite the system's philanthropic roots, however, the public account system of prison labor came, in the course of the Gilded Age, to bear a striking resemblance to contractual systems. In Pennsylvania, the state assumed the form of a large-scale commercial enterprise, consolidated its prison industries, applied the same principles of profit-making to prison life and administration, and put prisoners to work under much the same set of conditions as those to which their brethren were subject in the contractual prison factories. In some instances, the state's "warden and agent" was entitled to a slice of the profits, which, in effect, made him part contractor and part state agent. In other instances, wardens, though not formally entitled to a portion of profit, received some anyway. In principle, public account was not a variant of contracting; in practice, however, it became a Trojan horse by which many of contracting's methods – and, above all, the profit imperative – entered ostensibly noncontractual prisons.[54]

---

[53] Piece-price was used, for example, in Western Penitentiary, Pennsylvania, after 1869 and in Eastern Penitentiary after 1886; the Detroit House of Detention (under Zebulon Brockway); and, in the early 1880s, at the Elmira Reformatory (again, under Brockway). Gildemeister, "Prison Labor," 67.

[54] Of the 14,827 prisoners laboring directly under public-account, almost a third worked at quarrying, carving, and dressing stone or marble. The boot and shoe, brooms and brushes, clothing, and furniture industries, and farming and gardening each accounted for between eight percent and ten percent of public-account prisoner laborers. Report of the Secretary

By 1880, it was apparent that the states' rationalization of their prison labor contracts had revived and stabilized convict labor in almost every state in the union. Whereas, in 1875, prison industries had fallen all but idle, by 1880, the vast majority of fit and able prisoners were at hard, productive labor; most of them labored for private enterprise. All told, by the mid-1880s, approximately 45,000 prisoners – or almost four in every five – labored away on a daily basis for *private* interests, or a mix of public and private interests, under one or another of these prison labor systems. Two-thirds of these prisoners worked exclusively for private enterprise. More prisoners labored under the prison factory variant than either the piece-price or lease variants of the contract system: On any one day in the mid-1880s, just over 15,000 convicts labored in the prison factories, directly under the management of a contractor. Some 9,000 prisoners labored under the lease system of the South and a handful of Western states, and 5,500 prisoners worked under the piece-price system.[55] Regardless of the system under which contractors extracted their labor, prisoners everywhere were concentrated, as never before, in just a handful of industries or lines of work: Two in every three prisoners laboring under factory and piece-price contracts in the industrial states made footwear, stoves and hollow ware, harnesses and saddlery, or textiles.[56] Four in every five leased convict workers in the South and West worked the mines, laid railroad tracks, or tended the fields of commercialized agricultural interests.[57]

The publication, in 1887, of the U.S. Commissioner of Labor's voluminous study of the nation's convict labor systems confirmed that prison industries everywhere were booming: According to the Commissioner's report, American prisoners were making goods or performing work worth almost $29 million annually, a full $25 million of which were produced by prisoners working under a contract of one sort or another. Prison labor forces also appear to have grown since Reconstruction, and at quite a remarkable rate. Although the incompleteness of many states' prison records makes it impossible to track this growth with any precision, the most reliable prison

of the Interior, Vol. 5, U.S. Commissioner of Labor, "Convict Labor in the United States" (Washington: U.S. Government Printing Office, 1887), 80–1.

[55] Report of the Secretary of the Interior, Vol. 5, U.S. Commissioner of Labor, "Convict Labor in the United States" (Washington: U.S. Government Printing Office, 1887), 30–1.

[56] Over one-third of all contract prison laborers (5,950) worked in the boot and shoe industry; approximately ten percent made stoves and hollow ware (1,741); around eight percent (1,295) made harnesses and saddlery, and eight percent (1,276) made clothing. Report of the Secretary of the Interior, Vol. 5, U.S. Commissioner of Labor, "Convict Labor in the United States" (Washington: U.S. Government Printing Office, 1887), 170.

[57] In the mid-1880s, almost one-third of all leased prisoners were put to mining, more than a quarter built railroads, and just under a quarter were engaged in commercial agriculture. Brick-making and carriage and wagon manufacturing each accounted for about five percent of leased prisoners, and the rest were scattered between the lumber and stone industries and a handful of small-scale manufacturing enterprises. Report of the Secretary of the Interior, Vol. 5, U.S. Commissioner of Labor, "Convict Labor in the United States" (Washington: U.S. Government Printing Office, 1887), 171.

censuses of the period indicate that the number of prisoners being put to productive labor (whether for private or state-owned industries) may have increased as much as *seven-fold* in the thirteen years between 1873 and 1886 (from 6,544 prisoners to 45,277). The prison population, on the other hand, appears to have only doubled in the same period.[58] Not only had the raw number of prisoners being put to productive labor increased dramatically between late Reconstruction and the early Gilded Age, but a much greater portion of the country's prisoners were being put to hard, productive labor in the mid-1880s than had been the case in 1873. The era of large-scale, monopolistic, prison industry had dawned.

As well as being a remarkable transformation in and of itself, the resurrection, consolidation, and expansion of profit-oriented prison labor after 1876 was the catalyst for a series of profound changes in the field of American legal punishment. The effects of rationalization were felt, most immediately, by the convicts whose laboring energies the contractors sought to harness, and in the workshops, mines, and railroad camps in which those prisoners toiled. But rationalization also reverberated in other spheres of prison life and in the larger force field of American penal culture and politics. Critically, consolidation altered the delicate balance of power that had prevailed before the depression struck (in 1873) between government, as the imprisoning authority, and the private business interests that contracted for the labor of the state's prisoners. Here, it is important to recall that the chief motivation for diversifying contracts after the Civil War had been the desire among prison reformers, legislators, and prison administrators to hold the influence of any one contractor over prison industries – and prison life more generally – in check. By distributing prison laborers across many small businesses, states had been able to terminate or alter (and, importantly, threaten to terminate or alter) a particular contract, secure in the knowledge that, in so doing, only a small portion of the state's prison population would be thrown into idleness and a fraction of the state's revenue (from the sale of prisoners' labor) lost. When business was booming, as it was in the North between the end of the Civil War and 1872, such an arrangement gave the state a fair degree of leverage against contractors; in effect, the diversification of prison labor in the Reconstruction era had fostered a relationship in which the contractor needed the state more than the state needed any single contractor.

This relation of power was all but reversed when the states and counties consolidated their prison labor contracts after 1872. Consolidation effectively established monopolies and oligopolies in prison labor. Now, with large-scale prison contractors exercising control over much larger portions of a state or county's prison labor force than had been the case during Reconstruction, cancellation of a contract could mean idleness – with its attendant

---

[58] Wines, National Prison Association, *Transactions*, 1873; Report of the Secretary of the Interior, Vol. 5, U.S. Commissioner of Labor, "Convict Labor in the United States" (Washington: U.S. Government Printing Office, 1887).

disorders and scandals – for one-third, one-half, or even the entire population of a penal institution. As the power of cancellation, and of the threat
of cancellation, shifted from the state to the contractor, the penal arm of
government became far more dependent upon individual contractors – and
susceptible to their needs and demands. Indeed, the states' consolidation of
prison labor contracts created the conditions under which contractors were
able to influence, whether more or less directly, the way things were done
in the prisons. As we shall see, contractors wasted no time in exercising this
new-found influence, not only at the point of production proper (that is,
the prison factories, mines, fields, and so forth), but in matters of prison
governance, institutional discipline, and the political and legal spheres,
as well.

That John Sherwood Perry, Charles Bigelow, and other contractors would
seek to broaden their sphere of influence within prisons was consistent with
the general reason they had set up shop in the prison or leased convict laborers from the state in the first place: Contractors sought to turn a profit, and
to do so using the unfree labor of incarcerated convicts. The contractor's
relationship with prisons and prisoners was, first and foremost, pecuniary
in nature; he was an owner and operator of a business, who, like any other
proprietor, endeavored, above all else, to make a profit through and by the
laboring energies of his workforce. This is not to say that contractors had no
other motivations for entering the prison or were inherently unsympathetic
to the various, and contending, ends of legal punishment (such as the rehabituation of the soul, in the spirit of Benjamin Rush, or retribution in the
Kantian vein, or Bentham's deterrent effect): A few contractors endeavored
to treat their prison laborers with "humanity" and some, including Perry,
appear to have genuinely believed that putting convicts to hard industrial
labor for private enterprise was both morally and physically "good" for the
prisoners and fiscally advantageous to the state. (As we shall see, convict
laborers repeatedly and forcefully disputed such claims.) However, any sympathy the contractors may have felt for their convict workers or for the
supposedly higher moral mission of the penal system was incidental to their
principal concern: making their prison enterprises profitable.

Although few contractors penned sustained accounts of their reasons for
using convict rather than free labor, their somewhat fragmentary observations on the subject, combined with evidence regarding their conduct of
business in both the free and prison worlds, cast considerable light upon
their thinking. The apparent cheapness of convict labor (relative to free
labor) was one important motivation: The lower *price* of prison labor certainly drew contractors to the prisons. The careers of many prison contractors tended to confirm this. A number of prison contractors had experimented with various sources of cheap labor before finally settling upon
prison labor in the 1870s. After a controversial and failed "experiment" in
which he attempted to capture the greater New York laundry market via
the employment, first, of young female workers and then, cheap migrant
Chinese labor in his large, Belleville, New Jersey laundering facility, Captain

James B. Hervey signed a contract for the labor of 300 Sing Sing prisoners and transferred his laundry business to the prison in 1873.[59] In similar fashion, New York's Bay State Shoe and Leather Company experimented with other forms of cheap labor as a way of gaining a competitive edge against Boston shoe manufacturers.[60] Some contractors spoke openly of their search for cheap but easily disciplined workers, and of their preference for imprisoned over free labor. The Bay State Shoe and Leather Company's proprietor, Charles D. Bigelow, explained, "First I employed raw Germans, but found it difficult to compete with Boston with them. Then I took some boys from the Asylum for Juvenile Delinquents, who did very well."[61]

The perception of many contractors, in the 1870s and 1880s, that the overall cost of using convict labor was radically lower than the cost of employing waged labor, was well-founded. Although it varied by region, the *per diem* price of a prison laborer was typically anything from one-fifth to one-third the daily wage of a local free laborer in the same industry.[62] In some states, particularly in the South, the relative price of convict labor could be even lower: For example, in the mid-1880s, contractors in Georgia, Arkansas, Louisiana, and Kentucky paid anywhere between two percent and fourteen percent of the daily wages that local free laborers were paid in the same line of work. Even in the North, it was not unheard of for contractors to enjoy this magnitude of cost savings: A shoe contractor in a Massachusetts prison, for example, paid just six percent of the daily wage of a local free cobbler working on exactly the same tasks. Of course, commentators disagreed about the overall cost (as distinct from the price) of convict labor: Critics of the contract system often cited examples of prison factories in

59 *New York Times*, May 5, 1871, 8; Aug. 4, 1873, 8; Hervey was among the first employers in the East to retain Chinese laborers for factory work; in 1870, he recruited some sixty-eight Chinese workers from California for his Belleville, New Jersey laundry. See Frederick Rudolph, "Chinamen in Yankeedom: Anti-Unionism in Massachusetts in 1870," *American Historical Review* 53: 1 (Oct., 1947), 24.

60 Bigelow, in New Jersey, Prison Labor Commission, Report of the Commission on Prison Labor of the State of New Jersey, 1879, Legislative Doc. No. 37, 1880, 55, quoted by Gildemeister, "Prison Labor," 154–5.

61 Ibid.

62 Report of the Secretary of the Interior, Vol. 5, U.S. Commissioner of Labor, "Convict Labor in the United States" (Washington: U.S. Government Printing Office, 1887), Table X, 200. In the case of the Massachusetts shoe contract, the per diem price of state prison labor was 15¢ per prisoner per day, as compared with $2.40 per free cobbler per day. In the absence of company ledgers, it is impossible to say for certain how much contractors, in fact, paid for prison labor. There is some evidence that they paid less than the specified price: As Gildemeister notes, once the contract had been signed, the state often made concessions to the manufacturer, such as lowering the price of labor. My own research confirms that this was the case in a number of states, particularly where the state had contracted out all or most of its prisoners to just one manufacturer. In New Hampshire, for example, the state agreed to build new shops for a contractor who was already operating at the prison and wanted to expand his enterprise. Technically, the contractor was to "pay" the state for the construction and outfitting of the new shops, but the state permitted him to raise the money to do so by negotiating a fifty percent cut in the per diem price of his laborers: In effect, the state convicts themselves paid for the construction of the workshops.

which the convicts were put to work on the "latest labor-saving devices," which enabled the contractor to outproduce his competitors and, thereby, render the overall cost of convict labor even cheaper than its already heavily discounted price suggested. Others countered that the productivity and quality of convict workmanship were generally inferior to the work of free laborers, and that convict labor was therefore not always as inexpensive as its *per diem* price implied.[63] Regardless of where most commentators stood on this matter, however, they concurred that even where prisoners were less productive than free labor, or turned out work of inferior quality, the overall cost of prison labor was significantly lower than that of free labor. Indeed, a range of investigative reports, including Wines and Dwight's 1867 report, the exhaustive 1887 study by U. S. Commissioner of Labor, Carroll Wright (who, at that time, was a supporter of the contract system), and numerous state investigations confirmed that, even where prison labor was less productive and the work of lower quality, prison labor generally cost less than prison labor.[64] Regardless of how cheap prison labor "actually" may have been, contractors perceived that it afforded enough of a cost saving to give them a competitive edge over employers whose labor forces were made up entirely of waged laborers, and this made prison labor very attractive to them.

Although contractors' perception of prison labor as cost-effective was undoubtedly an important motivation for seeking it out, considerations of cost-accounting did not furnish the only, or even the most compelling,

[63] For example, the editors of *Scientific American* estimated convict labor had "an efficiency of only sixty per cent" of free labor, and the *Monthly Register* asserted that "under any system whatever convict-labor is only one-half as productive as free-labor." Neither journal disclosed the source of these estimates. "Labor in State Prisons," *Scientific American* LX:9 (Mar. 2, 1889), 136; "Convict Labor," *Friends' Intelligencer*, Aug. 18, 1888, 528. Working from the most systematic study undertaken in the period (the report of the U.S. Commissioner of Labor, Carroll Wright, in 1887), it appears that Gilded Age penal labor was very probably almost half again as productive as free labor: For every dollar paid in wages in the United States in 1880, there was $5.66 worth of product; for every dollar the contractor paid for convict labor (in 1885/86), there was $8.19 worth of product. Report of the Secretary of the Interior, Vol. 5, U.S. Commissioner of Labor, Convict Labor in the United States (Washington: U.S. Government Printing Office, 1887), 293.

[64] The per diem, per capita price paid for prison labor under every kind of contract typically ranged from one-third, and sometimes as little as one-fifth, up to one-half the daily wage of a free laborer in the same line of work. In 1871, the shoe contractor using inmate labor at the Randall's Island house of refuge for boys, for example, was paying a monthly, per capita price of $3.19 for his unfree labor, when on the outside, a month's worth of work from a free laborer would have cost him $17.34. In the mid-1880s, in shoe and boot manufacturing (which was the single largest prison industry), the daily price of prison labor under the industrial contract system cost anything from a quarter to two-thirds that of local free shoemakers (in Massachusetts and Connecticut, respectively). Even more so, under the convict lease variant of contract prison labor, the daily price of mining labor was anything from one-seventeenth to approximately one-half that of free mining labor (in Arkansas and South Carolina, respectively). *Annual Report of the Prison Association of New York*, 1870, 133; Report of the Secretary of the Interior, Vol. 5, U.S. Commissioner of Labor, "Convict Labor in the United States" (Washington: U.S. Government Printing Office, 1887), 210, 213.

reason for using convict labor. Contractors were also drawn to the penitentiary because prison industries seemed to promise a much higher degree of
control over workers and the production process than was ordinarily possible in the free world. In a related vein, contractors also conceived of many
and varied tactical uses to which they could put their unfree labor forces in
relation to waged laborers and trade unions. Unlike in free industry, both the
supply and the quality of imprisoned laborers could readily be made to hold
steady. This latter consideration repeatedly surfaced in discussions of prison
labor in the 1880s. In the deep South, in particular, the owners of railroad
companies and mining interests saw in prisoners a solution to the chronic
shortage, or spasmodic supply, of free laborers willing to submit to the slavish regimen of labor gang discipline and perform the often dangerous and
strenuous work of mining, laying railroads, draining swamps, and tapping
trees for turpentine.[65] As one journalist put it in 1890 (with regard to convict miners in Alabama): "three hundred men go to sleep at night...and
three hundred men get up the next day."[66] In some Northern states, as well,
contractors saw in prison labor a steadier and more easily replenished supply of labor. Sing Sing prison contractor, James B. Hervey (who, as we have
seen, had experimented with other sources of cheap labor before securing
a prison contract), lamented the difficulty of finding a steady and "trustworthy" supply of free workers: Typically, he complained, a young female worker
labored diligently in her first month at the factory, but, upon receipt of her
wages, "insisted on going home or to the nearest city to spend her earnings and her time."[67] For related reasons, Hervey's subsequent experiment
with Chinese workers "completely failed."[68] The significance of prisoners'
inability simply to up and quit the toil of the workshop for the pleasures of
the city – or even for the less onerous and better-paid workshop of the next
employer up the road – was not lost on contractors.

The importance contractors placed upon the constancy and steadiness
of the prison labor supply was registered in the terms and conditions of the
contract itself: contracts explicitly bound the state to maintain a steady supply of able-bodied prisoners. Critically, the contract might require not only
that the state replace a prison worker who, upon completion of sentence,
was released from prison, but any prison worker who was seriously injured
while working under contract, or fell ill or otherwise became incapable
of working. John Sherwood Perry's 1881 Sing Sing contract, for example,

[65] Ayers, *Vengeance and Justice*, 192–3; Karin A. Shapiro, *A New South Rebellion: The Battle Against Convict Labor in the Tennessee Coalfields, 1871–1896* (Chapel Hill: University of North Carolina Press, 1998), 49–50. As late as 1907, according to Brian Kelly, the operators of the Tennessee Coal and Iron Company in Alabama "considered 'regularity' one of the chief attractions of the convict system." Brian Kelly, *Race, Class, and Power in the Alabama Coalfields, 1908–21* (Chicago: University of Illinois Press, 2004).
[66] Harrison, "A Cash Nexus for Crime," *Birmingham Age-Herald*, Jan. 28, 190, quoted in Brian Kelly, *Race, Class, and Power in the Alabama Coalfields, 1908–21* (Chicago: University of Illinois Press, 2004).
[67] "Chinese Skilled Labor," *Scribner's Monthly* II:5 (Sep. 1871), 497–8.
[68] "The Sing Sing Prison," *New York Times*, Aug 4, 1873, 8.

provided that "in any case where a man so furnished to [the contractor] shall, after a reasonable trial be found unfit for the work, . . . another shall be substituted in his place;" in addition, Perry was "not to pay for any time lost by the men employed regularly . . . when such loss shall arise from sickness or any casualty beyond [his] control."[69] In effect, provisions such as these guaranteed that the state would furnish, and maintain at a constant level, a force of fit and able workers, and replace any prison laborer who fell ill, or became uncooperative or otherwise "unfit for work." Such terms promised a far steadier supply of fit and disciplined labor than could be achieved in the free world.

With the state bound to replace convicts who were injured in the course of their labors, the system also lacked the rudimentary checks that might have existed in a free workshop against the employer who chronically overworked or otherwise abused his workers. Under the conditions of labor scarcity and mobility that characterized Gilded Age economies, the industrialist worked his free laborers harder and longer, and disciplined them more stringently, at his own peril: His workers might simply move on. That dilemma was significantly relieved (though not entirely obviated, as we shall see) where the labor force was composed of a mass of perpetually confined, rightless, convicts. As John Sherwood Perry put it, in his typically direct manner, "(t)here is no intemperance, a minimum amount of sickness; there are no 'Blue Mondays,' and no strikes."[70]

By extension, prison industries promised contractors a much higher degree of control over the pace and general process of production than was the case with waged workers in free industry. Wholly dependent upon the state for the bare necessities of life, and socially and physically confined, prisoners were not merely a steady source of cheap labor, but also an unorganized and highly exploitable body of workers – unlike their increasingly assertive counterparts in the free world. Indeed, prisons promised contractors a refuge not only from the expense and inconstancy of free labor but from the various constraints and power struggles contractors often encountered in free workshops, mines, and plantations. Just as prisoners could not pack up their kit and hit road or rail in search of a better life, they could not very easily lay down their tools, unionize, and strike for higher wages, better working conditions, shorter work hours, and recognition of a union. In prison factories, piece-price workshops, and some of the lease camps, moreover, the state relieved the contractor of much of the time and money that he would otherwise expend on the supervision and discipline of his workers. Although, in a free factory, the employer was solely responsible for supervising and disciplining his laborers, in prisons that disciplinary work was shared with the state. Northern prison factory contracts usually provided

---

[69] Prison Labor Contract. Sing Sing. Stoves and Hollow-ware. Perry and Co, February 7, 1881, in New York Bureau of Labor Statistics, Annual Report (1883), 91–4 and Gildemeister, "Prison Labor," 257–60.

[70] Perry, quoted in Gildemeister, "Prison Labor," 70.

that the state's prison guards were to subject convict laborers to industrial work discipline, and at no charge to the contractor: As specified in Perry's 1881 contract, for example, the warden and agent of Sing Sing was to supply enough competent keepers, "at his own cost and charge," to "maintain perfect system and order among the men, and to compel industry and regularity during the time allotted to labor."[71] Thanks largely to the various practical and legal incapacities that a prison sentence inflicted upon the convict, this arrangement afforded the contractor far more flexible, coercive, and violent means by which to "compel industry and regularity" than were practicable in his dealings with waged workers. (This is not to argue that prison workshops and mines were power vacuums: Whereas the opportunity for organized, collective action of the sort free workers mounted may have been very limited, prisoners nonetheless skirmished with their overseers and prison keepers. Upon occasion, as we shall see in the next chapter, prisoners even engaged in full-scale strike and protest actions.)

As well as identifying prison labor as cheaper, steadier, and more easily disciplined than free labor, contractors in every region of the country saw in prison industries a potentially powerful weapon in their struggle against both the unionization of free labor and free workers' increasingly vocal demands for the eight-hour workday and higher wages. There were several well-known precedents for wielding convict labor as a weapon against waged labor: During the Civil War era, the New York manufacturer, I. G. Johnson had famously demonstrated convict labor's wider potential when, in response to a unionization drive among his free workers, he moved his operation *in toto* to Sing Sing prison and shortly afterwards crushed Local 11 of the Union of Iron Molders (see earlier discussion, p. 83). In 1863, the federal government had also employed – and conferred a measure of legitimacy upon – this combative labor relations tactic when it set prisoners from New York's Governors' Island to work as strike-breakers against some 3,000 longshoremen.[72] In the Gilded Age, as the union movement revived (following its near-collapse during the long depression of 1873–76), employers' use of convict labor to these ends proliferated. In the South, where unions were relatively weak and few in number, members of the burgeoning class of industrialists frequently used or threatened to use convict labor when free workers tried to unionize or act collectively to improve their lot. Free miners' strikes in Tennessee, for example, prompted the Tennessee Coal and Iron Company, and other Southern coal mining interests, to begin large-scale leasing of convict miners. As Karen Shapiro writes, the Tennessee coal

---

[71] Prison Labor Contract, Sing Sing. Stoves and Hollow-ware. Perry and Co., 1881, in New York Bureau of Labor Statistics, *Annual Report* (1883), 91–4, and Gildemeister, "Prison Labor," 257–60.

[72] During the Civil War, the U.S. government used prisoners from Governors' Island as strike-breakers when 3,000 New York longshoremen struck in 1863. Edwin G. Burroughs and Mike Wallace, *Gotham: A History of New York City to 1898* (New York: Oxford University Press, 2000), 884.

operators hoped that convict labor would not only "serve to reduce the wages they paid to free miners," but also "curb the miners' abilities to challenge the operators' labor practices."[73] Indeed, as Alex Lichtenstein writes, the Company went so far in its 1890 annual report to inform its shareholders that "'(i)n case of strikes . . . [the convicts] can furnish us enough coal to keep at least three of the Ensley furnaces running.'"[74]

In the North, prison contractors were among the most vocal opponents of labor unionization. Many were quick to recognize the disciplinary uses to which a prison labor contract could be put in their dealings with free labor, particularly when it came to free workers' efforts to unionize and engage in collective bargaining. New York's John Sherwood Perry, the oven manufacturer who enjoyed a near monopoly of Sing Sing's prison labor force, was a well-known antagonist of union organizers and child labor protection laws. Indeed, Perry went so far as to blame rising crime rates on the union movement. "Take the molders," he opined: "Formerly they employed boys as helpers, a hundred to a hundred men. The Trades Union forbade this. Hence, on every street corner are hundreds of idle boys, given up to crime." For good measure, Perry added: "Why are so many men, and such young men, in prison? It is from the action of the Trades Unions of this country."[75] It was in response to his struggles with the Albany Molders' Union, and that union's strike in 1876, that Perry turned to prison labor. Once installed at Sing Sing, he proceeded to break the local union.[76]

The Bay State Shoe and Leather Company, which went on to become one of the Gilded Age's largest contractors of prison labor, significantly expanded its operations in prisons following a series of organizing campaigns amongst its free workers, in the late 1860s. Shortly after co-signing a manufacturers' "Declaration of Independence," in which many New York area manufacturers announced their intention to resist any and all efforts on the part of labor "combinations" to influence wages and working conditions, the Company's proprietor acquired large contracts at the Brooklyn, Albany, and Rhode Island county penitentiaries, and the state prison at Sing Sing.[77] In a number of industries in the North, free workers reported that, in an effort to boost production and tighten shop floor discipline, employers threatened to close up free shops and relocate to a prison unless the workers speeded up production. The East New York Shoe Company made

[73] Shapiro, *A New South Rebellion*, 52–3.
[74] Alex Lichtenstein also notes that TCI frequently made use of additional convict labor in the mines in response to (and sometimes in anticipation of) a strike. Alex Lichtenstein, *Twice the Work of Free Labor: The Political Economy of Convict Labor in the New South* (London: Verso, 1996), 98, 102.
[75] "Discussion on Convict Labor," *Journal of Social Science*, May 1884.
[76] Panetta, "Up the River," 295.
[77] The Declaration read: "we do now declare our factories free. We will employ whomsoever we please, and at such rates as we may agree upon with the workmen and regardless of the dictation of any combination of men. . . ." *New York Times*, Dec. 31, 1870, 2.

good on precisely such a threat, closing its free workshops and setting up shop in the local prison.[78]

For free workers in some industries, the possibility of losing their jobs to forced labor of prisoners was reinforced by their employers' use of prison labor on certain, typically early, phases of the production process. Although some industrialists abandoned free labor altogether in favor of prison labor, many of the large-scale contractors of the Gilded Age employed a mix of free and imprisoned labor. Some (including Perry's oven-molding company in New York and the Sloss Coal Company in Alabama), integrated their prison workers into a production process that spanned the free and imprisoned worlds; typically, convicts worked on the earlier, and often less skilled, stages of production, and the unfinished goods were then sent on to be finished by skilled, free workers.[79] Others, including the Bay State Shoe Company, took integration a step further and brought hundreds of free workers into the state or county prison workshops, where they labored alongside or not far removed from convict laborers. At Kings County Penitentiary, Brooklyn, in 1880, upwards of 200 free female shoemakers passed through the penitentiary gates every day to work in the prison workshops of the Bay State Shoe Company;[80] likewise, the Midwestern shoe manufacturers, Selz, Schwab, and Company, and M. D. Wells and Company, put free labor to work at the Illinois state prison at Joliet and Wisconsin state prison at Waupun, respectively.[81] Variations of this practice were to be found in every region of the country: In the South, convict and free coal miners often worked for the same companies, as they did in the Pratt mines near Birmingham, Alabama in the 1880s, and on the Tennessee coalfields.[82] Sometimes, prisoners and free workers labored in separate parts of the mines and on different tasks. However, it was not unknown for convicts and free workers to labor in much closer proximity to one another, or even for free workers to sublet convict helpers from their employer. As free coal miners from Helena, Alabama testified before a U.S. Senate committee in 1883, a free miner could (and

---

[78] An employee of the East New York Shoe Company testified before the New York State Commission on Prison Labor that his employer told the workers to speed up production or he would "shut up the shop, and send the work 'up the hill.'" According to another employee, the company dismissed the free workers a week later. Quoted in Gildemeister, "Prison Labor," 154.

[79] For example, the Sloss Coal Company used convict labor in its mining camps and free labor to run its blast furnaces. W. David Lewis, "The Emergence of Birmingham as a Case Study of Continuity between the Antebellum Planter Class and Industrialization in the 'New South,'" *Agricultural History*, 68:2 (Spring, 1994), 62–80.

[80] *New York Times*, Feb. 6, 1880, 4. The practice was not unknown earlier, either. Seventy-five free workers joined hundreds of incarcerated boys who were laboring away for a shoemaking contractor at Randall's Island, in 1870. New York State Assembly Committee on Prison Labor, 1870, in *Annual Report of the Prison Association of New York*, 1870, 125.

[81] Gildemeister, "Prison Labor," 95. Gildemeister spells the company's name: "Sells." However the Illinois Supreme Court identified the company as "Selz." *Morris Selz et al v. Abijah Cagwin et al*, Supreme Court of Illinois, 104 Ill. 647; 1882 Ill. LEXIS 358.

[82] Testimony of John Rutledge, coalminer, Birmingham, Alabama, Senate Committee on Relations Between Labor and Capital, 1883, Vol. IV, 305.

frequently did) sublease a convict helper from his employer, at the cost of about a dollar per day, and put him to work on some of the heavier tasks of mining, such as loading and shoveling.[83] Where prisoners and free workers were integrated into a single business or its affiliates, an employer's threat to replace free employees with convicts must have carried considerable weight with his free workmen; after all, the employer had already shown himself more than willing to engage convict labor in other phases of his operation.

Between the political and tactical uses of prison labor, its cheapness and constancy, and the apparent ease with which it could be organized and disciplined, Gilded Age contractors and their critics alike came to see prison labor as a golden "business chance" and the unfree institution of the prison as the locus of the "freest" (or, as we might say today, most "flexible") labor market. Selz, Perry, Bigelow, and other large-scale prison contractors of the 1880s were not the first to seek competitive and tactical advantage in business through the retention of prison laborers: As we have seen, the earliest contractors had been drawn to the prisons for many of the same reasons. However, the structural changes that swept over prison labor contracting in every section of the country after Reconstruction and in the wake of the economic collapse of 1873 greatly enhanced the contractor's ability to realize what he took to be the full potential of his prison labor force. The pervasively monopolistic structure of the Gilded Age prison contract system and the states' increased dependency upon the one or two contractors who purchased the labor power of most or all of their prisoners allowed contractors a much freer hand in their dealings with prisoners and prison authorities than had previously been possible.

Most contractors wasted no time in flexing that hand. Consonant with their motivations for setting up shop in the prison in the first place, they embarked on a quest to reduce, still further, the costs of production in their prison industries, to perfect their control of the production process, and to make convict laborers as productive and as compliant as possible. Much of this effort took place at the point of production proper – in the workshops, mines, and fields in which the convicts toiled. In the prison factories of the North, for example, contractors brought in the latest labor-saving machinery and innovated new techniques for motivating convicts to work harder, longer, and more diligently. Increasingly, however, in the 1880s, contractors strayed out of the production sphere and into various areas of prison life and governance that, although not part of the laboring process in the strict sense, nonetheless directly or indirectly affected the prisoners' performance as laborers.

As contractors understood very well, what went on *outside* the workshops, mines, or fields (that is, at the point of production) partially conditioned what was possible within them: The quality and amount of prisoners' food rations; the hours of prisoners' rest and work; the kind and intensity of punishments meted out to disobedient, "soldiering," or clumsy convicts;

[83] Ibid.

the state keepers' conduct of general prison discipline; the supply, healthiness, and age of prison laborers; and the rules of prison life – all influenced the contractor's control over his operation and the quality and quantity of work he could extract from his laborers. Although, in most states during the Gilded Age, both statute law and the terms of the labor contract reserved these spheres of prison governance strictly to the state authorities, in practice, they proved wholly permeable to the contractor and the imperatives of profit-making.

Contractors' efforts to shape prison life and administration were most pronounced in the Southern lease camps, where the contractor took physical possession of the prisoners, as well as full responsibility for feeding, sheltering, and overseeing the prisoners' labor. As the extensive body of scholarship on Southern convict leasing illustrates, Southern Redeemer governments all but relieved the penal arm of the state of any practical role in the day-to-day government of its leased prisoners (save the role of replenishing the convict labor supply). In theory, state governments placed legal and administrative constraints upon the authority of the contractor in his dealings with prisoners and, by extension, extended certain rudimentary protections for the prisoners. Under the terms of many convict lease contracts, for example, the state reserved the right of disciplining and punishing the prisoner: State keepers, theoretically, were charged with these tasks; in many states, the lessee was also subject to laws mandating the "humane" treatment of prisoners. In practice, however, the lessee and his civilian foremen, rather than the state and its agents, routinely exercised power over much of the leased prisoner's waking and sleeping life. They exerted a tremendous degree of control over the convicts' lives: The quantity and quality of the meals and the hours of work, sleep, rest, and religious worship; the distribution of the leased workforce; the kind and intensity of punishments inflicted; convicts' health, and even the prisoner's life expectancy, all lay in the hands of the lessee and his overseers rather than with the state's agents and officers. Lessees commonly subjected their charges to working conditions and punishments that can only be described as violently abusive.[84]

The practical autonomy of the lessee was reinforced in the Southern courts, where jurists generally adhered to a "hands-off" policy with regard to the lessee's conduct of his prison labor force, the state's authority to discipline or farm out the discipline of its prisoners, and the prisoner's personal security and welfare. An 1871 Virginia Supreme Court case, concerning a convict laborer by the name of Woody Ruffin (a twenty-year-old former slave from Petersburg),[85] prefigured and exemplified the general position of the

[84] On conditions and discipline in the lease camps, see, for example: Lichtenstein, *Twice the Work*, 84–126; Curtin, *Black Prisoners and Their World*, 97–112; David M. Oshinsky, *Worse Than Slavery: Parchman Farm and the Ordeal of Jim Crow Justice* (New York: Free Press, 1996), Ch. 1; Ayers, *Vengeance and Justice*, 185–222; David M. Oshinsky, *Worse Than Slavery: Parchman Farm and the Ordeal of Jim Crow Justice* (New York: Free Press, 1996), 145–62.
[85] In 1869, Ruffin had been convicted of assault with intent to kill and sentenced to five years in the state penitentiary. *New York Times*, Feb. 11, 1872, 3. *Ruffin v. Commonwealth*, 62 Va (21 Gratt) (1871), 790.

Southern courts on these matters.[86] In 1870, the warden of the Virginia State Penitentiary at Richmond had dispatched prisoner Ruffin and several dozen other male prisoners to work camps owned and operated by Mason and Goach, a contracting company doing construction on the Chesapeake and Ohio railroad in Bath County (some miles away from Richmond).[87] That summer, while laying railroad tracks under the hot Virginia sun, Ruffin and some of his fellow laborers had made a break for their freedom. The railroad company's overseers thwarted the attempt, but not before one of their number, guard Lewis F. Swats, had been killed.[88] The railroad company immediately dispatched Ruffin back to the state penitentiary at Richmond, and he was soon tried before the city's Circuit Court for the murder of guard Swats. Throughout the trial, Ruffin insisted upon his innocence,[89] but the jury found him guilty as charged and he was sentenced to die on the gallows.

Fighting now for his life and not just his freedom, Ruffin appealed his case to the Virginia Supreme Court. Adamant that his client was innocent of murder, Ruffin's counsel argued that Virginia's bill of rights explicitly guaranteed any "man" prosecuted for a capital or other crime the right to a trial by an "impartial jury of his vicinage"; Ruffin's vicinage at the time of the alleged murder, counsel argued, had been Bath County, where Ruffin had been laboring at the time of the homicide, and not the city of Richmond, where he had been tried. The Supreme Court ought, therefore, to overturn the Richmond Circuit Court's verdict and order a new trial by impartial jury in Bath County. (Presumably, Ruffin's attorney was hoping that a new, Bath County jury would return a verdict of "not guilty.")[90] Writing for the Court, Justice Christian asserted that the Virginia penal code of 1860 clearly directed that the Circuit Court of the City of Richmond "shall have full jurisdiction of all criminal proceedings against convicts in the penitentiary."[91] The fact that Ruffin had been in the custody of a private railroad company, operating some distance away from the Richmond penitentiary at the time of the alleged murder, was immaterial: "If [a state prisoner] can be said to have a vicinage at all," wrote Justice Christian, "that vicinage as to him is within the walls of the penitentiary, which (if not literally and actually) yet in the eye of the law surround him wherever he may go, until he is lawfully discharged. . . ." (parentheses in original).[92]

---

[86] In some states, convicts did not suffer complete "civil death," per se, but severe civil disabilities. In 1889, for example, the Supreme Court of Georgia ruled that a person convicted of felony crime or treason was not *civiliter mortuus* in the State of Georgia and that he "might maintain an action for the injuries he received" while a prisoner. *The Dade Coal Company v. Haslett,* Sup Ct of GA, 83 Ga. 549; 10 S.E. 435; 1889 Ga. LEXIS 108; see also, *The Chattahoochee Brick Co. v. Braswell,* 92 Ga. 631; 18 S. E. 1015; 1893 Ga.

[87] *New York Times,* Feb. 11, 1872, 3.

[88] The guard's name in the court record was "Lewis F. Swats"; in the *New York Times* report of 1872, it appears as "Lewis Schwartz." (Feb. 11, 1872, 3).

[89] As reported two years later in the *New York Times,* Feb. 11, 1872, 3.

[90] The court records contain no information about Woody Ruffin's background, his race, or whether or not he was a former slave.

[91] *Ruffin v. Commonwealth,* 62 Va (21 Gratt) (1871), 790.

[92] Ibid.

Having ruled on Ruffin's vicinage, Justice Christian went on to refute the very principle upon which the substance of Ruffin's appeal depended: that was, the principle that, by simple virtue of being a man, Ruffin fell under the protection of Virginia's bill of rights as "a man" undergoing criminal prosecution. The Justice objected: "The bill of rights is a declaration of general principles to govern a society of freemen, and not of convicted felons and men civilly dead." As a "consequence of his [original] crime" – the one that had supposedly landed Ruffin in the state penitentiary in the first place – the prisoner had "not only forfeited his liberty, but all his personal rights except those that the law in its humanity accords to him. He is for the time being the slave of the State. He is *civiliter mortuus*; and his estate, if he has any, is administered like that of a dead man." Indeed, the prisoner was "in a condition of penal servitude to the State."[93] Having put Ruffin in his proper geographical, legal, and moral place, Justice Christian upheld Ruffin's conviction for the murder of guard Swats, and sentenced him to hang on February 9, 1872.

As it turned out, Ruffin was not hanged: Under circumstances that suggest the authorities may have harbored significant doubts about Ruffin's guilt, the Governor of Virginia commuted his sentence. (The original sentencing judge, the prosecuting attorney, prison warden, and a number of other "influential gentlemen" prevailed upon the Governor to commute his sentence – which he did, on the day Ruffin was to have been executed.) More generally, however, the case, and others like it, made it plain that neither private lessees of convicts nor the state authorities had much to fear from the law when it came to their dealings with prisoners. Whether the justices intended it or not, their rulings that Southern convicts lacked all or most civil rights (and implicitly cast doubt on whether the prisoner had even *the right to have rights*), served to lubricate the machinery of the extremely exploitative lease system. Imprisoned convicts appeared to possess few rights that the state, or anyone else, was legally bound to observe.[94]

Outside the South, the courts stopped short of declaring, with Virginia's Justice Christian, that convicts were "slaves of the state." Northern contractors rarely exercised as unchecked or as unmediated an influence over the lives and life chances of prisoners as was the case in the South; agents of the state continued to play an important role in the everyday life of the prisoner, and the rate of mortality for Northern prisoners was well below

---

[93] Ibid.

[94] *Ruffin* has often been used to support the view that the courts took an absolute, "hands-off" approach to prisons and prisoners in the nineteenth and early twentieth centuries. That claim overstates the courts' reluctance to intervene in the executive sphere of punishment and the prisoner's supposed absolute lack of rights. The courts did, in fact, hear prisoners' cases from time to time, which, in and of itself, constituted recognition of their right to bring suit; however, during the period in question, they rarely ruled in favor of prisoners. For a rejoinder to the "hands-off" thesis, see Donald H. Wallace, "Ruffin v. Virginia and Slaves of the State: A Nonexistent Baseline of Prisoners' Rights Jurisprudence," *Journal of Criminal Justice* 20 (1992), 333, 340.

that of Southern prisoners. Yet, in these regards, the Southern variant of contract prison labor was less an exceptional or "peculiar" penal system than the extreme limit of a national norm. Much as in the South, rationalization of the contract system in the Northern and Western states enabled contractors to exert considerable influence over the convicts whose powers of production – and enrichment – they sought to harness; indeed, from the earliest days of the Auburn-style prison labor system, contractors had looked for ways to extend and deepen their control over their convict laborers.[95] After 1876 and the rationalization of the contract system, Northern contractors slowly but surely intensified their hold over prisoners, taking steps to squeeze as much work as possible out of their laborers on the workshop floor, and extended their influence beyond the activity of labor proper to various other spheres of prison life and governance. Just as in the South, neither the state nor the courts actively sought to temper that endeavor. Indeed, they tended to facilitate it.

In the workshops proper, most Northern contractors introduced the latest labor-saving machinery and substituted a variant of the task system, known as "over-work" or "over-stint," in place of the "time" work of earlier eras. Originally an informal and illicit arrangement, contractors in some prisons (including Sing Sing) had experimented with over-stint as early as the 1840s. It was a crude, utilitarian technique of labor management, designed to motivate prisoners to higher levels of productivity by rewarding them for completing more work (or producing more goods) than a specified standard daily minimum, on one hand, and punishing those who failed to meet the minimum, on the other. Typically, contractors set two production levels – one was the bare minimum every prison laborer was to meet, and the other, a much higher "bonus" target. In theory, if a prisoner reached the bonus target, he or she would receive a reduction of sentence (through the acquisition of "good time"), or some extra tobacco or other desirable item; if a prisoner failed to meet the daily minimum or produced poor work, the overseer dispatched him or her to the state's guards for a dose of corporal punishment. By 1870, over-stint had become a more or less legitimate, and quite openly regulated, practice in most Northern prisons.[96] In New York, for example, contractors applied to prison authorities for special permits to give the prisoners gratuities, and were permitted to give prisoners a

---

[95] In New York's prisons in the early 1830s, contractors illicitly offered their prison laborers various incentives to work harder, better, and longer; according to the Prison Commissioners (who generally supported the prison labor system), contractors also sometimes caused the keepers to inflict stripes where, under the prison rules, none were due. Report of the New York State Prison Commissioners, January 29, 1835, republished in *Workingman's Advocate*, Feb. 14, 1835, 6, 27.

[96] In the transition to large-scale contracting, prison labor had been gradually reorganized from "time work" to "task work": rather than work for a fixed number of hours, prisoners were directed to produce a set number of items. *New York Times*, May 2, 1879, 2. According to Enoch Wines and Theodore Dwight, overwork had developed "unconsciously, without plan or design." Wines and Dwight, *Report on the Prisons and Reformatories*, 253.

range of necessaries, such as medicines and food, as well as what one warden described as "holiday delicacies," in return for overwork.[97]

In principle, the over-stint system offered the prisoner a means of improving his lot and, in some states, shortening his sentence. There is some evidence to suggest that at certain points and under certain conditions prisoners approved of the system. For example, in Ohio, in the 1860s, convicts reportedly supported this arrangement: but that was in a broadly diversified contract system, and not under the highly consolidated and rationalized contract system found in the Gilded Age.[98] After 1876, in those prisons in which a Pilsbury-style industrial system was in use – including prisons such as Sing Sing state prison and Albany county penitentiary – the contractors increasingly substituted nakedly punitive forms of coercion for reward- and incentive-centered techniques of motivation. In the late 1870s and 1880s, numerous witnesses wrote of the comparatively stringent industrial discipline the contractors imposed on prisoners in these institutions, as well as the ferocity and speed at which prisoners were now made to work. In many instances, bonus levels were set just beyond what prison workers were physically capable of achieving, but not so high that prisoners would not try to reach them. Motivated by the promise of better rations or earlier freedom, prisoners often labored to the point of extreme exhaustion, producing significantly more than the required minimum but often much less than the bonus level. In other cases, if prisoners attained the bonus level, the necessary minimum was subsequently raised to what had been the bonus level, and the bonus level raised safely beyond reach. According to one former Sing Sing prison officer, Elihu Campbell, when a Sing Sing prisoner managed to finish his daily task with a few minutes in hand and attempted to use that time to rest, the contractor's foreman would give him additional work; if the prisoner succeeded in finishing that work, his task for the following day would be raised; if he subsequently protested or refused to do the work, the task would be raised anyway "as a mode of punishment." Tasks "were continually raised as long as the man had life to hold out and perform those labors," the former officer testified.[99]

The contractors' drive to raise production levels had an immediate and palpable impact upon the bodies of convict laborers. A slew of investigators reported that convicts were being driven brutally hard and suffered

97 Lichtenstein, *Twice the Work*, 129. (Warden Gaylord Hubbell, 1866, cited in *Sing Sing Prison: Its History, Purpose, Makeup, and Program* (Albany: New York State Department of Correction, 1958), 22–3.

98 Overwork had not always been as exploitative as it became under the consolidated contract system. In the 1860s, Wines and Dwight considered Ohio's (which had the backing of the state legislature) favorably: Under the terms of the contract, prisoners were to perform a quantity of work equivalent to four-fifths the amount performed by a free mechanic in the same trade; the contractor would pay for any labor rendered beyond the four-fifths. This money was paid into the state treasury, where it was held without interest. The prisoner was entitled to withdraw funds for the purposes of supporting his family or purchasing books. Wines and Dwight, *Report on the Prisons and Reformatories*, 252.

99 New York (State) Assembly Committee on State Prisons (1883), 92.

unusually high rates of work-related accidents and illnesses.[100] Colonel John Lloyd Broome, who was dispatched by the U.S. Marine Corps to investigate the condition of federal prisoners whom the U.S. government had boarded out to the Albany penitentiary, described the scene he encountered:

> Each prisoner was working so violently, if I may so express it, and so rapidly as to excite my surprise that human beings should be compelled to work at so rapid and unreasonable a rate. I say 'compelled,' because the evidence was before me in the person of an overseer or disciplinary officer paid by the contractor, whose duty was, the Warden informed me, to keep the prisoners at work at that rate ten hours in summer and eight hours in winter, keeping their heads down and not looking up from their work, which I considered a most cruel requirement.[101]

Anyone who did look up from his work in the course of the day was summarily punished, he reported.[102] Shortly afterwards, a New York prison officer's characterization of the state of affairs at Sing Sing (again, under the Pilsbury system), echoed Broome's findings. When asked "by what rule these instructors undertook to regulate the amount of work which each man shall do?" the former Sing Sing officer replied: "None, except as long as life and body hold out; that seems to be the test."[103]

Judging by reports from Sing Sing and elsewhere, this "test" was commonplace in the prison factories of the 1880s. Prisoners working for John Sherwood Perry's stove-molding factory in the early 1880s, for example, were reportedly being worked to the point that they actually dropped faint and exhausted on the factory floor.[104] Although, in free industry, the chronic shortage and unsteadiness of waged labor, and the potential for industrial conflict, furnished at least a partial check against such obscene levels of exploitation, in the prison factories of the 1880s, the contractor did not have to worry too much about either losing his workforce or provoking a strike. With the state bound, under the terms of the contract, to maintain a steady supply of healthy, well-disciplined convict laborers, the contractor tended to work his convicts as hard as he needed to and without regard

---

[100] For example: Report of Colonel J. L. Broome, U.S. Marine Corps, to Secretary of the Navy, reprinted in *Annual Report of the Prison Association of New York*, 1879, 9; New York State Assembly Committee on State Prisons (1883), 7; Wines and Dwight, *Report on the Prisons and Reformatories*, 262.

[101] Broome estimated that prison cobblers were cutting and sewing twenty-five percent more shoes each day than a free workshop of the same size. Report of Colonel J. L. Broome, U.S. Marine Corps, to the Secretary of the Navy, reprinted in *Annual Report of the Prison Association of New York*, 1879, 9. Broome, a distinguished veteran of the Mexican and Civil Wars, served at the U.S. Marine Barracks in New York, Portsmouth, and Norfolk. As commanding officer of his detachment, he led the raids against the illegal whiskey stills in Brooklyn, New York in 1868 and 1870, and put down the whiskey riot of 1868. Register of the John Lloyd Broome Papers, U.S. Marine Corps Museum, Quantico, Virginia (Manuscript Register Series Number 6; no date; no page number).

[102] Broome to the Secretary of the Navy, 9.

[103] New York (State) Assembly Committee on State Prisons (1883), 93.

[104] New York (State) Assembly Committee on State Prisons (1883), 9.

for their welfare. Particularly when it came to the unskilled, highly mecha-nized, labor to which contractors tended to put prison workers, contractors had little incentive to nurture and protect their workers or to retain the same laborers over long periods of time: An exhausted and broken prison laborer, performing rudimentary tasks such as ladling molten iron, could be quite easily replaced with a healthier, fitter body drawn from the constantly replenished pool of newly committed prisoners. Contractors drove their prison laborers extraordinarily hard; they did so not because they sought to wreak vengeance on criminals or because they were sadistic or believed hard labor made good men out of bad convicts; they worked their prisoners to the bone because, under a system in which the state replaced, at no cost to the contractor, any and all broken, exhausted, sick, or disobedient laborers with fresher, fitter, more obedient ones, it made sound business sense to do so. The legal and practical structures of the Gilded Age penal systems fostered such conduct.

As well as driving their prison laborers harder and longer than had been possible under the more regulated contract systems of the Reconstruction era, the large-scale contractors of the Gilded Age increasingly put convicts to a variety of tasks that directly endangered life and limb. Being put to hard labor in a Northern prison factory often exposed the convict to dan-gerous substances or unsafe or faulty machinery and tools; prison labor's injury and occupation illness rates significantly rivaled those of workers in free factories. In Perry's oven-molding manufactory, for example, prisoners working in the polishing shop for any length of time inhaled large quantities of emery dust (generated by polishing the iron castings) and, consequently, developed serious respiratory problems.[105] Sing Sing's hospital recorded an unusually high number of severed feet and bodily burns among the prison's iron and stove workers, because of the company's use of inferior ladles that often broke, causing molten iron to course down the worker's legs and onto his feet.[106] The physicians' reports for the year in which the large Perry con-tract went into effect showed a tremendous upswing in both the number of prisoner requests for treatment by the prison doctor and the number of pris-oners actually treated: Between May and August of 1877, during the months in which Perry's iron-molding operation got up and running in earnest, the number of injuries treated in that workshop inclined steadily from 49 for the month of May to 715 for August – an increase of about 1,460% in a three-month period. With approximately 520 prisoners working in the shop by August, that was an injury rate of well over one treated injury per worker per month. (The surviving records do not indicate the precise nature of the injuries. However, in August, 1877, one in five [or 108] injuries were severe enough that the prison physician excused the wounded prisoner from labor altogether).[107]

[105] New York (State) Assembly Committee on State Prisons (1883), 22, 91.
[106] New York (State) Assembly Committee on State Prisons (1883), 61. In two days in 1881, for example, eight Sing Sing prisoners were treated for foot burns, 14–21.
[107] Sing Sing Prison Physician's Report, in New York State Superintendent of Prisons, Annual Report, 1876/77, 32.

Prisoners' increased vulnerability to overwork and serious industrial accidents and illnesses in the 1880s was reflected in – and compounded by – prisoners' lack of legal recourse in the event they suffered an industrial accident. This was true even where the accident may have been the direct result of negligence by the state or the contractor. One possible avenue of legal redress for prisoners lay in the protections afforded a servant in the master-servant relation. However, until the 1890s (when prison law began to change), most state courts denied that such a relation existed between the convict and either the state or the contractor. In 1881, for example, the Supreme Court of the State of New York ruled that the relation between contractor and convict was not one of master and servant, and that the convict, therefore, was not protected at law as a "servant" would be in relation to his "master."[108] In effect, the contractor, in his conduct of prison industries, was free of even the (admittedly, rather limited) legal constraints imposed by the master-servant relation, although the convict lost the benefit of that relation's protections.

New York's Supreme Court elaborated upon this principle, three years later, when a former prisoner, Warren E. Lewis, sued New York state for damages for serious injuries he had sustained while performing hard labor as a prisoner at the Elmira Reformatory for Boys in 1879.[109] Under the wardenship of Zebulon R. Brockway, that institution was operating a large-scale hollow-ware business on a piece-price basis: Young male prisoners labored away, for upwards of eight hours a day, casting molten iron, under state-employed overseers and instructors, in quantities and to specifications provided by private contractors. One such prison worker, Warren E. Lewis, upon discovering that a ladle in which he was carrying molten iron was defective and was likely to break and pour molten iron on himself and others, had appealed to his overseer (presumably, for a new ladle). The overseer did nothing, other than to compel Lewis to continue working with his cracked ladle; Lewis was later severely burned when, just as he had forewarned, the cracked ladle shattered, spilling the scalding iron down his legs and across his feet. Upon release from Elmira, Lewis sought damages for his injuries, under legal principles governing the master-servant relationship.

In court, Lewis's counsel argued that, although Lewis had been a prisoner at the time of the accident, he was protected by the master-servant relation, in which the state was Lewis's master and Lewis, the servant of the state. In light of the overseer's negligence, argued the attorney, the state owed the former prison compensation for his terrible injuries. In a unanimous decision, Supreme Court Justice Danforth found that no such master-servant relation existed between the state and its prison laborer: "The claimant was not a voluntary servant for hire and reward," he ruled, "nor was the State his master in any ordinary sense. [Lewis] was compelled to labor as a means

---

[108] *Cunningham v. Bay State Shoe and Leather Co.*, New York Supreme Court, 1881, reported in *The American Law Review* 2 (Dec. 1881) 811.

[109] *Warren E. Lewis, Appellant, v. The State of New York, Respondent* [No number in original] Court of Appeals of New York, 96 N.Y. 71; 1884 N.Y. LEXIS 469 (1884).

of reformation, and to endure imprisonment as a punishment and for the protection of the community." Justice Danforth went on to argue that the "cause" of the prisoner's injuries, lay – not with the state, or the irresponsible overseer, or the manufacturer of the defective ladle – but with the prisoner himself, and, in particular, with the crime he had committed and for which he was sentenced to imprisonment at hard labor in the first place: "While employed, [Lewis] was subject to such regulations as the keeper charged with his custody might, from time to time, prescribe, and if in the course of service he sustained injury, *it must be attributed to the cause which placed him in confinement.* He acquires thereby no claim against the State . . ." (emphasis added).[110] The prisoner, having committed a crime that was punishable by a prison term, was responsible for any accidents and injuries that might befall him in the course of his forced labor in prison: In effect, Justice Danforth claimed that Lewis had brought his devastating injuries upon himself.

Sophistic rulings such as these not only withheld from the convict the meager protections afforded by the master-servant relation, but suggested that the court would hold neither the state nor, by inference, the contractor responsible for injuries a prison laborer suffered while under the supervision of that state or contractor: Because the prisoner was in an *involuntary*, rather than a voluntary relationship, the law of master-servant relations did not pertain. (This arguably contradicted Danforth's other position – that the prisoner had, presumably through a voluntary act of crime, placed himself in the position of being injured in the first place). The federal courts also refused to protect prisoners at this time, though on different grounds: The handful of state prisoners who filed civil rights suits in federal court found their cases dismissed on the grounds that federal courts lacked jurisdiction over state prisons.[111]

---

[110] Ibid. In the late 1880s and 1890s, as contract prison labor became the object of a series of exposés, critiques, and large-scale protests, a number of courts in both the North and the South softened the positions found in *Ruffin* and in *Lewis*. In 1891, a Federal Court of Appeal ruled that a federal prisoner who was put to contract labor and who was injured on faulty scaffolding that the contractor had erected and that the prisoner was compelled to work on, was in a master-servant or employer-employee relationship with the contractor, and so, entitled to compensation for "the pain and suffering that he may have been subjected to from the time of the accident up to this time, and which may be caused to him in the future" and charged the jury to take loss of earning capacity into account in their calculation of compensation. Justice Chiras, in *Dalheim v. Lemon et al*, Circuit Court, D. Minnesota, Fourth Division, 45 F. 225; 1891 U.S. App. LEXIS 1733 (1891). Some state courts, however, stood firm: In 1890, for example, the Ohio Supreme Court ruled that no relation of master and servant existed between a contracted prisoner and his contractor: The plaintiff, a prisoner who had been severely injured when a poorly installed ceiling fan in the contractor's workshop fell out of its fixture, could not recover damages. *George W. Rayborn v. Alexander G. Patton*, State of Ohio, Court of Common Please, Franklin County, 1890 Ohio Misc. LEXIS 167; 11 Ohio Dec. Reprint 100 (1890).

[111] For useful overviews of the history of prisoner litigation, see Jim Thomas, *Prisoner Litigation and the Paradox of the Jailhouse Lawyer* (Totowa, New Jersey: Rowman & Littlefield, 1988), and John A. Filter, *Prisoners' Rights: The Supreme Court and Evolving Standards of Decency* (Westport, Connecticut: Greenwood Press, 2000).

In the 1880s, as the state courts reassured contractors and the state that they were not in a master-servant relation with their convicts, and federal courts refused to intervene, the everyday relations of authority and power in the workshops also began to change. In statute law, all matters relating to the disciplining of prisoners (including the imposition of punishment and the grounds upon which punishment might be meted out, the setting of prison rules, and the authority to enforce those rules) fell exclusively in the state's domain; the contractor and his civilian employees were simply to explain, demonstrate, and direct the process of production in the workshops. This neat distinction between the contractor's purview and that of the state was easy enough to draw in theory; on the factory floor, however, it proved little more than a flimsy fiction. The business of industrial production necessarily involved the contractor and his overseers and foremen in the disciplinary relations of the prison, at least to the extent that organizing and overseeing prisoners as they labored in the factories were concerned. Much as Colonel Broome had observed at the Albany penitentiary, civilians "paid by the contractor" started to play an enlarged disciplinary role in the prison workshop. The contractor's foremen and instructors determined the kind of work to be done and set the pace. Overseers and foremen employed by the contractor exercised considerable authority over prisoners by reporting, and threatening to report, prison laborers to the state's keepers for real or alleged incidents of slacking, disobedience, or poor workmanship. The states' guards still executed corporal punishment, but its imposition became tightly tethered to the contractor's setting of targets and standards, the prisoner's performance as a laborer, and the overseer's assessment of the quality and quantity of the prisoner's labor.

At the same time, in many prison factories, the state's prison keepers effectively became auxiliaries of the contractor – a relationship that many contractors affirmed and buttressed by putting the state's guards on the company payroll. In the 1870s and 1880s contractors commonly supplemented the wages of guards and other state officials.[112] Indeed, as one Sing Sing contractor put it in 1870, topping-up the keepers' monthly wage was a vital part of the contractor's business: "*(a)ll the contractors have to do this*" (italics in original).[113] (Sing Sing contractors did so to the tune of about $6 to $10 per guard per month).[114] In return, prison officers coordinated punishments with overseers and surveilled and recorded prisoners' work performances. Civilian foremen commonly referred prisoners to the state keepers for punishment, and pressured state officers to drive prisoners to higher levels of productivity through more liberal infliction of punishments. The contractor's

---

[112] The 1870 New York commission condemned the custom as nothing but "bribery." Report of the State Commission on Prison Labor (1871), *Annual Report of the Prison Association of New York*, 1870, 126.

[113] Report of the State Commission on Prison Labor (1871), in PANY, 26th (1870), 1871, 126.

[114] For a first-hand account of the contract industries at Sing Sing, told from the point of a prisoner, see Timothy Gilfoyle's vivid history, *A Pickpocket's Tale: The Underworld of Nineteenth-Century New York* (New York: Norton, 2006). Thanks to Timothy for sharing the manuscript.

overseer sometimes also questioned the guards' judgment of a worker's performance as "satisfactory."[115] Whether foremen and overseers directly requested the paddling or other punishment of a prisoner, as one of Perry's foremen reportedly did at Sing Sing in 1882, or the state's guards took it upon themselves to paddle supposed shirkers or disobedient prisoners, the infliction of punishments became closely tied to the prisoner's performance (or nonperformance) of his labors.[116]

The state's keepers began to work for the contractor in other capacities, too. Prison officers often found themselves obliged to assist the contractor and his foremen with clerical work and other tasks that were of service more to the contractor than to the state. By the early 1880s, Sing Sing's officers routinely performed a range of tasks for the contractor that, in many cases, interfered with their ability to fulfill the principal duties of state's keeper. Rather than being "constantly on their feet, strictly and vigilantly observing all the convicts" and in "constant readiness at all times for any exigency," as New York state prison rules mandated, some of the keepers spent their (and the state's) time doing paper work for the contractor. The keepers inspected convicts' work and maintained records of tasks, short work, and bad work – all of which was of much more importance to the contractor than to the state, and most of which fell outside the formal duties of state prison keepers. In effect, the keepers were furnishing the contractors with essential administrative labor.[117] Such an arrangement amounted to a tacit employment relation between contractor and state's guards. Contrary to law, it also made keepers answerable to two masters (the state and private business enterprise) and spliced what was supposed to be an undivided line of authority between the warden and his keepers.

As contractors, overseers, and keepers reinvented the relations of authority and loyalty in the prison in the 1880s, the formal and informal rules of the prison and the kinds and intensity of punishments meted out to prisoners also changed. Under the short-lived "reformatory" programs of the Reconstruction era, as we have seen, many prison authorities and rulebooks had treated the activity of hard labor as but one of several essential activities of the prison regimen; rudimentary schooling, reading, and religious education and worship were accorded equal, if not greater, importance. With the advent of large-scale, rationalized contracting in the mid-1870s, however, the observance of industrial discipline eclipsed all other disciplinary objectives

---

[115] James T. Cooper, officer at Kings County Penitentiary, complained of this to the New York (State) Assembly Committee on State Prisons [(1883), 205]. He noted, however, that he knew of one instance in which contractors had overridden a keeper's refusal to administer more punishment. Ibid, 205–6.

[116] According to testimony in 1882, one of Perry's foremen, on at least one occasion, ordered the paddling of a prison laborer. For similar reports, see Wines and Dwight, *Report on the Prisons and Reformatories*, 262; New York State Commission on Prison Labor, 7; Report of Colonel J. L. Broome, U.S. Marine Corps, to Secretary of the Navy, reprinted in *Annual Report of the Prison Association of New York*, 1879, 9.

[117] New York (State) Assembly Committee on State Prisons (1883) 97–9.

and became the foundation of prison order in general. Dutiful labor was frequently listed as the first and foremost rule of prison life. Under the Pilsbury system at the Albany county prison, for example, the rulebook (entitled, "Duties of Prisoners") made obedient labor the paramount requirement of prison life: "1. The prisoners are to labor faithfully and diligently, are to obey all orders promptly, and are to preserve unbroken silence."[118] Unsatisfactory work, accidents involving damage to machinery or materials, acts of insubordination, failure to meet task (that is, produce a set amount of goods on any one day), refusal to work, and sabotage became the most commonly punished offenses. Prisoners were also commonly punished for "insolence" to the "citizen" foremen, and for arguing with them.[119] In 1883, Sing Sing's prisoner pharmacist, who spoke German fluently and had acted as translator for the principal keeper on a number of occasions, testified that after locking a prisoner in position for a paddling, the keeper had instructed him to tell the prone prisoner, in German, that "he has fallen short of work and he must do his task, and if he don't do his task next time I am going to paddle him."[120]

As well as elevating strict industrial discipline to a position of paramount importance in the formal and informal rules of prison life, keepers ceased to enforce certain longstanding prison rules. At Sing Sing, for example, keepers no longer enforced the rule requiring that a keeper accompany any prisoner who, in the course of his work, had to move between workshops. Officers also ceased to enforce rules prohibiting instructors and officers from giving prisoners "gifts" or trading with or selling anything to prisoners, and rules requiring all transfers of prisoners between workshops to be approved by the warden, agent, or principal keeper.[121] In industries in which a degree of communication among workers, or between overseers and workers, was necessary, the oldest and most fundamental of American prison rules – the rule of silent labor – became all but obsolete. Although it remained on the prison rulebooks through the period, in many prisons it was enforced inconsistently, if at all. The advent of large-scale, highly rationalized prison industries had rendered these rules obsolete and even counterproductive; contractors quietly put them aside.

The kind and intensity of punishments meted out to prisoners, for transgressions real and imagined, also changed with the advent of large-scale contracting in the prisons of the Gilded Age. Three distinct kinds of punishments became commonplace: labor punishments, which made labor

---

[118] *Rules, Regulations, and By-Laws for the Government and Discipline of Albany County Penitentiary* (1868) [New York Public Library], 27. This rule, and the priority assigned it, remained on the books through 1882. See, *Rules, Regulations, and By-Laws of the Albany County Penitentiary for Its Government and Discipline* (1882) [New York Public Library].

[119] New York (State) Assembly Committee on State Prisons (1883), 40. Gilfoyle notes that a former Sing Sing guard tesitifed in 1882 that prisoners were punished for failing to make task; Gilfoyle, *A Pickpocket's Tale* (mss.), 33.

[120] New York (State) Assembly Committee on State Prisons (1883), 39.

[121] New York (State) Assembly Committee on State Prisons (1883), 96–7.

itself a punishment by raising the amount and intensity of work the convict was to perform; shock-oriented punishments, which took aim at the subject's central nervous system; and deprivative punishments, the more minor of which took away the hard-earned comforts of prison life (such as tobacco) and the most serious of which aimed to drain the prisoner of his will and capacity to avoid or disrupt labor. Although keepers had innovated some of these punishments in the wake of many states' prohibition of the use of the lash in prisons (in the 1840s and 50s), these forms of discipline were particularly well suited to the industrialized, large-scale contract labor system that came to dominate American prisons after 1876; indeed, in the Gilded Age these punishments underwent standardization, became a routine part of prison life, and displaced most of the older techniques of punishment.[122]

The punishment of harder, longer, labor became routine in the 1880s. Prisoners who accidentally ruined work or failed to make task were punished by the imposition of labor penalties that either raised the amount of labor to be performed on a daily basis or indirectly extended the convict's prison sentence. The standard labor penalties were loss of "good time" (which was typically earned in the workshops and which enabled convicts to shave weeks and even months off their sentence) and the raising of the minimum daily stint. Loss of good time lengthened the prisoner's sentence (and, by default, his time in the workshops); raising the daily stint forced him to speed up his work or face a more serious punishment such as a slugging or tricing. Often, the keepers combined labor penalties with the other kinds of punishment: When a prisoner failed to make task, he was required to make up the work the next day and was also subjected to a paddling.[123] Like the punishments of deprivation and shock, labor penalties were almost always meted out for offenses (whether real or imagined) that took place on the factory floor or otherwise arose in connection with the prisoner's performance of his labor "duties."

Shock punishments administered a swift, maximally painful but typically undebilitating, dose of physical pain to the prisoner's central nervous system. "Slugging," stringing-up (or tricing), and ice-bathing were the three most common techniques of the shock mode of punishment and they were routinely meted out to prisoners for poor work or disobedience in the workshops. Such punishments administered short, sharp, bursts of searing pain, and hinted at the physical devastation or death that would follow should the prisoner refuse or fail to render up the required quality and quantity of labor. At Sing Sing, Clinton, Elmira, and Albany prisons, a laggardly worker could find himself whisked out of the factory to a punishment room, where a guard locked him to the floor and wall, in a bent-over position, and administered a "slugging" to his bare buttocks with a wooden or thick leather

---

[122] See Gilfoyle for a discussion of the intensification of punishments under the Pilsbury system after 1879. Gilfoyle, *A Pickpocket's Tale* (mss.), 41–2.

[123] See, for example, the sworn testimony Elihu R. Campbell, a former state instructor in New York prisons, New York (State) Assembly Committee on State Prisons (1883), 87–9.

paddle.[124] At Sing Sing, under the Pilsbury system, approximately five to ten prison laborers were subjected to this punishment of "slugging" every day, except Sundays (when prisoners usually did not work). Except in cases of extreme injury or accident, prisoners were immediately returned to the workshop after the administration of shock.[125] The report of one former Auburn prisoner, in 1879, that he had received lashes for failing to produce his task of eleven iron hamboilers for his contractor was echoed in the testimony of many former convicts and guards.[126] Convicts who ruined materials, whether intentionally or by mistake, were also subjected to this kind of punishment. The experience of a prisoner-cobbler, who labored at inking the soles of shoes for a contractor at the Albany penitentiary, was not uncommon: As punishment for making a mistake in the inking process, he was fined a week's worth of tobacco; when he made a subsequent mistake, spilling the dark ink on the fine white lining of a shoe, the civilian instructor reported him to the keeper, whereupon the deputy warden promptly marched the prisoner out of the shop, shackled him to a wall, and administered fifteen lashes of a leather paddle.[127]

Other forms of shock punishment that became a fixture of American prison life during the Gilded Age included the particularly time-efficient punishment of stringing-up. The prisoner was "triced" up by the thumbs, with the help of fishing-line and a pulley mechanism attached to the ceiling of a purpose-built punishment room. At Sing Sing, this machine enabled the principal keeper to lift the prisoner clear off his toes, which resulted in nerve-tearing pain that the victim could endure only for a matter of seconds.[128] During the same decade, convicts in many American prisons

---

[124] Sworn testimony of Jules M. Columbani, former prisoner and former head pharmacist. Sing Sing hospital, before the New York State Assembly Committee on Prison Labor (1883), 4–5. Columbani testified that Sing Sing had two paddles, "one that is shown to the committee and the other is kept in hiding and is the actual instrument." The latter was reportedly a thick leather paddle, used on the naked buttocks of the prisoner; Columbani, who worked in the prison hospital, which was next to Sing Sing's paddling room, claimed he often heard the strikes of the paddle and then treated prisoners after the punishment. On one occasion, he testified, he heard guards administer 315 strikes to one convict, an African American man by the name of Louis; another convict, by the name of John Kehoe, reportedly received 315 blows on another occasion. New York State Assembly Committee on Prison Labor (1883), 5, 6, 37. See also sworn testimony of Richard Platt, 73; and sworn testimony of former prison officer Elihu Campbell, 107–8, 112. For testimony and reports of work-related paddlings at Elmira Reformatory for Boys, see *New York Times*, March 26, 1882, 1; Sep. 28, 1882, 5.

[125] New York State Assembly Committee on Prison Labor (1883), 74–5.

[126] *New York Times*, May 2, 1879, 2.

[127] Sworn testimony of former prisoner Richard Platt. New York State Assembly Committee on Prison Labor (1883), 72–3.

[128] *Sing Sing Prison: Its History, Purpose, Makeup, and Program* (Albany: New York State Department of Correction, 1958), 23; Colonel J. L. Broome, in his investigation of prisons for the Secretary of the Navy, reported that paddling was undertaken at Sing Sing, although the laws of the State of New York forbade the practice. Colonel Broome reported he subjected himself to the tricing punishment, and lasted forty seconds. Report of Colonel J. L. Broome, U.S. Marine Corps, to Secretary of the Navy, reprinted in *Annual Report of the Prison Association of New York*, 1879, 14.

were subject to the cold shower bath and variations of that technique. This punishment (which had first been used in the Boston House of Correction in the late 1830s and at Auburn prison after the formal abolition of the lash in the 1840s) combined nervous shock with a threat of imminent death by drowning: The keeper swiftly administered a massive shock to the victim's central nervous system by plunging him into a large vat of ice-cold water, and, by holding him under, communicated to the victim the ease with which the keeper might kill him. At Auburn prison, the practice had been combined with use of that old, pre-Revolutionary instrument of punishment – the stocks – and often to deadly effect. In the earliest days of its use, the prison physician reported that the victim was fastened into the stocks, which forced his head back, and then the keeper would "douche" him with ice-cold water. The doctor explained,

> The muscles involuntarily shrink from the application of cold. But [when in the stocks] they must bear the whole shock in all its severity. . . . The first effect is strangulation to a most painful degree. The next is aberration of mind, convulsions, congestion of the brain, liver, and bowels. The blood, receding from the surface, is thrown suddenly and violently upon these organs, and the above result is inevitable.[129]

Former prisoners also remarked upon the various uses of ice water as a punishment designed to shock the nervous system: John B. Reynolds, for example, recalled the occasional use of water torture in the Kansas State Prison in the 1880s. According to Reynolds, particularly recalcitrant prisoners were stripped, strapped to a wooden post, and then hosed at a pressure of about 60 pounds per square inch: "(a)s the water strikes the nude body the suffering is intense," Reynolds observed.[130] Such extreme forms of chastisement were not as commonly resorted to as others; they appear to have been reserved for prisoners who repeatedly, and flat-out, refused to work. One witness of a "bathing" in an Ohio prison noted that the prisoner was held down for some time, then allowed to breathe, and finally asked "whether he will consent to make bolts."[131]

The third kind of punishment to be refined and routinized in the industrial prisons after 1876 was based on the principle of deprivation. At its most extreme, it involved isolation, sensory deprivation, dehydration, and starvation. Although the shock punishment of a slugging or a tricing was relatively time-efficient and was meted out as a corrective to poor or slow work, or minor acts of insubordination, corporeal deprivation was generally a more serious punishment that was reserved for prisoners whom the keeper perceived to be deeply and willfully resistant to labor discipline. The prisoner was held for a matter of days or weeks in a stripped-down "dark

[129] Boston Prison Discipline Society, Fourteenth Annual Report (1839) 95; Twenty-Fourth Annual Report (1849), 49.
[130] John R. Reynolds, *The Twin Hells: A Thrilling Narrative of Life in the Kansas and Missouri Penitentiaries* (Chicago: M. A. Donahue, 1890), 94.
[131] Gildemeister, "Prison Labor," 117–8.

cell" or "dungeon" and put on a strict bread-and-water diet. Such punishment aimed at breaking the will of the prisoner by disorienting him and draining his energy. As Sing Sing's prisoner pharmacist testified in 1882, prisoners who flat-out refused to work were typically thrown in the dark-cell, and the length of confinement there was determined by the prisoner's "entire submission" to the labor regime.[132] Although deprivation, like shock punishment, had been in use in varied forms since the use of the whip had been prohibited in most state prisons (in the 1840s), the practice had been somewhat haphazard. In New York and elsewhere, before 1879, the dark-cell was typically a makeshift arrangement: The keepers adapted a regular cell as a deprivation cell, simply by blocking out all sources of light.[133] In the Gilded Age, the practice was refined and rationalized. In the 1880s, prison administrations constructed purpose-built dark-cells and dungeons. At Sing Sing, for example, the dark-cell was a tiny room on the ground floor of the prison, constructed out of four large flagstones – one for each wall – completed by a great iron door without windows.[134] (The room earned the named "the cooler" for its bone-numbing temperatures.) In these years, as well, the state began openly regulating the amount of bread and water to be supplied a dark-cell prisoner. What had been a makeshift and informal punishment before the 1870s became, in the great prison factories of the 1880s, a routinized, regulated, systematically *administered* form of discipline. Although most contractors were not personally or directly responsible for the invention of these punishments, the highly consolidated labor system of which contractors were the direct beneficiaries helped foster their proliferation and refinement. Whether or not such punishments did, in fact, make "good" workers of prisoners, contractors and their foremen made extensive, if indirect, use of these disciplinary tactics with that end in mind; contractors' implicit approval of these techniques of governance ensured their continuance.

Although the effects of the rationalization of prison industries were felt most keenly at the quotidian and administrative levels (and by the prisoners, keepers, and foremen who made the system "work") the states' adoption of Pilsbury-like labor systems had equally important consequences for the relationship between state government and prison contractors. As most Northern prisons consolidated their contracts and as prison industries became large-scale, monopolistic enterprises, the power relation between the state and the prison contractors began to shift. Although the contractors continued to need the penal arm of the state (as a procurer of labor), under the conditions of consolidation and oligopoly that prevailed in the Gilded Age, state government needed the contractor more. The state's growing dependency on the contractor was at once financial, administrative, and ideological. Although, in the mid-1880s, the Northern states' sale of prisoners'

[132] New York (State) Assembly Committee on State Prisons (1883), 52.
[133] Gilfoyle, *A Pickpocket's Tale* (mss.), 31
[134] New York (State) Assembly Committee on State Prisons (1883), 22, 25.

labor to contractors often did not cover the costs of running the prison, it nonetheless defrayed enough of the operating costs of imprisonment to make it essential. The country's factory contract prison system covered sixty-five percent of the ordinary running expenses incurred by state government (chiefly, the cost of feeding the prisoners) and fifty-six percent of total expenses (running expenses plus extraordinary repairs, construction, and so on); piece-price labor, which operated on a much smaller scale, generated enough income to cover twenty-three percent of the prisons' running expenses and twenty-one percent of total expenses. Under the lease system, the state had few, if any costs, and sometimes made a profit on the deal.[135]

Moreover, as the contractor's large-scale operation became the anchor of the prison's finances and as prison rules, punishments, and relations of authority came to serve the contract system, any sudden or unexpected withdrawal of the contractor promised to unleash a wide range of disorders in the prison. That the collapse of prison order during the long depression of the 1870s had triggered political crises in several states made it seem even more imperative that the state continue to attract, accommodate, and hold onto private enterprise.[136] When local and national labor movements once again revived their campaign against the contracting out of prisoners as laborers, prison wardens warned that to disband the system would be to plunge prisoners into idleness, ill-discipline, mental and physical suffering, and outright rebellion. Acutely aware of their dependency on particular contractors, high-ranking prison officials began arguing, in the 1880s, that the good order of the prison and the health and welfare of the prisoners depended on the continuation of the contract system. Although, just ten years earlier, most prison wardens and reformers had looked upon the contract system as an inherently abusive system that should be closely regulated and, ultimately, abolished, by 1885, most had come to see it as indispensable to the prison order (as we shall see in the next chapter).

Many contractors appear to have been well aware both of the imbalance in the power relation between themselves and the state and the perception of most penologists and high-ranking wardens that contractors were indispensable to the financial and disciplinary order of the prison. Contractors repeatedly sought to ensure that the state shouldered as much of the risk and as many of the costs of their business as possible. Events at the Kansas state prison typified this unequal relationship between state and contractor. In 1873, the Kansas Wagon Company signed a contract with the State of

---

[135] The lease generated 372% of the total expenses incurred by the states in running their lease penal systems, and 267% of total expenses (largely because the lease transferred the costs of feeding and housing prisoners from the state to the lessee). Report of the Secretary of the Interior, Vol. 5, U.S. Commissioner of Labor, Convict Labor in the United States (Washington: U.S. Government Printing Office, 1887), 296.

[136] Christopher Adamson, "Toward a Marxian Penology: Captive Criminal Populations as Economic Threats and Resources," *Social Problems* 31:4 (Apr. 1984), 435–58, 448; W. David Lewis, *From Newgate to Dannemora: The Rise of the Penitentiary in New York, 1796–1848* (Ithaca, NY: Cornell University Press, 1965), 267, 272–4.

Kansas for the labor of the state prisoners; as was quite common at that time, the contract stipulated that the contractor, and not the state, was to supply "all machinery."[137] Despite the fact that Kansas state law directed that the state prison operate a public-account labor system, and even though the state attorney general found that contract prison labor had no basis in law, the warden of the state prison signed a five-year contract. This illegal contract gave the Kansas Wagon Company the option to renew the contract for another ten years, and stipulated that neither the warden nor the state legislature could raise the contracted price of prison labor or divert that labor to other employers.[138]

Shortly after signing the contract, the Kansas Wagon Company insisted that the state pay for and install new machinery, enlarge the workshops, supply power, and prevail upon the Kansas Pacific Railway to lay a railroad switch between the penitentiary and its trunk line.[139] Although, under the terms of the Company's contract with the state, the state was not bound to supply the Company with machinery, the Kansas Board of Prisons agreed to do so. The Board, however, held fast in refusing to meet the Company's other demands. The Company's proprietor responded by swiftly dispatching a brief notice to the Board: "In accordance with the provisions of the contract of March 7, 1873," he wrote, "we hereby give notice that our contract will cease at the expiration of ninety days from this fifth day of August, 1873."[140] Having lost the contract and facing widespread idleness in the state prison, the Board immediately advertised for bids for the redundant prison labor. The Kansas Wagon Company privately placed bids and offered to pay what amounted to just half the price they had been paying for the labor of the prisoners under the original contract. Desperate to put their prisoners to work, the Board soon resumed talks with the Kansas Wagon Company; shortly afterwards, the state and the Company signed a new contract, the terms of which were exactly those the Company had demanded upon pain of canceling the original contract, and which the state had initially refused to entertain.[141]

Although the case of Kansas was particularly acute, much the same dynamic was at work in other prisons around the country. Contracts for prison labor frequently turned out to be binding only on the state. Because of the state's desperation to put its convicts to work (and to keep them there), contractors such as the Kansas Wagon Company were typically able to dictate the terms of the business arrangement, to renege on their contractual obligations, and to renegotiate contracts whenever a downturn in business or other contingency made it prudent for them to do so. Throughout the

---

[137] "[Signed] KANSAS WAGON CO," *Proceedings of the Annual Congress of the National Prison Association of the United States*, 1874, 317.

[138] Ibid., 315.   [139] Ibid., 315.

[140] Ibid., 317.

[141] Under the original contract, The Kansas Wagon Company was to pay the state 60¢ per skilled prison laborer per day; under the new contract, the Company was to pay the state 22¢ per day for the same skilled laborers.

period, contractors sued and threatened to sue over allegedly inadequate conditions, withheld full payment for labor, and, in financially difficult times, sought (and received) credit from the state. Furthermore, as Glen Gilde-meister notes, it was "not uncommon" for a contractor to refuse outright to pay for the labor for which he had contracted.[142] Particularly where all or most of an institution's prisoners were contracted out to just one con-tractor, state officials were inclined to make concessions in an effort to keep the contractor: Fearful that the contractor might simply up and quit (and, thereby, throw the prisoners into dangerous idleness), states often ended up capitulating to their demands and paying for the extension of workshops and the installation of machinery, boilers, or whatever else the contractor requested. Under the conditions of private monopoly that prevailed in the prisons of the Gilded Age, the contractors had the state over a barrel.

* * * * *

By the early 1880s, almost every state prison system in the country was func-tioning along the lines I have just described. Prison industries now operated on a large-scale, highly rationalized, and monopolistic basis; with but a few exceptions, the states had abandoned the "reformatory" or "progressive" rehabilitative programs of the Reconstruction era. In 1880, the new arrange-ments appeared to enjoy considerable legitimacy among the citizenry; at the very least, there was little evidence that either a critical mass of the population or a committed cadre of elite reformers was mobilizing against it. The various reform movements that had organized, in the early years of Reconstruction, against the practice of prison labor contracting and that had prompted state legislatures to rein in the contract system and establish refor-matory programs had all but withered away: In the course of the crushing depression of the mid-1870s, the reformist National Prison Association had lost all momentum, ceasing, at one point, even to convene its annual con-gresses. The workingmen's unions that had been the driving force behind various states' prison labor reforms had also all but collapsed during the long depression. In the absence of political pressure against contracting, and in the face of a mass of increasingly restive, idle prisoners, state legisla-tors reached out to those with enough capital and organizational heft to put whole prison populations back to work. In the service of bringing capital back into the prisons and keeping it there, the state gradually freed contrac-tors from most of the constraints to which they had been previously subject.

Market and prison now penetrated one another to a degree unknown in industrial Europe and unrivaled in antebellum America: Prison industries were pouring a comparatively larger volume and wealth of goods, miner-als and ore, and agricultural produce onto the markets than ever before. Within the prisons and lease camps, as we have seen, the profit motive had quite rapidly extended beyond the workshops and the production process proper to colonize domains of prison life, law, and governance that had

[142] Gildemeister, "Prison Labor," 38. See also, Adamson, "Toward a Marxist Penology," 448, and Lewis, *From Newgate to Dannemora*, 267, 272–4.

previously been relatively insulated from both the contractor and the profit principle. The great majority of American prisoners now spent most of their days working for large-scale private interests, producing tens of millions of dollars worth of goods on an annual basis. The distribution of convicts about the prison system; the amount and kind of food and medical attention prisoners received; the grounds upon which prisoners were punished and the kind of punishments meted out; the fealty of the state's prison keepers and relations of authority within the prison; and even the procedures by which prison sentences might be shortened or lengthened – all became subject to the contractor's efforts to raise his revenue and depress his costs.

Nowhere in the United States did the contractors or their foremen coax this valuable work out of the convicts via the gentler arts of persuasion. Although, as a whole, Southern lease convicts endured much higher levels of exploitation and brutality than other prisoners, convicts everywhere were put to sweated labor in the interests of profit (usually private), often under life-threatening conditions, and always upon pain of severe corporal punishment. Unshackled from most of the practical, political, and rudimentary legal constraints to which employers were subject in "free" industries, contractors worked with the state's keepers to drive unfree, rightless prison workers harder and longer than employers could work the waged laborers of the period. The least free of American institutions afforded the greatest possible freedom in the conduct of factories – and this is precisely what attracted contractors like John Sherwood Perry to the prison.

Under these new conditions, the prison's disciplinary regime took aim directly at the prisoner's body and threatened it with highly rationalized forms of torture, with the undisguised purpose of rendering hard, industrial labor the lesser of two pains. Here, and at every level of prison administration, the objective was not that of making perpetually docile "subjects" out of prisoners (as Michel Foucault argues was the objective of nineteenth-century penology) but of driving the body to render up immediate, unceasing, bountiful labor in the workshops. Both in practice and in the administrative imaginary, the prison became an amoral domain, dominated almost entirely by instrumental rationality. Prominent prison administrators, including New York prisons superintendent, Louis Pilsbury, now openly and publicly condemned reformatory and other "moral" approaches to incarceration, dismissing them as misguided "sentimentalism": Felons, Pilsbury declared, "have passed beyond moral influence," and "can only be governed by fear of bodily punishment."[143] Just ten years earlier, prison officials around the country had roundly condemned the contract system, publicly disavowed the penology of terror and the lash, and endeavored to outlaw the infliction of corporal punishments in the prisons; now, in 1880, such methods of prison governance were commonplace and generally uncontroversial.[144]

---

[143] *New York Times*, Feb. 6, 1880, 4.

[144] Pilsbury's comments did garner some criticism in the press, but it was quite tepid. For example, "The Treatment of Convicts," (ed), *New York Times*, May 7, 1881, 4; *Editorial*, Feb. 10, 1882, 4.

Finally, the key relation in the prison had ceased to be that between imprisoning state and convicted felon; it was now the relation between private contractor and convict laborer. Almost everywhere, the penal arm of government had been reduced to a mere instrument of private, commercial interests whose primary commitment was to the pursuit of profit. No longer the force lurking furtively "behind the throne" of formal state authority (as Wines and Dwight had cautioned in 1867), the contractor, and with him, the imperatives of large-scale capitalist industry, had emerged from the shadows to be crowned "sovereign" of the penal domain.

4

Disciplining the State, Civilizing the Market: The Campaign to Abolish Contract Prison Labor

> Sour bread, sour bread; no work, no work.
> Convicts' mess hall chant, Sing Sing Prison, 1870s

In the Gilded Age, contractors and their agents exercised power far more effectively than did the great mass of unfree, dependent prisoners in their charge; but they did not exercise it just as they pleased.[1] Rewriting the prison rulebooks, ordering speed-ups in production, and prescribing new ways of organizing and disciplining convict workers were easy enough; but actually implementing the rules and successfully subjecting the convicts (and the state's keepers) to the disciplinary rigors of the new regime posed a far more difficult set of challenges. In the early stages of restructuring (c. 1872–78), prisoners in every region of the country rebelled and struck against the reforms with an intensity and confidence unseen since the days of the early republican penitentiary and its feisty, rights-conscious inmates. Once the authorities put down these rebellions and submitted their prisoners to the discipline of large-scale industrial labor, they soon discovered that the very structure of the new, large-scale contract industries afforded new opportunities – and new means – of individual and collective acts of defiance. Indeed, the very success of the consolidated contract system was to have some deeply contradictory effects, including the destabilization of the system itself.

Nor were these the only difficulties with which large-scale contractors and the state authorities had to contend in the Gilded Age. Although barely perceptible before 1882, forces antagonistic to the consolidated contract system were quietly reviving and mustering political support for the abolition of contract prison labor. Beginning in 1878, isolated pockets of farmers and industrial workers around the country debated the contract prison labor system and organized local petition drives; some of these actions sparked investigations into the workings of the contract system. With the opening of these small but significant crevices in the otherwise solid supporting walls of the contract system, prisoners and the occasional prison guard found ways of relaying details of workshop discipline, corporal punishments, and the contractor's general conduct of operations to the press and various investigators.

---

[1] With apologies to Karl Marx ("The Eighteenth Brumaire of Louis Bonaparte," in *The Marx-Engels Reader* [New York: Norton, 1978], 594–617) and Michel Foucault, *Discipline and Punish: The Birth of the Prison* (New York: Vintage, 1979), espec. 135–257, 293–308.

Such revelations in turn fueled local anticontract labor efforts and hastened the formation of statewide, and eventually regionwide, anticontract labor campaigns. By 1883, in several Northern states, the contract prison labor system was in the grips of a full-scale crisis of legitimacy; within another seven years, the Southern lease variation of that system would also be in jeopardy of abolition. Although historians of punishment have all but ignored this rolling series of prison crises,[2] it constituted the single greatest watershed in the history of American legal punishment since the Jacksonian era and the states' wholesale adoption of prison labor contracting. It would climax in the destruction of the very foundation of the nineteenth-century American penal system and give birth to the progressive prison reform movement.

[2] With the notable exceptions of Glen Gildemeister (on the North) and Karen S. Shapiro, Alex Lichtenstein, David Oshinsky, and Edward S. Ayers (on the South), historians have all but ignored free workers' anti-contract labor campaigns of the 1880s and 1890s; moreover, none systematically discusses the wave of convict rebellions that preceded and often reinforced various local and national drives to end convict contracting. Gildemeister's ground-breaking doctoral dissertation includes a useful chapter on organized labor's efforts, in the industrial states of the North between 1866 and 1886, to abolish the contract system, and a brief assessment of their accomplishments; although Gildemeister does not consider the important differences between the prison labor politics of the Reconstruction Era and that of the Gilded Age, his study remains the only other detailed account of Northern free labor's response to prison labor. Ayers offers a brief but incisive discussion of Southern farmers' and workers' opposition to the convict lease system in the 1880s and 1890s, with particular reference to Georgia. Shapiro's *New South Rebellion* is a superb, book length-treatment of the free miners' campaigns against convict leasing in the Tennessee coalfields in the late 1880s and early 1890s; however, she situates the miners' campaigns firmly within the trajectory of Southern labor, rather than American penal, history; she is therefore not concerned with the long-term impact of that campaign on Southern penal practice. None of the otherwise excellent synthetic accounts of American prison history treats the convict rebellions or the Knights of Labor and trade union campaigns of the period 1876–1900 in any depth. David J. Rothman, for example, refers in passing to the existence of "political pressure exerted by free labor," and the turning of "solid public opinion" against the convict lease system, but does not elaborate. Nor, with the exception of Texas, does he consider the series of experiments in prison management that the abolition of contract prison labor sparked in the 1890s and 1900s. Another leading historian of progressive prison reform, Larry Sullivan, notes that "(p)erhaps the most significant development during the Progressive Era was the precipitous decline in convict employment," but does not explore the root cause of that decline or relate abolition to the progressive prison reform movement that followed on its heels. Notably, criminologists and penal historians of the 1920s and 1930s were well aware both of the history-altering impact of the anti-contract labor movement and of organized labor's continuing influence on prison law, policy, and theory after abolition. In 1934, for example, Blake McKelvey published a highly critical account of "the time when labor legislation first effectively invaded the field of prisons," in which he traced the roots of the prison labor problem of the 1930s to organized labor's campaigns against the contract prison labor system in the 1880s. Glen A. Gildemeister, "Prison Labor and Convict Competition with Free Workers in Industrializing America, 1840–1890" (Ph.D. diss., DeKalb: Northern Illinois Press, 1977; New York: Garland, 1987), 196–224, 255; Karin A. Shapiro, *A New South Rebellion: The Battle Against Convict Labor in the Tennessee Coalfields, 1871–1896* (Chapel Hill: University of North Carolina Press, 1998); Alex Lichtenstein, *Twice the Work of Free Labor: The Political Economy of Convict Labor in the New South* (London: Verso, 1996); David M. Oshinsky, *Worse Than Slavery: Parchman Farm and the Ordeal of Jim Crow Justice* (New York: Free Press, 1996); Edward S. Ayers, *Vengeance and Justice: Crime and Punishment in the 19th-Century*

The present chapter traces the roots, growth, and fruition of the movement to abolish contract prison labor.

* * * * *

From the earliest days of consolidation, in the mid-1870s, convicts in every section of the country engaged in diverse acts of resistance against the efforts of contractors and prison administrations to speed up production, cut costs (often by cutting back convicts' rations), impose a strict disciplinary regime, and punish disobedient or laggardly prisoners with a liberal dose of the lash, shock, or internment in the dark cell. Convict defiance ranged from individual and collective acts of theft, sabotage, arson, and self-inflicted injury (of the sort that made it impossible for the injured prisoner to continue working); through clandestine communication with the press and attorneys about conditions in the workshops; to various forms of collective action, including well-disciplined labor strikes and slow-downs, and spontaneous riots and brawls.

Of all the acts of defiance in which prisoners engaged during the Gilded Age, collective actions, such as riots and strikes, would prove to be the most troubling for contractors and prison authorities. Open, large-scale strikes and riots had not been unknown in American prisons before 1874. However, in the Gilded Age, an unprecedented number of prison "mutinies" (as the press typically referred to them) erupted around the country. Large-scale strikes and riots broke out in more than a dozen industrial prisons between 1879 and 1892; a number of smaller-scale strikes also took place in Southern lease camps. In both regions, rebellions caused production to grind to a halt, sometimes for several days at a stretch, and at considerable cost to both the contractor and the state (to whom the contractor typically passed on his losses). Many of the large-scale rebellions also had collateral effects: Most enjoyed enjoyed a considerable afterlife in the press, in the official and unofficial investigations that typically followed an uprising, and in organized labor's renewed campaign against the contract labor system. Despite the fact that the authorities always eventually broke the strikes and put down the riots, the experience and spectacle of rebellion taught prisoners, contractors, and wardens alike an important lesson. This was that, even within the high walls of a prison and with the state's keepers and militiamen at their disposal, the prison contractor lacked perfect control over his workers and his workshops.

In all likelihood, any mass of human beings, finding themselves subject to a markedly more coercive, violent, disciplinary order than the one to which they had been previously accustomed, would have tried by whatever

American *South* (Oxford: Oxford University Press, 1984); David J. Rothman, *Conscience and Convenience: The Asylum and Its Alternatives in Progressive America* (Boston and Toronto: Little, Brown and Co, 1980), 139–42; Larry Sullivan, *The Prison Reform Movement: Forlorn Hope* (Boston: Twayne, 1990), 37; Blake McKelvey, "The Prison Labor Problem: 1875–1900," *Journal of Criminal Law and Criminology*, 25:2 (July–Aug., 1934), 254–70; Philip S. Klein, "Prison Methods in New York State" (Ph.D. diss., Columbia University, 1920).

means available to repel, evade, or modify the imposition of such a regime. However, the men who populated the nation's prisons during the 1870s and 80s were particularly well-primed to resist the efforts of prison contractors and state authorities to impose the strict new regime that accompanied the advent of large-scale prison industries. Convict demography, the historical experiences that a significant portion of the men who were serving prison sentences at that time brought into prison with them, and the distinctive prison culture that had evolved during the reform-rich years of Reconstruction served to produce prison populations that were unlikely to capitulate to the new order without a fight. Indeed, in many states, in the 1870s, prisoners opposed the imposition of the new system openly, directly, and by all available means.

From 1865 through 1870, and for the first time in the history of the state prison systems, veteran citizen-soldiers made up a majority of prisoners in many states.[3] Immediately after the Civil War, in the Northern states, the courts had flooded the prisons with thousands of veterans (almost all of whom the U.S. Army and Navy had mustered out in 1865 and 1866, in the transition to peacetime). In 1866, Union veterans made up as much as ninety percent of the convict body in some institutions, and more than two-thirds in others. At the Massachusetts state prison in Charlestown, for example, 215 of the 327 convicts committed to the prison in the year ending October 1, 1866 were veterans of the Union army or navy. An even larger portion of new commitments to Eastern State Penitentiary were Civil War veterans: According to the warden, nine in every ten prisoners incarcerated at Eastern in 1866 had served during the war. Likewise, in several Midwestern states, former soldiers and sailors accounted for upwards of two-thirds of the entire prison population. The high ratio of veteran to nonveteran prisoners declined somewhat after the 1860s. Nonetheless, through the 1870s and into the 1880s, Civil War veterans retained a significant presence in the Northern prisons – typically accounting for more than half the total population of state prisoners.[4]

The prevalence of Civil War veterans within Northern prisons had a number of important consequences for contractors and prison authorities who sought to impose their strict new industrial system. When veterans were convicted of a crime and committed to prison, they did not check their memories of war, or their war-making skills, at the prison gates; their combat experience and the habits of military discipline entered prison with them. Equally, if not more importantly, imprisoned Union veterans, like their free compatriots, appear to have carried into prison with them a robust sense of themselves as citizen-soldiers who had risked life and limb in the causes of freedom and national reunification and, who, as a consequence

[3] F. B. Sanborn, "The Progress in Our Prisons," *Old and New*, 2:2 (Aug., 1870), 242. See Richard Severo and Lewis Milford, *Wages of War: When America's Soldiers Came Home: From Valley Forge to Vietnam* (New York: Simon and Schuster, 1989).
[4] Severo and Milford, *Wages of War*.

of such sacrifice, had acquired certain economic and social rights that fed-eral, state, and municipal government were duty-bound to recognize. The most pressing of the veterans' demands, in the period of Reconstruction, were the opportunity for gainful employment, decent working conditions and hours, and pensions for disabled veterans and soldiers' widows.[5] But as a slew of recent studies suggests, far from being the veterans' only claims upon government, these were simply the most commonly, and successfully, articulated of a series of demands that veterans pursued in the political and legal spheres in the late 1860s and 1870s. These issued from a deeply rooted belief among various communities of former Union soldiers that their collective sacrifice on the battlefield had earned them the full dues of republican manhood and citizenship – including honor and respect within their own communities and from the citizenry at large, the opportunity to choose an "independent" livelihood over the drudgery of waged labor, full participation in political and civic life, shelter and health care in old age and in times of high unemployment, and, in the case of black veterans, equal voting and related political rights.[6]

---

[5] As Theda Skocpol has shown, Union veterans wasted no time after the Civil War pressing the federal government to secure the full fruits of republican citizenship for war veterans, and for the widows and families of soldiers killed in the line of duty. Likewise, veterans, along with firefighters, were the first sections of the population to successfully press state and municipal governments to establish public pensions. In the lawsuits that later con-tested the extension of pension programs beyond Civil War veterans to other segments of the population, the courts' rulings often turned on the question of whether or not the contributions of firemen, teachers, and other non-veterans were equivalent to veterans' battlefield sacrifices, as contributions to the public good. Theda Skocpol, *Protecting Soldiers and Mothers: The Political Origins of Social Policy in United States* (Cambridge, Massachusetts: Belknap, 1995). See also, Susan M. Sterett, *Public Pensions: Gender and Civic Service in the States, 1850–1937* (Ithaca, NY: Cornell University Press, 2003); Donald R. Shaffer, *After the Glory: The Struggles of Black Civil War Veterans* (Lawrence: University Press of Kansas, 2004); and Eric Foner, *The Story of American Freedom* (New York: Norton, 1999), 100–14.

[6] Donald R. Shaffer, *After the Glory*; Richard Reid, "USCT Veterans in Post–Civil War North Carolina," in Keith P. Wilson, *Campfires of Freedom: The Camp Life of Black Soldiers during the Civil War* (Kent, Ohio: Kent State University Press, 2002); and Patrick J. Kelly, *Creating a National Home: Building the Veterans' Welfare State, 1860–1900* (Cambridge, Massachusetts: Harvard University Press, 1997). Veterans' political presence changed significantly in the Gilded Age. In the late 1870s–80s, the largest of the Union veterans' associations, the Grand Army of the Republic (GAR, est. 1866), revived as an organizing instrument of the Republican party; although it remained an advocate for veterans' pensions, in its new incarnation, it became a conservative patriotic society the leaders of which devoted much of their time and resources to memorializing the war – not as the war that ended chattel slavery, but as the war for the preservation of the republic. Black veterans of the Civil War were all but silenced within the organization after Reconstruction, and in some states the GAR made itself available during times of industrial conflict as a force of strikebreaking "patriots." Stuart McConnell, *Glorious Contentment: The Grand Army of the Republic, 1865–1900* (Chapel Hill: University of North Carolina, 1992). See also, Mary R. Dearing, *Veterans in Politics: The Story of the G.A.R.* (Baton Rouge: Louisiana State University Press, 1952); Larry M. Logue, *To Appomattox and Beyond: The Civil War Soldier in War and Peace* (Chicago: Ivan R. Dee, 1996); and David Blight, *Race and Reunion: The Civil War in American Memory* (Cambridge, Massachusetts: Belknap, 2002), 140–210.

As well as confronting large numbers of Civil War veterans, contractors and the authorities encountered a prison population in which significant numbers of long-term convicts had lived through the less industrialized, less violent, and more incentive-oriented contract system of the reformist Reconstruction era. In those years, as we have seen, prisoners had witnessed the introduction of rudimentary educational, religious, and vocational programs. In addition, official policy, and a new generation of reformist prison wardens, had actively promoted the principles of "moral suasion" over the more naked coercion of the lash and paddle, and passionately rejected the kind of prison order in which the contractor and his needs were the preeminent concern of prison governance. Under these reformatory policies, which were reinforced by the states' broader commitment to various kinds of social reform during Reconstruction, prisoners' moral standing in the community, though still relatively low, had risen. During the "long depression" of 1873–76, in the course of which many prison contractors had closed up shop, convicts in many Northern prisons had also become accustomed to exercising a relative degree of liberty within their institution (albeit under conditions of grinding poverty). The regime that prison administrators moved to introduce in the late 1870s rejected both the reformatory ethos of the Reconstruction era prisons and the various regulations aimed at limiting the scale and intensity of contractors' operations within the prisons. With its large-scale industries, punitive task system, liberal application of corporal punishment, and overriding doctrinal commitment to rendering the prison a secure and profitable institution, the consolidated contract system unambiguously threatened to lay waste not merely to prisoners' physical, mental, and spiritual welfare, but to their improving position in American society.

Unsurprisingly, large groups of these prisoners did all they could to prevent the new system from being established. Once the authorities had broken the first wave of strikes and rebellions and imposed the new regime, prisoners subsequently found new ways to frustrate, undermine, and, occasionally, assault the system. The particular triggering point of the rebellions and their outcome varied from state to state and among the different kinds of contract in use (that is, lease, time, or piece-price). But regardless of which part of the country or under which system convicts lived and worked, the rebellions invariably concerned the conditions under which they labored. Whether they toiled in the Southern lease mines or steelworks, Northern prison factories, or Western jute mills, the rebels took aim specifically at conditions or incidents directly connected with the operations of the contract labor system. In particular, almost all their grievances concerned the efforts of contractors to raise production levels, cut costs, inflict punishments, or a combination of these things.

A series of uprisings at the industrial Missouri State Prison in Jefferson City, beginning in 1874 (the same year in which the Missouri's Redeemer government adopted the convict lease system proper) and continuing into 1875, anticipated the general pattern of Gilded Age convict rebellions.[7] Like many prison uprisings, the 1874 protest began as a food riot in the mess hall. Following an apparent effort on the part of the overseers to work the convicts harder than usual, a large group of prisoners spontaneously rioted in the hall, claiming, in the words of one prisoner, that their food was "insufficient for hard-working men," and taking several guards hostage. As negotiations with the authorities got underway, the prisoners formed a leadership committee that then inspected the commissary and conversed with the president of the prison company (a Colonel Murphy) about the food problem. According to newspaper reports, Colonel Murphy assured the aggrieved prisoners that they would get all the good food they needed, whereupon the convicts promptly released their hostages and called an end to the action. The peace was short-lived, however; possibly emboldened by Murphy's apparent concession, prison laborers in the shoe shop of lessee August Priesmeyer and Co. staged another protest (the details of which remain obscure) later that day, in the course of which some of their number threatened to burn down the penitentiary if their demands were not met. This time the authorities responded with a general lockdown in the cellhouse, which they achieved with the aid of a small company of Jefferson City citizens who had rushed to the prison and leveled their guns at the rebellious convicts.[8]

It is unclear whether the prisoners found any real redress of their grievances that day. But in 1875, 300 of the leased convict cobblers armed themselves with hammers, knives, and pikes and again went on strike, once more in protest of the poor and meager rations. The strike quickly escalated, and within a matter of hours, about 500 prisoners had taken possession of the penitentiary and made hostages of some of the keepers.[9] One convict leader, a white man by the name of Henry Adams, enumerated the men's grievances: The food was not fit to eat; the hominy was "short," the Sunday soup "weak," and the apples riddled with worms; in sum, the men were being "treated like dogs." A tense standoff followed, as Governor Charles Henry Hardin, the state Attorney General, John A. Hockaday, and the lessees arrived to discuss the crisis. The state authorities soon found themselves having to contend not only with a rebellious mass of prisoners (who were now threatening to burn the prison to the ground), but an excited crowd of armed citizens who had, in the meantime, encircled the prison and made it clear they would shoot down the prisoners in the event of a mass break-out. Eventually, a small company of militia entered the prison, broke up the mass of striking convicts, and sent them back to their cells. By a local newspaper's account, "no blood was spilled" that day; the prisoners eventually all gave up

---

7 Because of the scale of the Missouri rebellions and the fact that, during Reconstruction, collective prisoner protests had been few and far between, the prisoners received quite a bit of local and national press – something that they apparently tried to put to their own use during the second rebellion.

8 *New York Times*, June 3, 1874, 1; June 20, 1874, 1.

9 According to the *St. Louis Republican*, 150 prisoners cooperated with authorities and refused to join the rebellion. *St. Louis Republican*, cited in *New York Times*, Jan. 24, 1875, 9.

and the volatile crowd of citizens dispersed. (The last convicts to concede defeat were the cobblers who had instigated and organized the strike. Blood was, in fact, eventually "spilled," when the state prison inspectors ordered the keepers to punish Henry Adams and another convict leader, Philip Noxon, to the full extent of the law: They were given seventy lashes and internment in the "blind [dark] cell").[10]

The other large-scale prison rebellions that erupted around the country between 1877 and 1892 were invariably triggered by efforts to speed up production; the implementation of cost-cutting measures (including a reduction or dilution of food rations, with no corresponding lowering of the daily task); an incident of a lashing, slugging, or interment in the dark cell; or a combination of these events. Convicts' demands followed much the same general pattern as found in Missouri: In almost every documented rebellion, the prisoners demanded more and better food, on the explicit grounds that they were hard working men who could only work if they were properly fed; an end to corporal punishments such as paddlings and the lash; a slower pace of labor; or a combination of these things. In many instances, the rebellions began as isolated, spontaneous riots and melées, only to escalate into more disciplined, prisonwide strikes in which certain leaders quickly emerged and became spokesmen for the greater mass of prisoners. Bread riots, in particular, often erupted in the mess hall or cellhouse without planning or forethought, but then quickly assumed a more disciplined form. Rioters typically forged a measure of solidarity among significant majorities of their number, appointed spokesmen, made demands, and attempted to negotiate with the authorities for relief.

Some months after the award of the massive stove-molding contract to John Sherwood Perry at Sing Sing in 1877, prisoners struck in solidarity with a prisoner who had just been brutally "paddled."[11] Eighteen months after the contract industries at Minnesota State prison at Stillwater were integrated into the massive North Western Manufacturing and Car Company, the prison was burnt to the ground in a fire that the authorities strongly suspected (but never proved) a group of prisoners had set.[12] Hundreds of prison workers at the Massachusetts state prison at Concord went on strike, beginning on Independence Day, 1882, and through the next several days;[13]

---

[10] The convict leadership included three white prisoners (most notably, Philip Noxon, the probable leader of the previous year's uprising, and Henry Adams) and a black prisoner whose name was (reportedly) Kemp Kollins. It is unclear what became of this last convict. A hardening of the authorities' attitudes was in evidence during the Missouri prisoners' second rebellion: Unlike the previous year, the wardens and lessees flat-out denied the convicts' charges of poor and inadequate food, and insisted that their rations were "both wholesome and adequate." The authorities also refused to negotiate with the prisoners – something they had been prepared to do the first time around. *New York Times*, Jan., 19, 1875; *St. Louis Republican*, in *New York Times*, Jan. 24, 1875, 9.

[11] *New York Times*, July 26, 1879, 1.

[12] Ted Genoways, *Hard Time: Voices from a State Prison, 1849–1914* (St. Paul: Minnesota Historical Society Press, 2002), 10–11, 67.

[13] *New York Times*, July 6, 1882, 2; July 7, 1882, 1; July 8, 1882, 5; July 9, 1882, 1; July 10, 1882, 1; and July 12, 1882, 2.

the following year, the Missouri state prisoners rebelled once more, burning down a number of the lease labor prison shops at the Jefferson City prison (including two of the much-hated shoe shops).[14] Similar events unfolded in the industrial prisons of New Jersey and Massachusetts: Prison laborers in the shoe shop at the Trenton state prison struck for heartier breakfasts in the winter of 1890[15] and, a few months later, upwards of a hundred shoe and harness makers at the Massachusetts state prison in Charlestown rioted, this time smashing machinery and completely demolishing their workshops.[16]

Prisoners working in the nation's largest industrial prison system, New York's, repeatedly rioted and struck. As noted earlier, in 1877, convict iron-workers at Sing Sing (where upwards of 900 men were now smelting and molding iron for John Sherwood Perry's oven-manufacturing business) struck. Like many other uprisings of the period, the rebellion was triggered by a paddling (and subsequent interment in the dark cell) dealt to a convict oven-molder on the grounds that he was shirking his work. After being punished for the transgression, John Barrett allegedly stabbed a guard with a modified mess-hall knife, fled into Perry's foundry, and successfully enjoined dozens of his fellow workers to strike. The keepers armed themselves with revolvers, eventually dispersed most of the striking convicts, and shot and killed Barrett (after he reportedly wielded a heavy hammer and ram against the officers).[17] Young male prisoners making hollow ware and brushware under the highly rationalized piece-price system that Zebulon Brockway had established at the Elmira Reformatory for Boys also struck tools and refused to work, in 1882.[18] Prison shoe-workers went on strike at Sing Sing in 1883,[19] and at Kings County penitentiary, in Brooklyn in the summer of 1885.[20] Like the Jefferson City rebellions of 1875–76, the trouble at Kings County began with an isolated strike by about 100 contracted men laboring in a single workshop; the men protested that the prison food was not giving them enough bodily strength and energy with which to perform a day's labor. Apparently galvanizing prisoners in other workshops to down tools and protest, the cobblers' strike quickly escalated into an all-out food riot in the cellblock, with hundreds of prisoners demanding that they "ought to

---

[14] Also the broom and harness shops. *New York Times*, Feb. 24, 1883, 1.

[15] *New York Times*, Mar. 30, 1890, 5. [16] *New York Times*, Aug. 8, 1890, 1.

[17] A coroner's enquiry later concluded that the keeper had acted in self-defense. (No convict testimony was admitted). The following day, the *New York Times* carried the story on the front page, announcing that Sing Sing had narrowly escaped a "sudden revolt." *New York Times*, July 26, 1879, 1.

[18] "The Abuses at Elmira," *New York Times*, Mar. 26, 1882, 1.

[19] *New York Times*, Mar. 15, 1883, 8

[20] *New York Times*, July 18, 1885, 3. At Kings County, there was some evidence to suggest that the guards conspired with prisoners against a new and unpopular disciplinarian warden. The theme of poor food and physical evisceration was of central importance in nearly all the strikes of the post 1870 period. Like the Jefferson City riots, and most of the prisoner rebellions of the post-Reconstruction period, the trouble at Kings County began with a strike by about 100 men in one workshop over the inadequacy of prison food and the consequent atrophy of bodily strength and energy.

have hash for breakfast when about to do a day's work." For three days, the prisoners yelled, "Hash! Hash!" (and, somewhat more cryptically, "We'll fix it in the morning!"). As in many of the other rebellions that took place in the industrial contract prisons, the Kings warden eventually restored order in the prison by orchestrating a show of force (in the form of a special detachment of the New York Police Department), and starving the weakened, and increasingly hungry, mass of striking prisoners into submission.[21]

Although open, large-scale acts of defiance occurred mostly in the contract prisons of the industrial states (most of which were in the Northeast and Midwest), prison strikes and rebellions were not unknown in other regions in the Gilded Age. The Far Western and deep Southern states also saw a number of prisoner rebellions – most of which erupted in the wake of the transition to one or another variant of the consolidated contract labor system. These regions' prison rebellions tended to be less well-documented than those in the Northeast and Midwest, but it is clear that even the country's most exploited and oppressed prisoners – the black men and women who toiled for convict lessees in the mines, swamps, and plantations of Florida, Georgia, Alabama, Mississippi, and South Carolina – struck, sometimes by the hundreds, for better food and the abolition of corporal punishment. Some took even more direct action, setting their prisons and mines on fire in protest at speed-ups and whippings.[22] Edward Ayers notes that, in at least one instance of convict rebellion in the South – a strike at the Rising Fawn Mines in Georgia in 1884 – the Governor of the state considered the uprising serious enough that he dispatched the militia and artillery to the site.[23] Similarly, in the Far West, prison laborers working the San Quentin jute mills struck twice in 1891, each time for more and better food, and once for the opportunity to air their grievances before the state board of prison directors.[24]

Understood as efforts to bring immediate and direct relief from the structures and conditions of which they were aggrieved, the Missouri, New York, and other prisoner strikes and protests of the 1870s and 1880s were manifest failures. The prison authorities did not concede to prisoners' demands and, in every instance I have been able to document, the authorities quickly, and forcefully, put down the rebellions (typically through a combination

---

[21] New York Times, July 18, 1885, 3.

[22] In 1886, 109 prisoners at Georgia's contract mine in Dade County refused to go back to work until the foremen was dismissed, food improved, and corporal punishment abolished. Lichtenstein, Twice the Work, 126. Within a year or so of the award of a contract for all of Alabama's state prisoners to the huge Tennessee Coal and Iron Company, prisoners responded to speed-ups and whippings by setting alight their mine, and refusing to return to work. Mary Ellen Curtin, Black Prisoners and Their World, Alabama, 1865–1900 (Charlottesville and London: University Press of Virginia, 2000), 130–5. For detailed discussions of the range of prisoners' resistance see Curtin, Black Prisoners and Their World, ch. 8, and Lichtenstein, Twice the Work, ch. 6.

[23] Ayers, Vengeance and Justice, 214. Rather than put the rebellion down by force, the troops starved the prisoners out.

[24] New York Times, Sep. 14, 1891, 2.

of a show of force and suspension of rations). More often than not, an insurrection not only failed to win any obvious measure of relief for the prisoners, but resulted in loss of life or limb, and extension of prison terms, for the participants. At the same time, however, the insurrections were neither without meaning nor entirely destructive to the prisoners' cause. Most immediately, strikes and riots were bad for the contractor's business: Rebellions disrupted production, however briefly, and, as we have seen, often led to the destruction of valuable machinery and materials. More subtly, strikes also taught an important lesson to contractors and prisoners alike: Convicts' laying down of tools and the consequent halt in production laid bare the contractors' unavoidable dependence upon their imprisoned workers, and persuasively negated the idea that convicts were powerless, broken men who could do nothing but toil obediently for their masters. In their collective acts of defiance, prisoners realized – and caused contractors to recognize – that far from having an entirely free hand within the prison factories and camps, contractors were subject, if only in some small degree, to a relation of dependency. Rebellions exposed a vital link between the conditions of prison life, on one hand, and the convicts' *ability and willingness* to work hard and well for their contractors, on the other. Prisoners possessed something that the contractors needed. Contractors were in the business of making commodities, extracting minerals and metals, or raising and harvesting produce, and for this they needed convicts to render up their labor. Even with the prison guard, state militias, local police forces, and armed possees at their disposal, contractors nonetheless depended upon two interrelated things: They required a significant degree of cooperation from the convicts, and they required, at the very least, the acquiescence of the citizenry at large to the prison labor system. Prisoners' strikes and rebellions reminded them of the first dependency; the newspaper stories and legislative investigations that generally followed upon the heels of any large-scale rebellion or other prison disorder underscored the second.

Although it is the case that the prisoners did not explicitly demand an end to their forced labor or the abolition of the contract system *per se*, they tended to take aim at its most injurious and unjust practices. The practices over which they were prepared to rebel (speed-ups, the administration of lashings and shocks, diminution of the rations) were not discrete or inessential features of the new, highly consolidated, contract system; rather, they were an intrinsic part of that system. Although rebelling convicts did not call for the outright abolition of the system, therefore, it was not the case that they were merely trying to ameliorate its worst excesses or reform it in such a way that its basic structure and operating logic were left intact: When convicts rebelled against speed-ups, beatings, and poorer rations, they contested, however obliquely, the system's foundational principle: that is, that the contractor had a free hand to raise production levels, cut costs, discipline his labor force, and maximize profits as he, and he alone, saw fit. Even with the full force of the state at his disposal, a judiciary that effectively adhered to a "hands off" doctrine in regard to prisons and prisoners, and a steady supply of fresh laborers, the contractor could not flex his hand just as he chose.

Prisoners had very few means available to them by which to contest or "negotiate" the conditions under which they worked; indeed, as we have seen, the lack of opportunity for organizing was among the characteristics of convict labor that made it very attractive to manufacturers who sought a freer hand on the factory floor. But prisoners were not entirely without means. Ironically, the very structure of large-scale prison industries both rendered the contractors more vulnerable to attack and made possible new, and potentially paralyzing forms of strike action. More so than the less specialized, smaller-scale industries of previous eras, Gilded Age contractors were vulnerable to a complete shut-down of their operation. As prisoners in a number of institutions appear to have grasped, the integrated nature of the contract industries and the division of labor into multiple, sequential phases not only vastly augmented production capacity, but rendered prison industries far more vulnerable to paralyzing attack. Under earlier versions of the contract system, labor had been less extensively divided and specialized and a disruption in one workshop or among one company of workers did not necessarily slow or halt the prison's industries *in toto*. Under the large-scale, integrated, and highly specialized structure of Gilded Age prison industries, small groups of convicts were able to halt production by disrupting just one phase in the sequence of production. Repeatedly, convicts were able to turn the large-scale, integrated nature of prison industry to advantage, whether by simply closing down one phase of production (as happened at Sing Sing in the foundry in 1877), or spreading word of a prisonwide strike along the production line itself.

It is very difficult to know whether contractors modified their approach to prisoners as a result of any given rebellion. Certainly, there is evidence that, in the wake of the strikes at Sing Sing in the late 1870s, the major contractor at that prison, John Sherwood Perry, commenced a public campaign in which he claimed that his system was firm, but humane (and, of course, the key to significant cost-savings for the people of New York).[25] Annual prison reports throw little light on the question of whether workshop conditions, food supplies, and disciplinary practices changed significantly following large-scale rebellions. Beyond prison walls, on the other hand, the rebellions had a profound and discernible impact. Although convict

[25] Perry was the most prolific of prison labor contractors, writing over a half-dozen articles in which he explained and defended his operations, and large-scale prison contracting more generally. See for example, John Sherwood Perry, *Analysis of the Vote on Prison Contract Labor Polled November 6, 1883, With Comments from Various Sources* (Albany, NY: Weed, Parsons, and Company, 1884); *A Few Considerations In Respect to Prison Labor* (Albany, NY: Weed, Parsons, and Company, 1878); *Letter to Hon. Louis D. Pilsbury, Superintendent of Prisons of the State of New York on Convict Labor* (Albany, NY: Weed, Parsons, and Company, 1880); *Prison Labor: An Argument Made Before the Assembly Committee of the Legislature of the State of New York On Prisons, March 7, 1883* (Albany, NY: Weed, Parsons, and Company, 1883); *Prison Labor in New Jersey, with a Letter from A. S. Meyrick* (Albany, NY: Weed, Parsons, and Company, 1883); *Prison Labor: Some Considerations in Favor of Maintaining the Present System* (Albany: n. p., 1883).

strikes and riots lasted, at most, just a few days, and typically failed to deliver any immediate relief to the prisoners, the insurrections nonetheless enjoyed a considerable afterlife in the press and in public discourse more generally. The prison "mutinies" of the Gilded Age invariably drew the attention of the press, labor organizers, and a growing cadre of middle class social critics. Press coverage of the rebellions, in turn, led prisoners to discover another means by which they could contest and undermine the prison order: They could smuggle out accounts of working conditions and abuses (real and imagined), or go to the press in person upon release from prison. In New York, a number of prisoners did this. In 1879, two years after the well-reported Sing Sing strike of 1877, prisoners recently released from Sing Sing and Auburn went directly to the press and warned that it was only a matter of time before prisoners would rebel again. One such prophet, an ex-prisoner by the name of William Hawley, turned up at the offices of the *New York Times* within days of being discharged from Auburn and testified to the illegal and routine use of the lash at Auburn, its grueling task system, the rotten, inedible food, and escalating rates of punishment. Reporting the story, the *Times* editorialized that if the "harrowing tales of life in that institution under its present management...are true, a general outbreak in the prison is to be feared."[26] (An "outbreak" did in fact follow, though not at Auburn but Sing Sing).

In many states, the convict rebellions helped reopen public debate over both the efficacy and the ethical value of the prevailing system of penal servitude. Reports of convicts' actions palpably refuted the claim of contractors and the authorities that their system imposed order in the prisons. In a related vein, the reports of beatings, shock treatments, and chronically overworked and underfed prisoners that invariably accompanied news of a prison rebellion contradicted one of the contractors' key claims – that their system was firm but humane. More than merely altering the free citizenry's perception of the prisons, stories of strikes and abuses prompted calls for legislative investigations of the prisons. News of prisoner rebellions and abuse scandals also helped revive organized labor's drive against contractual prison labor.

Repeatedly, as organized labor began to revive in the wake of the long depression of 1873–78, union leaders pointed to prisoner uprisings and associated reports of abusive punishments as positive proof of their long-standing complaint that convict labor competed unfairly with free. The contract system was injurious to prisoners because it broke them down physically and morally, labor leaders argued; it was injurious to free labor, precisely because it enabled contractors to exploit and drive convict laborers far beyond acceptable norms of humane and decent treatment, and to thereby sell their wares at prices that severely undercut those of the free manufacturer. As well as flooding the market with cheap, inferior goods and undercutting free labor, argued the President of the workingmen's Hatters'

---

[26] *New York Times*, May 2, 1879.

Association of the United States (E. L. Cornell) in 1879, the contract system was "demoralizing and brutalizing" the prisoner laborers who were subjected to it. [27] Labor leaders viewed prisoner insurrections as protests against
speed-ups and foremen who drove prisoners like slaves – and as bloody confirmation of the prison contractor's extreme and unjust advantage over free
industry.

Revelations about conditions in the nation's prison workshops, and about
the sheer scale and productive capacity of the new prison industries, catapulted the issue of contract prison labor to the agenda of urgent issues facing
the reviving labor movements of the late 1870s and early 1880s. In the last few
years of the 1870s, hundreds of local and national labor unions and workingmen's associations around the country flooded state legislatures with
petitions demanding immediate investigation of the contract system and an
end to unfair competition with convict labor. [28] Some unions sought direct
restriction of the system; some called for its outright abolition; and some
petitioned the legislature for laws that would indirectly destroy the system
by hobbling the contractors' ability to extract enormous profit from prison
laborers. (Petitioners in Massachusetts, for example, asked that the state fix
the price of convict labor at the average daily price of free labor; such a
stipulation, if enforced, would effectively destroy one of the chief sources of
profit for prison contractors – the comparative cheapness of prison labor). [29]
Those who ventured an alternative to contract prison labor argued that the
benefit of the convict's labor ought to go to the public, and the public alone:
Private interests ought not to benefit from the labor of those who had broken laws that were in principle enacted by and for the people, and they
certainly should not benefit at the cost of free workers. Rather, state government ought to take over prison industries, abolish the use of machinery in
prisons, and diversify prison production. [30]

[27] E. L. Cornell to the Joint Commission on State Prisons (of New Jersey, Connecticut, and
Massachusetts), paraphrased in *New York Times*, Nov. 14, 1879, 3.

[28] By contrast, unions did not take their campaigns against contract prison labor to the U.S.
Congress much before 1883. The topic of convict labor arose occasionally in House debates:
For example, in 1879, D. R. Streeter and C. F. Kenyon of the Chicago council of trade and
labor (representing twenty-seven unions) testified before a House select committee on
the long depression that the high concentration of convict labor in the shoe industry was
damaging free workers in the Chicago shoe industry; Charles H. Litchman, a Boston lawyer
sympathetic to shoe workers, also argued before the committee for the necessity of federal
action against convict contracting (although, when questioned by the committee, he was
vague as to under what power Congress might regulate the welfare of the states' prisoners).
However, before 1883 and the birth of a national campaign against the contract system,
labor leaders looked chiefly to the states for relief. See "Causes of General Depression
in Labor and Business; Chinese Immigration. Investigation by a Select Committee of the
House of Representatives Relative to the Causes of the General Depression in Labor and
Business; and as to Chinese Immigration." Dec. 10, 1879, 108, 121.

[29] Massachusetts Bureau of Statistics of Labor, Annual Report, 1879, in Annual U.S. Commissioner of Labor, Second Annual Report (1887), 329, 426–8.

[30] E. L. Cornell to the Joint Commission on State Prisons (of New Jersey, Connecticut, and
Massachusetts), paraphrased in *New York Times*, Nov. 14, 1879, 3. See also, Sperry to U.S.

Most of the anti-contract labor campaigns of 1876–82 were local in nature. However, as early as 1878, there were signs that statewide campaigns, and even a coordinated national effort, against the contract system were taking shape. Indeed, the prison labor issue was beginning to act as what Glen Gildemeister aptly characterizes as a powerful "catalyst and coagulant" of American labor organization.[31] At their convention in Reading in January 1878, the Knights of Labor formulated a Declaration of Principles, in which, amongst other things, they called upon the U.S. Congress "to prohibit this hiring out of convict labor."[32] In the early 1880s, as well, newly formed statewide unions, such as the Central Labor Union of New York, made the abolition of contract prison labor a central objective of their organization.[33] Over the next several years, the Knights made the abolition of contract penal servitude one of the key demands of their fledgling national labor movement; in its turn, the fledgling Federation of the Organized Trades and Labor Unions (hereinafter, FOTLU, which later became the American Federation of Labor) would aggressively pursue not only the abolition of all forms of contractual prison labor but the exclusion of convict-made goods from the open market.

Organized labor's protest over the contract system generated political pressure on state lawmakers to, at the very least, investigate the prison workshops. Between 1879 and 1882, in the face of mounting pressure from labor unions, concerned citizens, and former and current prisoners, many state legislatures opened investigations into their state's system of contract penal servitude and directed their superintendents of prisons to do the same; a number of state labor commissioners conducted studies of the impact of prison labor on local free workers. Massachusetts, New Jersey, Connecticut, New York, Michigan, California, Iowa, Illinois, and Ohio all conducted quite extensive investigations into what was beginning to be known, by 1879, as the "convict [or prison] labor question."[34] In addition, the legislatures

Congress, House Select Committee on the Causes of General Depression in Labor and Business, 1879.

[31] Gildemeister, "Prison Labor," 198.

[32] The Noble and Holy Order of the Knights of Labor, Declaration of Principles, Article 12, Reading, 1878, reprinted in Carroll D. Wright, "An Historical Sketch of the Knights of Labor" *The Quarterly Journal of Economics*, 1:2 (Jan. 1887), 137–68. The Knights' Declaration also included articles calling for an end to the employment of children under the age of fifteen in factory employment, the proscription of the importation of foreign labor under contract, and the socialization of telegraph, telephone, and railroad services. On the rise and fall of the Knights of Labor, with particular reference to New Hampshire, Vermont, Virginia, and Kansas, see Leon Fink, *Workingmen's Democracy: The Knights of Labor and American Politics* (Urbana and Chicago: University of Illinois Press, 1983).

[33] Gildemeister, "Prison Labor," 200.

[34] In 1878, the Massachusetts legislature authorized the state bureau of statistics of labor to make a "full investigation" into convict labor and to recommend legislation such as to "prevent competition" between convict labor and free industry. Massachusetts, resolution, April 8, 1878, quoted in U.S. Commissioner of Labor, Second Annual Report (1887), 328; labor commissioners in Michigan, California, Iowa, Illinois all investigated contract labor in 1884–1885.

of New Jersey, Massachusetts, and Connecticut convened a joint legislative commission on the subject of contract prison labor (in New York City) in 1879, and the prison commissioners of Kansas, Texas, and Colorado also filed reports in which they responded to organized labor's criticism of the contract system and explored its viability.[35] By 1882, almost two dozen states had conducted investigations into the contract system.

The hopes of organized labor and prisoners alike were bitterly disappointed by most of these investigations. With the exception of Ohio and California,[36] the reports' authors rebuffed the complaints of free workers that the contract system was inherently injurious to free and prison labor alike, and concluded that the contract system was no more injurious to either worker or prisoner than any other penal labor system would be. Connecticut's commissioners declared that the "evil" of overproduction would be the same under any prison labor system, whereas the New Jersey commission dismissed the alleged injuries of the contract system as more imaginary than real.[37] The northeastern states' joint committee asserted that although the concentration of prison laborers in any particular industry could injure the livelihoods of free citizens in that industry, this could be easily remedied: Apparently forgetting that, during the depression, the states had moved over to large-scale, monopolistic contracting largely in order to insulate prison industries from violent swings in the business cycle, they recommended that the states diversify and reduce the size of their industries. The committee

---

[35] All three states made minor alterations, but defended their various contractual arrangements as the best foundation for their prison system. Anne M. Butler, *Gendered Justice in the American West: Women Prisoners in Men's Penitentiaries* (Urbana: University of Illinois Press, 1997), 177–8.

[36] California was the only state where labor was strong enough, in the 1870s, to persuade the legislature to abolish the system, which the Constitution of 1876 mandated by the year 1882. The same constitution also forbade the use of Chinese prisoners in any form of productive labor, directed that prisons were to manufacture goods for use by the state and its agencies alone, and provided that prisoners were to manufacture only those goods (for state-use) that free labor was not already producing. Even in California, however, the contract system limped on, well past its official date of burial. Successive laws further restricted the sale of prisonmade goods (besides commodities to be used by state government) to crushed rock and jute grain bags, and regulated amounts and prices of both. Ohio's state assembly requested an investigation of the contract system in 1877; in a blistering assessment of contract prison labor, the commissioners charged that the system "leaves upon the state a fair escutcheon of the state a relic of the very worst form of human slavery" and "enables a class of men to get rich out of the crimes committed by others." The system was "pauperizing a large portion of our [free] laborers," and subjecting prisoners to "hopeless degradation." The report concluded that the state had "no right to make money out of prisoners at the expense of his reformation, much less delegate that power to other parties." On the contract in California, see Shelley Bookspan, *A Germ of Goodness: The California State Prison System, 1851–1944* (Lincoln & London: University of Nebraska Press, 1991). On Ohio, see Acts of 1889, ch. 264; Acts of 1893, ch. 42; Acts of 1895, ch. 208; Acts of 1897, ch. 97, cited "Summary of Convict Labor laws," U.S. Industrial Commission, 142; and Ohio State Assembly, Committee to Investigate Contract Convict Labor, reproduced in U.S. Commissioner of Labor, Second Annual Report (1887), 324–6.

[37] Quoted in New York State Superintendent of Prisons, Report of the State Superintendent of Prisons Relative to the Contract Convict Labor System in Response to a Resolution of the Last Assembly (March 25, 1880), 4–5.

also advised that the chronic problem of contractors' usurpation of disciplinary authorities of the state could be solved simply by stipulating in labor contracts that the state retain "absolute control" of prison discipline.[38] (In fact, most prison labor contracts stipulated that already – and were ignored with impunity). Prison commissioners in Kansas, Texas, and Colorado commended minor alterations to their systems, but nonetheless defended the contract system as the best foundation for their prison systems.[39]

In 1879, Massachusetts' State Chief of Labor Statistics, Carroll D. Wright, submitted an exhaustive study not only of his own state's prison labor practices, but those of the nation as a whole. Although he would later reverse his position (following workers' *mass* mobilization against the contract prison labor system, after 1882), Wright drew much the same set of conclusions as other investigators. He dismissed organized labor's call for abolition of convict labor as tantamount to demanding an end to prison labor in general, and derided as "socialist" the demand of Massachusetts workingmen that the state fix the price of prison labor at the same level as that of free workers. Wright conceded that the shoemakers' complaint of injurious competition from prison cobblers was somewhat warranted, but insisted that the problem could easily be solved simply by diversifying prison industries and ensuring that excessive numbers of prisoners were not concentrated in any one industry. Among many possible modes of prison administration, Wright concluded, the "contract system . . . is the wisest as a rule."[40]

In New York, where about a fifth of the nation's prison laborers toiled away, Prisons Superintendent Louis Pilsbury undertook two investigations of the highly rationalized system of prison labor of which he himself was the chief architect and champion. In April 1879, a month before the *New York Times* published convicts' reports of alleged abuses at Auburn and convicts struck at Sing Sing, Pilsbury submitted a brief report to the state Senate, in which he argued (echoing Carroll D. Wright of Massachusetts) for the contract system on the oft-repeated grounds that no better system had as yet been discovered.[41] Then, in the wake of news reports of brutality at Sing Sing and the revitalization of organized labor's drive against the contract system, the state Assembly requested that Pilsbury report more extensively on prison labor, "with the purpose of securing a greater variety and diffusion of employment in our State prisons and penitentiaries" and "substituting in part or whole for the present contract system, some other mode, form or kind of labor whereby the public interests may be secured and maintained without detriment to any one kind of labor or class of people."[42]

---

[38] Joint Special Legislative Committee of Massachusetts, New Jersey, Connecticut on Prison labor, in U.S. Commissioner of Labor, Second Annual Report (1887), 338.

[39] Anne Butler, *Gendered Justice*, 177–8.

[40] Massachusetts Bureau of Statistics of Labor, Annual Report, 1879, in U.S. Commissioner of Labor, Second Annual Report (1887), 329.

[41] Cited in U.S. Commissioner of Labor, Second Annual Report (1887), 309–11.

[42] Assembly Document No. 96, 21 May, 1879, in New York State Superintendent of Prisons, Report of the State Superintendent of Prisons Relative to the Contract Convict Labor System in Response to a Resolution of the Last Assembly (March 25, 1880), 1.

This time, Pilsbury (and the principal contractor at Sing Sing, John Sherwood Perry) went on the offensive, submitting a rigorous defense of the contract system in general, and a vindication of New York's particularly consolidated and highly industrialized version of it (the so-called "Pilsbury system"), in particular. Basing his report exclusively on the pro-contract reports of Massachusetts, New Jersey, and Connecticut, and prison contractors' own rather dubious "studies" of prison labor's impact on free labor, Pilsbury concluded that the system was working extremely well. He pointed to its profitability, arguing that the new system was saving the state of New York thousands of dollars per year. In an effort to refute the considerable evidence that the contract system displaced authority from the state's guards to the contractor's foremen and engendered a breakdown in prison discipline, he countered, "(t)he state retains absolute control"; the complaint that "the contract system interferes with the discipline of the prisons" was, in Pilsbury's view, an "erroneous impression."[43] On the question of free labor's indictment of the contract system on grounds of unfair competition, Pilsbury, like other prison commissioners of the day, merely insisted that it did not "interfere" with free mechanical industries any more than any other penal labor system would and that "the charge that contract labor materially interferes with free labor has not been proved."[44]

Much more than a defense of the system as an imperfect, though necessary, way of running the prisons, Pilsbury went on to argue that it was, in fact, a positive social good: The current arrangement not only "produces the best financial result" for the state treasury, he asserted, but it generated employment for free labor by raising the demand for raw materials, and supplying free workers with a range of unfinished, prisonmade goods that they could then finish. Free mechanics were simply deluded in their antagonism to convict labor, Pilsbury exclaimed; labor leaders misunderstood the causes of unemployment and declining wages: Mechanization of production and competition from skilled, cheap, *immigrant* labor, and not prison contractors and convict–laborers, were the true sources of free mechanics' pain.[45] Pilsbury concluded that there were no serious problems with the practice of selling the labor-power of prisoners to private interests, and made it clear that he had no intention of reforming, let alone abolishing, New York's increasingly controversial variant of that practice.[46]

---

[43] New York State Superintendent of Prisons, Report of the State Superintendent of Prisons Relative to the Contract Convict Labor System in Response to a Resolution of the Last Assembly (March 25, 1880).

[44] New York State Superintendent of Prisons, Report of the State Superintendent of Prisons Relative to the Contract Convict Labor System in Response to a Resolution of the Last Assembly (March 25, 1880).

[45] New York State Superintendent of Prisons, Report of the State Superintendent of Prisons Relative to the Contract Convict Labor System in Response to a Resolution of the Last Assembly (March 25, 1880), 6–9.

[46] New York State Superintendent of Prisons, Report of the State Superintendent of Prisons Relative to the Contract Convict Labor System in Response to a Resolution of the Last Assembly (March 25, 1880), 6.

The first round of official prison labor reports, in New York and elsewhere, had unambiguously rebuffed and dismissed the complaints of prisoners, workingmen and labor unions, and diverse private citizens outraged by the reports of prison abuses. But neither the unions nor prisoners resigned themselves to defeat. On the contrary, government's apparent deafness to complaints of brutality and unfair competition galvanized workers' and organized labor's resolve to overthrow the prison labor contract system. In the course of the 1880s, as labor organizations became bigger, better organized, more disciplined, and more truly national than ever before, local and statewide efforts to restrict or abolish contract prison labor became part of the first national, and truly mass-scale, campaign against the system. Labor organizations broadened their campaigns against the state's sale of convict labor, formulated and publicized a much more systematic critique of that practice, and worked to build a national movement for its abolition. They also engaged new tactics in their struggle (including, in at least two convict lease systems, bodily liberating convict–laborers from their prison stockades), mounting boycotts, and sponsoring legislation aimed at closing down the market for convict-made goods. Briefly, in 1886, the unions were also joined by a handful of manufacturers drawn mostly from the four industries in which large-scale contracting was making it difficult for smaller businesses to compete: stove, wagon, agricultural implement, and furniture manufacturing.[47]

The strategy of destroying the market for convict-made goods was adopted most widely and to best effect in the industrial states, where large-scale prison factories pumped several millions of dollars worth of consumer goods and construction materials onto the market every year.[48] A number of unions and local Knights' assemblies launched consumer and tradesmen boycotts of convict-made goods. A number of tradesmen's organizations banned their members from working with materials or goods processed or manufactured

[47] Gildemeister, "Prison Labor," 218–21. In the Midwest, manufacturers from the stove, wagon, agricultural implement, and furniture industries convened a region-wide conference in Chicago in 1886, established the National Anti-Contract Convict Labor Association (NACCA), and pledged to protest the U.S. government's purchase of convict-made goods. Contrary to Rosalind Petchesky's claim that manufacturers, rather than free labor, were responsible for bringing about the abolition of contract prison labor, manufacturers' active opposition to the contract system was both short-lived and ineffectual. As Gildemeister notes, the NACCA "arrived late on the scene and vanished as quickly as it appeared"; manufacturers tended to protest prison labor only during times of recession and to abandon their opposition whenever the economy rebounded (Gildemeister, "Prison Labor," 216, 220). Unlike organized labor, manufacturers' opposition to the system tended to be regionally focused and restricted to the handful of industries in which prison industries were prominent. Moreover, by 1886, and the founding of the NACCA, legislatures in the industrial states had either restricted or had begun to restrict prison labor contracting; the organization never met again. Both the scale and the timing of the Knights' and FOTLU's campaigns against the contract labor system strongly suggest that it was organized labor, rather than the scattered protests of a handful of manufacturers, that mobilized voters and legislators against the system and, ultimately, secured its abolition.
[48] See Chapter 3, in this book, at p. 90.

by convicts. The Chicago Building-Trades Council, for example, prohibited its members from handling "any material that is the product of convict labor,"[49] and the packing-trades councils organized against the sale of convict-made goods on the free market, and barred members from handling convict-made goods.[50] Various assemblies of the Knights and Labor committed to a consumer boycott of both convict-made goods and the merchants who handled such goods. In conjunction with these boycotts, the Knights and local unions called for a variety of laws, some of which aimed at rendering convict-made goods visible (so that consumers committed to boycotting the goods would know which goods to target) and others of which sought state regulation of distribution and sale of the goods. They drafted legislation requiring that goods made by prison labor be boldly branded with the words "Prison-Made" or "Convict-Made," laws mandating that convict-made goods be sold only wholesale, and regulatory laws requiring that persons dealing in convict-made goods obtain – and display prominently – a license to do so. These efforts aimed to hobble prison industries indirectly by constricting the various markets for convict-made goods and by channeling the growing popular antipathy toward prison contractors and convict labor into an effective consumer boycott of prisonmade goods.[51]

More traditional protests, aimed at the sphere of prison production proper, also proliferated in the 1880s, as individual trade unions attempted to exclude prison labor from particular trades or industries. In Massachusetts, printers took action when the mayor of Boston contracted out the city's printing jobs to convicts held on Deer Island; the same year, New York and Connecticut construction workers, stove-molders, shoe cobblers, and furniture makers protested contract penal labor (and, in particular, John Sherwood Perry's successful breaking of the stove-molders' union). Hat-makers and cigar-makers also sought statewide legislation prohibiting the use of prison labor in the manufacture of their products. Largely local efforts such as these were reinforced by the growth of two national, and initially complementary, labor organizations, the Knights of Labor and the FOTLU.[52] When 107 labor and trades leaders, drawn from local Knights of Labor assemblies and the printing, iron and steel, molding, glass, cigar,

---

[49] The Council also prohibited members from working on any building under police protection.

[50] This prohibition was applied to the particularly lucrative contracts for the World's Fair of 1892. Carl William Thomson, "Labor in the Packing Industry," *Journal of Political Economy* 15:2 (Feb. 1907), 88–108.

[51] For example, the Knights of Labor, Belle City Assembly 4516, committed such a boycott in 1886. (Gildemeister, "Prison Labor," 219).

[52] Although it lacked the organizational and financial structure of a modern industrial union like the American Federation of Labor, FOTLU's agenda foreshadowed that of modern industrial unions: Whereas the Knights of Labor drew mostly on older, agrarian republican values and sought long-range social change, FOTLU's objectives tended to be short-term and directed almost exclusively at the conditions of employment (principally, wages, hours, and employer liability) and external influences on those conditions (including various sources of cheap labor, including prison and Chinese immigrant labor).

and carpentry industries, met in Pittsburgh in 1881 to found the FOTLU, they enthusiastically adopted the prohibition of contract convict labor as one of a dozen-odd aims; two years later, John Jarrett, the president of the Amalgamated Association of Iron and Steel Workers, informed the U.S. Senate Committee on Relations Between Labor and Capital that the convict labor problem was so severe that it warranted national (that is, federal) legislation.[53] The Knights took the fight to the U.S. Congress in a more systematic fashion in 1885, as the country plunged into the second deep recession since the Civil War. Prominent Knights leader, Terence Powderly, drafted a bill that would ban the use of state and county prisoners on government works of any kind and direct the government to put free, unemployed men to work on these projects instead.[54] A year later, both the Knights of Labor and FOTLU announced nationwide campaigns against the contract prison labor system:[55] The Knights called upon their members everywhere to destroy the market for prisonmade goods and, to that end, to use "all honorable means at their command" to pursue legislation in their state legislatures compelling prison industries to brand their goods "prisonmade." In a detailed set of resolutions, the leadership recommended that any surplus money of the prisoner's labor be returned to the prisoner or prisoner's heirs and called upon the U.S. government to employ only free labor. In the same document, the Knights elaborated upon a possible alternative to the prevailing system of contractual penal servitude: The federal government might consider founding a penal colony for federal and long-term state convicts. True to the earlier, republican conviction that prisoners might yet be capable of self-improvement and civic virtue, the Knights suggested that such a penal colony could have some kind of promotion system that would enable a convict to shorten his or her term of servitude through good conduct.[56]

In the South, where the leasing out of small armies of convict–laborers and use of prisoners as strike-breakers was so endemic that free workers pragmatically hesitated to strike over any grievance whatsoever, popular action against the prevailing system of imprisonment at hard labor initially tended to take the form of petition to the state legislature or Governor. Free coal miners in Georgia and Alabama petitioned the state legislature against the use of convict labor in competition with free, and some 5,000 laboring men of the trades assembly at Wheeling, West Virginia,

---

[53] *New York Times*, Sep. 8, 1883, 8.

[54] Terence Powderly, address to Knights of Labor convention, Ontario, Canada, October, 1885, reported in *The Evening Star*, Washington DC, Oct. 7, 1885, 3.

[55] One vote shy of unanimity, the FOTLU delegates, who represented all skilled and unskilled, white and black, laborers and mechanics, voted for the prohibition of all Chinese immigration to the United States; they also called for a national bureau on labor. Philip S. Foner, *History of the Labor Movement in the United States*, Vol. 1 (New York: International, 1972), 519–24.

[56] Knights of Labor, recommendations, Oct. 1886, Richmond, Virginia, in U.S. Commissioner of Labor, Second Annual Report, 1887, 365; and *Evening Star*, Washington, Oct. 19, 1886, 5.

petitioned the state legislature for the abolition of the convict labor system.[57] Coal miners in Helena, Alabama (unsuccessfully) struck against having to work with convict miners[58] and in the mid-1880s, the free miners of Chilton County, Alabama, formed an association expressly dedicated to the over- throw of the use of convict labor in their industry.[59] In Texas, in the 1880s, granite cutters protested the use of convict labor in the construction of the new state capitol, at Austin, declaring that "freemen will not submit to the introduction of slavery into our trade under the guise of convict labor."[60] A hundred miles northeast of the state capitol, the townspeople and farm- ers of Hearne petitioned against pending increases in the number of Texas convicts leased out to large, privately owned plantations on the Brazos River bottom – and threatened to liberate the entire convict population if the plan went ahead.[61] The Texas Grange, Greenbacks, and Farmers' Alliance all called for an end to the use of convict labor in industrial and mechanical labor.[62]

Farmers and farm workers in several other Southern states also began protesting the system extensively in the mid-1880s. In Louisiana, the largely African-American workforce of cotton pickers, sugar cane cutters, and fruit and vegetable growers repeatedly petitioned against convict labor, and in the mid-1880s, African-American farmers of the Virginia Colored Farm- ers' Alliance organized against their state's convict lease system; various states' Farmers' Alliances followed soon afterward.[63] Free coal miners in Appalachian Tennessee also petitioned the courts, the Governor, and the legislature for an end to the use of prisoners as coal miners, negotiated directly with employers for an end to the practice, and worked with farmers' and workers' organizations to lobby the legislature to abolish convict leas- ing. By the mid-1880s, abolition of contractual prison labor had become an important plank in the electoral platforms of many Alliance and Populist candidates for state government; state branches of the Republican Party had also committed to abolishing the convict lease system.[64]

57 Gildemeister, "Prison Labor," 201.
58 Testimony of John Rutledge, coal miner, Birmingham Alabama, U.S. Senate Committee on Relations Between Labor and Capital, 1883, Vol. IV, 306. When the Senate committee pressed him on the Helena strike, Rutledge was reticent about the coal miners' reason for opposing working alongside the leased convicts: When asked, he replied, "Well, we didn't want them at all. Q: You wanted better company? A: Yes, Sir." Ibid., 306.
59 Shapiro, *New South Rebellion*, 239–40; Samuel L. Webb, "From Independents to Populists to Progressive Republicans: The Case of Chilton County, Alabama, 1880–1920," *Journal of Southern History*, 59:4 (Nov. 1993), 707–36.
60 Quoted in Robert Perkinson, "Birth of the Texas Prison Empire, 1865–1915" (Ph.D. diss, Yale University, 2001), 185.
61 Reported in *Evening Star*, Washington, Dec. 14, 1885, 1.
62 Perkinson, "Birth of the Texas Prison Empire," 191.
63 Shapiro, *New South Rebellion*, 240; William Edward Spriggs, "The Virginia Colored Farmers' Alliance: A Case Study of Race and Class Identity," *Journal of Negro History* 64:3 (Summer 1979), 191–204; Perkinson, "Birth of the Texas Prison Empire," 182–3.
64 For example, the Maryland Republican Party added abolition of convict contracting to its electoral platform in 1883. *Evening Star*, Washington, Sep. 28, 1883, 1.

Although most of the anti-contract labor efforts of Southern farmers and workers were initially confined to legislative politics, it was not long before free workers in two Southern states grew impatient with their state legislatures' apparent deafness to their calls for relief. Beginning in 1886, workers and farmers began to act far more directly and decisively against the practice of contracting out the labor of prisoners. Coal miners were particularly active in these states, mounting more than twenty strikes against the use of convict labor in the mining industry by 1900.[65] In 1886, the same year in which Knights of Labor announced a national campaign against contract prison labor and helped coordinate a wave of labor strikes around the country, free coal miners in Pulaski County, Kentucky took up arms, surrounded a stockade housing hundreds of convict strike-breakers, and demanded that the convicts be immediately returned to the state prison at Frankfort. After a tense confrontation with the militia, the free miners dispersed, but their action precipitated the passage, within a few months, of legislation confining prison laborers to within prison walls.[66]

The Kentucky miners' success emboldened them to assist their brethren across the border in Tennessee, where free miners had also been unsuccessfully petitioning the state legislature for relief from the Tennessee Coal, Iron, and Railroad Company's (TCIRC) large-scale use of convict labor in the coal fields.[67] In 1891, following several, fruitless years of petitioning and negotiation, and the Company's resorting to the use of convict strike-breakers, the free miners undertook a year-long campaign of direct action against prison labor contracting. They aimed to, quite literally, expel convict lease laborers from the coal fields. As Karin Shapiro has shown in her richly detailed history of this remarkable "New South rebellion," thousands of farmers, both black and white, rallied to the aid of the free miners (most of whom were white and members of the Knights of Labor and the United Mine Workers of America) in a large-scale campaign to end the lease. The miners and their supporters repeatedly armed themselves and emancipated convict–laborers from a series of stockades, putting hundreds on trains headed for Knoxville and the Nashville penitentiary. When the state called out the militia and attempted to enforce the company's contract, the miners were buoyed by a groundswell of support from thousands of Tennesseans – including the militiamen. The soldiers frequently expressed their sympathy for the miners, quietly took parole from the service, and, not uncommonly, threatened

<hr>

[65] Lichtenstein, *Twice the Work*, 96.   [66] Shapiro, *New South Rebellion*, 241.

[67] Shapiro, *New South Rebellion*, 241, Ayers, *Vengeance and Justice*, 215. For a polemical, if well-researched, account of contract convict labor, leased convict labor, and other forms of "direct forced" labor in post Civil War America, see Walter Wilson, *Forced Labor in the United States* (New York: International Publishers, 1933), 24–83. Wilson published his controversial study in the wake of the U.S. government's 1930 ban on the importation of goods made by Soviet forced labor; as Theodore Dreiser noted in his introduction to the book, Wilson's objective was to establish that "forced labor is one of the outstanding characteristics of the American business world, and of its colonial extensions." Theodore Dreiser, "Introduction" in Wilson, *Forced Labor*, 7.

to desert over the matter.[68] Lacking both the popular support and effective means by which to enforce the TCIRC's contract, state legislators were compelled to capitulate; by 1893, Tennessee's lawmakers were on the path to abolishing the practice of prison labor contracting.

The hundreds of thousands of farmers and workers who took action around the country against the contract prison labor system were clearly motivated, at least in part, out of a strong sense of self-interest: They repeatedly claimed that the private use of convict labor had a depressing effect on jobs and wages, and they frequently objected to employers' actual and threatened use of convict labor as a weapon with which to defeat organizing efforts, lower wages, raise tasks, and lengthen hours. Especially for the skilled mechanics of the industrial states, the prisoner–laborer embodied what many workers referred to as the automaton, the dependent industrial toiler who was put to work on highly mechanized forms of production and who, in effect, was reduced to little more than part of the machinery itself. These automata, free workers argued, at once threatened to deprive free labor of the value of their skills, a fair wage, and, perhaps too, their jobs. Workers commonly argued that industries and commercialized agricultural businesses run on cheap prison labor depressed wages for free workers in the same line of work; they also frequently asserted that elite business and planter interests were accumulating great wealth at the expense of small farmers and waged laborers.[69]

But self-interest was not the only consideration out of which workers and farmers mobilized in such force, and across such great cultural and geographical divides, against contract prison labor. Contrary to the claims of pro-contract lobbyists, such as Louis Pilsbury and John Sherwood Perry, something other than a crude calculus of economic self-interest was also at work here: Much as the Jacksonian mechanics before them, the farmers and workingmen of the Gilded Age objected to the contract prison labor system – and the larger edifice of servitude of which it was the foundation – on deeply embedded moral grounds. Their critiques of the system presented not only a claim concerning the economic injuries of prison labor but a series of religious, moral, legal, and political objections as well. While they took aim, in an explicit way, chiefly at the practice of selling the labor-power of prisoners to private interests, they also implicitly critiqued various of the legal, political, and disciplinary arrangements that reinforced that practice

---

[68] Shapiro, *New South Rebellion*, 211. See also, Ayers, *Vengeance and Justice*, 215–17; Lichtenstein, *Twice the Work*, 98–100; Pete Daniel, "The Tennessee Convict War," *Tennessee Historical Quarterly* 34 (1975), 273–92; C. Vann Woodward, *Origins of the New South, 1877 – 1913*, (Baton Rouge: Louisiana State University Press, 1971 [1955]), 232–4.

[69] The labor leaders who testified before the Senate Committee on Relations between Labor and Capital all noted that free workers' wages suffered when free labor was brought into competition with prison labor, which typically cost anywhere from a fifth to a third the price of free labor. See, for example, the testimony of P. H. McLogan (Chicago Trades Assembly and the Federation of Trade Unions) U.S. Senate Committee on Relations Between Labor and Capital (1883) Vol. I, 570, 581; John Jarrett (president of the iron and steelworkers' union), Vol. I, 1153–4; and Jeremiah Murphy (Railroad workers) Vol. II, 682.

and which, together, constituted the greater system of contractual penal servitude.

Although, in most instances, the abolition of contract prison labor remained only one of the goals of various unions and alliances of the 1880s and early 1890s, it was nonetheless an issue of key symbolic and organizational importance for workers and farmers.[70] From the earliest days of the contract system, the sale of prisoners' labor to private interests had cut against the grain of antebellum workingmen's dearly held beliefs concerning the meaning of a virtuous republic. Workingmen had been more or less content, for some years before the Civil War, to settle for a well-regulated, diversified system of prison labor; in the era of Reconstruction, they had spearheaded the drive to restrict, and ultimately abolish, prison labor contracting, and had met with a significant degree of success. As we have seen, however, these victories were all but reversed following the defeat of Reconstruction and the onset of the long depression of the 1870s. By 1880, a reviled institution that workingmen had believed to be in decline had rebounded and begun operating on a far larger scale, and far more profitably, they had ever seen before.

To an extent, workingmen's campaigns against convict labor were merely an extension of the older protests. By the same token, however, other events, some of which were strictly external to the advent of large-scale prison contracting, and some of which involved the nature of the contracting enterprise itself, imbued an old issue with new meaning and fresh urgency. Critically, the larger industrial field in which both imprisoned and free workers operated in the 1880s had changed substantially since the pre-war years. As it became apparent to many Americans, in the 1870s, that the industrial revolution was generating a more or less permanent class of wage earners, the hope of many antebellum workingmen that waged labor might be a temporary way station on an upward-leading path to small business ownership was increasingly contradicted by reality. In addition, the activity of work itself was undergoing deep change, both on the structural and experiential levels. With the completion of the nation's communications and transportation networks, around 1876, the technological innovations that had largely driven the first phase of the industrial revolution continued but were augmented with a series of radical financial and organizational innovations, both of which had profound and lasting consequences for skilled and unskilled workers.[71] In this second phase of the industrial revolution, industry was becoming at once far more capital intensive and its production

---

[70] In Philip S. Foner's words, competition from convict labor was "one of the most bitter complaints" of workingmen in the 1830s. It became even more bitterly contested as the second industrial revolution completed the displacement of the old, artisanal world in the decades following the Civil War. Philip S. Foner, *History of the Labor Movement.*

[71] Alfred Chandler remains the foremost historian of the managerial and technological innovations of the first and second industrial revolutions. For an assessment of industrial workers' responses to these changes, see David Montgomery, *Workers Control in America* (New York: Cambridge University Press, 1979), esp. Ch. 1, on the late nineteenth-century.

processes, far more specialized. For the first time, in an effort to benefit from the new economies of scale that highly capitalized systems of production afforded, industrialists strove to run their factories at maximum capacity and around the clock. As part of the general production-centered logic of Gilded Age industry, industrialists were also endeavoring to take control of one factor of production that still remained largely beyond their grasp: control over the activity of work itself, at both skilled and unskilled levels. Employers' drive for control, as David Montgomery has shown, extended to a bid for the power to determine the formal and informal rules of the workplace and an attempt to extract and transfer the considerable knowledge that skilled workers brought to and deployed on the shop floor to a new class of overseers: that of "managers."[72]

Especially for skilled workers, the prison laborer either embodied the automaton or a new, pernicious system of industrial slavery. John T. McEnnis, the author of a widely circulated critique of various forms of cheap labor (entitled "The White Slaves of Free America") wrote that, under the prison contract system, "the felons are mere machines held to labor by the dark cell and the scourge."[73] McEnnis and other labor leaders also repeatedly drew on the idiom of slavery in their description of the contract system and analysis of its evils. The FOTLU, for example, resolved at its first congress, that "convict or prison labor as it is applied to the contract system in several of the States is a species of slavery in its worst form; . . . it pauperizes labor, demoralizes the honest manufacturer, and degrades the very prisoner whom it employs."[74] In 1888, McEnnis characterized contract prison labor as a species of slavery and warned that "Slave labor should not be employed against free."[75] Through the turn of the century, the leadership of the American Federation of Labor would frequently refer to the prison labor system as "contract slavery."[76]

Repeatedly in the discourse of free workers and organized labor, the prisoner figured as a dependent, unfree laborer who at once threatened to deprive free workers of the value of their skills, a significant portion of their wages, control over the work process, and, perhaps too, their jobs. In addition, many labor leaders saw in the abject conditions and rightslessness of prison laborers the distilled essence of a deeply unjust set of social relations into which they believed the entire nation, and not just one section of the population, was in jeopardy of falling. With some minor variations, the theme of the anti-democratic nature of contractual penal labor recurred in workers' and farmers' discourse on the matter, across boundaries of

---

[72] Ibid.

[73] John T. McEnnis, *The White Slaves of Free America: Being an Account of the Sufferings, Privations, and Hardships, of the Weary Toiler of Our Great Cities* (Chicago: R. S. Peale and Co, 1888), 112.

[74] FOTLU, Convention Proceedings, 1881, 3. See also, J. J. Mudigan, of the Shoe Makers' Union, Central Labor Union rally, Cooper Union, Mar. 28, 1883 (reported in *New York Times*, Mar. 28, 1883).

[75] John T. McEnnis, *The White Slaves*, 113.

[76] See for example, American Federation of Labor, open letter to the U.S. Senate, republished in *Evening Star*, Washington, Sept. 17, 1890, 6.

community, region, race, and work culture.[77] In the industrial states, the larger system of penal servitude of which the contractual arrangement was the foundation, appeared to embody precisely the labor relation for which industrialists seemed to be striving beyond the prison walls, in their "free" factories. With its unfree, highly exploitable laborers, unbridled contractors whose principal objectives appeared to be the reduction of the laborer to a mere instrument of production, elevation of profit-making above all other concerns, and debased and debasing conditions of life and work, contract prison labor – and the large edifice of contractual penal servitude of which it was the foundation – became a potent symbol of a dystopic American future.

On this view, the prison–laborer's reduction to a so-called slave or cog in a money-making machine was threatening not only because of the crushing competition that the purchaser of such labor could bring to bear against free workers, but because it presaged an "industrial slavery" to which free, typically skilled workers felt they were liable to be reduced. That prison contractors had experimented with various other forms of cheap labor and repeatedly used and threatened to use prisoners as strike-breakers or replacement workers affirmed free workers in their view that industrialists wanted absolute control over the process and relations of production. Frequent revelations in the press of prison laborers' appalling conditions of work, horrific burns and other injuries, endurance of bloody corporal chastisements, and desperate rebellions, worked to harden the distinction that workingmen drew between themselves and imprisoned, emiserated laborers, and affirmed their belief that the forces of industrial slavery were on the march.[78]

Within this shared discourse of penal slavery, there were differences of emphasis, and these often corresponded to differences of geography, economy, and work culture. Many Northern critics of the system, including P. H. McLogan, of the Chicago Trades Assembly and the Federation of Trade

---

[77] Rosalind P. Petchesky, "At Hard Labor: Penal Confinement and Production in Nineteenth-Century America," in *Crime and Capitalism: Readings in Marxist Criminology* (Philadelphia, Pennsylvania: Temple University Press, 1993), 595–611; Gildemeister, "Prison Labor," Blake McKelvey, *American Prisons; A Study in American Social History Prior to 1915* (Chicago, Illinois: University of Chicago Press, 1936), 93–99; Ayers, *Vengeance and Justice*, 211–16. As Petchesky has commented, the leaderships of the labor and trade unions drew "a sharp distinction between 'voluntary' and 'involuntary' labor," and perceived convicts' interests as fundamentally opposed to their own. This perception, Petchesky points out, "precluded . . . helping the prisoners themselves to organize for improved wages and working conditions." Petchesky, "At Hard Labor," 599. The question of how nativism may have shaped organized labor's decision to resist rather than organize convict laborers (a disproportionate number of who were foreign-born) is deserving of further consideration.

[78] W. D. Mackenzie King, "The International Typographical Union," *Journal of Political Economy* 5:44, (Sep. 1897), 458–84; V. Lindholm, "Analysis of the Building-Trades Conflict in Chicago, for the Trades-Union-Point," *Journal of Political Economy* 8:3 (June 1900), 327–46; Roger Panetta, "Up the River: A History of Sing Sing in the Nineteenth Century," (Ph.D. diss., City University of New York, 1998), 293–9; Gildemeister, "Prison Labor"; Philip S. Foner, *History of the Labor Movement*, 125.

Unions, argued that contract prison labor transgressed the boundaries of what society could legitimately do in relation to free workingmen. Although society has the "right to imprison a man, and to see that he is employed during his imprisonment," McLogan argued, "still we don't believe that society has the right to go to work to imprison men, and clothe and feed them, and then hire them out as laborers, under contracts, at 40 or 50 or 55 cents a day..., and have them turn out by their labor all kinds of mechanical work, and throw that work into the market in competition with the work of the honest workmen."[79] Such a system was wrong and unjust. Many producers also saw in the country's ubiquitous, profit-driven systems of imprisonment an irreducibly immoral economy, in which convicts were reduced to slavery and in which the properly *democratic* state, which ought to be serving the citizenry at large, in essence exclusively served private, profit-making interests. Some, including George Blair, of the Knights of Labor, also pointed to the contractor's subversion of the procedures of justice: In the South, argued Blair in 1883, judges were routinely imposing long sentences for minor offenses purely to satisfy the contractors' prison labor needs.[80]

In Kentucky, Tennessee, Alabama, and other Southern states, farmers and workers commonly saw contract prison labor as first and foremost a threat to manly, republican independence. As Karin Shapiro has argued, Appalachian miners explicitly rejected socialism and embraced competitive capitalism, private property, and fair, free trade in the marketplace. The use of convict labor in the mines "threatened the image that (the) miners... had of themselves as independent, free men," as well as their conception of a democratic society.[81] Similarly, in Mississippi, the small farmers who opposed the state's convict lease system considered it a labor practice that unfairly swelled the coffers of big planters and commercial interests while depriving the small farmer of his means of independence.[82] Although Southern protestors believed that prisoners should, indeed, be put to work, they rejected the system that put them to work for private interests. Instead, they argued, prisoners should work solely for the state against the laws of which they had transgressed and to which they owed their subsistence.

For producers in every part of the country, however, contract prison labor both symbolized and instantiated the larger, anti-democratic forces that they saw at work in American politics and society as a whole in the 1880s, and which they associated directly with the rise of large corporations and trusts. When, in 1885, in the depths of a devastating economic depression, the federal government awarded a contract for construction work on a federal building to a company that employed convict workers, the affront to free workers was as much symbolic and moral as it was material. The award of the

---

[79] U.S. Senate Committee on Relations between Labor and Capital (1883), Vol. I, 570, 581.
[80] Blair, U.S. Senate Committee on Relations between Labor and Capital (1883), Vol. II, 40;
[81] Shapiro, *New South Rebellion*, 11, 238, 239.   [82] Oshinsky, *Worse Than Slavery*, 51–52.

contract for the rather modest task of adding a second floor to the U.S. Post Office in Peoria, Illinois, provoked a firestorm of criticism not just from local workingmen, but from labor organizations around the country.[83] "The sin of cheapness is becoming a national one," the Knights of Labor's Terence Powderly exclaimed, and it "must be punished in one way or another if persisted in. With the number of industrious men walking the streets of our cities and towns in idleness, it seems to me to be nothing less than criminal for government to award a contract to the employer of cheap labor, no matter whether it comes from the penitentiary or a foreign land."[84] That the federal government would retain a private contractor who used cheap, convict labor, rather than free workers, on a public works project took the inequities of the contract system to new, and highly symbolic, heights. "It is a serious matter," petitioned the Secretary of Philadelphia's Central Labor Union, "when the United States Government becomes a party to the vicious methods of corporate monopoly, using the cheap labor of the unfortunate criminal as a club to beat down the standard subsistence of industrious, law-abiding mechanics."[85]

Workingmen's and farmers' local and national campaigns began to bear fruit in some Northeastern and Midwestern states as early as 1883; at that time, many states undertook fresh, and more thorough-going, investigations of what the press was beginning to refer to as the convict labor question. Beginning with a groundbreaking legislative inquiry into the contract prison system in New York in 1883, legislature after legislature investigated the system. By 1887, all the industrial states, bar Indiana, had conducted an official investigation of prison labor.[86] Repeatedly, these investigations generated fresh evidence of systemic brutality in prison factories, mines, and camps. Some legislative committees concluded that the profitability of prison labor and contractors' increased demand for convict workers were, indeed, causing an increase in prison populations (much as the Knights' George Blair and other labor leaders claimed). In addition to degrading prisoners and "pauperizing honest labor," the Ohio legislative committee argued, the prevailing system of prison labor was also "in great measure,

---

[83] Among the organizations that formally petitioned the U.S. Senate in protest of the contract were the Philadelphia assembly of the Knights of Labor, the Stone-Cutters Union of Albany, New York, the Workingmen's Committee of Quincy, Massachusetts, and the District Assembly of the Knights of Labor in Richmond, Virginia. A group identifying itself simply as "the laboring class of Peoria" also protested the contract.

[84] Terence Powderly, address to the Knights of Labor convention, Ontario, Canada, October, 1885, reported in *The Evening Star*, Washington, Oct. 7, 1885, 6.

[85] W. H. Foster, petition to the Secretary of the Treasury, July 14, 1885; reproduced in Letter from the Secretary of the Treasury, transmitting, in response to Senate Resolution of January 20, papers relating to the employment of convict labor in the construction of a public building at Peoria, Illinois. February 2, 1886. Serial Set Vol. No. 2333, Session Vol. No. 1, 49th Congress, 1st Session, S. Exec. Doc. 59, Feb. 11, 1886, 9.

[86] Blake McKelvey, "The Prison Labor Problem," *Journal of Criminal Law and Criminology*, 25:2 (July–Aug., 1932), 255.

responsible for the over-crowded condition of so many of our penal institutions."[87]

Although the politicization of the convict labor question proceeded along various axes and within different timeframes across the several states in the 1880s, the state of New York, with its massive force of prison laborers and history of labor activism against contract prison labor, proved an early and crucial battleground in the national conflict over penal servitude. In 1882, Democrats set about exposing the brutal conditions of the prison that organized labor had come to despise above all others – Sing Sing, where 1,300-odd prisoners were now laboring away in the oven-molding factories of the union-breaking manufacturer, John Sherwood Perry. Following accusations in the *New York Herald* that the Sing Sing contractors had turned the prison into a miserable den of disease, sexual immorality, cruel exploitation, and political corruption,[88] the New York State Assembly appointed a special investigating committee. That committee's report corroborated and elaborated upon many of the *Herald*'s claims.[89] Publication of the report resulted in no immediate legislative action, but, by discrediting Louis Pilsbury's view that the system was working well, it did deliver the contract's critics an important moral victory. The tide of popular opinion had begun to turn against the system.

Later that year, the *New York Star* ran a series of eleven articles and editorials on prison conditions, in which it claimed that a significant number of New York state prisoners had died or attempted suicide after suffering "brutal and inhuman treatment," and that such treatment had been "brought about by the system of contract labor now in existence."[90] These articles prompted the New York State Assembly to convene an exhaustive and widely publicized investigation into the prison system. Through the first few months of 1883, committee members subpoenaed dozens of prison officers, contractors, convicts, ex-convicts, wardens, and prison physicians from around the state, and procured a mass of testimony on the contract system and its influence on prison and civilian life. The announcement of a thorough investigation into the contract system and the comprehensiveness of the subsequent investigative process, were, in and of themselves, moral and tactical victories for the thousands of prisoners and ex-prisoners, and tens of

---

[87] Ohio legislative investigative committee, quoted in *Proceedings of the National Conference of Charities and Correction*, 1887, 106. T. Thomas Fortune, before U.S. Senate Committee on Relations between Capital and Labor. A number of other legislators and prison reformers commented upon the commercialization of imprisonment and the impact of market forces on the incarceration rate. Henry W. Lord, for example, linked the history of the African slave trade and the Southern lease system; *Proceedings of the National Conference of Charities and Correction*, 1880, 38–9. In New York, Judge Nott testified that he was offered a commission on every prisoner he committed to the Albany penitentiary. See also Julia Tutwiler, "Alabama," in *Proceedings of the National Conference of Charities and Correction*, 1903, 26–7; "Convict Labor," *Annals of the American Academy of Political Science* 17 (Jan./May 1901), 369.

[88] NYSAD (1882) #131, 222–29. Cited in Panetta, "Up the River," 295–300.

[89] NYSAD (1882) #131.

[90] *New York Star*, Dec. 17, 18, 19, 20, 21, 22, 23, 24, 25, 26, 27, 1882. Cited and quoted in Report of the Committee, New York State Assembly Committee on State Prisons (1883), 1125–6.

thousands of free workingmen, who had variously struck, petitioned, and protested against the system over the preceding several years. The Assembly's decision to convene the committee, and the committee's admission of testimony from prisoners, guards, and labor leaders (and not just the contractors and prison authorities), telegraphed around and beyond the state of New York the news that prisons, although effectively managed by private industry, were nonetheless state institutions that, as such, were subject to the scrutiny and overhaul of democratically elected representatives.

The importance of the New York prison investigation and the likelihood that a negative report might finally spur the legislature to abolish or severely restrict the system were not lost on either the supporters or the opponents of contract prison labor. As the committee commenced its work, prisoners, labor leaders, prison contractors, the prison authorities, prison guards, and free manufacturers all strove to bring evidence to bear in their favor and to influence the committee's findings as to the "true" conditions of imprisonment under the contract system. Within the prisons, a fresh power struggle broke out as prisoners attempted to make their voices heard and the authorities moved to censure them. Despite the best efforts of Sing Sing's Warden Brush to suppress prisoner testimony, a number of prisoners clandestinely enlisted the help of a New York lawyer by the name of Michael H. Sigerson. Sigerson, a Democrat and associate of Tammany Hall, made at least two visits to Sing Sing in 1883, during which time convicts smuggled him a number of letters and petitions relating to prison discipline and conditions, and offered detailed accounts of brutal punishments that they alleged had been inflicted for work-related offenses.[91]

Armed with the prisoners' testimony, Sigerson appeared before the New York State Assembly investigating committee and accused authorities and contractors of treating prisoners cruelly and inhumanely.[92] His accusations, which were reported at length in the press, further emboldened the prisoners. Shortly after Sigerson testified, according to the Sing Sing warden, prison laborers began to be "insolent" and to assert that they were unfit for work; many walked out of their workshops.[93] When the committee convened at Sing Sing in February, unrest again broke out, and some prisoners demanded to meet personally with the committee. Warden Brush stated that the prisoners thought that by acting in this "rebellious" manner, they would be "doing their part" to ensure that "the contract system is broken up."[94] The warden promptly transferred those who had testified to the committee or communicated with Sigerson to the up-state prisons, on the grounds that "discipline could not be maintained if the convicts were allowed to do as they pleased." Immediately following that action, however, the unrest at Sing Sing escalated into what the *New York Times* declared was a "mutiny," when convict laundrymen went on strike. The number of prisoners refusing

<hr />

[91] *New York Times*, Feb. 18, 1883, 8; Feb. 20, 1883, 1; Feb. 23, 1883, 5; Mar. 3, 1883, 2.
[92] New York (State) Assembly Committee on State Prisons (1883), 632–8.
[93] *New York Times*, Feb. 20, 1883, 1.
[94] *New York Times*, Feb. 18, 1883, 8; Feb. 20, 1883, 1; New York (State) Assembly Committee on Prisons (1883), 632–8.

to work tripled (to 122), and then doubled again over the subsequent few days, when Sing Sing's shoeworkers and then a workshop of molders went on strike in support of the laundrymen. Warden Brush responded by locking up hundreds of prisoners in the cellblock, putting them on low rations (in the time-tested tactic of draining rebellious prisoners of their fighting spirit), and handing out fifty Winchester rifles to the guards. Clearly embarrassed by the prisoners' well-publicized and sensitively timed protests, Brush also made a series of press releases in which he blamed the insurrection on lawyer Sigerson's acceptance of letters from the prisoners, and banned Sigerson from ever again setting foot in Sing Sing prison.[95]

The credibility of both Brush and the contract prison labor system by which he stood were severely damaged by this and other testimony heard before the Assembly's investigating committee. Even though the committee was divided (along party political lines) on the question of whether the contract system should be abolished or simply reformed, the revelations of abuse made an obvious impact upon both the majority and minority reports. Although the majority reported, rather ambiguously, that the *New York Star*'s charges of brutal and inhuman treatment were neither "sustained by the evidence," nor, on the other hand "not proven," its authors went on to offer a damning description of the conditions under which the prisoners labored, before concluding that the contract system was unjust.[96] "[E]vils of the gravest character have prevailed in some of the prisons of the State, and particularly in the prison at Sing Sing," they wrote:

> Prisoners have been put upon task to which they were entirely unequal, and employed in forms of labor for which they had not fitness or adaptation. . . . It seems to have frequently happened that men were put upon work in which the average task was entirely beyond their power of performance. Failing to perform their task, they have, in some instances been subjected to punishment, and the punishment has diminished their already feeble energies, and made them still less equal to the work required of them. Thus punishment has followed failure, and renewed failure has followed punishment, until the unfortunate prisoner, in utter despair, has refused to work, and been ready to commit some deed of reckless frenzy, even the taking of his own life.[97]

Punishments, they concluded, had indeed been excessively severe, and sick men had been sent to the workshops instead of to the hospital. Moreover, "the interest of the contractor," they wrote, "is best served by the severer

[95] *New York Times*, Feb. 21, 1883, 5; *New York Times*, Feb., 22, 1883, 2.
[96] This was not the only ambiguity in the majority's report. In the same vein, the majority asserted that there was no evidence to suggest that contractors "(interfered) with the proper discipline of the prison, or (imposed) unreasonable tasks" upon the prisoners, but then asserted that "the contract system sustains intimate relations to the discipline of the prison, and especially in the matter of punishments." New York State Assembly Committee on State Prisons (1883), 1125–43. The majority members were: E. R. Keyes, Geo. Northup, Homer Emans, B. D. Clapp, James Geddes, James Taylor, W. S. Kelley, Godfrey Ernst. Taylor and Ernst also signed the much more sharply worded minority report.
[97] New York (State) Assembly Committee on State Prisons (1883), 1126–7.

forms of corporal punishment, such as paddling or showering, which generally result in prompt submission without seriously impairing the prisoner's ability to resume his work." Contractors, they argued, were motivated by self-interest and, naturally, made their best effort to "render the contracts remunerative." Under the contract system, "The labor of the prisoner is let or sold by the State with a view to the largest pecuniary profit. The prisoner thus finds himself in a situation of a hireling, not to say a slave, to serve mercenary ends, viz., first the pecuniary interest of the contractor, and, second, the pecuniary interest of the State." The contract system was inimical to what they described as the "reformatory" mission of the prison; the state took a paternal interest in prisoners, wrote the majority, whereas the contractor was a businessman, "not a charity," and his commitment was first and foremost to the profitability of his business.[98]

Despite advancing this damning critique, the committee's majority stopped short of characterizing the contract system as inherently abusive. Their position more or less encapsulated the view of most northern Republicans on the convict labor question in the 1880s and early 1890s. This was that the contract system might be in need of reform, but it was not intrinsically abusive, whether of prison or free labor, and it ought to be reformed rather than abolished. The committee concluded, "We deem it our duty to say, that this system of labor and discipline, as now established, in our judgment, fails to meet the just demands of a wise and effective prison regime."[99] Steering clear of recommending any substantive change to the system, the majority recommended that the state (once again) put the entire system under review and appoint another commission to frame a new, less injurious prison labor system.

The minority report, which much more closely echoed the state Democratic Party's position on contract prison labor, drew the conclusion to which the critical contents of the majority's report logically should have led, but did not. In a few succinct and sharply worded sentences, the minority concluded that Sing Sing was organized around "the single idea of making as large a financial showing as possible," and that the contract system was pernicious and deeply injurious to convicts and free industry alike. If legally permissible, all contracts should be immediately cancelled and the contract system, "wiped out" in its entirety.[100] Here was a clear affirmation of labor leaders' abolitionist position, and formal acceptance of prisoners' repeated contention that New York's contract system was cruel and unjust.

Regardless of the ambiguities in the committee's majority report, the sordid revelations of life at Sing Sing helped seal the voting citizenry's opposition to penal contract labor. The increasingly popular movement for the abolition of contract prison labor in New York also very probably received

---

[98] New York (State) Assembly Committee on State Prisons (1883), 1134–5.
[99] New York (State) Assembly Committee on State Prisons (1883), 1134–5.
[100] Minority Report, New York (State) Assembly Committee on State Prisons (1883), 1144–5. Members: Patrick H Roche, James Taylor, and Godfrey Ernst.

a boost from the various exposés of the brutalities of the Southern prison labor system that had appeared in the local and national press in the same year (1883). George Washington Cable, T. Thomas Fortune, and other critics of the Southern penal system were now drawing citizens' attention to the South's prison camps, and the particularly deadly strain of contractual prison labor (the convict lease system) to which thousands of Southerners were subject. In a widely circulated essay, which was later published in the *Century Illustrated Magazine,* Cable described conditions in the lease camps of twelve Southern states, presenting evidence to support his finding that, "from the Potomac to the Rio Grande," the lease system killed and maimed prisoners, taught cruelty, instigated false clemency, imposed illegal punishment, and "(seduced) the state into the committal of murder for money." Although Cable was not a critic of the North's system of contractual penal servitude, his indictment of the Southern system unavoidably recapitulated many of the same objections labor leaders made in their criticism of Northern prison practice.[101]

Northern and Southern variants of contractual penal servitude received further critical attention in 1883 from the U.S. Senate Committee on Relations between Capital and Labor, which commenced an extensive investigation into American labor relations that year.[102] Committee members heard lengthy testimony against contract prison labor from labor leaders, social reformers, and a small number of manufacturers who favored labor reform. T. Thomas Fortune, a former slave from Florida who had gone on to become a well-known writer and the editor of the *New York Globe,* decried what he called the "contract convict system" of the South. "It is not equaled in inhumanity, cruelty, and deliberate fraud in any other institution outside of Russian Siberia," he exclaimed, before describing some of the shocking treatment to which Southern convicts were subjected, including fatal

---

[101] Cable, like many middle-class critics of the Southern lease system, implicitly accepted the Northern variant of the contract system as a mode of prison administration. He commended the labor system in use in the Maryland state penitentiary, where prisoners cut marble, cobbled shoes, and manufactured stoves and hollow ware for private contractors, and argued that putting prisoners into a competitive relation with free labor was a "positive good": It teaches the "lazy" prisoner the value of "competing in the fields of productive labor," and therein reforms him. George Washington Cable, "The Convict Lease System in the Southern States," *Proceedings of the National Conference of Charities and Correction,*,1883, 265 –301. Later published in *Century Illustrated Magazine,* 27 (Feb. 1884), 582, and in Cable, *The Silent South* (New York: Scribner's and Son, 1885).

[102] The Senate Committee on Relations Between Labor and Capital (1883). The Committee's mandate was to conduct a wide-ranging investigation of the conditions, grievances, and strike actions of American labor and to "report what legislation should be adopted to modify or remove such causes [for strikes],... as well any other legislation calculated to promote harmonious relations between capitalists and laborers, and the interests of both, by the improvement of the industrial classes of the United States." Contract prison labor was just one of many grievances that the senators investigated; but organized labor's repeated, and widespread, condemnation of the contract prison labor system emerged as one of a handful of problems against which the Committee's Chairman, Henry Blair, argued both federal and state government should take some kind of action.

whippings and obscenely disproportionate prison sentences. The criminal laws of the South, he argued, had been "purposely framed to convict the negro, guilty or not guilty. . . . The object being to terrorize the blacks and furnish victims for contractors, who purchase the labor of these wretches from the State for a song. . . . (T)he whole system of contract labor is pernicious," he concluded.[103] Before the same committee, Carroll D. Wright, the Massachusetts chief of statistics who, only four years earlier, had dismissed organized labor's claims against the contract system and proclaimed it the "wisest as a rule," informed the Senate committee that although the contract system was good for the state treasury it was not the best means of reforming prisoners. Moreover, he confessed, it had, in fact, injured free workers in certain lines of work (most notably, the boot and shoe industry). The federal government, he concluded, would have to confront the problem sooner or later. The many critics of contract prison labor who appeared before the committee appear to have finally persuaded the chairman of the Senate committee (Senator Henry Blair) that the system was indeed unacceptable: "The method now acted upon is almost a guarantee that the man will continue in crime, no matter what good impulses may have been implanted during the time that coercion has compelled good behavior," Blair concluded; "the contract system – carrying the profit to the contractor – is, it seems to me, in the last degree objectionable."[104]

This slew of legislative investigations, and the revelations of abuse that surfaced in these inquiries, further stimulated popular support for the abolition of contract prison labor and fostered legislative initiatives to restrict or otherwise reform prison labor contracts. By 1885, in the North, the major political parties found they could no longer skirt the issue. In the South, the Texas legislature was the first of several states to restrict the contract system: In 1883, it prohibited the use of convicts in mechanical labor beyond the walls of the prison.[105] By 1892, and after the coalminers' rebellions in Kentucky and Tennessee, much the same state of affairs existed throughout the South.

In many Northern states, there unfolded a bitter struggle between Democrats and Republicans over contract penal labor, with the majority of the former committed to the system's overthrow and the latter favoring its retention or modification. When Democratic administrations opposed to the contract system won office in Massachusetts, New York, Pennsylvania, and Ohio, the stage was set for the dismantling of the contract system

---

[103] U.S. Senate Committee on Relations Between Labor and Capital (1883), Vol. II, 530.

[104] U.S. Senate Committee on Relations Between Labor and Capital (1883), 1883, Vol. III, 570. Senator Blair suggested a number of alternatives: He suggested that all American convict-made goods be exported to the "developing peoples of the world" as a way of avoiding the problems of which free American labor complained; he also argued that the prisoner be paid three-quarters of what an ordinary workman might earn (which would make prison labor less competitive), and that this would be the "strongest guarantee of reform."

[105] Perkinson, "Birth of the Texas Prison Empire," 184.

of imprisonment at hard labor.[106] In 1883, as New Yorkers learned about their own and other states' prison systems, their state legislators introduced no fewer than thirteen bills seeking to regulate or abolish contract convict labor, including one generated by the New York state Trades Assembly and sponsored in the state Assembly by the Democrats. This bill provided for the abolition of contracting and the creation of a handful of highly diversified industries to be run by and for the state; no industry was to employ more than fifty convicts at a time, and there was to be no production of "American manufactures" except for use by the state and its agencies. Surplus prisoners at Sing Sing and Clinton were to be put to work in the state lime quarries and iron mines, respectively.[107] Unable to settle upon any one of these bills, the Democratic legislature finally voted to send the question to the voters in the November, 1883 elections. The Republican editor of the *New York Times*, an antagonist of the workingmen's unions and supporter of the con-tract system, wrote in a tone of relief that the contract labor referendum would "have a tendency to draw out a larger vote in the country districts than any other issue to be decided in November. Tax-payers of both parties are generally opposed to taxing themselves a million a year, more or less, to maintain prison convicts in idleness." Indeed, he concluded, the citizenry would be so motivated to vote against abolition that they would turn out in droves (and, in so doing, also carry the Republicans to victory).[108]

New York voters did, in fact, turn out in large numbers on election day: Indeed, significantly more New Yorkers voted on the prison labor propo-sition than on any other proposition in the state's history.[109] But, contrary to the *Times'* prediction, the unprecedentedly high turnout did not secure the contract system. By a convincing ratio of two to one, New Yorkers voted to abolish the state's sixty-year-old system of contract penal labor.[110] A few months later, the state's Commissioner of Labor, Charles F. Peck, affirmed the wisdom of the voters' decision: In his first annual report he wrote: "The interference of the contract system with the discipline of prisons, wherever that system prevails, is well established [and] the reporting of convicts for

[106] Gildemeister, "Prison Labor"; McKelvey, "Prison Labor Problem," 255–6, fn 6. The Ohio Republican Party added abolition of the contract to its electoral platform in August 1883 – some time after the Democrats had pronounced it a key issue of the election. *New York Times*, Aug. 17, 1883, 1.

[107] *New York Times*, Jan. 25, 1883, 4.   [108] *New York Times*, Sep. 24, 1883, 2.

[109] *New York Times*, Nov. 10, 1883, 2.

[110] Of all New York voters, 405,882 voted for abolition; 266,966 voted against it. The *New York Times'* editor and other opponents of abolition, nonetheless explained the defeat as a consequence of the fact that the majority of voters were city dwellers and ignorant of penal matters. "We do not regard the vote as anything like a fair and full expression of the judgment of the people of the state," declared the editor of *The Independent*; "(a)nd even if it were, at least ninety-nine votes in every hundred would be without the requisite information to make them the expression of an intelligent opinion." Report of the House Committee of Labor, "Contract Convict Labor," April 1, 1884, 48th Congress, 1st Session, H. Rpt. 1064, 2; Panetta, "Up the River," 301; "Prison Contract Labor," *The Independent . . . Devoted to the Consideration of Politics, Social and Economic Tendencies, History, Literature, and the Arts*, 35:1827 (New York: Dec 6, 1883), 17.

punishment by contractors' agents, who have no interest in the reformation of the convicts, has been attended with widespread and shocking abuses and cruelties." The state should immediately assume complete control of its prisons and diversify prison industries so as to avoid undue competition with any section, whether skilled or unskilled, of free labor. "The profits of the labor of the convict belong to the state, the laws of which he has transgressed," not to private interests, Peck asserted; the state's labor contracts with Perry and Co., the Bay State Shoe and Leather Company, the New York Clothing Company, and every other private concern, were "illegal and void."[111]

After some months of legislative maneuvering (including a last-ditch attempt by Republicans to save the system), New York's Democratic Governor, Grover Cleveland, finally signed into law a bill prohibiting the renewal of all existing prison labor contracts and the signing of any new contracts. (Existing contracts were due to expire in or before March 1886; possibly in the light of legal advice, legislators stopped short of endorsing Labor Commissioner Peck's declaration that all outstanding contracts were null and void.)[112] In straightforward language, the new law mandated the abolition of the decades-old practice of selling the labor of prisoners to private interests. Although it was not written into the letter of the law, the law's dissolution of the foundational relation upon which the prison's finances, disciplinary regime, structures of authority, everyday life, and official doctrine had come to rest, effectively amounted to the abolition, not just of a labor practice, or even of the particular kind of contract system that Louis Pilsbury had shepherded into the prisons: it abolished the prison system that had first come into existence at Auburn in the 1820s, and which had gone on to be the general model for almost every other state prison system in the country. Abolition was a signal victory for organized labor in New York – and a galvanizing event for organized labor throughout the union. The law's passage reverberated across the country, and especially in the other industrial states, the penal systems of which were built upon the same contractual labor relation that New York legislators had just prohibited.

In 1884, the question of what, exactly, would take the place of the contract system – and the larger edifice of penal servitude of which it was the foundation – was not easily answered. What was clear was that New York's

[111] New York Commissioner of Labor, First Annual Report, (publ. 1884), reproduced in U.S. Commissioner of Labor, Second Annual Report (1887), 312–16.

[112] Laws N.Y. 1884, Ch. 21, §1 (the "Comstock bill"). The Republicans attempted to forestall abolition. The November 1883 elections had returned a Republican legislature, which appointed a prison labor commission with a mandate to review the contract system rather than find a substitute for it. However, when the committee was unable to report its findings within the time allotted, Democratic Governor Grover Cleveland and Democratic legislators deftly maneuvered to terminate the prison labor commission and initiate the abolition of contractual penal servitude. The legislature sent two bills to Cleveland: one renewing the prison commission's tenure, the other prohibiting the renewal of prison labor contracts. Cleveland vetoed the former and signed the latter. A few months later the legislature prohibited houses of refuge and reformatories from contracting out of the labor of their child wards. Laws N.Y. 1884, Ch. 470.

prison authorities, and the penal arm of the state now confronted a deepening fiscal, disciplinary, and ideological crisis, and that, now that organized
labor had been victorious in the state with the largest prison labor system,
contracting was likely to be further destabilized in other states. Prison officials and penologists around the country responded to the news with great
alarm. Just a few years earlier, most had dismissed as ridiculous free workingmen's calls for the abolition of contract prison labor. Then, as contract
abolitionism gained political traction and won victories in Ohio, New York,
and within federal government, the penal authorities were forced to recognize that, regardless of the merits of the arguments against contract prison
labor, the established penal system was in real danger of termination. Organized labor's challenges to the convict labor system and the question of how
prison administrators ought to respond to legislative initiatives to change
or abolish contract prison labor helped revive the National Prison Association, proceeded to dominate discussion at both the Association's annual
congresses and the National Conference of Charities and Corrections.[113]

In February 1884, when the passage of New York's abolition law appeared
imminent, the National Prison Association called an emergency conference
of prison officials to discuss the convict labor question.[114] The possibility
that New York might start a chain reaction of abolition across the country
prompted some of the most heated and impassioned debates in American
penological history. Penologists and prison officials disagreed over the questions of how to respond to the attacks upon contractual prison labor, whether
they should simply voluntarily drop contractual labor or reinvent and ameliorate it (so as to ward off legal abolition), and whether they should lobby
Congress and the state legislatures, or appeal directly to the citizenry, to save
contractual prison labor.[115] Regardless of where they stood on these questions, however, all prison administrators of the 1880s took as a self-evident
truth that the activity of productive labor was the indispensable foundation
of prison discipline and financial stability; almost all also assumed that the
only way to put convicts to productive labor was through some form or other
of the contract labor system. The possibility that order in the prison (or any
institution) might either rest or be made to rest upon some basis other than
productive labor was unthinkable.

To these wardens, and indeed, to nineteenth century society at large, the
very font of disorder was the absence of productive labor – or what they
referred to as "idleness." "I can think of nothing so near chaos," exclaimed
one prison warden before a meeting of the National Prison Association, "as a
prison with fifteen hundred men without labor. . . . It needs no argument to

[113] *Proceedings of the National Conference of Charities and Correction*, 1884–1900; *Proceedings of the
Annual Congress of the National Prison Association of the United States*, 1884–1900.
[114] "Special Conference of Prison Officials, New York City," *Proceedings of the Annual Congress of
the National Prison Association of the United States*, 1884.
[115] The following discussion is drawn from *Proceedings of the Annual Congress of the National Prison
Association of the United States*, 1880–1900, and *Proceedings of the National Conference of Charities
and Correction*, 1880–1900.

demonstrate that the worst thing in the world for a man who has the ability to work is *enforced idleness*.... In penal institutions especially it has been shown time and time again, that it leads to habits of immorality, to disorder, and riot, and in a large number of cases mental derangement and physical ruin."[116] For prison officials, productive labor was not just a means of generating wealth (although it was certainly that) or a way of maintaining discipline; it was the means to self-improvement and a necessary condition of salvation. Depriving prisoners of work was both cruel and unwise, many argued: "To deny him [labor] is like shutting out the light of heaven," one warden argued in 1884.[117] "So fraught with evil would this be," argued another warden,

> that I can not conceive that any intelligent man, having the good of his kind heart, could give it a moment's serious consideration. Idleness is the prolific cause of mischief and crime; in no place is this truth more shockingly demonstrated than inside prison walls. Language would fail to describe the horrors of a prison in which men have nothing to do. The fearful sights and sounds of which we read, in some prisons in South America and Mexico, would be reproduced.

Only Dante's Inferno would surpass the horrors of such a prison, he concluded.[118]

Added to this conception of the laboring origins of good discipline and moral order were the implicit assumptions of almost all prison authorities that prisons could not put convicts to work without the aid of private business in some shape or form, and in isolation of the market. Prison administrators disagreed on precisely what form the relationship between private capital and convict workers ought to assume, and how the entry of prison-made goods onto the market ought to be regulated, but almost no one envisioned a system in which private capital played no role whatsoever. In the 1880s, prison administrators were working within a concept of political economy in which state government was comparatively stripped-down, decentralized, and fiscally feeble. The British "state-use" model, in which the state assumed private capital's function as investor, producer, distributor, price-fixer, vendor – and *consumer* – of prisonmade goods, remained a wholly foreign concept in American penological circles.[119] Although many

---

[116] Warden Wright, *Proceedings of the Annual Congress of the National Prison Association of the United States*, 1894, 141–2.

[117] *Proceedings of the National Conference of Charities and Correction*, 1884, 328.

[118] Warden Patterson (New Jersey State Prison at Trenton), *Proceedings of the Annual Congress of the National Prison Association of the United States*, 1887, 120–1.

[119] In 1882, Charlton Lewis reported to the National Prison Association on his recent tour of English and Irish prisons, and commended the English "state-use" system. However he did not elaborate on its applicability in the U.S. context and it drew little interest from his fellow American penologists. *Proceedings of the Annual Congress of the National Prison Association of the United States*, 1882, 39–40. In 1884, at the emergency meeting of prison officials, Eugene Smith also commended the British system, with its state-use prison labor arrangement, as "beyond question of cavil the most perfect system of prison administration in the world." The states could adapt the system, but American federalism prevented its full application. Again,

American prison administrators were prepared to regulate and renegotiate the prison's place in the market, none pondered the possibility of withdrawing prisoners from the labor market altogether. The idea of closing the open market to convict-made goods struck most of these administrators as equally absurd.

A small minority of prison officials, most of whom hearkened from Pennsylvania, the only state whose government, as late as the 1870s, had resisted putting its prisons on a contract prison labor basis, rejoiced that contract prison labor was finally being discredited. Pennsylvania prison warden, Richard Vaux, argued before the National Conference of Charities and Corrections that the contract system, "necessitates association, with all its evils, and makes the convict a machine, cared for only with a view to keep up his physical capacity, forced to work not as a punishment, but for the profit of his employers, the State and the contractor."[120] George W. Hall, of the Philadelphia Prison Society, echoed the position of the Pennsylvanian penologists when he implored reformers and prison administrators: "*Have no contract labor in your penal institutions.*"[121] Through the 1880s, the Pennsylvanians commended their own "state-account" prison labor system, in which the state ran prison industries and sold the prison's product on the open market.[122]

The vast majority of prison administrators, however, responded angrily to the growing popular support for the abolitionists' cause. They denounced organized labor, resolved to protect the decades-old system of contract prison labor, and formulated strategies for its defense. For many of these prison officials, the attack upon contractual prison labor was an attack upon prison labor *per se.* To expel contractors from the prisons would be to destroy prison labor in general. The view of one prison administrator, Mr. Berry, was typical in this regard: "The doctrine that [New York] has been tempted to follow," he said in regard to New York's abolition law, "is not only unsound, but in every respect dangerous. It is not only that but unspeakably cruel toward the convict, who in the end is going to be made to bear the consequence of that legislation. If it results in enforced idleness on his part, then we may attempt to do what we will to supply the deficiency which that idleness will induce; and our ingenuity is not sufficient to do it, for there is nothing that can take the place of an opportunity to labor."[123] Berry

however, his colleagues did not engage him on the matter. Special Conference, National Prison Association, *Proceedings of the Annual Congress of the National Prison Association of the United States,* 1884, 132–6. American penologists only began to debate state-use in a serious way once the New York state constitution was amended, in 1894, to direct its use in all the penal facilities of that state.

[120] *Proceedings of the National Conference of Charities and Correction,* 1881, 255–6.
[121] George W. Hall, "Prison Discipline: A Paper from The Philadelphia Society for Alleviating the Miseries of Public Prison," *Proceedings of the National Conference of Charities and Correction,* 1885, 301–3.
[122] *Proceedings of the Annual Congress of the National Prison Association of the United States, Proceedings of the National Conference of Charities and Correction.*
[123] Berry, *Proceedings of the National Conference of Charities and Correction,* 1884, 327.

and others argued further that Pennsylvania's state-account system was an expensive and politically questionable alternative to the contract system. One critic estimated that the cost of putting New York on a public-account system would be approximately $1,000 per prisoner, or $3 million for the state – a sum that would have to be borne, he pointed out, by New York's taxpayers.[124] The state-account system was also morally questionable, according to most prison officials outside Pennsylvania: It is "wrong in principle for the government of a state or a nation to directly engage in manufacturing and commercial enterprise with funds forced by taxation from the pockets of the people."[125] (U.S. State Commissioner of Labor, Carroll D. Wright, also raised this objection).

Another supposed alternative to contract prison labor was championed by Zebulon R. Brockway, who was appointed superintendent of the country's first state reformatory for boys, at Elmira, New York, in 1876, and who went on to be known as the "father" of Progressive Era, rehabilitative penology.[126] Thanks to Alexander Pisciotta's nuanced history of the reformatory-prison movement, historians are familiar with Brockway's success as a pioneering and highly influential theorist of reformatory penology, as well as his failures at Elmira (where, under Brockway's superintendency, a series of abuse scandals rocked that institution – and Brockway's reputation – in the early 1890s).[127] What is less well known is that Brockway's emergence as a leading penologist in the 1880s proceeded amidst, and was deeply conditioned by, the crisis of prison labor that erupted in New York and elsewhere in that decade.[128]

Brockway's development as a penal theorist and administrator came in two distinct phases, both of which were deeply influenced by changes in

---

[124] Zebulon Brockway, *Proceedings of the National Conference of Charities and Correction*, 1883, 169–74.

[125] Brockway, *Proceedings of the National Conference of Charities and Correction*, 1883, 172; Wright, testimony to U.S. Senate Committee on Relations Between Labor and Capital (1883).

[126] Alexander W. Pisciotta, *Benevolent Repression: Social Control and the American Reformatory-Prison Movement* (New York: New York University Press, 1994), 3–4, 7, 28–32. See also, David J. Rothman, *Conscience and Convenience*, 32–35.

[127] Pisciotta, *Benevolent Repression*, 28–59.

[128] Pisciotta notes Brockway's prior experience with running prison industries, and notes that Brockway used repressive means toward the end of making "'machine men, but also proletarians'" (Pisciotta, *Benevolent Repression*, 22). However, he considers neither Brockway's critical role in the prison labor debates of the 1880s nor the impact of contract abolitionism on the Brockway's penology and the larger reformatory movement. Part of the difficulty here is that Pisciotta treats Brockway's career during the "golden age" of reformatory penology (1883–99) as following a single, unwavering trajectory. As I argue here, however, both Brockway's reformatory theory and his administration of Elmira underwent significant changes in 1888, once the legislature moved to scale back even the piece-price and state-account forms of prison industry. At least for the period 1876–88, Pisciotta's claim that the Michigan reformatory's heavily labor-oriented reformatory was markedly different to the Elmira model appears to be an overstatement: In light of the evidence regarding the sweated prison industries at Elmira and Brockway's own writings on prison labor during those years, hard, productive labor played a critical role in both the theory and practice of Brockway's reformatory penology. Pisciotta, *Benevolent Repression*, 29–30; 83–4.

the politics and law of prison labor. During the first phase, which stretched from 1851 to 1888, Brockway's penology was first and foremost a labor, rather than a medical or pedagogical, model of prison discipline. Like almost every other state prison in the country in the 1880s, Elmira's regime was grounded in the activity of penal productive labor and reinforced by an ideology that held that productive labor was good for state, taxpayer, and prisoner alike.[129] Although it is the case, as Pisciotta and others have pointed out, that Brockway helped author and, later, revived the National Prison Association's groundbreaking Declaration of Principles (of 1870), Brockway's interpretation of those principles and his practical administration of prisons placed a great deal more emphasis on the importance of productive labor in prisons than did its key author, the Reverend Enoch Wines.[130] Whereas, in the National Prison Association's original reformatory scheme, religious and educational programs, probationary and conduct mark programs, and the principle of self-regulation were accorded primary importance, in Brockway's rendering of this early formulation of reformatory penology, these techniques of prison governance played second fiddle to the activity and ideology of productive labor. The distinction between the reformatory penology articulated in the Declaration of Principles, and Brockway's own labor-centric version of reformatory theory, was a distinction that Brockway himself acknowledged. Indeed, he often asserted before congresses of his fellow prison administrators that productive labor was a new and very promising frontier in reformatory penology.[131]

Although Brockway was correct that productive labor played a less prominent role in the National Prison Association principles than in his own penology, he inverted the relation between productive labor and reformatory theory: In fact, the various educational, probationary, and incentive-

[129] Quoted in Pisciotta, *Benevolent Repression*, 22.
[130] For a discussion of the National Prison Association Declaration of Principles, see Chapter 3 in this book. Other key theorists of reformatory penology included Eugene Smith, New York City attorney and president of the New York Prison Association. Smith stressed that prison administrations needed to change the relation between the state and the prisoner; disabuse convicts of the idea that they were "slaves"; and lead prisoners to re-imagine themselves as "employés": "The relation of the State to the convict, in the matter of prison labor, should be changed, so far as proper prison discipline will admit, from relation of master and slave to that of employer and employé." Although historians have not considered Smith's writings in any depth, his work is important both as a precursor of Progressive Era penology and in its own right as an artifact of, and searching attempt to come to terms with, the Gilded Age's great crisis of imprisonment. See Smith, Special Meeting, National Prison Association February 27–29, 1884, 132–6; *Proceedings of the Annual Congress of the National Prison Association of the United States*, 1884, 82–3; *Proceedings of the National Conference of Charities and Correction*, 1885, 267–73.
[131] Although it was the case that Brockway gave much more prominence to the activity of productive labor than had the prisoner reformers of the Reconstruction Era, rather than labor entering reformatory penology as just another useful tool of prison management, it is more accurate to say that Brockway intended various educational, probationary, and incentive techniques to serve and reinforce a labor-based system of prison discipline.

oriented techniques with which he experimented at Elmira in the 1870s and 1880s served and reinforced the much older, labor-based system of imprisonment that he established at that prison. Until 1888, productive labor was the foundation, rather than a mere, supplemental, disciplinary technique, in Brockway's Elmira. Indeed, productive labor had long been the central, organizing principle of Brockway's method. Before arriving at Elmira, in 1876, Brockway had risen to prominence as a warden who, above all else, possessed both the skills and commitment to turning prisons into stable, profit-making institutions. Two decades earlier, he had entered prison administration as a clerk, manager, and deputy superintendent under Amos Pilsbury at the Albany County Penitentiary; here, he had helped run some of the most profitable prison workshops in the country (under the famous Pilsbury system). Subsequently, Brockway had applied his first-hand knowledge of that system first, to the Monroe County Penitentiary, in Rochester, New York, and then to the Detroit House of Correction in Michigan.[132] The profitability of Brockway's Monroe penitentiary industries established his reputation as an effective prison warden; "(t)his feature, more than any other, attracted outside attention," Brockway himself would later write, and was "the main consideration that induced the municipal authorities of Detroit, Michigan to tender me the position" at the house of correction.[133] At Detroit, in the 1860s, Brockway had repeated his earlier successes at Monroe, setting up a chair manufactory that, by 1865, was reported to be generating income in excess of four times the annual operating costs of the institution.[134] Although it was the case that, once the industries were up and running, Brockway had introduced some educational and inmate self-government programs at the House of Correction, he made it clear that he intended these to complement and enhance, rather than replace, his labor-based system of discipline. (Most blatantly, his appointment of prisoners to supervisory and instructional positions in the early 1870s, was first and foremost a cost-cutting measure – as the civilian foremen who struck in protest of his decision appear to have immediately grasped).[135] By 1870, Brockway was widely known as the man who had made Detroit's House of Correction, in the words of one supporter, "a source of reformation and a source of profit, at the same time."[136]

---

[132] Pisciotta, *Benevolent Repression*, 29–30. See also, Gildemeister, "Prison Labor," 59.

[133] Zebulon Brockway, *Fifty Years of Prison Service: An Autobiography* (Glen Ride, NJ: Patterson-Smith, 1969 [1912]), quoted in Paul W. Keve, "Building a Better Prison: the First Three Decades of the Detroit House of Correction," *Michigan Historical Review* 25:2 (Fall 1999), 5.

[134] Keve, "Building," 8.

[135] Harold M. Helfman, "Antecedents of Thomas Mott Osborne's 'Mutual Welfare League' in Michigan," *Journal of Criminal Law and Criminology*, 40:5 (Jan.–Feb., 1950), 597–8.

[136] *The Independent . . . Devoted to the Consideration of Politics, Social and Economic Tendencies, History, Literature, and the Arts*, 21:1098 (Dec. 16, 1869), 2. See also, Frederick H. Wines, "A Sabbath in Prison," *The Independent . . . Devoted to the Consideration of Politics, Social and Economic Tendencies, History, Literature, and the Arts* 22:1131 (Aug. 4, 1870), 8; *Scribner's Monthly* IV:4 (Aug. 1872), 504 (3 pages); "Prison Reform," *The Independent . . . Devoted to the Consideration of Politics, Social and Economic Tendencies, History, Literature, and the Arts*, 25:1263 (Feb. 13, 1873), 208; "The

When Brockway took up the reins of power at Elmira, then, he brought with him extensive experience in, and a well-known commitment to, the management of profitable prison enterprises.[137] By that time, he had also conceptualized and practiced a version of reformatory penology in which productive labor was the foundation of the disciplinary, moral, and financial order of the prison.[138] Much as the young prisoners of Detroit had done under Brockway, by the early 1880s, the young men at Elmira were laboring eight hours per day, under piece-price contract, and under threat of corporal discipline; like their older brethren at Sing Sing and Auburn, they worked in the large-scale industries of hollow-ware, shoe, boot, and broom manufacturing.[139] Brockway's commitment to labor-based penology, meanwhile, only strengthened during his first decade at Elmira. As organized labor's campaign against contract prison labor began to pick up steam in the early 1880s, Brockway insisted that "(e)mployment is essential to the penitentiary system for criminals. Without employment the system must be abandoned. When the prisoners of a penitentiary are left in idleness, the penitentiary proper no longer exists."[140] The reasons for the continuous employment of convicts, he continued, were perfectly straight-forward: "[c]riminals" were a "low bred class," "imbruted" by "squalor and vice," and "devoid of the common incentives to industry, to honesty, to honor." Incapable of voluntarily reforming themselves, prisoners would have to receive "compulsory assistance" in the form of constant labor, which would habituate them to "honest conduct" and "decent behavior."[141] Moreover, Brockway repeatedly reminded both his fellow administrators and the citizenry at large, the reformatory activity of productive labor generated necessary funds for the institution, and made it possible for the prisons to be self-sustaining.[142]

As it became clear that organized labor's opposition to contractual convict labor was not about to whither away, Brockway, like most other prison administrators, began directly engaging the problem of how to keep prisoners at productive labor in the event that contracting was prohibited. He responded to New York's 1883 referendum and the legislature's subsequent

Limitations of Prison Discipline," *The Independent... Devoted to the Consideration of Politics, Social and Economic Tendencies, History, Literature, and the Arts,* 25:1284 (July 10, 1873), 881.

[137] In the 1870s, following a series of legal and political problems arising from his management of the Detroit House of Correction, Brockway briefly left corrections to become vice president of the Michigan Car Company. Pisciotta, *Benevolent Repression,* 30.

[138] Pisciotta, *Benevolent Repression,* 199.

[139] *New York Times,* Apr. 29, 1881, 2. In 1882, a New York Assembly Committee investigated complaints of abuse at Elmira; a number of convicts testified that work in the hollow ware workshop was sweated, and that beatings were commonplace. Two civilian carpenters who had done work at the reformatory corroborated these claims. *New York Times,* March 26, 1882, 1.

[140] Brockway, *Proceedings of the National Conference of Charities and Correction,* 1886, 113–14.

[141] Brockway, *Proceedings of the National Conference of Charities and Correction,* 1886, 114; see also Brockway's article, "Needed Reforms in Prison Management," *The North American Review* (July 1883), 40–9, esp. 47.

[142] Pisciotta, *Benevolent Repression,* 199.

prohibition of the contract system in rather measured tones: Organized labor's campaign against contractual prison labor, he opined, was far more narrowly focused than Warden Berry and other prison administrators had assumed; there was no need for prison administrators to be unduly alarmed. Labor leaders were not seeking the abolition of prison labor *per se*, Brockway reassured his colleagues; rather, free workers were merely demanding an end to contractors' *direct* employment and management of prisoners inside the prisons. Prison labor could be reinvented and regulated in such a way that it pacified organized labor and prisoners, while remaining the vital center of prison life, economy, and discipline. The solution, Brockway declared, was his own piece-price system of prison labor: Under piece-price, the state put its prisoners to work under the exclusive supervision of state overseers, instructors, and guards; private business merely requisitioned goods for manufacture, which it then advertised, distributed, and sold on the market. Prison-made goods still entered the open market, and the contractors still paid, however indirectly, for the labor of the prisoners. But contractors would not directly oversee the production process. Such a system, Brockway argued, would meet with organized labor's approval; it would also keep prisoners at productive labor, secure the disciplinary and financial order of the prison, and eliminate the source of the cruel and inhumane treatment that was often meted out in the prisons when contractors were present. The Elmira Reformatory, Brockway argued, offered a model upon which other prisons could base their industries; Elmira offered an alternative, politically acceptable means of keeping convicts at productive labor.[143]

Through the mid-1880s, prison officials debated the respective virtues of Brockway's piece-price, Pennsylvania's state-account, and the ubiquitous contract prison labor systems. No one system emerged as the obvious choice. Penologists' lengthy, circular discussions at times appeared to exhaust the subject – and, more so, the discussants. Those opposed to the abolition of prison labor contracting pointed to the inconsistency in the piece-price and state-account positions: Neither system addressed the problem of the entry of cheap, convict-made goods onto the open market and, hence, failed to grapple with the problem of the stiff competition that prison labor posed to free workers in the same industry. Brockway's piece-price was "the contract system under another name," argued one school.[144] Similarly, Pennsylvania's state-account merely substituted the state for the private contractor, and offered organized labor little relief from the competition of which free workers complained. The substitution of the state-account or piece-price system of production for contractual labor would not appease the unions, one

[143] Brockway, in *Proceedings of the Annual Congress of the National Prison Association of the United States, 1883* 61–3; *Proceedings of the Annual Congress of the National Prison Association of the United States, 1884*, 147–8. See also, Brockway, in *Proceedings of the Annual Congress of the National Prison Association of the United States, 1885*, 205–10.

[144] Warden Patterson of Ohio, *Proceedings of the Annual Congress of the National Prison Association of the United States, 1883*, 140–1, 327–8.

critic added: "Your argument that convict labor is brought into competition with free labor, and [that] therefore a change of proprietorship should be made, amounts to nothing. It affects you just the same, whether the State shall manufacture or whether Mr. A. shall hire the labor. . . . you are walking around in a circle."[145]

In the mid-1880s, as penologists debated the question of how best to put convicts to productive labor, the chain reaction that many of them had feared would be triggered by New York's abolition bill got underway. North Carolina, in face of opposition to the use of prisoners in industries, moved to solve its "convict labor problem" by putting many of its prisoners to agricultural labor on a great, state-owned "plantation" on the Roanoke River.[146] In Minnesota, following the systematic campaigns of the St. Paul Trades and Labor Association, the legislature prohibited the signing of any prison labor contracts that competed with free industry; prisoners were to be put to work under the public-account system, manufacturing binder twine, which the state would then sell at cut-price rates to Minnesota farmers. (This scheme had the added advantage, from legislators' perspective, of breaking the much-detested "trust" in binder twine).[147] Illinois ratified a constitutional amendment banning contract convict labor. The Ohio and New Jersey legislatures enacted laws in 1884 abolishing the contract system. Other Northern, and some Southern, states enacted a slew of laws restricting both the conditions under which convict labor might be let or contracted out to private manufacturers and how and to whom convict-made goods might be marketed.[148] Prison officials' fierce debate over the advantages of

---

[145] *Proceedings of the National Conference of Charities and Correction*, 1884.

[146] In 1896, South Carolina prohibited the leasing out of convicts to any enterprise bar agricultural labor; in 1895 the legislature prohibited the private use of prison farm labor, effectively mandating a state-use system of farm labor. Jane Zimmerman, "The Penal Reform Movement in the South During the Progressive Era," *Journal of Southern History* 17:4 (Nov. 1951), 464–5.

[147] Ted Genoways, *Hardtime: Voices From a State Prison 1849–1914* (Minneapolis: Minnesota Historical Society Press, 2002).

[148] Alba M. Edwards, "The Labor Legislation of Connecticut," *Publications of the American Economic Association*, 3rd Series 8:3 (Aug. 1907), 217; New York's convict-made laws were passed in 1894 and 1896; the licensing law, which provided that retailers of goods made by convicts in other states must apply for and exhibit a license to engage in such commerce, was enacted in 1897: N.Y. Laws 1894 Ch. 698; N.Y. Laws 1896 Ch. 931; N.Y. Laws 1897, Ch. 415. The Supreme Court of New York ruled these laws unconstitutional, however. See *People v. Hawkins*, Sup. Ct. NY, 10 Misc. 65; 31 N.Y.S. 1894 NY Misc. LEXIS 888, Oct. 1894; *People v. Hawkins*, Sup. Ct. NY, 220 A.D. 494, 47 N.Y.S. 56; 1897 N.Y. App. Div. LEXIS 1770; *People v. Hawkins*, Sup. Ct. NY, 157 N.Y. 1; 51 N.E. 257, 1898 NY LEXIS 552 Apr. 16, 1898; People ex rel. *Phillips v. Rayness*, Ct. of Apps., N.Y., 64 N.Y. 93, NY 539; 92 N.E. 1097, 1910 NY LEXIS 883. In 1910, the Supreme Court of New York ruled the 1897 licensing law unconstitutional under the Fourteenth Amendment, on the grounds that a classification of goods by origin (i.e., penal labor), when applied to a vast variety of goods, was an interference with interstate commerce. The attitude of the courts was neatly summarized by the editors of the *Yale Law Journal* in 1897: "No Legislature, only Congress, can declare that convict-made goods are not articles of commerce and then discriminate against them or exclude them from the State by unfriendly legislation." *Yale Law Journal* 7 (Oct. 1897 – June 1898), 44–5.

a piece-price over a public-account prison labor system became increasingly moot, as states began to limit the production, importation, and circulation of any and all prisonmade goods. New York legislators considered a bill prohibiting outright the use of machinery in prisons (under any system of prison labor, including the state-account system). Bills regulating the traffic in convict-made goods soon succeeded in various state legislatures. In 1894, Ohio enacted legislation regulating the sale of convict-made goods, making it unlawful for any person to import convict-made goods without first acquiring from the Secretary of State a license to do so.[149] The following year, Indiana provided that all vendors wanting to sell convict-made goods had to be licensed by the state, and Connecticut enacted legislation that was originally designed to protect free cigar-makers and which prohibited the use of convict labor in the manufacture of drugs, food, cigars, tobacco, pipes, chewing-gum, or "anything used within or through the mouth."[150] (The one striking exception to the otherwise uniform retrenchment of contract labor was the state of Oregon: In 1895, that state went in the opposite direction to the rest of the country and leased out its entire state prison population to single private interest).[151]

New York's abolition of the contract system reverberated in the U.S. Congress, as well. Directly referencing New York's referendum and subsequent abolition of the contract system, the House Labor Committee began drafting legislation prohibiting the hiring out of federal prisoners, in early 1884. Repeating, almost verbatim, the arguments that workingmen and organized labor had advanced in New York during the run-up to the 1883 referendum, the Committee offered two reasons to support abolition: "The prisoners are treated as if they were so many dumb beasts, being driven to their daily tasks by men whose aim is to get a certain amount of work out of them each day," and "(t)he contract system works great injury to honest workers in many branches of industry."[152] Not content with merely putting the federal prison house in order, in the summer of 1884, the House Labor Committee extended the scope of its legislative intent to the states, as well: The committee submitted a bill to the House calling for an amendment to the U.S. Constitution prohibiting any *state* from contracting with any person or corporation to hire or contract out the labor of prisoners.[153] Twenty-four

---

[149] Shortly thereafter, Ohio's Supreme Court ruled that this law contravened the interstate commerce clause of the U.S. Constitution (*Arnold v. Yander*, 47 N. E. Rep. 50, cited in *Yale Law Journal*, 7 (Oct. 1897–June 1898), 44–5).

[150] William B. Shaw, "Social and Economic Legislation of the States in 1895," *The Quarterly Journal of Economics* 10:22 (Jan. 1896). 218–29; Edwards, "Labor Legislation of Connecticut," 217. In 1895, the Indiana legislature also directed that all convict-made goods be "plainly marked 'Convict-made.'" Ernest Bicknell, *Proceedings of the National Conference of Charities and Correction*, 1895, 346.

[151] Blake McKelvey, "The Prison Labor Problem," 265

[152] Committee on Labor, U.S. House of Representatives, "Contract Convict Labor," 48th Congress, 1st Session H. Rpt. 1064, April, 1884, 2–3.

[153] "Amendment to the Constitution of the United States," 2259, Session Vol. No. 7 48th Congress, 1st Session, H.Rpt. 2043, July 2, 1884, 1.

months later, a joint resolution of Congress directed the first federal Commissioner of Labor, Carroll D. Wright, to undertake a systematic study of convict labor in every state of the union; in its resolution, Congress specifically directed that the Commissioner report the methods under which convicts were employed "and the influence of the same upon the industries of the country."[154] Wright, who had investigated the impact of prison labor on free workers in Massachusetts in 1879, added to these tasks that of assessing "the influence that the labor of convicts . . . has upon free labor."[155] When Wright presented his exhaustive, 605-page report the following year, it confirmed at least part of what the Knights of Labor and the FOTLU had been arguing for the previous several years: The contract prison labor system, in all its various forms, had grown exponentially since the 1870s, it was remarkably profitable, and, in some sections of the economy, it was depressing wages. (However, at this point in time, Wright, unlike the unions, believed this could be ameliorated without abolishing contracting).[156]

With the election of New York's Democratic Governor, Grover Cleveland, to the U.S. presidency in 1884, the federal government proceeded to prohibit the leasing-out of federal prisoners (in 1887). The government then set about extracting federal prisoners from Southern lease camps and relocating them to Northern prisons.[157] Three years later, in an effort to end the practice of farming out federal prisoners to the states (which generally led to those prisoners being put to contract labor, in contravention of the 1887 law), Congress authorized the construction of three federal prisons and provided that the inmates were to work exclusively in the manufacture of government supplies.[158] The Republicans' Tariff Act of 1890 also delivered an important victory to organized labor by prohibiting the importation into the United States of any goods made by foreign convict labor.[159]

---

[154] Resolution of Congress, Aug. 2, 1886, reproduced in Report of the Secretary of the Interior, Vol. 5, U.S. Commissioner of Labor, Convict Labor in the United States (Washington: Government Printing Office, 1887), 3.

[155] Report of the Secretary of the Interior, Vol. 5, U.S. Commissioner of Labor, Convict Labor in the United States (Washington: Government Printing Office, 1887), 5.

[156] Report of the Secretary of the Interior, Vol. 5, U.S. Commissioner of Labor, Convict Labor in the United States (Washington: Government Printing Office, 1887), 371, 390–6.

[157] On the history of federal prisoners and corrections policy, see Paul W Keve, *Prisons and the American Conscience: A History of US Federal Corrections*, (Carbondale: Southern Illinois University Press, 1991). Although Cleveland was generally sympathetic to the anti-contract labor movement, he nonetheless vetoed a labor-supported bill, in 1887, that prohibited the government's use of any and all convict-made products on public works, on the grounds that its language was confusing. *Evening Star*, Washington, March 10, 1887, 1.

[158] U.S. Congress, Acts of 1890–91 (26 USS, 839). See also Acts of 1894–95, Ch. 189 (28 USS, 257).

[159] U.S. Laws of 1890, Ch. 1244, 26 Stat. 567, 624 (1890)]; Congress re-enacted this prohibition again in 1897, c.11, and in section 307 of the Smoot-Hawley Tariff Act of 1930. The latter added the "consumptive demand" caveat that the ban did not extend to foreign, convict-made goods that were in demand in the United States and which American industry did not produce "in such quantities in the United States as to meet the consumptive demands of the United States." Report to the Committee on Finance, U.S. Senate, and the

In these years, a number of other bills advancing and broadening organized labor's drive to close down contract prison labor were introduced into the House of Representatives. J. J. O'Neill of Missouri introduced a bill prohibiting the transportation across state lines of all goods made or extracted by prisoners,[160] and an Illinois Representative sponsored a bill aimed at extinguishing competition in the labor market between organized labor and prison labor. Representative Hopkins' bill provided that convicts be put only to that work they were "fitted" to perform, that they work no more than eight hours a day, and that prison laborers be paid the same wage as local, unionized workers received in the same line of work.[161] Hopkins' bill threatened to strip convict labor of two of its most attractive characteristics: cheapness and freedom from regulation. In the event, neither bill became law; O'Neill's was tabled and subsequently reintroduced repeatedly over the next several years. Nonetheless, a federal ban on the interstate commerce in prison-made goods remained a distinct possibility. Well into the 1900s and 1910s, representatives sympathetic to free workers and the American Federation of Labor introduced a steady stream of bills aimed at harnessing the power of federal government against prison labor contracting.[162] Carroll D. Wright's prediction that the national government would inevitably enter the fray was being borne out. Although a number of the bills were defeated or tabled, those that aimed at withdrawing federal prisoners from contract industries were passed. Moreover, the flurry of legislative activity introduced a significant degree of uncertainty around the future of contract prison labor, thereby further destabilizing the institution.

By 1895, the rising tide of protest had propelled legislatures and executives in almost half the states, and the U.S. Congress, to place restrictions of some sort or other on the contracting out of prison laborers to private enterprise. Every region of the country boasted at least two states whose legislature had mandated the abolition or severe restriction of the much-protested contract and lease labor systems. In the South, the convict lease became subject to the Democratic Party leadership's wider effort to win back the mass of disaffected white farmers and white workers who had flocked to support populist and Alliance candidates for local and state office in the

Committee on Ways and Means, House of Representatives, April 1995. U.S.-CHINA TRADE Implementation of the 1992 Prison Labor Memorandum of Understanding, Appendix I, 19.

[160] HR 8716, 1888. The preamble read: "A bill to protect free labor and the industries in which it is employed from the injurious effects of convict labor by confining the sale of goods, wares and merchandise manufactured by convict labor to the state in which they are produced." Any person who knowingly transports such goods across state lines would be liable to punishment of $250 or up to one year's imprisonment. It was first introduced in 1888 and reintroduced in 1894.

[161] *Evening Star*, Washington, May 12, 1888, 1.

[162] See for example, HR3928 (prohibiting federal government's employment of any person convicted of a crime and sentenced to imprisonment in any prison, penitentiary, or jail) and HR3286 (prohibiting federal employees from purchasing materials made in whole or in part by convict labor), 1890. *Evening Star*, Washington, Apr. 24, 1890.

1880s. The threat posed to Democrats was underscored in 1890, as the Farmers Alliances and surviving chapters of the Knights of Labor began talking of founding a third, nationwide party, in an effort to break the Democratic Party's hold on state and federal offices in the South, and the Republicans' domination of the North. Particularly in Georgia, Mississippi, and Tennessee, antipathy to the convict lease had proven an important rallying ground for cooperative, interracial political action among farmers and workers. A Democratic commitment to abolishing the widely reviled convict lease system promised to extinguish the source of one, particularly charged, grievance between two of the party's most important, and apparently alienated, constituencies (white farmers and white workers); more than this, it would also deprive white and black Southerners of some critical common ground.

Mississippi was the first state to abolish the convict lease outright when, in 1890, the Democratic legislature called a constitutional convention. A majority of the 135 delegates, a full 129 of whom were Democrats, voted for an amendment that provided, "no penitentiary convict shall ever be leased or hired to any person or persons, or corporation, private or public or quasi-public, or board, after December the 31st, A.D. 1894" (with the exception that the state could put its prisoners to work on public roads and public works). All extant leases were to be terminated by 1895.[163] The new constitution also authorized the state legislature to acquire and put prisoners to work on state farms.[164] In a tactic that would ultimately destroy the remnants of the Republican party in the South and render victorious the Democratic strategy of fracturing the interracial, class-based political alliance taking form in some farming and industrial workers' communities, the same constitutional convention also significantly tightened and extended restrictions on the franchise. The constitution not only added a poll tax and literacy test to the requirements for voting and registration (which, as is well-known, were chiefly aimed at black voters),[165] but also strengthened and extended the somewhat vague criminal disfranchisement provision of the old, 1868 state constitution. Under that constitution, all adult male residents, who were also citizens of the United States but who were not "idiots,...insane persons,...Indians not taxed" or persons "disqualified by reason of any crime," were entitled to vote (provided they were registered to vote, for which purposes they need merely recite an oath of registration). The 1890 constitution now explicitly disqualified an otherwise eligible voter from voting if he had a conviction for "bribery, burglary, theft, arson, obtaining money or goods under false pretenses, perjury, forgery, embezzlement or

---

[163] Constitution of Mississippi, 1890, Art. 10, §223–24.
[164] Constitution of Mississippi, 1890, Art. 10, §223–25.
[165] A poll tax of $2 was imposed on every adult male inhabitant of Mississippi and those who could not show proof of having paid their taxes were prohibited from voting. In order to register to vote, the intending registrant had to "be able to read any section of the constitution of this State; or...to understand the same when read to him, or give a reasonable interpretation thereof."

bigamy." Conveniently, this suite of disfranchisement grounds was to take effect eleven months ahead of the 1892 election. Equally fortuitously (for the amendments' sponsors, at any rate), the amendments were never put to popular vote for ratification: Had the state Assembly or Senate framed these amendments, they would have had to have been passed by a two-thirds majority in both houses *and* ratified by a majority of the voters.[166] But a constitutional convention of delegates wrote the amendments and no law required the amendments be returned to the voters for ratification. For obvious reasons, the delegates chose not to send the new constitution to the very people whose collective voting rights they aimed to abridge.[167]

In Tennessee, by the fall of 1892, free miners had removed the majority of Tennessee's prison miners and cost the TCIRC hundreds of thousands of dollars.[168] Following lobbying by organized labor in Nashville, the legislature enabled Tennessee's four major cities to reject the lowest bidder in city contracts if that bidder proposed using convict labor on the job.[169] After 1893, the state moved toward the abolition of the convict lease and the adoption of a state-use system under which prisoners would work for the state, mining and also processing coal within a prison owned and operated by the state; convict leasing was formally abolished in 1895.[170] Louisiana's convict lease ended the same year. By the end of the century, convict lease had been *formally* abolished in three Southern states and severely restricted in nine others. (As we shall see, *actual* abolition took longer). In 1892, the national Democratic party elevated the abolition of contract prison labor to its electoral platform.[171]

In New York, the state in which protest against contract prison labor had first attained critical mass, contracting slowly wound down after the passage of the abolition law in 1884. Piece-price continued in some prisons, and the legislature extended the term of some contracts when faced with a mass of idled prisoners. The legislature subsequently (in 1888) directed the governor to appoint a Prison Labor Reform Commission, the members of which it directed to investigate alternative prison labor systems. New legislation provided that wardens were to implement public-account systems, under which the state would supervise production and distribute goods on the open market. If wardens could not find enough work for the convicts

---

[166] Constitution of Mississippi, 1868, Art. 13.

[167] Constitution of Mississippi, 1890, § 241–44. See also, Oshinsky, *Worse Than Slavery*, 51–2.

[168] Shapiro, *New South Rebellion*, 253.

[169] The contract in question was for the construction of a new sewer line for the city; the passage of the law effectively extinguished the bid of the Tennessee Coal, Industry, and Rail Company – the same company that held an exclusive lease for the Tennessee state prisoners. The city's newfound ability to reject any bidder intending to use convict labor persuaded the company to withdraw its bid. As Shapiro puts it, under the new political conditions, the company "increasingly found reliance on unfree labor onerous." Shapiro, *New South Rebellion*, 215.

[170] Shapiro, *New South Rebellion*, 244–5. The state's coal prison enabled the state to become the leading supplier of coal and coke throughout the early twentieth century.

[171] *New York Times*, Jun 23, 1892, 1.

under this scheme, they could then engage in the piece-price variation of the contract system.[172] But in 1888, the legislature proscribed the use of motive power in prison industries and restricted prison workshops to the production of goods "commonly" consumed in New York's public institutions. This statute (known as the Yates law) effectively caused the closure of most prison industries (which had hitherto run on motive power). For the first time, the legislature appropriated funds for the development of new state-use prison industries – a total of $250,000 – and provided for the establishment of a requisition system under which state departments could order prison-made goods; however that sum fell well short of the amount needed to finance the new system.[173] The following year, the "Fassett law" provided that the few remaining contractors were to move to a piece-price system, that prisons were to use either this or a public-account system, and that the product of New York prison labor was no longer to be sold on the open market in New York.[174] Organized labor's efforts to restrict the distribution and sale of goods manufactured by out-of-state convict labor also bore fruit: Beginning in 1887, New York legislators enacted a series of laws mandated the branding of out-of-state prison goods: the words "CONVICT MADE," were to be boldly embossed in "grand primer Roman condensed capitals" on every prison-made product.[175]

Taken together, these acts effectively banned the piece-price system that many prison administrators in the industrial states had hoped would short-circuit the popular movement for abolition of the contract. The great champion of piece-price, Zebulon R. Brockway, was now far less sanguine about organized labor's intentions. Finally acknowledging that piece-price did not offer a politically acceptable solution to the prison labor crisis, after all, he angrily declaimed New York's bills as "class legislation," and declared that there was now an all-out effort abroad to "disorganize and destroy prison labor systems" *in toto*. In a final, desperate bid to save the piece-price system, Brockway proposed that the National Prison Association break with its longstanding tradition of nonengagement in the political sphere and work to build a federated, nationwide prison system; this prison federation, he asserted, would regulate competition among various states' prison industries and form a political coalition that would defeat any and all "class legislation" that might injure prison industries.[176] Meanwhile, in 1888, as the Yates law came into effect and his Elmira industries idled, Brockway scrambled to devise an alternative to his labor-based reformatory regime: It was at this point, and as a direct response to the collapse of his prison industries, that Brockway entered the second phase of his career as a leader of reform penology. He introduced at Elmira a modified version of West Point's system of

---

[172] Laws N.Y. 1886, Ch. 432, §1, §2, §4. Laws N.Y. 1887, chap. 464.

[173] Laws N.Y. 1888, Ch. 586 (the "Yates Law").

[174] Laws 1889, Ch. 382, § 1 (the "Fassett Law"). See also Panetta, "Up the River," 305.

[175] Laws N.Y. 1887, Ch. 323; Laws N.Y. 1894, Ch. 698; Laws N.Y. 1896, Ch. 931.

[176] *Proceedings of the Annual Congress of the National Prison Association of the United States*, 1888, 62–4.

military discipline, put prisoners to marching practice for between five and eight hours a day, and extended other, non-laboring disciplinary activities, such as athletics and baseball.[177] In effect, he inserted an ensemble of alternative disciplinary practices into the vacuum left by the productive labor regime that, down to 1888, had been the foundation of Elmira's famous reformatory method.

As in the past, Democratic lawmakers had been responsible for New York's slew of anti-contract legislation. Although, in the South, Republicans had long sought the abolition of the lease system, in New York and other industrial states, the Grand Old Party had steadfastly defended the principle of contracting. In the wake of New York's anti-contract legislation, however, a growing number of New York Republicans gradually committed themselves to what had proven to be a popularly-supported, and apparently irreversible, mandate to abolish contract prison labor. The urban and reform wings of the New York party now moved, on the eve of the pivotal elections of 1892, to add "restriction of convict labor" to the party's electoral platform. As part of the larger electoral strategy that the Republican leadership was pursuing across the industrial belt, and by which they aimed to draw industrial workers' votes from both the Democratic party and the Populist insurgency, the delegates to New York's 1891 Republican convention also added a platform that linked the party's longstanding support of tariffs (on imported goods that competed with American industry) with a commitment to protecting New York's free workers from competition from all foreign, convict, and contract labor. Over the opposition of New York's more conservative, up-state or country Republicans, the delegates resolved: "We favor such legislation as will protect the home industries of this state [from] unfair competition [with] prison labor."[178] The following year (1892) the Republican national convention included protection of free workers from convict labor in the party's platform.[179]

More than just a paean to industrial workers and the labor unions, the reform wing of the Republican party followed through on its commitment (the party's other ostensibly pro-labor platforms, however, did not fare as well).[180] After 1892, New York's Republican legislators moved to complete the termination of the last few, long-term prison contracts and to enshrine the abolition of contractual penal servitude in the state constitution. At the state constitutional convention of 1894, Republican delegate-at-large, John T. McDonough, introduced an amendment that would prohibit the sale both of convict labor to private interests, and of convict-made goods on the open market. Before a convention heavily dominated by Republican delegates, McDonough argued that prison labor had tended in recent years to migrate to those industries in which workers had no political voice.

---

[177] Pisciotta, *Benevolent Repression*, 22–3. [178] *New York Times*, Aug 6, 1891, 1.

[179] *New York Times*, May 6, 1892, 2.

[180] More than a dozen labor reforms were debated at the Republican-dominated state constitutional convention of 1894: The only proposed amendment to be carried was McDonough's amendment providing for the abolition of contract prison labor.

Hat-makers, shoemakers, and stove molders had all successfully mobilized to bring political pressure to bear against prison labor in their respective industries, he explained, but prison labor contracting had simply decamped from those industries and resettled wherever the civilian labor force happened to be unorganized and politically weak. In the Northeast, that "weak link" was textile manufacturing. Here, the civilian labor force was increasingly made up of a class of workers who lacked both voting rights and union representation – women. Noting that, earlier in the week, the delegates had decided against extending the suffrage to women and had, instead, promised to "take care of" New York's women, McDonough insisted that here was an instance in which the women of New York urgently needed the state's protection: By supporting his amendment for the prohibition of all forms of contract prison labor, the delegates would be looking out for women's best interests.[181]

The delegates debated McDonough's proposed amendment for a little over a day. Democrats supported it and counseled the Republicans to follow through on their electoral commitment to protect free workers from the competition of convict laborers. At first, Republicans were split on the issue. Joseph H. Choate (the Republican president of the convention), Charles R. Pratt, and a number of "country" Republicans argued against the amendment on the grounds that it was an issue properly left to the state legislature, and that abolition would "interfere with the efficiency" of the prisons.[182] Speaking for the amendment, Republican Elihu Root explained that, although originally opposed to abolition, he had since been persuaded that removing convict labor and convict-made goods from the open market was the logical corollary to that key policy of the national Republican party: tariff reform.[183] In the event, the majority of Republican delegates followed Root's lead; by fifty-eight to thirty-three, the convention voted in favor of McDonough's amendment to the state constitution.[184]

Unlike in Mississippi, New Yorkers were offered the chance to vote for or against ratification of this and other constitutional amendments. In November 1894, the electorate voted to ratify the amendment (and some thirty others with which it was "bundled"). The New York state constitution was amended to read: "after December 31, 1896, no person in any . . . prison, penitentiary, jail or reformatory shall be required or allowed to work while under sentence thereto at any trade, industry or occupation wherein or whereby his work, or the product or profit of his work, shall be farmed out, contracted, given or sold to any person, firm, association or corporation."[185] The amendment further provided that the legislature was to enact legislation providing for the "employment" of all New York state, reformatory, county, and local and prisoners and that nothing in the amendment

---

[181] *New York Times*, Aug 26, 1894, 8.   [182] *New York Times*, Aug 26, 1894, 8.
[183] "The New York Constitutional Convention," *Outlook*, Sep. 22, 1894, 461.
[184] "The New York Constitutional Convention," *Outlook*, Sep. 22, 1894, 461. Choate, and most country Republicans, on the other hand, voted against the amendment.
[185] Constitution N.Y. 1894, art. 3, § 29. Affirmed by Laws N.Y. 1896, Ch. 429.

was to be "construed to prevent the Legislature for providing that convicts may work for, and that the product of their labors may be disposed of to, the State, or any political division thereof." Under the terms of this section, then, all forms of contractual prison labor and the sale of prisonmade goods on the open market were prohibited, and the legislature was directed to keep prisoners at work, but only under a system in which the state was sole employer, producer, distributor, vendor, purchaser, and consumer of prisonmade goods.

$$* \quad * \quad * \quad * \quad *$$

With ratification of the amendment in New York, the longstanding, collective efforts of prisoners, labor leaders, workingmen, and others in that state to abolish contract prison labor had finally succeeded. The amendment promised to wrest the sphere of legal punishment – and the punished – from the hands of the contractors and the vicissitudes of market forces; it would also expel rightless, incarcerated offenders from the open labor market and prevent employers from wielding New York's convict laborers as a weapon against free workers (and from threatening or insinuating to do so). Here was a double prescription, inscribed in the highest law of the state, for, on the one hand, disciplining state government in regard to what it might and might not do with its convicts, and, on the other, civilizing the state's labor market. After two decades of strenuous lobbying, petitioning, and protest activity by free workers and the unions, the political battleground surrounding the state prisons finally fell quiet. The spiraling crisis of legitimacy in which the penal arm of state government had been caught since Louis Pilsbury had first introduced large-scale monopolistic contracting in the state prisons and John Sherwood Perry had landed his large-scale contract at Sing Sing, came to an end.

Inside the prisons and within the administrative ranks of the penal arm of the state, however, a different, though nonetheless destabilizing, crisis was gestating. As we have seen, contract prison labor had not been a mere, incidental attribute of the Gilded Age prison; it had been the foundation of a distinctive mode of legal punishment. Under the large-scale, monopolistic form that contracting had assumed in the Gilded Age, the contract prison labor system had colonized and conditioned every sphere of prison life: The prison's financial structure; its formal and informal rules; the division and use of time; the type and frequency of punishments meted out to convicts; the condition of prisoners' health, welfare, and morale; the convict's legal status; the official doctrines of punishment; the legitimating fictions of imprisonment; and, in some instances, even the flow of convicts in and out of the prisons, had all been heavily conditioned by the imperatives of the large-scale, industrial contract system.[186] These various spheres of prison life and administration had, in turn, reinforced and reproduced the contract system (including the contradictions of that system). By

[186] See Chapter 3 in this book.

abolishing the contract labor system and closing the open market to prison-made goods, New York had, however indirectly, set in motion the toppling of the established prison order, itself.

With no alternative system of prison labor in sight and under the continuing hegemony of labor-reformatory ideology, the penal arm of the state now faced a full-scale crisis of discipline, funding, and ideology. In the days following ratification of the new constitution and through the following year, New York's prison administrators, penologists, and Republican supporters of the contract system repeatedly warned the citizenry that their state was facing what one critic described as nothing less than an issue of civilization . . . a crisis of humanity. "In a year's time," he forewarned, "the prisons of the state will be crowded with idle men. How shall they be fittingly employed; how shall their welfare be conformed to the public weal?"[187] Reformers and administrators' desperate efforts, in the years after 1895, to answer this question and to contrive a constitutionally viable, labor-based disciplinary order for the prisons would spark the rise of the third great penal reform movement in the United States since the Revolution, and foster the articulation of a new, self-consciously progressive penology. Far from making a clean break from recent history, this progressive prison reform movement would be continuously shaped and motivated, both by its adherents' enduring faith in the transformative powers of productive labor, and by the political, legal, and moral constraints to which the popular campaign against contract prison labor had finally, and so decisively, subjected the penal arm of the state.

[187] Anon., "An Interior View of Prison Labor," *New York Times*, Dec. 29, 1895, 28.

5

A Model Servitude: Prison Reform in the Early
Progressive Era

(E)mployment is still enjoined upon the State; the contract system is prohibited. Thus the manner, but not the matter, of penal servitude is affected.

Justice Judson S. Landon, Supreme Court of New York, 1897[1]

In 1900, the state of New York sent an elaborate scale-model of one of America's oldest and most infamous prisons, Sing Sing, to the International Exposition in Paris. Meticulously crafted by a convict reputed to have learned the art of model-making in St. Petersburg, Russia, the structure was illuminated from within by tiny strings of light bulbs. These brightly alerted viewers to one of New York's latest penal reforms: the installation of electric lighting in Sing Sing's old stone cellblock. All underground pipes were clearly marked so as to advertise the recent installation of modern plumbing in administrative and industrial buildings. The intricate model also had automated front gates, which viewers could operate from within the model's tiny guardhouse, and movable alabaster walls that swung open to reveal the clean, bright interior of the model prison's cellhouse. Spectators were instructed that once the International Exposition was over, the model would be returned to the warden's office at Sing Sing, where it would be used as an aid for locating prison fires.[2]

---

[1] Landon also noted that the law effected "a mere narrowing of the employers of such labor, but no denial of the necessity, humanity or propriety of compelling or employing such labor." *Bronk v. Barckley*, 7, Sup. Ct. N.Y., 13 A.D. 72; 43 NYS 400; 1897 N.Y. App. Div. LEXIS 25.

[2] *Star of Hope* 1:2 (May 1899), 7. The convict craftsman went by the rather improbable name of John Howard. Prior to his conviction and imprisonment, Howard, a gifted organ builder, mechanic, and engineer who was born and raised in England, had helped install the great organ at the Winter Palace in St. Petersburg, Russia. Later, while incarcerated at Sing Sing in the 1890s (on unknown charges), Howard also designed and built a photomicrograph for use in the prison hospital, and two reed organs (one of which was reputed to be the largest in the world) in the prison chapels. New York prison authorities ensured these achievements received considerable publicity. *New York Times*, Aug. 14, 1899, 5; *New York Times*, Apr. 30, 1899, 4. (In an earlier article, the *New York Times* misidentified Howard as a native of Germany. *New York Times*, Jan. 24, 1897, 20). The New York State Prison Commissioners also sent issues of the prisoners' newspaper, *The Star of Hope*, to the Paris exposition. The paper's convict–editor later reported that the French prison authorities were so impressed with its value as an educational medium that they established a similar newspaper in their prisons. "Prisoner No. 1,500," quoted in James McGrath Morris, *Jailhouse Journalism: The Fourth Estate Behind Bars* (Jefferson, NC: McFarland and Co., 1998), 105.

Whether or not the Sing Sing miniature presented a "realistic" picture of life inside New York's prisons, circa 1900, it was a fitting emblem of the sweeping series of penal reforms upon which the Empire State had embarked just three years earlier, when the last few private contractors had finally vacated the prison factories. In prohibiting both the hiring out of prison labor to private enterprise and the sale of prisonmade goods on the open market, the McDonough amendment of 1894 had effectively set in motion the abolition of the foundation upon which New York's prisons had rested for almost three-quarters of a century. Ratification had also precipitated an urgent search for a new foundation for the state's penal institutions. With remarkable speed, after 1896, the agency charged with the task of reconstructing the state's postcontractual prisons (the New York State Prison Commission) had laid the groundwork for a new system: The Prison Commissioners had established a network of state-owned and operated prison industries, whose product was to be sold exclusively to other state departments and agencies. They had also implemented a case-history system, by which prison staff generated a record of the particular labor experiences, skills, health, family background, and reform potential of each and every prisoner, and provided for the classification and division of the entire state prison population into "grades" on the basis of these records. As part of their sweeping program of reconstruction, the Commissioners had also sanitized, electrified, and ventilated the old stone cellblocks; abolished many of the disciplinary techniques that had flourished under – and become emblematic of – the contract labor system (such as the infamous lockstep march, the silent rule, and paddling); fostered the adoption of a disciplinary regime grounded in a system of privileges, incentives, and probation; and established literacy and vocational classes for inmates.

As they pursued these reforms, the State Prison Commissioners forged a new way of thinking and talking about convicts and the appropriate means and ends of legal punishment. In the process, they also fleshed out a novel conception of the nature and responsibilities of the penal arm of the state, and, more generally, of the ethical and social functions of government. The "old system," as the Commissioners obliquely referred to the disbanded system of contractual penal servitude, was nothing better than a "species of slavery."[3] It had dealt with prisoners as though they were nothing more than a great mass of degraded, "slavish" brutes to be hired out, ruthlessly exploited for private gain, denied all protection of law, and humiliated and punished without compunction. Conversely, they argued, New York's new system treated convicts as individual "men," each with a distinctive history and set of skills, talents, and needs. Far from being the alienated refuse of society, the Commissioners insisted, New York prisoners were wards of the state and, as such, persons deserving of the firm and gentle guidance of the parental state; in the sphere of legal punishment, the state's duty, to prisoner and free citizen alike, was to nurture, educate, and instill the "manly" virtues

---

[3] *Superintendent of New York State Prisons, Annual Report* (1898), 7.

into its wards, with the objective of raising them to be healthy, employable, and law-abiding men. (With its sanitized cells, electric lighting, modern plumbing, and convict–craftsman, the Sing Sing miniature was thus both an apt instantiation of the Commission's reconstruction of the New York prison system and an impressive showpiece for that effort. Here was a model, not merely of a modern prison plant, but of an enlightened, new penology – one that the State Prison Commissioners hoped would revive the Empire State's long-since tarnished reputation as a leader in penal reform).

As historians of the Progressive Era will immediately recognize, New York's "Americanization" classes, prison sanitization programs, individual-ized case-history system, and publicity drives typified the methods and kinds of innovations that a new, self-consciously "progressive" prison reform move-ment championed in most non-Southern states after 1900. Equally, the Com-missioners' welfarist discourse articulated many of the key doctrines of what progressives, from Theodore Roosevelt to Thomas Mott Osborne, would come to refer to as the "new penology." Thanks to the extensive body of scholarly work on progressive prison reform,[4] the ideal and normative moral content of these and related progressive reforms are by now quite familiar: In the Northern states, in the first two decades of the twentieth century, a new generation of self-consciously progressive reformers aimed to turn the "nightmarish prison" inherited from the nineteenth century into a thera-peutic "community."[5] Theoretically, this prison community would "normal-ize" prisoners and adjust them for life on the outside, through educational, work, and recreational programs and with the help of individualized medical and psychiatric treatment; by normalizing imprisoned subjects – whether as efficient housewives and loving mothers, in the case of white women; domes-tic servants in the case of women of color; upright and gainfully employed breadwinners, in the case of men; or appropriately Americanized citizen–laborers in the case of immigrants from Russia and Southern and Eastern Europe – the new, progressive prison community would make good citizens of imperfectly socialized offenders.[6]

---

[4] The leading treatments of Northern progressive prison reform are: David J. Rothman, *Conscience and Convenience: The Asylum and Its Alternatives in Progressive America* (Boston and Toronto: Little, Brown and Co, 1980), espec. 117–58, and 379–424; Estelle B. Freedman, *Their Sisters' Keepers: Women's Prison Reform in America, 1830–1930.* (Ann Arbor: University of Michigan Press, 1981); Larry E. Sullivan, *The Prison Reform Movement: Forlorn Hope* (Boston: Twayne Publishers, 1990); Paul W. Keve, *Prisons and the American Conscience: A History of U.S. Federal Corrections* (Carbondale: Southern Illinois University Press, 1991). Blake McKelvey, *American Prisoners; a Study in American Social History Prior to 1936* (Chicago: University of Chicago Press, 1932). For the post-World War I period, see Estelle B. Freedman, *Maternal Justice: Miriam Van Waters and the Female Reform Tradition, 1887–1974* (Chicago: University of Chicago Press, 1996).

[5] Rothman, *Conscience and Convenience*, 17–32.

[6] Rothman, *Conscience and Convenience*, 118–28; Freedman, *Their Sisters' Keepers*; McKelvey, *American Prisoners*; Sullivan, *The Prison Reform Movement*. The term, "new penology" was widely used by progressives in the 1910s, to describe the new principles and doctrines of progressive prison reform. It was largely articulated by Northern prison reformers, social

Although the existing literature on these reforms remains indispensable to our understanding of Progressive Era legal punishment, with the notable exception of the Southern historiography, it has tended to obscure the political field within which progressive reform took shape and, most especially, the "prison labor problem" out of which the prison reform project grew in the 1890s. We still know relatively little about the relation of the so-called new penology to the old, labor-based penology that had flourished alongside the contract prison labor system in the Gilded Age; likewise, we have no account of the broader political and legal pressures to which progressive reform was subject through the 1900s and 1910s. As I argue in the pages to follow, in the few years either side of 1900, the Northern states' abolition or otherwise severe restriction of contract prison labor cast the penal arm of state government into a full-scale disciplinary, financial, and ideological crisis. This crisis proved the vital crucible of the great project of progressive prison reform, first in New York and eventually throughout the Northern states as a whole. Moreover, the prison labor problem – that is, the problem of how to revive productive labor in the prisons, amidst a deepening thicket of political and legal constraints upon the organization of that labor and sale of its product – remained the single most important preoccupation of Progressive Era prison reformers throughout the period (c.1896–1919). The effort to solve that problem lay at the root of the progressive prison reform project as a whole; moreover, reformers' perception that productive

scientists, and penal administrators, and it enjoyed its greatest support among lawmakers and social reformers in the Northern states. However, as the work of Alex Lichtenstein and Robert Perkinson suggests, when Southern states moved from the convict lease to the state chain gang and state penal farm systems (during the Progressive Era), their prison administrators and lawmakers soon picked up on the new penology's emphasis on the prison's normalization function, and proceeded to fuse that principle with Southern racial-segregationist doctrine. In ways broadly consistent with Northern new penology, penal administrators and lawmakers in Texas, Georgia, and other Southern states reasoned that their states were dutifully assuming paternal responsibility for their offenders, and making every effort to appropriately socialize their "wards"; they invariably insisted, however, that in the South this meant recognizing the distinctive needs and skills of the thousands of black convicts who made up the majority of the convict population: Specifically, black wards of the state needed to be put to the kind of agricultural, road, and other kinds of out-of-doors manual labor they were allegedly good at. Holding black convicts "indoors" in Northern-style prisons, on the Southern new penological view, was cruel and unnatural, and would only result in madness or premature death for the black prisoner; by extension, they asserted, the various recreational and vocational prison programs for which Northern penologists called had little application in the South. The Southern progressives' chain gang and the state penal farm, then, became the analogue of Northern progressives' educational, vocational, recreational, and psycho-medical prison programs. (As we shall see in Chapter 9, Southern penology amplified and refined the latent racial doctrines of Northern new penology; moreover, Northern progressives appear to have acquiesced to the Southern formulation of the new penology on the grounds that the South had a "peculiar" condition: the so-called negro problem. See, for example, Theodore Roosevelt, "The New Penology," *Annals of the American Academy of Political and Social Science* 46 (Mar. 1913). Alex Lichtenstein, *Twice the Work of Free Labor: The Political Economy of Convict Labor in the New South* (London: Verso, 1996), 152–85 and "Good Roads and Chain Gangs in the Progressive South: 'The Negro Convict is a Slave,'" *Journal of Southern History* 59 (Feb. 1993), 85–110; Robert Perkinson, "The Birth of the Texas Prison Empire, 1865–1915" (Ph.D. diss, Yale University, 2001).

labor was the only true basis for an effective and just system of legal punishment continuously shaped and informed both the moral ends and technical means of that project.

As we shall see, the effort to put convicts to productive labor was most visible in the early, formative period of progressive penal reform (c.1896–1913): In these years, progressives in three states – New York, Pennsylvania, and Massachusetts – spearheaded what would eventually become a nationwide effort to save prison industries by reinventing them in ways at once acceptable under law, in politics, and in accordance with established penological principles. Yet even at the high tide of progressivism (1913–19), when reformers articulated and pursued their most innovative programs, the quest to revive and sustain industrial prison labor remained a central preoccupation. In addition, in subtle, though unmistakable, ways, both the obstacles that reformers encountered in their earliest endeavor to revive productive prison labor and the frequently ironic consequences of that effort deeply conditioned the most novel and innovative of progressive penal reforms.

* * * * *

Even as reformers flooded cellblocks with electrical light, put prisoners to work white-washing moldy cell walls, and pronounced the old system dead and buried, the ghosts of contract prison labor stalked the prison halls. Although it was the case that, in the decade either side of 1900, New York and almost every other state had abolished or significantly scaled back the contractual system and the entry of prison-made goods into the market, no state had prohibited the activity of compulsory productive labor that contractors had introduced and entrenched at the heart of the American prison system. Despite the passing of its original master, compulsory productive labor remained firmly entrenched in penal law, discourse, and ideology. Leaders of the various popular movements for the abolition of contract prison labor had neither sought the abolition of compulsory productive labor in the prisons, *per se*, nor controverted the widely accepted penological principle that convicts ought to be subject to hard labor of some sort or other; indeed, through the 1890s and into the new century, most labor leaders considered it vital that prisoners be put to productive labor on the grounds that convicted offenders ought to live by the sweat of their brow rather than by the tax dollars of free citizen–workers.

The states' penal codes, the U.S. Constitution, the judiciary, prison administrators, state and federal lawmakers, and reformers, still conferred upon hard penal labor the full force of law. Even though many state legislatures scaled back or prohibited contracting in the 1890s, state law continued to require that convicts be put to hard labor of some kind or other. As the U.S. Industrial Commission reported in 1900, every state in the Union still mandated productive labor for their prison populations (which, in the view of the Commissioners was both morally just and sound public policy).[7]

---

7 United States Government. Industrial Commission. Report on Prison Labor, 56th Congress, House of Representatives (Washington, DC: Government Printers, 1900), 7, 20. The

Even in NewYork, where the McDonough amendment had prohibited labor
contracting in all state prisons, county penitentiaries, jails, and reformatories after December 31, 1896, the constitution nonetheless commanded
the state to find "employment" for its prisoners. As State Supreme Court
Justice Landon interpreted the amendment in an 1897 ruling, the law prescribed "a mere narrowing of the employers of such labor, but no denial
of the necessity, humanity or propriety of compelling or employing [it]."
(Under the Thirteenth Amendment to the United States Constitution, he
reminded the court, "(i)nvoluntary servitude for the punishment of crime is
permissible").[8]

Jurists, administrators, lawmakers, and, in all probability, a good majority
of the citizenry still reflexively identified legal punishment with the activity
of "hard labor." This identification was not simply descriptive in character
(in the sense that people understood that the legal consequence of conviction for felony crime was, as a matter of fact, subjection to hard labor); it
was also normative: Prisoners were to be put to hard labor because that was
what law-breakers deserved and because that was what a fair system of political economy demanded. Although some administrators and jurists placed
more emphasis on the punitive or retributive dimension of the offender's
"just deserts," most emphasized the allegedly redemptive and reformative
effects of industrial labor, and the political–economic principle that "honest
citizens" ought not to have to support the "dishonest" (through tax or other
public revenue). In addition, prison administrators and reformers everywhere still subscribed to the view that industrial labor was the primary, and
indispensable, foundation of prison finances and convict discipline. "No
fact has been more thoroughly demonstrated in prison administration,"
declared New York's Superintendent of Prisons, Austin Lathrop: "Convicts
in prison need constant employment at work, to save them from destructive moral and physical deterioration and degradation."[9] Even that small
minority of American prison administrators who favored the abolition of
the contract system did not question the assumption that industrial labor
was the cornerstone of prison order.[10] Indeed, well into the early twentieth
century, it remained an axiom of American prison administration that the

---

Commissioners wrote that putting convicts to labor was in the interests of discipline, health,
convict reformation, and fiscal economy.

[8] Landon also noted that the law effected "a mere narrowing of the employers of such labor,
but no denial of the necessity, humanity or propriety of compelling or employing such
labor." *Bronk v. Barckley*, 7, Sup. Ct. N.Y., 13 A.D. 72; 43 NYS 400; 1897 N.Y. App. Div. LEXIS
25.

[9] New York Superintendent of Prisons, Annual Report (1894); quoted in *New York Times*,
Jan. 31, 1895, 13. All three state prison wardens and Zebulon Brockway, Louis D. Pilsbury
(warden of the New York County Penitentiary), Warden Hayes of the Kings County Penitentiary, and W. M. F. Pound (secretary of the New York Prison Association) underscored
this principle in their testimony before the State Prison Commission and in statements to
the press. *New York Times*, Nov. 14, 1895, 9.

[10] In the late 1890s, NewYork's State Prison Commissioners were openly critical of contracting;
as more and more states abolished or scaled back contracting, prison administrators and

orderly, just, and financially sound prison was, above all else, a hive of industry; without a well-established, productive labor system, the prison could not help but descend into "enforced idleness," "chaos," and moral collapse.[11] The position of Charles E. Felton, Superintendent of Chicago's House of Correction, was typical: Prisons could only make a "new man" through habituating him to industry, Felton wrote in an article condemning New York's constitutional amendment; "Industry, forced if need be, is the greatest factor yet discovered in securing such change of habit.... Laxity in labor or discipline, in prison management, breeds disorder and that often creates revolt. It never breeds reform."[12]

In the 1890s, as state after state abolished or severely restricted the contracting system, prison administrators in three industrial states – New York, Massachusetts, and Pennsylvania – spearheaded the search for alternative labor systems for their prisons. Each state advanced its own solution to the prison labor problem, and each held up its particular approach as a model for others to follow. Scaling back its contract system in the mid-1890s, New York's oldest rival in the field of penology (Pennsylvania) crafted a modified public-account system. Under the traditional public-account arrangement (which Pennsylvania had utilized in the past), prisoners worked for the state and the state disposed of prison-made products on the open market. In the Keystone State's revamped version of this system, prisoners worked under state supervision and on state-owned materials, but their product was sold on the governmental and open markets under certain strict conditions aimed at ensuring prison industries did not undercut free industries. In the course of the 1890s, the legislature enacted a slew of laws regulating prison production in ways intended to protect free workers from competition: All prison-made goods in Pennsylvania were to be marked "convict made"; the hours of convict labor were restricted to a maximum of eight hours a day (1891); only a small percentage of a prison's inmate population were to work in any one industry (1897); and no prisoner was to work on "labor-saving

reformers appear to have gradually, if somewhat grudgingly, accepted the idea that contracting out the labor of prisoners was poor public policy.

[11] Although a growing number of administrators, following the work of Zebulon Brockway, countenanced the use of military drilling and other nonlaboring modes of discipline, like Brockway, they saw these strictly as a supplement of the labor-disciplinary regime, rather than a replacement for it. Various members of the New York Prison Association, including president William F. Rounds, repeatedly warned that the constitutional amendment would cast prisoners into systemic idleness. See, for example, address to the Municipal Conference (organized by the Reverend Dr. Parkhurst and the City Vigilance League), reported in *New York Times*, Jan. 18, 1895, 5.

[12] Charles E. Felton, "Prison Labor," *Lend a Hand* 17:6 (Dec. 1896), 440. (Originally presented at the annual meeting of the National Prison Association, Milwaukee, Wisconsin, September 1896). Every leading penologist of the late 1890s echoed Felton's criticism of New York's amendment and his assessment of the indispensable reformatory value of productive labor. See, for example, Eugene Smith, "Prison Labor," *Lend a Hand* 15:6 (Dec. 1895) 408 (originally a paper presented before the annual conference of the American Social Science Association, Saratoga, New York, 1895).

machinery" (1897).[13] By 1900, penologists and prison observers such as Carroll Wright were closely watching these developments with the view that Pennsylvania might be forging a viable alternative to the contract prison labor system.[14]

Massachusetts, another industrial state with a long history of working-men's activism against contractual prison labor, offered a second model. This "hybrid system," as Carroll Wright referred to it, combined elements of the contract, state-use, and Pennsylvanian state-account arrangements to produce a system of prison labor that Massachusetts prison officials claimed was at once fiscally viable, legally consistent, and acceptable to free workers. Under the hybrid system, the majority of prison laborers were to manu-facture goods for use by state departments, agencies, and institutions; any product that the state could not absorb was to be sold on the open market at prevailing wholesale prices. Unprepared to abandon the contract system altogether (chiefly because of the concern that state government might not always be able to keep convicts at labor, or need so many convict-made goods), Massachusetts law-makers allowed that a minority of prisoners could be put to work under the piece-price system (a variant of contract labor under which a private manufacturer bought and sold prison-made goods, but the state supervised the production process). They also provided that where the demand for prison-made goods was lacking on the state and open markets, as a last resort in the effort to keep prisoners at labor, prisoners could be worked under the old factory contract system and their products, sold on the open market.[15] As in Pennsylvania, the Massachusetts legislature aimed both to allow prison products to be sold on the open market and to insulate free workers from the deleterious impact of competition with prison labor. Prisoners were permitted to labor by hand only, and, after January 1, 1898, no more than thirty percent of the prisoners in any one institution could be put to work in any given industry.[16]

New York embarked on the most ambitious, novel, and widely scruti-nized of the three experiments. Ratification of the McDonough amendment

[13] In the 1890s, Pennsylvania also made arrangements for furnishing released prisoners with enough money to get back to their county or state of origin: Under the regulations, anyone living within five miles of the prison was to receive $5, and anyone beyond ten miles, $10. *Proceedings of the Annual Congress of the National Prison Association of the United States*, 1894, 77.

[14] Minnesota had operated a state-account system for some years as a way of indirectly subsidiz-ing the state's farming sector. Convicts at the Stillwater prison made the binder twine with which farmers tied crops and bales, enabling the state both to keep prisoners at work and to sell farmers the twine at extremely low prices. However, Minnesota had not dispensed with its contract system altogether: It was still putting anything up to half its prisoners to work under contract. Moreover, lawmakers and prison administrators in the industrial states did not regard Minnesota as a relevant model and tended, instead, to look at those states whose economies and political cultures resembled their own.

[15] Carroll Wright, *Some Ethical Phases of the Labor Question* (Boston: American Unitarian Asso-ciation, 1903), 184–5.

[16] Laws of 1887, in Harold E. Lane, "The State-Use System of Prison Labor in Massachusetts," *Social Forces* 19:1 (Oct. 1940), 59; *New York Times*, Jan. 2, 1898, 13. The 1898 law exempted the cane-seating and umbrella industries from the thirty-percent limit.

in 1894 affirmed that state's position in the vanguard of the national movement to put the unfree, sweated labor of prisoners entirely off limits to private industry; it also set in motion the first systematic attempt in the United States to construct a prison system in which government, rather than private interests, exclusively possessed, managed, funded, and profited from the labor of those undergoing punishment for crime. As well as explicitly directing the legislature to find (noncontractual) employment of some kind for the prisoners, the amendment authorized (but did not mandate) the adoption of a system of prison labor known as state-use. Under that system, prisoners worked exclusively for the state, producing various goods for sale to, and use by, government departments and agencies. In principle, most, if not all, the expense of running prisons would be met by the product of the convicts' own labor, but in such a way that their labor did not compete directly with that of free workers.

In June 1895, the legislature appointed an eight-member State Prison Commission and charged it with conducting an investigation into various systems of prison labor and recommending one for adoption.[17] After electing Lispenard Stewart, a well-known New York City lawyer, real estate developer, and reform Republican, president of the Commission, that body commenced an exhaustive investigation of the prisons and prison industries, gathering testimony from wardens, penologists, labor leaders, and local manufacturers. In late 1895, the Commission reported its findings and recommendations to the legislature. Against the position uniformly taken by New York's prison wardens, penologists, and Republican lawmakers, the Commission concluded that both the old contracting system and the public-account system (under which the state ran prison industries and sold its goods on the open market) were uneconomic to the state and injurious of free manufacturers and workers. "It is time to try another plan; to try the one provided for by the Constitution," the Commissioners informed the legislature: The state should put its entire workforce of state, county, and reformatory prisoners to work in the manufacture of goods for exclusive sale to state departments, agencies, and institutions. These institutions and agencies, and the 80,000 people who worked or resided in them, would easily absorb the product of the New York's 10,000-strong penal labor force, argued the Commissioners. If properly planned, they continued, this exclusive state-use system of prison industry would more than cover the costs of incarceration, while fulfilling the legal requirement that prisoners be put to "hard labor," the administrative imperative of maintaining discipline in the prisons, and the state's supposed moral duty to provide prisoners an opportunity for reform. The Commissioners concluded their report by

---

[17] The Commission was composed of representatives drawn from each of the state's eight judicial districts; Stewart served as president and principal champion of reform through 1903. *New York Times*, Feb. 28, 1895, 16; *New York Times*, Oct. 20, 1895, 19; *New York Times*, Dec. 30, 1895, 4. (Obituary), *New York Times*, Oct. 16, 1927, 31. The other members were: Nelson Davenport, William R. Remington, George B. Hayes, John Davenport, Augustus Sherman, Charles J. Boyd, and Robert Montayne.

recommending that their body be charged with the task of implementing such a system.[18]

In May 1896, after some desperate, last-minute attempts by New York's prison and penitentiary wardens and Republican lawmakers to repeal the provision of the McDonough amendment banning the sale of prison-made goods on the open market,[19] Governor Levi P. Morton signed into law two bills, both drafted by the Commission. One directed that all state, county, and reformatory prisoners be put to hard labor under the state-use system, beginning January 1, 1897; from that day all physically capable prisoners were to produce supplies for state institutions, departments, and divisions. The other empowered the Prison Commission to integrate all the state's various penal institutions into "one harmonious system," and to construct and manage the new, intragovernmental labor economy. In concert with the demands of free workers and labor leaders, prisoners were not to be worked more than eight hours a day, or on Sundays and public holidays.[20] The Commission immediately began planning for the January 1 transition from the old system to the new.

Neither the scope nor the novelty of the state-use labor system legislated for New York can be overstated. Although a few of the Western states had experimented with state-use before 1896, none had ever attempted to build as elaborate, as centralized, or as extensive a system as the one now mandated in New York. Nor had any industrial state endeavored to put its entire prison labor force on an exclusive, state-use basis.[21] Without direct recourse

---

[18] State Commission of Prisons, Annual Report, 1895 (1896). The Commissioners complained that the state incurred high costs retaining sales agents and that ongoing popular prejudice against prisonmade goods depressed the prices of those goods and, hence, prison revenues.

[19] New York Republicans, in conjunction with the wardens of the various state prisons, county penitentiaries, and reformatories, sought to restore the "public-account" or "state-account" system, whereby the state owned and operated prison industries but sold the product on the open market. Concurrent Resolution of the Senate and Assembly, Proposing Amendment to Article Three, Section Twenty-Nine of the Constitution, relating to Prison Labor [State of New York Assembly (April 24, 1895); State of New York Senate (May 14, 1895)]; *New York Times*, Oct. 20, 1895, 19; *New York Times*, Nov. 1, 1895, 13; *New York Times*, Nov. 14, 1895, 9; *New York Times*, Nov. 15, 1895, 4. Amendment of the state constitution, other than by convention, was a three-step process: It required majority support in the legislature through two successive sessions and then ratification by voters. The proposed amendment won support in both (Republican-dominated) houses in 1895, but the Republicans quietly dropped the bill the following year, in the run-up to the 1896 presidential election. There is some evidence to suggest that, in the course of this particularly bitter contest for the U.S. presidency, the national leadership of the Republican party determined that New York's prison labor bill would antagonize industrial workers whose votes the party was increasingly desperate to win. Certainly, organized labor vigorously opposed the proposed abridgement of the McDonough amendment and continued to lobby for federal laws against interstate commerce in prisonmade goods and prison labor contracting. *New York Times*, Dec. 11, 1895, 10; *New York Times*, Apr. 8, 1896, 8; *New York Times*, Apr. 21, 1896, 4.

[20] *New York Times*, May 6, 1896, 2.

[21] By 1900, about a dozen states had experimented with a limited form of the state-use system (beginning in 1887, when Nevada committed a portion of its prisoners to the production of government supplies). In Nevada, the system was at first restricted to the manufacture of

to private capital, with only a handful of outfitted workshops, and with the state advancing no seed capital, the Commissioners' task was to find a way, not only of equipping prison industries, getting them up and running, and organizing, training, and supervising a workforce of some 3,500 prisoners (held in four institutions scattered over many hundred square miles), but also of marketing, distributing, and selling prison-made goods to public schools, hospitals, city sanitation departments, and various other governmental customers. In effect, New York's legislation called for the establishment of a diverse, statewide business operation; the creation of a market for that business's products (within state agencies, departments, and institutions); and the fabrication, out of whole cloth, of a state bureaucracy, the task of which would be to continuously manage the new, state-use economy. In addition, the Commissioners were to take a motley collection of old and decaying prisons, each of which had been, for many decades prior, an isolated, autonomous institution subject to local political patronage practices and the peculiar needs of individual contractors, and integrate those institutions into a single, centralized, and bureaucratically administered prison *system.* In short, their charge was to build and manage a penal state.

Contemporary observers were fully aware of the novelty and ambitiousness of New York's program. Ten years earlier, at a time when popular campaigns against prison labor contracting were beginning to win legislative victories around the country and prison administrators began to cast around for an alternative prison labor system, penologists had agreed that the productive capacity of prisons far outstripped the capacity of government to absorb convicts' output; some observers, including the U.S. Labor Commissioner, Carroll Wright, had also pointed out that, under a state-use system, private manufacturers would lose lucrative contracts to the government – and so would likely oppose such an arrangement.[22] Officials' skepticism had not diminished with the passage of time: In 1896, the proposition that a state penal system, or even a single prison, *could* operate successfully on an exclusive state-use basis as mandated in New York, remained highly controversial. The New York Commissioners' report to the contrary, Carroll Wright still maintained that only a portion of prisoners would be needed to meet the

boots and shoes, which prisoners were to supply to all state inmates and wards; gradually, other products were added, including construction materials for use on state buildings. Wright, *Some Ethical Phases of the Labor Question,* 177–8; Certainly, prisoners in most regions of the country were increasingly likely to be laboring for the government in the 1890s, but until New York embarked on its reforms in earnest in 1896, state-use was a minor, and supplemental, penal labor practice. According to the Federal Industrial Commission's report on prison labor, in 1898–9, just five states (South Dakota, Idaho, Montana, Nevada, and New York) were working their prisoners exclusively in some form of state-use system. New York, however, was the only state in which state-use was *legislated* as the sole system of prison labor permitted; recently revised statutes in the other four states authorized one or more of the contract, lease, or public-account arrangements. U.S. Government. Industrial Commission. Report on Prison Labor, 56th Congress, House of Representatives (Washington, DC: Government Printers, 1900), 79, 145, 153–4, 161.

[22] Lane, "The State-Use System" *Social Forces* 19:1 (Oct. 1940), 56–7.

state's demand for goods and wares.[23] Both the New York Prison Association and the American Prison Association publicly and repeatedly decried the constitutional convention's vote to abolish contracting outright and made it clear that they considered the proposed state-use system doomed to failure. (One skeptical penologist from Pennsylvania scoffed, "New York thinks it has found a remedy and applied it and made it a success, but it may be a failure, as most of the experiments that have been made in New York in prison laws have been failures").[24] W. M. F. Pound of the New York Prison Association argued that only one-fifth of the prisoners could be put to work under the state-use system and went so far as to sponsor a bill authorizing the sale of prison-made goods on the open market.[25] Lending his support to Pound, the *New York Times* editor declared that "all competent authorities" on the subject of prison labor considered it "absolutely impossible" to keep all or even a "considerable part" of the state's prisoners at work under the state-use system; it simply would not work.[26] Even Levi P. Morton, the Republican Governor of New York (who pragmatically endorsed the Prison Commission's recommendations) admitted that it would be "no easy task to provide employment within the law, and to make the prisoners yield an appreciable portion of the cost of their maintenance."[27]

Whatever their position on the abolition of contracting and the adoption of an exclusive state-use system, labor leaders, penologists, and prison administrators throughout the industrial states fully grasped the significance of the pending experiment. In the eyes of labor leaders (especially those of the Knights of Labor and the American Federation of Labor [AFL]),[28] New York would be a vital test case, not only of the validity of the proposition that the prisons *could* be successfully operated entirely in the absence of private capital and in isolation of the open market, but, specifically, of the

---

[23] Note by Carroll Wright, *Some Ethical Phases of the Labor Question*,183. The Secretary of the Prison Commission estimated in 1896 that on January 1, 1897, 1,844 state prisoners and 1,251 county prisoners would be without work. Another 716 county prisoners would still be working under contracts (which were legal, because they were entered into before the amendment came into effect), but would eventually join the state-use work force as those contracts expired. *New York Times*, July 11, 1896.

[24] The critic, Michael J. Cassidy, concluded, with an air of envy and resentment, "Everything goes to New York and they take particular pains that everything shall go there. A person cannot go across the ocean unless he goes to New York first." *Proceedings of the Annual Congress of the National Prison Association of the United States*, 1897, 355.

[25] Noted in *New York Times*, Feb. 5, 1896, 4. The New York Prison Association later modified this view, claiming that only one-third of the prisoners could be put to manufacturing labor. *New York Times*, May 8, 1896, 4.

[26] *New York Times*, Feb. 5, 1896, 4.

[27] Governor Morton, Message to the Legislature, January 1895, reproduced in *New York Times*, Jan. 3, 1895, 10.

[28] The Seventh Annual State Congress of the Knights of Labor endorsed the State Prison Commission's 1895 report and recommendations regarding the establishment of a state-use system. *New York Times*, Jan. 15, 1896.

state-use system of labor in a large industrial state.[29] George Blair, the former president of the New York Workingmen's Assembly and a prominent
critic of prison labor contracting, enthusiastically endorsed the adoption of
the system, calling upon defenders of the old contract system not to condemn the new one "without a fair trial."[30] Prison administrators and other
critics, on the other hand, followed New York's foray into this uncharted
territory convinced that it would demonstrate decisively that prison labor
could not serve the ends of either reformation or economy when its product
was barred from sale on the open market. Despite his skepticism about the
capacity of New York's state government to absorb the product of a fully-
employed prison workforce, Carroll Wright nonetheless emphasized that
New York presented an important test case for state-use: "(t)he failure or
the success of [New York's] system must be taken as indicative of the failure
or success in the other States that provide for it; for the obstacles and the
disadvantages, as well as the advantages, of the system are on trial here more
perfectly, probably, than in any other Commonwealth."[31]

New York's Prison Commissioners and the Superintendent of Prisons,
Austin Lathrop, commenced their planning for the end of contracting and
the founding of the state-use system in late 1896. They began by surveying
the needs of their prospective "customers": that is, the various state, city,
and county agencies to which the prison commerce was now restricted.[32]
Working in concert with the newly established Board of Classification (composed of the Superintendent of Prisons, the State Comptroller, and the
Lunacy Commissioners), they surveyed all state departments, institutions,
offices, and buildings, and compiled lists of the manufactures each agency
required. The lists were exhaustive: As the Commissioners found, New York's

---

[29] Although, in the mid-1890s, a handful of other states had prohibited contracting outright,
the vast majority had not. Moreover, none (including the other strongly anti-contract state,
Ohio) had gone so far as New York to prohibit the sale of convict-made goods on the open
market or provide for an exclusive "state-use" system of prison labor.

[30] George Blair, "Another Word on Prison Labor," *North American Review* 64:6 (June 1897),
758.

[31] *Wright, Some Ethical Phases of the Labor Question*, 182. Wright considered Massachusetts a
test case as well, but emphasized that New York, as the first state to enact a complete
system of state-use, had "longer experience" with the system. Wright, who had worked
for the state of Massachusetts, in the capacity of Chief of the State Bureau of Statistics,
and conducted studies of prison labor on and off since 1879, initially appeared reluctant
to concede that New York had the leading-edge status in regard to prison labor reform:
Although Massachusetts differed from New York in both the letter and practice of prison
labor law, and New York was the first (and for a few years, the only state) to make state-use the
basis of the penal system, Wright nonetheless insisted before an audience at the National
Prison Association in 1899 that state-use was on trial in both Massachusetts and New York.
Carroll Wright, "Prison Labor," *Catholic University Bulletin* 7:20 (Oct. 1899), 403–23.

[32] New York State Commission of Prisons, Annual Report (1896), 15–17, 30–4. For a discussion
of the Commissioners' first attempts to set up a state-use system of prison industries (in
1896), see New York State Commission of Prisons, Annual Report (1897), 8–10, 18–19,
36–43.

state agencies purchased a wide range of goods every year, including printed forms, engraved photographs, park benches, office desks, school books, sash windows, envelopes, brooms, shovels, trash carts, enamel buckets, beds, sheets, uniforms, boots, and – every few years or so – voting booths, official ballots, and ballot boxes.[33]

Surveying the government's needs was straightforward enough, but actually establishing the infrastructure for the new system proved a much more complex task. Despite advance notice in 1896 of the prisons' pending transition to the state-use system, as of January 1897, not a single state agency had made a requisition for convict-made goods.[34] Although the state-use statute provided that prisons were to sell their goods on the state market and an 1896 law provided that state institutions (such as the prisons and hospitals) were to be supplied "so far as practicable" by prison-made goods,[35] no law unambiguously compelled all state agencies, departments, and institutions to purchase their wares from the prisons. Adding to the complexity of the task was a prison labor law, enacted in 1895 and sponsored by lawmakers sympathetic to the labor unions, that provided categorically that convict labor was not to compete with "honest free labor" (even under the state-use system); convict-made goods, destined for state departments of various kinds, were to be priced as closely as possible to free market prices.[36] As the Commissioners noted, this effectively deprived prison industries of their most important advantage over free manufacturers: low prices. These legal and practical difficulties were compounded by the fact that several of the new prison industries would have to be built from scratch: When the last few manufacturers exited the prisons in 1896, they had taken with them all their machinery, tools, and materials. Some of the old public-account workshops (which the state had operated after 1888) were still outfitted, but they were not necessarily suited to the production of the goods that would be needed under the new state-use system. As one Prison Commissioner reflected following his inspection of the state's quieted prison workshops in 1897, "prospects were indeed bleak."[37]

Prospects were made all the more bleak by a looming crisis of discipline within the state prisons. As contracting had wound down in the wake of the ratification of the McDonough amendment, administrators and prison keepers had found themselves with a growing mass of incarcerated men who had nothing to do and a lot of time on their hands. Industrial idleness in the prisons threatened far more than prison economics; as recent history had shown, if it continued for more than a few days, it was also likely to

---

33 New York State Commission of Prisons, Annual Report (1897), 36–9; Sherman to Lathrop, Jan. 7, 1897, cited in *New York Times*, Jan. 8, 1897, 3.
34 New York State Commission of Prisons, Annual Report (1897), 7.
35 Laws N.Y. 1896, Ch. 429.
36 Laws N.Y. 1895 Ch. 1026. The Commissioners reiterated their commitment to developing a penal labor system that did not compete with free labor in New York State Commission of Prisons, Annual Report (1896), 17.
37 New York State Commission of Prisons, Annual Report (1897), 7.

undermine the good order of the prison. In the great prison factories of the Gilded Age, New York's convicts had spent upwards of ten and even twelve hours a day laboring away for the contractor.[38] In and of itself, this activity had absorbed much of the convicts' energy, and subjected them to a rigorous variant of industrial discipline. But in addition, and as we have seen, the industrial prison labor system had also played an important disciplinary role outside the workshops and work hours: It had given rise to a distinctive corpus of customs, rules, and routines that were particularly well-suited to the needs of contractors and that served to reinforce the contract system itself. The structure of the daily regimen of eating, sleeping, and waking, the so-called "silent rule," the lockstep march, the single-file dining tables, and even the punishments meted out, had all been shaped by the needs of the contractor and his system of production.[39]

When, at certain points in the Gilded Age, the prison factories had fallen silent (as they had in many states during the long depression of the 1870s, and again, for six-odd months in New York in 1889, following the temporary suspension of many contracts), the authorities had lost not only the single most important disciplinary means at their disposal but the activity around which the prison order as a whole was structured. Sustained periods of idleness in the workshops rendered the labor-centric routines, rules, and rituals of prison life obsolete and even dangerous. During these times, keepers had often marched the convicts to the workshops, as normal, for the duration of the workday, although there was no work to be done; congregated in the idling workshops, prisoners had caused all manner of trouble for their keepers. Locking them down in the cells for long stretches of time and releasing them only for meals in the mess hall was

---

[38] In the mid-nineteenth century, American prisoners worked from dawn to dusk, averaging ten hours of labor per day, at least six days a week; outside of laboring hours, the prisoner's waking hours were organized around and for the activity of productive labor. There is some evidence to suggest that work hours extended after the Civil War, when large-scale industry moved into the prisons. At the height of Sing Sing's industrial career (in the late 1870s and early 1880s), prisoners were regularly working twelve- and fourteen-hour days, seven days per week. See Chapter 6 of this book. See also, Glen Gildemeister "Prison Labor and Convict Competition with Free Workers in Industrializing America, 1840–1890" (Ph.D. diss., Northern Illinois University, 1977), 88–9; W. David Lewis, *From Newgate to Dannemora: The Rise of the Penitentiary in New York, 1796–1848* (Ithaca, NY: Cornell University Press, 1965), 118–20; David J. Rothman, *Discovery of the Asylum: Social Order and Disorder in the New Republic* (Boston and Toronto: Little, Brown and Co, 1971), 104; *New York Herald* (Feb. 3, 1882), cited in Roger Panetta, "Up the River: A History of Sing Sing in the Nineteenth century," (Ph.D. diss., City University of New York, 1998), 107.

[39] This is not to say that prison stripes, shaved heads, and the lock-step did not have other disciplinary functions: As Gustav Radbruch was among the first to argue, these practices were intended to debase the prisoner socially, morally, and aesthetically and to dishonor him in general. Radbruch, "Der Ursprung des Strafechts aus dem Stande der Unfreien," which is reprinted in Radbruch, *Elegantiae Juris Criminalis* (Basel: Verlag für Recht und Gesellschaft, 1950), 11–12, quoted in J. Thorsten Sellin, *Slavery and the Penal System* (New York: Elsevier, 1976), viii. See also W. David Lewis, *From Newgate to Dannemora*, 118–23 and David J. Rothman, *Discovery of the Asylum*, 105–7.

another option. But in the past, when this had been tried, some had become ill from want of physical and mental activity, and many more had become insubordinate and restive. A number of the wardens who, in 1896–97, were bracing for the end of contracting and public-account industries, had first-hand experience of the 1889 shut-down; Warden Patrick J. Hayes of Kings County Penitentiary wrote that "the men became very uneasy and discontented."[40]

The specter of idleness and its associated disorders, in turn, posed a political challenge to the Commission, if only indirectly. The experience of the 1870s and early 1880s had palpably demonstrated that public revelations of convict revolts, rising insanity and suicide rates, and mass ill-health could quite quickly lay waste to political and administrative careers and lose state elections; indeed, in 1888, such episodes had helped plunge the penal arm of government into a full-scale crisis of legitimacy. Now, in late 1896, as the workshops once more fell quiet and prisoners had little or nothing to do, the potential for a second political crisis over the state prisons was significantly elevated. Indeed, there were signs that such a crisis was already afoot. The punishment ledgers for Auburn prison suggest that greatly increased numbers of prisoners were indeed flouting long-established prison rules – most particularly, the rule of silence; in particular, the ledgers suggested an upswing in the incidents of prisoner-on-keeper "insolence" and defiance.[41] On the eve of abolition, in December 1896, Warden Omer Sage of Sing Sing announced to the press that he would be keeping all of Sing Sing's prisoners locked in their cells and that unless the state put them to work, there would be "a large amount of suffering" among them.[42] Other wardens repeatedly cautioned (typically, in the press) that such disorders were likely to erupt as industry ceased at the prisons; some, such as Kings County's Warden Hayes, continued to openly assail the new policy as "flawed."[43] Beyond the prison walls, much as in past periods of idleness in the prisons, the press was charging that want of labor was causing disorder and even a "suicidal mania" in the prisons.[44] Three weeks after the cessation of industrial production at Sing Sing, Warden Omer Sage reported that, although the recent

---

[40] Patrick J. Hayes, quoted in *New York Times*, Jan. 24, 1897, 20.
[41] The Auburn punishment ledgers for the 1890s record an increased number of punishments for insolence. Auburn Punishment Ledger, Vol. 1, Oct. 7, 1870–July 9, 1895; Vol. 2, July 10, 1895- NYSA (RDCS) Auburn Correctional Facility, Inmate Punishment Ledger, 1872 (1870)–1941.
[42] *New York Times*, Dec. 31, 1896, 12.   [43] *New York Times*, Jan. 24, 1897, 20.
[44] Noted in New York State Commission of Prisons, Annual Report (1899), 55–6. See also, "Driving Convicts Crazy: Practical Operation of the New Law Requiring Idleness in the Penitentiaries: Insanity Nearly Doubled," *New York Times*, July 23, 1897, 9 and *New York Times*, Aug. 14, 1897, 10. The Commissioners refuted the reports, comparing hospital statistics for 1896 (the last year the contract labor system was in place) and 1897. However, their rebuttal did not hold water on two counts: Prisoners were already severely underemployed in 1896 because of the ongoing flight of contractors; furthermore, *bona fide* cases of insanity often went unrecognized by guards and the prison physician, who were inclined to interpret episodes of insanity among the prisoners as feigned. The figure that would be more telling

suicides could not be attributed to the lack of labor at Sing Sing, the new laws were nonetheless causing the prisoners to become "restless and quarrelsome," and that the number of *reported* incidents of insubordination was more than double the usual.[45] (The punishment ledgers for Sing Sing for this period are missing, so it is impossible to verify Sage's claim; however, the key point here is that such statements to the press added pressure to the already fraught situation confronting the Commissioners).

These problems put considerable pressure on the Commission and Superintendent Lathrop to get the state-use system up and running as quickly as possible. Between late 1896 and 1900, the Commission set about laying the four cornerstones of a new prison system. In January 1897, they set about gathering, organizing, and disciplining a stable, industrial labor force in the state prisons. At the same time, they moved to outfit the workshops for production, using their earlier survey of the projected needs of the various state department and agencies to determine what kinds of industries to establish. The Commission also took steps at this time to integrate each prison's industries into a centralized command structure subject to the Commission's oversight; that is, they endeavored to build a statewide penal bureaucracy through which their body could construct, monitor, and manage the new state-use industries. Finally, the Commissioners also introduced a series of supplementary activities in the prisons, all of which were explicitly or implicitly designed to engage and discipline whatever portion of state prisoners the new state-use industries might not, in practice, be able to absorb.

As they set about revamping the prison workshops in January 1897, the Commissioners resolved that, unlike under the old contract system, the prison industries would be organized on a statewide basis and managed jointly by the Commission and the Department of Prisons (both of which were based in the state capitol of Albany). As an integrated, coordinated statewide network, the state prison system would produce standardized goods according to strict specifications drawn up by the Board of Classification. Whereas, in the old public-account industries, the style and quality of prison goods had been "largely dependent upon the taste and fancy of each prison warden," as one Commissioner put it, the Board of Classification resolved to set quality standards, design specifications, and fix prices for all convict-made goods.[46] The Board carefully examined the entire range of existing prison manufactures (which numbered some 250), selected the best types and models, and drew up specifications for the style, dimensions, and quantities of all goods to be manufactured. As part of their plan to centralize industrial production, the Prison Commissioners also announced that they would institute an annual review of the state departments' estimates

here would be that of the number of prisoners disciplined for feigning. (As of the time of writing, the Sing Sing punishment ledgers are lost).

[45] *New York Times,* Jan. 24, 1897, 20.
[46] New York State Commission of Prisons, Annual Report (1897), 36.

of their needs for the next year, set production quotas, and then distribute materials and labor around the prison industries accordingly.[47] As a result of their lobbying efforts, the State Controller also announced that he would indirectly enforce the 1896 law requiring that state institutions (such as hospitals) purchase their needs, as far as practicable, from the state prisons: He would refuse to pay any bill for goods that could be made in the prisons but which the institution in question had instead purchased on the open market.[48]

By the spring of 1897, the Commissioners had got a number of state-use industries up and running; by the winter, according to Superintendent Lathrop, the State Prisons Department had received requisitions for goods valued at over $750,000. (Lathrop immediately released a press statement in which he claimed that the prisons were now self-supporting: The promised revenue of $750,000 would more than cover the $500,000 annual expenses of the state prisons; next year, he confidently asserted, would see revenues amounting to a million dollars).[49] Several hundred convicts at Sing Sing, Auburn, and Clinton prisons were now working producing a diverse range of goods for state agencies. Among other things, they crafted desks and chairs for the Executive Mansion in Albany, made brooms and mattresses for public hospitals, built trash carts for the New York City sanitation department, welded hundreds of lockers for the state armories, tailored thousands of uniforms for the National Guard, carved wooden ornaments for various departments, and produced masses of boots and striped uniforms for the state's penal institutions. A print shop at Sing Sing also began typesetting and printing various agencies' reports and bulletins, including the Prison Commission's own annual reports.[50] The Commission also prepared the print shop to print textbooks for the public schools,[51] and prisoners began production of an illustrated catalogue of prison wares (which was consciously modeled on catalogues such as Sears Roebuck's) for distribution to the prisons' new state customers.[52]

As part of the drive to establish a viable state-use prison system, the Commissioners needed to select, organize, train, and manage a workforce of prisoners. To this end, they undertook to classify and redistribute New York's entire population of some 10,000 incarcerated persons.[53] The principle

[47] Ibid., and New York State Commission of Prisons, Annual Report (1898), 18–19.
[48] *New York Times*, Jan. 24, 1897, 20.
[49] Austin Lathrop in *New York Times*, Nov. 19, 1897, 3. Lathrop, as we shall see, grossly overestimated the revenues from state industries (discussed subsequently, 262–3).
[50] New York State Commission of Prisons, Annual Report (1897), 19–37. In the late 1890s, the New York City government became the single largest purchaser of prison goods made at Sing Sing; the garbage carts were in particular demand as the city's sanitation services expanded.
[51] *New York Times*, Jan. 11, 1898, 3. Textbook production was contingent upon the passage of the free textbooks law; it was also bitterly opposed by New York's printers' and typesetters' unions (see 265, above).
[52] New York State Commission of Prisons, Annual Report (1898), 18.
[53] New York State Commission of Prisons, Annual Report (1896), 5–8; (1901), 15.

upon which they proceeded was that of "segregation" or "separation," as the Commissioners alternately called it. Their objective here was two-fold: They aimed to identify, in New York's various state prisons, county penitentiaries, jails, and lock-ups, all those sane, physically fit, adult men who were serving sentences of a year or more for felony convictions, and concentrate these men in the three state prisons (Auburn, Clinton, Sing Sing). At the Commission's behest, county penitentiaries and jails were ordered to immediately dispatch any felons serving over a year's sentence to one of the state prisons.[54] Meanwhile, in the state prisons, women and girls, the mentally and physically impaired, adolescent boys, those guilty of misdemeanors, and any other convicts who did not fulfill the new criteria for commitment to state prison were to be transferred out of the three state prisons and distributed to one or another of the new, specialized institutions that the State was in the process of building. (Previously, in New York, female felons had been held either on a different floor of the same prison, as at Auburn, or in a separate building, as at Sing Sing; under the guidance of the Commission, in the three decades after abolition of contracting, women convicts were gradually sifted out of existing facilities and dispatched to three new all-women prisons. Likewise the Commissioners provided for the transfer of any male convict who became insane *in the course of his incarceration* out of the state prisons and into the new Dannemora State Hospital in the Adirondack mountains).[55] The great mass of fit adult men who were now

54 Ibid. Although, under the law, all men convicted of felony crime were supposed to be housed in the state prisons, over the years they had been dispersed across New York's many local jails and county penitentiaries; now, as the Commissioners set about building their state-use industrial system, they moved to enforce the law. The Commission had begun laying the groundwork for this reshuffling of the prison population in 1896. Upon the Commission's recommendation, the New York legislature enacted legislation in 1896 requiring that anyone convicted of a felony crime be committed to a state prison or, if a woman or youth below the age of 21, to a boys' or women's reformatory rather than a county penitentiary. In addition, all New York penal institutions were to cease the practice of boarding other states' convicts. In 1895, a total of 900 convicts in New York's penitentiaries were being "boarded-out" by other states. New York State Commission of Prisons, Annual Report (1898), 11, 18. The same law also mandated the incarceration in state prisons of all convicts who had been sentenced in federal courts but hitherto incarcerated in local jails and penitentiaries.
55 In 1893, the Auburn Prison for Women had been established within the grounds of the men's prison and the state's 100-odd women felons eventually held there. The majority of women prisoners would be housed in one or another of the new, independent women's prisons by 1918; administrators would transfer the remaining few dozen Auburn women to a new women's reformatory at Bedford Hills, New York, in 1933. *D.O.C. s Today* (Dec. 1987), 10–11. *D.O.C. s Today* (Jan. 1988), 10. Penal administrators had already begun moving toward the classification and separation of convicts in 1892, when the state opened the Matteawan Hospital for the criminally insane. A prison for convicts marked as "mentally defective" was opened in 1921, when the Eastern Reformatory at Napanoch was converted to the Institute for Defective Delinquents (*D.O.C. s Today* [Oct. 1988], 14). Initially, this institution was under the supervision of the State Commission for Mental Defectives; it was then transferred to the State Department of Mental Hygiene (for three months in 1926) and was finally relocated to the new Department of Corrections in 1926. *D.O.C. s Today* (Feb. 1988), 15–16.

concentrated in the three state prisons was to provide the labor power for new, state-use prison industries.[56]

The effort to organize this industrial workforce brought all New York felons who were adult men under the direct jurisdiction of the State – in particular, under the auspices of New York's Prison Commissioners and the Superintendent of Prisons and his Prison Department[57] – and removed from the state prisons any and all out-of-state prisoners over whom the state possessed only vicarious authority. In effect, the Commissioners constructed a great, human centrifuge, by which imprisoned women, the insane, the young, short-term prisoners, and the ill and infirm were exiled to peripheral "hospitals", "reformatories," and "refuges" while 3,000-odd nominally fit and able men were gathered at the "state prisons" proper (that is, Clinton, Sing Sing, and Auburn).[58] Through both the early and later phases of the Progressive Era, it was this portion of New York's prison population with which the State Prison Commissioners, a succession of prison reformers, and lawmakers would be most concerned. Although the preponderance of prisoners in New York (approximately 6,400 of 10,000 in 1896)[59] were either female, infirm, young, or short-term or misdemeanor-related convicts, progressive prison reform was aimed first and foremost at the state prisons and at fit, able, adult men serving longer sentences. In popular and

---

[56] The Commissioners decided to make the state prisons the exclusive site of their industrial program both on jurisdictional and practical economic grounds: Although it was clear that state prisons fell directly under state jurisdiction, the county penitentiaries and local jails answered to county and local authorities. Furthermore, the county penitentiaries were populated mostly by those who committed misdemeanors, who served short sentences, rather than longer-term felons. The Commissioners considered the former, by dint of the shortness of their sentences, to make inefficient, unruly workers and a workforce that was prone to high turnover. As the Commission put it in 1898, "(t)he inmates of [county penitentiaries], being short-term men, cannot be successfully taught to perform skilled labor to any marked degree ... " It was also the case that at least three county penitentiaries still had labor contracts, which, by law, had to run their course; the state prisons, on the other hand, had no contracts in operation after January 1, 1897. With the exception of federal prisoners, only those convicted in the state of New York were to be held in New York institutions. Those convicted in other states and boarded out (at a fee) to New York institutions were to be returned to their state of origin. As of 1896, the federal government still had no civilian prison of its own, so it had boarded out convicted felons to state and county institutions; the new law provided that federal prisoners be transferred out of the county penitentiaries and into the state prison system. State Prison Commission, Annual Report (1898).

[57] Laws N.Y. 1896, Ch. 553. Cited in New York State Commission of Prisons, Annual Report (1896).

[58] Penal institutions for youth, women, the infirm, and those convicted of misdemeanors were no less restricted for their welfarist names: The thousands incarcerated every year at Dannemora "Hospital" and the women's "Refuge" were no freer to walk away from their institutions than were the felons of Sing Sing, Clinton, and Auburn "State Prisons."

[59] On October 1, 1896, there were 9,851 men, women, and youths in New York's penal institutions; 3,606 of these were state prisoners. In 1896, 130,245 people were committed to New York penal institutions. For a five-year study of New York's overall prison, penitentiary, reformatory, and jail population, see New York State Commission of Prisons, Annual Report (1902), 8–10.

expert discourse alike, the prison labor problem (or the prison problem, as it was also sometimes called) centered on this portion of the penal population, the state prisons in which they were now housed, and above all, the perplexing question of how New York's "useful" male convicts might be put to industrial labor.

Having separated out the healthy adult male felons from the rest and gathered these men at Sing Sing, Auburn, and Clinton, the Commissioners grappled with the task of making industrial workers out of them. They resolved that, "in connection with the productive industries required for public institutions," the convicts would be "classified and graded" into three hierarchical grades of laborers: Members of the first grade were to be assigned skilled labor and the second, semi-skilled work; both were also to be given compulsory education, physical training, and trades classes. The third grade would be assigned supportive menial and institutional labor.[60] The prisoners were to be distributed across these grades depending upon their case history and propensity for reform. The state legislature enacted the Commissioners' recommended "classification law" in 1897 and the latter promptly set about organizing the convicts for work in the new state-use system.[61] To this end, the Commissioners devised an examination system by which prison administrators would determine the supposed potential of each convict to reform himself and become an honest and industrious citizen upon his release. The prisoners who were determined to be the most susceptible to reform were to be employed and trained in the skilled trades or in office work.[62] Prisoners considered less susceptible – but nonetheless compliant – were to be employed in productive industries and to receive some industrial instruction. The lowest grade of convict, which comprised what one Commissioner referred to as "the incorrigible, vicious, and insubordinate," was to be confined and given such labor as Commissioners deemed appropriate – that is, the menial labor of quarrying stone, picking rags, or hauling trash. The classification law also conferred upon the Superintendent of Prisons the authority to transfer prisoners from one institution to another on whatever grounds he saw fit.[63]

As well as constituting a rudimentary division of labor, this grade and transfer system was the scaffolding for a new mode of discipline. Depending upon their conduct, convicts could be demoted or promoted between grades – and also transferred between prisons, upon the request of the Superintendent of Prisons. In allowing for the demotion and promotion of convicts between grades, the Commissioners strove to connect their labor

---

[60] New York State Commission of Prisons, Annual Report (1898), 19–21.
[61] Ibid.   [62] Ibid.
[63] New York State Commission of Prisons, Annual Report (1898), 19. Prior to 1897, the Superintendent had enjoyed the authority to move convicts according to the needs of prison industries: In practice, however, Superintendents had transferred very few prisoners out of the prison to which the sentencing judge had originally dispatched them. *Sing Sing Prison: Its History, Purpose, Makeup, and Program* (Albany: New York State Department of Correction, 1958), 23.

system with the newly instituted provisions for indeterminate sentencing, which had been provided for in law in 1889, but which had still not been widely implemented in the courts.[64] The 1889 law had authorized (but not compelled) judges to sentence convicts by providing a minimum and a maximum number of years to be served. Theoretically, a prisoner could be released after serving the minimum period specified, but he could also be forced to serve the full sentence. The law granted state-appointed officers the authority to determine exactly when, once the minimum sentence had been served, a prisoner was to be released. Now, in 1897, the Commissioners aimed to install a new disciplinary mechanism whereby early parole would be contingent upon a prisoner's "improvement" or progress toward rehabilitation: Hard work and obedience were to be the indices of such improvement. In conjunction with these arrangements, the Commissioners also recommended that a parole board be established for each prison (made up of the President of the Rison Commission, Superintendent of State Prisons, and the Warden), and review applications for early release. As the Commissioners explained in their 1899 report: "When (the prisoner) realizes that by industry and good conduct he can shorten his time, his *desire for freedom* impels him to make the effort, and when released on parole his dread of being returned to prison if he falls into idleness or into companionship of the dissolute keeps him under constant pressure to industry and honesty" (emphasis added).[65] As part of this effort to turn the prisoner's desire into a source of self-discipline, the Commissioners had also provided in their 1896 Prison Labor Law that industrious, obedient convicts would be paid for their labor, at a rate of up to ten percent of the total value of goods produced at the institution (approximately 2¢ to 5¢ per day); conversely, if the prisoner broke the rules, he could be fined 50¢. These earnings were to be paid to the convict upon release from prison.[66]

Herein lay a formula for a penal labor system that made use of softer (though potentially no less powerful) techniques of persuasion rather than the brute force and violent extractive methods associated with the contract prison labor system of the Gilded Age. The Commissioners sought to harness the convicts' "desire for freedom" and to mobilize this as a means of discipline in the prison workshops, in particular, and throughout prison life more generally. The Commissioners asserted that state-use was designed to stimulate the motivation and psyche, and not just the brute labor power, of

---

[64] Laws N.Y. 1889, Ch. 382, § 74; New York State Commission of Prisons, Annual Report (1901), 23. The practice was originally developed in reformatories for youth and adapted to adult prisons. For a detailed discussion of the Northern states' move toward indeterminate sentencing, see Samuel Walker, *Popular Justice: A History of American Criminal Justice*, 2nd ed. (New York: Oxford University Press, 1998), 99–103, 112, 113, 119–23. For an analysis of the theory of indeterminate sentencing and its place in the larger corpus of Progressive Era penal theory, see Rothman, *Conscience and Convenience*, 53–4, 59–61, 69–72.

[65] New York State Commission of Prisons, Annual Report (1899), 17.

[66] §108, Prison Labor Law, Laws N.Y., 1896.

the convicts.[67] Although elements of this particular constellation of penal techniques had been practiced in a haphazard way at Elmira Reformatory (and in some men's prisons before the 1890s), it was not until 1897 and the adoption of the state-use system that prison administrators attempted to implement them in any systematic manner.[68] Once more, it was through and by the great drive to reinvent prison labor, after 1896, that reforms that went on to become hallmarks of progressive penology (such as indeterminate sentencing and incentive-based disciplinary systems) were first systematically provided for in New York's prisons.

Setting the new state-use system in place required a reworking of the administrative structure of the state prisons, relations of authority, and, most acutely, the means of control. The enhancement, in the 1897 classification law, of the Superintendent's power to organize prisoners and transfer them among industries and between institutions significantly expanded the ambit of that office's authority over the state's convicts, and undermined that of wardens. The law licensed the Commission and the Superintendent of Prisons (and his Department of Prisons) to integrate the state prisons into a single network of specialized institutions around which convicts could be distributed and redistributed at the behest of the Superintendent – and it diminished each warden's formal authority over what had traditionally been "his" prison population. This had critical implications both for prison personnel and for the convicts; it changed both the mechanisms by which the practical fate of prisoners, for the duration of their sentence, would be decided, and the relations of power to which they were subject. The questions of where, for how long, and under what conditions a prisoner would serve his sentence ceased to turn solely on the discretion of the sentencing judge in a court of law. Now, a person convicted of felony crime and sentenced to serve time in prison was directly subject to the extrajudicial, administrative authority of the Superintendent of Prisons.

These new arrangements, under which the Superintendent of Prisons began to classify and transfer state prisoners, fostered (for the first time in New York penal history) a process of specialization among the state prisons. Each of the three prisons increasingly began to specialize in one of the three grades of prison workers. Within one year of the passage of the Classification Law, the Superintendent set about turning Sing Sing into a prison for first-graders; Auburn was to become a prison for the second grade; and the

---

[67] See, for example, *Annual Report, Superintendent of New York State Prisons*, (1897), 68; (1899), 14–16; (1902), 19–20, 78. In a note that foreshadowed the penal managerialism of the New Deal era, with its preoccupation with convict morale, the Commissioners argued for the relocation of prison executions far away from the general prison population: "The warden stated to your Commissioner how demoralizing was the effect upon the prisoners of an execution taking place within the prison walls." *Superintendent of New York State Prisons, Annual Report* (1900), 97.

[68] The Laws of 1892 specified the maximum term of a sentence and left it to the judge's discretion to determine the minimum term to be served. Laws N.Y. 1892, Ch. 662.

remote, alpine prison of Clinton, for the third.[69] In 1899, 251 prisoners were transferred out of Sing Sing.[70] Transfer now became a routine technique of prison administration: Especially after 1900, and with increasing frequency in the 1910s, each prison drafted large groups of prisoners several times a year for the purpose of concentrating "like" grades of prisoners in a particular state prison. This practice of transfer both firmed up the tendency to specialization within the prison system as a whole and hastened the integration of New York's men's prisons into a single network around which prisoners were moved at the behest of administrators. Critically, the transfer (or "draft") of prisoners became part of the emerging disciplinary regime; especially in the years after 1900, the mere *threat* or *promise* of transfer to a higher or lower grade institution, or a close or far-flung prison, would become an indispensable tool of penal discipline.

The adoption of this practice in turn fostered the creation of a system of prisoner records that was both far more detailed and far more important than the one used in the past. Previously, upon the commitment of a convict to prison, a clerk in the reception room recorded the name, religion, race, age, prison number (and, sometimes, marital status) of the incoming prisoner in a great leather-bound ledger; punishments meted out in the course of incarceration were recorded in another unwieldy tome, and in chronological rather than alphabetical order. As far as information about individual prisoners was concerned, the old contract-labor system of imprisonment required little more from the state than this very rudimentary system of record-keeping. Particularly under the highly exploitative, Gilded Age version of the contract system, the contractor's need for information about their prison-workers generally extended no further than the prisoners' physical fitness and capacity for hard labor on any particular workday. Nor did the state have any reason of its own to generate more detailed records: Through most of the nineteenth century, each prisoner's sentence had been fixed (or determinate), both in the sense that the judge's sentence was final and not subject to review by wardens or other state agents, and in the sense that it was the judge, acting in a court of law, and not state administrators, who determined in which prison or penitentiary a convict would serve time. Under these conditions, elaborate and easily accessible case histories, studies of convicts' work skills and educational levels, and even the need for accurate identification and punishment records made very little sense. Conversely, the distinctive state-use system that the Commissioners set about building after 1896 required solid, objective information about prisoners, their work and health histories, and their conduct while in prison; such information became, for the first time in American penal history, an administrative necessity.

Under the Commission's guidance, all prisoners were subjected, upon commitment to prison, to an extensive physical examination for the purpose

<hr />

[69] New York State Commission of Prisons, Annual Report (1898), 20, 21, 39.
[70] Superintendent of New York State Prisons, Annual Report (1899), 14.

of creating a "Bertillon" record. This anthropometric examination (which was invented by a French police inspector and statistician, Alphonse Bertillon, in Paris in the 1880s), consisted of a series of eleven standard-ized measurements of the convict's body, a photographic record of the pris-oner's distinguishing characteristics, and standardized notes written on a simple card, which could be sorted (according to the aggregate of the mea-surements) and stored in a filing cabinet.[71] The principles upon which the system relied were, first, that after the age of eighteen the body parts that were measured would not grow and, second, that the chances of any two people having exactly the same eleven measurements was one in four million. By 1896, the concept of "bertillonage" was quite familiar to Amer-ican prison administrators and had been put to use by a number of police departments: In 1888 and again in 1890, members of the National Prison Association and various administrators in New York had advocated the adop-tion of various kinds of identification techniques, including Bertillon's, on the grounds that accurate identification records would bring to light repeat offenders (who, until then, had been able to mask their identity, often by simply changing their name) and thereby facilitate the grade-based refor-matory system; a few years later Bertillon had demonstrated his system at the 1893 Columbian Exposition in Chicago.[72] The U.S. Army and a number of city police departments adopted the system shortly afterward.

Bertillonage promised to free prison administrators from reliance on slipshod court records, prisoners' own testimony as to their name, age, and criminal record, and "names, or . . . any data that is subject to change";[73] it would give prison administrators an "objective" identification of the pris-oner. Under the reign of the contractual system, however, state prison departments had been slow to adopt the system. In New York, it was only once the Commissioners set about devising their new, state-use system of prison administration that the Bertillon method was systematically applied: With its emphasis on the background, aptitudes, progress, and regress of the individual offender, the Commissioners' complex new system required,

[71] The measurements included the prisoner's height, length, and width of head, the left foot, the outstretched arms, the trunk (while seated), four fingers of the left hand, left arm, and length of ear. "The Registration of Criminals," *Proceedings of the Annual Congress of the National Prison Association of the United States*, 1888, 73. Other kinds of "signalment," as Bertillon referred to these objects of measurement, included eye color and distinguishing marks such as tattoos and moles.

[72] The method was first recommended at the 1888 annual congress of the National Prison Association, and again at the 1890 meeting. Joseph Nicholson, president of the Warden's Association and Superintendent of the Detroit House of Correction, National Prison Asso-ciation, 1888, argued for the utility of the system in relation to the reformatory system. *New York Times*, July 17, 1888, 2. See also, Allan Sekula, "The Body and the Archive: the Use and Classification of Portrait Photography by the Police and Social Scientists in the Late nineteenth and 20th Centuries," *October* 39 (Winter 1986), 16.

[73] Frederick G. Pettigrove, "What a Central System May do to Promote the Efficiency of Prison Methods," address to the Annual Conference of the American Prison Association, Albany, New York, 1906, in *Proceedings of the Annual Congress of the American Prison Association*, 1906, 152–3.

among other things, that administrators accurately identify the prisoner in question. In 1896, wardens and staff from New York's penitentiaries and prisons underwent a week-long training class (taught by a surgeon from the U.S. Army) at Sing Sing.[74] Each prison subsequently appointed a specially trained Bertillon clerk, whose task it was to record the presence of scars and other distinguishing features on the convict's body, take the eleven measurements, and photograph the subject's torso and head. Rather than simply recording this information in unwieldy leather-bound ledgers, the Bertillon clerks recorded information on file cards, which were then stored in vertical filing cabinets. Unlike the old ledger pages, these "fiches" could be located with ease, copied and sent out with the prisoner upon transfer, and, most critically, used to accurately identify a returning or "recidivist" offender.[75] (Felicitously, the demand for Bertillon blanks gave more work to the prisoners of Sing Sing's print shop). Eventually, after 1900, New York used these records to establish a central Bureau of Identification in the office of the Superintendent of Prisons in the state capital (Albany). Over the following decade, the Bureau endeavored to develop a uniform system of record-keeping by which to generate and collate information on the State's incarcerated population and exchange that information with other states.[76]

As part of this drive to accurately identify prisoners, the Commissioners also directed prison staff to put together information concerning the medical, laboring, and scholastic background of each prisoner so as to create an individual case history; this information was then to be used to determine in the prisoner's grade, prison, and, eventually, the duration of his sentence. Early release on parole was decided almost exclusively on the basis of these records. In this respect, the prisoner's history (at least as it was represented in prison records), became the basis upon which both his present and his future might be determined. That history was constantly unfolding as the prisoner served his sentence, labored or refused to labor, and followed or broke prison rules. Whereas, previously, the routines and rituals of a system of incarceration built upon large-scale labor contracting had acted to suppress the prisoner's particular history, the state-use prison was dedicated to representing and, ultimately, recreating convicts' identities.[77] As a result of

---

[74] *New York Times,* July 16, 1896, 3.

[75] The system was widely used by police departments throughout the United States between 1890 and 1930, and by the 1900s, prison departments. The New York State Department of Corrections discontinued its use in the 1930s, once it had rationalized its use of fingerprinting technology. For a discussion of bertillonage as a policing technique in France, see Sekula, "The Body and the Archive," 3–64. See also Simon A. Cole, *Suspect Identities: A History of Fingerprinting and Criminal Identification* (Cambridge, Massachusetts: Harvard University Press, 2001), especially 43–54.

[76] Annual reports of the Bureau of Identification were included in Annual Report, Superintendent of New York State Prisons, (1899–1927). In 1928, the Bureau of Identification was reorganized, expanded, and renamed the Division of Identification.

[77] Some kinds of information were standardized more quickly than others. Although prison demography was standardized quite early on in the administration-building era of

these initiatives, by 1899, New York state prisoners became some of the most documented, represented, and well-identified people in America.[78]

Although the drive to build a statewide prison *system* most palpably affected the prisoners at whom it was aimed, the Commissioners' program of reconstruction also carried implications for the hundreds of keepers and other prison staff who were now responsible, under the new system, for carrying out the directives of the Commission, the Superintendent, and the Board of Classification. If the Commission was to make an integrated, state-owned industrial system of New York's prisons and turn some 3,500 convicts into a well-disciplined industrial army for the state, it would also have to establish some kind of centralized command structure over the prisons and make loyal, effective, state servants of the keepers, wardens, and staff. As Lispenard Stewart and his fellow Commissioners appear to have understood very well, this meant, among other things, expelling the party patronage systems (chiefly Tammany Hall, and the country Republican machine, under which keepers and other employees had traditionally procured and kept their jobs) from the prisons and substituting in their place a hierarchical, state bureaucracy. It meant building a bureaucratic penal state, staffed by civil servants and subject to the central authority of the Prison Commission and Department of Prisons.

The legal foundation for making civil servants of prison staff had been partially laid in 1894, when New York's Constitutional Convention provided that all prison employees were to be made subject to the state's civil service rules. These rules specified that all appointments were to be made on the basis of the candidate's "fitness and merit" and under the auspices of the newly established Civil Service Commission.[79] Accordingly, in 1895, 333 people employed in the state prisons and reformatory (including prison chaplains, the state detective, wardens, clerks, stewards, manufactory purchasing agents, watchmen, foremen, and guards), officially became civil servants of the state of New York.

Conferring the legal status of civil servant upon prison keepers and other staff was relatively straightforward; however, turning them, in fact, into loyal servants of the state was a different matter. The Commissioners understood that just as the new state industries had to be built, and could not be simply conjured out of thin air by legislative fiat, the prison staff would have to be actively disciplined and remade as obedient and effective servants of

imprisonment, it took more than two decades to standardize the reports from each of the prison's industrial departments.

[78] There is a measure of irony in the fact that, on the whole, these records were very poorly cared for; in the case of New York, just a small portion of the mass of case histories, financial records, and official correspondence survive. Over the years, many records were lost to fire and neglect.

[79] Notably, only the guards (who numbered 280) were to be selected according to competitive exams: The Civil Service Commission could determine separate selection criteria for the other positions. The guards were to take a physical test and a ten-point reading, writing, arithmetic, memorization, and "judgment" test.

the state. Initially, the principal tactic by which the Commissioners aimed to establish centralized control over the prisons was that of routine inspection. Although directed by law to visit the prisons once a year, the Commissioners made inspections exhaustive and frequent. They divided up the prisons (and also the penitentiaries and jails) among themselves and proceeded to regularly inspect every nook and cranny of these institutions. In attempting to make prison inspections part of the routine of institutional life, the Commissioners hoped that they would gradually make their presence felt and enforce the changes they had mandated: As one Commissioner opined in 1901, "The very fact that these institutions are likely to be inspected at any time by State officials has a salutary influence on the officials in charge of them."[80] Spending upwards of a day at the prison, they collected all manner of information from admission registers, financial records, and hospital files, and inspected the cells, workshops, hospitals, and mess halls.

Routine inspection and reporting helped create what historians have described in other contexts as organizational memory.[81] The Commissioners gradually put in place a set of techniques designed to generate a regular flow of written information about prison operations that they hoped would enable them, over time, to make fully informed decisions about prison industries, staffing, the distribution of prisoners about the system, and the state prison budgets. Following each inspection, the Commissioner wrote up a detailed report, and the Commission's clerks in Albany subsequently compiled the recommendations and statistics into a single, lengthy report on the State's entire penal system. For the first time in their history, the prisons began churning out vast quantities of information (which was printed up by prisoners, of course). The Commissioners collated and presented their data in tables and written analyses that compared the operations of the prison from year to year. These reports contained detailed tables of the revenue from sale of manufactured goods for each prison and measured revenue against the cost of running the prison. The Commissioners also meticulously recorded the productivity, costs, and revenue of every prison industry, the distribution of prisoners in each industry, and the number of idle prisoners.[82] In theory, at least, the flood of information that swept

---

[80] New York State Commission of Prisons, Annual Report (1900), 8.

[81] See JoAnne Yates, "Investing in Information: Supply and Demand Forces in the Use of Information in American Firms, 1815–1920," in Peter Temin, ed., *Inside the Business Enterprise: Historical Perspectives on the Use of Information* (Chicago: Chicago University Press, 1991).

[82] Beginning in 1899, the Commissioners included statistics that broke down the cost of running the prison on a *per capita* basis. (The Commissioners estimated that the cost of incarcerating a person in Sing Sing at the turn of the century was approximately 37¢ per day, or $133 per year). Typically, the greatest cost of running the institutions was the salaries of employees. The cost of running Sing Sing in the first five years of the twentieth century declined slightly every year, from approximately $167,000 to $161,000 per year (a five-percent decrease). Officers' salaries accounted for approximately half the cost. The cost per prisoner remained relatively stable from 1899 through 1904, at approximately 37¢ per day. New York State Commission of Prisons, Annual Report (1899), 29; (1900), 13; (1901), 19; (1902), 19.

out of the prisons after 1896 would provide administrators an overview of the movement of people, goods, and money around the system, enabling them to plan and manage prisons – and prisoners – as a single, integrated system.[83]

Establishing industries, organizing a labor force, and subjecting the prisons to a centralized, bureaucratic mode of control were three cornerstones of New York's remarkable program of penal reconstruction; the fourth was disciplinary reform. As I have noted, the labor grade system became the scaffold for a disciplinary regime in which early release and payment of a tiny sum to prison laborers (which was indexed to productivity and payable upon release) were held out as incentives for obedience and industriousness. That arrangement fused an older, labor-based mode of discipline with more recent reformatory techniques and principles. It also assumed that state industries would be up and running and that most or all prisoners would be engaged in productive labor. Well into the first decade of the twentieth century, the Commissioners refused to capitulate to the prevailing opinion among prison wardens and penologists that the plan for state industries was not workable; the Commissioners (and Superintendent of Prisons) repeatedly and publicly insisted that success was just around the corner. At the same time, however, they quietly made allowances for the possibility that the new, state-use industries might not, in practice, be able to fully absorb the laboring energies of the state's entire penal population. They also grasped the basic moral of Gilded Age penal history that leaving prisoners with absolutely nothing to do, for anything more than a few days, was likely to cause all manner of disciplinary and political trouble. The Commissioners' effort to grapple with these problems fostered the development of a new disciplinary regime in the prisons and, eventually, the articulation of a new doctrine of legal punishment – the new penology.

At the same time as they argued that state government would generate enough demand to keep state prisoners at productive labor, the Commissioners quietly promoted and wrote into proposed legislation various provisions for putting large numbers of prisoners to both nonmanufacturing forms of labor and various nonlaboring disciplinary activities. Their most important fallback position, in the early years of the state-use system, was institutional construction and renovation work. In their original report to the legislature (in which they advocated the adoption of the state-use system), the Commissioners recommended that the state also build new cellhouses and install electric lights in the cells – and, conveniently, use convict labor in the construction.[84] A few months later, the Commissioners implicitly acknowledged that they viewed institutional renovation and construction

---

[83] In 1931, for example, the New York State Commission to Investigate Prison Administration and Construction projected the probable prison population through 1940 on the basis of the Commissioners' reports of the 1920s. *Report, Commission to Investigate Prison Administration and Construction* (Feb. 15, 1931).

[84] New York State Commission of Prisons, Annual Report (1895), cited in *New York Times*, Dec. 28, 1895, 3.

projects an alternative for industrial labor, when they advised that "in view
of the fact that all contract labor is to be abolished [in December 1896],"
all building work around the state prisons should be halted for the remainder of 1896 and saved for when there would be "many convicts free to labor
upon buildings."[85] Their state-use bill, in turn, stretched the term "state-use"
in the case of county and jail inmates well beyond its original emphasis on
manufacturing work to include labor on roads, buildings, drains, and other
public works in any town, county, or city.[86] In 1897, they further extended its
meaning, in a bill that authorized the use of convict labor on all state lands
near and around the prison at Clinton.[87] Like construction and related
building activities, educational classes were also briefly recommended in
the first report, and in such a way as to suggest that the Commissioners
viewed them as either strictly supplementary to the new industrial labor system, or a stop-gap solution in the event that state-use industries could not
keep New York's 3,500-odd state prisoners at full-time employment.[88]

The Commissioners were not alone in their efforts to stretch the meaning of "state-use" and generate alternatives to manufactory labor. Despite his
boasts to the press in early January of 1897, that he and the Commissioners
would have the new system up and running in just "three or four weeks,"
the Superintendent of New York's State Prisons, General Austin Lathrop,
also recognized the possibility the state would not be able to put all its prisoners to work under the new system. From quite early on in the planning
process, Lathrop made provisions for the introduction of supplementary
forms of work and educational programs.[89] In anticipation of the suspension of industries in January 1897, he established a class in carving and
free-hand drawing at Sing Sing Prison; a few days after the cessation of production at that prison he announced his intention to extend these classes
"as fast as is practicable." (This was the class in which the talented Sing
Sing model-maker was "discovered"). Lathrop also arranged to put large
numbers of idled prisoners at Auburn and Sing to work breaking stone
for road improvements across the state's cities, villages, and towns, dressing
stone slabs, building new floors in all the prisons, and outfitting workshops
for the new state-use industries.[90] One year into the new regime, Lathrop,

---

[85] Resolution of the State Prison Commission, reported in *New York Times*, Feb 27, 1896, 3.

[86] Bill reported in *New York Times*, Jan. 28, 1897, 4; Feb 4, 1897, 4. Previously, the law restricted
the use of convict labor to state-owned land that was uncultivated. Squatters (many of whom
had likely served sentences at Clinton Prison and then settled the land upon release from
prison) had cultivated tracts of state land near the prison, thereby disqualifying it from
cultivation by prison labor.

[87] *New York Times*, Jan. 28, 1897, 4.

[88] New York State Commission of Prisons, Annual Report (1895), cited in *New York Times*, Dec.
28, 1895, 3.

[89] Fives weeks into the new regime, the *New York Times* reported that Lathrop "thinks the
question of the employment of convicts is practically solved . . . [the state-use industries]
will furnish employment for all." *New York Times*, Feb. 4, 1897, 4.

[90] Austin Lathrop, press release, Dec. 31, 1896; quoted in *New York Times*, Jan. 1, 1897, 6;
"Convict Labor Problem," *New York Times*, Jan. 7, 1897, 9.

while still insisting that state-use industries promised to be a great success, was nonetheless giving fresh emphasis (in his public addresses and reports) to the "educational and reformatory aims of the law."[91] Subsequently, in 1900, prisoners of the second grade and many of the first found themselves extending and repairing Sing Sing's crumbling Northern wall. They quarried and cut stone from an adjoining lot, laid bricks and stone into the wall, and worked away until the entire compound was once again securely enclosed (two years later).[92] Prisoners were also put to work tearing down old buildings on the prison grounds, rebuilding the power plants, erecting new buildings, grading prison grounds, and laying walkways and wagon roads through the prisons. In addition, convicts scrubbed their workshops daily – and whitewashed them twice a month.[93]

In a similar vein, as prison industry wound down in late 1896, New York's wardens, who uniformly opposed the McDonough amendment, nonetheless began innovating and cobbling together other activities as alternatives to manufactory labor. At Sing Sing, a month into the state-use experiment and with hundreds of idle prisoners on his hands, Warden Omer Sage put prisoners to work carving and stock-piling flagstones for future construction projects; he also enlarged the carving and freehand drawing class for prisoners. Notably, he dispatched prisoners of the first grade – precisely those convicts who were supposed to make up the skilled labor force in the new manufacturing system – to the class. Construction labor and schooling, Sage explained, were undertaken with the "chief object of the prison law" in mind: This was "to give the prisoners work to do, and to teach them some trade by which they can support themselves after they are discharged from custody."[94]

As 1897 wore on and upwards of ninety percent of the prisoners continued to have little or no manufacturing work, the authorities extended these programs.[95] In late January, Sage established literacy and arithmetic

---

[91] *New York Times*, Jan. 29, 1898, 4.

[92] New York State Commission of Prisons, Annual Report (1901), 14, 97; (1902), 20–2.

[93] Superintendent of New York State Prisons, Annual Report (1902), 100.

[94] Omer Sage, quoted in "How to Employ Convicts," *New York Times*, Jan. 24, 1897, 20. (The drawing and modeling classes were taught by a convict whom Sage claimed had "graduated with honors from an art school in Rome, as a modeler, sculptor, and carver").

[95] Prior to the 1890s, there had been a few attempts to instruct prisoners in literacy. English-language literacy rates in the prisons had traditionally lagged well behind civilian rates. In the mid-nineteenth century, when ten percent of the adult white population were unable to read and write, the Sing Sing chaplain had reported that approximately half of the new inmates were unable to read and write. *Sing Sing Prison: Its History, Purpose, Makeup, and Program*, 17. In 1847, the agent and warden of Sing Sing hired two civilian teachers to teach the prisoners English reading and writing: These teachers stood on a cell gallery at night and instructed the men locked in their cells. The same year, New York state became the first to make annual appropriations for the development of prison libraries and to provide libraries with nonreligious texts. When Wines and Dwight toured American prisons in 1867, they found that small libraries existed in all state prisons in the North, but that these tended to be stocked only with religious texts. Indeed, in 1860, Sing Sing Prison had become one of the first prisons in the country to have books other than the Bible or related religious texts in

classes, and shortly thereafter extended their enrollment.[96] Wardens at Sing Sing and elsewhere also moved to give prisoners more to read and to extend prison libraries at this time, as well. Never one to mince words, Kings County's Warden Hayes made the rationale for introducing reading, and other educational programs, quite clear: "if we cannot give a man work to do, we try and keep his mind occupied."[97] Hayes, who was very much a product of the contract prison labor era of legal punishment, was hardly persuaded, however, that "mental employments" such as reading could substitute in any substantial way for the discipline of industrial labor. Such activities were of limited application in the prisons, he argued, "for there are many prisoners who cannot read. In my experience I have seen convicts so ignorant and stupid that they did not known [sic] enough to walk up stairs and turn to the right, or to the left, without guidance."[98] Hayes also applied what he believed to be a far more effective means of control: He put his 1,000-odd convicts to drilling and counterdrilling, 100 at a time, at 140-minute stretches, in the penitentiary yard.[99] In 1897, about ten percent of state prisoners were attending school lessons and smaller numbers started in trades classes in furniture-making, drawing, and carving.

Heading into the new century, alternative disciplinary activities such as these only continued to assume greater importance in the scheme of reform. As salvaging full-time industrial labor for the prisoners proved a slower, more arduous task than the Commissioners had imagined, and as the Wardens and Superintendent scrambled to find ways of occupying thousands of inactive men, the original concept of state-use began to change in subtle but important ways. The dawning realization among the Commissioners that the plan to make state-use industries the foundation of a new penal order probably was not as successful as they had projected led them to heighten their emphasis on various alternatives to the disciplinary activity of industrial labor and to forge new techniques of penal discipline. The Commission, wardens, and Superintendent continued to extend inmate-taught literacy and rudimentary educational programs at Auburn and Sing, and eventually established prison schools. Americanization programs, nominally aimed at assimilating immigrant prisoners, were also established. In 1903, such a program was introduced at Sing Sing for the purpose of instructing immigrants in the English language and the "customs of the country." A similar program operated at Auburn, and shortly thereafter the first prison building devoted to scholastic learning (rather than trades instruction) was built alongside the Sing Sing hospital (in 1905).[100]

its library. In 1868, the total number of books in all American state prisons was estimated to be 15,250. Approximately one-third of these were in New York prisons. McKelvey, *American Prisoners*, 42, 58. However, prison libraries underwent no appreciable expansion during the Gilded Age.

[96] Sage considered the Sing Sing art and carving school the most successful of the prison's departments. *New York Times*, Apr. 30, 1899, IMS 4.

[97] Patrick J. Hayes, quoted in *New York Times*, Jan. 24, 1897, 20.

[98] Ibid.   [99] Ibid.

[100] *Sing Sing Prison: Its History, Purpose, Makeup, and Program*, 17, 18.

Although these programs proliferated largely as a result of the continuing difficulties encountered in the effort to find manufacturing work for the prisoners, the Commissioners nonetheless explained that such innovations were an indispensable part of their new, state-use system of imprisonment. Educating and training prisoners, they argued, would enable those prisoners to fill the shoes of the civilian foremen and instructors who had supervised production under the old system; this, in turn, would save the state a considerable sum of money. Moreover, literate, skilled prisoners made better workers, and better workers made better citizens.[101] In the last year or so of the nineteenth century, this latter consideration, especially, dominated official discourse about New York's prison system; even the disgruntled wardens came to explain and justify their use of alternative disciplinary programs in a more ethical, and less narrowly instrumental, register. The Commissioners and Superintendent Lathrop increasingly spoke of the prison's principal mission being reclamation of convicts as productive, "manly" citizens. As one Commissioner put it in 1899, the objectives of imprisonment were now to "restore the prisoner's manhood" and to make of him an industrious, law-abiding citizen.[102] "Few prisoners are so totally depraved," he continued, "that they have not left within them some traces of honesty, – some sparks of manhood."[103]

"Manhood," in the Commissioners' usage, consisted first and foremost in a man's ability and willingness to earn an "honest" living through industrial or craft labor, and enough of a wage that he might support his family upon release from prison. The Commissioners pointed out that an ex-prisoner who was unable to work was likely to be dependent and consequently vulnerable to being drawn back into criminal activity; crime, in this view, was damaging not only to its immediate victim, but to the convict, his family and, ultimately, the state itself.[104] Here, as throughout their reform work, the Commissioners drew on established reformatory principles;[105] like Zebulon Brockway before them, they considered the disciplining experience of productive labor the single most generative source of convict resocialization. However, two years into the state-use experiment, as it became evident that getting state industries up and running was going to be far more difficult, and take a lot more time, than originally projected, the Commissioners' discourse began to change: The project of building manly citizens slowly became detached from the productive labor process to which it had been so tightly welded in the reformatory penology of the Gilded Age, and was gradually fused to the alternative disciplinary activities with which the Commissioners and wardens had been supplementing productive labor. As the

[101] New York State Commission of Prisons, Annual Report (1898), 20–1.
[102] New York State Commission of Prisons, Annual Report (1900), 14–15. See also, Superintendent of New York State Prisons, Annual Report (1897), 67, 68; (1898), 20–1, 50; (1899), 14–16, 18 (1903), 97; (1904), 18.
[103] New York State Commission of Prisons, Annual Report, (1898), 55; (1899), 14–15.
[104] New York State Commission of Prisons, Annual Report (1898), 55; (1899), 14–15.
[105] See, for example, New York State Commission of Prisons, Annual Report, (1897), 67, 68; (1898), 20–1, 50; (1899), 14–16, 18 (1903), 97; (1904), 18.

prison labor problem appeared far less soluble than the Commissioners had estimated, reformatory penology increasingly emphasized the preparatory and therapeutic mission of legal punishment and de-emphasized the supposedly life-altering experience of productive labor.

Rather than insisting that it was only or chiefly in the workshops that prisons made men of prisoners, in the late 1890s, the Commissioners began arguing that other spaces of the prison (including the mess hall, the classroom, the cellblocks) and other kinds of disciplinary activity were crucial to the process. The Commissioners imagined a prison in which every sphere of everyday life was redesigned around the principle of sparking "the spirit of manhood" in the convicts and "[showing] them the way to a better and manlier life."[106] "It is the duty of the State," one Prison Commissioner insisted, "to keep [the prisoners] in as good physical condition as possible, so that at the expiration of their terms they may be able to engage in some occupation which will afford them a livelihood and enable them to support themselves and their families. This is not only a matter of great importance to the prisoners themselves but is of economy to the State."[107] It followed that the prisoner should not be physiologically or psychologically debilitated upon his release from prison. Cleaner prisons, better food, exercise, education, medical services – and not just productive labor – would ensure that convicts were made into men, and thereby reclaimed as productive, law-abiding citizens.

They began, in 1899, by abolishing many of the rules of the old system, including the commonplace practices of shaving prisoners' heads, dressing prisoners in striped uniforms, and forcing prisoners to march in lock-step fashion (whereby men shuffled chest-to-back in an awkward and confined manner, with heads turned sideways and downwards, and hands on the waist of the man in front). Such practices were directly counter to the restoration of manhood, argued the Commissioners, as they were "un-necessarily humiliating and degrading." The traditional striped uniform, which indicated the prisoner's conviction record (by number of stripes), constituted a humiliating "advertisement" of the prisoner's former and, supposedly, unmanly, life. Convicts should instead wear plain military-style uniforms and, in their movements between cells, messhalls, classrooms, and workshops, march as men marched – that is, two by two in military formation, with heads held high and no bodily contact between them. Such marching, wrote the Commissioners in 1899, "tends to manly appearance and deportment."[108] By 1907, when the silent rule was finally abolished across the entire state prison system, almost all of the last vestiges of the old industrial prison discipline had dissolved.

In the arena of alternative labor activities, such as construction and renovation of the prison buildings, the Commissioners increasingly made a

[106] New York State Commission of Prisons, Annual Report (1898), 55; (1899), 14–15.
[107] New York State Commission of Prisons, Annual Report (1903), 78.
[108] New York State Commission of Prisons, Annual Report (1899), 14–15.

virtue of necessity. What had originated as make-work schemes became an expanded effort to "sanitize" and upgrade the prison plant in the name of making manly citizens of the convicts. Prisoners were put to work on the infrastructure of the new system, building administrative blocks, hospitals, chapels, workshops, kitchens, and messhalls. Of particular concern here were the old stone cellhouses (Sing Sing's in particular) that earlier generations of state prisoners had constructed in the 1820s and 1830s. Arguing (with considerable merit) that "small, damp, and illy ventilated" cells enfeebled and broke down the bodies of citizens-in-training, the Commissioners called for the complete renovation of the aging cellhouses in the name of reform: They requested the demolition of the old stone cellwalls and their replacement with clean, sanitary steel cells; the widening of windows; installation of ventilation systems; and the construction of a fireproof iron roof in the cellblock.[109] The number and complexity of these construction projects provided occupation for hundreds of otherwise idle prisoners.

Building on the innovation of literacy classes and other "mental occupations," the Commissioners also fostered the activities of reading and writing among prisoners more generally. In the contract prison labor era, convicts had been allowed no or only very minimal letter-writing privileges. In the transition to state-use, letter writing became a privilege that was conferred on a state prisoner according to how much of his sentence he had served. Under this arrangement, a prisoner serving his first year was entitled to write one letter per month; in his second year, a prisoner could write one letter every two weeks, and any prisoner with a good disciplinary record who had served five or more years was entitled to write once per week. The Commissioners also supported the improvement of prison libraries and opened a new library at Sing Sing, complete with 10,000 books all "properly shelved, classified, and indexed," and a brand new catalogue.[110]

It was as part of the larger effort to foster alternative means of discipline in the prisons that prison administrators invited prisoners to establish New York's first state prison newspaper. In 1899, the first edition of the *Star of Hope* rolled off the printing press at Sing Sing.[111] One of a dozen prison newspapers founded across America in the late 1890s, the *Star of Hope* was written and printed by convicts, and was distributed free of charge to every convict in the state's prisons. Its pages contained puzzles; poems; an "Open

---

[109] New York State Commission of Prisons, Annual Report, (1899), 70.
[110] New York State Commission of Prisons, Annual Report, (1903), 79.
[111] The editor of the *Star of Hope*, known only as "Sing Sing Prisoner No. 1500," later wrote that the idea of publishing a prison newspaper was his own, and that the Superintendent and warden of Sing Sing welcomed his suggestion. *No. 1500, Life in Sing Sing* (Indianapolis, Indiana: Bobbs Merrill, 1904), 90. Prisoners at Elmira Reformatory began publishing a newspaper, *The Summary*, for Elmira convicts and their families in 1883. Through the 1880s, its print run was limited to just 225 copies. "Edited by Convicts," *The Journalist* 8:4 (Oct. 13, 1888), 11 (thanks to Lara Vapnik, History Department, Columbia University, for this citation). See also James McGrath Morris, *Jailhouse Journalism: The Fourth Estate Behind Bars* (Jefferson, North Carolina: McFarland and Co., 1998), 103–5.

Parliament"; prisoners' writings on the latest penal reforms; and local Sing Sing news. By 1900, it was also carrying news of all the other New York state prisons. The prison newspaper's moniker encapsulated the psychological principle of the new disciplinary regime, according to which the prison ought to stimulate the convict's desire for freedom and to rekindle convicts' doused sense of hope (for the future). Like many of the other measures the Commissioners had undertaken, the newspaper was explicitly conceived as a critical element of the greater project to assimilate convicts as manly citizens: By writing, printing, reading, and responding to the newspaper, convicts would be inducted into a prison version of the public sphere, in which men engaged in reasoned debate about the world. Warden Sage put it this way: "Its aim and scope will be to furnish the inmates with a summary of the news of the world, and to stimulate interest among the men toward higher and nobler mental training." The new Superintendent of Prisons, Cornelius V. Collins, affirmed this opinion, adding that "the paper affords a salutary occupation for a great many prisoners and is a healthful stimulant in the mental activity of the contributors and, in a lesser degree, of all those who read the paper." In addition, Collins touted the paper's physical properties ("neatly printed and its proofs well read") as exemplary of the high standards of good craftsmanship to which all convicts should aspire: "It is," he exclaimed in 1900, "a constant pattern of good work to all the prisoners."[112]

Finally, beginning in 1899, the Commissioners undertook to extend quasi-legal protections and entitlements to the prisoners, and to extend avenues of redress in instances of abuse at the hands of keepers and wardens.[113] Up until 1899, prisoners' only means of redress in the event of unauthorized physical abuse had been to seek the permission of the warden to pursue the grievance. Given that the warden was often implicated in the alleged abuse, prisoners were put in the absurd position of seeking redress from their aggressor or his supporters. In the Commissioners' view, beatings and physical humiliation were not simply inhumane; such treatment was emasculating, inconsistent with the prison's citizen-making duty, and entirely prejudicial to the reconstruction of convicts' manhood. They argued that "abuses result largely from the fact that prisoners are without redress, and it is even impossible for prisoners to make a complaint other than to the very officials who may have been guilty of, or responsible for, the misconduct charged."[114] The solution they offered was to open up the prison to what they called light and publicity: Specifically, the judiciary, the

---

[112] New York State Commission of Prisons, Annual Report, 16. Praising the quality of New York's prison newspaper, the editor of the *New York Times* described it as "embarrassingly well-written and edited." *New York Times*, June 20, 1899, 6.

[113] Here, it is important to recall that guards, wardens, and many American citizens still considered certain forms of corporal punishment to be legitimate, although all forms were increasingly under attack from penologists.

[114] New York State Commission of Prisons, Annual Report (1899), 18.

governor, and the central prison authorities should be given the authority to investigate claims of unauthorized physical abuse. Insisting that an incarcerated person was nonetheless a citizen and, as such, a person entitled to certain protections,[115] they provided that prisoners were to be allowed to send sealed letters to the governor, a county judge, district attorney, the superintendent of prisons, and the Commissioners. The Commissioners made it clear in their report for 1899 that they intended this innovation to have an additional disciplinary effect: In theory, establishing independent channels of appeal would invert the most basic relation of surveillance in the prison (the keepers' supervision of prisoners) and subject the keepers to a degree of oversight. Knowing that prisoners had a newfound power of report, the keepers would then be less inclined to engage in illegal, abusive treatment of their charges. As the Commissioners confidently asserted, "the mere possibility of appeal would, in large measure, prevent... abuses."[116]

By 1900, New York's ambitious experiment in a state-use system of imprisonment had brought about sweeping changes at all four levels of prison labor, discipline, administration, and penological doctrine. New York's prisons had ceased to be semi-autonomous institutions organized in service of the profit imperative of the private contractor; the product of prison labor no longer entered the open market. Under the State Prison Commission's ambitious program of reconstruction, the prisons had also been integrated into a new, statewide penal bureaucracy, within which each institution played a specialized and subordinate role; prisons – and their convicts and staff – had become linked in a bureaucratic chain of specialized penal institutions. Many of the longstanding rules, routines, and rituals of imprisonment were being dropped: Administrators swept away the old penal tactics of the silence rule, striped uniforms, and lockstep march, and laid the foundations of a disciplinary regime that was more therapeutic than production-based, and which purported to make manly citizen–workers of prisoners by treating them as men. In official prison discourse, convicts had ceased to be the "civilly dead" refuse of society whose proper fate was to be driven to hard sweated labor at a profit, and had been reborn as "wards of the state" and American citizens-in-training. The state, on this view, now owed a positive duty to nurture, train, and prepare its wards for worker–citizenship.

The combined efforts of the Commissioners, Superintendent Lathrop (and his successor, Cornelius V. Collins), and the wardens to put the prisons on a state-use basis had also generated occupations – of various kinds – for the majority of state prisoners. By the end of 1897, the Commission was able to report that two-thirds of New York's 3,500-odd adult male prisoners were spending at least some of their waking hours in employment.[117] Indeed,

[115] Ibid.   [116] Ibid.
[117] New York State Commission of Prisons, Annual Report (1897), 11.

according to one Prison Commissioner, the overall employment rate for state prisoners had rebounded to pre-abolition levels: "All of the convicts in the State Prisons, with the exception of the sick, the crippled, the weak in mind and body," he boasted, "are now given employment."[118] Strictly speaking, prison labor, of the sort that prisoners had undergone in the contracting era had not rebounded: Whereas the vast majority of prisoners performed full-time industrial labor under the old system, under the new, they were more likely to do construction work, engage in daily institutional labor (such as hauling trash, cleaning, and cooking), or take classes. Nor was the labor fulltime. Still, several hundred were engaged in manufacturing labor for the state, and in the broadest sense of the term, the majority of state prisoners indeed had some kind of employment. Moreover, a New York state legislative committee had reported positively upon the new penal arrangements and their impact on free labor. Although full employment of state prisoners had not yet been attained and the financial results were "as yet inadequate and unsatisfactory," "greater experience and organization" would soon obviate these problems.[119]

Politically, the new, "New York system," as this particular formulation of the state-use prison was known by 1900, was beginning to stabilize and even win some new adherents. Finally acknowledging that they probably would not be able to overturn or modify the McDonough amendment, W. M. F. Rounds and the New York Prison Association slowly turned their lobbying energies to extending trades education in the state prisons: In late 1899, a special committee (members of which included Jacob Riis and Eugene Smith) set about drafting a bill for the establishment of a system of trade schools in the prisons.[120] Although many Southern, and some Northern, members of the National Prison Association remained adamantly opposed to New York's system, a number of well-known critics of it softened and even reversed their position. The president of the association, Roeliff Brinkerhoff, for example, heartily endorsed the system at the 1897 annual congress of the association, in Austin, Texas, and encouraged Texas (and other Southern states) to adopt it.[121]

---

[118] New York State Commission of Prisons, Annual Report (1897), 10. The statement exaggerates the amount of laboring going in the prisons: The commissioner was counting convicts who were not engaged in productive labor and whose work tasks were often far from defined, and he was ignoring the fact that the hours that prisoners worked were much fewer than under the contract system. Although prisoners tended to have employment, they continued to be severely underemployed.

[119] The Peterson committee also reported that New York's free laborers were not suffering competition from convict labor and that, as administrators overcame the teething problems of the new system, the system would "demonstrate within a few years the wisdom of those who caused its adoption." Quoted in Wright, "Prison Labor," *Catholic University Bulletin*, 5 (1899).

[120] *New York Times*, Nov. 12, 1899, 16.

[121] *Proceedings of the Annual Congress of the National Prison Association of the United States*, 1897. Southern members of the association replied that New York and other Northern states that

Most critically, the states of Pennsylvania and Massachusetts abandoned their own experiments (in public-account and "hybrid" labor systems, respectively) and endorsed and followed New York's lead. After 1897, Massachusetts slowly adopted most of New York's arrangements, including legislation compelling first state, and eventually, all county and city governments, to purchase their needs from the Massachusetts State prisons.[122] By 1910, almost all of that commonwealth's prison industries operated on a state-use basis. Much as in New York, a State Prison Commission worked regularly with officers from the various government departments to determine the design and quantity of goods to be produced and consumed by government.[123] Pennsylvania's penal industries (which were organized under the public-account system) failed to thrive, largely as a result of ongoing public antagonism toward convict-made products and the difficulties inherent in putting thousands of prisoners to work on nonmechanized forms of manufacturing. In late 1898, after conducting an extensive enquiry into the penal labor systems of other States, a dispirited Pennsylvania legislative committee reported that there was but "one gleam of light"[124] in the field of prison labor: New York. It appeared that New York had put prisoners to work for the state without objection from free labor, the committee reported; finding no objections to the system, the committee unanimously recommended that Pennsylvania adopt the New York system.[125] In the course of the next several years, Pennsylvania moved (if haltingly) toward a state-use model of prison labor explicitly based on that of their historic rival. Eventually, the Pennsylvania legislature mandated an integrated, state-use system modeled directly on New York's. Much as in the Empire State, a Prison Commission

had abolished or scaled back contracting seemed unconcerned about the costs to the state of dropping contracting. Robert Perkinson notes that the Governor of Texas, in rebuffing the President's admonition to consider adopting New York's system, added that his state's penal system had its own peculiar problems (namely African Americans, Mexicans, and "hardened" frontiersmen, and warned against any outside intervention in what he argued was an essentially "local" issue. Perkinson, "Birth of the Texas Prison Empire," 211–12. Charlton Lewis, a long-time member of the New York Prison Association, was one exception to the general tendency, among Northern administrators in the late 1890s, to reconsider the state-use system: Describing the McDonough amendment as a "blot" upon New York, he dramatically vowed to fight idleness among the prisoners "to the death." *Proceedings of the National Conference of Charities and Correction*, 1898.

[122] Lane, "The State-Use System," 60.   [123] Ibid.

[124] Wright, *Some Ethical Phases of the Labor Question*, 197.

[125] The way was partially cleared for Pennsylvania to fall into line with the New York model as the last of the older generation of prison wardens left prison service. In 1900, commentators remarked upon the death of Michael J. Cassidy, Eastern Penitentiary's long-standing stalwart of the Pennsylvania's "separate" system and antagonist of both contract and state-use labor, that "now, after Warden Cassidy's death, the [separate] plan may be dropped" ("Prisoners," *The Charities Review* 9 (Apr. 1900), 67–8). A few years later, prison labor was restricted still further, when the state prohibited the employment of prisoners beyond the prison walls. Finally, in 1915, Pennsylvania provided for the establishment of an integrated, state-use system modeled after New York's and, like the latter, to be administered by a Prison Commission. Barnes, "Economics of American Penology," 618.

was established and entrusted with planning and administering the new system.[126]

New York's system received additional support and publicity from organized labor, a growing number of penologists, and the federal government as well. Upon the ratification of New York's McDonough amendment in 1894, Samuel Gompers had informed delegates attending the AFL's annual convention in Nashville that, although the "evils" of the convict labor system had been modified only slightly in most states, New York "has proved the best solution thus far attained." Observing that many different approaches to prison labor, including the public-account system and convict-made labeling laws, were failing to solve the problem of unfair competition, Gompers went on to recommend the widespread adoption of New York's system: "It is urged," he continued, "that this system be extended to all other States as one of the best means to solve the problem." While stopping just shy of an unqualified endorsement, Gompers nonetheless noted that New York's state-use law "is a long step toward the solution of the problem of employing convicts in productive occupations with a view to minimizing the competition of their product with that of free labor."[127] By all accounts, Lispenard Stewart, the president of the State Prison Commission, worked hard to solidify the support of the Knights of Labor and AFL for the state-use system: When the Commission first investigated possible labor systems in 1895, they consulted with labor leaders; and, again, in early 1897, as they began setting up state-use prison industries, Stewart met with union leaders in the relevant industries. Stewart repeatedly assured labor leaders that, although, under law, prisoners had to be put to hard labor and it was the duty of the Commission to apply the state-use system of labor, his commission intended to run prison industries in ways that did not injure free workers. In turn, local labor leaders encouraged a version of the state-use system that put prisoners chiefly to institutional and unskilled forms of labor (including roadwork).[128]

---

[126] Pennsylvania's law was enacted in 1915. Barnes, "Economics of American Penology," 618; *Report of the Penal Commission on the Employment and Compensation of Prisoners*, Feb. 15, 1915, 8; Acts of the General Assembly, 1915, 656 ff. The law, however, did not make it compulsory for state, county, and city government to purchase their needs from the prisons. Albert H. Votaw, in advising Pennsylvania on the creation of a state-use system, cited New York's solution to the problem of a market for prisonmade goods: "The Mayor of Buffalo," he suggested, "cannot order a desk or chair for his room unless he has first made a requisition on the manager of prison products in the State of New York.... We must have some such a system in this State before there will be any successful operation of the laws on this subject." Albert H. Votaw, *Penal Legislation in Pennsylvania*, 1915, 12–13. Quoted in Harry Elmer Barnes, "The Economics of American Penology as Illustrated by the Experience of the State of Pennsylvania," *Journal of Political Economy* 29:8 (Oct. 1921), 637.

[127] Samuel Gompers, Report to Seventeenth Annual Convention, American Federation of Labor, Nashville, Tennessee, 1897, quoted in United States Senate, Committee on Interstate Commerce, Interstate Commerce in Convict-Made Goods, (Washington, DC: Government Printing Office, 1914), 52.

[128] For example, in March 1897, Stewart met with representatives of the National Lithographers' Union and the New York Typographical Union to hear their concerns regarding the

As New York's state-use experiment progressed and the Commission gradually extended the concept of "state-use" to embrace various kinds of unskilled labor, and vocational and educational classes, Gompers's initial, rather tepid support of the system became an unqualified endorsement. Between 1897 and 1904, under Gompers's leadership, the AFL formulated a position on the prison labor problem that held that prisoners ought not to be idle and that the New York system was the best means by which prisoners could be both put to labor and prevented from competing openly with free labor. As Gompers wrote in his Labor Day editorial in the *American Federationist* (1904): "Of course, no sane, thinking, humane man wants the convicts in our prisons to remain idle . . . [convicts] should be employed, but employed by the state direct on its own account, and with a view of benefiting both the state and the convict without injury to the free citizen."[129] The *American Federationist* and other labor publications now offered New York's state-use legislation as a model prison labor law, reproducing the state's constitutional amendment and various passages from the official state prison reports and arguing strenuously that New York had, in fact, forged a viable alternative to contracting. (In addition to promoting New York's prison labor laws, the AFL also continued to pursue federal legislation prohibiting the transportation of prison-made goods between States).

Organized labor's elevation of New York to the position of model for all the states was completed in 1906, with the publication of a special report by Collis Lovely, of the Shoe Workers' union. Lovely undertook an investigation of some twenty-eight American state prisons in the official capacity of state investigator for Missouri's Department of Labor. In his report, he made the case that contracting, which was still in effect in many states, had created a new form of human slavery more cruel and unjust than chattel slavery before the war. Assessing various states' efforts to palliate the abuses of prison labor, he concluded that no state, besides New York, had succeeded; the New York system distinguished itself as an unqualified success. New York had removed all competition between prison goods and the product of free labor and had thereby enabled the abolition of cruelty, corruption, and graft. New York's system was the "most equitable, the most practical and the nearest to the highest ideals of progress and civilization." Indeed, Lovely concluded, in a phrase that could have as easily been uttered by a New York State Prison Commissioner, New York's system was "destined to revolutionize the entire prison administration of our country."[130]

The view that New York state had found the answer to the prison problem was reinforced by no less an expert in the field than Carroll D. Wright. Initially leery of the state-use concept (chiefly on the grounds that it would be

print shop at Sing Sing. *New York Times*, Mar. 17, 1897, 7; *New York Times*, Mar. 18, 1897, 5; *New York Times* Mar. 22, 1897, 10; *New York Times*, July 23, 1897, 9.

[129] Samuel Gompers, Editorial, *American Federationist* 11: 9 (Sept. 1904), 774–6.

[130] Collis Lovely, *The Abuses of Prison Labor* (Unknown, republished in *Shoeworkers' Journal*, ca. 1909), 3–32.

a drain on the public purse), by 1899, Wright was arguing that the citizenry was ready to give up its insistence on making prisons self-supporting; American prisons, he approvingly informed the National Prison Association, were in the throws of evolving from the contract system, through public-account, to state-use. (He also made the astute observation that by forcing the abolition of contracting, the much-maligned leaders of organized labor were indirectly responsible for the introduction and extension of reformatory principles in many prisons).[131] Three years later, in a book entitled *Some Ethical Phases of the Labor Question*, Wright devoted a long chapter to "The Ethics of Prison Labor." He argued that, although many states had made progress solving the prison labor problem, New York was the only one to have established a system that both kept prisoners almost constantly occupied and made workingmen and manufacturers almost universally satisfied. Above all, New York had solved the problem of insufficient demand: By authorizing any agency or department of the state, and not just the prisons, to purchase their needs from penal industries, the Prison Commissioners had broadened the real market for prisonmade goods. (Wright criticized Massachusetts, which had also moved to state-use by this time, for having failed to broaden the state market for convict-made goods).[132] Moreover, New York's trade classes had enabled the absorption of surplus, idle prisoners.[133]

Wright went on to explain that New York had demonstrated the certain advantage of the state-use system and was finding ways of overcoming the difficulties inherent in the state-use system (such as unsteady demand for prisonmade goods, lack of skilled labor forces, and ongoing public sentiment against prisonmade goods). "(T)hese difficulties are likely to disappear," he opined, and "(t)here are no permanent disadvantages to the system.... (t)here are only temporary obstacles."[134] Finally, the New York system presented a solution to the political pressure that had been a constant in the penal sphere since the 1830s. "If ... satisfaction [with the system] becomes general," he concluded, "our legislatures will be relieved of great pressure from two avenues of approach. The paid lobbyist of the contractor will not be found in the lobbies of the legislature, nor will the committees of labor unions be found antagonizing them. The subject itself will be eliminated from public discussion in large measure."[135] In short, New York's Commission had solved the political, disciplinary, ethical, and economic problems posed by the abolition of contracting and open-market sales of prisonmade goods.

[131] Carroll Wright, *Proceedings of the Annual Congress of the National Prison Association of the United States*, 1899.
[132] In addition to the limitations noted earlier, Wright pointed to Massachusetts' omission of city and other subcounty political divisions from the state-use market. *Some Ethical Phases of the Labor Question*, 186.
[133] Wright, *Some Ethical Phases of the Labor Question*,184.
[134] Wright, *Some Ethical Phases of the Labor Question*, 188, 193.
[135] Wright, *Some Ethical Phases of the Labor Question*, 194.

Finally, in 1902, the New York system (and, implicitly, organized labor's continuing charge against all forms of contracting) received official, federal endorsement in the U.S. Industrial Commission's report on the state of convict labor. The first systematic investigation of convict labor undertaken since Carroll Wright's groundbreaking study of 1886–87, the report condemned without qualification all variants of prison labor contracting and endorsed New York's prison labor law as a model for the nation.[136] In a chapter entitled "The Convict-Labor Problem," the Commissioners wrote that prison labor "is a subject linked in the great chain of circumstances called the 'labor question.'" The linkage, they implied, was fair competition: "Competition with free labor exists and has been and can be made severe by the use of [contracting and public-account] methods now in vogue." Underselling on even a small scale, they argued, badly affected the entire market. Like the Supreme Court of New York, the Commissioners did not dispute that the decades-old practice of imprisoning convicted offenders and putting them to hard labor served the interests of justice and of policy; prisoners ought to work so that they might support themselves and be rendered obedient and tractable while in prison and industrious and useful members of society upon release. But such work ought not to be undertaken with the primary aim of profit and ought to be reserved to the state. In words that echoed those of New York's Prison Commissioners, the Commission argued that the state had both a right and a responsibility to take charge of its own convicts: Contracting amounted to a shirking of that responsibility. The Commission concluded that competition with free labor could be substantially reduced, though not eradicated altogether, while at the same time prisoners were put to work. In this regard, New York offered a way forward.[137] (The Commissioners also recommended that Congress apply what they described as the noncompetitive theory of convict labor and interdict the interstate commerce in prisonmade goods. This amounted to an implicit endorsement of the AFL's call for federal legislation protecting states that had banned

---

[136] In 1898, Congress provided for the establishment of an Industrial Commission, charging it with the tasks of investigating the nation's manufacturing and agricultural sectors and subsequently recommending legislation that would "harmonize conflicting interests" and be "equitable to the laborer, the employer, the producer, and the consumer." U.S. Government. Industrial Commission. Report on Prison Labor, 56th Congress, House of Representatives (Washington, DC: Government Printers, 1900), 5. Modeled on the English Labor Commission, the Industrial Commission's mandate was to investigate a range of questions, including immigration, labor, agriculture, manufacturing, and convict labor, and to recommend the passage of federal legislation as well as uniform laws at the state level. Its members (Senators, Representatives, and Presidential appointees), spent two years exhaustively researching the state of American industry and agriculture and considered the convict labor question serious enough to devote one entire volume of its findings to that subject, as well as dozens of pages in the separate volumes on *Manufactures* and *General Business*. (In endorsing New York's law, they added a proviso, drawn from Pennsylvania's penal law, that prisoners were not to work any labor-saving machines, bar those powered by foot or hand. Ibid, 15).

[137] U.S. Government. Industrial Commission. Report on Prison Labor, 56th Congress, House of Representatives (Washington, DC: Government Printers, 1900), 7.

contracting from the indirect competition caused by the importation of prisonmade goods from other states).[138] The apparent success in New York, and organized labor's ongoing championing of the New York system, induced lawmakers and prison administrators desperate for a solution to their own prison labor problem to adopt the system. In the decade or so after 1902, five states formally adopted a New York-style state-use system (Missouri, Ohio, Wyoming, and California, and New Jersey [the last two, at the instigation of governors Hiram Johnson and Woodrow Wilson, respectively]).[139] Others, such as Massachusetts and Pennsylvania, gradually moved to state-use. Some twenty-one other states provided for exclusive state control of prison *production*, and another eight states made government the sole consumer of prisonmade goods.[140] In only four states did private contractors retain sole control of the industries of the state prisons (Vermont, Connecticut, Delaware, and Maryland).[141] County

---

[138] Ibid, 15.

[139] The formal abolition or restriction of contracting took place several years before actual abolition. Ohio introduced a limited form of state-use by 1908 and gradually extended the system across all its penal institutions. James A Leonard, "Reformatory Discipline and Industries," *Proceedings of the National Conference of Charities and Correction*, 1898, 191–8. California moved very slowly and unevenly to enforce its abolition law. That state's 1876 constitution had mandated the termination of all prison labor contracts by 1882 and forbidden the entry of prisonmade goods onto the market. Yet, as Shelly Bookspan notes, the laws were only ever imperfectly enforced: When the state did not buy prisonmade goods, the prisons' Board of Directors sold the goods on the open market; hundreds of prisoners at Folsom still had little or no work; and, contrary to the state Constitution, Chinese prisoners were being put to productive labor in San Quentin's jute bag factory. See Shelley Bookspan, *A Germ of Goodness: The California State Prison System, 1851–1944* (Lincoln & London: University of Nebraska Press, 1991) 39–41; see also Benjamin Justice, "A College of Morals: Educational Reform at San Quentin Prison, 1880–1920," *History of Education Quarterly* 40:3 (Autumn, 2000), 282–3. Acts of 1889, Ch. 264, cited in U.S. Government. Industrial Commission. Report on Prison Labor, 56th Congress, House of Representatives (Washington, DC: Government Printers, 1900), 142. In the mid-1890s, Michigan was putting the majority of prisoners to work on contract, state-account, and piece-price plans, but under these conditions, one Warden complained in 1894, there was enough labor for only 600 of the 850 prisoners. The contractors worked 150 men for a half day every second day, while "(i)n trying to carry on any industries on state account we find a difficulty in employing all the labor and in selling the product we manufacture." Warden Chamberlain, *Proceedings of the Annual Congress of the National Prison Association of the United States*, 1894. Chamberlain reported the following year that the Michigan prisoners preferred working on contract, rather than state account, as they received a portion of their earnings under the former. *Proceedings of the Annual Congress of the National Prison Association of the United States*, 1895, 72–3. In Indiana, in 1899, the law provided that only half of the convicts could be employed on contract and that all contracts were to expire by October 1, 1904. As that date approached, however, the legislature extended the limit another six years, to October 1, 1910. Reported in *Proceedings of the National Conference of Charities and Correction*, 1903, 50. The Illinois General Assembly voted to abolish contract penal labor in 1894, but the system lingered on, in various forms, until 1931. L. Mara Dodge, "Her Life has Been An Improper One: Women, Crime, and Prisons in Illinois, 1835 to 1933," (Ph.D. diss., University of Illinois at Chicago, 1998), 438.

[140] E. Stagg Whitin, *Penal Servitude* (New York: National Committee on Prison Labor, 1912), 7.

[141] The Maryland legislature passed a law banning contract penal labor in 1888, following organized labor's campaign against the system, and provided for a state-account system;

penitentiaries registered a similar shift: Private concerns controlled penal industries in the penitentiaries of only five states; county government and private contractors shared prison production in the penitentiaries of just eighteen states.[142] By 1923, fifty-five percent of all prisoners working in productive labor were working under a New York-style, exclusively state-use system;[143] that percentage steadily inclined through the 1920s and, by 1935, almost all prisoners engaged in productive labor were employed under some version or other of state-use, and none worked under lease.[144] The national political parties, meanwhile, had also adopted state-use in their electoral platforms. In 1912, Theodore Roosevelt and his Progressive Party included in the official party platform "the abolition of the convict [contract] labor system; substituting a system of production for governmental consumption only."[145]

It was with some justification, then, that the Prison Commissioners and Superintendents who dispatched the Sing Sing scale-model to the Paris Exposition in 1900 offered their exhibit as positive proof of the Empire State's leadership in the arena of reform. By all accounts, New York had successfully made the preliminary transition to an exclusive state-use system of imprisonment; New York administrators had reinvented the means, ends, and scope of state use; in the course of trying to solve the prison labor problem, they had laid the groundwork for what one observer described as a system for "the utilization of the human energy stored up in the prisons of the state."[146] Labor leaders, a growing number of Northern penologists, federal investigators, and even New York's rivals in penal reform now held up the New York system as a model solution to the vexing prison labor problem.

At the same time, however, prisons consisted not only of electric lighting, administration blocks, industrial machinery, filing cabinets, rulebooks, and obedient subjects. Real flesh-and-blood prisons could not be reconstructed with the same ease and degree of control that the skilled craftsman exercised over his scale-model. Within prison walls congregated a mass of convicts and keepers who, at critical junctures of the nineteenth century, had shown themselves ready and willing to contest efforts to bring about systematic changes in prison life and labor. Equally, beyond the walls, various communities of citizens had proven themselves more than capable of mobilizing to influence their state's system of legal punishment. As convicts, guards, and certain segments of the citizenry immediately sensed, New York's

---

however, Governor Jackson vetoed the bill on the ground that no appropriation was made for funding the establishment of state-account prison industries. Reported in *Proceedings of the National Conference of Charities and Correction*, 1888, 333.

[142] Whitin, *Penal Servitude*, 45–7.

[143] *The Wall Street Journal*, July 17, 1933, 6.

[144] See later, Chapter 10, 460.

[145] Progressive Party platform, adopted at the national convention, Chicago, 1912; quoted in Theodore Roosevelt, "The New Penology," *Annals of the American Academy of Political and Social Science* 46 (Mar. 1913), 4.

[146] *New York Times*, Feb. 15, 1899, 6.

prison reform program carried important implications not only for convicts and keepers, but for New York's political structure, the exercise of the powers of government, and the relations between state and citizenry. For free workers and the leaders of organized labor, the drive to build a state-use system was generally welcome; nonetheless, through the turn of the nineteenth century, the unions continued to monitor and indirectly shape the contents of reform. For others, the various reforms proposed for New York's prisons constituted an assault upon their deeply ingrained sense of what was permissible – and impermissible – in the realm of legal punishment and in the field of governance more generally. Indeed, almost immediately upon beginning their work in the prisons, New York's prison reformers encountered resistance, outspoken opposition, and subterfuge. Far from quickly and successfully recasting the prison system as a perfectly administered and politically stable penal state, the Commission's reforms had set in motion a fresh series of confrontations over the means and ends of legal punishment.

6

Uses of the State: The Dialectics of Penal Reform in Early Progressive New York

> Reform is on the wing, and those in highest authority will undoubtedly see to it that small, inefficient men will be eliminated from the state's service ... thereby giving the wards of the state all the opportunity for reform.
>
> Sing Sing Convict, No. 1500, Editor, *Star of Hope* (1899)

While it has been the convention among historians to use the term "prison reformers" to describe the loose coalition of penologists, social philanthropists, and administrators who undertook the reconstruction of imprisonment in most Northern states between 1896 and 1919, it is more accurate to say that the prisons were reformed as much by convicts, guards, wardens, labor organizers, manufacturers, workingmen, and political leaders as by these so-called reformers. Indeed, along with the usual penologists and prison administrators, these people were the coauthors of the rituals, rules, and routines of the modern American prison.[1] Just like Benjamin Rush, Thomas Eddy, and others who, a century earlier, had met with considerable resistance in their endeavors to realize the strange new punishment of confinement to hard labor, the administrators who undertook to reinvent prisons along state-use lines in the early Progressive Era (c. 1896–1913) encountered stiff criticism and persistent attempts to subvert or modify their reform measures, both within and beyond the prison walls. Inside the prison, the efforts of administrators to erect a new order upon the ruins of the old sparked fresh forms of resistance and a series of confrontations among convicts, guards, wardens, and administrators over the appropriate means and ends of the new penal order. At times demonstrative and violent and, at

---

[1] I use the term, "modern American prison" loosely to denote the institutional arrangements that prevailed in most Northern state prisons and the federal prisons from approximately 1920 through until the early 1960s, and which elaborated and reworked the logic of the state-use system of imprisonment with which New York had experimented between 1895 and 1917. Most Northern (and some Southern) states adhered to some version or other of that system until the early 1960s, at which time prisoner rights movements undertook their own great reform project: rolling back arbitrary, bureaucratic forms of power in the prisons (of precisely the sort that progressives had championed) and enforcing the rule of law in prisons. For a first-rate study of two states outside the industrial belt that improvised some of the same disciplinary techniques and ideological forms as the Northern states in the interwar years, see Ethan Van Blue, "Hard Time in the New Deal: Racial Formation and the Cultures of Punishment in Texas and California in the 1930s," (Ph.D. diss., University of Texas at Austin, 2004).

other times, subtle and discursive, the responses of convicts and guards to administrators' innovations forged a new prison order that both drew on and undermined, the sanitized, "civilized," reformatory penal system provided for in law and policy. Outside the prison, meanwhile, workers, the political machines, voters, and, to some degree, industry, exercised various degrees of influence over the implementation of the reforms.

Despite the high walls of the prison and the persistence of laws mandating the separation of the convict from society, prisoners, guards, and administrators by no means confronted one another in a social or political vacuum. Just as in the past, when legal punishment had become embroiled in controversy in times of massive structural change and deep social conflict (for example, during the decline of the agrarian world, the rise of large-scale, industrial capitalism, and following the overthrow of chattel slavery), the prison was a critical referent, and even a lightning rod, in the much larger debates taking place around America over the meaning of a just economy and society, and the proper means and ends of government. These debates sprang forth from what Alan Trachtenberg has described as the colossal historical forces that were unleashed by an ascendant corporate capitalism between 1880 and 1910. Much as the collective work of Daniel T. Rodgers, Robert Johnston, and other recent revitalizers of Progressive Era historiography has revealed, a wide cross-section of American society, including farmers, industrial workers, cosmopolitan philanthropists, members of a rapidly expanding middle class, and small business owners, saw in the advent of an industrial, free market society varying measures of danger and opportunity.[2] In trade union halls, club rooms, universities, taverns, international congresses, boardrooms, churches, temples, and factories, they debated the merits and problems of a society, the combined cultural, organizational, and material capital of which, in theory, enabled breathtaking advances toward the collective improvement of American (and even global) society, but which was also increasingly dominated by "the trusts" and subject to deep cyclical depressions, a creeping commodification of everyday life, structural poverty, and large-scale, frequently violent, industrial conflict.

The ensuing discourse touched upon a wide range of questions, including the fate of the new immigrants who were settling in the larger cities, provisions for public health and schooling, poverty among small farmers, and relations between labor and business; but front and center in these discussions remained the question of the meaning, methods, and duties of democratic government in the face of the powerful new social forces at work in American society. For a growing mass of professionals, managers,

---

[2] Daniel T. Rodgers, *Atlantic Crossings: Social Politics in a Progressive Age* (Cambridge, Massachusetts: Belknap/Harvard, 1998); Robert D. Johnston, *The Radical Middle Class: Populist Democracy and the Question of Capitalism in Progressive Era Portland, Oregon* (Princeton, NJ: Princeton University Press, 2003); Michael McGerr, *A Fierce Discontent: The Rise And Fall of the Progressive Movement in America, 1870–1920* (New York: Free Press, 2003); and Alan Dawley, *Changing the World: American Progressives in War and Revolution* (Princeton, NJ: Princeton University Press, 2003).

social philanthropists, and the college-educated, the proposition (advanced chiefly by American economists trained in Germany)[3] that state agencies should be staffed by trained experts and subject to civil service rules resonated as a potentially fruitful means by which government might "rationally" and "efficiently" generate knowledge concerning certain social problems, recommend policy, and distribute and manage resources. Members of the reform wing of the Republican party, and a small but growing independent cadre of well-heeled Northern Democrats, increasingly argued that such bodies marshaled and effectively deployed the necessary resources with which to carry out the will of the legislature; rational state bureaucracies, they asserted, would empower the people and perfect democratic government. Upon their initiative, a number of states, including New York, and the federal government established investigative and advisory commissions (including the New York State Prison Commission, in 1895) to this end, and gave these bodies broad powers. However, the decision, by a growing number of state and local governments, to delegate the use of collective resources and the powers of government to expert, nonlegislative bodies struck many citizens, and the champions of machine patronage, as inherently undemocratic. In particular, those who supported the older, patronage method of raising votes and dispensing public resources took issue with the advocates of civil service reform and progressive state-craft of the sort that promoted the values of efficiency and administration by duly trained experts in government. In many parts of country, they resolved to defeat such measures.

In New York, as in most other industrial states, prisons were central to these larger turn-of-the-century debates over democratic governance as objects, sites, and ultimately, instruments of struggle. As the central authorities pursued state-use, people on both sides of the walls struggled to define and realize the appropriate uses of the state. The struggle unfolded along two different, intersecting, axes. Prisoners, many of whom were cognizant that both legal punishment and ideas about the state and political economy, were undergoing a fundamental reconfiguration, began to forge a series of tactics by which to press bureaucrats, wardens, guards, and, eventually, voters to improve food, eliminate the use of the whip, baton, and dark cell, and grant convicts greater liberty of the person. At the same time, the efforts of the Prison Commission and State Prisons Superintendent to set up the state-use system and implement new bureaucratic ways of organizing prisons and prisoners (described in the previous chapter) repeatedly came up against the local, more personal power relations and patronage structures that had more or less dominated New York politics – and prison administration – since the mid-nineteenth century. Machine "bosses" and others committed to the distinctive "state of courts and parties" (as Stephen Skowronek has described it)[4] that had thrived on American soil through much of the

---

[3] Rodgers, *Atlantic Crossings*, 110.
[4] Stephen Skowronek, *Building a New American State: The Expansion of National Administrative Capacities, 1877–1920* (New York: Cambridge University Press, 1982).

nineteenth century, were ill-disposed to the rational, bureaucratic state that middle-class progressives increasingly demanded. Between these two axes of struggle, the prison (and the larger penal state of which it was a part) became an intensely contested institution in the early Progressive Era; in the course of this extended period of contestation, the Commission's great reform initiatives would be abridged and transformed.

Rather than narrating this history as the story either of the failure of early progressive prison reform or of the defeat of idealistic progressive reforms by the cold, hard imperatives of prison administration, the present chapter explores the series of power struggles that the drive for reform set in motion. It also fleshes out an account of the new prison order that those struggles, over time, engendered. As I argue in the present chapter, the diverse efforts of prisoners, keepers, and wardens to reinvent the relations of everyday prison life, in the wake of the abolition or severe restriction of contractual prison labor, transformed the objective structures, subjective experience, and official doctrines of imprisonment in enduring ways.

A note about New York's place in the larger arena of American penal politics is in order here. The struggles I describe in the following pages occurred on a larger scale and were more widely publicized in New York than in other states; they also unfolded earliest in New York, largely because that state was in the vanguard of the movement to establish a state-use prison system. However, the differences were more those of intensity and timing than of kind. Indeed, as we have seen, the practice and politics of imprisonment had been surprisingly similar among the industrial states for some decades: Prior to 1895, all but one industrial state had run their prisons on one or another variant of the contract system; all had been subject to mounting political pressure to abolish prison labor contracting (and the competition between free and convict labor); and, in the first few years of the 1890s, all had to scale back prison production. Most had proceeded to reconstruct their penal systems according to some version or other of New York's state-use system. Equally, the kind of localized, patronage-based system of prison administration found in the Empire State was by no means peculiar to New York: Rather, it was ubiquitous. In whatever state they proceeded, Prison Commissions intent upon building strong penal bureaucracies confronted the resolute opposition of people who were firmly invested in the patronage system – and who faithfully argued that their system was the true, democratic way of organizing and using government. For their part, as we'll see, prisoners in other states found in many of the reforms a useful resource on which to draw. Indeed, thanks largely to the proliferation of convict newspapers and the promotion of reading and writing in most Northern prisons, New York's well-publicized reforms themselves became an important conceptual resource upon which prisoners around the country drew in their engagement with their own administrators and keepers.

Almost immediately following their first attempts at reform, in 1896 and 1897, members of New York's Prison Commission and Prison Department found themselves in a series of dialogical contests with the very people at whom their reforms were primarily aimed. Convicts appropriated the conceptual reservoir and many of the rhetorical tactics of the reconstructors in an effort to improve their lot as they (and not élite reformers) thought best within the limitations imposed by life in prison. Framing their own demands for change in the very rhetoric of manly reform that the Commissioners and other high level prison administrators had authored, prisoners frequently and loudly announced that reform was on the wing, and challenged the state to actively realize its responsibilities to its penal wards.

Prisoners had an ambiguous relationship to reformist administrators and to their reforms in general. Recognizing that the reworked concept of the state-use prison system could work both for and against them, prisoners resisted certain innovations, subverted some, and wholeheartedly supported others. As the pages of the prison newspaper, *The Star of Hope*, suggest, prisoners generally supported those reforms that they believed would improve many of the daily conditions of incarceration: For example, many took advantage of liberalized rules of religious worship, which made attendance at services voluntary and added Jewish and Catholic services to the traditional Protestant ones. Most critically, with the liberalization of writing and reading privileges, literate convicts forged an intramural discourse about the nature of crime and the rights and duties of convicts and the state. Perhaps more than anything else, the advent of literacy among the majority of convicts and convicts' immediate embrace of reading and writing privileges changed the workings of discipline in the prison and helped inaugurate a new relationship between the state and the convict.

Whereas only ten percent of New York's state prisoners could read or write in the 1840s, by 1903, approximately eighty percent of the convict population could either read or write.[5] Prisoners immediately took advantage of the liberalized rules regulating reading. After 1896 and through the 1900s, Sing Sing convicts borrowed approximately a thousand books from their newly refurbished library every week. There is no way of knowing which or how many prisoners borrowed books, but it is evident that they were reading books, journals, and magazines on a wide range of subjects, including philosophy, history, and current events (such as the Spanish-American War).[6] Prisoners who had once relied upon incoming inmates, the contractor's foremen, and the prison authorities for news of the world were now able to gain knowledge directly (and legitimately) through the refurbished prison library.[7] Perhaps unsurprisingly, the expansion of libraries soon sparked debate among penologists over the appropriateness of certain books and newspapers for a prison readership: For example, the Auburn and Sing Sing

---

[5] In 1903, the Commissioners reported that 1,057 of Sing Sing's 1,300-odd prisoners could either read or write. New York State Commission of Prisons, *Annual Report*, (1903).

[6] To my knowledge, none of the catalogues from this period has survived.

[7] In 1846, Sing Sing prisoners were allowed two visits per year; in the 1880s, they were allowed one every two months. *Sing Sing Prison: Its History, Purpose, Makeup, and Program* (Albany: New York State Department of Correction, 1958).

prison libraries were prohibited from subscribing to socialist publications (and, after 1905, particularly those of the newly-formed Industrial Workers of the World).

Convicts who could write also took advantage of liberalized letter-writing rules to communicate with family and friends on the outside. In the late 1890s, letter-writing privileges were extended and convicts could write their monthly letter as well as special letters to officials. Under this system, Sing Sing's 1,400-odd convicts were writing more than 1,500 letters per month by the early 1910s. Expanded libraries and literacy also helped diminish the isolation of the majority of prisoners not only from the world, but from each other; for the first time in American state prisons, conditions existed for the creation of a discursive community among convicts. The publication of the convict newspaper, the *Star of Hope* (the first issue of which rolled off the press in 1899), was critical in the formation of this discursive community: Every convict in the State was given a copy of this biweekly paper, and although there is nothing to indicate what proportion of convicts contributed to the paper, many of the sections were written by convicts. The editor received a steady flow of contributions from the convicts. In its second year of publication, the editor received 1,384 contributions (April 1900-April 1901), and he published all but 242 of them.[8]

The *Star* had four separate constituencies of readers and writers – penal bureaucrats, convicts, wardens, and civilian penologists – and each mobilized the newspaper to its own ends. As noted earlier, administrators considered the introduction of the newspaper a humane reform: In theory it would not only engage the convicts of Sing Sing's often-idle print shop in productive labor, but promote convict literacy in the service of rehabilitation to manly citizenship. It also had important administrative implications, chiefly as a useful medium through which authorities could communicate with convicts *en masse*, but also as a way of advertising the Empire State's progressive penal system to the world. In practice, these objectives were realized to some degree: Warden Sage and subsequent wardens frequently used it as a forum to explain changes in the rules, and the convicts of the print shop were kept in relatively steady employment.

From the beginning, however, the *Star of Hope* was something more than simply a sign and tool of administrators' top-down reform effort: It educated convicts about their legal status as well as about contemporary criminology, penology, and reform initiatives, and legitimized a certain kind of debate and dissent among convicts about questions of crime and punishment and their own fate as convicts. Many of the newspaper's commentaries explained and analyzed current penal legislation and contemporary criminological and penological theory. In particular, the convicts devoted space to debunking the "born criminal" theories of the Italian criminologist, Cesare Lombroso (described in the first issue as "the new Caesar who rules Rome"), Max Nordau, and Henry Boies, and arguing in favor of the sociological proposition

[8] *Star of Hope*, 3:1 (Apr. 20, 1901), 1.

that crime was the product of environment.[9] As prisoner #2300 put it: "Although I cannot claim to know as much about some things as Professor Lombroso, yet from an intimate knowledge of the professional criminal, it seems to me that the theories emanating from his 'giant intellect' are simply fine spun nonsense." Asserting that criminals were created by the environment in which they lived, the convict proceeded to point out that law-abiding Virginians were descended from Seven Dials harlots and Newgate thieves, Louisianans from Parisian "female prisoners," and Australians from convicts.[10] As the convict–contributors to the *Star* were probably well aware, Lombrosian theories of congenital criminality provided a rationale for the *permanent* incarceration of all convicts: If criminality could not be cured or treated, then the state would have no choice but to sequester permanently its criminals, and programs aimed at the humane amelioration of prison conditions in the name of rehabilitation would be endangered. Consequently, convicts (and some élite prison reformers) criticized such theories repeatedly and vociferously.

The *Star* also carried extensive commentary on parole law and other legal developments of concern to the convicts. These articles effectively provoked convicts to become conscious of themselves as the subjects of an

---

9 Cesare Lombroso, Max Nordau, and Henry Boies all subscribed to the theory that criminals were a distinct biological class of atavistic human beings who had either failed or ceased to evolve along with the law-abiding people of Northern European descent. These theorists wrote of criminality with a vocabulary that closely resembled that of biological race theory: Lombroso's well-known study of male convicts (*L'homme Criminel*, 1887; full citation given later in this note) implied a distinction between two classes of people he described as "criminals" and "the white race," respectively: "(N)early all the different kinds of sensibility, tactile, olfactory, and of the taste, are obtuse in the criminal.... Their physical insensibility recalls quite forcibly that of savage peoples, who can face, in the initiations to puberty, tortures which a man of the white race could never endure" (quoted in David Arthur Jones, *History of Criminology: A Philosophical Perspective* [Westport, Connecticut: Greenwood Press, 1986], fn. 127). Boies wrote in 1893 that it is "established beyond controversy... that criminals and paupers, both, are degenerates, the imperfect, knotty, knurly, worm-eaten, half-rotten fruit of the race" (quoted in Lawrence M. Friedman, *Crime and Punishment in American History* [New York: Basic Books, 1993], 142). Both criminologists asserted that these characteristics were biologically inherent. Robert A. Nye makes the argument that in France, the discourse of degenerative criminality arose from and in turn sustained the élite's fear of national decline in the wake of the French defeat in the war with Prussia. Nye, *Crime, Madness, and Politics in Modern France: the Medical Concept of National Decline* (Princeton, NJ: Princeton University Press). For an insightful and wide-ranging study of this and related discourses of degeneration in the European context, see Daniel M. Pick, *Faces of Degeneration: a European Disorder, c.1848–c.1918* (Cambridge and New York: Cambridge University Press, 1989). See also Cesare Lombroso, *L'homme Criminel; Étude Anthropologique et Médico-legale* (Paris: F. Alcan, 1887); Lombroso, *Crime, Its Causes, and Remedies* (Boston: Little, Brown, and Company, 1911); Lombroso and Guglielmo Ferrero, *The Female Offender* (Littleton, Colorado: 1980 [1895]). Max Nordau, *Degeneration* (Lincoln: University of Nebraska Press, 1993 [1895]). Henry Martyn Boies, *Prisoners and Paupers: a Study in the Increase of Criminals and the Public Burden of Pauperism in the United States; the Causes and the Remedies* (New York: Putnam, 1893); Boies, *The Science of Penology: the Defense of Society Against Crime* (London and New York: G. P. Putnam's, 1901).

10 *Star of Hope* 1:2 (May 1899), 5.

administrative state and educated them about how changes in the law might affect them. The *Star's* convict readers made it clear that they wanted as much information as possible on pending legal and administrative reforms. Following an editorial on the new parole law, convicts began writing letters to the editor, replete with questions and opinions about suggested innovations. In representing legal and criminological debates and answering convicts' questions, the *Star* helped to bring its prisoner readership into consciousness about progressive reform and their legal rights *viz. a viz.* the state.[11] (By the same stroke of the pen, however, the editor [Sing Sing prisoner number 1500] was careful to follow the implicit directive of the Superintendent of prisons and refrain from directly criticizing penal laws or court decisions in the pages of his paper).[12] The newspaper also helped make convicts aware that they were incarcerated, not in a single, semi-autonomous prison in which the warden had sole authority, but in an integrated, bureaucratic statewide penal system that was subject not only to the local authority of wardens, but to the authority of central bureaucrats as well as courts of law. Both the implicit and explicit content of the newspaper fostered this awareness: In its second year of publication, the *Star of Hope* contained separate reports written by prisoners at Auburn, Clinton, Napanoch, and the Women's Prison at Auburn with news about those institutions; it also began to publish articles from other prison newspapers around the nation as well as occasional reports on foreign prisons. The newspaper even facilitated the dissemination and standardization of the distinctive prison lexicon that nineteenth-century prisoners had created, and the distinctive genre of prison humor, throughout the state prisons: The first issue carried a guide to prisoner slang, written by Sing Sing prisoner #1535, who intuitively grasped the concept that language is a vessel of culture and a strategy of survival in prison. He wrote:

> (A)lthough our language may be corrupted and our vocabulary twisted by these scentless roses, culled from some dead or foreign living language, still there are words we do understand and they inspire hope, give expression to the thought that a respectable existence is possible, even after prison, and give force to the sentiment of the poet who wrote that "No state was ever lost that once we've seen; We always may be what we might have been."[13]

Another convict columnist, bringing news of changes at Sing Sing to his convict readers, playfully referred to Sing Sing as a hotel currently undergoing various improvements for the comfort of those who are permanent residents of the season. Among these was the new guardhouse, described as the "Hotel á la Francaise" (sic): "Incidentally," he warned, "we might say, for fear that some of our residents will entertain an error, and be brought

---

[11] See, for example, *Star of Hope* 1:1 (April 1899), 1:2 (May 1899), 440; 3:1 (April 1901), 5–6.

[12] *Star of Hope* 1:15 (November 1899), 8.

[13] *Star of Hope* 1:2 (May 1899), 5. The glossary included the following: term: a bit; thief: grafter; coffee: bootleg; tea: hops; easy work: graft; letter: stiff; a man mentally deranged: bug; guard: screw; inmate: bloke; search: frisk; complainant: copper; doctor: croke.

into subjection by accidentally dropping into the café, that our officers are solely the patrons. No ménu (sic) provided for the general public."[14]

Columns such as these helped foster a coherent, if censored and self-censoring, discursive community of convicts that was transmural in character; furthermore, it incited convicts to think of themselves as members of a distinct group that was national, even international, in nature and as people whose status and fates were linked. Perhaps most critically, the *Star* provided convicts with a language and a forum in which they could press their own demands for penal reforms – both the far-reaching and more mundane. The "Open Parliament" section became a forum for a host of minor complaints about Sing Sing's rules and conditions. One convict complained about the new rule that permitted convicts to play their musical instruments for a few hours in their cells at night before the two bells signaled a return to silence: One neighbor, he lamented, had been "after that 'Bowery Girl'" for months, while another was being "persistent in his efforts to be 'Put Off at Buffalo.'" The humorous tone of this convict's letter was repeated in many of the columns and editorials, and was one tactic by which convicts presented their complaints in such a way that affirmed the authority of the warden while pressing him to take action on their behalf. The "Rumors" column in particular made dozens of cryptic and less cryptic criticisms about the mundane aspects of prison life. At one point, the columnist noted that it had been whispered about the dilapidated grounds of Sing Sing that "a number of our yard buildings are not modern."

The tactic of humor was very likely born of strict censorship rules, both self-imposed by the convicts and enforced by prison administrators, which made direct criticism of prison administrators both unwise and subject to being struck from the paper. Although there are no surviving records of the process by which the *Star of Hope* was edited (apart from #1500's autobiography, which he wrote while still incarcerated and subject to the rules of censorship),[15] it seems probable that prison administrators ensured that the editor would be a "responsible" convict who would publish editorials that were sympathetic to their management of the prison. When an editor did engage in direct criticism, as the *Sing Sing Bulletin* editor Charles Chapin (former editor of the *New York World*, who was convicted of murder and sentenced to life at Sing Sing in 1918) did in the early 1920s, publication was suspended.[16] Administrators also headed off rigorous criticism by demanding that all correspondents identify themselves by name and convict

[14] *Star of Hope* 1:1 (April 1899).

[15] #1500, *Life in Sing Sing* (Indianapolis: The Bobbs-Merrill Company, 1904).

[16] The *Sing Sing Bulletin* succeeded the S*tar-Bulletin*, (which resulted from the 1918 fusion of the Mutual Welfare League's *Bulletin* and the original *Star of Hope*. Much to the chagrin of New York's penal administrators, Chapin turned the *Sing Sing Bulletin* into an advocate for prisoner rights, including the convict wage movement. Lewis E. Lawes, *Twenty Thousand Years in Sing Sing* (New York: Ray Long and Richard Smith, 1932), 223–35. See also Chapin's account of his time in Sing Sing, *Charles Chapin's Story: Written in Sing Sing Prison* (New York: G. P. Putnam's Sons, 1920), and James McGrath Morris, *The Rose Man of Sing Sing: A True Tale*

number: What was standard practice in civilian newspapers – the act of identifying oneself – undoubtedly had a far more inhibitory effect on men and
women subject to incarceration.

Humorous provocation was one technique of criticism (as well as a means
of building solidarity in the face of adversity) that escaped censorship.
Another was the practice by which editors and columnists deployed the
new ideals of bureaucratic reform in the service of pursuing the amelioration of certain prison conditions. This strategy, which became commonplace
in prisoner newspapers in the 1900s, included the tactics of mirroring the
rhetoric of efficiency and manliness back on the circular bureaucracy, and
citing leading penologists and circular bureaucrats in support of certain
requests.[17] In the first issue of the *Star*, and in almost every subsequent
one, the editor not only affirmed the wisdom of the Commissioners, but
condemned guard brutality in terms that were far bolder than those of
the Commissioners. He began by commending the recent improvements in
the prison library, sanitation, food, and religious services. Repeating verbatim the sentiment of the Commissioners on the question of the prisoner's
manliness, he affirmed their position that the lowest type of human being
always has left a spark of manhood, before launching into a critique of
guard brutality: "The time has passed when unsympathetic officials should
be given opportunity to swing their batons promiscuously over those under
the state's care, merely to gratify their own personal ambition by exercising
undue authority." Deploying the bureaucracy's rhetoric of efficiency and
humane penology once more, he went on to embrace the Commissioners'
reforms and concluded by asserting that it was consistent with the Commissioners' logic that guards who behaved brutally be dismissed.[18]

Another, closely related tactic was that of holding state government to
its agents' aspirations that the Empire State be the most advanced in the
nation, if not the world: "Advancement" being a relative concept in this
case, the convict contributors to the *Star* began to report on developments
in other states' prison systems as a means to prod administrators into action.
In 1899, for example, convict #1122 reported that since 1888, the convicts
at the prison in Stillwater, Minnesota, had been organizing a Chautauqua
Literary and Scientific Circle. The Circle had six classes of six students, each
of whom would read, write, deliver, and debate papers, essays, and fiction.
Every student delivered a paper every ten weeks, and every three months,

of Life, Murder, and Redemption in the Age of Yellow Journalism (New York: Fordham University Press, 2003), 103.
[17] *Star of Hope* 1:2 (May 1899), 3–4.
[18] The editor may well have been implicating warden Sage in his statements, for in the same issue of the *Star of Hope*, Sage announced his resignation from the wardenship in such a way as to suggest that he himself may have been one of the "small, inefficient men" at whom the prisoner editor directed his ire. While maintaining he had tried to make Sing Sing a modern and model prison, Sage elliptically noted that he was nonetheless compelled to "yield to the logic of events." It was at this point that he stopped just short of apologizing to the prisoners for any injustices he may have perpetrated against prisoners. *Star of Hope* 1:2 (May 1899), 3.

the thirty-six members were allowed to convene to present poetry, music, and recitations. In recommending that Sing Sing immediately set up such a circle, as well as trades and general education classes, the author quoted directly from the State Prison Commissioners' Report: "There is now no reason why trades classes should not be established at SS [Sing Sing] and education be made compulsory and a general reformatory treatment put in operation."[19]

In a constant flow of articles such as these, as well as a slew of letters to officials, the convict contributors to New York's first prison newspaper set in motion a tactic that successive generations of convicts would repeatedly deploy.[20] The seminal fiction of the reworked doctrines of state-use – that the advanced state was one that guaranteed the humane treatment of its convicts, while the "barbaric" state was that which undernourished, brutalized, and drove them like slaves – carried with it the potentially radical implication that incarceration *per se* was an inherent contravention of inalienable human rights. Whether or not convicts fully grasped this potential, many of them recognized that the nascent penal state was deeply invested in portraying itself as humane, and that consequently it was possible to effect change in the prison system by drawing attention to various forms of inhumanity inflicted in the state's prisons. Subsequently, convicts entered into an ongoing struggle with guards, bureaucrats, and legislators to define the meaning of "inhumane." The newspaper was one vessel that was peculiarly well-suited to this purpose; it took its place alongside the older practices of riot and food strike as a means of expression.

The creation of a discursive community of convicts who could not only read and write but were also conversant with criminology and state penal law, in turn, provoked a response from guards, wardens, and central administrators. They quickly grasped that the literate and knowledgeable prisoner who was engaged in a statewide discussion with other convicts was a different kind of subject from the civilly dead, hard-toiling convict of the old contract-labor–based prison system. As they appear to have comprehended, the prisoners' embrace of reading and writing privileges fostered a new means by which convicts could criticize or otherwise seek to influence reform, and by which they could organize collectively to these ends. Literate prisoners could write about the prison and its abuses; there was the possibility that they

---

[19] *Star of Hope* 1:2 (May 1899), 3.

[20] Although none of their correspondence has survived (as far as is known), many convicts began to write up their ideas for reform and send them to the Superintendent of Prisons (and presumably the Commissioners as well) in the late 1890s. Reported in the *Star of Hope* 1:2 (May 1899), 7. This was a precursor of more sustained efforts on the part of convicts to influence both the enactment and interpretation of penal legislation. In 1915, for example, Sing Sing and Auburn convicts retained an attorney and took the Superintendent of Prisons to court for having miscalculated the duration of sentences under new parole law (see Chapter 6). Beginning in the 1920s, small numbers of convicts educated themselves in law and undertook individual legal actions on behalf of their release (see Chapter 7). This process of legal education and action was critical to the transformation of convicts' juridical status from aliens to wards of the state who possessed certain rights.

were in communication with civilians about crime; and there was substantial evidence that convicts were also smuggling notes to each other, which constituted a breach of the tenacious, if ailing, rule of silence.[21] The most obvious and immediate response of prison administrators was their establishment of new rules around the activity of reading and writing. Beginning around 1900, prisoners were explicitly prohibited from writing to, or receiving mail from, another prisoner or an ex-prisoner. Letters to prisoners containing what authorities referred to as "criminal news" were outlawed, and all correspondence was monitored by an official "Correspondence Censor" (who was to work with the aid of a staff of three convicts). Moreover, keepers were to strictly monitor the supply of paper (for writing): At Auburn in the early 1900s, prisoners were assigned a set number of blank pages each month for letter writing and borrowing another convicts' was prohibited. The severity of the punishment for an offense suggests the weight attached to the effective regulation of writing: Those who borrowed or otherwise procured extra paper illicitly were locked up in the dark cell for a few days.

A much less obvious, but arguably more portentous response to prisoners' newfound ability to critique and report on developments in the prisons, was the administrators' performance of accountability. Beginning in the late 1890s and continuing through the 1900s, wardens and bureaucrats from the Prison Commission and Prisons Department went to great lengths to explain their reforms to convicts and to respond to their criticism. In part, this was born of the theoretical tenets of their penology, which posited that in order to make men of convicts, convicts must be reasoned with, but it was reinforced and made more urgent by convicts' practical efforts (most conspicuously in the pages of the *Star of Hope* but also in special letters to officials) to hold the penal state to its chief administrators' word. If convicts were to be treated as men, their ideas were to be taken seriously: Prison administrators became ensnared in their own logic. For the first time in prison history, wardens and bureaucrats began to explain and justify their actions to the convicts.

At first this occurred in the pages of the *Star of Hope*, which afforded the most direct access to the mass of convicts. In 1899, for example, warden Sage felt obliged to respond to convicts' complaints about a modification to the labor classification system, which displaced many convicts from their old work companies: Explaining that he had no control over the changes, the warden nonetheless proceeded to try to appease the prisoners by promising to find work for the excluded convicts as soon as possible.[22] On another occasion, the warden went so far as to express regret over some of his disciplinary decisions. In an almost farcical inversion of the principles of

---

[21] As the rule of silence was increasingly undermined at Auburn, through the passing of notes, talking, and singing, the guards disciplined a number of prisoners for note smuggling. (Others were punished for singing, whistling, and talking). See Auburn Punishment Ledgers, Vols. 1–2 (Oct. 7, 1870–Jan. 16, 1904). NYSA (RDCS) Auburn Correctional Facility, Inmate Punishment Ledger, 1872(1870)–1941.

[22] *Star of Hope* 1:1 (April 1899), 7.

the emergent new penology, he pleaded in the pages of the *Star* that he (too) was human and, therefore, fallible: "It is reasonable to assume that I have sometimes erred, for I am human. If I have done anyone an injustice, I sincerely regret it." In subsequent years, this performace of accountability was extended to large, often celebratory gatherings of convicts and administrators at which the warden, Commissioners, Superintendent, and even the Governor of New York went to great lengths to impress upon the convicts that the state was truly responsive to their plight (See Chapters 8 and 9). That the officials' apparent accountability was staged and at times flimsily disingenuous mattered little: In perpetuating and re-affirming the fiction of humane, accountable treatment of convicts, convicts repeatedly sought to hold the statesmen to their word; the dialogue of power continued and the relations of imprisonment underwent subtle changes along the way.

The fate of other prison reform initiatives followed much the same plotline. Prisoners resisted certain innovations in the management of the prison, most notably the creation of the classification system and the new techniques of information gathering that arose alongside it. Where, traditionally, convicts had been assigned to the prison's various labor companies according to the warden's whim and their performance as laborers, the new classification system assigned convicts on the basis of their conviction records. The system worked well for first offenders, who were assigned to the better companies of the First Grade (which also had priority for drawing and craft classes) while it penalized prisoners with two or more convictions who had been doing skilled work in the industries and prison offices prior to the adoption of classification. (The new system required that they be demoted to the Second or Third Grades of labor). As a rule, the convicts preferred laboring in the First Grade companies and, consequently, this reorganization of prison labor caused considerable consternation among some of the displaced prisoners at Sing Sing.[23] Despite the protests of some of the demoted convicts and the warden's promise to try to redress the grievance, the new system became further entrenched. Prisoners about to serve second or third sentences responded by concealing their conviction records in large numbers: At Auburn, in one five-month period in 1908, at least thirty prisoners were punished for having lied about their conviction records upon commitment to Auburn.[24] One new prisoner refused to answer the clerk altogether. He was subsequently held in the dark cell for an undetermined number of days and, soon after that, transferred to the Third Grade prison at Clinton. By linking a convict's record to his placement in a work company, the new classification system incited concealment, while the weakness and inflexibility of the prison's information networks meant that there was a reasonable

---

[23] *Star of Hope* 1:1 (April 1899), 7.
[24] Auburn Punishment Ledger, Vol. 3 (June 28, 1902–July 19, 1912). See entries Dec. 5, 1907–May 5, 1908. NYSA (RDCS) Auburn Correctional Facility, Inmate Punishment Ledger, 1872(1870)–1941.

chance that the convict's official record would remain undiscovered, either permanently or for a long period of time.

More than anything else, the convict's tactics of *silence and dissimulation* exposed an obstacle in the way of creating an institutional memory for the state's prisons: To a large degree, and despite the introduction of bertillonage, the intelligence-gathering system was still in large degree dependent on the cooperation of convicts. Although the advent of a state penal bureaucracy had engendered the development of new techniques of collecting, representing, and storing information about prisoners, through the first decade of the twentieth century, prison officials relied upon convicts to provide the information upon which managerial decisions would be made. Although the identification of prisoners had been "objectified," the internal collection of other information about prisoners – and hence the enterprise of constructing case records for each prisoner – involved interviewing every incoming convict. Upon commitment to prison, a clerk asked the prisoner a number of questions relating to his conviction and sentencing, and entered the information volunteered by the prisoner in the admission register. At some point, the prisoners' testimonies were compared to an official record, but without filing technologies, the cross-checking of records proved cumbersome and haphazard.

As bureaucrats discovered the weaknesses of their techniques and the strength of prisoners' will in the early 1900s, they hastened to develop new and more flexible methods of recording, duplicating, and transmitting information about convicts, thereby lessening the bureaucracy's reliance on prisoners' oral testimony. By 1920, most prisoners found they had little to gain (with regard to classification) by lying or withholding the truth about their conviction records. Even so, the project of constructing case records continued to necessitate some form of confession from convicts, particularly once psychological and psychiatric assessments were added in the late 1910s. Silence remained one of the most critical, and most severely punished, acts of insubordination; the refusal of a prisoner to answer the clerk's questions might appear to be an act of no consequence, yet as both administrators and convicts grasped, the fabric of the new penal bureaucracy might be easily unraveled by pulling on the single thread of refusal to cooperate. (There is some evidence to suggest that as late as 1921, at least one of the state prisons had difficulty positively identifying all its prisoners: As Denis Brian recounts, when a Sing Sing prisoner by the name of J. Cohen had completed his sentence and was due for release, warden Lewis E. Lawes reportedly had difficulty figuring out which of the five Sing Sing convicts by that name was the man to be released).[25]

Although historians now have at their disposal a range of archival sources with which to flesh out an account of the convicts' various responses to penal reform and their struggles to negotiate and change everyday life in

---

[25] Denis Brian, *Sing Sing: The Inside Story of a Notorious Prison* (New York: Prometheus Books, 2005), 122.

the prison, the responses of those who were charged with carrying out the reforms – that is, the keepers and various civilian staff – are much more difficult to access. Little is known about the hundreds of men who guarded the prisoners of New York at the turn of the century: Even their names, ages, terms of employment, and residence are mostly absent from the surviving records. The keepers are also more or less absent from the Commissioners' reports for the 1890s and 1900s. (It would not be until the late Progressive Era that penal administrators and élite reformers such as Thomas Mott Osborne and Hastings Hornell Hart would comment in any sustained way about keepers and their role in prison reform; when these reformers did begin to consider the question, it was largely because of a series of scandals that made it clear that many keepers were highly resistant to progressive prison reform and fully capable of sabotaging it).[26] These archival lacunae are mirrored in the absence of autobiographical writings by keepers: Although the reform efforts of the postcontracting period gave tremendous stimulus to prisoner-authored memoirs, essays, and newspaper articles in the 1890s, it appears not to have had the same effect on the keepers. There is no genre of guard writing from this period to match the extensive body of literature penned by convicts.

These methodological difficulties notwithstanding, a few traces of the guards, and of their relations with the Commissioners and other central administrators, have survived from the early Progressive period, chiefly in the reports and recommendations of the Commissioners and Superintendent. As we have seen, these high-ranking prison administrators undertook to make efficient civil servants out of the keepers; they also had to find a way

---

[26] A few penologists argued for guard training in the early 1900s; most notable among these was C. E. Haddox, the spokesman for the National Prison Association's (NPA) Committee on Prison Discipline, who spoke at length about the need to train guards at the NPA's annual conference in 1906: "If convicts are to be gradually educated and turned from crime unto virtue . . . it must be through the agency of officers, themselves disciplined, educated, and schooled in self-control." Guards were to maintain discipline and reform prisoners in part by setting an example. To this end, Maddox suggested that a national training school be set up, and that guards be required to read criminological theory as well as muck-raking literature such as Charles Reade's "It Is Never too Late to Mend." (See *Proceedings of the Annual Congress of the National Prison Association of the United States*, 1906, 268–71). However, there was no sustained discourse about guard training in the United States until the 1910s, and no systematic attempt to set up state guard training schools until the 1930s. The first empathetic analysis of the role of guards was offered in 1922 by Frank Tannenbaum in *Wall Shadows*, when he noted that the keepers were not free men, and that they were brutalized by the prison system into acting sadistically toward prisoners. Ten years later, Tannenbaum added that the guards were "watched by the warden and the principal keeper on one hand and by prisoners, who are always scheming to break the prison rules, on the other. . . . The keeper is caught in a vortex that either tends to make a brute out of him or to make him dishonest." Tannenbaum, *Wall Shadows: A Study in American Prisons* (New York and London: G. P. Putnam and Sons, 1922), and *Osborne of Sing Sing* (Chapel Hill: University of North Carolina Press, 1933), 32. Plans for guard schools were floated in the 1920s, but it was not until the 1930s that New York state guards received any serious training, when the Central Guard School opened for instruction at Wallkill Prison (discussed in Chapter 10).

of working with the keepers to carry their various reforms forward.[27] As a whole, the reports made clear that Lispenard Stewart and others were much quicker to recognize the humanity of prisoners than that of the guards. Middle class and élite reformers typically characterized the guards as brutes of a worse character than the prisoners, and although they did not view the guards' alleged brutishness as somehow inherent, they did tend to characterize these employees as the unsavory dregs of the lowest social classes. The low esteem in which bureaucrats and penologists held guards was echoed in the guards' conditions of work. Although, under law, they were civil servants and employees of the state, guards worked relatively long hours for the times (twelve hours) and earned relatively low wages through the 1890s and 1900s. (Typically, at any one of the prisons, twenty-four guards worked the day shift, and four, the night. They were not unionized, and would not try to unionize until the 1920s).

The records also make clear that the keepers resisted many of the reforms that the Commission and Superintendent sought to implement after 1896. The guards resisted the attempts to de-legitimize certain kinds of corporal punishment (the whip, baton, and stringing up) to make civil servants of them, and to subject them to new forms of surveillance and control. Guards were particularly critical of élite reformers' opposition to the use of certain forms of corporal punishment. In most American prisons during the nineteenth century, as we have seen, guards had tended to rule with baton and whip; they summarily meted out blows for real and imagined transgressions of rules, and reported prisoners to the principal keeper for a host of more severe corporal punishments. In the punishment of more serious transgressions of prison rules, the guards relied heavily on the dark cell, in which convicts were interred for three or more days without light and only one gill of water. As penologists and bureaucrats increasingly criticized the dark cell practice, guards – and some wardens – defended it not only as indispensable to prison order but as a humane form of punishment. Principal keeper Coultry's defense of the dark cell and the cuffing of convicts to walls at Clinton prison was typical: Such discipline, he told investigators, did the prisoners no harm.[28]

The guards resisted attempts to police and subject them to a bureaucratic mode of control; in turn, the Commissioners and Superintendent sought to counter their resistance. In the early days of the reform drive,

[27] I have found little evidence of how guards were recruited, their age, and former occupations (if any). That the New York state legislature enacted laws in 1903 protecting guards who were veterans of the Spanish-American War suggests that a significant number of guards may have been drawn from the armed forces. Georg Rusche and Otto Kirchheimer note that in Europe in the early twentieth century, guards were "recruited from retired noncommissioned officers of the army and navy who have a claim on the state," and that before World War One, prison administrators justified this hiring practice "on the ground that the work was quite simple." Georg Rusche and Otto Kirchheimer, *Punishment and Social Structure* (New York: Columbia University Press, 1939), 156. Laws N.Y. 1893.
[28] Thomas Coultry was known among the Clinton convicts as the "Czar of Russia," and was investigated on a number of occasions on charges of brutality.

wardens and guards of some institutions were less than cooperative with the Prison Commissioners: When investigating Commissioners turned up at the prisons without scheduled appointments in 1895, for example, a number of prison officials barred them from the prison grounds. Once they had gained entry, the Commissioners sometimes experienced difficulty in gathering information about the operations of the prisons, as some prison staff refused to provide relevant documents and give oral reports. Following a number of such incidents, in 1896 it became a misdemeanor punishable by a fine of $100 for any prison or jail officer to bar entrance or refuse to give information to a Commissioner. The same law empowered the Commission to compel witnesses to produce relevant papers and to be examined under oath.[29] The Commission welcomed this law, viewing it as vital to the extension of bureaucratic means of control over the prisons, because it invigorated the element of surprise inherent in unscheduled inspections. Yet, even after its passage, keepers continued to withhold their full cooperation. Exasperated by such stonewalling, the Commissioners sought tougher laws against guards' obstruction of penal administration.[30] The passage of the Moreland Act in 1907 added sharper teeth to the investigative authority of the penal bureaucracy (and to the Executive branch of State government in general). Under this Act, commissioners and officers appointed by the Governor were given wide-ranging (and extrajudicial) powers to investigate the management and affairs of any department, board, bureau, or commission of the state. This included the state prisons and, in principle, investigators were given the authority to subpoena not only employees but prisoners and any books or papers deemed relevant, as well.[31]

The Commissioners' estimation that surprise inspections and the newly legislated authority to subpoena would have an effect on guards and wardens proved, in other respects, correct. Yet the effect was not always the salutary one they desired: Guards, civilian employees, and, upon occasion, wardens simply learned to cover up malfeasance and abuse in a more effective manner. Often, this involved threats of violence against would-be informants, and the internment or isolation of potential informants in punishment cells for the duration of the investigation.[32] Over the next several decades, countless

---

[29] Laws N.Y. 1896, Ch. 430, §7.
[30] New York State Commission of Prisons, *Annual Report* (1900), 8.
[31] Laws N.Y. 1907, Ch. 539. For the history of the investigative commissions appointed under the Moreland Act, see Ernest Henry Breuer, *Moreland Act Investigations in New York: 1907–65* (Albany: University of the State of New York, 1965).
[32] See discussion of this problem in a transcript of an investigation conducted by the New York State Commission of Prisons in 1915. In the Matter of A – B. F – , New York State Prison Commission, transcript of testimony taken at Clinton Prison, Dannemora, New York (June 7, 1915), 67. OFP, MSS64, Box 272, Org. Recs. Note: New York state law requires that prisoners' names not be used until seventy-five years have passed. However, even where the records are more than seventy-five years old, I have erred on the side of caution and used prisoners' names only where the documents are not marked confidential *and* where their names have also appeared in public documents (such as newspapers) in such a way as to suggest explicit or implied consent to being identified publicly. In ambiguous cases, I have

commissions of enquiry ran into silence and subterfuge when trying to investigate alleged abuses in New York's prisons.[33] This was particularly true in the case of investigations into repeated allegations of brutality at Clinton Prison, where the tight-knit community of guards and civilian employees (many of whom were related by blood or marriage) became renowned for losing incriminating evidence upon news of an impending visit by the suit-and-briefcase Commissioners from Albany.[34] Not only did investigators have little luck in eliciting testimony from guards but, recognizing the more proximate power of the keepers, convicts repeatedly proved reluctant to expose abuses.

As certain kinds of corporal punishment became illicit, guards became more careful about the conditions under which it was meted out; specifically, they ensured that there were no witnesses to the punishment. The transcript of one convict's testimony in a 1915 investigation into guard brutality at Clinton illustrates the problem well:

[Commissioner]: Will you tell us with regard to any other mistreatment of other prisoners?
[Prisoner]: There are other men that will be coming in here after me who can tell you.
[Commissioner]: You never saw that (beating)?
[Prisoner]: No, nobody ever sees it but yourself.[35]

The surveillance of prisons and the policing of brutality also gave birth to the familiar tactic of "hiding" those convicts likely to offer up damaging testimony to visiting investigators. The same convict who testified in 1915 to the isolated nature of illicit punishment went on to inform the

erred on the side of caution, substituting initials for names (for example: In the Matter of A – B. F –).

[33] Furthermore, there were a number of instances in which investigators found proof of malfeasance, but nonetheless concluded in their official reports that all was well. Despite accepting evidence that implicated the principal keeper (Thomas Coultry) of Clinton in the beating and death of one prisoner, and evidence of extensive use of restricted diets and isolation as punishment, George Blake concluded: "Clinton Prison seems to be conducted along lines as humane and capable as the conditions permit." Two years later, when the Prison Commissioners heard evidence of beatings, cuffings, and the abuse of tuberculosis patients at Clinton, they concluded that the charges of cruelty were not sustained, except as to the degree of punishment administered. Papers Relating to George Blake's Special Commission to investigate Prisons, Reformatories, and the Office of Superintendent of Prisons, NYSA, Governor's Office Records, Investigation Case Files of Charges and Complaints Against Public Officials and Agencies, 1857–1919, A0531 Box 41; and In the Matter of A – B. F – , New York State Prison Commission, transcript of testimony taken at Clinton Prison, Dannemora, New York (June 7, 1915), 67, OFP, MSS64, Box 272, Org. Recs.

[34] This was generally true with regard to official investigators. Every one of the three special Governor's Commissions, a Senate Commission, and six or more Grand Juries conducting investigations into New York State prisons between 1911 and 1913 ran into these problems, as did the Prison Commissioners' investigation of violence at Clinton in 1915, and Governor Roosevelt's investigation of the 1929 Auburn riots.

[35] In the Matter of A – B. F – , New York State Prison Commission, Transcript of testimony taken at Clinton Prison, Dannemora, New York (June 7, 1915), 91. OFP, MSS64, Box 272, Org. Recs.

Commissioners that when the Blake Commission (a special commission of enquiry appointed under the Moreland Act) had investigated Clinton for several days in 1913, the principal keeper had locked him in a punishment cell for two months, effectively disappearing him and his testimony. Rather than eliminating the corporal punishment of convicts, such treatment became more secretive in the course of this power struggle between guards and investigators; when, in the late Progressive period, the higher penal authorities gave up trying to regulate corporal punishments and outlawed them altogether, the bodily chastisement of prisoners would take on new and bloodier forms.[36]

Even the most rudimentary requirement of a bureaucracy – that there be a clear chain of command, supported by written directives and subject to verification – was frustrated in practice. Although the Commissioners attempted to surveil guards and establish systems for monitoring prison operations and generating and gathering information, they did not develop reliable techniques for communicating orders and policies down the prison hierarchy. In the 1900s, communication between wardens and guards, and guards and prisoners, remained oral, thus forming a fatally weak link in the bureaucratic chain. There were a few isolated attempts by wardens to convey orders to prisoners through the written word: Most notably, the wardens at Sing Sing made use of the prisoner newspaper to reiterate certain rules and to convey information that hitherto, they would have repeated to individual prisoners in a series of personal interviews.[37] But it was not until the 1910s that bureaucrats and wardens first attempted to replace informal oral communication between wardens and guards with systematic, written (and thereby traceable), orders and bulletins.

Upon occasion, the prison wardens, who stood to lose much of their former power under the new bureaucratic scheme of administration, also stymied the efforts of the Commissioners. As has been noted, the Commissioners took steps to restrict the scope of the wardens' authority after 1896: Although the warden retained the authority to hire and dismiss guards, only those guards who had passed civil service requirements could be hired. Similarly, through the 1900s and 1910s, the warden's authority to dismiss guards was increasingly subjected to regulations and laws. In 1909, the Civil Service Laws were amended so as to make it more difficult for wardens to dismiss guards who were veterans of the Spanish-American War: They could be dismissed only on the grounds of incompetence or misconduct and only after the warden had conducted an internal investigation and hearing.[38] Although wardens did, in fact, experience a diminution in their authority

---

[36] Blake Commission.
[37] The *Star of Hope* had a special section, the warden's "Bulletin," for this purpose. Warden Omar V. Sage noted in the first issue that rather than granting personal interviews to a group of disgruntled prisoners who wanted to talk with him (because they had been demoted by the Superintendent of Prisons from the industrial workshops to maintenance duties) he would communicate with them through the pages of the *Star of Hope. Star of Hope* 1:1 (April 1899), 7.
[38] Laws N.Y. 1909, Ch. 15.

to hire and fire staff, they held on to others of the powers that the Com-missioners (and the legislature) had attempted to take away from them. The traditional arrangement by which wardens had controlled the award of prison contracts for food and other necessaries, for example, proved to be tenacious: Despite administrators' attempts to centralize the finances and purchases of the prisons, wardens retained practical control over con-tracts for food and other prison supplies well into the 1910s.[39] (As well as structurally compromising administrators' control of prison management, this arrangement fostered another axis of unchecked influence in prison administration: Prison supply contracts were often extremely lucrative, and local businesses (and even large-scale meatpacking companies as far away as Chicago) frequently held an active interest in the careers of particular wardens. On at least one occasion, after 1900, one such outside business concern attempted to influence the appointment – and dismissal – of New York's prison wardens).[40]

Wardens also acted, in these years, to subvert the new prisoner classifi-cation laws, which, in principle, gave prison bureaucrats the power to dis-tribute prisoners into work companies as they, rather than the warden, saw fit. Under the new classification scheme, wardens stood to lose one of the key disciplinary techniques at their disposal under – the threat and reward of allocation to particular companies – as well as an important part of their formal, discretionary authority. As the pages of the *Star of Hope* suggest, the warden of Sing Sing believed that, at the very least, he had to be seen by the convicts to be responsive to their complaints and requests. During down-turns in the workshops, for example, when prisoners had little work to do, a succession of Sing Sing wardens announced they would "try" to increase employment; wardens also explained and justified their decisions, and those of their superiors, through the medium of the prison newspaper. Wardens' resistance to losing the power of allocation culminated in substantial modi-fications being made to the classification law, such that the Superintendent of Prisons returned to wardens the authority to demote or promote convicts on the basis of their behavior; wardens were thus able to regain control of a crucial tool of discipline – and much of their former authority.

The formal position of state prison warden, and the procedures by which they were hired and fired, also remained beyond the reach of the penal reconstructors. As the Commissioners and Superintendent struggled to rein

---

[39] In 1915, a Senatorial enquiry into the Office of the Superintendent of Prisons recom-mended centralizing this authority in the hands of the Superintendent, on the grounds that ordering supplies in bulk would be more economical. (The New York state hospitals had already changed to this system, whereby the State Board of Charities negotiated food contracts). Critical Statement (on the) Superintendent of State Prisons, 1914–16 (no page numbers), Appraisal Reports of Staffing at State Agencies and Institutions, Confidential Working Papers, New York State Senate Committee on Civil Service, NYSA, Leg. Recs., Box 1.

[40] See, for example, Blake's investigation of Sing Sing in 1913 and the investigation of New York State Senate's Committee on Civil Service, 1914–16.

in the wardens' autocratic authority and submit them to bureaucratic discipline, the authority to appoint and dismiss wardens continued to reside with the Governor. In theory as well as practice, bureaucrats exercised little influence over the appointment of wardens through most of the 1900s. As a position under the exclusive control of the Governor of New York, wardenships remained subject to the spoils system, with the consequence that changes in government helped ensure a high turnover of appointees.[41] Scandals around a particular warden's management of his prison continued to be stirred up by whichever party was in opposition, in order to discredit the government's credibility in general (see subsequent discussion).

The patronage-bound nature of the wardenship, in particular, points to the much greater conflict in which prisons became enmeshed after 1896. The importance of the prison as an institution of patronage linked to the distribution of jobs, money, and votes meant that élite reformers who attempted to integrate the prisons into a single bureaucratic penal state had to negotiate not only with convicts, guards, and wardens, but the leaders of the political machines that had traditionally exercised considerable influence over prison appointments. The Commission-led efforts to put the state prisons on a rational, bureaucratic basis, together with the related civil service reform efforts in various state departments, ran into considerable resistance from both the wing of the Republican party known as the "Platt machine" (after its leader, Senator Thomas C. Platt, a former convict lessee and president of the Tennessee Coal and Iron Company during the convict-lease coalfield wars of 1892)[42] and the powerful Tammany Hall section of the Democratic party. Indeed, on the key question of progressive reform in government, these otherwise mutually antagonistic machines pragmatically forged an informal and, in the eyes of reformers, distinctly unholy, alliance.[43] With

[41] Sing Sing, in particular, was subject to a high turnover of wardens. In the 1870s, six men held the position; some of these wardens lasted for only a year. For most of the following decade, the position was held by one person (A. A. Brush), but the rapid turnover of wardens resumed in the 1890s, when four men held the wardenship between 1890 and 1894. The wardenship stabilized somewhat after 1894 and remained relatively stable through the first decade of the twentieth century, when just three wardens managed Sing Sing with tenures of between four and eight years each. The traditional pattern resumed, however, when, in the 1910s, no fewer than ten men held the position. In 1920, Lewis Edward Lawes was appointed warden, and he held the position for twenty-one years – longer than anyone before or since. There is some evidence to suggest that wardens may have tended to have policing or military backgrounds: Warden John Kennedy was a former New York City policeman, warden Lawes was an army major and former prison guard, and Auburn's Warden Jennings had served in World War One. *Sing Sing Prison: Its History, Purpose, Makeup, and Program* (Albany: New York State Department of Correction, 1958), 23.

[42] Platt served as president of the highly controversial company from 1889 through the coalfield wars of 1892. *New York Times*, Aug. 16, 1892, p. 1. For a discussion of Platt's remarkable skills as a machine politician, see Harold F. Gosnell, "Thomas C. Platt – Political Manager," *Political Science Quarterly* 38:3 (Sep. 1923). 443–69.

[43] There is evidence that, in 1894, for example, Platt and Tammany's Senator David Hill cut a deal by which they traded key appointments on legislative committees; rumors of a Tammany–Platt bargain persisted through the next several years. Reform Republicans

increasing ferocity, after 1894, the machines dedicated themselves to fighting the managerial restructuring of state government. In 1895, members of the Republican machine attempted to thwart the implementation of the constitutional amendment mandating the integration of keepers and other state prison employees into the civil service. Machine lawmakers informally requested of Superintendent Lathrop that he delegate the distribution of positions at Clinton Prison to the local Republicans; when Lathrop refused, on the grounds that the law forbade it, the machine mobilized against him, calling for his resignation and setting in motion a Governor's investigation into the management of each of the three state prisons.[44] In addition, the Commissioners frequently encountered difficulties in securing state monies to pay for the reforms they had recommended, even when the legislature had already voted in favor of the reforms. Occasionally, when monies were appropriated for projects, they were diverted to other prison projects considered to be more pressing, or simply withheld from immediate use.[45] In the early 1910s, chronic underfunding of the prisons would reach crisis proportions, causing near starvation in the prisons.

The forces of bureaucratization encountered other obstacles as well, and not just in the prison proper. The clerical workers appointed to the expanding penal bureaucracy in the state capitol were as ill-disciplined in the ways of bureaucracy as were the guards and wardens. In addition, the prison Commissioners ran into technical difficulties in getting a properly functioning bureaucracy up and running. The Commissioners' early efforts to develop the kind of bureaucratic information technology called for by the state-use system, proceeded in a haphazard fashion. In the 1890s, there were still few means of duplication, short of using a blotter or writing the record out again by hand. For the first twenty years of the twentieth century, the state's record keeping system was a cumbersome and confusing hybrid of both rudimentary and more complex bureaucratic practices. The central Bureau of Identification's records system came under frequent criticism for being incapable of generating fast, accurate information about the prison population. Apart from the Bertillon files, which established the identity of a convict on the basis of bodily measurements and distinguishing marks, the standard bureaucratic techniques of assembling individual convict files, making use of index cards, and vertical filing technologies were still not in regular use as late as 1915.[46]

(most conspicuously, Theodore Roosevelt, who owed his rise in the state Republican party to Platt but then broke with him) often asserted the two machines were linked. *New York Times,* Jan. 11, 1894, 8. *New York Times,* Mar. 14, 1895, 3; *New York Times,* June 4, 1898, 6.

44 *New York Times,* Nov. 22, 1895, 1.

45 For example, the legislature authorized the building of a new iron roof for the Sing Sing cellhouse in 1901, but by 1903, the work was still not underway. New York State Commission of Prisons, *Annual Report* (1903), 19. Commissioner John P. Jaeger complained in 1905 that, although the state legislature had appropriated $100,000 for improvements at Sing Sing the year before, the Governor of New York had withheld the money "due to pressing needs at other institutions." New York State Commission of Prisons, *Annual Report* (1905), 94.

46 Critical Statement (on the) Superintendent of State Prisons, 1914–16 (no page numbers), Appraisal Reports of Staffing at State Agencies and Institutions, Confidential Working

More than this being a simple case of inadequate or poorly applied technology (although, it was partly that), the disorderly and inefficient nature of the information system was a symptom of a far more insoluble problem confronting the Commissioners: a deeply entrenched culture of patronage and informality among state employees, and their instinctive resistance to being turned into good bureaucrats. Indeed, the existing machinery of the bureaucracy was jammed for most of the 1900s and early 1910s by the very staff charged with running it. Like prison guards and wardens, the central offices' clerical workers conceptualized and executed their jobs in the personal, familiar, ways of the older, patronage-style of organization. Detailed evidence of this began surfacing in the 1910s, following an investigation by legislators who correctly apprehended that the principles of bureaucratization and of civil service, which the state had adopted in the 1890s, had hardly been realized in practice. According to the State Senate Committee on Civil Service (the members of which filed confidential working papers in March 1916), although the staff of the Bureau of Identification were generally hard-working, the office was run on the "big family idea" wherein there was little specialization of tasks and employees were assigned work regardless of their titles. No records of the workers' attendance and punctuality were kept, and there were no rules pertaining to vacations and sick leave. The Senators took especial exception to the Bertillon clerk, who had been on leave since becoming "mentally deranged . . . due to a certain brain disorder" three months prior, yet was still collecting his wages. Moreover, the technology of bureaucratic order was inadequate. The filing system was creating redundant information, and the format for the industrial reports from Sing Sing, Auburn, and Clinton, varied significantly, making collation difficult. Of further concern to the investigators was the fact that one of the most critical roles of the office, the identification and tracking of convicts, was compromised by "a certain amount of friction" between the head of the Bureau of Identification and the fingerprint indexer. In all earnestness, the Committee recommended that, "From the stand point of proper administrative control, with a view toward increased efficiency in this bureau, it would seem that this matter of unharmonious action between these two employees should be carefully investigated and a definite policy carried out." Finally, the Senators criticized the traditional practice whereby each warden purchased food supplies for his prison. The Senators concluded their working papers by recommending that the office disestablish certain positions, standardize reporting procedures, centralize prison finances, and install that iconic recording device of modern management, the punch-in time clock.[47] As the

Papers, New York State Senate Committee on Civil Service, NYSA, Leg. Recs., Box 1. See also Jo Anne Yates, "Investing in Information: Supply and Demand and Forces in the Use of Information in American Firms, 1815–1920," in Peter Temin, ed., *Inside the Business Enterprise: Historical Perspectives on the Use of Information* (Chicago: Chicago University Press, 1991).

47 Critical Statement (on the) Superintendent of State Prisons, 1914–16 (no page numbers), Appraisal Reports of Staffing at State Agencies and Institutions, Confidential Working Papers, New York State Senate Committee on Civil Service, NYSA, Leg. Recs., Box 1. Note:

Senators' lament attests, although the technology of bureaucratic surveillance had been imagined and many of its critical components developed, successive attempts on the part of high-ranking administrators to build the system had been repeatedly foiled.

The new system of state-use industries, which the Commissioners had intended would fill the disciplinary and financial abyss left by the abolition of contract penal labor, suffered a similar fate between 1896 and 1910. Although the Commissioners and Superintendent worked hard to rekindle prison industries along the state-use lines prescribed by law, the problem of generating enough state demand for prisonmade goods persisted through the period. Although, by 1900, a number of state industries were up and running in the prisons, their workforces had labor enough only for three or four hours of the day.[48] Successive reports by the Commissioners, Superintendent of State Prisons, and outside observers acknowledged the underemployment of the prison manufacturing workforce but invariably concluded that this was largely attributable to teething problems and that it was only a matter of time before the industries would be fully operational. By 1913, however, most prisoners laboring in the workshops still had, at best, five hours of work each day.[49] (This did not stop members of the Prison Commission from claiming that, with proper business management, prison industries could make the prison self-supporting in a few years").[50] Moreover, earnings from the state prison industries at no point approached the amounts necessary to make the prisons self-sustaining. In the early 1890s, before the McDonough amendment prohibiting contracting and public-account industries was ratified and prison industries began to wind down, the earnings brought in by the state prison industries annually covered anything from two-thirds to three-quarters of the total maintenance and operating expenses of the three state prisons.[51] In the fifteen years following the introduction of state-use (1897), conversely, New York's prison industries generated revenue worth no more than one-quarter of prison expenses, and very frequently much less than that. Despite Superintendent Lathrop's claim, in 1897, that revenues from state-use industries would generate a sixty-percent profit for the state that year, the three state prisons, in fact, lost more than

the Senate Committee undertook a special confidential investigation of Sing Sing; however, two of the report's three sections went missing and have not been recovered. In the surviving section, the Senators objected to the warden's unofficial appointment of his confidential agent as deputy warden and his subsidization of the salaries of the agent and his private secretary.

[48] W. M. F. Rounds, quoted in *New York Times*, Nov. 12, 1899, 16.

[49] Report of the Committee of Industries of the Commission of Prisons, 1913, quoted in *New York Times*, Apr. 8, 1913, 3.

[50] Report of the Committee of Industries of the Commission of Prisons, 1913, quoted in *New York Times*, Apr. 8, 1913, 3.

[51] In 1889, the state had established public-account industries alongside existing contract industries. Earnings over operating expenditures for the three prisons (excluding extraordinary expenses such as the loss of a workshop to fire) were as follows: 1891: $275,325/$408,060; 1892: $344,436/$484,935.

$560,000.[52] At first, Lathrop and the Commissioners put this loss down to the ill-effects of the new branding law, which required that all goods made in New York prisons be stamped "CONVICT MADE," and the necessary initial outlays incurred in getting prison industries up and running. Six years into the state-use system, however, the annual earnings of prison industries amounted to just over $94,000,[53] while the state spent more than $500,000 on the prisons' operating costs; in 1911–12, fifteen years into the state-use system, the prisons brought in a record $190,000. However, in the same year, expenditure on the prison maintenance costs totaled just under $750,000.[54]

There were a number of reasons that, as a whole, state-use prison industries never allowed the prisons to be self-sustaining. Some of the difficulties encountered were technical or instrumental, but the most insurmountable were political and, in some instances, moral in nature. Goods made in the state prisons competed with goods manufactured in the other state institutions that had also had to move over to the state-use system in 1896; to compete, the state prisons lowered their prices, and in some instances, simply lost their state-use contracts to other institutions.[55] In addition, prison administrators were repeatedly frustrated by the general lack of state infrastructure, including roads, communications networks, and fiscal capacity. Although the political pressure brought to bear by the unions was the single most important constraint upon the new state-use industries, the lack of state infrastructure added considerably to the difficulty both of the task of building competitive state-use industries and the effort to set in place bureaucratic forms of control over the prisons. Regular inspections of the state prisons, which was intrinsic to the workings of the nascent penal bureaucracy, were frequently hampered by the horrendous logistics involved in moving around New York state at that time. The state prisons were anywhere from 250 to 300 miles apart from each other, and at least 125 miles from the state capitol at Albany. In 1900, there was no direct rail route between Clinton and the state capitol, nor between Clinton and the other prisons. Many of the roads were rough and the routes between prisons, circuitous. Although

---

[52] *New York Times*, Nov. 19, 1897, 3; "State Prison Deficiencies," *New York Times*, Jan. 29, 1898, 4.

[53] Superintendent of Prisons, *Annual Report* (1902). For some unexplained reason, there was a major discrepancy between the value of goods produced and the earnings realized.

[54] Earnings slipped the following year (1912–13), to about $140,000, while annual expenses escalated to over $810,000 (almost six times the amount earned). Well after the state-use system had "teethed," then, it was neither profitable nor constant in the degree of its losses. Superintendent of Prisons, *Annual Reports*, 1891, 1892, 1894, 1895, 1897, 1898, 1901, 1903, 1913. A 1911 investigation by a special Governor's commission found that prison labor's contribution to the total cost of maintaining the state prison system was a mere fifteen percent. Report of the Commission to Investigate the Department of State Prisons (William Church Osborn, George E. Vann Kennan, John D. McMahon), December 1911, quoted in *New York Times*, Dec. 11, 1911, 5.

[55] Cornelius V. Collins, the Superintendent of Prisons, complained of this in Superintendent of New York Prisons, *Annual Report* (1899). For example, Manhattan State Hospital began manufacturing its own clothing, and the Kings County Penitentiary took away Sing Sing's contract for New York sanitation workers' uniforms in 1898.

the gasoline automobile had been invented (in 1893), its use was still not widespread, and would not be commonplace until the 1910s. All this made it quite difficult to regularly transfer convicts around the system, particularly in the case of the remote Adirondack prison of Clinton, and difficult to maintain routine, frequent inspections of the prisons.[56] The integration and centralization of the prisons proved to be an elusive goal; much as the new Superintendent of Prisons, Cornelius V. Collins had warned in 1900, New York's prison industries had little chance of competing against "modern business" in which "the movement in all branches . . . is towards consolidation and concentration."[57]

In addition, the demand for prisonmade goods was never steady or bountiful. Despite the 1896 law directing state institutions to purchase their needs from the state prisons (as far as practicable), many institutions continued to purchase goods on the open market, much as they had always done. As the director of one such institution, the Northern New York Institution for Deaf-Mutes, put it, public institutions did not want to use prisonmade stuff.[58] (In this instance, the attorney-general exempted the institution on the rather dubious grounds that it was not fully public – although built entirely with state monies, its title was in a private board of trustees).[59] Prison administrators could not purge from the collective psyche the "taint" of convict labor, which the unions had so effectively publicized through boycotts and petitions against prisonmade goods in the 1880s and 1890s. National Guardsmen in some towns refused to wear prisonmade uniforms, and not because the garments were poorly made but because they were made by dishonored and dishonorable men.[60]

Above all, state-use industries suffered from pressures that were political in nature. Even though, with the enforcement of the McDonough amendment, the state had formally met organized labor's longstanding demands that contractors be removed from the prisons and prisonmade goods from the open market, local labor unions and manufacturers moved to oppose the use of prison labor in the production of certain "state-use" goods, as well. Ironically, the state-use prison labor law threatened to deprive workers in certain industries not just of higher wages but of their jobs as well. Whereas, before the state-use prison labor law came into effect, a significant portion of New York's prisonmade goods were exported out of the state, with the passage of the law, all the state's prisonmade goods were to be disposed of within New York borders: The prisons were authorized to sell goods only to

[56] The Commissioners wrote that they found the journey to far-flung Clinton long and exhausting. (In the 1850s, it sometimes took up to forty hours to travel from Albany to Clinton; although roads had improved a great deal by the 1890s, Clinton remained relatively isolated).

[57] Superintendent of New York State Prisons, *Annual Report* (1899), 11, 20. Collins also pointed out that prison industries were hampered, relative to free industry, by the fixed cost of prison labor.

[58] *New York Times*, Jan. 25, 1897, 1.   [59] *New York Times*, Jan. 25, 1897, 1.
[60] *New York Times*, Dec. 15, 1897, 6.

the public institutions of the state.[61] Free manufacturers that supplied the state now faced a substantial (and, potentially, complete) loss of business. In early 1897, as the state Prison Commissioners publicized their plans for state industries, both organized workers and employers in the industries likely to be affected mobilized to avert a possible loss of contracts to state prisons. The unions, especially, moved swiftly and effectively. Workers in the highly skilled printers' and bookbinders' unions led the way. Upon hearing that the Commissioners were contemplating establishing a printing industry at Sing Sing for the purposes of supplying the state's stationery and printing needs, the printers' union immediately drafted a legislative bill prohibiting the use of prison labor in any and all printing work for state departments and municipal offices (with the exception that prison presses might print documents for their own institution).[62]

Frustrated but undeterred, organized printers soon stepped up and widened their campaign. The Bookbinders' Union, Allied Printing Trades, Typographical Union, and Central Labor Union moved to block the Commissioners' initiative to put prisoners to work printing school grammars, spelling books, and arithmetic texts. Building on the logic of the unions' ongoing consumer boycott of prisonmade goods, one labor leader argued: "If union men will not wear prison-made clothes, their children also should not read prison-made books."[63] Within days, the campaign broadened to other industries, including the clothing business. Legislators sympathetic to organized labor called for a special legislative committee to report on "whether it is wise" to have all public institutions supplied exclusively by the prison labor. As State Senator John Francis Ahearn (a powerful Tammany Hall politician and ally of skilled labor) grasped very well, "the extension of convict employment to new industries, including the manufacture of blankets, cloth, woolens, shirts, stockings, ties, woodenware, the printing of books, reports and documents, will eventually take the State and the cities . . . out of the open market as purchasers of supplies."[64] Just as organized labor had argued that prison labor contractors squeezed free workers, labor leaders now warned that the proposed system of state-use industries "will deprive honest labor of employment in the ever-narrowing channels of legitimate trade . . . "[65] In connection with this issue, other Tammany Hall lawmakers, including State Senator Jacob Cantor, intimated that the campaign to restrict state-use industries might be stepped up to include an attack on the legitimacy of the Prison Commission itself: If the legislature continued to delegate important questions to unelected bodies such as the Prison

---

[61] Austin Lathrop noted this difficulty in 1897. *New York Times*, Feb. 24, 1897, 3.

[62] Submitted to the Tenth Annual Convention of the New York State Branch of the American Federation of Labor, January 1897 (cited in *New York Times*, Jan. 13, 1897, 15). See also, *New York Times*, Mar. 1, 1897, 4.

[63] "Against Labor in Prison," *New York Times*, Feb. 22, 1897, 3; "Printing in State Prisons," *New York Times*, Mar. 5, 1897, 4.

[64] Senator Ahearn, resolution, quoted in *New York Times*, Mar. 11, 1897, 5.

[65] Senator Ahearn, resolution, quoted in *New York Times*, Mar. 11, 1897, 5.

Commission, Cantor exclaimed, the state might "soon be governed, not by the Legislature but, by these commissions."[66]

It was in the midst of this mounting opposition that Lispenard Stewart and his Prison Commission agreed, in March of 1897, to consult with organized labor about the proposed prison industries; from that point on, Stewart, and New York's prison administrators more generally, began emphasizing the need for a system of prison industries that did not conflict with the interests of the free workmen of New York.[67] The day after the meeting, the Commission quietly announced that it would be impracticable for legislative and departmental printing to be done in the prisons.[68] A year later, state law restricted prison printing to the production of documents that directly related to the penal system; all other state documents were to be printed by civilian industry using union labor.[69] From there, other prison industries were subject to much the same rule. The clothing companies at Sing Sing, the members of which worked around the clock stitching thousands of military uniforms during the first few months of the Spanish–American War, lost much of that lucrative contract to free industry. Manufacturers and free workers producing a range of goods for the public schools also lobbied the state Prison Commission, in protest at the loss of contracts,[70] and school superintendents became increasingly resistant to having to purchase chairs, tables, and other supplies from the prisons. Some organized workers even quietly took direct action against prison-made goods; as one New York City union leader strongly intimated in 1908, the union men who handled supplies for municipal and county departments saw to it that any and all goods bearing the prison-made brand failed to reach their destination.[71] In 1900, the legislature passed a bill authorizing public schools to purchase their furniture on the open market.[72] Organized labor's allies in the legislature introduced a bill exempting the Board of Health from having to purchase its needs from the state prisons.[73]

The opposition of various sectors of free labor and manufacturers to the use of prisoners in productive labor in competition with free would continue through the 1910s and 1920s, effectively hobbling the ambitious efforts of New York's administrators to build a new, politically acceptable system of imprisonment at hard labor. Although no longer available to industrialists bent on breaking unions, prison labor continued to be the object of

---

[66] Jacob Cantor, paraphrased in *New York Times*, Mar. 12, 1897, 5.

[67] The meeting was reported in *New York Times*, Mar. 17, 1897, 7.

[68] *New York Times*, Mar. 18, 1897, 5.

[69] New York State Commission of Prisons, *Annual Report* (1899).

[70] *New York Times*, Nov. 13, 1897, 2.   [71] *New York Times*, June 18, 1908. p. 6

[72] Although the school superintendents complained about poor construction, delayed delivery, uncompetitive pricing, and failure to build to specifications, it is clear that they resented having to purchase from the prisons, period. *New York Times*, Nov. 2, 1898, 9; *New York Times*, Dec. 13, 1898, 14, Dec. 15, 1898, 12; *New York Times*, Dec. 24, 1899, 8.

[73] *New York Times*, Mar. 2, 1898, 4.

strenuous objection by organized labor and, now, the manufacturers who had been locked out of the penal labor market by the abolition of contract penal labor. As one exasperated penitentiary administrator put it, "Every industry we tried to start seemed to conflict with somebody. I couldn't find work for our people, and they were getting crazy." (Like a number of state wardens, this one partially solved the disciplinary dimension of the problem by putting prisoners to work breaking stone).[74] By 1899, even the use of prisoners in institutional construction work came under fire from local unions. Here, however, Lispenard Stewart drew a line: Pointing out that such labor was constitutionally permissible, he insisted, "The present system was adopted in obedience to the desire of the labor organizations of the State and had their indorsements [sic]."[75] Following Stewart's lobbying, Governor Theodore Roosevelt reinforced this position shortly afterward, when, in a characteristic display of his rhetorical skills, he vetoed the school furniture law on the grounds that it was the work of "the furniture trust" and went against the interests of the State.[76] These instances of officials' refusal of efforts to restrict or close down state-use industries were few and far between, however. They did very little to prop up the state-use industries. (Indeed, Theodore Roosevelt went on, as President of the United States, to issue an executive order of considerable consequence to the state-use system: He ordered that no convict labor was to be used on federal government works).[77] Subject to this multiplicity of pressures, the state-use industries failed to generate the level of revenue, and the labor-based system of discipline and reform, that the Commissioners and Prisons Superintendent had envisioned for New York.

Although the prisons did not conform to many of the Commissioners' expectations, neither did prison life go on as it had before 1896: Things did change, if not according to the official prescription. The old penal regime, with its distinctive set of rules, rituals, and practices, had all but disappeared by 1910. There were important shifts in the experience and conditions of imprisonment, as well as in the complex power relations of everyday prison life. The massive amount of institutional, construction, and demolition work around the prisons (which originated, as we have seen, in the inability of industries to absorb the prison population) resulted in extended, sanitized, and reorganized buildings and grounds. Such work kept the vast majority of prisoners at labor through the early 1900s. Gradually, prisoners tore down many of the older buildings, centralized each prison's power plants, and erected new buildings. The Sing Sing hospital, pharmacy, and doctor's offices, which were located on the top floor of the newly completed building,

---

[74] Commissioner of Charities and Correction Burton, quoted in *New York Times*, Oct. 9, 1897, 9.

[75] Stewart in *New York Times*, Apr. 6, 1899, 8.

[76] Theodore Roosevelt, quoted in *New York Times*, May 7, 1900, 5.

[77] Executive Order, reported in *New York Times*, May 24, 1905, 16. The order was aimed at the use of *contracted* prison laborers, but appears to have been applied to all prison laborers.

opened in 1899. When the roof and upper floor were damaged by fire the following year, hundreds of prison laborers were set to building a new iron roof (which was fireproof) over the block, and the building was reopened in 1903. Prison laborers also demolished some of the old workshops, graded the grounds, and built walkways and wagon roads through the prison in 1900. The construction of a new visiting room for prisoners' wives, family members, and attorneys got underway in 1904. In the early years of the twentieth century, and for several years hence, more prisoners were put to labor on the grounds and buildings than in any other prison operation. (In Sing Sing's case, such work provided occupation for approximately one-third of the population).

In the early 1910s, this trajectory was extended when state prison administrators also saw an opportunity to solve two problems in one fell swoop: By organizing road gangs of state prisoners, they could improve the state's inadequate road system and further absorb the underemployed energies of the prison population. The Superintendent put several companies of prisoners to work laying roads as part of the nationwide Progressive Era project known as the Good Roads Movement. Under that program, prisoners in several dozen states (including Colorado, Oregon, New Mexico, Wisconsin, Georgia, and New Jersey) went to work laying and Macadamizing highways and byways. Like administrators elsewhere, New York's prison authorities reasoned that not only did such work help create a much-needed network of roads across the state but that the prisoners' exposure to outdoor labor and fresh country air would be beneficial to their health and morals.[78] (As Charles Henry Davis, a prominent leader of the Good Roads Movement put it, rather than submit prisoners to cruel idleness, "We should turn on the light; we should give men sunshine, the free air and fields of the country. We should have, and thus give, hope, faith, help.... *via* good roads...").[79] Notably, administrators in New York and other Northern states found a way around the objections that the cost of guarding road gangs would be exorbitant, and that manacling and chaining prisoners constituted a return to slavery: The answer was the so-called "honor system." Under the honor system (which was developed in Oregon in 1912, and eventually widely adopted outside the South), between 50 and 200 prisoners went out "on their honor" to the roads, at a month at a time, under no official or only limited armed guard; unarmed trusties directed the work, which, if properly performed,

[78] Thomas J. Tynan, "Prison Labor on Public Roads," *Annals of the American Academy of Political and Social Science* 46 (Mar., 1913), 58–60; Joseph Hyde Pratt, "Convict Labor in Highway Construction" *Annals of the American Academy of Political and Social Science* 46 (Mar., 1913), 78–87; Philip E. Bauer, "One Year of the Honor System in Oregon," *Annals of the American Academy of Political and Social Science* 46 (Mar., 1913), 105–10; "Good Roads and Convict Labor," *Proceedings of the Academy of Political Science in the City of New York* 4:2 (special issue; Jan., 1914); Alex Lichtenstein, "Good Roads and Chain Gangs in the Progressive South: 'The Negro Convict is a Slave'," *Journal of Southern History* 59 (Feb., 1993), 85–110.

[79] Charles Henry Davis, Forward, "Good Roads and Convict Labor," *Proceedings of the Academy of Political Science in the City of New York* 4:2 (Jan., 1914), 243.

was rewarded with "good time" (that is, the shortening of the sentence) and other incentives.[80]

Organized religion made deeper incursions into the prisons in the late 1890s, as the administration proceeded to provide services for Jewish and Catholic convicts (as well as extending the traditional Protestant services). Attendance was voluntary. At Sing Sing in 1899, and through the 1900s, Catholic and Protestant services were held every Sunday, and every second Saturday, Jewish prisoners could attend synagogue, which was held in the Protestant chapel. Some convicts attended Mrs. Anne Field's bible class, which was held once per month, and Catholic convicts talked with two visiting Sisters of Mercy on a monthly basis.[81] Besides offering the prisoners moral instruction and spiritual consolation, the church services, classes, and visits provided prisoners with an opportunity to engage in social activity and to hear some news of the outside world: As the warden's frequent reiteration of the rule prohibiting talking and whispering during the services suggests, many of the prisoners who were ostensibly gathering together to commune with God were also using the occasion to communicate with one another.[82] The Protestant services often included talks by civilian speakers who addressed the prisoners on a range of worldly topics. Organized religion thereby became part of the general trend toward exposing the prisoner to worlds other than that of the prison and, by the same token, rabbis, clergy, and Christian laity were exposed to the conditions and problems of imprisonment.

The restructuring of the prison labor companies, and the convicts' disgruntled response to it, also resulted in substantive change in the everyday life of the convicts. Whereas the prisoner had once worked alongside prisoners regardless of their record, crime, or disciplinary record, he was now segregated in companies with prisoners whose conviction records were similar to his own. As the Superintendent of Prisons had directed, the majority of first-time prisoners were separated from the other convicts. But the separation was never more than partial, in part because there was not enough work for the skilled First Graders. Indeed, at the turn of the century, about three of every ten Third Grade men were not working in the productive industries and offices of the Third Grade. They often joined prisoners of the Third Grade working in the old quarry adjoining Sing Sing, where they cut stone for use in institutional and local construction. Others of the Third Grade did yard and institutional work, such as white-washing the prison walls, hauling garbage, cooking, and improving institutional roads.[83]

---

[80] Philip E. Bauer, "One Year of Honor System in Oregon" *Annals of the American Academy of Political and Social Science* 46 (Mar., 1913), 105–08; Sydney Wilmot, "Use of Convict Labor for Highway Construction in the North," *Proceedings of the Academy of Political Science in the City of New York* 4:2 (Jan., 1914), 6–68.

[81] M. Xavier and M. Theresa counseled convicts. *Star of Hope* 1:1 (April 1899), 7.

[82] *Star of Hope* 1:1 (April 22, 1899), 7; and 1:2 (May 1899), 7.

[83] Figures are taken from the New York State Commission of Prisons, *Annual Reports*, 1899–1905.

Little is known about the third and lowest grade of Sing Sing prisoner – the prisoners who had served upward of two previous prison sentences. Some were in the "Idle Company." The Idle Company was, in certain respects, a punishment company. Its members were physically fit prisoners; invalid prisoners belonged to a separate company for "invalids." Where prisoners in the industries might have periods of idleness and slowness in their workshops or around the institution, the men in Idle Company were prevented from working, or doing anything whatsoever. As the prisoners' newspaper attests, most prisoners would rather have done some kind of work than nothing at all, and both they and the guards considered demotion to the Idle Company an extremely punitive measure.

The grade to which a prisoner was assigned not only determined the kind of work he would do, but other aspects of his incarceration as well. Reforms, such as abolition of prison stripes and the introduction of letter writing, were generally introduced as privileges that the warden could suspend as punishment or reward for good behavior. As noted earlier, the majority of prisoners of the Third Grade were entitled to training and education. They were also the first prisoners to benefit from the extension of various privileges. When the disciplinary techniques consonant with the old system of contract labor were abolished, they were often selectively abolished for the Third Grade, ahead of the rest of the prisoners.[84] Sing Sing's First Grade men, for example, stopped lockstepping in 1897; the rest of that prison's convicts stopped in 1899, and Auburn followed suit in 1901. The division of prisoners into groups with greater and fewer privileges was to become a hallmark of the new disciplinary order; moreover, following complaints and insubordination over the new classification system, the method of allocation to a company was altered so as to reward convicts for good behavior and demote them for poor conduct. This meant that many of the prisoners with two or more convictions ended up back in the more desirable work companies, while first-timers who misbehaved were demoted. This was the first of many systems of reward and privilege with which wardens and bureaucrats would experiment in the early twentieth century.

Eventually, the majority of prisoners within a single institution shared the same privileges; but there was also always a minority of convicts within each prison from whom privileges were partially or entirely withheld. Their presence within each prison was crucial to the disciplinary logic that was slowly but surely taking root in the prisons. They provided a visible reminder to prisoners that failure to cooperate would return them to the unprivileged conditions of the so-called "old system." They also provoked the specter of a return to the old system for all prisoners, not just the uncooperative ones, and hence had the disciplinary effect of causing prisoners to bring pressure to bear on reluctant prisoners. This effect was most starkly demonstrated

---

[84] With the introduction of grades, it became necessary for guards to be able to distinguish more easily between men of different grades. Hence, each grade of Sing Sing prisoners initially wore a particular style of uniform and a number of stripes corresponding to the grade. Stripes were first abolished in 1899 at Auburn and at Sing Sing in 1900.

in an internal disciplinary hearing at Sing Sing in 1915, involving a prisoner who was thought to have destroyed important papers that documented alleged corruption in the prison industries. He was examined by fellow prisoners of the Judiciary Board:

Q(uestion): Were you here under the old system?
A(nswer): No.
Q: Then you haven't any idea what the old system means.
A: I have an idea.
Q: Under the old system a man was strung up by the thumbs; it was the rule of gun and club. If we return to the old system, which you are helping, they will take it out on us with a vengeance.[85]

This logic also became generalized to the institutional level. The bureaucratic oversight and the system of privileges that emerged at Auburn and Sing Sing did not develop at Clinton in this period. As training, education, and other privileges were extended to the majority of prisoners in other state prisons, and third-timers were transferred and concentrated at Clinton, the Clinton convicts became the least privileged, and most deprived, in the state.[86]

It was at this point in New York prison history that the well-known practice of maintaining one particularly terrible prison as both a deterrent to disorderly conduct in the other prisons and a repository for allegedly insubordinate prisoners developed.[87] Clinton came to be known in the first twenty years of the twentieth century as the "Klondike," "Siberia," and "Dark Hole of Calcutta"; it became the most feared prison in the system. The concentration of third-termers at Clinton caused that prison to develop a reputation as the prison of hardened criminals, and few of the labor, health, and punishment reforms that were instigated at the other prisons were extended there. Stories of guard brutality as well as violence among the convicts at Clinton circulated among prisoners of the other prisons, while one infamous principal keeper became known as "the Czar of Russia."[88] Consequently, convicts

---

[85] Sing Sing Prison Judiciary Board: Testimony taken in case of R – P – , #65748, Oct. 27, 1915. OFP, MSS 64. Box 276 Org. Recs., Misc.

[86] The Prison Commissioners justified this arrangement in 1915, when they noted that the Clinton men were quite possibly incapable of conducting themselves properly under the system of privileges in operation at Auburn and Sing Sing. In the Matter of A – B. F – , New York State Prison Commission, transcript of testimony taken at Clinton Prison, Dannemora, New York (June 7, 1915), 91. OFP, MSS64, Box 272, Org. Recs.

[87] The transfer of troublesome prisoners was commonplace by 1915. As Superintendent of Prisons, John Riley, would instruct the warden of Sing Sing, "you understand that in the case of prisoners who fail to comply with the prison regulations, you should submit their names and I will immediately order their transfer to Clinton. It is not necessary in matters of discipline to await the regular transfers, which should, as near as possible, provide for a carload." John Riley to Thomas Mott Osborne, Albany, Feb. 19, 1915, OFP, MSS64, Box 276, Org. Recs.

[88] New York State Prison Commission. In the Matter of A – B. F – , New York State Prison Commission, Transcript of testimony taken at Clinton Prison, Dannemora, New York (June 7, 1915), 91. OFP, MSS64, Box 272, Org. Recs.

in the other New York prisons attempted to avoid transfer to Clinton, while wardens and guards threatened uncooperative convicts with a one-way trip to the Adirondacks.[89]

The transcript from a disciplinary proceeding against a Sing Sing prisoner in 1915 conveys the meaning that convicts attached to Clinton in the early twentieth century and its place in the new style of discipline that followed on the heels of the reorganization of Sing Sing, Auburn, and Clinton into first-, second-, and third-grade prisons respectively.

Q(uestion): Ever hear of Clinton prison?
A(nswer): Yes
Q: Ever hear anything good about it?
A: No.
Q: Dan [the prisoner's friend] has been there?
A: Yes.
Q: When a man gets drafted to Clinton, especially a first-timer, the first thing they say of that man is 'You don't belong here.' They think a man has been sent up there for correction; they certainly correct you.[90]

Under the same logic of incentive to orderliness, the prison at Great Meadow, which was opened in 1911, came to be seen as perhaps the best prison in which to serve a sentence, due to its modern architecture (there was no stone cellblock as there was at Sing Sing, Auburn, and Clinton), proximity to New York City, and the system of privileges.

Closely related to the punitive system of transfer were new rules relating to the punishment of transgressors within each prison. The punishment ledgers suggest that Auburn developed a methodical and well-worked-out system of formal punishment. Punishment in the contracting era had typically consisted of a summary clip on the head with a baton, a paddling or other shock-based treatment, and/or isolation in a dungeon or dark cell. The dungeon was a basement room with no light and little air, whereas the dark cell was a cell made of sheet iron and deprived of all light sources. It contained only a bucket and a tin can for water, and very little ventilation. Typically, a heavy wooden door closed over the barred door of the cell, depriving the occupant of all light and causing the cell to be stifling. With the introduction of work grades, indeterminate sentences, and parole in the 1890s, prisoners' formal punishment consisted both in time in the dark cell

---

[89] See subsequent discussion, Chapters 4 and 6. Sing Sing Prison Judiciary Board. Testimony taken in case of R – P – , #65748, Oct. 27, 1915, OFP, MSS 64, Box 276, Org. Recs. The Prison Commission found evidence of beatings and cuffings at Clinton in 1915. The principal keeper, Thomas Coultry, was quite forthright about the practice of cuffing prisoners' hands behind their backs and forcing them to stay standing in their cells. At least two prisoners provided testimony, but only on the condition that they receive protection. In the Matter of A – B. F – , New York State Prison Commission, Transcript of testimony taken at Clinton Prison, Dannemora, New York (June 7, 1915), 91. OFP, MSS64, Box 272, Org. Recs.

[90] Sing Sing Prison Judiciary Board: Testimony taken in case of R – P – , #65748, Oct. 27, 1915. OFP, MSS 64. Box 276 Org. Recs., Misc.

and loss of compensation, good conduct marks, or privileges. (Although there is little written about the conduct marks, it seems likely that a prisoner could be demoted a grade after losing a certain number of marks, and that this influenced the prisoner's chances of early parole.)[91] A prisoner interned in either the dungeon or dark cell was also placed on a restricted diet of bread and water: Until 1913, dark cell prisoners were officially allowed no more than one gill of water per day; the Superintendent of Prisons, John Riley, increased the official ration to three gills in 1913.[92] (Of course, there is no way of knowing if prisoners actually received the water to which they were entitled.)[93] According to the records of formal punishment at Auburn, the dungeon was used much less frequently after the 1890s and incarceration in the dark cell had become the most common form of punishment by the turn of the century. At Auburn, internment in the dark cell also carried with it a fine: A prisoner lost 50¢ – or the equivalent of thirty-four days' worth of prison wages – for every day spent in the cell.[94]

In the early 1900s, Auburn prisoners were formally punished for talking in workshops, disobedience, making noise, feigning insanity, and insolence by being placed in a dark cell for a few days.[95] Prisoners punished for insolence generally spent up to three days in the dark cells, while those alleged to have feigned insanity were held up to eleven days. Assault on a prison guard was taken very seriously: In 1900, one Auburn prisoner was held for thirteen days in the dark cell, and when he was reported one year later for threatening an officer, he was held in a dark cell for sixteen days and had six months of good time deducted.[96] In a number of cases, prisoners who had been sent to the dark cells for feigning insanity were ultimately transferred to the asylum. As the punishment ledgers record, these prisoners were invariably transferred out of the prison, either to Clinton or to the Dannemora prison hospital. The questions of whether their insanity was real or imagined, and, if real, whether or not it developed as a result of spending long spells on

---

[91] Since the 1870s, the vast majority of prisoners who were formally punished were incarcerated in special punishment or dark cells. At Auburn, the official name for these cells in the 1880s had been the dungeon. See Chapter 3, supra, for a discussion of the particular place of dark cell punishment in the contract labor regimes of the Gilded Age.

[92] Rudolph W. Chamberlin, *There Is No Truce: The Life of Thomas Mott Osborne* (New York: MacMillan, 1935), 252.

[93] Records also use the term "jail" when referring to the punitive incarceration of a prisoner: The jail was probably a standard cell, possibly the prisoner's own, and disciplined prisoners would be held there in solitary confinement for a few days.

[94] Chamberlin, *There Is No Truce*, 254. Prisoners were paid 1.5¢ for a day's labor.

[95] Auburn Punishment Ledger, Vol. 1 (Oct. 7, 1870–July 9, 1895) and Vol. 2 (Apr. 26, 1895 – Jan. 16, 1904), NYSA (RDCS) Auburn Correctional Facility, Inmate Punishment Ledger, 1872(1870)–1941. At Auburn Prison, women's transgressions of the rules were more severely punished than were men's: Typically, where men would get three days in the dark cell for insolence or talking, and ten or more days for assault, women were held in dark cells for between seven and fifteen days for the offenses of quarreling, writing notes, insolence, and vile language.

[96] J – M – , #25914, Auburn Punishment Ledger, Vol. 2 (Apr. 26, 1895 – Jan. 16, 1904).

restricted diets in the dark cells, are difficult to answer.[97] Whatever the case may have been, the punishment for a person thought to be feigning insanity was relatively severe, and typically it resulted in several days' isolation in a dark cell or the dungeon. In the eyes of guards, the convict who was either insane or simply staging insanity was unmanageable either way: His state amounted to a refusal to submit to the will of the guards.[98]

While the nature of prisoners' labor underwent these changes and the architectural disorder of the 1870s and 1880s was replaced by a modern architecture of incarceration, the great cellblocks in which state prisoners spent all of their sleeping – and even some of their waking – hours survived more or less intact. The use of iron and steel in cell construction had begun in American prisons in the 1880s.[99] However, the old stone cellblocks such as those in use at Auburn, Sing Sing, and Clinton were costly and difficult to renovate: It took two years of intensive labor, for example, for Sing Sing's masons to enlarge the windows a few inches in two wings of the cellblock. Consequently, prisoners at Auburn, Sing Sing, and Clinton continued to be housed in the original, if slightly altered, stone cellblocks through the 1900s.[100] Every prisoner was locked up nightly in a cell measuring 7'3/4" by 6'1/2" by 6,' and, as noted earlier, he was increasingly likely to be sharing that small room with another prisoner. Despite repeated calls for the replacement of the cellblock's wooden roof (and not withstanding the return from Paris of the prized scale-model of Sing Sing) the cells continued to be a fire hazard; the fact that every cell had to be unlocked and locked by hand meant that it took twenty-four guards at least one hour to unlock the cells. Quick evacuation was impossible: At night, when only four guards were on duty, evacuation would have taken upwards of six hours.[101] These conditions were made even more dangerous by the fact that the prisoners often lit small fires in their cells to reheat cups of bootleg, the bitter prison brew

---

[97] J – S – , #20996, got eleven days in the dark cell for feigning insanity, and fewer than three days for offenses such as insolence, and disobedience while marching. Auburn Punishment Ledger, Vol. 2 (Jan. 25, 1902); G – W – , #26359 got ten days in dark cell, Auburn Punishment Ledger, Vol. 2 (Apr. 22, 1901); E – S – got only four days for feigning insanity; Auburn Punishment Ledger, Vol. 2 (Jun. 14, 1900); W – B – , #26665, spent eleven days in the dark cell and lost sixty days, on Jan. 25, 1902. (He was finally sent to the asylum, Apr. 7, 1902). On the same day, Jan. 25, 1902, C – E. S – was punished in the same amount for "feigning," and he, too, was later sent to the asylum; Auburn Punishment Ledger, Vol. 2 (Jun. 14, 1900).

[98] New York State Commission of Prisons, *Annual Report* (1897), 55–6.

[99] Blake McKelvey, *American Prisons; a Study in American Social History Prior to 1915* (Chicago: University of Chicago Press, 1936), 155.

[100] Adapting the masonry of the cellhouse to contemporary sanitation and housing standards would be costly and difficult: Plumbing, airshafts, lighting, and enlarged windows had to be cut through thick granite stone. The early nineteenth century builders of prisons had built the Auburn-style cellblocks to last: Their monumental proportions resisted most attempts at remodeling, and although legislators could be persuaded to provide for their alteration, they resisted their outright demolition and replacement.

[101] New York State Commission of Prisons, *Annual Report* (1901), 86–7.

that passed as coffee.[102] Despite the fact that this was against the rules and prisoners were frequently punished for the offense, the practice continued. The fire risk was further compounded by some prisoners' use of oil lamps as reading lights after the new electric lights were turned out each night. [103]

One thing that did not change in any marked degree was the central structural technology of prison architecture: the cellhouse. Conditions in the cellblock at Sing Sing, which had earned among the prisoners the epithet "Bastille on the Hudson," and among élite reformers, that of "dungeon," continued to degenerate, claiming the good health of countless prisoners and outlasting the careers of even the most dogged of reform-minded administrators. Through the 1890s and well into the 1910s, there was no plumbing for either sewerage or running water in the cells: Each cell had a bucket, which the prisoners emptied every morning (except Sundays and holidays) into the Hudson River.[104] The number of hours spent in the cells exceeded the hours that prisoners spent there under the old contract prison labor regime: Whereas convicts had once spent between nine and twelve hours a night in the cells, after 1895, Sing Sing prisoners were locked in their cells from 3 P.M. every weekday until breakfast the following morning – usually a period of fifteen hours or more. Prisoners also spent all of Saturday night, Sunday (save an hour for chapel), and Sunday night in the cells; if Monday happened to be a public holiday, prisoners typically would not leave their cells again until Tuesday morning. On "holiday" weekends, therefore, prisoners ended up spending upward of sixty hours in the cells.[105]

Longer hours in the cellhouse had important implications for prisoners' health. Although it is impossible to assess with any degree of precision the overall health of the prisoners in the period in question, there is evidence to suggest that certain kinds of diseases plagued prisoners much more frequently in the years after the transition to state-use than before.[106] In the late 1890s and 1900s, the Commissioners repeatedly described Sing Sing's

---

[102] Convict #1535, "Knowledge in Prison," *Star of Hope* 1:1 (April 1899), 5. Prison coffee was infamously bitter, and quite possibly toxic. At Clinton, the 3,700 cups of "coffee" that prisoners drank daily was made from just six pounds of coffee beans mixed with six pounds of chicory. Papers Relating to George Blake's Special Commission to Investigate Prisons, Reformatories, and the Office of Superintendent of Prisons, NYSA, Governor's Office Records, Investigation Case Files of Charges and Complaints Against Public Officials and Agencies, 1857–1919, A0531 Box 41.

[103] New York State Commission of Prisons, *Annual Report* (1903), 20.

[104] This was confirmed by an investigator from the New York State Department of Health in 1915: C. A. Holmquist, "Preliminary Report on Inquiry into the Hospital and Medical Work of Sing Sing Prison," New York State Department of Health (February 1915), 2. OFP, MSS64, Box 276, Org. Recs.

[105] Westchester County Research Bureau, "Some Facts About Sing Sing Management: Bulletin 1" (unpublished report, c. 1915), 2. OFP, MSS 64, Box 276, Org. Recs.

[106] Much of the evidence is anecdotal and contradictory, and there are no reliable doctor's records for the 1890s and 1900s. The Commissioners' reports were sometimes self-congratulatory about the prisoners' health and welfare, which they proclaimed were markedly improved every year, thanks to implementation of their recommendations, and sometimes they were riddled with contradiction: One Commissioner might describe the

cellblock as poorly ventilated and disease-inducing, connecting the raised incidence of tuberculosis to its damp, miasmic airs.[107] In 1910, Doctor J. B. Ransom, who was the director of the Clinton hospital, estimated that the rate of death from tuberculosis in New York's prisons was three to four times higher than that for the general population.[108] Independent investigators often remarked on the gray pall of the prisoners at this time. What is clear is that prisoners incarcerated in the damp cellblock at Sing Sing suffered from a high rate of respiratory afflictions and that large numbers of Sing Sing men were transferred to the new tuberculosis hospital at Clinton. Located high in the Adirondacks, the hospital's dry, clean air was thought to be the best aid to curing consumptive prisoners; at the very least it quarantined ill prisoners from the healthy. Between 1904 and 1913, 804 convicts were transferred from Sing Sing to the Clinton hospital; the prison doctor estimated that most of these prisoners had developed tuberculosis while at Sing Sing.[109] In these years, a number of epidemics also broke out at the prisons: Sing Sing suffered an outbreak of typhoid in 1900, and Auburn was struck by a smallpox epidemic shortly thereafter.

As the foregoing discussion suggests, both the legal punishment of imprisonment at hard labor and the official doctrines of state-use imprisonment underwent profound alteration between 1896 and 1913. In some respects, attempts to reconstruct the prison along bureaucratic, state-use lines succeeded. Whereas for most of the nineteenth century, the prison had effectively been the exclusive domain of a warden who was more or less independent of supervision from any kind of state bureaucracy, by 1910, New York's prisons were interlinked as a series of specialized institutions over which the Commissioners and Superintendent exercised some degree of power. These administrators had also fairly effectively separated men, women, mentally ill, young, and ill prisoners from each other, expelled from New York's prison other states' convicts, and broken the mass of imprisoned adult men into three distinct categories of offenders. Just as the Commissioners had provided, prisoners were now moved around the system on a fairly routine basis, and although bureaucratic techniques of surveillance and statistical analysis continued to be rather crude and open to subversion, prison administrators generally had a much better sense of "who" was in the prisons. Although prisoners remained caged by night in the dreaded old cellhouses, various other practices that the Commissioners took to be the badges of the old regime (i.e., the rule of silence, the lockstep march, striped uniforms, summary corporal punishment, and the near-perfect autocracy of wardens), had

---

health of the prisoners as excellent, while, in the same report, another might describe the convicts as enfeebled.

[107] See, for example, New York State Commission of Prisons, *Annual Report* (1901).

[108] National Committee on Prisons and Prison Labor. OFP, MSS64, Box 271, Org. Recs.

[109] George Blake to William Sulzer, May 24, 1913. Papers Relating to George Blake's Special Commission to Investigate Prisons, Reformatories, and the Office of Superintendent of Prisons, NYSA, Governor's Office Records, Investigation Case Files of Charges and Complaints Against Public Officials and Agencies, 1857–1919, A0531 Box 41.

been done away with. Prisoners were now subject to a system of incentive, deterrence, bureaucracy, and indeterminate sentencing; if their immediate fate still rested with the keepers, their long-term prospects rested with the penal bureaucrats from Albany.

In other respects, however, the attempt to reconstruct New York's system of imprisonment at hard labor had failed dismally in its own terms. The new prison industries hardly defrayed the costs of incarceration, were prone to legislative prohibition, and were increasingly subject to legal restriction. Although lawmakers had limited the ambit of guards' and wardens' formal authority and provided for their subordination to central administration, administrators had failed to make fully obedient civil servants of them. At the same time, attempts at bureaucratization had deepened the antagonism between prisoners and their keepers, as keepers connected encroachments upon their authority with the emergence of prisoner voices in the *Star of Hope*, the occasional civilian newspaper, and (theoretically) in the letters of complaint that convicts were now entitled to write to administrators and judges.[110] Prison investigations and folklore attested that as bureaucratization proceeded, the corporal chastisements that élite reformers had held to be inhumane and barbarous, persisted, intensified, and proliferated. Such informal punishments were not simply the residue of the old system, as administrators and élite prison reformers often insisted. Nor were they the outcome of some inherent tendency of prison administrations to revert to what David J. Rothman has characterized as the "convenience" of a crude custodialism.[111] Rather, the terrible, secret acts of violence that arose in the prisons after 1895 were the consequence of the power struggle that unfolded between administrators and keepers as the former strove to make subordinates of the latter, and to enlist the prisoners in their endeavor. Ironically, as the Commissioners made corporal punishment illegal, and as Clinton prison became known among the convicts as the terrifying "Klondike" of last resort, the violence of the old system was remade. Much like the striped uniforms that had been officially discontinued only to be retailored as lining and sewn into the new military-style prison uniforms prescribed by the Commission, the vestiges of the old system that administrators had so fervently condemned were reinvented and woven into the new.[112]

---

[110] No. 1500 noted that although the Superintendent of Prisons and Sing Sing's warden supported the establishment of a prison newspaper, the guards were aghast: "Of all things that a prison keeper fears," he wrote, "nothing is so terrible as the newspaper." No. 1500, quoted in James McGrath Morris, *Jailhouse Journalism: The Fourth Estate Behind Bars* (Jefferson, NC: McFarland and Company, 1998), 104.

[111] David J. Rothman, *Conscience and Convenience: The Asylum and Its Alternatives in Progressive America* (Boston and Toronto: Little, Brown and Company, 1980), 5–8.

[112] Lewis Woods, a journalist who spent three days working undercover as a prisoner in Sing Sing in 1915, noted that the old prison stripes now lined the gray prison uniforms. Lewis Wood, "Former Celebrities in Prison Tribunal" *Tribune.* c. Jan. 20, 1915, newspaper clipping, in Clippings, OF Papers, MSS64, Box 342, Memorabilia, Scrapbooks, Prisons, Jan. 1 1915–Nov. 10, 1915. The prisoner's clothing allowance was officially extended in the early 1900s, with convicts being entitled to more clothing and more frequent replacement of their worn

The failure of state-use to materialize, in its original conception, and the proliferation of various new forms of suffering and violence in the prisons were not the results of some kind of struggle for dominance between the imperatives of administrative efficiency and the ethical ideals of prison reform in which the administrative was triumphant (as Rothman has argued was the fate of progressive prison reform in general).[113] As we have seen, and as the Commissioners themselves made clear, bureaucratic administration was itself failing quite badly. Inadequate technical or instrumental means (such as unreliable identification systems) and the presence of practical obstacles (such as the dispersed nature of the prison system) played a role in that administrative failure. But these were not the chief sources of frustration. Rather, various communities of people who, for a variety of reasons, saw fit to contest and modify the plan of reform, changed and imposed a series of constraints upon it. On the inside, the guards, wardens, and clerical workers who were supposed to be administrating the system, and the convicts who were supposed to be the objects of their administration, resisted, subverted, and sometimes just ignored the directives that arrived from on high. Here, the Commissioners and Superintendent repeatedly bumped up hard – less against the high walls of the prison than the accumulated weight of years of habituation among guards to what they took to be the natural order of things in the prisons, and the prisoners' overriding desire to improve upon their own relatively powerless and degraded position. On the outside, loyalists to the spoils system deprived the nascent penal state both of the full extent of funding that was needed to build the infrastructure of the new system, and of the political independence and constancy of operations that, in principle, are necessary to any rational bureaucracy. Finally, organized labor

out clothes and shoes. Under the new regulations, prisoners were allowed one gray coat every two years; one pair of gray trousers every year; one pair of summer trousers; one pair of shoes every nine months; two suits of underwear upon commitment and one new suit every year; one pair of socks every four months; one 'hickory' shirt per year; and one towel every six months. Although it is unlikely they received their full entitlement, the quality of inmate clothing was improving. "Some Facts About Sing Sing Management, Bulletin 1" (unpublished report, c.1915), 6, Westchester County Research Bureau, OFP, MSS 64, Box 276, Org. Recs.

[113] Rothman, *Conscience and Convenience*, 5–7. Rothman argues that custodial convenience trumped progressive ethical reform (or "conscience"): "What remained was a hybrid, really a bastard version [of the original progressive project] – one that fully satisfied the needs of those within the system but not the ambitions of reformers" (Rothman, *Conscience and Convenience*, 7). In light of the archival evidence I present here, however, Rothman arguably carves too a deep line between administrators and reformers: As we have seen, progressive reform, in its early phase, originated from within the administrative, penal arm of government. In progressivism's later phase, it was hard to distinguish between reformers (who often became state Commissioners and wardens) and administrators (who grappled firsthand with the disciplinary, fiscal, and ideological vacuums left by contracting). Moreover, the custodialism to which Rothman refers itself has a highly contested history, as we have seen: What worked in one age, for reasons of politics and popular morality, was contested or subject to failure in another. As historians of punishment, we need as much to explain transformations in the techniques, ideologies, and politics of custodialism, as changes in the means, ideals, and trajectories of supposedly "conscientious" reform movements.

and a handful of manufacturers succeeded in persuading state and federal legislatures to exclude prison labor from working in key segments of the burgeoning market in state-use goods. Those few state-use prison industries that did generate significant amounts of labor and revenue were repeatedly the victims of their own success.

With the acute insight of a person with first-hand, bodily knowledge of the workings of power in the prisons, Sing Sing convict #1500 captured the nature of the difficulties with which progressive administrators and penologists were being forced to grapple: "Sing Sing, like Great Britain," he wrote, "is governed by precedent that has the authority of law. It has no written constitution nor digest of its form of government but it has an enormous body of unwritten law which the prisoner can most easily learn by transgressing." So, too, he might have added, the ambitious prison reformer. In early progressive New York, the Commissioners, Superintendents, and lawmakers who sought to solve the prison labor problem and reconstruct the penal arm of the state from top to bottom, rewrote the formal laws of imprisonment; but, not unlike the newly committed inmate, they soon discovered and found themselves constrained and challenged by the prison's far more powerful, customary law. By 1910, the reconstructors had just begun to glimpse the extent and resilience of established penal culture, the deep power struggles that the reform effort seemed to be setting in motion, and the irreducibly political nature of their task. As we shall see in the next chapter, events that unfolded in and around Sing Sing's old "bastille" in the summer of 1913 would unambiguously demonstrate the power and tenacity of the prison's institutional culture and throw into high relief the bitterly contested political terrain of Progressive Era penal reform.

7

American Bastille: Sing Sing and the Political Crisis of Imprisonment

Come up her (sic) and write us up. . . . They are starving us. Give it a good write up in your paper.

Unidentified Sing Sing prisoner, to reporters, 1913[1]

In the early 1910s, the mounting internal crises of New York's prisons fused with the escalating struggle over the structure and purpose of government to produce a highly combustible alloy. That alloy exploded at Sing Sing in the summer of 1913. When Sing Sing's convicts threw their inedible rations through the windows of their cellblock, they catapulted the internal crisis of imprisonment over the walls of the institution and into the public sphere. Conscious of the presence of the press just beyond the prison walls, the defenestration of the "bastille" amounted to a disciplined, if spontaneous, protest against the conditions of imprisonment. Making emissaries of the reporters, prisoners effectively broadcasted an ultimatum to the prison bureaucrats, state legislators, New York's Governor, William Sulzer, and the free citizens of New York: Prisoners would not cooperate with a regime that had been progressively malnourishing, overcrowding, and sickening them. The act of breaking hundreds of windows with missiles of bread so stale it could shatter thick glass rudely punctuated the prisoners' point: The state would have to provide its convicts with edible food and ameliorate living conditions at Sing Sing or face collective, and quite possibly spectacular, acts of defiance.

As convicts, guards, newspaper reporters, and administrators correctly comprehended, the prisoners' demonstration was not just another convict food riot; both its causes and meaning made it much more serious than the raucous melées that had occasionally erupted in Sing Sing's mess halls during the previous few decades. The protest occurred at the end of a day of unrest in the prison and was followed by four more, in the course of which the prisoners went on strike, burnt workshops to the ground, passively resisted their keepers, demanded improved food, and called upon administrators to modify the much-hated practice of transferring prisoners to the remote prisons of Auburn and Clinton.[2] The riot erupted in the midst of a

---

[1] *New York Times,* July 23, 1913, 1.

[2] The pages of the *New York Times* offer the fullest account of the Sing Sing protests. *New York Times* (July 23, 1913), 1; (July 24, 1913), 1, 2; (July 25, 1913), 1, 2; (July 26, 1913), ed. 6,

political brawl that was being waged 125 miles away, in the state capitol of Albany. In the spring of 1913, Tammany Democrats and the New York Republican party had sided against "independent" Democratic Governor, William Sulzer, over Sulzer's charges that both Tammany and Republican prison authorities had systematically, and even criminally, mismanaged New York's prisons over the previous several years. Just six weeks before the Sing Sing rebellions, the State Controller, a Tammany man and vehement critic of Governor Sulzer, had suspended all funding of the prisons in retaliation for Sulzer's handling of the prison inquiry. The Controller's action had had an immediate impact on the prisons: Guards worked without wages, the prison pantries grew bare, and the prisoners had even less labor to do than usual. After six weeks of these conditions and no signs from Albany that the deadlock would be broken, the prisoners had taken matters into their own hands.

Clearly, the extraordinary circumstance of the suspension of prison funds played a precipitous role in the Sing Sing rebellion. Yet, the deeper roots of the rebellion lay in the spiraling crisis into which the prisons had descended after 1896 (when contract prison labor was abolished in New York) and in an internecine, state-wide political struggle that had escalated after 1902. Inside the prisons, two decades or more of declining conditions in the cellblock, diminished work assignments, and increasingly antagonistic relations among guards, prisoners, and administrators had brought the prison to the brink of rebellion at least three years before the defenestration. Rather than diminishing the chance of direct confrontation between prisoners and prison authorities, the administrators who sought penal reconstruction after 1896 had fortified prisoners' willingness to press for change; administrators had also lent prisoners (however inadvertently) a language of humane penal reform and the means by which to make themselves heard, effectively putting them in touch with a growing, and highly receptive audience of progressive reformers. Outside the prisons, administrators' struggle to rebuild the prison system along bureaucratic lines had fueled a political conflict over the questions of how and by whom the prisons – and the penal arm of the state, more generally – ought to be run. In seeking to reconstruct New York's prison system in the years following the abolition of contract penal labor, progressive reformers and administrators had declared war on the spoils system of penal management and had redoubled their effort to discipline the mass of prison keepers who refused to submit to "management."

As administrators and their unruly prison keepers understood very well, the attack on the prison's spoils system and its informal, personal ties of patronage was just one maneuver in a much larger campaign against the long-established forces of machine patronage and popular-democratic "boss" politics. Waged intermittently since the 1870s, this campaign consisted of the efforts of a loose conglomeration of professionals, civic

14; (July 27, 1913), Sec. I, 1; (July 28, 1913), 1; (July 29, 1913), 2; (July 30, 1913), 4; (Aug. 1, 1913), 16.

reformers, and industrialists to establish "efficient, managerial government." A diversity of political and ethical visions characterized these reformers' conceptualization of the task before them. Nonetheless, what they
shared in common was a strong commitment to unseating what Francis
Parkman once described as "King Demos"[3] – that is, the white working class
(and often heavily immigrant) Democratic political machines that came to
dominate urban politics in nineteenth-century America – as well as other,
Republican versions of "machine boss" politics. In the late nineteenth and
early twentieth centuries, most Northern states witnessed some variation of a
reform campaign aimed at hobbling the urban machines and the spoils system of government. In New York, following the success of the anti-Tammany
crusader, Samuel Tilden, in effectively breaking the power of Tammany
Hall's "Boss" William Tweed in 1872, [4] civic reformers had slowly but surely
initiated a series of reforms that foreshadowed the "managerialism" and
"efficiency" movements of the Progressive Era. Despite Tweed's demise,
Tammany Hall soldiered on and proved resilient enough that, in the 1890s,
a new species of "independent" Democrats and Republicans renewed the
effort to rid the Empire State of the "looters" and "spoilsmen" of both Tammany and Platt's Republican machines.[5] No department or section of local
and state government, including the prisons, was overlooked in reformers'
renewed drive against King Demos. By 1910, reformers had effected considerable structural change in various government agencies (including the
penal system): Within many of the Northern states, they had laid the foundations of governmental bureaucracy in state charities, hospitals, and prisons;
expanded the administrative reach of state and city government through
the reform of welfare, policing, sanitation, and penal agencies; and defined

[3] Francis Parkman, quoted in Samuel Haber, *Efficiency and Uplift: Scientific Management in the
Progressive Era, 1890–1920* (Chicago: University of Chicago Press, 1964), 100.
[4] Tammany Hall was founded as a benevolent association in New York City in 1789. In the years
1821–1872 and 1902–32, Tammany was a major or the principal controlling force not only in
local politics, but also in state and city criminal justice, welfare, and employment. Ward leaders commonly acted as advocates for individuals in legal proceedings, judicial appointments
turned on the candidate's loyalty to Tammany, and, true to its origins as a benevolent society,
Tammany provided food, aid, and employment for its supporters as well as a particular kind
of amative bond between supporters and party, which has been described by one observer
of the period as "political friendship." These personal, local bonds of patronage were considered a hallmark of democratic practice by many working class people in New York and
in other "machine" cities such as Kansas City, Missouri and Philadelphia; such voters considered managerialist drives to make democracy "efficient" through the bureaucratization
of the state and the severance of party politics from employment, welfare, and criminal justice, as inherently anti-democratic. Mary Kingsbury Simkhovitch, "Friendship and Politics"
Political Science Quarterly 17:2 (June 1902), 189–205; Richard Oestreicher, "Urban Working
Class Political Behavior and Theories of American Electoral Politics, 1870–1940," *Journal
of American History* 74:4 (Mar. 1988), 1257–86; Robert F. Wesser, *A Response to Progressivism:
The Democratic Party and New York Politics, 1902–1918* (New York: New York University Press,
1986); Daniel Czitrom, "Underworlds and Underdogs: Big Tim Sullivan and Metropolitan
Politics in New York, 1889–1913," *Journal of American History* 78:2 (Sep. 1991), 536–58.
[5] Walter Wilson, *Forced Labor in the United States* (New York: International Publishers, 1933),
63–4.

and attempted to regulate social hygiene. In New York, reformers had also established state committees to improve housing; set up a New York City Board of Public Improvements, with authority to coordinate public works; enacted legislation directing that state contracts be awarded to the highest bidder (rather than the one with closest ties to the political victor); and formally made civil servants of thousands of state and city employees.[6]

The commission and civil service reformers enjoyed a number of legislative victories in the decade either side of 1900. At the same time, however, within the various state agencies and institutions, they had encountered persistent, if local and relatively unorganized, resistance to their attempts to purge government administration of politics.[7] After 1902, especially, these local acts of resistance, and the increasingly widespread perception that the managerial reformers were anti-democratic, became rallying points for the ailing party of Tammany Hall. Freshly invigorated by former and current state employees' mounting disaffection with the reform program, Tammany Democrats once again sprang to life as a major force in New York politics and the indefatigable defender of machine democracy. As administrators and civic reformers lobbied for punitive legislation against uncooperative prison guards and other civil servants, and secured passage of groundbreaking laws such as the Moreland Act of 1907 (which authorized executive agencies to subpoena and otherwise discipline civil servants),[8] the stage was set for another confrontation between the adherents of two quite distinct and mutually antagonistic practices of democracy. As we shall see, that a critical battle in this larger confrontation directly concerned New York's penal system and was eventually waged in and around the "Bastille on the Hudson," was neither accidental nor politically inconsequential.

*   *   *   *   *

Sing Sing was no ordinary American prison; although, through much of the nineteenth century, its contract prison labor system, strict corporal regimen, and general mode of administration made it indistinguishable from most other industrial state prisons, Sing Sing had occupied a particularly prominent and symbolically laden position in the collective imaginary of legal punishment. The "resort of a great city's felons," as Frank Tannenbaum, the eminent Columbia University historian and one-time penitentiary inmate

---

[6] Haber, *Efficiency and Uplift*, 7–45, 100–01. For accounts of government reform at the state and local levels in New York, see J. Hampden Dougherty, *Constitutional History of the State of New York*, 2nd ed. (New York: The Neale Publishing Company, 1915); David Hammack, *Power and Society: Greater New York at the Turn of the Century* (New York: Russell Sage Foundation, 1982); H. Paul Jeffers, *Commissioner Roosevelt: The Story of Theodore Roosevelt and the New York City Police, 1895–97* (New York: J. Wiley and Sons, 1994); Adonica Yen-Mui Lui, "Party Machines, State Structure, and Social Policies: the Abolition of Public Outdoor Relief in New York City, 1874–1898," (Ph.D. diss., Harvard University, 1993); Martin V. Melosi, *The Sanitary City: Urban Infrastructure in America from Colonial Times to the Present* (Baltimore and London: Johns Hopkins University Press, 2000).

[7] Discussed earlier, Chapter 6.   [8] See above, 255.

once described it,[9] Sing Sing had been the object of scrutiny, debate, and conflict from its earliest days. Although, in the first few years of its career, leading penal reformers had hailed it as a model republican institution, Sing Sing subsequently developed a lasting reputation at home and abroad as what Dorothea Dix characterized as the harshest prison "north of the Mason and Dixon line."[10] In the 1830s, Alexis de Tocqueville and Gustave de Beaumont had helped spread the prison's fearsome reputation in reporting that order there was established and maintained by liberal doses of the lash and the keepers' systematic effort to break every prisoner's spirit.[11] Sing Sing went on, after 1840, to become the target of diverse social movements, including a nationwide crusade against corporal punishment, a series of workingmen's campaigns against contract prison labor, and various evangelical efforts to spiritually "awaken" the republic's wayward men. As the prison labor contract system became ever more deeply entrenched in the early Gilded Age and John Sherwood Perry proceeded to break the stove molders' union (using Sing Sing prisoners), Sing Sing became, in the eyes of skilled workingmen everywhere, a particularly potent symbol of industrialists' desire to crush organized labor and of the state's complicity with employers' allegedly nefarious intentions. Repeated scandals and investigations into Sing Sing and alleged abuses there in the 1870s and 1880s had kept the prison on the front pages of the New York newspapers. Now, in the early Progressive Era, following the abolition of prison labor contracting, Sing Sing would once again be in the public eye, as the institution in which progressive prison reform would be put to the test. In 1913, it would become a critical referent in a heated debate over the appropriate means and ends of legal punishment in the postcontractual era, the proper form and function of the penal arm of the state, and, ultimately, the meaning of democratic governance.[12]

As we have seen, everyday life in New York's prisons changed substantially following the exit of the private contractors in the 1890s and the suspension of the sale of prisonmade goods on the open market. Although living

---

[9] Frank Tannenbaum, *Osborne of Sing Sing* (Chapel Hill, NC: University of North Carolina Press, 1933), 109. In 1914, Tannenbaum was convicted in New York City on charges arising from his leadership of the "Army of the Unemployed" (whose 190-odd members Tannenbaum led into New York City churches during the recession of 1914, so that they might assert their "right" to food and shelter) and sentenced to one year's imprisonment. Tannenbaum wrote about his experiences in the Blackwell's Island penitentiary in *Wall Shadows: A Study of American Prisons* (New York and London: G. P. Putnam's Sons, 1922). For a wide ranging discussion of Tannenbaum's life and work as activist and scholar, see Charles Hale, "Frank Tannenbaum and the Mexican Revolution," *The Hispanic American Historical Review* 75 (1995), 215–46.

[10] Dorothea Dix, *Remarks on Prisons and Prison Discipline in the United States* (Montclair, NJ: Patterson Smith, 1967 [1845]), 16.

[11] Gustave de Beaumont and Alexis de Tocqueville, *On the Penitentiary System in the United States and Its Application in France*, trans. Francis Lieber (Carbondale: Southern Illinois University Press, 1964), 73, 162–5.

[12] The challenges to and partial collapse of productive labor in prisons after 1880 in New York and other states are discussed in Chapter 4 of this book.

conditions in all the state prisons declined in the wake of abolition, Sing Sing was hit particularly hard. After 1896, the prisoner's existence at Sing Sing was demonstrably more miserable and his life prospects, poorer, than at any previous point in the prison's history (besides the period in which the Perry contract was in place). Relative both to civilians and prisoners in other Northern states, Sing Sing's prisoners were unhealthy, underfed, and inactive. They had substantially lower life expectancy and far higher disease rates than civilians and, more than ever before, they endured some of the worst conditions to be found in an American penal institution outside of the South. This was largely attributable to the fact that every prisoner spent three-quarters of his time locked in one of 1,200 cells, each of which measured seven feet deep by six feet wide and six and one-half feet high. Constructed fifty years earlier out of slabs of granite stone quarried from the banks of the Hudson River, the cellhouse floor was mounted directly on the damp, low-lying banks of the river, with the result that, over the years, the walls, ceilings, and floors of the cells had become perpetually moist to the touch. The natural humidity of the structure was abetted by its double shell design, whereby the block of 1,200 cells stood free within a larger stone building, ensuring that very little sunlight and even less fresh air penetrated the cells. As the practice of doubling the surplus of prisoners together in these dank cells became the norm in the 1890s, Sing Sing convicts contracted a range of pulmonary, upper respiratory, and dermatological diseases.[13]

Efforts to bureaucratize and sanitize the state prisons, which had begun in earnest following the departure of the last few private contractors in 1896, had done little to ameliorate the basic living conditions at Sing Sing. More often than not, attempts by the New York State Prison Commission to improve conditions were defeated by the unwieldy masonry of the cellhouse, the poorly drained site upon which the prison lay, and the legislature's reluctance to fund the costly work of altering the heavy stone walls. Where alterations were made, the solution to one problem spawned another, as was made strikingly evident by the authorities' failed attempt to improve the air quality of the cells by drilling ventilation shafts through the granite walls in the late 1890s: As vermin claimed the shafts as byways into cells, the prisoners demonstrated their preference for stale air over roaches and rats by blocking the shafts with clothing, books, and any material they could smuggle out of the prison workshops. The occasional effort to clean up the cells by whitewashing the walls was invariably defeated by the rapid return of mildew.[14]

---

[13] James W. White, a progressive investigator, claimed that between 1910 and 1912, Sing Sing's hospital records proved that prisoners were contracting syphilis after commitment to the prison, basic principles of quarantine were not adhered to in the hospital, the prison physicians were constantly absent, and nefarious operations had been performed on unwilling prisoners. James W. White, "Facts About Sing Sing" (unpublished report, ca. 1914), OFP, MSS64, Box 276, Org. Recs.

[14] Presentment of the Westchester Grand Jury to the June Term of the Supreme Court in the Matter of the Inquiry into the Conditions of Sing Sing Prison, 1913; see also Sing Sing

The dilapidated condition of the Sing Sing cellblock did not go unremarked. As poor design and makeshift solutions combined to defeat successive attempts at sanitation through the late 1890s and prisoners had little work to do, the cellhouse emerged in prisoners' narratives as an object of undying loathing. Its captives spoke of long days and longer nights spent in cramped, overcrowded, vermin-infested cells, and of the inexorable wasting away of body and spirit these conditions engendered. In their daily conduct and in the pages of the *Star of Hope*, prisoners made it clear that they would rather do even hard labor – such as quarrying stone or heaving coal – than spend time in the cells.[15] But most prisoners could do little more than find the legitimate means to evade the cellhouse for an extra hour or two each week. Refusal to return to the cells at the end of the workday was one form of protest, but it was perilous, as the authorities were quick to use violent means to enforce a lock-down of the entire prison population.[16] With its double-locked cells and solid stone walls, the cellhouse remained the ultimate guarantor of prison security.

Prisoners were not the only people to register their distress at the Sing Sing cellhouse. Since the publication of Dorothea Dix's survey of American prisons in 1845,[17] prison reformers had intermittently criticized its conditions and called for its sanitization. Around 1900, however, élite social reformers from a variety of civic organizations elevated their intermittent criticism into a vociferous campaign to demolish the cellhouse altogether. For these reformers, unlike previous ones, the cellhouse was both a practical threat to the lives of convicts and the symbolic embodiment of a penal system that was outmoded, barbaric, and corrupt. Pointing to the penal bureaucracy's studies of Sing Sing's disease rates, the dilapidated condition of the cells, and the number of hours convicts spent in the cellhouse, members of the New York Prison Association joined other prison reformers in petitioning the legislature that the cellhouse posed a threat that was simultaneously biological, moral, and economic. With Cornelius V. Collins' annual reports on the cellhouse in hand, they set about publicizing the view that the

---

Prison reports in New York State Commission of Prisons, *Annual Report* (1897, 1898, 1899, 1900, 1901, 1902, 1903, 1904, 1905).

[15] Donald Lowrie, *My Life in Prison* (ca. 1912); Anne Porter Lynes Field, *The Story of Canada Blackie* (New York: E. P. Dutton and Co, 1915); selections, *Star of Hope*, 1–3 (1899–1901), discussed earlier, 243.

[16] The "lock down," by which the entire prison population was locked in the cells, remained the cornerstone of prison order through the early twentieth century. Whenever there were signs of trouble in the workshops or mess hall, the prison authorities responded by sending all the prisoners back to their cells, where they could be secured and counted. Most critically, from the point of view of prison order, the cellblock isolated prisoners from one another – or, at the very least, separated prisoners into pairs of cellmates – and enabled reliable technology (the building), rather than fallible and costly human labor (prison guards), to enforce order. Only once the prisoners were safely under lock and key in the cells was the possibility of escape or riot arrested. Any hint of refusal to return to the cells was met with uncompromising force. Tannenbaum, *Wall Shadows: A Study of American Prisons*, 23. *

[17] Dorothea Dix, *Remarks on Prisons.*

high incidence of tuberculosis, pneumonia, and skin and rheumatoid diseases among Sing Sing prisoners posed an imminent threat not only to the convicts but the citizens of New York: Diseased convicts, they argued, were carrying contagion back to the City of New York after release from prison, thereby endangering the population at large.[18] Whereas, in the early 1830s, state officials had proudly shown Sing Sing to visiting European statesmen, travel writers, and scholars as proof of America's enlightened republicanism, the prison now enjoyed a reputation as the incubator of disease, hopelessness, and moral corruption. As investigators repeatedly claimed, Sing Sing's cellblock was a "disgrace" to the Empire State, and it should be demolished as soon as practicable. In a lament typical of the times, John P. Jaeckel, the new president of the New York State Prison Commission, wrote in 1904:

> It is an axiom that the State of New York has failed to keep pace with the advanced demands of public sentiment in the housing of its criminal classes, and has, no doubt, through a narrow and false sense of economy, tolerated a dangerous condition by continuing in service of this old, obsolete and inhuman receptacle in which human beings are cast to acquire disease and stimulate criminal tendencies. These conditions have lasted for many years, and the early dawn of the twentieth century should witness a complete revolution of the sheltering of criminals.[19]

As these reports suggest, not only the condition of the cellblock but its symbolic meaning was changing in the early twentieth century. At various points of its eighty-year history, Sing Sing Prison had served as the embodiment of – and symbol for – immorality: Identifying it as the fullest expression of industrial wage slavery in the 1830s, workingmen had flooded the state Senate with more petitions than had ever been submitted on any other topic; antebellum evangelists of the campaign against corporal punishment had indicted Sing Sing as a sinful transgression of a Divine right over life and death; and in the 1870s and 1880s, manufacturers' organizations in pursuit of a free market held up Sing Sing's convict contract labor system as the worst example of state-sponsored monopoly and market bondage.[20] Then, after 1896, as administrators set about reconstructing the penal system, Sing Sing – and the cellhouse in particular – came to signify much more than the degeneration of convicts' strength and health. It became the emblem of the barbaric, old system, the continued existence of which enforced and legitimated a corrupt political order. Much as the republican revolutionaries of late-eighteenth-century France had seized upon the Bastille of the Bourbons as a monument to the evils of the *ancien régime*, élite penal

---

[18] As early as 1895, investigative committees such as the New York state Assembly Committee on Prisons, recommended that Sing Sing be replaced. Reported in the *New York Times* (May 3, 1895), 5.

[19] New York State Commission of Prisons, *Annual Report* (1896), 39–40; (1901), 18–21; (1902), 97–100; (1903), 18–20, 78. Jaeckel succeeded Lispenard Stewart in 1903; he was also the State Treasurer.

[20] Discussed earlier, 155.

reformers of the early twentieth century assailed the Sing Sing cellhouse as the embodiment and enforcer of an outmoded, unjust political order: The cellblock symbolized precisely the corrupt politics and decrepit state that progressive reformers sought to overthrow. Such a bastille would admit of no effective renovation, they argued: Like the old political system for which it stood, it would have to be destroyed and replaced.[21]

By this time, the Superintendent of State Prisons, Cornelius V. Collins, had also begun to favor the replacement of Sing Sing – albeit on the more obviously instrumentalist grounds that leaving Sing Sing and constructing a new prison might be an opportunity to generate sorely needed employment for prisoners (in construction work), to establish more efficient industries, and to advance the centralization of the penal arm of state government. In 1904, after several frustrating years trying to establish state-use industries and render them profitable, Collins began to search out a more systematic solution to his prison labor problem. Persuaded that the task of managing the prisons and their industries was greatly hindered both by the unions and the decentralized character of the prison system, Collins recommended to the state senate that the majority of state prisoners be put to work digging some thirty million cubic yards of stone, located just four miles north of Sing Sing on the western shores of the Hudson River. Consistent with state-use law, most of this stone would be sold to the state for use in its good-roads program, he noted; in addition, "(t)he income to be derived from the sale of the stone to state, county, and town officials should be sufficient to pay for the maintenance of the prisoners engaged in its production."[22] In thinking through this scheme, Collins struck upon the idea that he could also solve the administrative problem through the construction at the quarry of one, huge prison, to hold the entire populations of Sing Sing and Auburn; these older prisons could be sold, he suggested, and the profits applied to the cost of building the new "central prison."[23]

Shortly after receiving Collins's report, the legislature directed the Governor to appoint a Commission on Prison Improvement, the task of which it was to investigate the condition of existing prison buildings and Collin's proposed central prison. The five-person commission (members of which included Collins, the two other state Prison Commissioners, and a long-time critic of the Sing Sing cellhouse, Samuel J. Barrows [of the New York Prison Association]), eventually recommended that New York replace both Auburn and Sing Sing prisons, but with two prisons, rather than the one large-scale central institution that Collins had originally suggested.[24] In their report,

---

[21] *Star of Hope* 1: 2 (May 1899), 7.

[22] Special Report of Superintendent of State Prisons and State Engineer and Surveyor, New York State Senate, January, 1905 (quoted in *New York Times*, Jan. 26, 1895, 5).

[23] Special Report of Superintendent of State Prisons and State Engineer and Surveyor, New York State Senate, January, 1905 (quoted in *New York Times*, Jan. 26, 1895, 5).

[24] The Commission gave a number of cost-related reasons for rejecting the central prison proposal, none of which is very persuasive; it seems likely that the Commissioners, who were drawn from both western and eastern New York, could not agree on a central site.

the Commissioners strongly affirmed the view that both the Sing Sing and Auburn cellhouses were unfit for human habitation and the source of a wide range of illnesses among the prisoners; they estimated that it would cost at least $2 million to upgrade the existing cellhouses, whereas two new state-of-the art prisons, complete with improved administrative, medical, educational, and industrial buildings, could be constructed, by convict labor, for just under $4 million (excluding the savings realized by sale of the old prisons).[25]

The legislature voted in support of the recommendation and the Commission announced an architectural competition to secure a design for what they claimed would be "the most modern and best equipped prison in the world." Thirty-four architects submitted plans and the Commissioners eventually chose the design submitted by a local architect by the name of William J. Beardsley: The new prison would have enameled steel cells (which were easier to clean than stone or brick), plumbing in the cells, cell closets with noiseless rolling doors, and a pillarless mess hall and chapel that could easily seat the entire prison population while affording the guards an unobstructed view of the convicts. Beardsley also provided for the installation of advanced telephone systems and "push-button annunciators" in all the cells. Sing Sing's ugly thicket of work sheds, stone cellhouse, and obscure alleyways would be replaced by a simple, uncluttered compound in which surveillance and sanitation were intrinsic to the design. According to the Commissioners, such "advanced" design would lead penologists "from all parts of the United States...Europe, South America and even Japan and China" to observe its operation. Closer to home, the prison would be seen by "the thousands of people traveling up and down the Hudson River" as a "monument" to the state's advanced form of government. The Prison Improvement Commissioners seemed certain that Beardsley's prison would make the Empire State a leading penal innovator once again.[26]

In the meantime, the Commissioners located a suitable plot of land, some fifteen miles up the Hudson River from Sing Sing, on a site adjoining Bear Mountain. The Legislature acted the next year, establishing yet another commission (the Commission on New Prisons, whose members were drawn from the old Prison Improvement Commission) to oversee the project, and appropriating $75,000 for the purchase of the land.[27] Work on the site got underway in the summer of 1908. Fifty Sing Sing convicts and a handful

[25] *New York Times*, Jan. 29, 1906, 6.

[26] Quoted in New York State Commission on New Prisons, *Annual Report* (1906) (Albany, NY: J. B. Lyon, 1907).

[27] The legislature passed a law in 1906 that provided for the replacement of Sing Sing and the establishment of a prison commission to find and develop a suitable site. Laws N.Y. 1906, Ch. 670. The members of the New York State Commission on New Prisons were Samuel J. Barrows, John G. Wickser, Cornelius Collins, Edwin O. Holter, and Elisha M. Johnson. It is worth noting that from the beginning, these Commissioners frequently articulated the importance of publicizing their work: Their first report was rushed out on the evening of January 11, 1907, to be released for the morning edition of the newspapers. New York State Commission on New Prisons, *Annual Report* (1906) (Albany, NY: J. B. Lyon, 1907), 1.

of guards traveled daily by steamship to Bear Mountain, where they began clearing and grading the heavily forested land in preparation for the construction of the new prison. Over the next two years, work on the new prison continued apace. By 1909, 150 Sing Sing convicts were living and working on the site under the supervision of Bear Mountain's first warden. They excavated and graded a roadbed for a trolley line that would stretch from the West Shore railroad to the prison site, erected power and telephone poles along the roadbed, built a power house, barn, and ice house, installed a gravity water supply to carry water from the mountain to the prison, erected temporary barracks, and build a sixteen-foot wooden stockade around the prison site.[28]

As it turned out, Sing Sing was not to be replaced by the Bear Mountain prison; despite a significant investment of time, capital, and convict labor, no felon was ever committed there. From the moment that the architectural competition was announced, the Bear Mountain prison became ensnared in the larger, ongoing struggle in New York politics over state resources and the rules by which those resources should be distributed. Some days after the Commission selected Beardsley's plan, a minority of the Commissioners came out publicly to declare it wildly flawed, and accused their fellow Commissioners of cronyism in the award of the contract. Beardsley, it turned out, had no practical experience in prison construction but was rumored to be a near relative of one of the Commissioners. When pressed, the Chairman of the Commission refused to release the suspect plans to the public – or even allow the dissenting members of his Commission to access them again.[29] Subsequently, the State Architect, and eventually the American Institute of Architects, pronounced the plans flawed, and the Commission's conduct, unethical; a group of New York City architects (many associated with the leading firms, including that of the distinguished architect, Benjamin W. Morris) subsequently brought suit against the state, seeking a cessation of construction and the termination of the Commission itself.[30]

At the same time, other, politically influential, segments of the community had mobilized against the Bear Mountain prison-building project. A chapter of the Sons of the American Revolution sought to bring political and moral pressure to bear against the Bear Mountain prison, on the grounds that it was being constructed on the site of the Revolutionary Era forts of Clinton and Montgomery, and that a massive and bloody battle in the war for independence had taken place there in 1777. To build a prison upon that hallowed land, the Sons argued, would be to "desecrate this battlefield, christened by the blood of our Revolutionary heroes."[31] The Scenic and Historic Reservation Society added weight to this objection, repeatedly

[28] New York State Commission on New Prisons, *Annual Report* (1908), 7–8; (1909), 4.
[29] *New York Times*, Aug. 6, 1908, 4.
[30] Among other things, the suit charged that the legislation establishing the Commission did not authorize the appointment of an architect, and that Beardsley's appointment was null and void. The *New York Times*, July 11, 1908, 14; Dec. 9, 1908, 3.
[31] *New York Times*, Jan. 26, 1908, C8.

petitioning the legislature against the pending construction and arguing that the entire Bear Mountain area should be preserved as a state park.[32] Under increasing pressure, the legislature slowed in its appropriation of monies for the work at Bear Mountain. Finally, all construction was abandoned in 1910, when Mary W. Harriman (widow of the railroad magnate) made it a condition of her bestowing upon the state a large tract of the Hudson shoreline and more than $2 million that the state abandon construction of the Bear Mountain prison.[33] Shortly thereafter, the land was absorbed by the Parks Department, and Bear Mountain was eventually opened to civilian recreators as part of the Palisades Park. The convict prison builders rejoined their fellow convicts back at the dismal "Bastille on the Hudson."

Undeterred, the Commission on New Prisons immediately began looking for a new site for Sing Sing's replacement. With an initial legislative appropriation of $60,000, the Commission purchased a large tract of swamp and arable land at Wingdale, sixty-nine miles up the Harlem Railroad from New York City. Planning for the construction of "Harlem Prison" began at Wingdale in mid-1910.[34] For a second time, however, the effort to replace Sing Sing encountered major political difficulties. Initially, there were delays in work on the site, caused partly by the ongoing objections of the State Architect, Franklin B. Ware, to Beardsley's controversial blueprints. After working out a compromise with Ware, the Commission finally commenced the construction work in late 1910. More ominous, however, was the outcome of the 1910 state and mid-term Congressional elections. The Republican party's sixteen-year tenure in the Governor's office came to an abrupt end when New York voters elected a Tammany Democrat, John A. Dix, over the Republican candidate, Henry L. Stimson. The Democrats also swept the New York state legislature and the U.S. House of Representatives; indeed, across the country, as Theodore Roosevelt bluntly called it, the Democrats whipped the Republicans "to a frazzle."[35]

In New York, the Democrats' electoral triumph threw into question not only the fate of the Wingdale prison, but the structure and staffing of the penal arm of the state and the direction of the state's ongoing program of prison reform, more generally. In his first "appeal to the people," Governor Dix voiced his opposition to precisely the kind of state commission that progressive state-builders had championed, arguing that such bodies were unaccountable to voters and thus anti-democratic;[36] in the ensuing months, as he disassembled several commissions, he also quietly rolled back the ambit of the civil service law, exempting some 224 positions from civil service rules. In effect, Dix freed such positions, and the process of hiring and firing

---

[32] *New York Times*, Jan. 26, 1908, C8.   [33] *New York Times*, Jan. 7, 1910, 3.

[34] The abandonment of Bear Mountain and commencement of work at Wingdale was directed by the legislature in 1910. Laws N.Y. 1910, Ch. 365. At Wingdale, the Commissioners set about building Beardsley's original prison, with only a few modifications.

[35] *New York Times*, Nov. 9, 1910, 1. Democrats also won gubernatorial races in New Jersey, Ohio, Massachusetts, Indiana, and Connecticut.

[36] *New York Times*, Feb. 3, 1911, 3.

people in those positions, from the rules and regulations of bureaucratic control and returned them to the arena of spoils politics.[37]

In regard to New York's penal system, the new Governor's first move was to purge the upper ranks of the civil service and various government commissions of Republicans. Two weeks into his tenure, Dix announced that he would be conducting investigations into all state departments, including the Prison Department, and that he had asked the long-time Superintendent of Prisons, Cornelius V. Collins, to resign his post. Shortly afterward, his Prison Commission commenced an inquiry into the management of all the state prisons (and, in particular, Sing Sing).[38] Collins, a Republican who had been Superintendent of Prisons since 1897 and had served on every major prison commission in the state since 1901, at first ignored the request for his resignation. However, as the Dix Prison Commission commenced its investigation, he resigned all his positions – and made preparations to leave for Havana, Cuba with William Beardsley (where he hoped to build for the Cuban government the prison he had failed to build at home).[39] As the Governor announced this investigation into the state prisons, a political scandal over the purchase of the Wingdale site the previous year also broke: It became clear that a local businessman had bought up the land, in partnership with the son-in-law of an influential Republican State Assemblyman, on the expectation that the abandonment of Bear Mountain might present them an opportunity to sell the land to the state at a tidy profit. (In the event, the speculators probably made about seventy-five percent on their investment; they defended their actions as nothing worse than "smart business").[40] Soon afterward, the Governor purged the higher administrative wing of the penal state of all Republicans, installing Democrats in the positions of State Prison Commissioner, Superintendent of Prisons, and all three prison wardenships.[41] Finally, Dix requested that the remaining Commissioners of New Prisons tender their resignations; when they refused, he ousted them and then promptly declared that there was no immediate need for a new prison.[42]

While the administrative positions in the penal arm of the state were being "Democratized" along Tammany lines, work on Harlem Prison had continued apace. In the last few weeks of 1911, just as the prison was nearing completion, Governor Dix ordered its construction halted. Dix's new Superintendent of Prisons, Colonel Joseph Scott, announced that Harlem Prison would not be completed and that a new cellblock was to be built at

---

[37] Report of the Executive Committee of the Civil Service Association, quoted in *New York Times*, May 9, 1912, 6.

[38] *New York Times*, Jan. 11, 1920, 2; *New York Times*, Apr. 11, 1911, 2.

[39] *New York Times*, Mar. 18, 1911, 8. I have been unable to verify whether Collins and Beardsley made any headway with their Cuba plan.

[40] The state paid a total of $75,000 for land that the speculators bought for approximately $34,000. *New York Times*, June 9, 1910, 2; Apr. 11, 1911, 1.

[41] *New York Times*, Apr. 27, 1911, 4; *New York Times*, Oct. 18, 1911, 20.

[42] *New York Times*, Oct. 11, 1911, 20.

Sing Sing instead.[43] Much to the frustration of members of the New York Prison Association and many other prison reformers, Harlem Prison stood empty for years (and was finally transferred to the Department of Mental Hygiene in the 1920s). For a second time in fewer than ten years, a replacement prison for Sing Sing had been planned, partially built, and abandoned; fifteen years after penal bureaucrats had first condemned it, Sing Sing's cell-block still housed one-third of all the state's prisoners, and not a single state prisoner was ever held in what was supposed to have been the "most modern and best equipped prison" in the world.[44]

The fact that in 1912, more than 1,400 convicts were still being locked up in Sing Sing's oft-condemned bastille for more than half their waking hours, suggests the limits of the power of penal reformers in the early Progressive Era, the failure of their effort to build a bureaucratic penal state that was politically neutral (or even merely perceived as such), and the continuing importance of party politics to New York's state penal system. By the same token, that the state had authorized and funded the replacement of Sing Sing at all was highly significant and bore important consequences, both for the terms of the political and moral debate over legal punishment and the ongoing power struggles taking place on the ground, in the prisons themselves. Both the passage of the legislation authorizing the construction of a prison to replace Sing Sing and the fanfare with which the Commissions on Prison Improvement and New Prisons announced its programs signaled to convicts and citizens alike that the state – for the time being at least – agreed with penologists and social reformers that Sing Sing was a disgraceful, shameful, and inhumane prison in which to house its felons. In subsequent years, the relevant legislation and commission findings would be repeatedly cited by those seeking the abolition of Sing Sing, in such a way as to add weight to the demand that Sing Sing should go. In directing that Sing Sing be replaced, the legislators had helped delegitimize the ongoing use of the Sing Sing cellhouse and they had implicitly, if unintentionally, lent convicts a modicum of moral authority (and perhaps too, the confidence) with which to criticize or even resist their internment in the bastille. As the prisoners were probably well aware, the state was becoming ever more ensnared in a contradiction of its own making.

It was in the course of the construction efforts at Wingdale during 1910–12 that the series of localized conflicts over the management of New York's prisons began to escalate into full-scale political struggle. With the final victory in New York, in 1896, of the foes of contractual prison labor, prisons and prisoners had receded significantly, although not entirely, from popular

---

43 Much to Dix's consternation, the private contractor constructing the Wingdale prison intermittently forged ahead despite the Governor's order. Once construction actually ceased on the site (in mid-1912) and the state settled the contract with the construction company, the total cost of the project amounted to over $300,000. *New York Times*, Dec. 28, 1911, 8; Report of the Commission on New Prisons, *New York Times*, July 17, 1913, 2.

44 The only prison to be built and opened in these years was the one at Comstock, New York (Great Meadow), which opened in 1911.

discourse; to the extent that there was a public discourse of legal punishment in New York in the first decade of the twentieth century, it mostly
centered on the so-called prison labor problem and was authored largely
by administrators, labor leaders, penologists, and philanthropists. With the
handing over of the reins of political power to Tammany's John A. Dix,
in 1911, however, prisons and prisoners were thrust once again full-square
into the public consciousness. Governor Dix's order to halt all work on
the Harlem Prison was one of several steps his administration took against
efforts to reconstruct the prison system along the managerial lines to which
Lispenard Stewart, Cornelius V. Collins, and other reformers had hewed
over the previous decade and a half.

Unsurprisingly, Tammany's efforts to pare back the civil service rules
and, more generally, halt the long-term effort of independent (or "county")
Democrats and urban Republicans to curtail patronage and spoils-based
state-craft, met with immediate and considerable resistance. Counterattacks
came from a variety of quarters, including from within the Democratic party
itself. There followed several years of remarkably bitter and highly publicized struggles over penal reform and the penal state. A slew of highly
politicized commissions of inquiry, grand jury indictments, civil legal proceedings, and muckraking exposés unleashed a steady torrent of stories and
images of prisons, prisoners, and keepers into the public sphere. No fewer
than three special Governor's commissions, a Senate commission, and six or
more Grand Juries conducted investigations into conditions in the New York
state prisons. The first round of inquiries, prosecuted by Dix and his Tammany Democrats, resulted in the dismissal of two wardens, the indictment
of the Superintendent of Prisons (Cornelius V. Collins), and substantial lawsuits against a number of officials, including the former Secretary of State, G.
C. Kellog.[45] This combative series of investigations, which were thoroughly
reported in the daily press, together with the news that an expensive state
facility (Harlem Prison) sat empty at Wingdale, began to awaken the citizens of New York to the internal crisis of the prisons. By 1912, Sing Sing
was once again on its way to becoming an object of considerable popular
concern.

In the wake of Dix's remarkable rollback of recent reforms, independent, county, and self-identified "progressive" Democrats began mobilizing

---

[45] The first commission of inquiry (the Dix Commission, to which Governor Dix appointed
William Church Osborn and George E. Van Kennan) investigated Sing Sing following complaints that employees had been coerced into making contributions to political campaigns
(*New York Times* [Mar. 15, 1913], 4). The Dix Commission found this to be the case, and also
criticized the prison's accounting methods. Subsequently, Warden J. D. Frost and Clinton's
Warden F. D. Cole were forced to resign. A year later, New York state successfully sued the
former Secretary of State and G. C. Kellogg for alleged fraud in the sale of coal to Clinton and Sing Sing Prisons. More damaging still, the Superintendent of Prisons, Cornelius
V. Collins, was indicted by the Washington County Grand Jury for larceny and forgery
in connection with his administration. *People v. O'Brien* [and Kellog], Sup. Ct. N.Y., App.
Div., Third Department, 157 A.D. 119; 141, N.Y.S. 1046; 1913 N.Y. App. Div. LEXIS 5920
(May 7, 1913); White, "Facts About Sing Sing," 1–3.

against the Governor and the leader of the Tammany machine, Charles F. Murphy, whose support had been critical to Dix's election. As soon as a few months into Dix's administration, some party members publicly charged him with incompetence; others, including Senator Franklin D. Roosevelt and his ally and friend, former New York Civil Service Commissioner, Thomas Mott Osborne, aimed their ire – and organizing power – against Murphy, as the alleged "boss" behind Democratic party nominations and Dix's policy of rolling back civil service reform.[46] Through much of 1912, these factions waged a rancorous struggle for control of the party, almost coming to blows at the Democratic State Convention in October.[47] By then, U.S. Congressman William Sulzer had emerged as the favored candidate of independent and progressive Democrats. Sulzer spoke of the need for the managerial, meritocratic reconstruction of state government in general, and of the scandal-plagued prisons and highway departments in particular. Styling himself as a Samuel Tilden for the 1910s, he courted the votes and financial donations of New York City's professionals and élites as well as the support of its Italian and Jewish immigrant communities, and native-born skilled workers. Repeatedly insisting he was "unbossed," he promised to bring "economy" to government, end the alleged fleecing of New York's taxpayers by state contractors and politicians (exemplified by the losses incurred over the abandonment of Harlem Prison), and establish minimum wages for laborers in certain industries. He would be a "reform Governor," he proclaimed, and one who would put an end to spoilsmanship once and for all.[48]

When the delegates to New York's State Democratic Convention finally came to vote on a candidate for Governor, in October 1912, no fewer than thirteen nominees threw their hats in the ring. Tammany's Charles Murphy, perhaps shrewdly sensing the change of winds, and wanting to counter the charge of Osborne and others that he was the party's puppet master, declared he would not vote. In the first round, the majority of votes were closely divided between Dix and Sulzer, with neither receiving the necessary

---

[46] Thomas Mott Osborne and Franklin D. Roosevelt established a group of independent Democrats, known as the Empire State Democracy, precisely for the purpose of reining in Tammany Hall.

[47] *New York Times*, Oct. 3, 1912, 2.

[48] Early in Sulzer's Governorship, a number of political commentators expressed reservations about his apparent embrace of progressivism. The editors of *The Nation* ribbed him for his "little affectations" and "amusing by-play of being 'just Bill,'" and pointed to the disjuncture between Sulzer's rhetoric and his actions: While advocating the extension of meritocratic civil service practices in the first days of his Governorship, he proceeded to appoint party politicians with no administrative experience to the Civil Service Commission. In short, *The Nation* asserted that despite representing himself as an anti-Tammany Democrat, Sulzer was duplicitously cooperating with Tammany and was showing signs of being as much a machine politician as those he denounced. The editors put it vividly, if artlessly: "If Governor Sulzer is honestly to fight Tammany there must be real blood, and at the end a real corpse." *The Nation* got its "corpse," but not the one for which its editors had hoped. *The Nation*, 96 (Jan. 9, 1913), 27–8.

majority to win. Gradually, in the course of balloting, however, a number of
rural counties that had supported other candidates swung their support over
to Sulzer. After two such rounds, Murphy signaled his support for Sulzer, and
the fourth round increased Sulzer's lead. Dix conceded, and the Democrats
put forward an avowedly progressive Democrat as their candidate for the
governorship of New York.[49] Gathering the support of a broad cross-section
of the electorate (and an official endorsement from Samuel Gompers and
the American Federation of Labor), and capitalizing on internal divides
within the Republican party and the splitting effect of the Progressive party,
Sulzer won the election.[50] As voters carried Woodrow Wilson to the White
House in a landslide victory over Taft and Roosevelt, Sulzer handily beat his
Republican and Progressive opposition by margins of about fifty and eighty
percent, respectively.[51]

Very soon after Sulzer's inauguration, the new administration began its
promised managerial overhaul of state government and, especially, the controversial prisons department. The Governor initiated a series of investigations and dismissals that were putatively aimed at purging the penal system
of political corruption and solving the Sing Sing problem. In March, 1913,
Sulzer set about installing his supporters in important prison positions. He
began by asking the Superintendent of Prisons to appoint one of his Democratic allies, Charles F. Rattigan, to the wardenship of Auburn. When Superintendent Scott, an appointee of the Dix administration, refused to appoint
Rattigan, Sulzer dismissed Scott on the grounds of nonfeasance and neglect
of duty. Scott's Chief Clerk (John G. McDowell) was dismissed shortly thereafter.[52] Twenty-four hours later, under the sweeping authority of the Moreland Act of 1907, Sulzer commissioned a special deputy attorney-general,
George Blake, to undertake a thorough investigation of the prisons, reformatories, and construction projects as they had operated under the administration of Superintendent Scott and his wardens. Pending the approval of
the Senate, the Governor also nominated an anti-Tammany Democrat and
Judge, John B. Riley, to fill the position of Superintendent of State Prisons,

[49] *New York Times*, Oct. 3, 1912, 1.   [50] *New York Times*, Oct. 12, 1912, 9.
[51] *New York Times*, Nov. 6, 1912, 1.
[52] The Governor charged Scott with the following: (1) nonfeasance and neglect of duty:
that Scott appointed Frederick Mills as Sales Agent of the State Prison Department, and
he had an interest in a company that competed with prison manufactures. Scott did not
fire Mills when he found out. (2) Appointing an underqualified physician, James V. May,
to Matteawan, although several others, including Dr. Amos Squire, outperformed him in
the examination for office of superintendent. (3) Subsequently appointing Dr. May to
the presidency of the State Commission of Prisons and installing Dr. John W. Russell to
Matteawan, who then allowed Harry Thaw (who was well-known to New Yorkers as the
murderer of the eminent architect, Sanford White) to change his own medical record so
that it recorded him as sane, thereby securing his freedom. And finally, (4) allowing Thaw
to continue to conduct business transactions from Matteawan. Charges Against Colonel
Joseph F. Scott, Albany, March 12, 1913. NYSA Governor's Office Records. Investigation
Case Files of Charges and Complaints Against Public Officials and Agencies, 1857–1919.
A0531. Box 40.

and appointed one of his own political advisors as acting Superintendent in the interim.[53]

The summary dismissal of Superintendent Scott and his Chief Clerk, together with Sulzer's nomination of an anti-Tammany Superintendent, inspired vociferous protest from Republicans and Tammany Democrats alike. With Scott gone, Sulzer successfully opened up the prison wardenships to his unmediated influence. But by law, the Senate had first to confirm the Governor's nominee. Tammany Democrats and Republicans in the Senate immediately registered their protest at Scott's dismissal by refusing to confirm Riley's nomination and resolving that Scott had been a successful Superintendent who had improved prison conditions. The conflict deepened as the outgoing Chief Clerk, John C. McDowell (whom Sulzer had dismissed on the dubious grounds that McDowell had told the Governor to "go to Hell") publicly criticized Sulzer for replacing Colonel Scott with "an inexperienced subaltern from his own office," and for "pursuing [a] headlong course, disregarding precedent, and ignoring the law."[54] By the end of March, Sulzer's avowed campaign against machine politics and patronage was increasingly beginning to resemble the very spoils practices he had so loudly decried.[55]

As the Tammany Democrats protested Sulzer's dismissal of Colonel Scott, Sulzer charged his Special Commissioner, George Blake, with the task of investigating the prisons on the grounds that they had become enmeshed in the practices of graft. Blake, a court reporter for the New York City newspapers and editor of Sulzer's Congressional speeches,[56] rushed through the State's prisons in April and May of 1913, collecting oral testimony from critics of the previous administration. As Blake filed his reports in Albany, Sulzer and his aides maintained a steady stream of press releases in which they condemned past management of the state prisons and construction projects. (Notably, the Governor's office never released the reports themselves). Quoting Blake at length, they described the financial and disciplinary practices of the previous administration as "criminal." According to the Governor's office, Blake had found evidence of widespread mismanagement of the prisons and prison construction, including a $500,000 loss in the construction of a new prison (Great Meadows) at Comstock, in Washington County, because of over-charging by contractors and flawed design and construction. Great Meadows had originated as a hospital under the management of the State Lunacy Board; built in the early 1900s, the uncompleted hospital was eventually handed over to the Prisons Department with the view that it could serve as a minimum-security prison farm for younger, first grade convicts.

---

[53] *New York Times*, Mar. 15, 1913, 4.
[54] Charges Against Colonel Joseph F. Scott, Albany, March 12, 1913. NYSA Governor's Office Records. Investigation Case Files of Charges and Complaints Against Public Officials and Agencies, 1857–1919. A0531. Box 40.
[55] *New York Times*, Mar. 15, 1913, 4.
[56] George W. Blake, ed., *Sulzer's Short Speeches* (New York: J. S. Oglivie Publishing Co., 1912).

Much like the Bear Mountain and Wingdale developments, Great Meadows had been mired in political intrigue from the day the state had purchased the land on which the hospital was to be built. The original site had originally been purchased from long-time Republican state legislator, railroad developer, and Superintendent of Prisons, Isaac V. Baker. According to the Governor's office, investigator Blake found that over the years the state had paid $92,000 for land that was worth only $30,000. Once the Prisons Department took it over, contractors had proceeded to erect a cellblock, one wing of which was built on quicksand; within months of the wing's completion the walls of the building had cracked. Furthermore, Blake had found that the inner walls of the guardhouse were "fragile and combustible," and that the prison's water supply was unfit for human consumption. Finally, $30,000 had been paid for a prison road that was never laid.[57]

In assigning the blame for what they claimed was an expensive, crumbling prison, the Governor's office declared Blake's report proved that not only the contractors responsible for the construction of Great Meadows, but the Tammany Democrats' State Architect (Franklin B. Ware), the State Controller, and the Superintendent of Prisons were complicit with an expansive prison "ring" that encompassed local elected officials, builders, designers, and suppliers.[58] According to the Governor's office, Blake had proven that the project was nothing more than an elaborate act of "theft": as one contractor swore in an affidavit: "My opinion is that this is the worst job I ever saw, and no honest inspector, understanding his business, should have passed the work."[59]

As Blake worked his way around the state prisons, the Governor's office reported that he had found mounting evidence of corruption, which the office proceeded to offer up in a steady stream of press releases to the New York newspapers. At Auburn Prison, Blake was said to have found evidence of brutality, violation of the law, waste, and general incompetence.[60] In particular, the Governor's office singled out the Auburn physician (John Gerlan) for illegal and brutal treatment of prisoners, and criticized former Superintendent Scott and Warden Benham for allowing this treatment to continue. In addition, Blake was reported to have criticized the ongoing use of dark cells, the practice of having convict nurses in the women's prison attend pregnant convicts, and the management of the prison's food supply. The office gestured toward the influence of Tammany Hall, stating that Blake had found that certain unnamed men "allied with some strong influence

---

[57] Blake's report had no official title and went missing in July 1913; no copies are known to have survived. Its contents appeared chiefly in the press releases made by the Governor's office, although, as will become evident, it is unclear whether the press releases were a full and fair representation of the report. Hereafter it will be referred to as the "Blake Report." Blake Report, quoted in *New York Times*, Apr. 14, 1913, 1.

[58] Blake Report, quoted in *New York Times*, Apr. 14, 1913, 1.

[59] Blake Report, quoted in *New York Times*, Apr. 14, 1913, 1; *New York Times*, May 11, 1913, II, 14.

[60] *New York Times*, Apr. 28, 1913, 1.

in New York" were purchasing underpriced convict-made products, which they then illegally sold for a profit on the open market, while overcharging the prison for delivery costs.[61]

The office's assessment of Clinton Prison followed the same tack: The prison's industries were improperly managed and the prison was generally subject to "bad business methods." But the Governor's office was careful to exempt Clinton's Warden Kaiser from criticism, instead laying the blame with the former Superintendent of Prisons.[62] The flurry of press releases from the Governor's office strongly implied that the penal system was riven-through with corruption, and that such malfeasance was the progeny of Tammany politicians' efforts to divert honest citizens' hard-earned wages to Tammany's contributors and voters.

According to the press releases from the Governor's office, Blake's harshest criticism was reserved for the most scandal-plagued of New York's prisons: Sing Sing. He accused Sing Sing's Warden John Kennedy (a Tammany Democrat) of pilfering prison supplies, fostering cruel treatment of the convicts, and chronically mismanaging prison finances. According to the Governor's office, Blake found that "warden Kennedy has violated the law, he has permitted the creation and continuance of unbusinesslike methods and has caused the State to lose thousands of dollars in a way that points directly to graft. He has made no efforts to protect the men from disease or vice, nor any efforts to produce better conditions in this prison."[63] Just as penal bureaucrats and élite reformers had done at the turn of the century, Blake singled out the stone cellblock, condemning it for causing rheumatism in the convicts and implicitly pointing to the existence of sexual relations between convicts: "The worst feature of the prison management cannot be discussed in any public document." Appealing to his readers' subscription to one of the most sacred precepts of American legal justice, he wrote that the internment in the cellhouse, in and of itself, constituted cruel and unusual punishment. Finally, the Governor's office charged that former Superintendent Scott knew of conditions such as these but had done nothing to ameliorate them.[64]

Having flooded the New York press with reports that the state prison system was enmeshed in graft and Tammany cronyism, in May of 1913, Governor Sulzer moved to consolidate his position. Bypassing the uncooperative Senate, Sulzer took advantage of its May recess and went ahead and appointed his supporter, Judge John B. Riley, as Superintendent of Prisons against the wishes of the Senate.[65] Tammany was quick to protest that this action was in defiance of the state constitution, which required the "advice and consent" of the Senate regarding any appointment. Meanwhile, Republican legislators, concerned about the Executive's usurpation of the legislature's authority, were quick to lend support to the Tammany Democrats.

[61] New York Times, Apr. 28, 1913, 1.
[63] New York Times, May 12, 1913, 4.
[65] New York Times, May 27, 1913, 7.
[62] New York Times, Jun. 2, 1913, 4.
[64] New York Times, May 12, 1913, 4.

Sulzer countered that the consent of the Senate was only necessary while the legislature was in session, and proceeded to announce the formation of an eleven-member Prison Reform Commission charged with a thoroughgoing investigation and reconstruction of the prisons. The commission, made up of anti-Tammany Democrats including Thomas Mott Osborne, Prisons Superintendent John B. Riley, and Margaret Wilson (Woodrow Wilson's daughter), were given broad investigative powers to

> examine and investigate the management and affairs of the several State prisons and reformatories, and departments thereof, the prison industries, the construction and plan for adequate prison facilities, the employment of convict labor, and all subjects relating to the proper maintenance and control of the State prisons of the State of New York.[66]

Suffering from the revelations of the Blake Commission and having been outmaneuvered by the Governor with regard to the Superintendency of John Riley, Tammany Democrats went on the offensive. At Sing Sing, Warden Kennedy called upon the Westchester County Grand Jury to conduct an investigation of his prison. Kennedy did so not to expose abuses in the prison but to clear his name. He refuted most of Blake's accusations about his management, insisting that he had "never accepted a dollar of graft in (his) life," and claimed that some of the problems, such as the disease rates and the dilapidated cellhouse, were the fault of the prison structure itself and not his management of the prison. Further, he countered that Blake's investigation had been unfair and that the Grand Jury should examine the financial books for themselves.[67] That Kennedy, and not Sulzer, first called for a Grand Jury investigation, suggests that Kennedy was quite confident that Blake's accusations would prove unfounded; the fact that Westchester County's district attorney was a Tammany Democrat seems the likely source of such confidence. However, before the Grand Jury had completed its investigation, Governor Sulzer summarily dismissed Kennedy from the Sing Sing wardenship, citing Blake's report as substantive evidence of mismanagement in and of itself.

Meanwhile, in the capitol, State Controller William H. Sohmer, a Tammany Democrat, insisted that the Governor had acted unconstitutionally in appointing a Superintendent during the Legislature's recess and that, consequently, the appointment was null and void. From there on in, Sohmer announced, no state monies would be distributed to the prison department and requisitions would not be honored. The Controller was true to his word:

---

[66] A twelfth member was appointed soon afterward. The Committee members were Thomas Mott Osborne (Chairman), George Kirchwey, John B Riley, Edward Bates, Mary Garrett Hay, Howard T. Mosher, Hannah Blum, Charles M. Hough, E. Stagg Whitin, Madeleine Z. Doty, George W. Perkins, and Margaret Wilson. William Sulzer, Announcement of Appointment of Prison Reform Commission, June 13, 1913, NYSA, Governor's Office Records, Investigation Case Files of Charges and Complaints Against Public Officials and Agencies, 1857–1919, A0531, Box 41.

[67] *New York Times*, May 13, 1913, 7.

Beginning in June 1913, Sing Sing and the other state prisons, county penitentiaries, and local jails operated without financial resources: Guards and civilian employees could not be paid, and the wardens were having to borrow on credit to feed the convicts. Underfed convicts and unpaid guards were now drawn into the breach of a mounting political crisis.

As Sing Sing's funds dried up and the state government entered deadlock, the Westchester County Grand Jury concluded its investigation of former Warden John Kennedy's management of Sing Sing prison. Reporting to the State Supreme Court on June 19, the Jurors confirmed much of what Blake had asserted about the prison: Their report was perhaps the strongest attack made on that prison in its eighty-eight year history. The Jurors presented a long list of abuses: Among other commonplace practices at Sing Sing, the Grand Jury singled out the use of the dark cells, which consisted of eight hard-walled and two padded cells, as forms of "suffocation." Prisoners, who were typically locked up in these cells for three days, but sometimes ten days at a time, often lost their sanity, became emaciated, and, upon occasion, committed suicide. The medical facilities were found to be inadequate, the bedding, rotten (having been stored alongside vegetables in the cellar), and the convicts' clothing perennially damp because of the dilapidated state of the prison laundry. [68]

The Grand Jury's most pointed attack was reserved for the cellhouse – the so-called bastille. As investigators before them had done, the Grand Jurors emphasized that the cellhouse was a site of extreme biological and criminal contagion. They reported without qualification that "the cells are unfit for the housing of animals, much less human beings": The cells were so damp that it was possible to "wet one's hand" by touching the wall, and vermin "swarmed" in the cells. Disease, they claimed, was transmitted from one prisoner to another through the use of a single bucket of water, which was passed between cells, and into which each prisoner dipped his tin cup. Furthermore, each cell afforded only 168 cubic feet of air, which fell well below the minimum of 400 cubic feet specified by the New York Board of Health for lodging houses in New York City. The most critical problem at Sing Sing, as the Grand Jury saw it, was the doubling of prisoners together in the cells. With one prisoner to a cell, the prison could house 1,200 prisoners in the cellhouse and another 135 in a makeshift dormitory in the Chapel hall. However, with a prison population that sometimes numbered 2,000

---

[68] In the Matter of the Inquiry into the Conditions of Sing Sing Prison (1913), 8–9, Westchester County Grand Jury, Presentment to the June Term of the Supreme Court, 1913, OFP, MSS64, Box 278, Org. Recs. A subsequent (and unpublished) report by the Westchester County Research Bureau affirmed the jury's finding, suggesting that the rate of insanity among prisoners was directly related to use of the dark cell. In 1913, the year in which unusual numbers of Sing Sing prisoners were interned in the dark cells, forty-eight (or 3.3%) of the prisoners were found to be insane. Following the formal prohibition of dark cell punishment in late 1914, the number fell to 27 (or 1.8%) of the prison population. "Some Facts About Sing Sing Management, Bulletin 1" (unpublished report, 1915), Westchester County Research Bureau, 7, OFP, MSS64, Box 276, Org. Recs.

and never fell below 1,450 in the early 1910s, anywhere between 330 and 1,330 prisoners were typically doubled together in cells that were thought to be unfit for one convict, let alone two.[69]

Critically, the Grand Jurors innovated the usual refrain of penal reformers that the cellblock's disease-inducing condition was a moral disgrace to the state: They wrote, "We find young boys condemned to room with habitual criminals and creatures who make a practice of sodomy.... We find Negroes and whites have shared the same cells. Immoral practices obtain among many of the convicts; acts of sexual perversion are taken for granted; sodomy is rife."[70] Continuing in the same vein, they reported that the bath house was too small and lacking enough shower heads for each prisoner to shower individually: Three or four convicts were typically bathing under one shower, and "The steamed and cloudy condition in the bath house and the crowding of the men under the shower afford an opportunity for perverts, thus screened from observation, to practice acts of sexual degeneracy."[71] Finally, the Jurors reported that prisoners who had been healthy upon commitment to Sing Sing were contracting gonorrhea and syphilis in the prison, a sure sign of the existence of sexual relations among prisoners. They concluded, "It is imperative that space be provided for the proper segregation of those suffering from venereal and skin diseases, as well as for the seclusion and medical supervision of degenerates."[72]

This was the first time in public discourse that a report about a New York prison contained an explicit and sustained discussion of prisoners' sexual habits; although Blake and other prison investigators had alluded to "unspeakable (and) unnatural acts," the Grand Jurors made sex between prisoners one of the principal grounds of condemnation.[73] At a time in

[69] Westchester County Grand Jury, In the Matter of the Inquiry into the Conditions of Sing Sing Prison (1913), Presentment to the June Term of the Supreme Court, 1913, OFP, MSS64, Box 278, Org. Recs.

[70] They added that in the makeshift dormitory located in the hallway to the Chapel, "immorality abounds, disease is fostered, criminal propensities cultivated and inculcated." Westchester County Grand Jury, In the Matter of the Inquiry into the Conditions of Sing Sing Prison (1913), 8–9.

[71] Ibid, 8–9.

[72] Ibid, 9. Their tone of moral outrage aside, the Grand Jurors were in all likelihood correct in their apprehension of the existence of not only sexual relations, but a sex market, in the prisons. Fragments of evidence from the records of prison disciplinary hearings in 1914 and 1915 confirm that sex among prisoners was happening, that in some cases it was physically coercive, and that in others it was not. In many instances, sex was traded for food or money. The records also suggest that in the case of coerced sex, any prisoner who complained to the warden or sought protection was likely to be severely disciplined, while the alleged attacker – or attackers – would probably not be disciplined at all. Investigator James W. White noted that in 1912 and 1913, Warden Kennedy had sometimes sent the complainants, not the alleged attackers, to New York's most feared prison – Clinton. White's position was echoed by many penal reformers. James W. White, "Facts about Sing Sing" (unpublished report, ca. 1914) OFP, MSS64, Box 276, Org. Recs.

[73] The hostile and alarmist tone of the Grand Jury's report also anticipated what historians have described as the "homosexual panics" that took place in American cities after World

which even the mention of same-sex sexual relations (or "inversion," in the medical terminology of the day) were considered unacceptable in respectable public discourse, the Jury's extensive report of prison sexuality was an exceptionally bold indictment of Sing Sing and, by implication, the state: Not only was the state seen to be incubating disease, it was inciting what in the Jurors' view were immoral sexual practices of various kinds, including the most depraved sexual "perversion" of all. The charge of sodomy made the Grand Jury's report even more damning than Blake's and broadened and deepened the moral scope of the struggle over Sing Sing, prisons, and state government: No longer a minor and repressed element of public discourse about prisons, sexual relations between prisoners would prove to play a critical role in the conflict. Sing Sing's bastille, in the meantime, became synonymous with sodomy.

The Grand Jury report was surprising in another important respect: Contrary to former Warden Kennedy's expectation that he would be vindicated, the Jurors held him personally responsible for many of the abuses. They concluded their report with the indictment of Kennedy, the storekeeper, the kitchen keeper, and two other employees for failing to perform their duties under the prison regulations: Specifically, they indicted Warden Kennedy on six counts of misdemeanor, including "putting prisoners suffering from contagious disease in cells with sound prisoners, putting whites and Negroes together, putting degenerates and those morally sound together, [and] putting men in dark cells without examining them to see if they were fit to stand punishment." Finally, Kennedy was charged with "having kept the prisoners . . . with improper and insufficient clothing, unclean and damp bedding, and with blankets that were washed but once a year."[74] Under present conditions, the use of the cellhouse might be unavoidable, the Jurors seemed to be arguing, but the manner in which convicts were distributed throughout was a matter of legal responsibility, and Kennedy had not fulfilled his duty as warden. The Grand Jury's final recommendation confirmed something that penal reformers had been asserting since the turn of the nineteenth century: Many of Sing Sing's problems were endemic and the prison should be abandoned altogether; a new prison should be built – and occupied. Jury report in hand, Governor Sulzer dismissed the remaining indicted staff.

With the return of the Grand Jury's indictments, Tammany Democrats had suffered their most serious setback to date. Moreover, Sing Sing was now firmly ensconced in an increasingly bitter political struggle over the objectives, procedures, and administration of the agencies of government. Tammany immediately launched an aggressive campaign to undermine Blake's report, Sulzer's administration of the prison system and the state, and

War I. For a discussion of the New York panic, see George Chauncey, *Gay New York: Gender, Urban Culture, and the Making of the Gay Male World, 1890–1940* (New York: Basic, 1994).
[74] Hyman S. Gibbs and Frederick Hahn were the storekeeper and kitchen keeper, respectively; *New York Times*, July 11, 1913, 7.

managerial reform more generally. Within days of the Grand Jury indictments, Tammany senators established a committee to investigate the use of
state funds by the State Board of Charities, the Hospital Commission, and
the Superintendent of Prisons. In an extraordinary session of the state legislature, the Frawley Committee (named after its Chairman, James J. Frawley)
was granted wide-ranging authority to investigate various state agencies as
well as Sulzer's campaign finances and his alleged use of patronage to win
votes for his Direct Nomination bill, which was then before the legislature.[75]
For the first two weeks of July, the Frawley Committee doggedly pursued
Governor Sulzer with the intent of publicly discrediting him and the reform
program for which he supposedly stood. According to the *New York Times*,
"It was understood thoroughly in the Capitol that the investigation . . . was
conceived for the purpose of giving the Governor a black eye in retaliation
for the bitter attacks he had made not only on Charles F. Murphy, Tammany
Leader. . . . but also on the Legislature itself."[76] The manner in which Sulzer
had bypassed the Senate in order to appoint his Superintendent of Prisons,
as well as his managerialist emphasis on an activist Executive, was accurately
understood as a breach of established legislative procedure.

   Convening in the first week of July 1913 under the close scrutiny of
the daily press, the Frawley Committee immediately narrowed its sights on
George Blake and his investigation of the prisons. Frawley began by requesting that Blake account for his expenditure of monies from the $50,000
prison-investigation fund that Governor Sulzer had set up for him, and
then proceeded to scrutinize the credibility of George Blake's report. In
the course of these hearings, the Committee attempted, for the first time in
New York's history, to subpoena the Governor. When the Committee failed
to locate Governor Sulzer (who was on his way to Gettsyburg for the July
4th celebrations), his secretary was subpoenaed instead, and commanded
to produce Blake's original reports (seven in number), all relevant correspondence, and the letter notifying the State Controller of Blake's appointment.[77] It is probable that Frawley suspected that Blake's reports had been
doctored by the Governor's Office before being selectively released to the
press. It remained the case that no one outside of the Governor's office had
ever seen Blake's original reports, raising the possibility that the office had
fabricated, withheld, or embellished evidence from the reports. Whatever

---

[75] In many states, the direct primary was one of the managerialists' most important weapons
in their attack on urban machines. However, in many instances, the machines proved adept
at adapting the primary to their own ends. The historiography of progressive electoral
reform is vast, but for useful overviews see James Gimpel, "Reform-Resistant and Reform-
Adopting Machines: The Electoral Foundations of Urban Politics," *Political Research Quarterly*
46:2 (June 1993), 371–82; Richard L. McCormick, "The Discovery that Business Corrupts
Politics: A Reappraisal of the Origins of Progressivism," *American Historical Review* 86:2 (Apr.,
1981), 247–74; John F. Reynolds and Richard L. McCormick, "Outlawing Treachery: Split
Tickets and Ballot Law in New York and New Jersey, 1880–1910," *Journal of American History*
72:4 (Mar. 1986), 835–58. and Robert F. Wesser, *A Response to Progressivism*.

[76] *New York Times*, Jul. 3, 1913, 8.

[77] Sulzer's secretary was Chester C. Platt. *New York Times*, July 4, 1913, 1.

the case, there ensued a tense and public confrontation between the Governor's secretary and the Committee, during which the secretary flatly refused to produce the papers in question, insisting that in any event, he knew the whereabouts of only three of the seven reports. Sulzer, whose reputation as a reform Governor was in danger of being undermined in the face of his secretary's refusal to render up public documents, returned to Albany and promised full and complete cooperation with the Committee: The relevant papers would be presented immediately.[78]

The significance of the missing reports became clear as the Committee's inquiry proceeded. Certain of the missing papers related to the funding arrangements for Blake's investigation, over which there was now fundamental disagreement: Although Blake insisted that the Governor had provided that he be recompensed $25 a day and railroad expenses, the Controller's office maintained that the terms of Blake's appointment had not provided for compensation for anything save itemized expenses. After the Controller had declined to pay Blake for anything but the documented expenses, Blake produced a letter of appointment in which the Controller was directed to recompense him for all his expenses, itemized or otherwise. When the Controller questioned the authenticity of the letter, Blake and Sulzer admitted that the letter they had produced was an antedated letter of appointment they had substituted for the original. They defended their action on the grounds that the substitution had taken place with the full knowledge of the Controller; the Controller flatly denied this.[79]

As well as establishing that the Governor and his Special Commissioner had "substituted" official correspondence, in the first few days of the Frawley inquiry it also became clear that Blake could not fully account for his use of the $50,000 prison investigation fund. On July 3, Blake appeared before the Frawley Committee and testified that he had drawn approximately $4,000 in a two-month period, for which he could not account. When questioned about the use to which he put this money, Blake simply stated that he could not remember, and that no law required him to keep books. This admission was exactly the kind of evidence for which Sulzer's opponents were searching: The fact that Blake had not properly accounted for his expenses enabled Frawley to undermine Sulzer's championing of efficient, accountable government: The graft hunters were now the hunted. As Counsel Richards put it, "Did you think that was a proper thing for you to do? You have been unsparing in your criticism of other officials who have been deficient in that respect." By the end of the first week of the inquiry, even the editors of the *New York Times*, who had been very sympathetic to Blake and the Sulzer administration, had implicitly and conspicuously criticized the integrity of the Governor's anti-graft crusade. The newspaper's front-page headlines for July 4 were unambiguous: "KEPT NO BOOKS ON GRAFT HUNT FUND."[80]

[78] *New York Times*, July 6, 1913, sec. II, 10.   [79] *New York Times*, July 25, 1913, 2.
[80] *New York Times*, July 16, 1913, 1.

These were not the only embarrassing findings to surface in the course of the Frawley Committee's hearings. More damaging yet was the Frawley Committee's discrediting of the dubious testimony upon which Blake had based his finding that the prison construction project at Great Meadow had cost the State $500,000 in graft. It transpired that several of the well-publicized accusers of graft were of very dubious credibility: At least two of Blake's "expert witnesses and investigators" turned out to have had little experience in prison construction or the financial administration of large institutions. Among these, one alleged "expert investigator," Wallace B. Hunter, was revealed to be a well-known Albany lobbyist, former restaurateur, and one-time director of "fake circuses." Another expert witness was Blake's brother-in-law, one Henry Leeds, who had little or no knowledge of prison construction, but was paid $130 a week for his expertise anyway. As these details came to light, the Governor's initial promise to cooperate with the Committee became a flat refusal to present documentation of any kind. Subsequently, most, if not all, of the relevant material had become "lost" by July 7.[81]

By the end of the second week of its inquiry, the Frawley Committee had mounted a strong case that Blake's findings were based on "belief, vague suspicions, and rumors." It had almost entirely discredited both Blake and the Sulzer administration, and it had embarrassed the friends and supporters of managerial reform. Editors once sympathetic to Sulzer, such as the editor of the *Times*, now grudgingly lent support to Senator Frawley's triumphant proclamation that Blake and his Commissioners "are a pack of scoundrels of the worst type" (as well as to Frawley's rather more mirthful jibe that Blake's brother-in-law was "the biggest boob" the Senator had ever seen). The *Times*' editors did not parse words: "GREATMEADOW LOOT CHARGES SHATTERED: Blake Admits He Based Report of $500,000 Prison Graft on Rumor and Suspicion," ran the headline on July 17.[82] Blake's investigation was slipshod, wrote the editor, and compared unfavorably to Samuel Tilden's investigation of the Tweed Ring forty years earlier.[83]

Within seven months of his inauguration as Governor, Sulzer's crusade against the "thieves and robbers" of machine politics had been turned inside out and his own moral character, impugned. The crisis within the Democratic party was of such magnitude that it threatened to catapult the Republicans back into power, as that party moved to contrast the relatively stable years of Republican rule in New York with the Democracy's. (As one Republican Senator gleefully announced to the press, the formally discredited Superintendent, Republican Joseph Scott, had been "the best prison Superintendent the State ever had").[84] Managerial reformers were now faced with recuperating the credibility of their programs while neutralizing their

[81] Leeds had not only extended his services to the Blake Commission, but the Westchester Grand Jurors who had indicted Sing Sing's Warden Kennedy and the other prison officials. *New York Times*, July 16, 1913, 1.
[82] *New York Times*, July 17, 1913, 2.   [83] *New York Times*, July 19, 1913, ed., 6.
[84] *New York Times*, July 17, 1913, 2.

principal mouthpiece. Although commending Sulzer for initiating an anti-graft campaign, the editors of the *New York Times* nonetheless criticized him for choosing the wrong aides and advisers and for being calculatingly self-interested in his pursuit of the Tammany "thieves." In the face of a hostile Tammany legislature, the editor lamented, the Governor "needs help, [yet] he calls upon men who get him deeper into trouble." Although the editor wrote that it was too late for Sulzer to rectify the problem, it was rapidly becoming clear to managerial reformers (particularly Thomas Mott Osborne and others of the Sulzer-appointed Prison Reform Commission) that Sulzer was a liability to the cause of meritocratic, efficient, government. The position of the *New York Times'* editor was unequivocal: Sulzer would have to correct his mistakes or lose the support of the reformers who had been instrumental to his success at the ballot box.[85]

As Sulzer and the cause of managerial reform were being assailed, the conditions of Sing Sing and the larger question of the state's duties toward its felons had briefly slipped out of public discussion. Although the Blake report had been discredited with regard to its claim of corruption in prison construction, the basic finding that conditions at Sing Sing were degraded to the point of moral abasement had gone unchallenged. There had been some debate as to the placement of responsibility for those conditions, but no one had questioned the conclusion that conditions at Sing Sing were as Blake (and the Westchester Grand Jury) had said they were. The evidence that Sing Sing was indeed an infectious, run-down prison was widely accepted – even by the indicted Warden Kennedy. No elected representative was likely to contest the Sing Sing reports, and although managerial reformers' commitment to Sulzer was waning, their determination to overhaul Sing Sing and the penal system was undiminished.

It is perhaps unsurprising, therefore, that immediately following his public drubbing and in the face of political collapse, the embattled Governor attempted to return the subject of New York's infamous bastille to the center of the debate. On the same day upon which the Frawley Committee finally destroyed the credibility of Blake's expert witnesses, Sulzer addressed the state legislature on the subject of Sing Sing. He condemned Sing Sing in the strongest terms as intolerable, and declared that "immediate action is demanded both by the dignity of the State and by every feeling of humanity on the part of its people." Following the speech, Sulzer's supporters in the legislature introduced bills in both houses to enable the replacement of Sing Sing. The bills were passed, but modified so as to ensure the Governor would not control the construction of Sing Sing's replacement.[86]

The passage of these bills may have conveyed to the people of New York that the crisis of government had been averted, but thanks to the continued suspension of funds to the Prison Department, food and industrial supplies were running low at Sing Sing and the keepers and staff were entering their sixth week of unremunerated work. To make matters worse, the prison had

[85] *New York Times*, July 19, 1913, ed., 6.   [86] *New York Times*, July 17, 1913, 2.

been without a warden for several weeks, since Sulzer's abrupt dismissal of the Tammany-supported John Kennedy. With the dismissal of the store-keeper and the kitchen keeper following their indictments on June 19, the prison had few staff with the requisite experience in preparing food for a large mass of people. That the dismissed staff had also been operating an illicit market for food in the prison made their departure all the more prob-lematic in the sense that the trade in contraband, upon which the good order of the prison depended in no small degree, had been severely dis-rupted. Dozens of convicts who had acted as suppliers in the illicit trade had lost the means by which they sustained their relatively privileged positions in the prison. Regardless of whether the state Controller consciously aimed to foster the conditions under which the prisoners might rebel (as penal reformers would later claim), his suspension of prison funds created a very volatile situation at the prison. On July 9, 1913, when Kennedy's replace-ment, James M. Clancy, arrived at Sing Sing to take up the wardenship, he found the prison in the midst of one the worst crises of its eighty-eight–year history.[87]

Warden Clancy took immediate action: Making use of the power of trans-fer – one of the most significant innovations of penal bureaucratization in the 1890s[88] – he consulted with Superintendent Riley and together they compiled a list of 185 convicts to be transferred out of the prison.[89] Trans-fer to up-state Auburn or Clinton Prisons was generally unpopular among the Sing Sing convicts: According to newspaper reports, when news of the impending draft filtered through the prison, convict laborers in the mattress workshop set a fire that could be seen for miles up and down the Hudson River.[90] As the prison alarm sounded, the guards responded in the usual way – by emptying the workshops and enforcing a lock-down in the cells. The prison fire company, made up of fifteen convicts, together with 200 convicts selected by the keepers, battled the flames with the aid of

---

[87] Clancy was an anti-Tammany Democrat and a real estate assessor from the Bronx. Con-cerned that Clancy might soon become frustrated with trying to reform Sing Sing, the Governor requested that he post a $50,000 bond, on the understanding that he would forfeit it in the event that he resigned without the Governor's consent. The legality of this agreement was dubious, in light of a recent (April 1913) finding of the New York Court of Appeals that "(t)here is no provision (in the public officers' law) requiring the acceptance of such resignation to make it effective." Quoted in *New York Times*, Oct. 31, 1913, 9.

[88] Originally introduced (in 1895) to facilitate the flexible distribution of convict laborers throughout the State's prisons, prisoners had quickly come to resent the administrative technique of transfer. See Chapter 5 in this book.

[89] To my knowledge, neither these lists nor any archival material (other than the official reports) relating to this episode of Sing Sing's history have survived. Riley and Clancy rep-resented this draft as a response to the Westchester Grand Jury's charge that overcrowding was leading to all manner of immorality and disease. However, it seems probable that the transfer was also aimed at removing those convicts who had been loyal to former warden Kennedy and who had lost their privileges in the prison following the crack-down on the illicit prison economy.

[90] Although it seems likely that the convicts of the mat making shop planned and lit the fire, there is no definitive evidence.

100 volunteers from Ossining's local fire companies. By the end of the evening, the fire had razed the northern gate of the prison and more than one-third of the workshops, including the cart and wagon shop and the paint shop. As a large audience of newspaper reporters and villagers gathered on the hill overlooking the prison, the remaining 1,250 convicts began to yell from their cells in what the *New York Times* described as a "wave... of shouts, oaths and imprecations." According to the reporter for the *Times*, the prisoners were not yelling out of fear of the fire, which the wind was carrying away from the cellblock; rather they decried Warden Clancy and the conditions of their incarceration, and challenged the newspapermen to enter Sing Sing to "see for yourselves" the conditions in which the state's felons were being held.[91]

The demonstrations that followed lasted four days and filled the front pages of the local and national press. A direct outgrowth of the struggle to determine the new political order, the crisis was set to test the effectiveness and legitimacy of those proponents of managerial reform under whose authority Sing Sing was formally managed. The prison now ceased to be simply a rhetorical instrument or a metaphor for an immoral and outmoded political order; as food, supplies, and wages ran low, and as convicts lit fires, went on strike, and hurled "bread," Sing Sing became both an instrument of force and a critical arena in which the battle was to be fought. The circle of combatants had extended to include not only the political parties and their factions but the convicts and guards whose practical fate partly hinged on the result of the political struggle. As the firemen fought the flames in the prison yard, the outcome of the riot was by no means clear: The visible and well-publicized nature of the state government's loss of control over one of the nation's oldest and most infamous prisons simultaneously presented the gravest of threats and the most promising of opportunities for the forces of managerial government. On the one hand, the riots called into question the managerial state's ability to maintain control of its prisoners and to do so in a way that was consistent with its humane prison policy. In this regard, the Sing Sing rebellion tested the authority and legitimacy of the reformist/administrative mode of government. On the other hand, the riots, triggered as they were by the suspension of funds by a Tammany controller and following on the heels of revelations of abuse, corruption, and excessive suffering at the prison under a Tammany-backed warden, also presented the managerialists with an unprecedented and fully dramatic opportunity to discredit Tammany and the spoils system of government.

The convicts' noisy protest continued long after the fires had been extinguished. The next morning, after breakfast, 213 convicts from the destroyed workshops found themselves without work. The warden ordered them set to work clearing the rubble, but when it became clear that the debris was too hot to move and that consequently, the convicts had no work to do, the guards attempted to return the convicts to their cells. Faced with the

<hr>

[91] *New York Times*, July 24, 1913, 1–2.

prospect of spending twenty-four hours or more in the cells, the convicts refused to move from the site of the smoldering ruins, protesting that as they had broken no prison rule, they should not be locked up in the cells. (Once again, prisoners insisted on enforcing what had become an unwritten law of the prison, that breaking prison rules was the only grounds upon which a prisoner should be locked in his cell outside of evenings and Sundays.) Rather than force the prisoners back into the cellhouse, Warden Clancy negotiated an agreement by which the convicts would be locked in the cells only until lunch time. The convicts moved back to the cells peacefully and, as Clancy had agreed, they were allowed to join the other 1,200 convicts for lunch in the mess hall.[92]

After lunch, Clancy's guards again tried to return the men to their cells. Once more, the majority of them resisted; instead of marching back to their cells, they ran to the coal pile in the prison yard, where they garrisoned themselves and began throwing large chunks of coal at the guards, yelling their refusal to return to the cells. As Clancy approached the convicts and negotiated with them once more, the convicts won permission to stay outside the cells for the afternoon, and went to the cells as usual at the end of the day, having collected their rations of bread. It was on this, the second night of demonstration, that an unknown number of convicts staged the bread-throwing protest that sent more than 200 window panes crashing into the prison yard below.[93]

Once the lock-down of the bread-throwing convicts had been completed, Superintendent Riley and Warden Clancy set about identifying the "trouble-makers" who had garrisoned themselves at the coal pile the previous day and added their names to the list of convicts who were to be immediately removed from the prison. There was one difficulty with this strategy of drafting the convicts to other prisons: The Controller's freeze on money for the Prison Department meant that there were no funds with which to pay a railroad company for transporting 300-odd convicts to Clinton and Auburn. Despite the urgency of the situation (or perhaps, because of it) the acting state Controller and Tammany leader of Westchester County, Michael J. Walsh, refused to honor the Superintendent's requisition for transportation costs on the grounds that John Riley's appointment to the Superintendent's position was illegal. Without the requisition, Warden Clancy was unable to move the convicts.

Consequently, on Thursday, the 300 prisoners listed for transfer to Clinton and Auburn were held in the cells. Included in this 300 were eighty-odd convicts from the knitting shop. Clancy detained these convicts, having received what he claimed was a tip-off that they were planning to light fires. Despite Clancy's precautions, mattresses were set alight in the knit factory that day. The convict fire brigade soon extinguished the flames, but within hours, 100 convicts of the shoe-making company went on strike and forcibly detained the convict they believed to have been the informant. According to

[92] Ibid.   [93] Ibid.

the *New York Times* reporter, one half of the shoemakers were striking against what they described as the rotten food, and the others were demanding that the release of the 300 convicts who were being held in the cells. Venturing into the shoe shop, Warden Clancy negotiated with the shoemakers, but ultimately refused to release their comrades. He then locked the striking shoemakers in their workshop and placed dozens of armed guards around the building. The strikers remained locked in until lunchtime, when they were marched to the mess hall under armed guard. Refusing to work, they elected to return to the shop to continue their strike. Finally, upon pain of forfeiting their supper, they marched back to their cells at 5 P.M. On the way back to the cells, a group of convicts broke marching formation and severely slashed the head of the lone man who had resisted the convicts' call for a strike and whom the other prisoners suspected of being an informant. The prisoner, a black man by the name of Texas Jack, died of his wounds shortly afterward.[94]

By Thursday evening, the convicts appear to have succeeded in conveying to the warden, the prison bureaucracy, and the citizens of New York that the lack of decent food and many other conditions were at the root of their grievances. That day, the Superintendent of Prisons publicly conceded that because of the removal of the prison cook and assistant, the meals were not as they should have been, and he made arrangements to improve the food *post haste*. Meanwhile, in Albany, the attorney general informed the state Controller that the Superintendent's appointment was legal: Funds were to be freed up immediately. The convicts and warden appeared to have reached a turning point by the end of this, the third day of protest. The next morning, the fourth day of the trouble, the entire prison population was kept in the cells while the first sixty convicts to be transferred up-state were shackled, hand-cuffed in pairs, lined up, and marched to the Ossining railway station under armed guard. Outside the prison gates, a crowd of photographers and village sightseers (most of whom were women) awaited them. The convicts angrily rushed the crowd and the guards reportedly followed suit, smashing one photographer's camera. All the way to the station, the convicts exchanged insults with the crowd; finally they mounted a special rail car attached to a regular train and departed for Auburn Prison. That evening, as they pulled into Auburn, they were surrounded by a crowd of 1,600 or more townspeople. But where they had been rowdy and defiant in the streets of Ossining, the transferred convicts were calm as they were marched into Auburn Prison.[95]

These developments notwithstanding, the people of Ossining were becoming increasingly fearful of renewed trouble and a general prison break; the guards began to agitate for armed reinforcement, with the result that the Ossining Town Supervisor, John F. Jenkins, requested that the Eighth Division of the New York State Naval Militia (stationed at Ossining) be

94 Ibid.
95 *New York Times*, July 25, 1913, 2; July 26, 1913, 14.

put on alert, along with the National Guard companies of Yonkers and White Plains. Notably, there was persistent and well-publicized confusion over the question of which officials had the authority to mobilize the Militia and Guards. This became clearer as both the warden and Superintendent Riley distanced themselves from Jenkins' requests to deploy the troops, insisting to the press that Town Supervisor Jenkins had overreacted. As it turned out, Jenkins was a Tammany ally, whose brother, George Jenkins, was the State Controller's representative at Sing Sing.[96] After the Tammany-allied warden, John Kennedy, had been dismissed, Kennedy had stayed on in Ossining, where he had conducted a series of clandestine meetings with Jenkins, Jenkins' brother, and certain Sing Sing guards.[97] The role of Kennedy and his allies in precipitating the protests or attempting to exacerbate them is difficult to determine: What is clear is that these Tammany allies did, in fact, try to regulate events at Sing Sing and that their actions tended to excite fears of a full-scale uprising. As details of Sing Sing's shadow government came to light in the daily press, the free citizenry was left with the distinct impression that the state had not only lost control of its prison, but had forfeited the command of its armed forces.

Back at Sing Sing, the official agents of the state began to reassert their control after three days of rebellion. Warden Clancy slowly moved the prison back into its usual routine. Four hundred convicts from the knit, shoe, and clothing shops continued to be locked in their cells twenty-four hours a day (they remained there for six days) while the rest of the convicts were released from their cells in staggers and put to work. Despite his supposed opposition to the use of dark cells, and in defiance of New York State law, Warden Clancy locked ten convicts in the dark cells (which were located beyond the cell block, on a level with the river) where they remained on a bread-and-water diet for some days.[98] Over the next week, a further 110 convicts were transferred to Auburn, Clinton, and Great Meadow, and the Westchester Grand Jury prepared to investigate Sing Sing once more in order to establish the cause of the riots and identities of the arsonists.[99] Five days after the prison workshops had gone up in flames, Sing Sing was peaceful once more. Food supplies were restored, the guards were back on the payroll, and convicts thought to have been supportive of the Tammany/Kennedy regime had been drafted up-state. Moreover, Sulzer's Warden Clancy had been seen to take control of a volatile prison population and bring it under control with almost no loss of life. In the meantime, at least, Sulzer's prison administration had been seen to perform well.

[96] *New York Times*, July 25, 1913, 2; July 26, 1913, 14.
[97] *New York Times*, July 28, 1913, 1.   [98] *New York Times*, July 29, 1913, 2.
[99] The majority were sent to Auburn; those second and third term convicts considered intractable were transferred to Clinton, while a number of first termers were sent to the state's new prison, Great Meadow. (Given that this was by far the most preferred prison among the prisoners, these convicts were quite probably being rewarded for their efforts to fight the fires and break the strikes). *New York Times*, Aug. 1, 1913, 16; *New York Times*, July 28, 1913, 1.

In hindsight, it might be argued that, judged by its duration and the extent of the damage done to persons and prison property, the rebellion of 1913 was a rather minor event. Once the bread had been thrown, the windows shattered, the fires extinguished, and the suspected ring-leaders shackled and freighted up-state to Auburn Prison, the warden and guards had been able to restore the prison to its proper order rather swiftly; it was only a matter of days before the prisoners were put to work repairing the physical damage. By the standards of previous prison uprisings, it had also been remarkably bloodless: Only one person (the prisoner suspected of being an informant and known only as Texas Jack) lost his life. Although they had access to work tools and materials that might have been easily fashioned into weapons, the convicts had not attacked guards or taken them hostage; rather, they had eluded their keepers and thrown a few lumps of rock and coal at them when ordered to return to cells. Above all, the prisoners had made no attempt to break out of the prison, even though the north gate had been destroyed and the prison was, consequently, rendered insecure.

However, from the point of view of the political and moral legitimacy of the prison authorities and, by extension, Governor William Sulzer's administration, the Sing Sing rebellion had been a very significant, and dangerous, occurrence. In putting the old bastille to work for themselves, the convicts had expropriated not only the stone edifice of the prison proper but a popular emblem of the state's absolute and, as Alexis de Tocqueville and Gustave de Beaumont once famously noted, despotic power to subjugate any freeman adjudged felon.[100] In so doing, the convicts had thrown the absoluteness of that power into grave doubt. That they had done so in front of a newspaper-reading audience of several millions compounded the crisis, for not only had the state lost control of its convicts, it had been seen by a mass audience to have done so. Worse still, at least from the point of view of the Sulzer administration, the convicts' palpable corroboration of their claim that the state was starving them baldly contradicted the state's much-touted, and avowedly progressive, penal policy. Far from being among the most orderly and civilized prison systems in the world, as governors and prison Commissioners had repeatedly boasted since the transition to the state-use system of imprisonment in 1897, Sing Sing had been shown to house an unruly and, apparently, thoroughly emiserated, rabble.

Equally significantly, the riots at Sing Sing received a great deal of attention from the regional and national press. As the convicts' solicitation of reporters suggests, the press served as something more than a documentary agency: The presence of large numbers of photographers and journalists just outside the prison entrance influenced the actions of both convicts and keepers, who were aware that they were participants in a penal drama that was being followed by hundreds of thousands of daily newspaper readers in

[100] "While society in the United States gives the example of the most extended liberty, the prisons of the same country offer the spectacle of the most complete despotism." Beaumont and Tocqueville, *On the Penitentiary System*, 79.

New York City and beyond.[101] More than simply a means of broadcasting, the mass press became a coauthor in this penal drama, for the presence of photographers and reporters palpably influenced the character of the protests and of their suppression. The convicts appear to have been as aware of the need to court public interest – and ultimately, support – as were the Albany politicians and the Sing Sing administration. Not only did they stage theatrically effective protests such as the bread-throwing demonstration, which caught the attention of the press, they explicitly invited journalists into the prison to hear their demands. At one point, many of the 300 convicts who were detained in the cells prior to transfer shouted to the reporters, "Come up her (sic) and write us up.... They are starving us. Give it a good write up in your paper. They have locked us in and won't let us out."[102] In this respect, convicts strove to use the press to bring public attention to what they considered to be a gross injustice against them. That the bread riot occurred in the bastille (rather than in the yard or mess hall, where prison riots more typically took place) meant that the convicts were easily secured by a lock-down; but the dramatic act of breaking its windows carried images of the controversial stone edifice – and prisoners' protest of it – onto the front pages of the newspapers. The prison administration also recognized the very public nature of the riots, and of the important role the press might play in informing the outside world about events. Warden Clancy went to some lengths to master the flow of information through the press (for example, he made frequent press releases and took measures to ensure that neither guards nor convicts spoke to the press without his consent), and former warden Kennedy, lurking nearby in Ossining, also appears to have attempted to influence not only the event of the riot but its representation. In this respect, the Sing Sing riots and the responses of present and former prison authorities to the riots, were as much a battle over meaning and representation as a struggle over food, conditions, and poor prison administration.

The substance of those contested representations discloses that all concerned had perceived a marked shift in commonplace assumptions about the acceptable level of depredation to which a convict should be subjected. Eighteen years after the New York State Prison Commission had first insisted that convicts were "wards of the state," who, as such, were entitled to protection and certain basic rights, convicts were becoming accustomed to seeing themselves as wards and bearers of certain entitlements more or less guaranteed by the state. Moreover, the prisoners had calculated that free citizens might very well be sympathetic to their plight. The careful manner in which Clancy and Superintendent Riley deployed force against the convicts and sought to impress journalists with their nonviolent riot control, suggest that the prison authorities recognized that neither a bloody end to the protest nor the unchecked decline in prison conditions to which the prisoners

[101] The *New York Times* noted that the photographers and journalists "all were favorites with the convicts." *New York Times*, July 25, 1913, 1.

[102] *New York Times*, July 24, 1913, 1.

referred would be acceptable to many of the citizens of New York. Clancy repeatedly assured the press that no guns were drawn during the rebellion (despite the fact that several of the workshops and the prison proper were, in fact, surrounded by armed guards), and in his press releases he underscored the point that he negotiated with the convicts.[103] This is not to say that the authorities' actions were entirely cynical or pragmatic: Rather, the kinds of violence that were openly deployed little more than twenty years earlier could not be used in 1913 without risk of severe criticism. At the very least, the state could not be seen to be spilling the blood of its "wards" in the absence of an extremely good reason to do so.

By the same token, the question of whether or not the state possessed the ability to contain the convicts was very critical. At stake was the state's ability to monopolize the legitimate use of violence: The July 24th front page headline of the *New York Times*, which read, "SING SING REVOLTS AND CONVICTS WIN,"[104] put the citizenry on notice that the state had lost control in its own prison. The spectacle of the state's loss of control and the fear on the part of Ossining's townspeople and the crowd of reporters (and perhaps, too, the thousands of newspaper readers) that the convicts were about to execute a mass breakout, were critical dimensions of the Sing Sing crisis. Although prisoners made no attempt at escape, the guards, villagers, and the pro-Tammany supporters repeatedly commented to the press that a mass break was imminent. As a reporter from the *New York Times* commented, after the first day of protest, guards and villagers warned journalists that an "outbreak might be reasonably expected anytime within the next few days." This fear heightened when, without the consent of Warden Clancy, the National Guard was put on alert – and the newspapers informed about it.[105] Yet the prisoners had made no such attempt. Although the convicts had caused a break down in prison order, nothing they said or did, either at the beginning of the protest or the end, nor anything in the prison's recent history, warranted such intense concern. With armed guards and vigilantes staked out around the prison, the prisoners were far safer inside the prison than out: Indeed, the only prisoners to leave Sing Sing were not escapees but convicts who were forcefully transferred to Auburn at the request of the warden and the Superintendent of prisons. Despite the evidence, however, the townspeople and newspaper reporters were convinced that an escape was likely to occur (so much so, that the newspapers reported that property values around Ossining had plummeted during the trouble). Citizens appear to have been concerned that, instead of fleeing the state or going to ground, escaped prisoners would unleash a frenzy of vengeful violence

---

[103] According to the *New York Times*, Clancy then met secretly with the indicted former warden, John S. Kennedy, in a hotel in Ossining, and a local banker and Democrat, Henry M. Carpenter. (Kennedy and Clancy claimed to have met quite by accident.) At this meeting, Carpenter claimed that the riots had been the direct outcome of attempts by Charles Murphy and Tammany Hall to wrest control of the prison from the reform Democrats. *New York Times*, July 27, 1913, I: 1.

[104] *New York Times*, July 24, 1913, 1.   [105] *New York Times*, July 25, 1913, 1.

against the persons and property of Ossining and the surrounding area. Such a response suggests that the villagers, many of whom had fathers or brothers or neighbors who worked in the prison, tacitly acknowledged that the convicts had suffered very badly while in Sing Sing – much as George Blake and the Grand Jury had claimed – and that prisoners might consequently wreak violence upon them in revenge for all the years of mistreatment endured at Sing Sing.

The villagers' fear was potentially very damaging for Sulzer and the system for which he stood, for it signaled a breakdown in local citizens' faith that the state could provide for their security. From the point of view of Governor Sulzer, Warden Clancy, and other prison administrators, the riots, the widely reported fears among citizens, and the shadowy involvement of a previous regime, suggested that immediate action had to be taken to reassert control in the prison. This would involve undertaking preventative measures such as punishing the instigators (both real and imagined) and reforming certain conditions, such as the inedible food. Most critically, Clancy and the penal bureaucrats acted to bring publicity about the prison under control. This meant tightening the bureaucracy so as to diminish the flow of informal news within and beyond the prison and securing and intensifying the flow of official information.

The day after the protests ceased, Clancy traveled to Albany to discuss the previous weeks' events with Governor Sulzer and Superintendent Riley. He requested the replacement of certain employees whom he thought to be politically aligned with Tammany. In service of a more easily controlled guard corps, he suggested that a pension system be put in place so as to allow him to retire certain guards and make new appointments. He also requested that the state employ more civilian clerks so that the administrative affairs of the prison were not in the hands of convict clerks. More than fifteen years into the project of bureaucratization of the state prison system, the prison stenographer was a convict, and convicts operated the telephone system and opened the mail. One of the most basic requirements of a smoothly functioning penal bureaucracy – the flow of information around the prison and up to the central administration – had yet to be realized. Moreover, those channels of communication that the Lispenard Commission and Superintendents Lathrop and Collins had succeeded in establishing were in the possession, not of prison administrators (or even the keepers), but the convicts. Clancy was adamant that closing what he referred to as the underground information bureau would be critical to ensuring that another crisis did not break out: Civilians seemed to know as much about events in the prison as did the prison staff, and this had made the prison almost impossible to manage.[106]

Upon his return to Sing Sing, Clancy set about realizing some of his objectives. In effect, he picked up the mantle left by Collins and others of the first generation of penal reformers and set about a flurry of activity at the prison.

[106] *New York Times,* July 29, 1913, 2.

Having learned that information was a matter of security and, hence, of political survival, he was careful to publicize his reforms and to conceal certain of his more punitive measures. He informed newspaper reporters that he was going to offer the convicts what he called a square deal: He would call the spokesmen for various sections of the prison population together to hear grievances; he would then offer to erase all the disciplinary marks against the convicts (bar those against convicts accused of setting fires and assault) if they would promise to behave well. He also announced that he had written a report to present to the Westchester Grand Jury in order to pursue indictments for the assaults and fires.[107]

Clancy's efforts to extinguish the crisis at Sing Sing were not limited to press releases. He and Superintendent Riley also set about overhauling the everyday life of the prison. With prison funds freed up thanks to the order of the attorney general, they secured funding to clean, replaster, and paint the cells, and to replace some of the cell bedding. They also began to overhaul the prison's antiquated plumbing system and built a new bath house to relieve the overcrowded conditions complained of by the Westchester Grand Jury. In accordance with the recommendations of the State's Prison Reform Commission and on the example of the Good Roads prison work in other states, Clancy established an "honor" company of prisoners who were set to work picking apples in an orchard beyond the prison walls. As penal reformers had been suggesting for some years, Riley and Clancy also made provision for convicts to meet in private with their legal counsel in a special room. Most importantly, from the convicts' point of view at any rate, they reduced the hours that prisoners spent in the cellhouse on Sundays and holidays.[108] Clancy also ended the practice of disciplining convicts by interring them in the dark cell and improved conditions for the prisoners on death row. (This included replacing with plates and bowls the old tomato cans in which the prisoners ate their food). As a consequence of Clancy's programs, by the end of 1913, Sing Sing convicts were spending eighteen hours in their cells on Sundays instead of twenty-one, and they were spared the twenty-four hour lock-down that typically occurred on state and federal holidays.[109]

As Clancy slowly ameliorated conditions at Sing Sing, the twelve members of Sulzer's Prison Reform Commission proceeded with their investigations of the prisons, while the discredited George Blake attempted to salvage his tattered reputation by reiterating his original judgment of Tammany's Sing Sing. The Sulzer administration had survived the Sing Sing crisis; but the Frawley Committee had effectively undermined the Governor's credibility and generated talk of impeachment. In August 1913, when the committee presented evidence that William Sulzer had, in fact, expropriated campaign donations in the run-up to the gubernatorial elections the previous year, the

[107] *New York Times*, July 26, 1913, 14; July 29, 1913, 2; July 30, 1913, 4.
[108] This was achieved in part by instituting Sunday dinners in the mess hall.
[109] James W. White, "Facts about Sing Sing," 4a–4j.

state Assembly impeached him; in October, the New York Court of Appeals confirmed that Sulzer was indeed guilty on three of the charges of impeachment.[110] Much to the disgust of Sulzer's supporters, it now seemed very probable that Sulzer had stolen Democratic party money, fabricated and destroyed evidence of prison graft, and lied under oath.

That it was the champion of machine politics, Charles Murphy, and his fellow Tammany Democrats who had brought the misdeeds to light constituted a double blow to the cause of reform. Now, with a leading advocate of managerial government impeached and dispatched, Charles Murphy was set to sweep the New York City mayoralty elections: Independent Democrats (and advocates of the managerial state more generally) needed a success and they needed it promptly. This time they would be helped by a powerful coalition of prominent industrialists, jurists, philanthropists, progressive lawmakers, and intellectuals who had been mustering their collective resources with the intention of delivering the prison, once and for all, from the vise grip of "politics." In the wake of the twin crises of Sing Sing and Sulzer, they resolved to tackle the financial, disciplinary, and ideological problems that the abolition of contractual prison labor had set in motion twenty years earlier – and which now threatened to overwhelm not just the many and varied progressive prison reforms of the previous decade, but the drive to build a progressive penal state.

[110] For a discussion of the impeachment, see *The Nation* 97 (Oct. 23, 1913), 376–7.

8

Changing the Subject: The Metamorphosis of Prison Reform in the High Progressive Era

Our principal trouble in prison reform is that reforms have been patchwork. The time has come, it seems to me, for thorough-going studies followed by thorough-going reform.

Theodore Roosevelt, "The New Penology" (1913)

In the fall of 1913, the defenders of progressive statecraft engineered a remarkable opportunity to reverse their losses and advance their cause when an ordinary laborer by the name of Tom Brown was committed to the New York State Prison at Auburn. On its face, Brown's incarceration was routine: Upon entering the administration building, he was allocated a prisoner number – #33,333X – which the Prison Clerk recorded, together with details of his conviction, in the prison Admissions Ledger. Brown then answered questions put to him by one of the prison medical orderlies. The orderly noted on an index card that the new prisoner was a widower, laborer, and father of four, with a high school education. Prison officials then prepared Brown's person for incarceration: A convict–barber trimmed his hair and shaved off his thick moustache, an office clerk took his finger prints, and the Bertillon clerk examined, photographed, and measured his body, noting that the new prisoner's distinguishing features included a large scar and six small tattoos on his left bicep. Brown then exchanged his civilian attire for prison shoes, underwear, and the standard-issue coarse gray uniform. Finally, a guard handed him a copy of the *Rules and Regulations for Inmates of the New York State Prisons*, and escorted him to his cell, where he was to remain until the following morning. With the turn of a key, the transformation of one more American citizen into a prisoner of the state was complete, and a fairly typical convict began serving a rather ordinary prison sentence.[1]

But the headlines of the local and national daily papers for the following day revealed that the incarceration of Tom Brown had been anything but

---

[1] I have reconstructed Osborne's "commitment" to prison with the help of the following sources: Tom Brown, Medical Record, OFP, MSS64, Box 268, Org. Recs.; Rudolph W. Chamberlin, *There is No Truce: The Life of Thomas Mott Osborne* (New York: Macmillan, 1935), 245; Thomas Mott Osborne, *Within Prison Walls: Being A Narrative of Personal Experience During a Week of Voluntary Confinement in the State Prison at Auburn, New York* (New York and London: D. Appleton and Co, 1914). The prisoner was probably handed a copy of the newly revised *Rules and Regulations for Inmates of the New York State Prisons*, adopted November 1, 1912. (Superintendent of Prisons, New York State: 1912), OFP, MSS64, Box 268, Org. Recs.

routine. The *New York Journal* put it most dramatically: "Millionaire Head of Penitentiary Commission Takes his Place in Auburn, as Thomas Brown, and Works at Sorting Straw – Has Receiver of Stolen Goods for His Mate at Table – Eats Plain Fare and Seems to Like It – Shut Off From World."[2] As the *New York Times*, the *New York Journal*, and dozens of other newspapers reported that day, "Tom Brown, Auburn Prisoner #33,333X," was in fact Thomas Mott Osborne, and Osborne was neither a laborer nor a convicted felon, but the wealthy New York manufacturer, philanthropist, and progressive Democrat whom Governor Sulzer had recently appointed Chairman of the State Prison Reform Commission. The mysterious tattoos recorded by the prison Bertillon clerk turned out to be the marks of a Harvard man, and not those of a common laborer.[3] Under the alias, Tom Brown, and after several weeks of secret planning, Thomas Mott Osborne had commenced a week of voluntary incarceration as part of an elaborate and well-publicized study of prison conditions in the state of New York.[4]

No doubt, for many newspaper readers, the dramatic revelations concerning Tom Brown's true identity seemed bizarre and without context. But for attentive observers of public affairs, Osborne's widely publicized "bit" at Auburn capped a series of remarkable events that had transpired in and about American prisons over the previous year. When Thomas Mott Osborne donned the garb of an incarcerated laborer in the fall of 1913, it was already clear that the year would be a watershed in the annals of the penal history both of New York and of the country as a whole. The rebellion at Sing Sing in July had provided palpable proof that New York's oft-touted prison reforms of the previous fifteen years had not succeeded nearly so well as state officials had led the public to believe. Indeed it amplified and brought to

---

[2] *New York Journal* (Sep. 30, 1913). Osborne hired a press agency to clip articles pertaining to his incarceration and subsequent career as a prison administrator. They are collected in his scrapbooks, OFP, MSS64, Box 342.

[3] It turned out that, unlike his prison mates, Auburn prisoner #33,333 was not subject to all the rules laid down in the State Prison Rulebook: Upon commitment, Osborne was allowed to retain his wedding ring; he was permitted writing materials in his cell (which he put to use writing a journal that became the basis of his book, *Within Prison Walls*); perhaps in recognition of his gentility, Osborne was allowed to keep personal toiletries in his cell; and he was able to follow news of his incarceration by reading a daily newspaper that was delivered to his cell every morning. Chamberlin, *There is No Truce*, 245.

[4] Although Osborne had initially wanted neither the prisoners nor the guards to know his true identity, he was dissuaded from this course of action on the grounds that the prisoners would inevitably discover his true identity, and that consequently, he would fail to win their trust (Chamberlin, *There is No Truce*, 241). It seems probable that Superintendent Riley and other officials also wanted to avoid a situation by which the guards or prisoners might unknowingly rough-up the Chairman of the Prison Reform Commission. This fear may well have been borne out a few months later, when Madeline Z. Doty and Elizabeth Watson (fellow members of the New York State Prison Reform Commission), underwent a week of voluntary incarceration in the women's prison at Auburn. Unlike the case in the Osborne investigation, the guards did not know the true identities of the investigators. The women only completed three of the seven days they had intended to spend in the prison, finding their treatment as prisoners too harsh to endure. See Doty's account, *Society's Misfits* (New York: Century Co, 1916).

public notice a troubling fact that prison administrators around the country, and the Governors and lawmakers to whom those officials answered, had known for some time: The Empire State's answer to the vexing prison labor problem (that is, the state-use system of imprisonment) was failing, both in its own terms and by any measure of good governance. In no industrial state had the primary objective of the state-use system – to find full or near-full industrial employment for state prisoners – been realized. Indeed, the cumulative weight of evidence in New York, Massachusetts, California, and elsewhere strongly suggested that, under prevailing political conditions, the industrial state-use system was not an effective solution to the problem.

Some commentators, including the editor of the *New York Times*, were by now plainly exasperated: "as a matter of fact," the editor quipped in 1912 – and with no small hint of vitriol – "the convict labor problem is one quite beyond solution in any other way than by eliminating the convicts and so the problem."[5] Many other observers, including Chicago's leading penologist, Dr. F. Emory Lyon, admitted in more measured tones that despite the recent period of experimentation with prison industries around the country, "the problem of prison labor has nowhere reached a satisfactory solution."[6] Expert and official discourse on the matter had proliferated steadily through 1912 and 1913. As the wider political struggle over machine politics and the proper means and ends of government began to spiral into a full-scale crisis in the Empire State, prison administrators and social reformers had penned a slew of books and leaflets calling for a radical change in the states' approach to prisons and prison labor. Governors, lawmakers, and national political leaders (including Theodore Roosevelt and Woodrow Wilson) pronounced the prison labor problem one of the key social questions of the age, and state officials from every region of the country converged at national conferences to exchange ideas on what to do next.[7]

Within this crucible of intense activity, exchange, and discourse, key tenets of established penological dogma began to melt away, and a new progressive prison reform movement was forged. Incited by the deepening crises into which state penal systems everywhere seemed to be falling, reformers from every state outside of the South resolved to confront the prison labor problem once and for all. A younger generation of progressive reformers stepped forward to elaborate and implement what would prove to be some of the most innovative and enduringly controversial reforms in American penal history. New York's Thomas Mott Osborne, who had had some limited experience in prison reform prior to his appointment to

---

[5] *New York Times*, May 4, 1912, 12.
[6] F. Emory Lyon, "The Payment of Prisoners," *Journal of the American Institute of Criminal Law and Criminology* 3:1 (1912), 36.
[7] See for example, *Proceedings of the National Conference of Charities and Correction*, 1911. In those states in which the lease or contracting system lingered, there was an upsurge in the abolition effort: Arkansas Governor George W. Donaghey received national publicity when, as an explicit protest against the legislature's failure to abolish the lease, he pardoned and released some 360 prisoners. *New York Times*, Dec. 17, 1912, 1.

Sulzer's Prison Reform Commission, would quickly become the most influential, and certainly the most controversial, leader of the new, "new penology." His stint as Tom Brown (and his account of his experience, *Within Prison Walls*, which he rushed into print three months after his "release" from prison) drew considerable attention to many of the new ideas being generated in penal circles; it also helped catalyze the new progressive prison reform movement.[8]

The present chapter fleshes out the genesis and development of this new reform movement in the high Progressive Era (ca. 1913–17). It is the first of three chapters that, taken together, re-situate the most famous progressive penal initiatives in the highly charged political context in which they came to life, and within the longer *durée* of labor ideology and penal labor politics with which the younger generation of reformers were compelled to grapple. It traces the rise to national prominence of a diverse reform coalition known as the National Committee on Prison Labor, and fleshes out Osborne's related efforts, in New York in 1913 and 1914, to define and confront the prison labor problem in the country's oldest state prison, Auburn. The subsequent chapters address the remarkable set of experiments that took place at Sing Sing Prison under the joint direction of Osborne and the National Committee on Prison Labor in 1915–16, and these experiments' place in the larger, national arena of high progressive prison reform. These chapters' principal focus is the massive reform effort that unfolded in the largest and most widely scrutinized of the Northern penal states. The Empire State was the site of some of the most renowned, well-funded, and fully realized penal reforms of the late Progressive Era. At the same time, however, events in that state did not occur in a vacuum. As I shall argue here, they unfolded against a backdrop of nationwide agitation and struggle over the complex moral and political issues engulfing the state penal systems in the early 1910s. That backdrop influenced the form and content of reform in New York; and, as in earlier watershed periods of American penal history, New York's experiments would, in turn, have important repercussions well beyond the state's borders.

Although previous scholarly accounts have touched upon the younger progressives' efforts to revive prison labor and establish prison industries, they have considered the prison labor problem as just one among many preoccupations of the reformers.[9] As I argue here, however, the prison reform

---

[8] See note 1 in this chapter.

[9] For example, see David J. Rothman, *Conscience and Convenience: The Asylum and Its Alternatives in Progressive America* (Boston and Toronto: Little, Brown and Company, 1980), 140–3. "In sum," Rothman concludes with regard to progressive prison labor initiatives, "one more reform hope was disappointed." Larry Sullivan notes that "the most significant development during the Progressive era was the precipitous decline in convict employment." However, he does not elaborate on the broader social forces behind the decline, the multifaceted struggles over prison labor, or its significance, beyond the fact that "the lack of activities to fill the prisoner's time became a problem." Sullivan, *The Prison Reform Movement: Forlorn Hope* (Boston: Twayne, 1990), 38–40.

movement of the high Progressive Era grew out of a much longer engagement with that problem, and was continuously conditioned by it. Unlike
their predecessors, Osborne and his contemporaries did not construe the
prison labor problem in the narrow terms of how to put prisoners to the
hard labor prescribed by law; nor did they cast their task merely as that of
building efficient prison industries (although, as we shall see, they were certainly committed to having prisoners perform some kind of useful labor).
Chastened by the experience of their immediate predecessors and incited
by the escalating prison crisis, the new generation of progressives conceptualized their task, first and foremost, as that of discovering the means by
which they might instill in prisoners a recognition of the value and benefits
of gainful employment, *under conditions that had rendered full-time industrial
employment in the prisons all but impossible.* Recognition of the limitations of
the original, state-use plan of imprisonment sped the articulation of the
"new penology" and the discovery of novel modes of discipline. It was in the
course of this confrontation with the old, labor-based disciplinary system,
that a new concept of human subjectivity – whether of persons captive or
free – and a new strategy of governance were wrought.

* * * * *

By the crisis-ridden summer of 1913, a small but growing number of prison
administrators, lawmakers, and social reformers had begun to question not
only the efficacy of existing state-use prison systems but the twin assumptions at the heart of Northern penal doctrine and ideology:[10] These were,
that the activity of hard productive labor was the natural and indispensable
foundation of prison discipline, finances, and moral reform, and that the
state had both a right and a duty to compel prisoners to perform such labors.
As we have seen, both these deeply normative assumptions had survived the
abolition of contract prison labor more or less intact; the first generation of
progressive prison reformers had self-consciously conceptualized their task
as one of salvaging full, productive employment in the prisons. However,
like any other ideological fiction torn loose from the thing it explains and
justifies, the tenacious grip of these "self-evident truths" upon the minds
and souls of penologists began to slacken in the early 1910s; as many state
prisons headed into a second decade of relative industrial idleness, official
pronouncements concerning the "inevitable delays" and "teething problems" of the new state-use industries grew fewer and far less audible.

The earliest signs that a major ideological shift was underway came
in 1910, when a diverse group of citizens incorporated an organization
under the name of the National Committee on Prison Labor (which was
renamed the National Committee on Prisons and Prison Labor [NCPPL],

---

[10] As we have seen, during the period of Reconstruction, penal reformers in both the North
and South placed considerably less emphasis on productive labor as a reformatory agent
than was the case both before and immediately after that period. Even the most innovative
of Reconstruction's prison reformers, however, still took for granted that productive labor
was essential to the prisoner – and the prison.

in 1914). Drawing together progressive prison administrators, members of the National Federation of Women's Clubs, trade union leaders, jurists, employers, social scientists, a handful of philanthropists, and progressives from both major political parties, the Committee announced its intention to investigate the prison labor problem broadly and systematically and to promote appropriate remedies.[11] Like many other progressive coalitions that were emerging at that time, the Committee proceeded, between 1910 and 1913, to document and publicize the problem and to recommend and foster the enactment of enlightened legislation in the field. Led by its energetic young director and progressive economist, twenty-nine-year-old Dr. E. Stagg Whitin,[12] the Committee systematically tracked official discourse on prison labor around the country, generated national surveys of relevant legislation and the political parties' platforms, published a slew of leaflets and books, formulated state and federal policy initiatives, organized national conferences at which governors, lawmakers, and penologists came together to

[11] The Articles of Incorporation are reprinted in The National Committee on Prisons and Prison Labor (NCPPL), "The Use of Prison Labor in U.S. Government Work," NCPPL, Prison Labor Leaflet No. 44, 1918. See also, "National Committee on Prison Labor," *Journal of the American Institute of Criminal Law and Criminology* 1:3 (Sep. 1910), 459. The NCPPL was originally founded on the initiative of women workers of the Baltimore textile industry (which faced stiff competition, in a number of states, from prison labor). During a strike, in 1909, the workers approached Helen Varick Boswell, who chaired the social and industrial committee of the General Federation of Women's Clubs, for support in their cause. Boswell responded by bringing pressure to bear on the Department of Labor to conduct an investigation, and initiating the founding of an anti-contract labor lobbying group – the National Committee on Prison Labor. The group soon applied itself to the twin tasks of abolishing contracting and establishing exclusive state-use systems of prison labor around the country. By 1915, a number of well-known progressives had served on the Committee's executive board. These included Thomas Mott Osborne, George Kirchwey (Dean of the Columbia University Law School), Julia Jaffray, Frederick A. Goetz (a Columbia University dean), Charles B. Davenport (one of America's leading eugenicists), Dr. Hastings H. Hart, Samuel McCune Lindsay, James C. Egbert (Dean of Engineering, Columbia), Charles Henry Davis, and a number of leading attorneys and judges (George Foster Peabody, William H. Wadham, and George Gordon Battle). On the NCPPL's origins, see Julia Jaffray, in *New York Times*, Mar. 22, 1936, N6, 1.

[12] Ernest Stagg Whitin, a Columbia University Ph.D. and instructor in "social legislation," was a progressive economist with a background in labor and welfare policy. Before cofounding the National Committee on Prison Labor, he served on the New York Welfare Commission and in the New York State Department of Labor. He was also the secretary of the National Civic Federation, where he worked in the cause of pacifying industrial relations and establishing more cooperative relations between organized labor and business. Whitin wrote prolifically and organized tirelessly in the cause of progressive prison reform throughout his career. He published three books, and numerous articles and leaflets, on the question of prison labor and reform between 1912 and 1914, organized a number of national conferences on the topic, served on the federal War Industry Board's prison labor committee during the Great War, and was a senior labor advisor in the American delegation to the Paris Peace Conference. Whitin, *The Caged Man: A Summary of Existing Legislation in the United States on the Treatment of Prisoners* (New York: The Academy of Political Science, 1913); *Penal Servitude* (New York, National Committee on Prison Labor: 1912); *Prison Work* (Boston: American Unitarian Association, c.1915), 1–2, OFP, MSS64, Box 271, Org. Recs.; *New York Times*, Feb. 12, 1946, 28 (Whitin obituary).

discuss prison labor, and strove to mobilize public opinion in support of what members argued was a workable and just solution to the prison labor problem.[13]

The reform program the Committee eventually pursued was three-pronged: It opened, in 1910, with the aim of persuading state and federal government to complete the abolition of the country's remaining contract prison labor systems and adopt the basic legal framework of the state-use system.[14] This objective affirmed the general direction of early Progressive Era prison reform and did not challenge, in any obvious way, the ideological presuppositions of that system. The Committee's elaboration of the purpose and the organization of that state-use system, however, broke decisively with established convention. Rather than simply substituting the state and its agencies for the contractor and open market (as the first wave of progressive prison reformers had aimed to do), the Committee called upon the states to change the structure, meaning, and objectives of the activity of prison labor, as well. Specifically, the Committee urged the states to abolish *forced* labor in the prisons. Whitin argued in his groundbreaking work, *Penal Servitude*, that compelling prisoners to labor was tantamount to "economic slavery," and that such slavery was both manifestly unjust and demonstrably contrary to the process of rehabilitation. A prison-based species of slavery still thrived throughout the union, he insisted, because the profit imperative continued to reign supreme in prison administration, even where the state had replaced the contractor. Although adoption of the state-use system had mitigated some of the evils associated with the sale of prisoners' labor to private interests, it "in no vital way [affects] the economic injustice always inherent in a slave system": State-use merely transferred the profit motive to government.[15] Rather than compel prisoners to labor, the Whitin and the Committee as a whole concluded, the state should motivate convicts to labor, chiefly by offering them the incentive of a wage and by reconfiguring the activity of labor as a process of training and instruction, rather than of production and profit-making. As Whitin saw it: "The payment of a wage to the convict as a right growing out of his production of valuable commodities . . . tends to destroy the state of slavery." "Adequate industrial training . . . under proper

---

[13] The Committee published two, sequential series of pamphlets. The first ran from 1912 to 1913 under the title, "National Committee on Prison Labor, Prison Labor Leaflets, Nos. 1–22." The second ran from 1914 to 1919, under the title, "National Committee on Prisons and Prison Labor, Prison Leaflets, Nos. 1–65." The Committee used the first leaflet series to publish, among other things, the proceedings of a prison labor conference jointly sponsored with the American Academy of Political and Social Science in 1913. (The proceedings are also collected in the *Annals of the American Academy of Political and Social Science* 46, Prison Labor (Mar. 1913), 1–167.

[14] Committee member J. Lebovitz advanced this theme in a pamphlet circulated among the penologists, prison administrators, and lawmakers who gathered in Washington, D.C., in the fall of 1910, for the eighth International Prison Congress. J. Lebovitz, "The Importance of the Prison Labor Problem," (New York: National Committee on Prison Labor), 1910.

[15] Whitin, "Prison Labor," *Proceedings of the Academy of Political Science in the City of New York* 2:4, 161.

instructors, encouraged by a fair wage," he insisted, was the only means by which both the disciplinary and the long-term reformatory objectives of the penal system could be met.[16]

The third element of the Committee's reform program emerged more slowly than the others, but represented another important departure from early progressive penal ideology. In 1912, Whitin and other members of the NCPPL's executive committee began tentatively advancing the idea that prison labor, even in its reconstructed, waged, form, ought to be thought of as just one among several means of disciplining and reforming prisoners. Making disciplined citizen–workers out of prisoners remained the central preoccupation of the Committee's penology, but the Committee increasingly placed less emphasis on the decades-old idea that the activity of productive labor was the sole foundation of discipline and reform. Various activities, such as education and physical exercise, which the early progressives had viewed strictly as useful supplements to a labor-based disciplinary regime, slowly shed their supplicant status. At the same time, what it meant to "be" and "become" an ideal citizen–worker also began to change.

In 1912, the Committee commenced its most concerted drive yet to promote these ideas among the citizenry, persuade lawmakers to act, and build the organizational muscle necessary to the task of securing systematic reform across the several states. Working closely with the American Academy of Political and Social Science, Whitin and his fellow organizers staged a large-scale convention devoted to the topic of prison labor and featuring governors, unionists, and prison administrators from all around the country, whose ideas and local experiments in the field were consistent with the Committee's general program for reform. Theodore Roosevelt warmly endorsed the general program of reform (which he referred to as the "new penology"), and lent his name to the cause. For the first time in several years, the annual congress of the American Prison Association (which was attended by prison officials from thirty-eight states) foregrounded the prison labor problem as the most urgent issue for action.[17] A number of state officials, including the Governor of West Virginia, traveled to New York to work with Whitin to draft prison labor legislation for their states.[18] Through the spring of 1913, Whitin and other members also lobbied hard among churches and civic groups to raise awareness and support for the Committee's critique of existing policies and its program of reform. That approach bore fruit in May of 1913, when the annual meeting of the Quakers announced the launch of a "new abolition movement" to overthrow "convict slavery."[19] Finally,

[16] Whitin, "Prison Labor," *Proceedings of the Academy of Political Science in the City of New York* 2:4, 161; Whitin, letter to the editor, *New York Times*, Apr. 15, 1911, 12.

[17] The National Prison Association changed its name to American Prison Association in 1908. "American Prison Association," *Journal of Prison Discipline*, March 1913, 50 and *Annals of the American Academy of Political and Social Science* 46, Prison Labor (Mar. 1913), 1–167.

[18] *New York Times*, Nov. 16, 1913, XX11.

[19] *New York Times*, May 27, 1913, 11. The following year, the American Unitarian Association published more than 10,000 copies of Whitin's critique of prison labor, *Prison Work* (Boston: American Unitarian Association, c.1915), 1–2, OFP, MSS64, Box 271, Org. Recs.

as Governor Sulzer's office began to publicize George Blake's findings of alleged malfeasance and abuses in New York's Tammany-controlled Prisons Department, the Committee leadership approached Governor Sulzer and persuaded him to appoint a Prison Reform Commission for the purposes of conducting a full-scale investigation of the state prisons, their labor system, and their administration. Sulzer obliged, appointing his ally in the attack on Tammany, Thomas Mott Osborne, to the chairmanship of the new commission and E. Stagg Whitin to the position of secretary. (A number of other Committee members were appointed to the twelve-person commission, as well).[20]

Momentum continued to build in the weeks before the trouble began at Sing Sing. In time for Bastille Day, the National Committee on Prison Labor announced what they hoped would be a groundbreaking lawsuit in the field of legal punishment. In a Rhode Island court, the Committee's attorneys (George Gordon Battle and Columbia University Law School Dean, George W. Kirchwey) challenged the constitutionality of a state law authorizing the contracting out of prisoners as laborers, and sought the recovery of wages from a contractor to whom the state had sold the labor of dozens of prisoners. The Rhode Island State Constitution of 1847 was one of just three state constitutions that prohibited slavery outright, making no exception whatsoever for penal slavery. In *Anderson v. Salant*,[21] Battle and Kirchwey put E. Stagg Whitin's concept of penal servitude to work, arguing that the contracting-out of convict William Anderson's labor, with no remuneration for the prisoner, rendered him a slave; such an arrangement was thus illegal and the plaintiff was entitled to recover wages for his services. Designed as much to draw public attention to the cause of convict labor reform as to secure relief for Anderson and his fellow prisoners, the Committee's lawsuit received considerable publicity in newspapers and journals. A full-page feature article, complete with photographs and drawings depicting convict laborers at toil around the country, appeared in the *New York Times*, and the case received considerable coverage in numerous other publications.[22] When *Anderson v. Salant* finally made it into the Rhode Island Supreme

---

[20] The Prison Reform Commission was instructed to "examine and investigate the management and affairs of the several State prisons and reformatories, and departments thereof, the prison industries, the construction and plan for adequate prison facilities, the employment of convict labor, and all subjects relating to the proper maintenance and control of the State prisons of the State of New York." Sulzer appointed eleven members to the Prison Reform Commission June 13, 1913; the commission was announced to the public on July 7, 1913. Prison Reform Commission, NYSA Governor's Office Records. Investigation case Files of Charges and Complaints Against Public Officials and Agencies, 1857–1919, A0531, Box 41, Folder: Appointed Prison Reform Commission.

[21] *William E. Anderson v. Gabriel Salant, et al* [No number in original] Supreme Court of Rhode Island, 38 R.I. 463; 96 A. 425; 1916 R.I. LEXIS 8 (1916).

[22] *New York Times*, July 13, 1913, SM13; "Convict Labor in the United States; Resolved: That unpaid convict labor is slavery and should be abolished in the United States. Brief for the Affirmative. Brief for the Negative," *The Independent... Devoted to the Consideration of Politics, Social and Economic Tendencies, History, Literature, and the Arts*, Aug. 28, 1913, 3.

Court, the justices ruled against the prisoner. (They found that the contract did not cast Anderson into a condition of "slavery," as Battle and Kirchwey had defined it, and that, in any case, the framers of the Rhode Island constitution had had "in mind slavery as it . . . existed in some of the states of the Union [in 1847] and as it had existed in this State" – that is, the constitution proscribed only the chattel slavery system of the sort found in the Old South and in pre-abolition Rhode Island).[23] This defeat notwithstanding, the suit had attracted considerable (and generally sympathetic) publicity for Whitin, the Committee, and their case for prison reform.

The great rush of organizing and publicity around penal servitude in 1912–13 established the Committee as the most authoritative prison reform group in the country; Whitin, Kirchwey, and other executive board members were now consulting with lawmakers and governors around the nation. The Committee had also laid the groundwork for more direct influence over penal policy in New York (through the establishment of the Prison Reform Commission). When the convicts at Sing Sing subsequently rose up in protest of their living conditions and the penal arm of New York's government was seen to be on the verge of collapse, conditions were ripe for the initiation of reform. Planning began in earnest, between the Prison Reform Commission and the National Committee on Prison Labor, for a full-scale campaign to abolish the last remnants of penal slavery and reinvent imprisonment in New York. When the state Assembly finally impeached Governor Sulzer in August 1913, the pressure on the independent wing of the Democratic party to salvage its reputation must have been immense. Osborne's "bit" at Auburn was both the opening maneuver in the mounting campaign to reform the state's penal system and a well-timed effort to counter the charge that independent Democrats, like the machine politicians they professed to despise, were little better than thieves and "spoilsmen."

When Osborne assumed the identity of Tom Brown in September of 1913, it was not the first time a well-known public figure and ally of prison reform had undergone voluntary incarceration. At least two state Governors (in Arizona and Tennessee) had done so the previous year, in the name of first-hand investigation of prison conditions.[24] But unlike his predecessors, Osborne entered Auburn with a clear vision of what needed to be done, an acute sense of the power of publicity, and the implicit backing of a

[23] *Anderson v. Salant*, 481.
[24] Governors G. W. P. Hunt of Arizona and Benjamin W. Hooper of Tennessee underwent voluntary incarceration in 1912, as part of well-publicized efforts to bring voters' attention to bear on their reform programs; prison investigators Madeline Z. Doty and Elizabeth Watson committed themselves to the women's prison at Auburn in 1913; Frank Tannenbaum (who served a real sentence the New York City penitentiary in 1913), also went undercover as a convict at Sing Sing in 1915, as did journalist Lewis Wood. For accounts of some of these experiences, see *New York Times*, Dec. 24, 1911, 3 (Hooper); *New York Times*, Mar. 27, 1912, 1 (Hunt); Madeline Z. Doty, *Society's Misfits* (New York: Century Co., 1916); Lewis Wood, "Sing Sing's Shops Show New Spirit" *New York Tribune* (Jan. 19, 1915); "Former Celebrities in Prison Tribunal" *New York Tribune* (Jan. 20, 1915), in OFP, Clippings, MSS64, Box 342, Memorabilia, Scrapbooks, Prisons, Jan. 1 1915-Nov. 10, 1915.

well-organized and well-respected prison reform group (the National Committee on Prison Labor). For Osborne, entering Auburn was the first step toward overhauling the conditions and everyday practices of incarceration in New York state's prisons; for the impeached Sulzer and besieged Superintendent Riley, Osborne's prominence as a progressive philanthropist and wealthy up-state Democrat with powerful political and business ties promised to bolster the former Governor's flagging support.

Osborne's background in business, politics, and social reform, his considerable personal charisma, and his press-worthy flare for the dramatic, made him peculiarly well-suited to the task of spearheading New York's prison reform movement. Born in Auburn, New York (in the shadow of the famous prison) on the eve of the Civil War, Osborne's life spanned the period in which familial, proprietal capitalism first characterized American market relations, and was subsequently eclipsed by the practices and ideology of large-scale corporate capitalism. His family was of the proprietal class that had dominated American business in the mid-nineteenth century but which had begun, by the end of the Gilded Age, to cede ground to the great corporate and financier classes. His father, D. M. Osborne, owned and managed a prosperous mower and reaper manufacturing business, and after graduating from Harvard University in the early 1880s, Thomas took over its directorship. Under Thomas's direction, the company expanded and eventually opened offices and warehouses in San Francisco, the mid-western United States, Hamburg, Paris, Odessa, Sydney, and Buenos Aires.[25] In 1903, amidst the frenzy of business mergers that broke out across the United States that year, Osborne sold the company to J. P. Morgan (who purchased it for his International Harvester Company). After that, Osborne continued to hold a handful of presidencies of smaller companies, and he founded a newspaper, *The Auburn Citizen*. He also accelerated his involvement in state and national politics.

Like most men of his generation and class, Osborne was active, from an early age, in national, state, and local politics, chiefly as a "county" Democrat. In a party dominated by Tammany Hall (at least within New York state), he had met with greater success as a minor political appointee than as a candidate for electoral office. In the 1880s, he supported the Democrat Grover Cleveland in his run for the Presidency; he later ran (and lost) the race for Lieutenant Governor of New York as the Democratic nominee in 1894. In the 1890s, he joined others of his class in denouncing Tammany Hall and the trusts, and he temporarily deserted the Democrats when they nominated the tabloid magnate, William Randolph Hearst, for Governor in 1906. (The Republican victor in that election, Charles Evans Hughes, rewarded Osborne with his most important government appointment to date: Public Service Commissioner.) In 1910, Osborne had sought the Democratic nomination for the Governorship of New York, but lost it to the Tammany-backed John A. Dix. Convinced that Dix, and Tammany Hall, were destructive both

[25] Bibliographical notes, OFP, MSS64, Catalogue, 2.

toward his party and progressive government, Osborne then proceeded to work closely with the young senator from Hyde Park, Franklin D. Roosevelt, to rein in the power of Tammany leader Charles Murphy and to promote civil service reform, open party conventions, and stronger executive commissions within the Democratic party. Establishing a club for progressive Democrats (known as the Empire State Democracy), the two men worked closely together through 1912 to get the party to drop John Dix from the ticket and crush the power of Charles Murphy.

Throughout his political career, Osborne had been active in the progressive cause of restructuring local and state government around principles of bureaucracy and efficiency. When elected mayor of the city of Auburn in the early 1900s, he had restructured the municipal administration of that town according to conceptions of municipal efficiency. In 1907, in the capacity of public service commissioner, he investigated the safety and efficiency of the New York railways. Adopting an investigative technique that would later make him famous as a prison reformer, Osborne donned the rags of a hobo and rode the rails of the New York Central Railroad, surreptitiously observing and recording the work of the train crews.[26] Before entering Auburn Prison as "Tom Brown" in September 1913, Osborne had also had some experience in prison reform. Although he would later claim that it was not until 1912, when he read Donald Lowrie's autobiography, *My Life in Prison*,[27] that he decided to concentrate his political efforts on systematic prison reform, by that time he had already published in the field of penology and requested (of Governor John A. Dix, in 1910) an appointment to the superintendency of state prisons. (Dix appointed a Tammany ally, instead, and offered Osborne the minor position of Commissioner in the Forest, Fish, and Game Department). Most critically, Osborne had also served fifteen years on the board of the George Junior Republic, a private reform school for indigent and "wayward" boys and girls located outside of Ithaca, in up-state New York.

Founded in the twilight of the Gilded Age, the Republic was both a backward-looking and an innovative institution. Breaking decisively with established pedagogical principles, the philosophy of its founder and namesake, William R. George, was that children could only become good citizens through active participation in the kinds of civil, political, and economic institutions they would have to engage with in the adult world. Only

---

[26] Osborne recommended that the number of workmen in the crews be maintained, as smaller crews would make the railways unsafe.

[27] Donald Lowrie, *My Life in Prison* (New York and London: Mitchell Kennerley, 1912). First published in serialized form in the *San Francisco Bulletin*, 1911, Lowrie's account was among the better known of the many prisoner narratives that began to appear in the early 1900s. As historian Frank Tannenbaum, one of Osborne's biographers and a close friend, put it, Lowrie's book "crystallized all of (Osborne's) previous experience and reflections. . . . After that, every time he appeared in public to deliver an address he chose to speak about prisons and prison problems." Frank Tannenbaum, *Osborne of Sing Sing* (Chapel Hill, NC: University of North Carolina Press, 1933), 63.

through participatory learning would the children become productive, self-governing citizens. To that end, George organized the Republic as a simulacrum of republican society. The children lived in large, family cottages, under the "parental" eye of an adult woman (and, sometimes, her husband); attended regular "town meetings"; exercised the rights of citizenship in regular elections for a president, cabinet, and two attorneys general (one for the boys and one for the girls); were offered handicraft and farm labor in return for a wage paid in tin tokens; and kept shop, paid rent, and banked their tin-token savings. Breaking from conventional pedagogies of the authoritarian rod-and-cane persuasion, this system of self-government was relatively radical for its time. But at the same time, it honored and served a decidedly conventional value: that of living by the sweat of one's brow. The Republic's motto was "Nothing without Labor," and its social system enforced that principle without compromise. The amount and quality of a child's work determined the amount of wages he or she received; in turn, the amount of a child's income determined the quality of the cottage he or she could afford – and the amount of food he or she ate. As the British penal reformer, Sir Evelyn Ruggles-Brise, approvingly observed following a visit to Republic, if the children chose to be idle, they simply starved.[28]

Osborne appears to have been deeply influenced by his involvement at the Republic. He wrote the laudatory introduction to William R. George's lengthy book on the institution, and presented a paper on penology to the National Prison Association, in 1904, in which he adapted the theory of self-government to adult penology: Prisons, argued Osborne, in echoes of George, ought to teach convicts how to choose between honesty and crime, and between work and idleness. In a subsequent address to the Association, Osborne went on to argue: "Society must brand no man as a criminal; but aim solely to reform the mental conditions under which a criminal act has been committed."[29] Osborne continued working these themes in public addresses on penology, including one in Syracuse, New York, in which he joined other prison reformers of the day in indicting the prisons for treating prisoners "like wild animals," and for "(brutalizing) the men and the keepers."[30]

By 1912, then, Osborne had acquired both a degree of familiarity with penal matters and an ambition to secure a position of power from which

---

[28] William R. George, *The Junior Republic: Its History and Ideals* (New York and London: D. Appleton and Co, 1910); Evelyn Ruggles-Brise, "An English View of the American Penal System," *Journal of the American Institute of Criminal Law and Criminology* 2:3. (Sep., 1911), 366–7; Ugo Conti and Adolph Prins, "Some European Comments on the American Prison System," *Journal of the American Institute of Criminal Law and Criminology* 2:2 (July 1911), 199–215.

[29] *Proceedings of the Annual Congress of the National Prison Association of the United States*, 1906. In this regard, Osborne had a poor sense of history: The first prison theorists had argued for incarceration as an alternative to what they viewed as the barbaric and retaliatory practices of earlier systems of justice. See Georg Rusche and Otto Kirchheimer, *Punishment and Social Structure* (New York: Columbia University Press, 1939) 141.

[30] *Proceedings of the Annual Congress of the National Prison Association of the United States*, 1904; Frank Tannenbaum, *Osborne of Sing Sing*, 62.

he might initiate and oversee reform. With the election of Sulzer to the governorship of New York in 1912, Osborne was finally able to secure an official appointment in the prison system (that is, as chairman of the Prison Reform Commission). Seeking to consolidate his position, he also successfully lobbied Governor Sulzer to appoint his long-time friend and political ally, Charles Rattigan, to the wardenship of Auburn. As one of Osborne's biographers put it, Rattigan was the Democratic boss of Cayuga County and Osborne's right-hand man.[31] By September 1913, with a close friend installed at Auburn and the chairmanship of the State Prison Reform Commission under his wing, Osborne was finally in a position to initiate the process of reform in the New York prison system.

When he entered Auburn as Tom Brown, Osborne set out to achieve a number of things. By making use of a methodology that sociologists would later refine as the participant–observer method,[32] Osborne undertook to study the daily life of the prison to better understand what he called "prison psychology." He reasoned that such a study would enable him to devise a program of reform that took account of the psychological effects of incarceration and replace what he viewed as the purely punitive aspects of imprisonment with corrective techniques that would break what he took to be a "cycle of revenge." Only by suffering the deprivations of the prison, Osborne

---

[31] Chamberlin, *There is No Truce*, 238–40, 239. Chamberlin was an unabashed champion of Osborne and his programs, and his biography must be read with this in mind. He had some difficulty reconciling Osborne's anti-Tammany rhetoric with Osborne's method of procuring the wardenship for Rattigan. Chamberlin justified Osborne's actions on the grounds that Osborne needed a trustworthy man in the position, and that Rattigan's appointment only "*looked* like a political appointment," but was really done with the best interests of prison reform in mind (his emphasis). Chamberlin, *There is No Truce*, 239.

[32] David J. Rothman cites Osborne as probably the first practitioner of "participant-observation." However, it should be noted that unlike contemporary practitioners of participant-observation, Osborne did not adhere to any particular methodology. Unlike the academic sociologists and cultural anthropologists of the 1920s and 1930s who developed participant-observation as a set of standard techniques, Osborne, Doty, and other prison investigators of the 1910s made no claims as to the scientific validity of their studies. In this regard, their studies of prisons fell somewhere between naturalist fiction, in which authors narrated stories about various milieus on the basis of their informal studies of the communities in which they had lived, and the sociological methodology of participant-observation. Moreover, some years before Osborne undertook his study of Auburn, the Columbia University anthropologist, Franz Boas, had made extensive use of a participant-observer methodology in his studies of the Inuit, the Bella Coolas, and the Kwakiutls. As Osborne undertook his studies of Auburn, Elise Clews Parsons, a follower of Boas, observed and wrote about the élite milieu in which she moved in Washington, D.C. Whatever the roots of participant-observation and Osborne's relation to it, the principle from which ethnologists, naturalist writers, and amateur social investigators of the 1900s and 1910s proceeded was much the same: This was that the empirical methods of observing and living among communities (whether primitive, élite, working class, or incarcerated) would provide evidence to support the irreducible unity of humanity. Paul Atkinson, *The Ethnographic Imagination: Textual Construction of Reality* (London and New York: Routledge, 1990); Rosalind Rosenberg, *Beyond Separate Spheres: The Intellectual Roots of Modern Feminism* (New Haven, Connecticut: Yale University Press, 1981); David J. Rothman, *Conscience and Convenience: The Asylum and its Alternatives in Progressive America* (Boston: Little Brown, 1980), 119.

argued, could he begin to understand the effect of incarceration on prisoners. As he said to the 1,400 prisoners gathered in the Auburn chapel the day before he entered Auburn as Tom Brown:

> ...deep down, I have the feeling that after I have really lived among you, marched in your lines, shared your food, gone to the same cells at night, and in the morning looked out at the piece of God's sunlight through the same iron bars – that then, and not until then, can I feel the knowledge which will break down the barriers between my soul and the souls of my brothers.[33]

In seeking to dismantle the barriers between his soul and those of the prisoners, Osborne also strove to remove what he perceived as the far more enduring barrier that stood between society and prisoners. In his study of Auburn and in all his subsequent prison work, Osborne proceeded on the assumption that poor conditions existed in the prisons because prisoners were effectively screened off from society and that, consequently, society was unaware of the degrading state of the prisons. If society only knew the truth, he reasoned in the best traditions of progressive muckraking journalism, it would press prison administrations and the state government to reform the prisons. Of course, by "society," Osborne was not referring in the widest sense to all inhabitants of the United States, or even all adult U.S. citizens. Rather, he referred to members of America's bourgeoning middling and élite classes, whose active membership in political parties and civic clubs, and participation in public discourse about the meaning of government and its realm of activity, made them highly influential in the formation of public policy. It was the support of these classes, rather than that of native and immigrant workers, that Osborne (and his backers in the National Committee on Prison Labor) sought to harness in the attempt to reform the prisons of New York.

In seeking their support, Osborne and his supporters on the National Committee on Prison Labor adopted the familiar technique of other progressive reformers of the era – the investigative exposé – as the means by which to document "the truth," and thereby engage middling and élite Americans in the work of reforming the prisons. They made use of newspapers and silent movies to bring his conception of the truth about prisons to the attention of the public. In this respect, Osborne's voluntary incarceration was orchestrated as a dramatic event that would be publicized in the pages of the mass press, as well as in his own writings.[34] Osborne himself

---

[33] Later, Osborne would compliment himself on having changed the written speech from "God's sunlight" to "the piece of God's sunlight" that a small, barred cell window affords the prisoner.

[34] Some months later, Osborne would open Sing Sing Prison to journalists and arrange for them to join prominent penologists, business leaders, and civic leaders in tours of the prison. He also made two moving pictures on the subject of Tom Brown's incarceration at Auburn, and wrote and appeared in a dramatic film shot on location at Sing Sing Prison. In his film ("The Right Way," dir. Sydney Olcott, Producers' Security Corporation [1921]) the old system of stripes, lockstep, and silence is depicted as cruel and unjust, and is ultimately abolished by a new warden who sets up a convict self-government league. The film received

brought some measure of expertise to his press campaign, having founded a newspaper (*The Auburn Citizen*) in 1905, through which he had promoted Democratic candidates running in local and national races. The National Committee on Prison Labor, meanwhile, had ample experience catching the attention of the press. They did not have to do a great deal of work to attract the attention of the press to his Auburn study. Indeed, upon hearing news of Osborne's impending investigation, the press, and a number of photographers and silent film-makers, requested that they be allowed to accompany him into Auburn in order to document his incarceration.

Osborne declined these requests, noting that the presence of journalists and film-makers would disrupt the everyday life of the prison and thereby defeat the purpose of the study. However, he did arrange for press releases to be made through the office of Warden Rattigan during his incarceration, and journalists were permitted to tour the prison. (At least two groups did so; Osborne gleefully reported that, shorn of his moustache and dressed in the ill-fitting prison uniform, not a single visitor managed to identify him from among the 1,400 prisoners).[35] It was in order to facilitate the discursive objectives of the study that Osborne circumvented the prison rules governing the acts of reading and writing: Unlike Auburn's prisoners, he was provided with pen and paper in his cell, and a morning newspaper was delivered to him daily. (By that time, prisoners were entitled to receive one "reputable weekly newspaper," whereas the highest grade were entitled to a daily, tri-weekly, or semi-weekly paper, provided it was not "sensational").[36] The waiver of the reading and writing rules meant that Osborne was able to both keep the journal that later became the basis for his approximation of a prisoner narrative (*Within Prison Walls*), and stay abreast of what was being said about his study in the newspapers.[37]

In undertaking the Auburn study, Osborne explicitly sought out, and then narrated, not simply the experience of everyday life at Auburn, but the terrors of incarceration. The press articles and *Within Prison Walls* told of Osborne's horrified responses to the depravations of prison life. According to Osborne, among the most horrifying moments were his first night in prison, overhearing a beating in the cells, and a night spent in a "dark (punishment) cell." As had been the case in the nineteenth-century prison, the dark cell was the linchpin in the disciplinary regime of most American

---

excellent reviews within the motion picture industry, and *Variety*'s reviewer described it as "a kind of propaganda for the Osborne method . . . but written and acted out in a thoroughly dramatic way." *Variety* (Nov. 13, 1921). See also *Billboard* (Nov. 5, 1921) and *Wid's Daily* (Nov. 13, 1921).

35 Chamberlin, *There is No Truce*, 246.

36 Rule 27 of the *Rules and Regulations* regulated newspaper subscriptions. Rule 31 regulated the possession of writing paper, and expressly prohibited prisoners to use the paper on which *the Star of Hope* was printed for anything but its official purpose. *Rules and Regulations for Inmates of the New York State Prisons*, Superintendent of New York State Prisons (adopted 1912), ix.

37 *Within Prison Walls* (supra., fn 1) is the only (known) surviving account of Osborne's week in Auburn Prison.

prisons in the 1910s: Prisoners who breached the rules were officially held there for between one and ten days, and unofficially, for much longer periods of time, and put on a barely subsistent bread-and-water diet. In 1913, there were at least five such cells in use at Auburn, and Sing Sing had eight, as well as two padded cells.[38] More serious transgressions of the rules were punished by internment in them. Located between the noisy power generators and the execution chamber, the Auburn cells' solid steel walls blocked out all sources of light and fresh air, and prisoners commonly complained of losing all sense of time and space while incarcerated there. In addition to the deprivation of light, fresh air, and bedding, each prisoner was given a bucket, a tin cup, and the three gills (1.5 cups) of water to which he was officially entitled each night.[39]

Osborne was well aware that his experience and documentation of the evils of the prison system would be incomplete without an investigation of the Auburn dark cells. Consequently, toward the end of his week in the prison, he arranged with Warden Rattigan to be detained in a dark cell. In his effort to experience as many of the commonplace practices of incarceration as possible, he committed the kind of transgression that would normally result in such punishment: He refused to work. On cue, a guard escorted him to the punishment cells, and locked him in a cell (which, it turned out, had been specially cleaned for him). According to the original arrangement, Osborne was supposed to spend just three hours in the dark cell. But when his time was up he insisted that he spend the night there, as three hours had not been long enough to "(taste) the bitterness of solitary."[40]

By his own account, Osborne was terrified by that night in the dark cell. Despite the knowledge that he was to be interned only for twelve hours and that he was not, in fact, a prison convict, Osborne claimed that he nearly became insane while there. In somewhat turgid, but nonetheless evocative, language he told the press and his readers of his having become feverishly delirious during the night, and of swiping futilely at the vermin that crawled all over his body. Only by talking to a prisoner held in a nearby dark cell was he able to retain his sanity. In corroborating the assertion of reformers that the dark cell made rehabilitation of a prisoner impossible, he insisted that the cell had virtually broken his spirit and temporarily instilled in him a heartfelt hatred of the guards and of society: When the guard came to release him in the morning, he reported, what had been an intuitive dislike for the guards had hardened into defiance of all authority. After he was discharged from prison (the following day), Osborne made a press release about his time in Auburn, in which he condemned prisons for what he described as their "cruel slavery." He singled out the dark cell as one of the principal

[38] In the Matter of the Inquiry into the Conditions of Sing Sing Prison, Westchester County Grand Jury, Presentment to the June Term of the Supreme Court, 1913, OFP, MSS64, Box 278, Org. Recs.

[39] Prisoners were allowed one gill until 1913, when the Superintendent of Prisons, John Riley, increased the official ration to three gills. Chamberlin, *There is No Truce*, 252.

[40] Osborne, *Within Prison Walls*, Ch. 13 "A Night in Hell."

evils in the New York state prison system: Both its use as a punishment for refusing to work and the peculiar psychic pains it inflicted affirmed that the prison labor system was in fact a system of slavery, much as Whitin and the National Committee on Prison Labor had claimed. Moreover, Osborne argued, the worst effect of the dark cell was that it caused prisoners to hate society and predisposed them to commit subsequent crimes against their object of hatred.[41]

Osborne's night in the dark cell predictably supplied him with the experiential evidence by which to write a forthright condemnation of its use, but it also appears to have caused him to undergo a conversion-like experience: Osborne reported he had been touched by the hand of God that night in the dark cell at Auburn. In *Within Prison Walls*, he wrote that upon returning to his regular cell in the morning, he knelt and prayed, "May I be an instrument in Thy hands, O God, to help others see the light, as Thou hast led me to see the light. And may no impatience, prejudice, or pride of opinion on my part hinder the service Thou hast given me to do."[42] Although, like many progressive reformers, Osborne had been cut from the mold of protestant social reformism and had always brought a Christian humanist ethics to bear in his philanthropic work, after his night in the dark cell he began to conceive of his reforms as part of a Divine mission: As he saw it, the treatment of prisoners was not only a secular problem for the experts of social efficiency, psychology, and pedagogy, but a deeply moral problem in which the forces of evil were arrayed in epic struggle with the good. Prison reform would require him to possess the undying zeal of a missionary and an acute knowledge of human psychology.

As well as being an amateur study in psychology and a spiritually transformative experience, Osborne's week in Auburn was the first step in his plan to foster support among the prisoners for a self-government league and recreation program at Auburn. Critical to the project of prisoner self-government, as Osborne saw it, was the consent of the prisoners to proceed with the experiment. Although, as noted earlier, Osborne had conceived of the idea of self-government well before entering Auburn, he went to great lengths to persuade convicts, prison administrators, and civilians alike that the impetus for self-government came from the prisoners. His week in Auburn provided the stage for this simulation. When he entered Auburn as Tom Brown, Osborne not only pursued the prisoners' consent to the idea of setting up a self-government league, but sought to generate a belief among the prisoners that the idea had originated among themselves. He placed a great deal of emphasis on this matter, because he believed that prisoners would reflexively resist self-government if the impetus for its creation were seen to originate with the prison authorities. If prisoners believed self-government to be of their own making, they would more likely lend their support. (This was broadly consistent, as well, with the "penal slavery"

---

[41] Quoted in *New York Times* (Oct. 6, 1913). See Scrapbooks, OFP, MSS64, Box 342.
[42] Quoted in Chamberlin, *There Is No Truce*, 259.

abolitionism espoused by Osborne and the National Committee on Prison Labor, and their effort to replace external, top-down models of discipline with a system of internal and incentive-based discipline).

Tom Brown wasted no time initiating a discussion with the prisoners on the question of self-government. On the morning following his commitment, the Superintendent of Industries assigned him to the weave shop, where he befriended his work partner and long-term prisoner, Jack Murphy. Osborne recounts in *Within Prison Walls* that as they conversed while weaving rattan into baskets, he mentioned to Murphy that Superintendent Riley was considering establishing some kind of recreational activity for prisoners on Sunday afternoons, but that the Superintendent was uncertain how this "freedom of the yard" would be supervised, as Sunday was the guards' day off. According to Osborne's account of this conversation, when he mentioned to Murphy the idea of having the prisoners supervise themselves, Murphy suggested the means by which this could be organized: A good conduct league could be set up among the prisoners, and the privileges of participating in Sunday recreation would be contingent upon good standing in the league. The problem of Sunday policing would be solved by the league providing its own officers to supervise recreation. Murphy's suggestions neatly mirrored Osborne's own ideas about reform. As Osborne's sympathetic biographer and friend, Rudolph Chamberlin, later put it, in the course of this conversation, "(t)he basic principles of the Mutual Welfare League had been drafted – ostensibly by a convict, in reality by Osborne himself." Over the next several years, however, Osborne repeatedly praised prisoner Murphy as the originator of the plans for self-government.[43]

Osborne was released from Auburn, on Sunday, October 5. By the end of his week in prison, he had labored at weaving baskets and heaving coal, conversed with a prisoner about the concept of self-government, struck tools, and struggled through a night in the dark cell. Daily, he had marched in military formation between cellhouse, mess hall, and workshop, eaten his meals in silence while seated single-file in the mess hall, and suffered severe indigestion from drinking the prison "coffee." Locked up by night in his cell, he had written about all of this, as well as of the terrors of isolation, the long nights in the cell, and guard brutality, in the pages of his journal. When he left Auburn seven days after first entering the place, he was convinced that he had experienced, and now thoroughly understood, the reasons why prisons were failing to reform prisoners and reduce crime.

As Osborne had planned, he had also sparked a mass press event of national proportion, drawing both the ire and support of newspaper editors and journalists across the United States.[44] Among the newspapers and journals whose editors wrote favorably of Osborne's experiment were the *Outlook*,

---

[43] Ibid.

[44] For example, *New York Sun*, *The Republican* (Denver, Colorado), *New York Herald*, *New York World*, *Syracuse Herald*, *Albany Argus*, *New York Press*, *Brooklyn Union*, and *New York Times*. Articles from these and many more newspapers are collected in Osborne's scrapbooks, OFP, MSS64, Box 342, Scrapbooks.

The Independent, Saturday Evening Post, Current Opinion, the *New York Tribune, Boston Transcript,* and the *Christian Science Monitor.*[45] Critics of Osborne's study remarked that the well-heeled Osborne could not possibly know what it meant to be a prisoner: He was not, they insisted, a real prisoner, but, as the *New York Times* put it, an "amateur prisoner."[46] Although the *Times* was not entirely condemnatory of Osborne, describing his study as "well-intended, and yet ill-advised," other observers openly ridiculed him. Former U.S. President, William Howard Taft, for example, denounced Osborne from a pulpit in New Haven, dismissing the investigation as little more than sensationalism and "brotherhood gone mad."[47] Many editors in the press reported that the methodological premise of Osborne's study – to experience the psychology of the prison first hand – was inherently flawed.

Regardless of their view of the experiment, editors grasped the point that the voluntary commitment of a member of New York's élite to a state prison was eminently newsworthy. They comprehended that Osborne's "bit" as Tom Brown constituted a remarkable drama of American class relations – and class transgression. As the headline of the *New York Tribune* announcing the incarceration of the "Millionaire Head of Penitential Commission," suggests, it was the idea that the well-heeled Osborne was voluntarily subjecting himself to the plain food, rough company, and menial labor of a class of people well below his station in life that captured the imagination of newspaper editors and journalists. The theme of class transgression was repeated in most of the stories: An article in the *Rochester Union* criticizing Osborne's entry to Auburn described him as "the millionaire student of prison reforms." Many of the papers drew attention to the refined Osborne's consumption of the coarse fare of prison food, while skeptical cartoonists pictured him being waited upon in his cell, supping wine, and savoring caviar. To some, Osborne's communing with convicts was titillating; to some it was a worthwhile investigation of prison conditions; to others it was appalling, or simply misguided. Whatever their stance, it was Osborne's transgression of social hierarchy that appealed to editors: Osborne had struck a nerve.[48]

Osborne had also struck a nerve with several of the editors of prisoner newspapers around the United States. Many shared the skepticism of the civilian press about the ability of Osborne, as an outsider (and an élite one, at that), to experience prison as prisoners did. The prisoner–editor of *Good Words,* a paper published at the federal penitentiary in Atlanta, protested that this "penitentiary Columbus" had merely made a "trip to Tophet, with

45 "Mr. Osborne Goes to Prison," *Outlook,* Oct. 11, 1913, 228; "A Voluntary Convict," *The Independent . . . Devoted to the Consideration of Politics, Social and Economic Tendencies, History, Literature, and the Arts,* Oct 16, 1913. 76:3385, 114; "New Revelations and Criticisms of our Prison Methods," *Current Opinion,* Dec. 1913, 427–8; others collected in OFP, MSS64, Box 342, Scrapbooks.
46 *New York Times,* Oct. 5, 1913, 12.
47 Osborne, paraphrasing Taft, *New York Times,* Jan. 11, 1914, 8.
48 Osborne's scrapbooks, OFP, MSS64, Box 342, Scrapbooks.

a string tied to himself."[49] In language that conjured images of Dante's brief tour of Hell, he continued that Osborne had reached only the "outer threshold of the actual infernos in which all *bona fide* convicts live." Unlike the editors of the civilian press, however, this prisoner–editor insisted that Osborne's enumeration of the bodily and mental injuries sustained by prisoners had missed the crux of the prisoners' suffering. The prisoner wrote, "The mere physical part of it is nothing. . . . It is not only, or chiefly, that [the prisoner's] body is afflicted with punishment, his nerves racked with fears and his mind crazed with strain; it is that he is unceasingly conscious that he is a slave in the blackest sense of the word."[50] The simple, powerful idea that the physical conditions of incarceration are of secondary importance to the fact of incarceration *per se* was a point that Osborne, the new penologists, and most free Americans would never fully appreciate. At the same time, many convicts appear to have grasped that although inadequate in certain key respects, Osborne's sympathetic effort to understand and publicize the pathologies of the prison system had brought tremendous attention to bear on the terrible conditions of the prisons and that Osborne, himself, appeared to be coordinating a fresh reform effort. Much as New York prisoners had applauded the efforts of Superintendent Collins and Lispenard Stewart to abolish stripes and the lockstep fifteen years before, and had eagerly redeployed the language of reform in service of further amelioration, the prisoners of Auburn openly embraced Osborne and his work.

Osborne commenced the work of reforming Auburn along new penological lines two months after his release from that prison.[51] In early December 1913, he prevailed upon Warden Rattigan and Superintendent John Riley to allow him to organize prisoner self-government at Auburn. Over a three-week period, beginning in late December 1913, Osborne met regularly with the Auburn prisoners and oversaw the creation of what came to be known as the Mutual Welfare League (MWL). He began by addressing the Auburn prisoners *en masse* in the chapel in late December 1913, and informing them

---

[49] In their writings about prison, convicts of the late-nineteenth and early-twentieth centuries frequently referred to prison as "hell upon earth," Tophet, and Dante's Inferno. Tophet was the Old Testament name of a place near Gehenna, or in the Valley of the Son or Children of Hinnom, which was southwest of Jerusalem. According to Jeremiah 19: 4–7, Jews made human sacrifices of their sons and daughters to "strange" gods (such as Molech, the God of the Ammonites) at Tophet. The *Concise Oxford Dictionary of Current English* (2nd ed., online) notes that later, people from Jerusalem used Tophet as a place in which to discard their refuse, and it came to symbolize the eternal torments of Hell. Over time, the name came to signify "a place, state, condition, or company likened to hell . . . A 'hell upon earth' . . . (and) a place or state of wild chaos and warring elements; a roaring furnace; a raging whirlpool, a maelstrom." John Bunyan, in *Pilgrim's Progress*, for example, referred to Tophet as Hell. *Holy Bible*, Revised Standard Version (Philadelphia: A. J. Holman Company, 1962); *Oxford Companion to the Bible* (New York: Oxford University Press, 1993); Joan Comas, *Who's Who: The Old Testament* (Oxford: Oxford University Press, 1993), 215.

[50] Editorial, *Good Words*, quoted in *Atlanta Journal* (Nov. 1, 1913), OFP, MSS64, Box 342, Scrapbooks.

[51] Before doing so, he took a six-week business trip to Europe.

of his conversation with prisoner Jack Murphy, and the plans for the new organization. Elections were to proceed with the purpose of electing a body of delegates that would act as a "constitutional convention" entrusted with the task of drawing up a constitution and rules for the prisoner organization.[52] In effect, Osborne was recreating the political "state" of the George Junior Republic in a state prison.

When election day rolled around on December 26, 1913, 1,285 of Auburn's 1,382 prisoners voted in their workshops for delegates. Each prisoner wrote the name of a prisoner from his work company on a specially prepared voting form and dropped it into a sealed box that was carried from shop to shop by the prison clerks. The votes were then counted in the warden's office by the warden's secretary, the prison's Bertillon clerk, and two prisoners. The names of the forty-nine delegates elected to frame the prisoners constitution were announced that evening. Two days later, the forty-nine delegates of the constitutional convention met in the chapel to debate the form and purpose of their new organization. Warden Rattigan called the meeting to order, informed the prisoners that they would be allowed to meet "in secret," and then departed with the guards. This meeting of prisoners without guard supervision was unprecedented. Osborne stayed with the delegates and was elected Chairman of the meeting,[53] whereupon he proceeded to set out the three questions to be addressed by the constitutional convention of prisoners: He asked, who should be a member of the league? What should the organization do? How should executive officers be selected from among the delegates? The delegates agreed that membership of the organization should be extended to all prisoners other than those undergoing punishment in the isolation cells. Prisoners were to join by taking a pledge. Following this discussion, Osborne selected from among the forty-nine delegates twelve prisoners to draw up the constitution and bylaws of the society.[54]

The forty-nine prisoner delegates concluded this first meeting by drafting a letter to the state's Superintendent of Prisons, John B. Riley, in which they hailed him as the visionary and architect of the tentative reforms at Auburn. They congratulated Riley for having personally "inspired among the officers

[52] From notes probably written by Auburn Prison's stenographer, S. L. Richards (Dec. 22, 1913), OFP, MSS 64, Box 269, Org. Recs.

[53] Minutes of the Meeting of the Delegates Elected by the Inmates, Dec. 28, 1913, OFP, MSS 64, Box 269, Org. Recs.

[54] Osborne – and his biographers – maintained that the impetus for the reforms came from the prisoners themselves. In *Within Prison Walls*, as well in his public lectures and other writings, Osborne emphasized the extent to which the idea came from the prisoners (one prisoner in particular, Jack Murphy), and represented his own role as one of simple facilitation of the prisoners' will to organize. Such a representation indicates the desire of Osborne (and other progressive penologists) to indicate to the public that prisoners were capable of generating and supporting democratic institutions, which, for Osborne, was the measure of a prisoner's potential fitness for citizenship. However, as the pages that follow establish, Osborne took a far more active role in organizing the league (writing its constitution and guiding its operation) than he ever acknowledged.

and prisoners of [Auburn Prison] a new and kindly spirit of physical, moral and humanitarian progressiveness." Continuing in a register designed to assure Riley of his place in history, the prisoners wrote that his support "warrants the hope of more considerate management and supervision of the whole personnel of the said Prison than that which has obtained in all the previous history of prison conduct."[55] As though to hold Riley to his word – or warranty, as the prisoners' language infers – Riley was told that the prisoners would be sending him an engrossed copy of their resolutions "as a souvenir to recall the inauguration of a more promising future for those who for so many years have been considered outside the pale of human kinship." The next day, the prisoners sent this letter and the engrossed copy of their first resolution to the Superintendent in Albany.

The letter's lofty language, its authors' celebration of Riley as an enlightened humanitarian, and the appeal to Riley's sense of his own historical importance were rhetorical techniques that the league organizers would repeatedly deploy in addressing officials. As we have seen, since at least 1899, prisoners at Auburn, Sing Sing, and other institutions had appropriated the officials' language of progress and humanitarianism as a technique in affirming certain prison practices and in requesting new reforms (see Chapter 3). The authors of the letter to Superintendent Riley knew very well that he had simply rubber-stamped a proposal that had originated with someone else, and for which he could take little credit. Nonetheless, the experiment of setting up a prisoners' league could not proceed without his consent, and was more likely to succeed in the long-term if it received the active support of Riley and the carceral bureaucracy. Consequently, in this, and in many subsequent letters and publications, the prisoners attempted to convince Riley – and other officials – of the historical significance of the reform and of the prestige it would accrue to the administration. In an era in which state governments strove to be at the forefront of "humanitarian reform," rhetoric such as this remained one of the critical weapons in the rather limited arsenal available to prisoners in the struggle to improve their lot. Unlike the riot and the strike, this strategy was not likely to provoke bloody repression and it presented prisoners not as violent, dangerous convicts who needed to be screwed down, but as reasoning human beings who would cooperate with the prison regime if treated as such. Of course, unlike the riot or strike, the polite letters of prisoners could be easily ignored.[56] However, for a time, at least, the prisoners met with some success: Soon thereafter, Superintendent Riley began boasting to the press of "his" reforms at Auburn.

55 Minutes of the Meeting of the Delegates Elected by the Inmates, Sunday, Dec. 28, 1913, 22, OFP, MSS 64, Box 269, Org. Recs.
56 Of all the letters written to bureaucrats and government officials in New York state, only the correspondence accompanying requests for the governor's pardon and restoration to citizenship have been archived. Access to these letters, regardless of the year in which they were written, is restricted by statute; no researcher – scholarly or otherwise – has yet succeeded in gaining access to them.

From the beginning, the prisoner delegates set out to record their organizing efforts: At their first meeting, they immediately appointed the warden's stenographer, prisoner S. L. Richards, as official clerk of the organization. Over the following months, Richards proceeded to generate a
stack of minutes and reports that meticulously chronicled the rise of the
inmate organization. These records provide tremendous insight into the
chronology of events, the points of conflict among the prisoner delegates,
and Osborne's role in fostering the organization. On a deeper level, they
also afford a rare glimpse into the workings of authority in the prison, the
relations between guards and prisoners, and the day-to-day concerns of prisoners in the 1910s. As with any archival material, it should be noted, the specific conditions under which these invaluable records were created must be
borne in mind. The minutes are incomplete and they are silent on certain
critical issues that arose in the prisoners' meetings. Secretary Richards was
extremely cautious in his reporting of certain discussions that took place
among the prisoners. For example, he frequently omitted lengthy discussions about socialist organizers in the prison (to whom the league leadership
were opposed), disciplinary arrangements, and relations with the authorities. Whether through his own volition or because of instructions from the
delegates, it is clear that conversations on these and other strategic matters
were selectively and carefully reported.

This incompleteness serves to negatively document an important aspect
of incarceration in the 1910s: Few prisoners wanted their opinions on guards
and problems such as theft and violence in the prison to be recorded in writing, despite the assurances of Warden Rattigan that their meetings would
proceed in "secret." As Richards and his fellow organizers appear to have
been aware, the new "openness" of prison authorities and the opportunity to
organize without official surveillance brought with it new dangers: Putting
details of guard brutality, official corruption, and prisoner rule-breaking in
writing could lead to retribution, on the part of the authorities, and possibly
even bring an end to reforms. In fact, Richards' cautiousness was vindicated
two years later when the "confidential agent" of the Superintendent of Prisons surreptitiously removed papers from Sing Sing with the intention of
finding incriminating evidence about the Sing Sing MWL. Following the
agent's botched attempt, officers of the Sing Sing league destroyed most of
the league's disciplinary records.

Two days after the forty-nine prisoner legislators had first met to discuss the framing of a constitution, Osborne's handpicked "Committee of
Twelve" convened in the warden's office to discuss the creation of a prisoner
league.[57] This was the first of five intensive meetings that took place over the
first week of the New Year, 1914. By the end of that week, the Committee had
hammered out a blueprint for the organization, disciplinary procedures,
and new privileges for Auburn prisoners. Once again, the prisoner delegates were allowed to meet without the warden and the guards in attendance,

---

[57] Minutes of the Meeting of the Committee of Twelve, Dec. 30, 1913, OFP, MSS 64, Box 269,
Org. Recs.

and Osborne convened as Chair. The twelve delegates discussed the transfer of certain police powers from the guards to prisoners, the establishment of freedom of the yard (by which prisoners would be allowed an hour or two a day to socialize and exercise in the prison yard), and the election of delegates to the league's governing body. They also discussed the procedures for electing representatives to a prisoner legislature and compared different electoral systems. The committee heard one delegate, Shea, report on the Commission system of voting used in Iowa and other states, and after some discussion, they agreed to adopt this electoral method as the most democratic means of setting up their organization. Another election would be held in which prisoners of every work company would vote for company representatives (the number to be determined according to the size of each company), who would then convene as a general commission or governing body for the league. Toward the end of this meeting, the first draft of a constitution and bylaws for the still unnamed prisoner organization was presented and discussed. It is unclear who authored this draft, but it is likely that Osborne influenced its contents, as it conformed to many of his ideas about the prisoner league. The draft provided for the mode of election (commission system), and the appointment of a secretary and a sergeant-at-arms for the organization.[58] With regard to the league's bylaws, this first draft stated that the organization's rules were to be the rules laid down by the New York State Prison Department for the administration of Auburn Prison.[59] In other words, the league would adopt the official prison rules as its own.

As the meeting progressed, the question of rules, and the larger question of which they were a part – police powers in the prison – quickly became the central issue of contention among the delegates. These questions arose as the Committee of Twelve began to discuss the way in which they would organize one of the most sought-after privileges: freedom-of-the-yard. This privilege was keenly pursued for the reason that it would alleviate one of the most repressive and despised practices of incarceration: the sixteen and one-half hours every prisoner spent in his cell each day between the hours of 3 P.M. and 7:30 A.M.[60] Although the Committee took it for granted that procuring

---

[58] Minutes of the Meeting of the Committee of Twelve, Dec. 30, 1913, 9–10, OFP, MSS 64, Box 269, Org. Recs.

[59] Minutes of the Meeting of the Committee of Twelve, Dec. 30, 1913, 10, OFP, MSS 64, Box 269, Org. Recs.

[60] In the 1910s, prisoners were gradually allowed greater time away from the cellhouse. Typically, prisoners were locked in their cells from 3:00 P.M., upon the end of their workday, until 7:30 the next morning. It was not until 1913 that the convicts in all New York Prisons were taken out of their cells on Sundays, when the Superintendent of Prisons (John B. Riley) instituted dinner in the mess halls. Typically, prisoners would leave their cells for Sunday breakfast, remain under guard in the workshops until 12:00 midday dinner, and then return to the cells at 1:00 P.M. The following year, Sing Sing's warden McCormick added a daily supper in the mess hall from 4:30 P.M. to 5:30 P.M. Athletic contests were organized for Saturday afternoons, and occasionally on Sunday afternoons. In 1915, under Osborne, industries began to run until 4:00 P.M. in the summer, and prisoners were given an hour of time in the yard. They attended supper from 5:15 P.M. and were then locked in

freedom of the yard for all prisoners was of primary importance, the question of who would supervise the prisoners during yard recreation became
the subject of protracted debate among Committee members. The crux of
the question related to the disciplinary role of guards and the assumption of
limited police powers by prisoners. Some delegates argued that the presence
of guards during yard recreation would be necessary for the protection of
the prisoners. They affirmed the position of delegate Shea, who had argued
that every institution – even a "peanut stand," as he put it – needed a system
of authority. "I have seen the time, and it was a bad time in prisons," warned
delegate Cameron, "when there was (sic) no officers in the hall."[61] Delegates worried that the absence of guards would lead to abuse and violence
among prisoners; in the 1910s, guards might assault prisoners, but in the
interest of maintaining order, they generally ensured that prisoners did not
assault each other. (Prison administrations had not yet fully discovered the
usefulness of prisoner-on-prisoner violence as a technique of prison government).

Implicit in the delegates' discussion (and made more explicit in the many
debates that were to follow) was the prisoners' recognition of the fact that
freedom of the yard was likely to generate more labor for guards, without
increasing their wages. Guards were already working six days per week, on
twelve-hour shifts. Whereas only six guards were needed on duty once the
prisoners had been locked in their cells for the night or on Sundays, many
more would be needed to supervise 1,400 prisoners in the yard. Although
élite prison reformers rarely took guards into account in their attempts to
reconstruct prison life, prisoners were well aware of the need to win over
guard support for reforms, or, at the very least, ensure guards were not
actively opposed to the reforms. As delegate Shea had pointed out the day
before, it was critical to gain their sympathy, as the guard "is the power down
in the shop and the man behind the power of the 'reprimand' or the 'chalk-
ing in'. . . . Unfortunately (the guards) have us in their power."[62] Increasing
the guards' labor would probably alienate them at the most sensitive stage
of the league's development. Shea continued:

> I do not want any more privileges if it is (sic) to extend the hours of the
> keepers. They feel disgruntled enough now and the success of this organization

their cells from 6:30 to 8:00 P.M., whereupon they attended the evening entertainments or
classes. Under Osborne, prisoners spent not only longer labor hours out of the cells, but an
extra forty to fifty hours out of the cells. Beginning in the summer of 1915, however, newly
committed prisoners of the "awkward squad" were held in their cells continuously for two
weeks, except for one hour in the morning and one hour of exercise in the evening. They
were fed an evening meal consisting simply of bread and tea, which was served in their
cells. "Some Facts About Sing Sing Management: Bulletin 1," Westchester County Research
Bureau (unpublished report, 1915), 2.
[61] Minutes of the Meeting of the Committee of Twelve, Dec. 30, 1913, 4, OFP, MSS 64, Box
269, Org. Recs.
[62] Minutes of the Meeting of the Committee of Twelve, Dec. 30, 1913, 4, OFP, MSS 64, Box
269, Org. Recs., 14–15.

depends upon the good will and support of the keeper. Now we have got to face these things. It is all right for us to say he is not in this thing, and we dont (sic) want to support him, but there he is with that blue coat and that stick. They constitute authority and we have got to work in concert with them because he (sic) is a part of our life and his (sic) attitudes towards anything that is to be done for us must be considered.[63]

Shea went on to argue that the guards were hoping that the reforms would benefit themselves as well as the prisoners and that if the reforms did in fact benefit guards, they would be both invested in having the prisoner organization succeed, and less inclined to report prisoners for breaches of prison rules.[64]

In light of these considerations, a delegate who was one of Osborne's principal supporters (delegate Barr, a teacher in the school company), suggested that the prisoners devise a method to police themselves during recreation. Each prison company should elect two prisoners to act as sentries, guarding the entrances to alleys and shops, just as prison guards were posted during work hours. Despite initial opposition to Barr's suggestion, he ultimately prevailed. This was largely because his suggestion met with Osborne's approval, and, perhaps recognizing the real power relations of the situation, the Committee tended to defer to Osborne's opinion. It became evident in the subsequent meetings of the Committee of Twelve in the first week of 1914 that Osborne envisioned a new mode of penal discipline whereby the prisoners would take responsibility not only for policing during freedom-of-the-yard, but for much of the daily order in the workshops, mess hall, and marching lines. He viewed prisoner police powers as part of the greater project of fostering what he called "self-discipline" and loyalty among the prisoners. Furthermore, he linked the introduction of exercise and education programs with prisoner police power: Participation in such activities was a privilege or liberty, in Osborne's view, and such privileges and liberties should only be extended where prisoners undertook to police themselves.

Ultimately, Osborne prevailed upon the delegates not only to set up a system of prisoner supervision during freedom-of-the-yard, but also to vest in the prisoner league the police powers of citation, prosecution, and punishment. In this vein, he insisted to the twelve constitution framers that the prisoner society should set up a disciplinary body to "try" prisoners who had abused newfound liberties such as freedom-of-the-yard. A court adjudicated by prisoners was legitimate, he argued, because when prisoners break the rules, "they have committed an offense not against the warden, but against you."[65] Meeting with resistance from the delegates, Osborne went on to argue that privileges such as freedom-of-the-yard could be conferred only

[63] Minutes of the Meeting of the Committee of Twelve, Dec. 30, 1913, 13–14, OFP, MSS 64, Box 269, Org. Recs.
[64] Minutes of the Meeting of the Committee of Twelve, Dec. 30, 1913, 14–15, OFP, MSS 64, Box 269, Org. Recs.
[65] Minutes of the Meeting of the Committee of Twelve, Dec. 30, 1913, 5, OFP, MSS 64, Box 269, Org. Recs.

in return for prisoner responsibility – specifically, collective responsibility for ensuring the rules were not broken.

In attempting to convince the Committee of the advantages of trans-ferring police powers to prisoners, Osborne argued that prisoner police powers would break what he viewed as the perpetual and destructive oppo-sition between guards and prisoners. Osborne's program in general aimed to break down the oppositional relationships of guards to prisoners, and of criminals to citizens, by making incarceration a cooperative enterprise among all concerned. He reasoned that only when prisoners cooperated with their own reform and citizens cooperated with prisoners by renouncing revenge and supporting penal reconstruction, would prisoners be rehabil-itated and crime, controlled. Here, Osborne echoed the thinking of con-temporary penological theorists who advocated reconstructing prisons as educational institutions, and treating prisoners as students in need of train-ing in the skills of labor, economy, and democracy. For this purpose, prisons must be clean, safe, and healthy environments that were conducive to edu-cation.[66]

In trying to convince the twelve prisoners of the legislative committee that they should create prisoner police and disciplinary tribunals, Osborne argued that prison relations were analogous to pedagogical relations. He insisted that the relations between guards and prisoners are "exactly as in any school." He continued, "(t)here is the false view of the teacher and the false view of the scholar. The false view of the teacher is that he must emphasize his authority from above; the false view of the scholar is that as long as he is under tyrannical authority the scholars must band together

---

[66] Osborne's emphasis on cooperation over conflict, and his efforts to dismantle oppositional relations, resonated with that of another leading institutional innovator of the 1910s: Freder-ick Winslow Taylor. Published in the same year in which Osborne entered Auburn prison, Taylor's *Principles of Scientific Management* elaborated organizational techniques aimed at forging cooperation between labor and capital in search of increased surplus. As has been pointed out, Taylor did not so much invent the techniques for which he is famous, as collate and popularize existing practices as a standardized set of managerial techniques. Much as Taylor claimed that his theory of scientific management was at once ethical, politically neu-tral, and efficient, Osborne maintained that his penology was "neutral" in the sense that it would work for everyone: It would improve conditions for guards as well as prisoners; it would make healthier, more cooperative prisoners; guards would cease to be subject to vio-lence from prisoners; the rate of recidivism would decline, and ultimately, social efficiency would improve. Notably, the work of both Taylor and Osborne appealed to Henry Ford, who made extensive use of both sets of ideas in his "White Palace" auto-assembly plant in Michigan (see later in this book, Chapter 9). Neither Taylor nor Osborne's theorization of worker and prisoner psychology took account of the larger structural relationships that existed between subordinates and superiors; rather, they attempted to adapt behavior – and ultimately bodies and psyches – as a means to improving and supporting the existing sys-tem. Frederick Winslow Taylor, *Principles of Scientific Management* (Easton, Pennsylvania: Hive Publishing Company, 1986); Thomas Mott Osborne, "Prison Efficiency" (paper read before the Efficiency Society, September 19, 1915); *Society and Prisons* (New Haven, Connecticut: Yale University Press, 1916); and *Prisons and Commonsense* (Philadelphia: J. B. Lippincott, 1924).

against the teacher."[67] The correct view, as Osborne saw it, was one in which there was no need for authority to be exercised from above; rather, prisoners must exercise it upon themselves, in concert with the administration's wish for order. Osborne held that guards and prisoners wanted the same thing, even if they did not know it: order and rehabilitation. Invoking the new penological principle that prisoners should act and be treated as men, he argued, "You are either going to be ruled by arbitrary power, or else you are going to rule yourself and assist those whom you select." Then, in a refrain he was to repeat at critical junctures in prisoner discussions about the creation of the league, he asked, "In other words are you going to be held as slaves, or are you going to be treated as men?"[68]

If being treated as men involved spending less time in the cells, the opportunity to organize recreational and sporting activities, and improved food and sanitation, then prisoners wanted to be treated like men: of the benefits of such reforms, they needed no convincing. But they were not so easily persuaded by Osborne's psychologistic vision of the prison as a cooperative venture between guards and prisoners, and the meeting drew to a close with no resolution on the question of prisoner policing. At their second meeting, held on New Years Day, 1914, Osborne once again presided as chairman and exerted influence on the matter of policing. Again, he linked the liberalization of prison discipline to the prisoners' ability to conduct themselves in an orderly manner. He insisted, "the rules you make must be subject to the Prison rules.... The Prison Rules must hold. What we all hope, I presume, is that the prison rules will be generally relieved or put aside just as fast and just as far as you show you can handle yourself."[69] The question of prisoner disciplinary tribunals arose and, again, the Committee made little headway toward a proposal: The delegates floated two ideas and Osborne, a third. One delegate (Hodson) suggested that the governing body of forty-nine delegates could also preside as a grievance committee to hear cases arising from the breach of rules; another argued for a military-style court to be presided over by a prisoner chairman and in which the prisoner sergeant-at-arms would "prosecute" prisoners thought to have broken the rules. Osborne rejected the latter proposal outright and offered a modified version of the former: Rather than have the governing body act as a grievance committee, the governing body should elect five of its members to constitute a grievance committee.

The Committee of Twelve did not resolve the matter of police power that day, but resumed their discussion of this critical aspect of prison life the next day. Secretary Richards did not report much of this discussion. In those parts of the discussion that were reported, the prisoners argued at

[67] Minutes of the Meeting of the Committee of Twelve, Dec. 30, 1913, 9, OFP, MSS 64, Box 269, Org. Recs.

[68] Minutes of the Meeting of the Committee of Twelve, Dec. 30, 1913, 6, OFP, MSS 64, Box 269, Org. Recs.

[69] Minutes of the Meeting of the Committee of Twelve, Dec. 30, 1913, 4, OFP, MSS 64, Box 269, Org. Recs.

some length about which prisoners were to be authorized to report prisoners to the grievance committee for transgressions of the rules. The critical questions were: If prisoners were to assume responsibility for many aspects of discipline, which prisoners were to exercise police power, how would they be appointed, and to whom would they report incidents of rule-breaking? Those prisoners who were familiar with the prisoner police practices of Elmira Reformatory, where the warden appointed prisoner–guards who then became the warden's informants and enforcers, were particularly leery of conferring police powers on fellow prisoners. Prisoner police, they argued, acted as rats for the administration. In floating an alternative means of policing, delegate Williams of the Idle Company, prisoners in which were either unable to work or had been punitively prohibited from working, suggested that the league adopt a jury system of policing, in which every prisoner would be eligible for police duty and would be appointed by random selection of his name from a membership list. These prisoner officers would have police power over the entire prison population. But delegate Barr of the School Company (who was one of Osborne's principal supporters), argued vigorously that such democratic methods would lead to "weak-minded" prisoners being placed in positions of authority over the rest. Other delegates insisted that whoever the prisoner officers were, their police powers should extend only to those men in their own work company, and they opposed Williams' jury system on the basis that prisoners from one company would exercise authority over prisoners from another.[70]

In the course of this argument over prisoner policing, the implicit tensions in – and limits of – the delegates' embrace of egalitarian principles became obvious: Any system of policing that conferred upon men from one company authority over the members of another was likely to upset the unspoken hierarchy between companies. As noted earlier (in Chapter 5), some companies had higher status than others. The weave shop was considered low status, as the labor was thought to be that of women, and consequently inappropriate for men. More than simple sexist prejudice was at work in the prisoners' low estimation of the weave shop: Prisoners commonly believed that whereas the print shop, the state shop, and certain of the industrial shops would equip them with skills that would make them employable outside the prison, the weave shop equipped prisoners with skills in what had become a women's industry on the outside; hence, such skills would be useless in the search for gainful employment upon release. Given the rigid segmentation of the free workforce along the lines of sex, the prisoners' resistance to working in the weave shop was based on an accurate estimation of their chances of employment on the outside. (Although the labor

---

[70] Another Osborne supporter, delegate Shea, joined the fray, making a rather weak argument that Williams's jury system would generate a great deal of clerical work given that the membership lists were to be constantly updated as prisoners entered and left the prison. Minutes of the Meeting of the Committee of Twelve, Jan. 2, 1914, 1, OFP, MSS 64, Box 269, Org. Recs.

of the kitchen shop was also the kind of labor typically done by women, the work conditions, better meals, and sociable atmosphere made that company popular among the prisoners). Under the jury system of policing, the prisoners of Williams' lowly Idle Company or the feminized weave shop might exercise authority over the more privileged prisoners of the print shop or the state shop.

As the twelve delegates failed to resolve this critical question of policing, discussion stretched into a third day. Finally, Osborne raised an objection that apparently laid to rest Williams' egalitarian jury method of policing: Under the jury system, black prisoners (whom Osborne described as "objectionable men" in the context of their assumption of police powers) could conceivably exercise authority over white prisoners.[71] Osborne's invocation of the specter of black American prisoners exercising authority over white Americans was his final effort to convince the all-white delegates that Williams' jury system would overturn the hierarchy among prisoners. Whether persuaded by his comment, or by his ability to effectively veto any developments with which he did not agree, the Committee resolved that the elected company delegates would be given police powers only over the members of their companies. (As black prisoners were concentrated in the idle and unskilled companies, this meant that the vast majority of white prisoners, who were in other companies, would not be subject to their jurisdiction). In this important respect, the prisoner system of authority recognized the existing hierarchies of race and labor among prisoners, and further entrenched them.

Five days after convening their first meeting, the Committee of Twelve had finally generated a proposal for a system of prisoner policing. They had also discussed the question of prisoner adjudication of grievances at length.[72] Building on Osborne's plan to set up a grievance committee consisting of five delegates, the Committee of Twelve resolved after a lengthy, and largely unrecorded, discussion that there would be eight grievance committees made up of five delegates each, and that these would be put on a revolving schedule to hear both prisoner grievances and reports from the police-delegates of rule-breaking in their companies.[73] The Committee further provided that the prison administration would deal with more serious cases – though the delegates had not yet established the criteria by which an offense would be considered serious.

---

[71] Minutes of the Meeting of the Committee of Twelve, Jan. 4, 1914, 11, OFP, MSS 64, Box 269, Org. Recs. It is worth noting that although the idle company re-elected Williams as a delegate in the elections for the Mutual Welfare League governing body, Williams lost his position a few weeks later because he was transferred out of the company. The conditions of his transfer are unclear. Minutes of the Meeting of the Executive Committee of the MWL, Feb. 10, no page number, OFP, MSS 64, Box 269, Org. Recs.

[72] Minutes of the Meeting of the Committee of Twelve, Jan. 2, 1914, 3–5, OFP, MSS 64, Box 269, Org. Recs.

[73] Minutes of the Meeting of the Committee of Twelve, Jan. 2, 1914, 8, OFP, MSS 64, Box 269, Org. Recs.

Finally, on January 4, the twelve prisoner legislators convened one last time in the warden's office. In the presence of a journalist whom Osborne had invited to the meeting, Osborne read the members the various proposals they had drafted as part of a constitution in the course of the week. The legislators had one hour to consider and vote on the draft before they were scheduled to report back to rest of the forty-nine delegates of the constitutional convention, who were waiting for the Committee in the chapel. Many of the articles of this original draft became part of the final "Constitution and By-laws" of the Auburn league; and later, a number of other prisoner leagues around the United States adapted this statement of principles to their own institutions. The first article provided that the society's motto would be, "DO GOOD: MAKE GOOD," and the second announced that, "The object of the League shall be to promote in every way the ture (sic) interests and welfare of the men confined in prison. By gaining for them the largest practical measure of freedom within the walls to the end that by the proper exercise of freedom within the walls within restrictions that they may exercise worthily the larger freedom of the outside world."[74] This early draft also established the commission system of government, an executive committee (to be elected by the governing body), biannual elections, and the revolving, five-member grievance committees. Despite continued dissent from Williams and the Idle Company, the draft constitution provided that delegates were to have police authority only over their companies, and delegates would elect a prisoner sergeant-at-arms.

Under pressure of time, the Committee hurriedly considered the draft and made some minor alterations. The delegates' discussion of the draft constitution suggests that the constitution and bylaws were designed both to establish certain new practices and to render them legitimate, not only in the eyes of prisoners but in the eyes of the warden, the Superintendent of State Prisons, the guards, the press, and the voting public. Aware of the presence of a journalist in the room, Osborne warned the Committee that the use of the term "freedom" in the statement of objectives might "scare (outsiders) to death." Delegate Shea concurred, remarking that the public would be "afraid that we would be going to hang around their houses at night." Consequently, the Committee amended the article to read: "OBJECT: The object of the League shall be to promote in every way the ture (sic) interests and welfare of men confined in prison."[75]

At Osborne's instigation, the draft constitution also provided that all prisoners elected to office be required to take an oath: Delegates would promise to promote "friendly feeling, good conduct and fair dealing among both officers and men to the end that each man after serving the briefest possible term of imprisonment may go forth with renewed strength and courage to

[74] Minutes of the Meeting of the Committee of Twelve, Jan. 4, 1914, 1, OFP, MSS 64, Box 269, Org. Recs.

[75] Minutes of the Meeting of the Committee of Twelve, Jan. 4, 1914, 1–2, OFP, MSS 64, Box 269, Org. Recs.

face the world again." Notably, prisoner delegates were to take the oath in the chapel, before an assembly of all the prisoners. Furthermore, the warden, and not the chaplain, would administer the oath. The warden's involvement in the proceedings would constitute a show of official support for the league, suggested Osborne, and it would give the delegates more respect in the eyes of the men.[76] Although Osborne did not say so, the administration of the oath was designed not only to establish the legitimacy of the prisoner government in the eyes of prisoners, and to lend it the authority of the administration, but to further imbricate the prison administration in the process of reform. In this vein, Osborne also quietly but firmly pressed the committee to further solidify the support of Superintendent Riley and warden Rattigan by having the league confer honorary (league) membership on them. The delegates agreed with Osborne, and, a few weeks later, of their own accord, they made the principal keeper and the prison doctor honorary members as well. The draft also provided that all Auburn prisoners be eligible for membership in the league, and that they could join by signing a pledge in which they promised to "faithfully...abide by [the league's] Rules and By-Laws."[77]

Having hurriedly debated and passed thirteen resolutions in less than an hour, Osborne, the journalist, and the Committee of Twelve concluded their meeting and set out for the chapel, where the rest of the forty-nine delegates awaited their report. At this gathering of delegates, Osborne again took the floor, and proceeded to explain the Committee's resolutions. He read the proposed constitution and bylaws to the delegates, and then explained the reasons for establishing an Executive Committee of the league.[78] Osborne told the assembled delegates that the Executive Committee would perform one of the most important functions of the league: It would act as an intermediary between the prisoners and the warden. When prisoners had a grievance about the prison conditions such as poor food or inadequate clothing, rather than organize a strike, Osborne emphasized, they should bring it to the attention of the Executive Committee of the league. The

---

[76] Minutes of the Meeting of the Committee of Twelve, Jan. 4, 1914, 6, OFP, MSS 64, Box 269, Org. Recs.; By-Laws of the Mutual Welfare League (MWL), Auburn Branch, Article III (1914), OFP, MSS64, Box 270, Org. Recs.

[77] Minutes of the Meeting of the Committee of Twelve, Jan. 4, 1914, 3, OFP, MSS 64, Box 269, Org. Recs.; By-Laws of the MWL, Auburn Branch, Article III (1914), OFP, MSS64, Box 270, Org. Recs. After the league had been in operation for a year, the pledge was altered to embody the principles of self-government and to warn prisoners of the consequences of breaking the law after release from prison. Every prisoner wishing to join the league had to pledge that "It is my duty to live for the mutual welfare of society, and: Should I be arrested and convicted again after leaving this Prison in a fair and impartial trial which calls for a States' (sic) Prison sentence, I call upon the State to bring forward this pledge and sentence me to the full limit of the law. I take this pledge because as a member of the MUTUAL WELFARE LEAGUE, Auburn Branch, I must be done with the life that is a detriment to the mutual welfare of society." Pledge of Membership, MWL, Auburn Branch, OFP, MSS64, Box 269, Org. Recs.

[78] If the Committee of Twelve had, in fact, discussed the formation of an executive committee in their first four meetings, little of their conversation was recorded by the stenographer.

Executive Committee would then bring the problem to the warden's notice. Osborne noted that this approach would also protect prisoners from gaining reputations among the guards as complainers.[79]

Just as prisoner policing had proven to be the most contentious question among the twelve delegates of the Committee, the forty-nine delegates debated prisoner–guards and prisoner disciplinary tribunals at length. Osborne informed the delegates that freedom-of-the-yard was to be granted on Sunday afternoons: The prison guards would be withdrawn from the yard and put on wall patrol: "The state," argued Osborne, referring to the prison guards, was duty-bound to "patrol its property, patrol its wall and see that you don't get away. . . . the state will patrol the walls, that is their business, but inside the walls it is up to you."[80] Each delegate's police authority as an "assistant sergeant-at-arms" was to extend only over the members of his company, except on occasions when the entire prison population would be mixed in together, such as the athletic competitions planned for July 4, Independence Day.[81] Osborne told the delegates that although most prisoners would not cause trouble in the yard, a few men would be waiting for an opportunity to start a fight. Others would try to dodge the head count at the end of the day, and there would be "attempts at that proposition" of sexual liaison. Osborne implored the delegates to ensure that no fights broke out among the prisoners at recreation: The success of the league, he told them, rode on the conduct of the prisoners in the yard. Osborne then floated the idea that every delegate should wear a badge or insignia to "show his power." Delegates should not have resort to guns and sticks, he argued; instead, their persuasive power was to flow from their league badges, backed up by "bare knuckles" and the aid of other prisoner officers, if necessary.[82] Osborne concluded his explanation of prisoner police powers by imploring the delegates to cooperate with the prison administration in its crack down on the smuggling and use of opium in the prison.[83]

The forty-nine delegates of the constitutional convention proceeded to debate the proposed system of policing and the rest of the draft constitution. Whether or not the word, "prisoner," should be part of the league's official name, or be given constitutional expression in any way, was the subject of extensive debate. The issue was framed as a question of whether the prisoners should define themselves as prisoners or as men. The debate over this question amounted to a problem of tactics in the contradictory struggle of prisoners to win for themselves improved conditions in a total

[79] Minutes of Meeting of forty-nine Delegates, Jan. 4, 1914, 6–7, OFP, MSS 64, Box 269, Org. Recs.

[80] Minutes of Meeting of Forty-nine Delegates, Jan. 4, 1914, 14, OFP, MSS 64, Box 269, Org. Recs.

[81] Minutes of Meeting of Forty-nine Delegates, Jan. 4, 1914, 13, OFP, MSS 64, Box 269, Org. Recs.

[82] Minutes of Meeting of Forty-nine Delegates, Jan. 4, 1914, 14, OFP, MSS 64, Box 269, Org. Recs.

[83] Minutes of Meeting of Forty-nine Delegates, Jan. 4, 1914, 14, OFP, MSS 64, Box 269, Org. Recs.

institution. In the course of the discussions over the wording of the constitution, it became apparent that the constitution was a multivalent document intended for many different audiences. On one level, the document was to be made public as a manifesto for prison reform: A member of the press had been present at at least one meeting, and a copy would be forwarded to others. In light of this, secretary Richards vociferously opposed the use of the term "prisoners" in connection with the league, arguing that the prisoners should refer to themselves as "men." "I think we should not appeal to the men outside as 'prisoners' but as 'men,'" Richards insisted, "Man to Man is my idea." On another level, the delegates recognized that the constitution must persuade prisoners that the league was worth joining. Richards, again arguing against the use of the term, "prisoners," put it in a way that resonated with the *Good Word*'s analysis of the peculiar effect of incarceration on the consciousness of the prisoner:

> I am a prisoner, I know it, but I am only a prisoner for a short period during the day. If you go to a new man and aks (sic) him to join a Prisoner's League, he says, Oh, why don't you let me alone and let me forget that I am a prisoner once in a while. I myself when I go to my room at night and lay down on my bed forget that I am a prisoner, as I do when I am working during the day time. I know I am a prisoner, but I want to forget it as much as I can, and I don't care to have the word thrust upon me on every occasion that I turn around.[84]

Richards prevailed, and the word was dropped from the final version of the constitution in favor of "men."

The delegates' resolution to remove from the document any reference to themselves as prisoners mystified the real relations of incarceration by obfuscating the objective fact of the prisoners' forced detainment within well-patrolled prison walls. However, the prisoners also implicitly acknowledged those relations, by writing a constitution that was aimed at winning the support of the people who had the power to change the conditions of incarceration. Finally, as the constitutional convention drew to a close, the men behind bars agreed on the name of their new organization. Having started with fifty suggestions for a name for the new league (including one honoring Osborne – the "Tom Brown League"), the forty-nine delegates eventually decided to name their organization the "Mutual Welfare League." With the thirteen resolutions agreed to, the constitutional convention was dissolved and the delegates prepared to address the prison population at large the following day.

Exactly three weeks after Osborne had first addressed the Auburn prisoners and announced plans to set up a prisoner organization, all but a few of the 1,400 prisoners gathered in the chapel to hear about the formation of the MWL and its constitution and bylaws. For the first time in the history of Auburn prison, the guards withdrew from the chapel, leaving Auburn's prisoners to conduct their meeting without supervision. Osborne, chairing the meeting once again, read the draft of the constitution and bylaws

---

[84] Minutes of the Special Meeting of the Committee of Twelve, Jan. 5, 1914, OFP, MSS 64, Box 269, Org. Recs.

to the assembled prisoners and then put it to a vote. According to secretary Richards, the prisoners unanimously endorsed it, whereupon the first
election for the MWL was announced for January 15. Upon the initiative
of Osborne, a motion was passed to thank Warden Rattigan for allowing
the prisoners the opportunity to form a league, and, at this peculiar prison
rally, where prisoners discussed liberty while men with "sticks and bluecoats"
patrolled outside, the prisoners of Auburn concluded their assembly by rising to sing the anthem, "My Country 'Tis of Thee."

The deliberations of the Committee of Twelve and the forty-nine delegates over the previous week had revealed the tensions and contradictions
that were inherent in the practice of prisoner self-government. In their
efforts to graft the organs of democracy onto the prison body, Osborne and
Warden Rattigan were masking the real relations of power in the prison.
Most critically, although Osborne and his supporters insisted that the impetus for the league had come from the prisoners themselves, it is clear that
Osborne had instigated and guided its creation. The authority to organize
this prison-based representative democracy emanated from the warden and
the Superintendent of Prisons, and its survival depended upon the continued support of both. Although the prisoners elected delegates to frame
a constitution, and delegates argued over the critical questions of policing and discipline, Osborne's selection of a special (and small) committee
of drafters, his marshaling of the discussions, and the defeat of dissenting
opinion, make it clear that Osborne and his supporters were engaged in an
elaborate staging of democracy. In this respect, prisoner self-government was
instigated from the top down; it was not an organic or democratic movement, and it certainly was not generated from below – that is, from within
the prisoners' ranks – as Osborne claimed.

One incident in particular provides a remarkable illustration of
Osborne's mystification of the operations of power in the prison. This incident involved him masking his own relation to the prisoners: During the New
Year's Day meeting of the Committee of Twelve, Osborne had suggested that
the warden, Superintendent Riley, and himself be made honorary members
of the league. In response to this suggestion, delegate Cameron noted that
this was a good idea, and that "It is too bad that (the) idea did not originate
with one of us [the prisoners]." When Osborne retorted, "I am one of you,"
Cameron rejoined, "– Without the coat," whereupon Osborne reached for
a prisoner's regulation coat and exclaimed, "I will put on the coat. I have it
here. Here goes." Of course, as Shea and his fellow prisoners no doubt knew
full well, coat or no coat, Osborne was not a prisoner but an élite reformer
whose opinion invariably trumped that of the prisoner delegates. At the end
of that particular meeting, "Tom Brown" took off the prison coat, uttered
words that only a freeman would – "I must be going" – and walked out of
the prison the same way he had entered it – a free citizen.[85] (Perhaps the

---

[85] Minutes of Meeting of Forty-nine Delegates, Jan. 4, 1914, 19, OFP, MSS 64, Box 269, Org.
Recs.

irony of the incident was not lost on secretary Richards, who reported the conversation in full).

As he made clear in the prisoner meetings, Osborne sought to make an inherently coercive institution into a cooperative one. His recourse to ped-agogical penology missed the point that delegates repeatedly made about the prison's inherently violent character, its high mortality rate, and its inci-dence of injury and disease. At one point during the New Year's Day meeting, the delegates discussed the procedure by which an elected delegate could be relieved of his duties should he be beaten, die, or be taken ill. A few moments later, Osborne, who had had little to add to this discussion of the peculiar violence to which prisoners were subject, offered the term limits of the student body at his *alma mater,* Harvard University, as a model of elec-toral fairness.[86] Although the prisoners seemed not to agree with Osborne's argument that guard–prisoner relations were falsely oppositional, they did grasp the relations of power that existed between Osborne and themselves: They disagreed over certain issues, but they never drew attention to the incongruity or simple absurdity of some of Osborne's analogies, nor did they vote against his suggestions.

As the fate of the league attests, the new techniques of cooperation con-stituted a novel form of carceral coercion, and these practices obfuscated the real power relations of the prisons. As will become evident, prisoners were able to put the league and the new privileges to their own uses, but these were always circumscribed by the fact that prisoners were physically held in a carceral system they could not leave, and that, as delegate Shea put it most precisely, prisoners at any and all times remained subject to the guard with "that blue coat and that stick."

However, all this is not to say that prisoners had no use for Osborne or the league; on the contrary, it generated new possibilities for prisoners' ongoing attempts to improve their lot and to hold the state to its official policy of amelioration, on both an individual and collective basis. As noted earlier, the prisoner delegates were particularly attentive to the need to win some measure of approval from the guards. The delegates carefully phrased their initial requests to the warden in such a way as to recognize the hierarchy that existed between warden, guards, and prisoners. Typically, the warden issued orders to guards, who then relayed these to prisoners. In avoiding a breach of this practice, the delegates rephrased one delegate's motion that the warden be asked to grant each prisoner permission to converse during the entertainments that were planned for New Year's Day. Instead of ask-ing the warden to directly communicate with the prisoners, thereby absent-ing the guards from this one small, but significant, attempt to change the rules, the delegates requested that the warden make the guards the subject

---

[86] Osborne commented that, at Harvard, the student government had a rule limiting officer-holders to three consecutive terms; this ensured that "mediocre" people would not serve multiple terms. Minutes of the Meeting of the Committee of Twelve, Jan. 1, 1914, 6, 8, OFP, MSS 64, Box 269, Org. Recs.

of the communiqué. As their motion put it, "a committee of one (should) be appointed to ask the warden to instruct the officers not to report a man for talking during the entertainment on New Year's day."[87] This was the first of many attempts to enlist the guards in the league experiment by confirming their place in the hierarchy of prisoners, guards, and warden.

As the foregoing discussion suggests, prisoners were probably aware of some of the contradictions in Osborne's program, and they were under no illusions as to Osborne's own institutional authority over them. Although many of the delegates were skeptical of the cooperative model of prison reform, it seems probable that they nonetheless supported Osborne's suggestions with the hope that his reforms would lead to some amelioration of the material deprivations of prison life. Prisoner delegates also worked with existing hierarchies to bring about changes for the prisoners instead of tackling the existing prison hierarchy head-on. Indeed, in the months to follow, the leadership of the MWL took swift disciplinary action against any prisoners who attempted to take more direct action, such as striking, to effect change in the prison.

In three short weeks, the disciplinary techniques of Auburn Prison had been transformed. The first election for officers of the MWL took place as scheduled on Thursday, January 15. In the days leading up to the election, hundreds of prisoners took the oath and signed up as voting members of the MWL. By January 12, more than 1,300 of approximately 1,400 prisoners had signed up to vote.[88] On Thursday afternoon, the warden excused the prisoners from work, and the prison clerks carried a single ballot box from shop to shop, as the prisoners recorded their vote on the official ballot paper and deposited it in the sealed box. As each prisoner voted, a clerk checked his name off against the register of members. By dinner time, the clerks had counted the votes, in the presence of two prisoner witnesses, and had announced the names of the forty-nine delegates who were to comprise the first governing body of the MWL.[89] Eight members of Osborne's Committee of Twelve were re-elected to the league.

A few days later, all the prisoners gathered in the chapel for the swearing-in of the newly elected delegates. With the green and white ribbons of the league pinned to their lapels (Osborne had selected these colors for their signification of hope and truth), the forty-nine delegates performed the oath of office administered by the warden. One by one, they read aloud the oath:

> I solemnly promise that I will do all in my power to promote in every way the true welfare of the men confined in Auburn Prison; that I will cheerfully obey and endeavor faithfully to have others obey the rules and Regulations of the duly constituted prison authorities, and that I will endeavor in every way to

---

[87] Minutes of the Meeting of the Delegates Elected by the Inmates, Dec. 28, 1913, 21, OFP, MSS 64, Box 269, Org. Recs.

[88] Report on membership and poll lists, Jan. 12, 1913, OFP, MSS 64, Box 269, Org. Recs.

[89] Report of voting, Jan. 15, 1914, OFP, MSS 64, Box 269, Org. Recs.

promote friendly feeling, good conduct and fair dealing among both officers and men to the end that each man after serving the briefest possible term of imprisonment may go forth with renewed strength and courage to face the world again. All this I promise faithfully to endeavor. So help me God.[90]

Then the prisoners were treated to a number of pep talks from guests such as Major Hunter of the Salvation Army, who condescended to congratulate them on their "little by laws," and Henry J. McCann, of the New York State Board of Parole, who challenged the newly enfranchised prisoners to "look at things differently" through reading the works of the "greatest men on earth" – William Shakespeare, John Milton, and Benjamin Franklin. Although the league had invited the Governor of New York to the inauguration ceremony, he was not in attendance. Osborne read a telegram from him in which he apologized for his absence, but stopped short of explicitly endorsing the league.[91]

Shortly after the swearing-in ceremony, the governing body elected an Executive Committee from among its members. In the early months of 1914, the new Executive Committee met regularly in the office of Warden Rattigan and heard prisoners' complaints and requests that had been forwarded by the delegates. Meeting without the presence of guards or other officials, secretary Richards recorded the requests and the actions taken by the Executive. The prisoners' requests and complaints might at first appear excessively mundane in character, but they addressed and attempted to change the daily conditions of incarceration in Auburn. For example, one delegate requested that sand be sprinkled on the slippery winter walkways; others, that hot water be made available in the old hospital, and that the prisoners be allowed to talk in the workshops. The prisoners of the coal company requested new boots, and the ill and aged prisoners of the Invalid Company requested that their quarters be cleaned and painted. One group of prisoners requested that the men seated at the back of chapel for entertainments be seated in the front the next time, and that prisoner musicians of the newly established prisoner orchestra be allowed one hour away from their cells for music instruction and playing every night. One prisoner who was having trouble sleeping requested that the guards desist the practice of shining their flashlights into the cells at night.[92]

The Executive delegates deliberated upon these and dozens of other requests pertaining to the everyday conditions of the prison, three or four times a month. Typically, they either declined the request, instructed secretary Richards to take up the matter with the warden, or sent the appropriate delegate back to the prisoners with other suggestions for action. The Executive Committee decided to take no action over a prisoner's request to install

[90] By-Laws of the MWL, Auburn Branch, Article VIII (1914), OFP, MSS64, Box 270, Org. Recs.
[91] Minutes of the First Meeting of the MWL, Jan. 18, 1914, OFP, MSS 64, Box 269, Org. Recs.
[92] Minutes of the Meeting of the Executive Board of the MWL, Feb. 17, 1914, 1–2, OFP, MSS 64, Box 269, Org. Recs.

electric lights in all shops and another request for more winter clothing, and they agreed that the warden had made it clear that he did not intend to allow a commissary or canteen to be set up. With regard to the nightly invasions of torch light into the prisoners cells, the Executive Committee allowed the request that the practice desist to go no further, noting that it was a necessary "precautionary measure . . . to see that the men in the rooms were all right and . . . to guard their health." (This may also be further evidence of the Executive Committee's attempt to police – or, at the very least, be seen to be policing – sexual relations between prisoners.) Rather than ask the warden to create more space in the overcrowded mess hall, the committee instructed the prisoners that the problem would be corrected if the prisoners simply refrained from putting their elbows on the table.[93]

The Executive Committee also dealt with more systemic problems that were brought to their attention by prisoners. For example, in early April, 1914, the Committee appointed a number of subcommittees to investigate certain prison conditions, such as the state of the cots. They also conducted their own investigations of efficiency in the shops, and appointed a subcommittee to talk to the deputy warden about improving the quality of trade instruction in the workshops.[94]

A close reading of the reports and minutes of these early days of the Executive Committee's activities suggests that the secretary and stenographer, prisoner S. L. Richards, became a critical member of the league: Not only did he author dozens of reports, he liaised with the warden and various league committees, and typically presented the warden with the prisoner requests that had been filtered through the Executive Committee. In addition, Richards convened the grievance committees and filed prisoner appeals to the governing body. He also frequently addressed the prisoners at mass meetings and was the only prisoner to address an audience of guards, officers, and their families at a benefit show put on by the prisoners in March of 1914.[95] As the warden's stenographer, he had a prior relationship with the warden, and he quickly became a channel of communication between the league leadership and the administration. Richards' importance to the league as the archivist, emissary, publicist, and counsel was testified to on at least two occasions, when he threatened to resign unless the Executive followed his prescribed course of action: On both occasions, the delegates conceded to Richards. [96]

The governing body of the league met far less regularly than did the Executive Committee. Constitutionally, the league's secretary was directed

[93] A minority of requests were of a more personal nature. Minutes of the Meeting of the Executive Board of the MWL, Feb. 10, Feb. 17, Mar. 15, Mar. 31, 1914.

[94] Report and Minutes of the MWL's Committee to Investigate Workshops and the Conditions of Industries, Sept. 23, 1914, OFP, MSS 64, Box 269, Org. Recs.

[95] Report on the MWL Benefit/Entertainments for Officers and Employees, Mar. 26, 1914, OFP, MSS 64, Box 269, Org. Recs.

[96] Minutes of the Meeting of the Executive Committee of the MWL, Mar. 31, 1914, OFP, MSS 64, Box 269, Org. Recs.

to call the forty-nine delegates together once a month. The body met mostly to hear appeals from prisoners who had been brought before the grievance committees, pass changes to the bylaws as they were recommended by the Executive, and, most importantly, introduce and organize entertainments for the prisoners. It was the prisoner delegates of the Governing Body who worked to introduce Auburn's first sustained program of entertainment and recreation. In the first few months of 1914, they organized choruses, a band, and an orchestra, all made up of prisoners, and proceeded to arrange shows and concerts for the prisoners. They also organized athletics and baseball.[97]

One of the first actions the delegates of the governing body undertook was to organize a day of entertainment to mark Abraham Lincoln's birthday on Sunday, February 12.[98] It was no coincidence that the delegates selected Lincoln's birthday as the day upon which to organize their first program of entertainment. Lincoln's significance among the prisoners as the "emancipator of the slaves," made the prisoners' commemoration of his birthday an important statement about what prisoners hoped was the death of the old prison system and the birth of the new. Furthermore, as Osborne and his prisoner supporters had impressed upon the governing body, Sunday's entertainments would be an acid test of the league's ability to maintain order among the prisoners and to prove their fitness for "liberty." As Osborne put it, Lincoln's birthday celebrations would provide the prisoners with an opportunity "to show that they could behave themselves and act like men."

In preparation for the event, townspeople from Auburn helped decorate the chapel and a make-shift orchestra was thrown together. The day was given over to lectures, music, and dramatic performances. In the morning, prison guards marched the members to the chapel, where they listened to musical performances by prisoners, including a selection from the newly established prisoner orchestra, songs by the "Black Pearl Quartette," and the "Golden String Octette's" mandolin and guitar music. Between performances, league delegates addressed the prisoner audience, paying homage to Osborne and explaining the objectives of the MWL. After eating lunch in the mess hall, for the first time in Auburn's history, prisoner delegates, rather than prison guards, escorted the prisoners back to the chapel. Richards reported that the escort proceeded without incident, and that the prison guards claimed they had never seen the prisoners walking in such an orderly fashion.

Once seated in the chapel, prisoners heard a piano and violin recital by civilian musicians provided by Osborne and his associate, Peter Kurtz, and after that, two penologists, Dr. Mosher and E. Stagg Whitin of the National Committee on Prisons and Prison Labor addressed the men. (No record

---

[97] Minutes of the Meeting of the Governing Body of the League, Feb. 6, Feb. 11, Feb. 14, Feb. 15, Mar. 28, 1914.

[98] At this point (Jan. 18), the proceedings of the league and its activities become faint to the historian's eye; there is no trace of delegate Richard's meticulous minutes or any other reports of the prisoner meetings that took place between January 18 and February 6.

of the addresses survives).[99] Following these addresses, secretary Richards gave a speech in which he inevitably likened "Osborne, the Emancipator of the Prisoner" to "Lincoln, the Emancipator of the Slave." In his report of the day's events, Richards referred to himself in the third person, noting that "the Clerk's" speech "brought forth continued applause, which showed that the men really appreciated all that was being done to make their lives cheerful and to bring them to a full realization of what their duty was." Lincoln's Birthday had concluded without incident; the prisoners had shown themselves fit to be granted the "liberty" of entertainment.

For the first three months of its existence, the prisoners' recreation was restricted to Sunday afternoon entertainment in the chapel and athletics events to mark holidays such as Independence Day and Lincoln's birthday. By May, 1914, prisoners were regularly watching moving pictures supplied free of charge by the Auburn Film Co. Notably, efforts of the league to secure freedom-of-the-yard on Sundays met with no success in the early months of the 1914. It seems probable that questions of policing continued to make daily yard recreation seem difficult to organize. The question of discipline and prisoner policing continued to be the object of debate among the prisoners in the early months of the league's activities. The league officials began to grapple with the transition to a new disciplinary regime almost immediately upon taking office. One of the earliest problems to arise was the relationship between the prisoner grievance committees and the prison's formal disciplinary apparatus. Since 1870, formal punishment had followed the procedure by which guards stationed in the workshops cited prisoners for transgressions (whether real or imagined) and reported them to the principal keeper. The principal keeper would then determine if and how the prisoner was to be punished, and record the name and number of the prisoner, the guard's explanation of the offense, and the prescribed punishment in a hefty, leather-bound tome, which bore the title, Punishment Ledger.

Early in 1914, the Governing Body of the League passed a new bylaw that required delegates to report to the league clerk (Richards) any and all reports made by the guards to the principal keeper. As a result, prisoners who were punished by the principal keeper were now also liable to punishment by the prisoner grievance committee. Consequently, double punishment for the same offense happened on a number of occasions: One of the first cases the grievance committee dealt with involved a league delegate whom a guard had reported to the principal keeper for fighting with another prisoner. The grievance committee decided that both the delegate and the prisoner should be immediately removed from office, and that neither be allowed to attend the upcoming entertainments on Lincoln's birthday. This punishment was in addition to that meted out by the principal keeper: According to the entry in the principal keeper's Punishment Ledger, these prisoners had already

---

[99] E. Stagg Whitin, *Prisoners' Work* (Boston: American Unitarian Association, c.1915), 1–2, OFP, MSS64, Box 271, Org. Recs.

been punished in accordance with the Rules for State Prisons by losing sixty good conduct marks each.[100] In the days following the formation of the league, prison guards continued with the traditional practice of reporting prisoners to the principal keeper, while the league delegates also began to report prisoners to the prisoners' grievance committee for breaking the rules. In order to prevent double punishment, Warden Rattigan ordered the principal keeper to turn over disciplinary cases described as "minor" to the prisoner grievance committee for deliberation. The warden's plan generated a hybrid disciplinary mechanism whereby both guards and prisoner officers were instructed to report transgressions to the prisoner grievance committees. This constituted a highly significant alteration of prison disciplinary procedures. Furthermore, the manner in which the change was brought about illuminated the way in which authority operated within the league, and between the league and the administration. The idea originated with Warden Rattigan; Osborne then called the Executive Committee together in order to "air the authorities' plan." The Executive delegates, implicitly accepted it by resolving to ask the governing body to amend the league's constitution so as to accommodate

---

[100] Auburn Punishment Ledger, NYSA (RDCS) Auburn Correctional Facility, Inmate Punishment Ledger, 1872 (1870) – 1941; Minutes of the Meeting of the Governing Body of the League, Feb. 6, 1914, 2, OFP, MSS 64, Box 269, Org. Recs. *The Rules of the Board of Parole for State Prisons* (1912) established a uniform system of mark-deduction for all New York state prisons (as provided for in Laws N.Y. 1907, Ch. 467). Initially, the principal keeper's Punishment Ledger and the typed minutes of the grievance committees generated very different kinds of accounts of offenses. The inmate grievance committees had an air of secrecy; the records consist of reports typed up by Richards which were then presented to the governing body. Whereas the principal keeper recorded the character of the offense, sometimes to such a degree of detail that the "vile language" attributed to an prisoner was recorded word for word, the grievance committee minutes and reports rarely recorded the alleged offense with any specificity. Wheras the principal keeper wrote up prisoner offenses, the league records instead noted the existence of prisoner complaints – that is complaints of one prisoner against another or against the league. In the case of the sparring delegate, for example, the minutes convey no sense of the circumstances of the transgression. Even when the former delegate came to appeal the grievance committee's ruling, a description of the character of his actions was markedly absent from the minutes; his sudden withdrawal of the appeal under pressure from Osborne further testifies to the careful and selective reporting of the MWL's grievance proceedings. Although the former delegate appealed the case to the governing body, Osborne prevailed upon him to accept his punishment and withdraw the appeal. Osborne, who represented the delegate before the governing body, told the delegates that the former delegate's withdrawal was a "manly straight forward exhibition of courage." Given that in the middle of discussing the former delegate's case, the governing body voted to prohibit "political faith" and "political principles" from league proceedings, it seems likely that the former delegate's conflict was connected to a conflict over politics. After a few weeks of operation, and once the jurisdiction of the prisoner tribunals had been established, however, the grievance committees became more specific about most of the more mundane cases. More serious cases, such as those involving sexual relations, continued to be reported in a vague manner. See for example, Minutes of Grievance Committee Number Three, Feb., 26, 1914; Minutes of Grievance Committee Number Four, Feb. 27, Mar. 4, Mar 14, 1914; Minutes of Grievance Committee Number Four, Feb. 27, 1914, OFP, MSS 64, Box 269, Org. Recs.

the new plan. The next day, when Executive delegate Shea explained the plan to the delegates of the Governing Body, and asked for their support, he was effectively presenting the legislative body with a *fait accompli.* As he informed the governing body, the administration was already in the process of setting up a detention room in which prisoners who had been found guilty by the principal keeper would await a grievance committee hearing. Shea's request that the delegates amend the league's constitution was hence a matter of form – an interesting and important matter of form, nonetheless.[101]

The delegate legislators were given twenty-four hours to consider the *fait accompli.* The next day, the governing body underwent the first of several crises over the issue of discipline and the relationship of the administration to the league. Notably, the meeting began not with a debate about the proposal, but with a vote in favor of the new disciplinary regime. This was quickly followed by a telling resolution: Any delegate who detrimentally criticized another delegate, or made any "unwarranted criticisms" of the governing body following a meeting of that body, should be reported to a grievance committee for disciplinary action.[102] Therein followed considerable, but predictably unreported, discussion of the new system. Within a few days of its inauguration, the governing body was threatening to fragment over the question of police powers. In the course of the meeting, it emerged that delegate Norton of state shop "A," together with certain other unnamed delegates, had questioned the legitimacy and fitness of some of the Executive delegates. Upon hearing this, the legitimacy of the Executive Committee was put to a vote, and affirmed by thirty-seven votes to nine. Then, in what must have been an action designed to intimidate the dissenting delegates (in light of the censorious new rule), the Executive Committee (or, more probably, Richards) asked each delegate, one by one, whether or not in that delegate's view, the Executive delegates were fit for office. Not a single delegate took issue with the fitness of the Executive delegates.

There is little in the way of archival material to suggest what the prisoner population in general may have been saying and doing about the disciplinary changes at Auburn at this point. However, evidence of considerable consternation about the operation of the grievance committees seeped through Richards' carefully constructed minutes and reports of the meetings of the Executive Committee and governing body. According to Osborne, in the early, precarious days of the prisoner discipline system, prisoners were refusing to attend the grievance hearings both as witnesses and accused offenders. Osborne explained the prisoners' refusal of the grievance committees as a protest against double punishment, which had occurred with some frequency in the first four weeks of the grievance committees' operation. The

[101] Minutes of the Meeting of the Executive Committee of the MWL, Feb. 13, 1914, 1–8, and Minutes of the Meeting of the Governing Body of the MWL, Feb. 14, 1914, OFP, MSS 64, Box 269, Org. Recs.
[102] Minutes of the Meeting of the Governing Body of the League, Feb. 15, 1914, 1–2, OFP, MSS 64, Box 269, Org. Recs.

grievance committees were aware of the problem of double punishment, and tended to be more lenient on those prisoners who had already been reported or punished by the principal keeper. Typically, instead of suspending these prisoners from the league, the committee reprimanded them and elicited promises of better behavior. On at least one occasion, the prisoner committee reprimanded two prisoners who had already spent three days in the dark cells and lost ten days good time. In the same session, the prisoner jurists announced that they would ask the principal keeper to treat two other prisoners, who had been reported for fighting, leniently. (It is likely that the principal keeper accepted their recommendation, as no record of the prisoners' offense was entered in the ledger).[103] Although the grievance committee's punishments were light, evidence from the Punishment Ledger and the grievance committee minutes lends support to Osborne's argument that the prisoners were resisting the new system because of its tendency to punish offenders twice over.

However, a speech given by the prisoner Osborne had befriended during his investigation of Auburn – Jack Murphy – suggests that the prisoners were objecting to something much more intrinsic to the new prisoner policing system. The prisoners of Murphy's weave shop met on at least three occasions to air their concerns about the new disciplinary system. At one of these meetings, Murphy implored them to accept the new system. It is clear from his speech that the primary point of conjecture among the prisoners was the very existence of prisoner police powers. Prisoners were protesting that regardless of their shape or form, the prisoner police apparatus engendered "ratting," or reporting fellow prisoners to the authorities. In his explanation of the system, Murphy passionately refuted this charge and insisted that reporting other prisoners to a prisoner delegate was not equivalent to "ratting." Ratting, he argued, was pernicious because it was secretive and anonymous; the league system of reporting an offender to a delegate was ethically defensible because the complainant would have to sign his name to his complaint, and the charge – and its source – would thus be transparent.

Judging by what Murphy had to say to the prisoners next, the prisoners also objected to the system because it appeared to be aimed at punishing transgressions of the more minor prison rules, which, under the old system, might not be punished. In other words, extending police powers to delegates constituted more than a transfer of authority: It meant an expansion of policing and surveillance. Murphy assured the weavers that he would only ever report them for the serious offenses of fighting, stealing, and "acts of degeneracy"; he would never report them for what he himself would not want to be reported for.[104] In addition to defending the prisoner self-government

[103] Minutes of the Hearing of Grievance Committee Number One, Feb. 16, 1914, OFP, MSS 64, Box 269, Org. Recs.; and Auburn Punishment Ledger, NYSA (RDCS) Auburn Correctional Facility, Inmate Punishment Ledger, 1872 (1870)–1941.

[104] Jack Murphy, untitled speech, Auburn Prison, Feb. 18, 1914, 5, OFP, MSS64, Box 270, Org. Recs.

as ethical, Murphy also told the prisoners that reporting was dutiful because it served the interests of the league to suppress and discipline those who broke the rules. If fighting, stealing, and degeneracy (sexual relations among prisoners) were allowed to go on under the new system, he reasoned, the league (and all the privileges that accompanied it) would fail. Like Osborne and the league leaders, Murphy had a keen sense that the publicity that the league had already begun to generate in the mass media would affect its future. He argued before the prisoners of the weave shop:

> The league now in its infancy is the cynosure of the eyes of all the prison authorities in the U.S. and also of those in the more progressive lands of Europe. If our league ends in failure, which we are determined it shall not, the promotion of the prisoner's welfare in all penal institutions will be woefully retarded. An opportunity such as that now within our reach, an opportunity for aiding the unfortunate prisoners everywhere, will not come again, perhaps, for a whole century.[105]

If Murphy had one eye fixed on the publicity of the mass press, the other was focused on the men's conduct – and their sexual relations in particular. "I'm not blind, fellows, as to what is going around in this prison," he insisted, "and let me tell you, no set of degenerates is going to turn this League into a red-light League, if I can prevent it." He argued that if fighting, stealing, and sex continued under the liberalized regime, newspapermen would write stories of gangs and degeneracy at Auburn based on the tales of former prisoners, and the state would have no choice but to destroy the league and return to the old system.[106]

Shortly after Murphy addressed the prisoners, Osborne was prompted to call a special general meeting of the entire MWL membership (ninety-five percent of the prisoners), for Sunday, February 22, to discuss the arrangement. According to an essay Osborne wrote a few years later, he called the meeting because the prisoners whom the guards and delegates had reported to secretary Richards for rule-breaking had been refusing to attend the grievance committee hearings. Furthermore, other prisoners were declining to appear as witnesses, on the grounds that some of their number were being punished twice, and some of the grievance committees had refused to hold hearings when the cases involved prisoners who had already been disciplined by the principal keeper. After three short weeks of operation, many prisoners, according to Osborne, wanted the league to relinquish all disciplinary authority, on the grounds that self-government had simply intensified punishment.[107]

---

[105] Murphy was appointed sergeant-at-arms in July 1916. He received many letters of congratulation from prisoners upon being appointed. *The Bulletin*, MWL, Auburn Branch, 3:6 (July 15, 1916), OFP, MSS64, Box 270, Org. Recs.

[106] Jack Murphy, untitled speech, Auburn Prison, Feb. 18, 1914, 5, OFP, MSS64, Box 270, Org. Recs.

[107] Minutes of a Special General Meeting, MWL, Auburn, Feb. 22, 1914, OFP, MSS64, Box 269, Org. Recs.; Auburn MWL2/MSW/2/pp.14–15. In 1924, Osborne incorporated the

The refusal of prisoners, and even some of the delegates, to proceed with certain cases had created a crisis of legitimacy for the league, and threatened to arrest the entire program of so-called self-government. As Osborne had reiterated to the prisoners, recreational privileges and other liberties were to be extended only as fast as prisoners (by which Osborne meant the league officers) assumed disciplinary responsibility for themselves: The failure of the new apparatus of prisoner discipline would diminish the likelihood that athletics, shows, and movies would continue. This moment of conflict between many of the prisoners on the one hand, and Osborne and the league leadership on the other, is highly instructive about the relationship of the league to the general prison population: Unlike the impetus for the new system of government, prisoners' resistance to the novel disciplinary arrangements originated among their number. Instigated from above, the league was confronting resistance from below as a result of the intensification and extension of policing that the new hybrid disciplinary system was engendering. As well as disrupting Osborne's vision of a system of prisoner government based in liberties and responsibilities, the prisoners' refusal threatened to overturn the founding myth of the league's democratic origins, and hence its legitimacy. Prisoners' opposition to the policing arm of self-government required Osborne, the league leadership, and the warden to act swiftly.

At the special mass meeting called by Osborne, 1,300 prisoners debated the question of prisoner policing for three long hours. Although they met without the presence of guards, what they said never made it onto the record; secretary Richards, consistent with his previous excision of much of the discussion pertaining to prison discipline, did not transcribe the substance of the discussion – though he did remark, perhaps with unconscious wit, that the discussion constituted "something unheard of in history."[108] As a result of the long discussion, the prisoners concluded the meeting by voting for a disciplinary system that would ensure prisoners would not be punished twice for the same offense: The grievance committees were given jurisdiction over all cases of prison discipline other than those of deadly assault on one prisoner by another, assault on a guard, refusal to work, strikes, and attempts to escape.[109] Both guards and prisoner delegates were to report minor transgressions to the grievance committees. Osborne and his league supporters hoped that this division of disciplinary authority would end the problem of double punishment and secure the support of the mass of prisoners for the league's disciplinary tribunals.

manuscript into his book *Prisons and Commonsense*. His interpretation of the prisoners' resistance to the MWL disciplinary proceedings was that the prisoners wanted to shirk their responsibilities and enjoy their privileges. Osborne, *Prisons and Commonsense* (Philadelphia: J. B. Lippincott, 1924), 81.

[108] Minutes of a Special General Meeting, MWL, Auburn, Feb. 22, 1914, OFP, MSS64, Box 269, Org. Recs.

[109] Minutes of a Special General Meeting, MWL, Auburn, Feb. 22, 1914, OFP, MSS64, Box 269, Org. Recs.; Auburn MWL2/MSW/2/14–15; and Tannenbaum, *Osborne of Sing Sing*, 92–3.

With the formal transfer of minor disciplinary cases to the prisoner grievance committees in late February, the committees set up a revolving schedule whereby one committee convened between 9 A.M. and 1 P.M. every work day.[110] Typically a grievance committee would hear cases three to seven days after the incident. In practice, cases involving workshop behavior such as shirking, fisticuffs, talking on line, and bad language tended to qualify as minor, whereas cases in which prisoners were thought to be challenging the guards or threatening the general order of the prison were dealt with by the principal keeper. The vast majority of formal punishments administered by the principal keeper were related to discipline in the workshops: Refusal to work and fighting in the shops were the most common grounds for official punishment. He also continued to punish prisoners for possessing contraband, and any prisoner who created a serious disturbance among the other prisoners. In the ensuing months, the principal keeper disciplined far fewer prisoners than usual: For example, in the month immediately following the transfer of minor cases to the prisoner committees, he disciplined only eleven prisoners; in each of the previous months he had typically disciplined thirty.[111]

As the prisoner grievance committees became part of the everyday life of the prison, the committees began to develop their own bureaucratic procedures, by which they produced standardized reports of the hearings. The reports of these sessions were framed in a paralegal language, and made use of certain of the inventions of the carceral bureaucracy – most notably, the prisoner identification numbers. Secretary Richards recorded the substance of each complaint, the reported prisoner's explanation or admission of guilt, and the action, if any, taken by the presiding grievance committee.

Upon first view, it would appear that the grievance committees had a limited range of sanctions they could apply to prisoners they found guilty. The committee often extracted a promise from the offending prisoner that the offense would not be repeated; sometimes they reprimanded and warned the guilty prisoner. More frequently, prisoners were punished by being barred from attending an upcoming concert or show in the chapel. Working on the principle of withholding new-found privileges, the committee also began to suspend prisoners from the league – and, in some cases, expel members altogether. This effectively excluded the prisoner in question from all recreational activities. Most significantly, suspension or expulsion placed the prisoner in a separate system of discipline: The principal keeper's discipline of dark cell and loss of good time. One prisoner, who quit the league following a confrontation with his company delegate (in the course of which

---

[110] Tannenbaum, *Osborne of Sing Sing*, 92–3.
[111] Auburn Punishment Ledger, NYSA (RDCS), Auburn Correctional Facility, Inmate Punishment Ledger, 1872 (1870) – 1941. Four of the eleven prisoners were punished for violation of parole; the others were punished for transgressions including refusal to obey orders, threatening to "punch (a guard's) face off," fighting, making a knife, abusive behavior and walking out of court, and causing trouble in the mess hall.

he reportedly tore his MWL membership badge from his lapel and threw it in the delegate's face), was subsequently interned in the dark cell on at least three occasions by the principal keeper. Had this prisoner remained a member, two of his three offenses would most likely have been heard by the grievance committee, and he would not have spent so much time in the dark cell.[112]

It appears that the first prisoner to be suspended indefinitely from the league was a prisoner who was found guilty of writing and passing what Richards described in the minutes as a licentious note to another prisoner (who, incidentally, had been recently suspended for three months for fighting). In suspending the note writer, the Committee remarked that the content of the note, which was read aloud at the hearing but not reproduced in the minutes, was of "such a nature as would tend to create a continual disturbance in the shop," and that the prisoner should also be transferred to another shop. Other prisoners were suspended indefinitely for fighting and one prisoner, suspended for being "simple-minded." Prisoners brought before a grievance committee developed certain tactics to minimize their punishment. Invoking their manliness by drawing attention to their honesty, a number admitted guilt (sincerely or otherwise) and were rewarded by more lenient punishments. After a few weeks, the grievance committees also began handing over prisoners found guilty of certain offenses to the principal keeper for punishment: For example, in June, a grievance committee asked that the principal keeper lock up one prisoner.[113] (The nature of his offense is unclear).

Despite the new division of disciplinary authority between the committees and the principal keeper, as might be expected, tension between the two disciplinary arms persisted. After a few weeks of the new system's operation, the principal keeper began to punish larger numbers of prisoners on the grounds that they had been insolent to guards: This offense was clearly considered to be a more serious offense, though it was not formally listed by the warden as an offense punishable by the administration.[114] Insolence typically consisted of a prisoner swearing at a guard or back-chatting him. A prisoner who not only refused to work but swore at a guard was likely to end up being penalized more severely than the prisoner who would not work.

The principal keeper also kept track of the grievance committee proceedings, and upon occasion requested permission from the warden to further

[112] Minutes of a Meeting of Grievance Committee Number Three, Feb. 21, 1914, OFP, MSS64, Box 269, Org. Recs.; Auburn Punishment Ledger, NYSA (RDCS), Auburn Correctional Facility, Inmate Punishment Ledger, 1872 (1870)–1941.

[113] *The Bulletin*, MWL, Auburn, 1:8 (June 12, 1914), OFP, MSS64, Box 270, Org. Recs.

[114] Sometimes the guards recorded the alleged insults in some detail: The guards recorded that one prisoner attending school, for example, allegedly called his teacher a "god-damned liar" and told him "'to go fuck himself,' as teacher wasn't trying to instruct him." Other times they simply noted that the prisoner had used "vile language" or "indecent language" to an officer. Auburn Punishment Ledger, NYSA (RDCS), Auburn Correctional Facility, Inmate Punishment Ledger, 1872 (1870)–1941.

punish a prisoner who had already been punished by a grievance committee. For example, just days after the new disciplinary division was instigated,
the deputy warden asked the warden's permission to further punish by fine
two prisoners who had already been disciplined by a grievance committee.
When they were alerted to this request, the league's Executive Committee
struck a compromise by which the principal keeper would fine the prisoners
only if they got into any more fights during the proceeding two months. The
principal keeper agreed to this compromise. But judging from a comparison
of the official punishment ledger and the grievance committee records two
months down the road, although the majority of prisoners reported for rule
breaking were being disciplined by the grievance committees alone, some
prisoners were still being punished twice: The principal keeper was locking
some prisoners in the dark cell for offenses for which they had already been
punished by a grievance committee.

The arrangement by which both guards and prisoners now reported
minor infringements to a committee of prisoners put the guards in an
unusual relationship to the prisoners. Both Osborne and the league's leadership understood that the cooperation of the guards would be as crucial
to the success of the new disciplinary system – and to the league – as was
the cooperation of prisoners. By early March, tensions between guards and
delegates were mounting over the division of disciplinary authority, and the
situation was exacerbated by the quarantine of Auburn Prison following an
outbreak of small pox in the central New York area. Recognizing the guards'
mounting disaffection for prisoner self-government, the governing body of
the league acted to appease them by holding a benefit show for the guards
and civilian employees of the prison.[115] Once the small pox quarantine had
ended, some 800 guards, employees, and their families attended an evening
show in the prison chapel, where they were treated to a round of minstrelsy,
an olio of songs and skits, and a performance of the official MWL march by
the league orchestra. League officials ushered the audience of law enforcers
and their families to their seats, and secretary Richards appealed to the audience for donations. The program offered up the evening's fare as a token
of "appreciation for the co-operation of the official force" and a step toward
establishing "more cordial relations between (the officers) and the MWL."
In his report of the evening's activities, Richards proclaimed that the show
"marked the beginning of a new spirit among both officers and men, and
will be long remembered."[116] A few days after the benefit, the governing
body followed up on their effort to secure the support of guards by asking
Osborne to meet with the prison officers and employees to determine their
views and suggestions about the league.[117] At the same time, the Executive

---

[115] Minutes, Grievance Committee Number Five, MWL, Auburn, Mar. 14, 1914, OFP, MSS 64,
Box 269, Org. Recs.
[116] Report on the Benefit for Officers and Employees, MWL, Auburn, Mar. 26, 1914, OFP, MSS
64, Box 269, Org. Recs.
[117] Minutes of a Meeting of the Governing Body, MWL, Auburn, Mar. 30, 1914, OFP, MSS 64,
Box 269, Org. Recs.

attended to their relations with the guards' chief executive – Warden Ratti-gan – who had fallen ill, by sending him flowers and a get-well note.[118]

As the league delegates attempted to secure the support, or at the very least, the acquiescence, of the guards and employees, they also began to quietly pressure the administration to change the kinds of punishments meted out to prisoners by the principal keeper. On March 31, the Executive Committee passed a motion condemning the conditions endured by the prisoners who were locked in their cells (or "square chalked"). It is unclear what the condition of life was like for these prisoners, beyond the fact that they were held continuously in their cells; what is certain is that the league leadership was concerned about the condition of these prisoners, and they took a number of steps to reform the conditions of their punishment.[119]

The alliance between the administration and the league leadership was further cemented in the summer of 1914. Summer was traditionally the sea-son in which prison discipline broke down and in which riots and strikes broke out. In 1914, the threat of prisoner restiveness fused with the emer-gence of socialist activism in the prison workshops to produce the specter of immobilized prison industries and a militant prisoner body. In the face of militant resistance, the league officials joined the administration in crushing socialist organizing in the prison shops. Judging from secretary Richards' elliptical reporting of one incident in particular, at some point during the summer, Warden Rattigan had prohibited prisoners from subscribing to cer-tain socialist publications, and the Superintendent, Riley, had written a letter to the league affirming Rattigan's action. In June, one prisoner reported to the governing body that certain MWL members had been seen wearing the red lapel ribbon of socialism and another reported that "socialist agitation" was occurring in some of the prison workshops. Upon hearing this news, the governing body voted unanimously that socialist organizing be stopped, and further, that any member who would "infuse into our League political, racial or creed prejudice shall be guilty of conduct unbecoming of League members." Such conduct made a prisoner liable to expulsion to the segrega-tion company, and certain suspension of all privileges. As well as prohibiting socialist organizing, a majority of the delegates on the governing body rec-ommended that any prisoner who refused to work or fought with another prisoner be automatically expelled from the league for six months.

The allusion to "racial and creed prejudice" is not illuminated anywhere in the archive, and it appears that what was of utmost concern to the govern-ing body was not racism or religious intolerance, but the presence of socialist activism in the prison. The week following the governing body's prohibition of socialist organizing and prejudice, an unusual number of prisoners were expelled from the league: Thirteen of twenty-six men who appeared before

---

[118] Minutes, Grievance Committee Number Five, MWL, Auburn, Apr. 13, 1914, OFP, MSS 64, Box 269, Org. Recs.

[119] Again, the report of this discussion is thin, and Richards did not put these conditions into writing. Minutes of a Meeting of the Executive Committee, MWL, Auburn, Apr. 7, 1914, OFP, MSS 64, Box 269, Org. Recs.

the grievance committees were permanently removed from the league.[120] It is not clear exactly why they were expelled, but it seems probable that they were punished for promoting strike activity. It was at this point that the league leadership moved to tighten its disciplinary hold on the prisoners. At the same time as cracking down on prisoners they viewed as subversive, the governing body also made it much more difficult for prisoners who had been suspended or expelled by a grievance committee to appeal to the governing body. The body also made a formal request to the warden that a section in the North wing of the prison serve as a segregation unit for expelled members.

The administration followed the recommendations of the governing body and set up the segregation unit in the summer of 1914; prisoners in this unit became known as the segregation company. All prisoners who were suspended or expelled from the league were hitherto consigned to this company as part of their punishment, and they had little or no contact with the rest of the prison population. They were deprived of most of the activities organized by league membership, which effectively meant that they could not participate in any of the sports and other recreational activities going on in the prison. Up to 100 prisoners occupied the segregation unit. The league leadership did not, however, abandon the segregated prisoners entirely. They took steps to ensure that conditions in the segregation wing met certain standards: Within two months of establishing the segregation company, the governing body set up a committee to investigate it. The leadership also made provision for the re-entry of suspended (but not expelled) league members back into the general prison population. They recommended to the governing body that all "sentences" handed down by the grievance committees be indeterminate and that a prisoner "parole board" be set up to interview the suspended prisoners on a weekly basis, with the view of integrating the disciplined prisoners back into the general population.

Following the election of a new set of delegates in July, 1914, the governing body investigated the possibility of relieving the idle boredom of the prisoners in the segregation company, by establishing some kind of labor for them. Following the Executive's suggestion, they also created a parole board, which began to parole the prisoners back into the general prison population. The parole boards were composed of three delegates who met with the suspended members of the segregation company once a week, in order to make recommendations to the Executive Committee about who, if anyone, should be restored to the league (and hence, the general prison population). In its first week of operation, the board recommended that nine men be restored; the Executive Committee accepted six of the nine prisoners, and placed them on probation back in the general prison population.[121]

---

[120] *The Bulletin*, MWL, Auburn, 1:9 (Jun. 20, 1914); 1: 10 (Jun. 29, 1914), OFP, MSS64, Box 270, Org. Recs.

[121] *The Bulletin*, MWL, Auburn, 1:15 (Aug. 1, 1914), OFP, MSS64, Box 270, Org. Recs.

As well as being a critical element of the Osbornian program of prisoner self-government, the development of the prisoner grievance committees and the parole board was understood by many of the leaders of the league to be a model system of how the American criminal justice system of police, courts, and prisons should work. In a reversal of the fiction of rehabilitation whereby the state undertook to reform convicts, the prisoners of Auburn attempted to reform the state – and its courts and prisons – by demonstrating that indeterminate sentencing, probation and parole, and healthy prison conditions would effectively rehabilitate prisoners who had transgressed the rules. Hence the league leadership adopted the principles of the new penology in its treatment of transgressors. As one delegate put it, "This is the plan that we prisoners are trying to have the people of the outside world adopt and it is up to us to show them that it is the proper method of handling the subject."[122]

The league leadership also grasped the state's use of prisoners in the laying of new roads in the summer of 1914 as an opportunity to educate the outside world about the correct way to treat prisoners. In late summer, a number of Auburn prisoners were organized into six road-building gangs and sent out beyond the prison walls into central and upstate New York to assist the state with its "Good Roads" construction program. One such road gang, named the Honor Camp, was organized by the league. These prisoners set up camps and labored away from the prison for up to three months at a time, some under the watch of only one guard, and without the leg irons of the chain gangs of many of the Southern states. The leadership of the MWL considered these camps to be critical in the struggle to win public support for the reforms at Auburn: In their eyes, it gave the prisoners the opportunity to do work that was socially useful, and the relatively low level of surveillance demonstrated to the world that prisoners could be trusted to conduct themselves in an orderly way when given some degree of liberty.

Arguing that the gangs would be "carefully watched throughout the country," the leadership urged the prisoner road workers to prove their working skills to the world. The leadership promoted the gangs to prisoners as an opportunity to regain fitness and health before release: "Instead of being confined in a three by seven [cell], you are given a chance to breathe the fresh air," wrote secretary Richards. The rigors of roadwork would put the prisoners in "better physical condition to face the battle with the outside world when released." In particular, the leadership supported one camp, known as the "Honor Camp," where prisoners labored under a regime modeled upon the league. Osborne donned his old Tom Brown uniform and joined these prisoners as they labored on the roads, on at least two occasions. Like many of the reforms connected with prisoner self-government, he ensured that the road camps attracted substantial media attention, much of it supportive. At one point, the well-known aviator, Johnson, visited the Honor Camp, where he was presented with an MWL button, whereupon

[122] *The Bulletin*, MWL, Auburn, 1:15 (Aug. 1, 1914), OFP, MSS64, Box 270, Org. Recs.

he announced he would take the button "higher than it ever has been before."[123]

The league began to publish its own news sheet, *The Bulletin*, in April of 1914, as a means to communicate operations of various league committees to the prisoners. This weekly news sheet was written and edited by clerk Richards, and was delivered to the prisoners every Saturday. It carried the minutes of MWL meetings, a lost and found section, notices about past and upcoming sporting and entertainment events in the prison, and disciplinary instructions from the delegates. It also reported disciplinary action taken against prisoners by the grievance committees. As had been the case in the *Star of Hope*, the paper published at Sing Sing in the early 1900s (see Chapter 5), the prison administration increasingly made use of it as a medium of communication with the prisoners. By December 1914, Warden Rattigan, and even the Superintendent of Prisons, John B. Riley, communicated orders to the prisoners via *The Bulletin*.

The Bulletin also became the central means by which the league leadership reiterated certain rules and requested compliance by prisoners. These often pertained to minor questions of conduct: Among other things, prisoners were frequently told to "please refrain from groaning when the film breaks" during the moving picture shows, to keep their feet off of the freshly painted chairs in the chapel, and to desist spitting tobacco juice on the chapel floor (which was expressly prohibited by the official Rules for State Prisons).[124] They were also warned against talking between cells and pushing on line. Often, the requests were accompanied by a reminder that prisoners were being frequently observed by visitors to the prison, and that prisoners' disorderly and impolite behavior might prejudice civilians against the league. Occasionally, the editor spoke out against more serious transgressions of rules: For example, following reports of fighting in the yard in May, the editor quipped, "Behave like gentlemen. . . . If you want to fight, go to Mexico." (The U.S. had recently gone to war against Mexico's new republican government).[125] These requests reflected the league leadership's intent to ensure the orderly conduct of prisoners; they also suggest the extent to which the leadership's objectives coincided with those of the prison administration. For example, in noting that prisoners seemed to be afflicted by imaginary ailments, the leadership set up an "anti-doctor" league, and insisted that prisoners seeking medical attention fill out the appropriate form.[126] Like other leadership actions, this was intended to put a halt to practices that interrupted the daily discipline of prison life.

The league's role in developing athletic and sports events at Auburn was perhaps one of the most enduring legacies of the Auburn experiment: In these activities, prisoners and administrators alike had found a disciplinary

[123] *The Bulletin*, MWL, Auburn, 1:18 (Aug. 22, 1914), OFP, MSS64, Box 270, Org. Recs.
[124] Rule 34, Rules and Regulations for Inmates of the New York State Prisons, 1912, OFP, MSS64, Box 268, Org. Recs.
[125] *The Bulletin*, MWL, Auburn, 1:6 (May 30, 1914), OFP, MSS64, Box 270, Org. Recs.
[126] *The Bulletin*, MWL, Auburn, 1:10 (June 29, 1914), OFP, MSS64, Box 270, Org. Recs.

alternative to the unreliable prison labor system that had proven so vulnerable to ongoing political attack after the abolition of contract labor. Most of the organizing efforts of the governing body of the league were devoted to establishing various kinds of recreational events for prisoners, and sometimes guards. The first athletics competition at Auburn was scheduled for May 30. A notice in *The Bulletin* announced that prisoners interested in competing should preregister for the events. Prisoners could compete in a tug of war, the fat man's race, a guards-versus-prisoners sprint around the prison yard, and a number of other novelty races. Prisoners competed in teams for their cell wing, and a member of the Commission for Prison Reform donated a trophy for the victorious wing, as well as $100 to purchase several smaller prizes for individual champions.[127] Columbus Day was celebrated with pie-eating contests, egg races, the usual sports events, and a human version of coconut shi – the "African Dodger" where prisoners threw objects at a prisoner and won a cigar if they hit him. Although prisoners initially competed for their wing of the cellhouse, by October, the organizational basis for team competition had been altered: Prisoners played for teams that were nationally and racially defined. On Columbus Day, for example, the all-white U.S. citizens of the "American" team engaged in a furious tug-o-war with the "Italian" team. Every week, *The Bulletin* reported on the games and athletics, in a manner that mimicked but also employed irony regarding the sports commentary of the civilian press: A prisoner reporting on one of the athletics days noted that the activities at "Welfare Park," (that is, the prison yard) were attended by "the usual holiday crowd."[128]

During the summer of 1914, the governing body also organized five baseball teams, two of which were named after Osborne. In observance of the prison hierarchy, these teams were organized according to race and nationality. The various shows put on by prisoners were also organized by national and racial categories. Unfortunately, few descriptions of these shows have survived, but it is evident that the prisoner audience was entertained most Sunday afternoons by groups such as the "Neapolitan Street Singers," the "Society Garibaldini del Mare," the "Irish Comedians," and the "Colored Players." There were a number of skits involving blackface minstrelsy, and various kinds of cross-dressing performances, including a skit by "White and Co" entitled, "A Southern Cotton Field." The prisoners also organized a glee club. The prisoners had substantial support from outsiders in these endeavors: Civilian groups such as the Bayliss-Hicks Players and the Pals performed for the prisoners through the summer of 1914, and local civilians helped the prisoners with the construction of props and scenery for the league productions. Not uncommonly, guards put together acts for the prisoners, and on more than one occasion, had their children perform skits at Sunday entertainments in the chapel. The Auburn Picture Company

[127] *The Bulletin*, MWL, Auburn, 1:6 (May 30, 1914), OFP, MSS64, Box 270, Org. Recs.
[128] *The Bulletin*, MWL, Auburn, 1:21 (Sep. 12, 1914), OFP, MSS64, Box 270, Org. Recs.

donated a movie projector, and the prisoners began to regularly view moving picture shows. As prisoners, outsiders, and guards began to donate money to the league, and as the league began to raise funds, the Executive opened a bank account at the local National Bank of Auburn. (The Executive also secured an attorney in Auburn for legal advice in league matters).[129]

* * * * *

With the establishment of the league, the institution of recreation, and the restructuring of police powers, everyday life at Auburn prison had been radically altered by June of 1914. Male prisoners had begun to compete in athletics and baseball; and were participating in musical bands and shows. As prisoners participated in these new activities, they were spending less time in their dank cells than they had since prison industries had boomed before the abolition of prison labor contracting. The Superintendent of Prisons, John Riley, had offered some reprieve from the long hours in the cellhouse the year before the MWL had been set up, when he instituted a midday Sunday dinner in the mess hall. But it was not until the advent of Tom Brown's installment at Auburn that the hours spent in the cells were radically diminished by the institution of sporting events and entertainments on Sundays, extended workshop hours on week days and Saturdays, and, eventually, freedom-of-the-yard. In the next six months, the governing body and Executive of the league would undertake a number of new projects: In July, ongoing problems in the foundry workshop were brought to the attention of the Executive. The members decided to conduct a thorough investigation of the shop.[130] Other investigations were made of the efficiency of the shops. League leaders continued to pursue the amelioration of prison conditions: Following the expulsion of several men from the road gangs, the Executive asked the sergeant at arms and Richards to investigate conditions at the camps. The leadership also began to organize evening lectures in late 1914. Prisoners were not compelled to attend these lectures, but many did.[131] After almost two decades of searching for an alternative to the system of imprisonment at hard contract labor, a solution that appeared acceptable to convicts, administrators, and guards alike seemed to be taking shape in New York's oldest state prison. (A few tentative reforms also got underway in the women's prison at Auburn, although not on the same scale as in the men's prison: In February, 1914, the women prisoners were allowed their first-ever dance).[132]

---

[129] Almost every issue of *The Bulletin* reviewed or advertised shows, movies, and athletics. *The Bulletin*, MWL, Auburn, 1:2 (May 2, 1914) – 3:1 (May 5, 1916), OFP, MSS 64, Box 269, Org. Recs.

[130] Report and Minutes of the Committee to Investigate Workshops and the Conditions of Industries, MWL, Auburn, Sep. 23, 1914.

[131] Outside speakers addressed them on subjects ranging from travel in Spain to bird watching, the Mexican War, music, and history. *The Bulletin*, MWL, Auburn, 1: 25 (Oct. 10, 1914); 1:34 (Dec. 12, 1914); 1:41 (Feb. 16, 1915), OFP, MSS64, Box 270, Org. Recs.

[132] *New York Times*, Feb. 15, 1914, 10.

Osborne and his fellow Commissioners had also carefully publicized the reforms underway at Auburn. Although they waited, initially, for the elections to be organized and for the MWL to be up and running, they proceeded to generate a steady flow of press releases through the winter and spring of 1914. Newspapers as far away as California carried news of the Auburn experiment.[133] They tirelessly delivered addresses to various civic and religious groups in an effort to generate moral and financial support for their work. In the lower Hudson Valley, in the meantime, not much had changed; the recently riotous institution of Sing Sing remained internally and politically unstable. Indeed, the Democratic administration of acting-Governor Glynn was receiving as much criticism for its failures at Sing Sing as it was support for the changes at Auburn. In September 1914, as Auburn convicts sat down to a rare dinner of chicken, cranberry sauce, celery, and bread rolls, prepared in honor of the first anniversary of Tom Brown's commitment to Auburn, Superintendent John Riley asked Osborne to head an effort to transform America's most infamous prison into a stable, well-managed institution: "Rich Man As Warden," ran the headline in the *Los Angeles Times.*[134]

---

[133] See, for example, *New York Times,* Jan. 19, 1914, 2; Feb. 15, 1914, 10; Mar. 7, 1914, 20; June 1, 1914, 6; *New York Times,* Oct. 10, 1914, 12; *New York Times,* Nov. 27, 1914, 6; "Voluntary Convict is Champion of Prisoners," *Los Angeles Times,* June 14, 1914, VI7.

[134] *Los Angeles Times,* Nov. 29, 1914, 13.

9

Laboratory of Social Justice: The New Penologists
at Sing Sing, 1915–1917

Men can stand vermin and dirt and disease, but they cannot survive injustice.

Thomas Mott Osborne (1914)[1]

The received historiographical wisdom about the prison reforms of the high Progressive Era (1913–19) holds that the new penologists sought to remodel the prison on society and that they did so out of the conviction that prisoners could be rehabilitated if, and only if, the prison *socialized* them to be honest, self-governing citizens.[2] Certainly, this is how the new penologists understood and represented their mission: Just as William R. George, in the 1890s, had imagined he was constructing an authentic replica of the American republic at George Junior,[3] when Thomas Mott Osborne fostered the establishment of voting, prisoner government, entertainments, schooling, and athletics at Auburn Prison in 1913, he did so in the belief that he was replicating as nearly as possible the true relations of free society. Osborne appears to have genuinely believed that if prisoners partook in the same kinds of activities in which the free citizenry engaged, they would become good and productive citizens.

In the early 1910s, however, the society upon which Osborne and other new penologists claimed to be modeling the new American prison was far different from the one they imagined. Whereas the new penologists conceived of an America in which labor and capital, men and women, Catholics, Jews, and Protestants, teachers and pupils, immigrants and natives, and white men and black men had broken their "falsely" antagonistic bonds and realized

---

[1] Thomas Mott Osborne, Address to the City Club, New York City, quoted in *New York Times*, Jan. 11, 1914, 8.

[2] David J. Rothman argues that prison reformers of the Progressive Era "reversed" the principles of Jacksonian penology, which had held that the prison should be an "antidote to the community." Progressives endeavored to "model (the prison) on society: it was not to be an antidote to the external environment, but a faithful replication of it." David J. Rothman, *Conscience and Convenience: The Asylum and its Alternatives in Progressive America* (Boston and Toronto: Little, Brown and Co., 1980), 117–18. Frank Tannenbaum, Estelle Freedman, and Lawrence Friedman make similar observations. Frank Tannenbaum, *Wall Shadows: A Study of American Prisons* (New York and London: G. P. Putnam and Sons, 1922); Estelle B. Freedman, *Their Sisters' Keepers: Women's Prison Reform in America, 1830–1930* (Ann Arbor: University of Michigan Press, 1981); Lawrence M. Friedman, *Crime and Punishment in American Society* (New York: Basic, 1993).

[3] Discussed earlier, 330–31.

their common interests, the society in which Americans actually lived and worked in the early 1910s was in the throes of widespread, and frequently violent, upheaval. The industrial states were undergoing what Alan Dawley has described as the most severe industrial relations problem in the [contemporary] Western world.[4] Between 1909 and 1914, hundreds of thousands of laboring men and women around the United States struck, picketed, and marched for higher wages and better conditions, and a revolutionary new labor movement, spearheaded by the Industrial Workers of the World, successfully mobilized new communities of workers – including immigrants, migrants, and African Americans – whom the American Federation of Labor (AFL) and other established labor unions had failed to organize.[5] In New York City and other Northern cities, meanwhile, immigrant women and the college-educated "New Woman" of the middle-class, were making a dead letter of the decades-old American gender conventions of separate spheres and female chastity. These women and their male allies confronted a revived social purity movement, the crusaders in which saw in women's entry into the worldly and traditionally masculine spheres of commerce, politics, and extramarital sexuality the impending decline of American civilization.[6] In the South, meanwhile, the criminal, though rarely policed, practice of lynching was claiming, on average, at least one victim (almost always a black man) every week.[7] The Knights of the Ku Klux Klan were slowly reviving, this time in places like Detroit and Portland and not just Alabama and Mississippi; hundreds of thousands of middle- and lower-middle class Americans were committing themselves to securing "native, white, Protestant supremacy" over Jews, Negroes, foreigners, socialists, and Catholics.[8] Finally, in many parts of the country, the political system was far from the civil, deliberative, and truly republican democracy that supposedly

---

[4] Alan Dawley, *Struggles for Justice: Social Responsibility and the Liberal State* (Cambridge, Massachusetts: Belknap/Harvard University Press, 1991), 84.

[5] In New York, in 1909, thousands of women shirtwaist makers went on strike; two years later, thousands more Chicago clothing workers went on strike in what became known as "the rising of 50,000"; and through 1912 and 1913, spontaneous strikes for higher wages, together with dozens of pickets and marches organized by the Industrial Workers of the World, took place across the industrial states. Dawley, *Struggles for Justice*, 84.

[6] Kathy Peiss, *Cheap Amusements: Working Women and Leisure in Turn-of-the-Century New York* (Philadelphia: Temple University Press, 1986), 88, 95, 101–3; Nancy Cott, *The Grounding of Modern Feminism* (New Haven, Connecticut: Yale University Press, 1987).

[7] Lynching peaked around 1890, when 139 African Americans and 52 Euro-Americans were lynched that year. In the 1910s, lynch victims were almost always African American, and between 50 and 73 African Americans were lynched every year. Orlando Patterson, *Feast of Blood: Consequences of Slavery in Two Centuries* (New York: Basic, 1998), 177. See also, Leon F. Litwack's excellent introductory essay in James Allen, *Without Sanctuary: Lynching Photography in America* (Santa Fe, NM: Twin Palms, 2000); Stewart Emory Tolnay, *A Festival of Violence: an Analysis of Southern Lynchings, 1882–1930* (Urbana: University of Illinois Press, c1995); W. Fitzhugh Brundage, *Under Sentence of Death: Lynching in the South* (Chapel Hill: University of North Carolina Press, 1997).

[8] Kenneth T. Jackson, *The Ku Klux Klan in the City, 1915–1930* (New York: Oxford University Press, 1967).

served as a model for progressive prison reform: Since 1902, a momentous political battle had been waged in the Northern states, as Charles Murphy and other adherents of old-style machine politics recovered from a series of defeats and returned to fight the political equivalent of a war of attrition against the partisans of progressive government.[9]

This America was not the model upon which the prison reformers of the high Progressive Era based their program of reform. The "society" they sought to replicate in prisons existed, but it existed only in reformers' ethical imagination. The new penology was one articulation of progressives' deeply normative vision of a just society. Although the exact contents of that vision varied (as the rich and recently revived historiography of the Progressive Era confirms),[10] at its heart were certain core tenets concerning human nature, morality, and good government. The just society was one in which social relations of all kinds were cooperative rather than antagonistic in nature; where individual and collective morality was developmental, rather than inherent or divine in origin, and was acquired through participatory forms of learning; where being a citizen meant, above all, being a gainfully employed man, actively engaged in the electoral process, and managing one's wages with one's immediate family in mind; and where a paternal state pooled and distributed the legal, technical, and material resources necessary to the task of extinguishing poverty, dangerous working conditions, toxic foods and drugs, and all other material impediments to individual and social flourishing.

In 1914, at Auburn Prison, Thomas Mott Osborne and the Prison Reform Commission had gone some way to constructing a "prison community" on the basis of these general principles; as we have seen, the reforms, which the Prison Reform Commission had carefully marketed to the press, had met with significant interest and a degree of enthusiasm among the public. However, as Osborne and his allies at the National Committee on Prisons and Prison Labor (NCPPL)[11] understood it, Auburn was merely a first, tentative experiment by which they might test the political and institutional waters of a far more systematic and innovative set of reforms. Although well known among penologists and penal administrators, Auburn was nonetheless a backwater, and an institution whose place in the public consciousness was marginal, at best. Sing Sing, conversely, had the potential to be a showpiece laboratory for reform. With its international reputation, scandal-bound past, and proximity to a major metropolis, the "bastille on the Hudson" presented

---

[9] Discussed earlier, 241–42, 259, 281–83, 291–310.

[10] See especially, Daniel T. Rodgers, *Atlantic Crossing: Social Politics in a Progressive Age* (Cambridge, Massachusetts: Belknap/Harvard, 1998); Robert D. Johnston, *The Radical Middle Class: Populist Democracy and the Question of Capitalism in Progressive Era Portland, Oregon* (Princeton, NJ: Princeton University Press, 2003); Michael McGerr, *A Fierce Discontent: The Rise And Fall of the Progressive Movement in America, 1870–1920* (New York: Free Press, 2003); and Alan Dawley, *Changing the World American Progressives in War and Revolution* (Princeton, NJ: Princeton University Press, 2003).

[11] Formerly, the National Committee on Prison Labor.

Osborne and the NCPPL with a remarkable opportunity to demonstrate before the nation the transformative power of a systematic application of the new penology. Mustering a remarkable coalition of industrialists, union leaders, philanthropists, educators, financiers, jurists, filmmakers, journalists, physicians, and psychiatrists to the cause, in 1915, the NCPPL turned Sing Sing into a laboratory, not merely of prison reform, but of social justice. The pages that follow recount the story of that remarkable (although largely forgotten)[12] experiment, and of the final, and uncommonly bitter, political confrontation it precipitated.

*   *   *   *   *

In the wake of the uprising at Sing Sing in the summer of 1913, Warden James M. Clancy had moved to ameliorate the conditions to which the prisoners had so strenuously and so publicly objected. He ordered the painting and replastering of many of the cells and the replacement of the prisoners' moldering bed linen with new, dry sheets. He also arranged for prisoners to spend a few hours less each week locked down in the cellhouse. By the end of 1913, prisoners were spending approximately twelve percent less time in their cells than previously. The food was also improved, and the prisoners on death row (who had been eating the lowest grade of food) were now treated the same as other convicts. In a bid to find more work for the prisoners, Clancy put several dozen to work picking apples in the orchard beyond the prison walls. With few prison guards to spare, the warden instigated an "honor system" of discipline for the apple-pickers (similar to the one that Osborne had introduced at Auburn, and with which Oregon, Colorado, and a handful of other states were experimenting with the "Good Roads" gangs); Clancy also planned the formation of similar honor companies inside the prison walls.[13]

Despite Clancy's efforts to alleviate conditions at the prison, however, Sing Sing remained an unstable and violent institution. According to the hospital records, the prisoners were sustaining more incision and stab wounds from fights and assaults than they had under the wardenship of Tammany's John S. Kennedy.[14] Although the number of hours spent in the cells had been reduced, the practice of double-celling convicts continued: Indeed, in the nine months following Clancy's arrival at Sing Sing in July 1913, the

---

[12] As of going to press, no scholarly account of the Sing Sing experiment has been published. Rothman notes it, but only briefly and without reference to the political context in which it was conceived (and to which it would fall victim). David J. Rothman, *Conscience and Convenience*, 119–22; 131–2.

[13] At the request of Superintendent Riley, the warden arranged for prisoners to be served a Sunday dinner in the mess hall. James W. White, "Facts About Sing Sing" (unpublished report, ca. 1914), OFP, MSS64, Box 276, Org. Recs.

[14] In 1915, the Westchester County Research Bureau examined the Sing Sing hospital records, comparing numbers of emergency cases, incision, and stab wounds for the years 1911–15. This report is the only record of these injuries known to have survived. "Some Facts About Sing Sing Management: Bulletin 2" (unpublished report, 1915), 3, Westchester County Research Bureau, OFP, MSS64, Box 276, Org. Recs.

prison population had increased by ten percent (150 convicts), while available bed space had remained the same. Furthermore, the phenomenon that independent Democrats and progressive state-builders had condemned as corruption continued to pervade the prison industries and offices.[15] According to an investigation undertaken by James White, civilian employees were shirking their work and appropriating state property and labor for their own purposes. The civilian foreman of the cart and wagon shop, for example, made use of convict labor and the state's time to invent and build a specialized sanitation truck, to which he affixed a sign that read "patent pending," before driving it to New York City in the hope of selling a fleet of the trucks to the city's Street Cleaning Department. (Apparently no deal was struck: In the best traditions of the shoddy quality of goods made by forced labor, the truck broke down on the way to New York and once more on the journey back to Sing Sing. It subsequently underwent "constant repair and overhauling").[16]

In the prison storehouse, there were more serious problems. According to investigator White, who carefully reviewed the prison's official Quotation Records and store ledgers (subsequently destroyed), the Chicago meatpacking company that supplied Sing Sing was awarded the prison's contract although other companies had made more competitive bids. Furthermore, the company was routinely underdelivering the orders to the tune of several thousand pounds of meat per year. According to White, the storehouse logs suggested that only two-thirds of the meat paid for was ever received and weighed in by the storekeeper. Once the meat reached Sing Sing, the prison storekeeper then relayed only some of it to the kitchen keeper, illegally retaining a portion, which he then sold to convicts for cash. (When Tammany's John S. Kennedy had been warden, according to White, he had drawn almost three times his legal quota from the store). As a result of these practices, in 1914, there was still an illicit market for meat in the prison, and, according to investigator White, this in turn stimulated a market for sex: Underfed young men, deprived of their full ration, routinely "sold their bodies" to get money for extra food. Although an advocate of progressive reform, after several months of effort, Warden Clancy appeared to have only a little more control over the prison than he had had during the rebellions of 1913.[17]

Clancy's difficulties stemmed in large part from the ongoing political struggle between Charles Murphy's Tammany Democrats, on one side, and Governor William Sulzer and the independent Democrats, on the other. Sulzer's impeachment in the fall of 1913 did not resolve the much larger

---

[15] "Some Facts About Sing Sing Management: Bulletin 2" (unpublished report, 1915), Westchester County Research Bureau, OFP, MSS64, Box 276, Org. Recs; and White, "Some Facts About Sing Sing," 4a–4j.

[16] "Some Facts About Sing Sing Management: Bulletin 2" (unpublished report, 1915), Westchester County Research Bureau, OFP, MSS64, Box 276, Org. Recs; and White, "Some Facts About Sing Sing," 22.

[17] White, "Some Facts About Sing Sing," 28–38, especially 36, 38.

conflict in which Sulzer had been merely one protagonist among many, and Sing Sing remained as deeply enmeshed in the conflict as ever before. Both Sing Sing's fiscal controller, George Jenkins, and the state controller were Tammany men who were singularly uninterested in supporting either Clancy or his reforms, and even though the state attorney general had ordered the restoration of funding to the prison following the 1913 rebellions, the struggle between Tammany and independent Democrats for ascendancy in state government continued to be played out over the fiscal management of Sing Sing. Almost all of Clancy's requests for extra funding for prison improvements were bluntly refused. Ironically, given his progressive credentials, Clancy also found himself impeded by the Civil Service Law, which provided that the prison wardens could not summarily dismiss guards and civilian staff. These laws, which were among the most significant triumphs of the progressive state-builders of the 1890s, protected many of the Tammany employees who actively opposed Clancy and the forces of administrative reform from summary dismissal. Throughout his tenure at Sing Sing, Clancy complained bitterly of the "underground information bureau" by which his plans for change, telephone conversations, and correspondence were constantly leaked to his Tammany opposition in Albany. Unable to build a staff of loyal supporters and facing another funding crisis, Clancy found himself stonewalled at every turn.[18]

Within three months of taking up his appointment, Clancy decided to resign from Sing Sing. His letter of resignation came shortly after his patron, Governor William Sulzer, had been impeached and on the eve of the hotly contested municipal elections in New York City (in which Tammany's leader, Charles Murphy, was a front-running candidate). In the run up to the election, the disgraced Sulzer attempted to discredit the Tammany senators who had impeached him; this inevitably led Sulzer to Sing Sing, where a former Tammany state senator (Stephen Stillwell) was serving time for bribery. It is likely that Sulzer conscripted Warden Clancy in this endeavor by asking him to help procure damaging testimony from Stillwell, of the sort that would irreparably damage the Tammany machine. At some point in October 1913, Warden Clancy arranged and presided over a clandestine meeting between the ex-senator (convict Stillwell) and Clancy's longtime friend and Sulzer-confidante, John A. Hennessy, and allegedly offered Stillwell a full pardon in return for testimony against Stillwell's Tammany friends. In a murky intrigue of political double-crossing and simple blundering, the deal, and Warden Clancy's alleged role in brokering it, was exposed when Hennessy went to press with his "evidence."[19] Implicated in the illicit activity, Warden Clancy

---

[18] The Westchester County Bureau reports include useful comparisons of the wardenships of Kennedy, Clancy, McCormick, and Osborne. See "Some Facts About Sing Sing Management: Bulletins 1–5" (unpublished reports, 1915), Westchester County Research Bureau, OFP, MSS64, Box 276, Org. Recs.

[19] Whether it was out of impatience or sheer duplicity, Hennessy released what he claimed were the detectaphone transcripts of his conversation with Stillwell, along with a letter allegedly authored by the ex-Senator, while Stillwell was still in prison. Subsequently, the

immediately denied the authenticity of the detectaphone transcript and the letter, and angrily denied any role in the affair. When a *New York Times* journalist put it to Clancy that the intensity of his anger implied support for Tammany, Clancy immediately gave Superintendent Riley notice of his resignation.[20]

Superintendent Riley, however, refused to accept the resignation, and publicly reminded the warden that he had posted a $50,000 employment bond to be forfeited upon an unapproved resignation. Grudgingly, Clancy remained in the position and drew up plans for the establishment of new workshops and a recreation and drill ground at the prison. Five months later, and ever more deeply mired in the problems of Sing Sing, Clancy offered his resignation once more, citing the legislature's refusal to grant him the necessary funds for the workshops and grounds, and the latest political scandal to unfold at Sing Sing. (On this occasion, Clancy had attempted and failed to mediate between political enemies over the celebrated case of Lieutenant Charles Becker, the former New York policeman twice sentenced to death for murder and who was widely reputed to have been framed). Perhaps sensing that reform at Sing Sing would be impossible as long as Clancy was warden, Superintendent Riley finally accepted the besieged warden's resignation and began the search for a successor to fill one of the nation's most challenging and scandal-prone wardenships.[21]

In the weeks immediately following Clancy's resignation, prisoners threatened to rebel as they had the summer before. The possibility of another rebellion was underscored in late April, when 180 convicts of the knit shops went on strike, and rumors of more widespread action were heard around the prison. The heightened unrest at Sing Sing and continuing pressure from Tammany prompted Governor Glynn and Superintendent Riley to appoint a Tammany Democrat to the Sing Sing wardenship. The new warden, Thomas McCormick, was a close political ally of Michael Walsh, the acting state controller and Tammany leader of Westchester County who had withheld funding from Sing Sing the previous year and precipitated the worst Sing Sing riot in living memory. By July 1914, Tammany controlled Sing Sing once again.

Despite being opposed to Osborne and other reformers associated with the new penology, the new Tammany warden adapted many of the reformers' techniques to Sing Sing. McCormick's activism may well have been driven by the knowledge that the independent Democrats controlled the administration of Auburn Prison, and that their Prison Reform Chairman (Osborne), was engaged in a bold and well-publicized experiment at that

Governor's office of pardon claimed that Stillwell's application had never reached the office. Hennessy's actions enraged Warden Clancy. For a detailed account of this intrigue, see *New York Times*, Oct. 29, 1913, 1–2; Oct. 30, 1913, 2; Oct. 31, 1913, 9.

[20] *New York Times*, Oct. 29, 1913, 1.

[21] In the spring of 1914, the legislature ignored Clancy's recommendations. He had asked for several thousand dollars for fire protection, $10,000 to build three shops to replace some dilapidated buildings; and $10,000 to extend the prison wall so as to create a drill and recreation area for the convicts. *New York Times*, Apr. 6, 1914, 1.

prison; it was also the case that, regardless of the political and ethical commitments of the wardens, the disciplinary crisis brought on by the long-term decline of prison labor called for innovation, if the prisons were to remain calm and orderly institutions. Shortly after arriving at Sing Sing, Warden McCormick founded a "Golden Rule Brotherhood" that strongly resembled Auburn's Mutual Welfare League (MWL) – except that it reflected a political process and form of government more in keeping with the machine mode of politics. Like the MWL, the Brotherhood had a governing body, an executive, and committees to organize activities such as athletics, baseball, and entertainment.[22] However, unlike the Auburn League, the electoral process of the Sing Sing Brotherhood was indirect: Although, initially, all prisoners were eligible for membership (as at Auburn), they voted for a president who then single-handedly selected his executive committee (unlike at Auburn, where delegates elected the executive). Where the Auburn league had no president, the Sing Sing Brotherhood had a president who was all-powerful and an executive that answered directly to him. Whereas the Auburn system approximated the reformers' ideal of modern political organization, the Sing Sing system reproduced the boss structure of its Tammany administrators.

At the same time as fostering a prisoners' version of the urban political machine, McCormick worked toward establishing various disciplinary activities as alternatives to labor. In 1914, and for the first time in Sing Sing's history, prisoners organized athletic events, baseball, screenings of motion pictures, and entertainments. These activities, together with the relocation of suppertime from the cellblock to the mess hall, meant that the convicts were spending one hour less in the cells each day than previously. McCormick also formally abolished the silence rule in the mess hall, permitting the convicts to talk while they ate, and dropped the punishment of isolation in a dark cell. Like Osborne at Auburn, McCormick put a company of prisoners to work on New York's roads.[23]

Although conditions improved substantially at Sing Sing under Warden McCormick, and the prisoners were much less restive than they had been a

---

22 The Golden Rule Brotherhood's "golden rule" was: "Do Unto others as you would have them do unto you." Its motto was, "Preach, Publish, Practise It." As the constitution of the Brotherhood put it, the organization aimed "To preach, publish a d (sic) practise the spirit and principles of manhood, conduct and mutual good-will." Constitution of the Golden Rule Brotherhood of Sing Sing Prison (ca. 1914), OFP, MSS64, Box 270, File: Organization Records, Mutual Welfare League, Sing Sing Prison, Golden Rule Brotherhood, 1914–15.

23 In the summer of 1914, sixty prisoners were organized into a road camp ("Camp McCormick"), which was put to work on the Kaaterskill-Cleve road near Palenville, New York. Unlike the Auburn Honor Camp, which Osborne had helped organize, conditions at the McCormick Camp were poor. The camp was makeshift, with prisoners sleeping in open-air bunk houses without hot water or bed linen and the food was of very low quality. Eventually, the Highway Department took over the preparation of food and started to supply the road workers with a better diet. Dinner consisted of three ham sandwiches, coffee, and an orange. Inspection of Sing Sing Road Camp (unpublished report prepared by Philip Klein, Sep. 21, 1914), OFP, MSS64, Box 276, Org. Recs. *Star-Bulletin*, 19:3 (August 1917), 7; "Some Facts about Sing Sing Management: Bulletin 1" (unpublished report, 1915), 1–5, Westchester County Research Bureau, OFP, Box 276, Org. Recs.

year earlier, Sing Sing continued to be the subject of well-publicized scandals. Just as Tammany Democrats had tried to pry the prison out of the hands of independent Democrats, the latter sought to wrest control of the prison from the former. With this in mind, Governor Glynn appointed a special commissioner, Stephen O. Baldwin, to investigate warden McCormick in October 1914, following reports that McCormick was consorting with certain wealthy convicts. Baldwin found that McCormick had been using a prisoner, former bank president David A. Sullivan, to drive him around Westchester County in the warden's new automobile.[24] Furthermore, it became apparent that the warden had been chauffeuring Sullivan, and that the prisoner had been seen drinking sodas and transacting personal business in Yonkers. On one occasion, McCormick had reportedly allowed Sullivan to take a four-hour trip to New York City unattended. Furthermore, Baldwin reported, McCormick had acquired the money with which he had paid for his expensive new automobile from a dubious and possibly illegal source: He had borrowed it from Sing Sing's banker-convict. On Baldwin's advice, acting-Governor Glynn suspended Warden McCormick from office in October 1914.[25]

It was at this point in Sing Sing's troubled history, with increasingly critical reports of the state's administration of the prison appearing in the local and national press and the passage of four wardens through the prison gates in as many years, that Thomas Mott Osborne became interested in taking on the wardenship of the prison. He had spent much of the summer of 1914 overseeing the development of the MWL at Auburn Prison and, consistent with the NCPPL's national drive to put prisoners to work on the highways, the creation of convict road gangs in central New York. When McCormick was suspended from the Sing Sing wardenship in October, Osborne's supporters, as well as several hundred prisoners at Sing Sing, urged him to consider taking up the wardenship. The prison administrators in Albany also encouraged Osborne to seek the position: Besieged by successive scandals over Sing Sing, Superintendent Riley needed a warden who would both put a stop to the corruption and insubordination (or, at least end the publicity), and provoke positive reviews of his superintendency. Acting-Governor Martin Glynn, meanwhile, was facing a difficult election battle in November 1914 for the Governor's office: The bitterly divided Democratic party seemed likely to lose to the Republican candidate, Charles S. Whitman, the district attorney of New York City. Under siege both within their own party and by the Republicans, Riley and Governor Glynn looked to Osborne for some traction. They had been impressed by his masterful orchestration of the publicity around the Auburn self-government reforms, and the apparent good order of that prison. Osborne now became the great hope of the independent Democrats.

[24] Sullivan, the former president of the Union Bank, was convicted of appropriating $20,000. *New York Times*, Oct. 25, 1914, 1.
[25] Report of Commissioner Stephen O. Baldwin on Inquiry into Sing Sing Prison (typed manuscript), Oct. 13, 1914, OFP, MSS64, Box 276, Org. Recs. See also, *New York Times*, Oct. 26, 1914, 4; Oct. 27, 1914, 5; Oct. 28, 1914, 1; Oct. 29, 1914, 1.

On Election Day, the Republican Whitman defeated Martin Glynn, thereby throwing Osborne's offer of the Sing Sing wardenship into doubt. Osborne immediately met with governor-elect Whitman to gauge whether his work at Sing Sing would receive the Governor's support. In the months leading up to the election, Whitman had toured Auburn Prison and responded very positively to Osborne's reforms; according to published reports, Whitman now declared he had every confidence in Osborne, and assured the reformer of his full support.[26] (That a Democrat, Osborne, received the blessing of a Republican, Whitman, was something of a coup for independent Democrats, and progressive state-builders more generally, as it suggested that the appointment was in no way partisan). In the meantime, 250 Sing Sing prisoners had signed petitions imploring Osborne to accept the post. As one petition read, Osborne should "put into practice the many excellent ideas you have concerning PRISONS AND PRISONERS" (caps in original).[27] Osborne accepted the wardenship shortly thereafter. "I am not unaware of the many difficulties connected with the position," wrote Osborne in his letter of acceptance, "but the possibilities of service seem great enough to more than counter-balance them."[28] Upon receipt of the news, the *New York Times* underscored what was at stake: Under the front-page headline, "OSBORNE SETS UP CONVICT REPUBLIC," it declared, "Sing Sing Prison is to be the ideal penal institution in the State, or the reform plans of Warden Thomas Mott Osborne ... must be pronounced a failure" (caps in original).[29]

Osborne's appointment to Sing Sing constituted a significant triumph for the champions of the new penology, in general, and for the NCPPL, in particular. E. Stagg Whitin and his fellow reformers at the NCPPL now had an unprecedented opportunity to develop and apply their principles in a thoroughgoing manner. As Whitin, put it: "When Osborne went in as Warden of Sing Sing we obtained a laboratory for working out many of the propositions in which [we] have been interested but have been desiring scientific application."[30] More than simply a laboratory, Sing Sing became an exhibition of the new penology in action and a showpiece for its supporters' plans to spark a systematic overhaul of the nation's penal systems. Under Osborne and with the help of the NCPPL, Sing Sing quickly became a model prison and the institution at the heart of the new penologists' publicity machine. It also became a rallying point for a powerful coalition of civic volunteers,

[26] *New York Times*, Nov. 20, 1914, 1; Thomas Mott Osborne, address to the congregation of the Church of the Ascension, reprinted in *New York Times*, Dec. 7, 1914, 8.

[27] Petition to Thomas Mott Osborne from Sing Sing Prisoners (undated, ca. November 1914), OFP, MSS64, Box 276, Org. Recs.

[28] According to Osborne's biographers, Whitman gave his consent, and on November 30, 1914, Osborne took up residence at Sing Sing as the prison's thirtieth warden and agent. *New York Times*, Nov. 20, 1914, 1.

[29] *New York Times*, Dec. 9, 1914, 1.

[30] Minutes, Meeting of the National Committee on Prisons and Prison Labor (hereafter, NCPPL), Apr. 13, 1915, OFP, MSS64, Box 270, Org. Recs.

penal reform groups, academics, and businessmen who embraced the new penology as the penal "science" appropriate to America's advanced industrial society. The Bastille was now in the hands of penology's vanguard, and that vanguard was becoming increasingly well-funded and supported.

The NCPPL, the leaders of which had already been quite active in the Auburn experiment, now stepped full square into the light as an organizing base and clearing-house for Osborne's reforms at Sing Sing. Within weeks of Osborne's installation at Sing Sing, members of the NCPPL set up committees to work on industrial and educational programs for the prison and invested the first of many substantial amounts of money and voluntary labor into Sing Sing. They were aided in this work by a second organization, the Joint Committee on Prison Reform (JCPR), which had been founded in March 1914 following a series of meetings held by the New York and New Jersey sections of the Women's Department of the National Civic Federation.[31] Formed in the midst of the internecine scandals over Sing Sing, the JCPR's larger objectives conformed to basic new penological principles, including "the elimination of politics from the management of correctional institutions" and the establishment of convict self-government, just compensation for prisoners, and systematic training for wardens and guards.

From the beginning, the JCPR identified "the Sing Sing problem" as its most pressing concern. In the weeks after Osborne took up the wardenship, JCPR members began organizing traveling exhibits, retained a filmmaker to make documentary and educational films about the MWL and life in prison, and ran a number of very successful fundraising events on behalf of the Sing Sing reforms. They also helped to found a third support committee in November, 1915, following a JCPR-sponsored conference on Sing Sing, at the Hotel Belmont; this committee became known as the New York State Prisons Council and it proceeded to marshall support for the Sing Sing reforms from its plush offices at 605 Madison Avenue. Eventually, the Council raised funds for Sing Sing by inviting the general public to subscribe to its local "Welfare League Association." As the leadership saw it, these local support committees were essentially, the outside, popular complement of the MWL inside the prisons and a means of galvanizing public opinion in support of the convict leagues and the new penology in general.[32]

In 1915 and 1916, this coalition of new penologists proceeded to plot out six interlocking fields of action in and around Sing Sing. These were prisoner self-government, labor and labor education, financial education, sexuality and mental health, race relations, and relations among keepers,

---

[31] Its members included Katherine B. Davis, Mrs. William Emerson; George W. Kirchwey; Adolph Lewisohn; Seth Low, ex-officio president of the National Civic Federation; and E. Stagg Whitin. The JCPR's membership overlapped with that of the NCPPL but was not entirely the same.

[32] The original Council members were Osborne, Wickersham, Dr. Walter B. James, Alice Preston, Judge William H. Wadhams, Arnold W. Brunner, Geo. Kirchwey, Dean F. A. Coetz, and E. Stagg Whitin. Most of these reformers also belonged to either the JCPR or the NCPPL. The Council set up offices at 605 Madison Ave., in New York City.

administrators, and prisoners. By simultaneously acting in these fields, the new penologists hoped to rapidly set in place a comprehensive set of programs that would ensure the majority of convicts became manly citizens, who, upon release from prison, would participate in the civilian economy as waged producers, consumers, financial planners, and husbands and fathers. Outside the prison, the new penologists launched a series of aggressive publicity campaigns that were designed to educate civilian Americans about the immorality and inefficiency of the "old system" and the promise of the new penology to make America a stronger, safer, socially just nation.

The first major reform measure undertaken at Osborne's Sing Sing was to transform former Warden McCormick's self-government league (the Golden Rule Brotherhood) into a MWL along the Auburn lines.[33] Much as he had done at Auburn, Osborne organized constitutional conventions and elections.[34] He also sent for a delegation of Auburn convicts to go down to Sing Sing to consult with the Sing Sing prisoners about how best to operate a league. Elections were held, and within a few weeks, Sing Sing prisoners began organizing convict-taught classes along the Auburn lines; the league's entertainment committee was bringing in outside performers, musicians, lecturers, and films; and various other league committees were consulting with the warden on matters ranging from religious services to the beautification of the prison graveyard. As summer approached, the convicts established a baseball league (outfitted thanks to the New York Yankees' donation of a complete kit of gear and uniforms for twenty-eight players), organized baseball and athletic competitions, and hosted visiting civilian teams.[35] The band practiced its marches and the 250 convicts of Sing Sing's first Choral Society sang for the prison. Sing Sing convicts also organized a knitting class to supply clothing for the Polish victims of the Great War. Convict "judiciary" committees began to convene in the Chapel, and convicts and guards took their minor complaints (such as spitting in the Chapel, impertinence, and disorderly behavior), to the "court" for adjudication. The league set up a garden committee that, thanks to donations of plants and tools by *New York*

33 The organization retained the name "Golden Rule Brotherhood" for some time, but eventually changed in to "Mutual Welfare League, Sing Sing Branch."

34 Osborne's first step was to transform warden McCormick's "Golden Rule Brotherhood" into the "Mutual Welfare League, Sing Sing Branch." As at Auburn, the prisoners were invited to convene without guards and discuss plans for setting up the new league. Few records from these meetings have survived, but newspaper reports, the new MWL constitution, and the transcripts of several prisoner disciplinary tribunals suggest that the Sing Sing League operated in much the same manner as the Auburn branch. The critical difference between the Auburn and Sing Sing branches of the MWL was the rule governing eligibility for membership. At Auburn, any prisoner could join the league upon taking an oath; at Sing Sing only those who could read, write, and speak the English language were eligible to join. This had been the case with the Golden Rule Brotherhood, and the rule was carried over into the new constitution, which was written in March of 1915. This rule effectively excluded twenty percent of the prisoners, most of whom were Italian, German, Polish, and Russian immigrants.

35 *New York Times*, Aug. 28, 1916, 9; *New York Times*, Apr. 30, 1916, 15; June 21, 1915, 16; Apr. 26, 1915, 16; Apr. 27. 1915, 10.

Garden Magazine, began planting flowers and shrubs for the first time at Sing Sing.[36] Within four months of Osborne's arrival at Sing Sing, the league was operating much as Auburn's did, and the everyday life of the prison had been transformed.[37]

With the support of his new penological coalition, Osborne then set about restructuring the prison's industries and training programs. Working in conjunction with the prisoner MWL, the reformers instigated procedures by which incoming convicts would be assigned to "suitable" labor in the prison, selected for industrial training classes, and matched with prospective employers upon release from prison. With money provided by the NCPPL,[38] the MWL set up an employment bureau at Sing Sing in January 1915. This bureau, which consisted of two league officials (prisoners) and the prison agent, Charles Blumenthal, segregated every incoming convict in the "Awkward Squad" for the first two to four weeks of his sentence, and interviewed him for the purposes of matching him to a suitable work company. Following several weeks of interviewing and instruction, the "awkward" convict was then assigned to the appropriate work company on the basis of the bureau's assessment of his mental and physical condition.[39]

In attempting a comprehensive reconstruction of Sing Sing's labor companies, Osborne sought both the financial and practical aid of big business and the consent of the trade unions and the American Federation of Labor. In accordance with the progressives' conception of the need for cooperation among the state, labor, and capital, the NCPPL's employment bureau actively pursued the involvement of the AFL in the restructuring of work companies at Sing Sing. The new penologists were aware that the support, or at least neutrality, of organized labor would be essential to their efforts.[40] Moreover, they recognized that organized labor was more likely to support the programs if prisoners were able to join trade unions either while still incarcerated or upon release. Almost immediately following Osborne's appointment at Sing Sing, the NCPPL consulted with Collis Lovely (the vice-president of the Boot and Shoe Workers International Union) and Hugh Frayne (the New York representative of the AFL), about the restructuring

---

[36] Report of the Outside Branch of the Mutual Welfare League (hereafter OBMWL), (prepared by Arthur Wood, 1916), OFP, MSS64, Box 269, Org. Recs.

[37] Tannenbaum, *Osborne of Sing Sing,* 124–33. Few documents pertaining to the Golden Rule Brotherhood have survived. Tannenbaum's account is based on interviews and first-hand observation.

[38] Including a donation by Mrs. A. D. Smith, the wife of future New York Governor, Al Smith. "MWL Employment Bureau" (NCPPL pamphlet, Feb. 1915), OFP MSS64, Box 271, Org. Recs.

[39] "MWL Employment Bureau" (NCPPL pamphlet, Feb. 1915), OFP MSS64, Box 271, Org. Recs.

[40] Since the 1830s, organized free workers had protested the use of convict labor in direct competition with free labor: As the new penologists were acutely aware, organized labor's opposition to contract prison labor and to the sale of convict-made goods on the open market had effectively led to the destruction or, otherwise, severe scaling back of prison industries in New York and elsewhere (see earlier discussion in Chapters 4 and 5).

of prison industries. Subsequently, in January 1915, for the first time in Sing Sing's history, unionists went to Sing Sing Prison to discuss prison industries and labor with the convicts. In the presence of officials from the NCPPL, the unionists and convict leaders of the league discussed the question of whether or not the unions should organize convicts. By the end of this meeting, the labor organizers had assured the league that any prisoners who were "properly trained" could join up while still incarcerated, and that the AFL would work out a method by which the prisoners could pay their membership dues. The minutes of this significant meeting have not survived, but judging from newspaper accounts of the interviews, it is likely that Collis Lovely openly solicited convict membership in his union: The union, he promised, would protect the prisoner member from "evil influence and the opposition of enemies." The problem with the unions' offer of membership to "properly trained" prisoners, was that it was difficult to fulfill the criterion of proper training at Sing Sing. The industries were outmoded by free market standards, and the few industrial education classes in existence did not afford adequate instruction.[41] Apparently acknowledging the limitations of the proposal, the AFL subsequently undertook to help Osborne and the NCPPL overhaul the prison industries. Shortly following the initial visit of Lovely and Frayne, a delegation of AFL leaders joined Osborne and the NCPPL's Frederick Goetz and E. Stagg Whitin in Albany to discuss a comprehensive program of labor reform in New York's state prisons.[42]

Osborne and Whitin pursued material and political resources from industry as well. A number of American business leaders were quick to support Osborne – in both the financial and discursive senses. In the weeks following Osborne's installation at Sing Sing, leading industrialists and financiers convening in New York for a meeting of the U.S. Industrial Relations Committee discussed the question of convicts and their rehabilitation. Henry Ford (of the Ford Motor Company) testified that former convicts from Sing Sing could and should be "reclaimed" as responsible citizen–workers.[43] Convinced of convicts' potential as disciplined consumers and producers, Ford was joined by John D. Rockefeller and a number of New York City stockbrokers and bankers in donating substantial amounts of money, equipment, expertise, and publicity to the Sing Sing experiment. As negotiations continued with organized labor, Ford and a number of other large industrial corporations worked on arrangements both to train convicts and to provide

---

[41] "MWL Employment Bureau" (NCPPL pamphlet, Feb. 1915), OFP, MSS64, Box 271, Org. Recs.

[42] *Evening Post* (NY), Feb. 2, 1915, OFP, MSS64, Box 342, Scrapbooks.

[43] *New York Times*, Feb. 17, 1915, OFP, MSS64, Box 342, Scrapbooks. Very little is known about the extent of the involvement of large American corporations in prison reform before World War II. The newspaper reports, correspondence, and prison bulletins discussed here suggest that further research into this question is much needed. In particular, evidence of employment schemes such as that of the Ford Motor Company suggest that the relationship between the rise of the mass carceral state and Fordist forms of industrial organization warrants further analysis.

them with employment upon release. In April 1915, Western Union Telegraph installed equipment at the prison and started a training class in telegraphy for sixty prisoners. The Pennsylvania Railroad Company also began to recruit New York prisoners for employment upon release, and sent an Italian-speaking employee to instruct the Italians at Sing Sing. The well-known New York stockbroker, Frank M. Dick, donated equipment for a mechanical drawing room, automobiles for instruction in car assembly, and typewriters for the stenography class. Dick also waged a campaign to have other businesses set up employment schemes.[44] By October, 1916, Sears Roebuck and Co, Pullman, Burroughs Adding Machine, Packard Motor, Emerson Drug, Pittsburgh Coal, Carnegie Steel, Winchester Repeating Arms, and a number of other large national companies had joined Ford and International Harvester in seeking ex-convicts for employment.[45]

Of all the companies involved in the reforms in New York State, the Ford Motor Company was perhaps the most deeply engaged. Henry Ford took an immediate interest in Osborne's work at Sing Sing. In February of 1915, he boasted that he could "guarantee to take any convict from Sing Sing and make a man of him." A few weeks later, he toured Sing Sing's workshops and addressed the prisoners, and then made arrangements with Osborne for former Sing Sing convicts to go west to Detroit to work in his auto-plant.[46] Shortly after Ford's visit to Sing Sing, Osborne began sending the Ford Motor Company the records of every prisoner about to be released, and Ford's Sociology Department used these to create a "card index" of prospective employees. Ford's eastern agents then commenced interviewing those newly released convicts the Sociology Department deemed potentially suited to labor on the auto assembly line. If a convict were hired, he was given a new set of clothes, a new legal name, and a one-way ticket to Detroit.[47] Osborne's friend and ally, Warden Charles Rattigan, also instituted the scheme at Auburn Prison, and throughout 1915 and 1916, a steady stream of ex-convicts headed west for employment.[48] A number of ex-convicts also began working on Ford's Long Island assembly line.[49] In the meantime, it was reported in the newspapers that Henry Ford had written to a number of other Midwestern manufacturers, encouraging them to initiate similar prison schemes.[50]

[44] *The World*, Apr. 13, 1915, OFP, MSS64, Box 342, Scrapbooks.

[45] Henry Ford, quoted in *New York Times*, Oct. 22, 1916, 12.

[46] Upon returning to Detroit, Ford's secretary wrote Osborne that his employer had found Sing Sing "splendid," and he invited Osborne to visit the Ford plant in Detroit as there "is much we can bring you in your magnificent work." C. A. Brownell to Osborne, Detroit, May 13, 1915, OFP, MSS64, Box 114, Correspondence.

[47] *New York Times*, Feb. 17, 1915, OFP, MSS64, Box 342, Scrapbooks.

[48] *The Bulletin*, Mutual Welfare League, Auburn Branch (Jun. 3, 1916), OFP, MSS64, Box 270, Org. Recs.

[49] Shortly after Henry Ford visited Sing Sing, Osborne began personally referring prisoners to the manager of the Ford factory in Long Island City, New York. Osborne to Gaston Plaintiff (Ford Motor Company, Long Island City), Ossining, May 15, 1915, OFP, MSS64, Box 114, Correspondence.

[50] *New York Times*, Feb. 17, 1915, OFP, MSS64, Box 342, Scrapbooks.

It is difficult to estimate what proportion of the convicts of the state of New York secured work at the Ford factories in Detroit or on Long Island. Although Henry Ford spoke publicly about his interest in reclaiming convicts by giving them employment upon release, the Ford Motor Company was less than open about the specific details of its arrangements with Sing Sing and Auburn. When the *New York Times* sought confirmation of the Sing Sing scheme, the head of Ford's Sociology Department refused to acknowledge that an official arrangement existed, and simply noted that former convicts from Sing Sing and other prisons were arriving daily at the Ford's "Crystal Palace" in Michigan.[51] The following year, however, S. S. Marquis of Ford's Education Department was far more explicit about the arrangement. In a private letter to Auburn's Warden Rattigan, he explained that the company's policy was "to take on as large a number" of former convicts as possible and that the company was receiving many applications from convicts from Auburn, Sing Sing, and other New York state prisons. Although he did not specify how many prisoners were arriving each day, he did comment that too many convicts from Auburn Prison were now arriving at the factory without having first received an offer of employment. (He instructed the warden that only those prisoners who had been given a written offer before leaving prison should go west to Detroit).[52]

Just as the new penologists argued that industrial corporations were essential to the restructuring of convict laboring practices, they actively sought the involvement of civilian educational institutions in the development of academic and vocational courses at Sing Sing. They did not have to lobby hard. In the early months of 1915, as Osborne commenced the reform of Sing Sing, the élite activists of the NCPPL and the JCPR were joined by faculty from the schools of law, education, science, and engineering at Columbia University. With the encouragement of Osborne, these academics set up educational classes at Sing Sing and provided the support committees with meeting and fundraising space (most notably, Columbia's Earl Hall).

[51] John R. Lee, head of the company's sociological department, said there was no special arrangement, and Ford's secretary, E. G. Leibold, said he "knew of no such agreement." Quoted in *New York Times*, Feb. 17, 1915, OFP, MSS64, Box 342, Scrapbooks. It is possible that the Ford employees' secretiveness about the convict employment scheme arose from frequent and recurring rumors that the company was building a private security force of ex-convicts. Frank Browning and John Gerassi argue that Ford went on to hire more than 8,000 convicts in the 1930s, many of whom worked for the company's security force (the Service Department) as "corporate vigilantes." In 1935, the New York City newspaper, *PM*, carried a story about one former employee, Ralph Rinear, who confirmed many of the rumors about Ford's force of ex-convicts. Browning and Gerassi, *The American Way of Crime* (New York: G. P. Putnam and Sons, 1980), 393–4, 405. The company still appears to view records pertaining to the employment of convicts as confidential: Although there is evidence (most notably the correspondence between the company and New York prison wardens) that arrangements of some sort existed, Stephen's Meyer's otherwise thorough study of Ford's Sociological Department does not discuss the hiring of convicts, which implies that such records are not readily available. Stephen Meyer, *The Five Dollar Day: Labor, Management, and Social Control in the Ford Motor Company, 1908–1921* (Albany: State University of New York Press, 1981).
[52] *The Bulletin*, Mutual Welfare League, Auburn Branch (June 3, 1916), OFP, MSS64, Box 270, Org. Recs.

Their work enabled Sing Sing to offer convicts a comprehensive education. Moreover, the involvement of Columbia academics, as well as people with higher degrees from other prestigious institutions, conferred intellectual and ethical credibility on the Sing Sing experiment.[53]

With the aid of voluntary labor from Columbia, the Massachusetts Institute of Technology, and the convicts themselves, Osborne initiated Sing Sing's first comprehensive educational and training classes. In March 1915, Professor Egbert of Columbia University's Extension Department began developing plans for a night school. By April 1915, members of the NCPPL's education committee, which included Columbia faculty and worked in consultation with Prof. Egbert and the Dean of Teachers College, James Russell, had arranged English literacy classes at Sing Sing by day, and a night class in automechanics.[54] Over the following year, the NCPPL organized several other classes: Sing Sing's first class in telegraphy, taught by a volunteer civilian with a degree from MIT, was underway by February 1916, by which time dozens of prisoners were enrolled in classes in civics, drafting, physics, English literature, and history.[55]

One of the most striking aspects of these new penological reforms at Sing Sing is that all were undertaken without formal funding from the state: The new industries, classes, and recreational activities were almost entirely funded by the NCPPL, philanthropic reform groups, and American corporations. This support extended to the supplementation of civilian employees' wages: In October 1916, for example, the NCPPL's education committee decided to supplement the Sing Sing industrial instructor's salary. It also included tools, materials, and teaching aids; the NCPPL provided Sing Sing with a large number of textbooks, an automobile and parts for the workshop, and a printing press for Auburn Prison. It also provided the convicts' new "Aurora" band and orchestra a complete set of musical instruments, valued at $3,000, and employed a military band leader to train the musicians.[56]

The new penologists solicited the involvement of capitalists, educators, and elite philanthropists in their reforms at Sing Sing because they realized both that little financial support would be forthcoming from the state, and that "at any and at all times, the latch-key is on the outside" of the prison (as Henry Ford's secretary once pointedly remarked to Osborne). Former prisoners were less likely to offend again if they had secure employment, they argued, and the most efficacious way of providing employment was to

---

[53] In early 1915, the NCPPL sought to capitalize on Columbia's support by making press releases that emphasized what one leading member described as the university's semi-official cooperation with Osborne. Dr. E. Stagg Whitin made a press statement on April 13 announcing Columbia's support: "Columbia University has for weeks been co-operating semi-officially with Warden Osborne in his development of trade education at Sing Sing Prison." *The World*, Apr. 14, 1915, 18, OFP, MSS64, Box 342, Scrapbooks.

[54] *The World*, Apr. 14, 1915, 18, OFP, MSS64, Box 342, Scrapbooks.

[55] *The Bulletin*, Mutual Welfare League, Sing Sing Branch (Feb. 14), 1916, OFP, MSS64, Box 269, Org. Recs.

[56] Minutes of a Meeting of the Executive Council, NCP(PL) (Oct. 31, 1916), OFP, MSS64, Box 271, Org. Recs.; President's Report, NCPPL, 1917, OFP, MSS64, Box 342, Scrapbooks.

involve large companies such as Ford and Western Union, which, unlike New York's divided state government, had the capacity and will to revamp prison industries and to absorb significant numbers of ex-convicts. Moreover, the tremendous support accorded Osborne by capitalists, academics, and civic reformers allowed him to bypass the fraught and highly politicized process of requesting funding from the Tammany-dominated Controller's office and the state legislature: Osborne could effect sweeping changes without permission from Albany politicians and bureaucrats. By freeing Sing Sing from Tammany's purse strings, the new penological coalition significantly reduced the influence of Tammany Democrats on prison life. At the same time, in disregarding the usual legislative channels by which to procure funding for development, the new penological coalition insulated the prison from democratic processes, whether those processes were dominated by old-style machine politics or the progressive, commission-driven style of government.

While the new penologists and the Ford Motor Company and other corporations sought to restructure Sing Sing's industries and make arrangements for postrelease employment, the AFL became increasingly cautious about participating in industrial and labor reform at Sing Sing. By April 1915, the AFL's New York representative, Hugh Frayne, was circumspect when asked by the *New York Times* about the extent of the AFL's commitment to prison reform: Avoiding the question, he merely noted that should the AFL join the reform efforts at Sing Sing, it would do so in a sustained and systematic manner, and not in the "hit-or-miss" approach of Ford and the other corporations.[57] Frayne's appraisal of industrial reform at Sing Sing was accurate: The development of Sing Sing's industrial training was patchy, being mostly confined to telegraphy and automobile assembly. The labor unions did not become fully involved; the records suggest that the only convicts to join a union were a handful of musicians from Sing Sing's new "Aurora Band," who went on to find union-listed employment after their release from prison.

The new penologists' efforts to find postrelease employment for former prisoners were more sustained, and former convicts helped administer the new scheme. In February 1916, ex-convicts set up the Outside Branch of the Mutual Welfare League (OBMWL). Its aims were to help former prisoners to find employment and to generally assist them. A number of elite reformers supported the Outside Branch through fundraising and organizing. The bureau was staffed by former prisoners, in office space provided by the New York Prison Council on 28th Street in New York City, and prominent penal reformers sat on a number of the Outside Branch's committees. Only the most cursory of documents pertaining to the Committee's operations have survived, but these suggest that by mid-1916, the Employment Committee was operating a large-scale job-search service for New York convicts. Working in conjunction with the "inside" league, in one month alone (April 1916) they sent out 1,200 letters seeking employment and received 300 favorable

57 *The World*, Apr. 14, 1915, 18, OFP, MSS64, Box 342, Scrapbooks.

replies, with offers of jobs in a number of American cities.[58] The NCPPL also expanded its involvement in the placement of former convicts in 1916, by which time its Committee on Employment had three subdivisions: one to find openings, another to match prisoners with employers, and a third to assist families to find employment. The Committee's new Employment Bureau in New York City began working in conjunction with the Outside Branch to find work for former prisoners: In the first nine months of 1916, these efforts resulted in the employment of 411 former prisoners.[59]

The restructuring of labor and training, and the establishment of job placement programs at Sing Sing, were a critical aspect of the new penological strategy to socialize convicts as manly worker–citizens in an industrialized economy. A second, related, field of action was that of personal financial responsibility. At Sing Sing, the new penologists set about disciplining prisoners as consumers and small investors capable of providing for their immediate needs while planning for the future: In other words, prisoners had to be taught not only how to make a wage, but how to save and spend it. As the authorities understood it, the convict was a citizen-in-training, and the best way to train a citizen was "to teach [him] the basic principles of monetary systems on larger scales . . . and teach economy."[60] This principle, which Osborne had first encountered while on the board of the George Junior Republic for children, now became a critical part of the experiment at Sing Sing.

Here, Osborne and his supporters took the idea of "modeling the prison on society" to an entirely new level: They set about simulating what they imagined to be the ideal conditions and relations of civil society. Beginning in 1915, every prisoner at Sing Sing was paid a wage in the specie of token aluminum coin and paper notes bearing the imprint Mutual Welfare League ("MWL"). Each convict was to be assured a minimum weekly wage of $6 but, in the spirit of Taylorist conceptions of motivation and incentive, additional income would be accrued by extra output. The prisoner was then to use his earnings to pay for what Osborne called the "cost of living" at the prison. Over the next year, Sing Sing prisoners proceeded to pay for breakfast (10¢), dinner (25¢), and the barber, laundry, bath, hospital care, and clothing. Convicts also paid weekly cell rental, or, as Osborne described it, room rental, which ranged from $1 to $1.60 per week. In seeking to simulate the civilian economy as nearly as possible, the rent for cells on the upper tiers, known as walk-ups, was lower than for those on the lower tiers, just as in Manhattan's tenements. As some convicts made and saved more of

[58] The wages ranged from between $9 and $22 per week. Report, Outside Branch of the Mutual Welfare League (hereafter OBMWL) (ca. December 1916), OFP, MSS64, Box 269, Org. Recs.

[59] Report, Outside Branch of the Mutual Welfare League (hereafter OBMWL) (ca. December 1916), OFP, MSS64, Box 269, Org. Recs.

[60] Report from the Treasury Department, Mutual Welfare League, Sing Sing Branch (ca. May 1916), OFP, MSS64, Box 270, Org. Recs.; *New York Times*, Oct. 10, 1915, OFP, MSS64, Box 270, Org. Recs.

their token wages, they could rent a more expensive room; those whose productivity fell off, or who spent their tokens unwisely, faced the possibility of having to give up better cells for worse ones.

It was estimated that the average cost of living was $4.65 per week, which left the convict with a surplus of at least $1.35. Consequently, to complete the simulation of a civil economy in which prisoners would be disciplined as consumers and producers, Osborne opened Sing Sing's own "Self Government Bank and Insurance Company." Nine prisoners were appointed directors, all of whom had to be stock holders in the bank (their capital consisted of league tender), and convict customers were provided with deposit notebooks, similar to those used by civilians.[61] Prisoners could deposit and withdraw their "money" from the bank, and they could also purchase health and accident insurance, which would cover the costs of any unforeseen medical expenses. As one of the convict Treasury officials put it, business was "conducted on the same basis as any bank on the outside, having the appearance of a real bank with all the small signs and advertisements found in any well conducted banking establishment." Mirroring the new penological rhetoric back on its authors, the convict treasurer continued:

> To note the eager expression upon the men's faces as they appear before the receiving teller's window with their small deposit books, would convince you that they are being taught responsibility which the actual handling and earning of money produce in a man, and that responsibility and thrift they are forming in here, and absolutely essential to every man will, we presume, continue upon a man's release.[62]

Notably, Osborne made no formal provision for taxation; however, the prisoners set up an approximation of a taxation system, by which they required every league member to donate one month's wages to the league every year, for the purpose of setting up a memorial fund to pay for the funeral of any deceased convict whose family could not or would not pay for a civilian funeral and burial.[63]

Whether or not the Sing Sing prisoners in fact became well-disciplined consumers and producers, as the new penologists and convict stock holders purported, they made great use of the Self Government Bank. By May 1916, $31,424.41 league "dollars" were on deposit, and between two-thirds and three-quarters of the prisoners had accounts at the bank, most of which contained between ten and fifty league "dollars."[64] Previously, when they had

---

[61] Report from the Treasury Department, Mutual Welfare League, Sing Sing Branch (ca. May 1916), OFP, MSS64, Box 270, Org. Recs.; Statement, Self Government Bank and Insurance Company, Mutual Welfare League, Sing Sing Branch (May 2, 1916), OFP, MSS64, Box 270, Org. Recs.

[62] Report from the Treasury Department, Mutual Welfare League, Sing Sing Branch (ca. May 1916), 3, OFP, MSS64, Box 270, Org. Recs.

[63] Untitled report, re. establishment of MWL memorial fund (undated), 1, OFP, MSS64, Box 270, Org. Recs.

[64] Statement, Self Government Bank and Insurance Company, Mutual Welfare League, Sing Sing Branch (May 2, 1916), OFP, MSS64, Box 270, Org. Recs.

been paid by the state, prisoners had earned 1.5¢ (U.S. legal tender) per day, and this money had been payable upon release from prison. To make the incentive as strong as possible, Osborne and the league leadership discussed ways of facilitating a similar redemption system for the token wages. It was not clear how this would be facilitated, until October 1916, when the NCPPL set about raising money for this purpose. With the help of the Outside Branch of the League, which donated $1,000 to the fund, the NCPPL raised over $10,000 in legal tender.

The third, and equally critical component of the new penological disciplinary regime at Sing Sing was the development of techniques aimed at the discovery, classification, and eradication of sexual relations among prisoners. Sex had almost certainly been going on in prisons since the first prison was built. But the opportunity for sex had probably been much more restricted in the hard-labor prisons of the nineteenth century;[65] and when hard industrial labor collapsed in many American prisons, as the contract system was dismantled, opportunities (and perhaps prisoners' energy) for sex were greatly multiplied. Prison administrators of the early twentieth century appear to have known that prisoners were having sexual relations with one another. Nonetheless the subject was not openly discussed or theorized in any sustained manner. This began to change in the 1910s. From the point of view of a penology committed to the socialization of prisoners as self-governing manly citizens, sexual relations between men posed a particularly urgent problem. Through the lens of the prevailing gender ideology of early twentieth century (as George Chauncey has documented it),[66] sex between men was intrinsically emasculating of at least one partner – the supposedly passive "receiver," whether or not the sex was consensual. Such a feminized position, as it were, contradicted precisely the ideal of manly subjectivity that the new penologists sought to realize in prisoners. Added to this difficulty was the problem of "manly discipline": The new penologists hued to an ascending, middle-class view that, rather than reflexively act on their sexual passions, men ought to channel or sublimate those passions into activities deemed socially or personally useful. On this view, then, the active or penetrative partner, although supposedly the masculine partner in the act, was failing to exercise manly self-discipline; he, too, presented a challenge to the manly ideal. In their Sing Sing laboratory, Osborne and his

---

[65] There is some evidence that Sing Sing prisoners engaged in sexual relations with each other in the 1870s and 1880s: In 1871, Warden Gaylord B. Hubbell reported the prevalence of "great abuses" in the prison, and the 1882 New York Special Assembly Committee (which was appointed to investigate charges of corruption and immorality at Sing Sing) reported that "sodomy" was practiced at Sing Sing. Timothy Gilfoyle, *A Pickpocket's Tale: The Underworld of Nineteenth-Century New York* (New York: Norton, 2006) (unpublished mss., Ch. 7); NYSAD (1882) No. 131, 222–9. For an extended discussion of sexual practices at Sing Sing in the 1870s and 1880s, see Gilfoyle, *A Pickpocket's Tale* (mss., Ch. 7). See also Roger Panetta, "Up the River: A History of Sing Sing in the Nineteenth Century," (Ph.D. diss., City University of New York, 1998), 299.

[66] George Chauncey, *Gay New York: Gender, Urban Culture, and the Making of the Gay Male World, 1890–1940* (New York: Basic, 1994).

fellow penologists proceeded to drag prison sexuality into the light of day, examine it, and "cure" it.

Fragments of evidence from the New York prison records of the early 1910s suggest that sex among prisoners at Sing Sing and elsewhere had been happening for some years. In some instances, it involved physical coercion, but in many it did not. As James White's report had suggested, sex was being traded for food or money as a matter of course.[67] Various reports also suggested that, before Osborne arrived at Sing Sing, such relations mostly went unpunished, and that when a person was punished in connection with prison sex, it was usually in connection with a sexual attack. It was not the aggressor, however, who received the punishment: Any prisoner who complained to the warden that he had been coerced into sex, and any prisoner who sought protection from coerced sex, was likely to be severely disciplined, while the alleged attacker – or attackers – would probably not be disciplined at all.[68] (One of Osborne's predecessors at Sing Sing, Warden John Kennedy, had sometimes gone so far as to send the complainant, rather than the alleged attacker, to New York's most feared prison – Clinton). Similarly, when Superintendent Riley heard of cases of sexual assault occurring during Osborne's wardenship, he proceeded to order the transfer of the complainants to Clinton, which suggests that the punishment of the complainant was standard practice. Indeed, it is likely that the act of complaining, and not the act of sodomy *per se*, was cause for punishment in prisons of the 1900s and early 1910s.

Osborne and the new penologists broke with the usual approach to prison sex, and on a number of counts. First and most conspicuously, Osborne discoursed at some length – and in public – on what had thitherto been the taboo topic of sex in prison; in true progressive style, Osborne argued that in order to solve the problem, one had first to study and understand it. Describing sex between convicts as "vile" and as a "problem…which should no longer be ignored," Osborne made it clear that he considered sex between men to be one of the most serious and little-understood problems of the American prison. In his early speeches and writings on the topic, Osborne drew distinctions between different kinds of men who engaged in sex with other men. On the one hand, he explained to members of the NCPPL, there was the man who "allows himself to be [sexually] used"; on

---

[67] See Golden Rule Brotherhood transcripts. A convict nurse testified to the convict court that examinations for evidence of anal penetration were not unusual in the prison hospital. He had personally assisted at a dozen such procedures. In a report to Warden Osborne, the Sing Sing convict stenographer claimed that sodomy had gone on before Osborne's arrival, but that it had been "*UNDER COVER*" – and added that Osborne had given the prisoners "a chance to work and play and thus find a natural outlet for the excess animal vigor" (emphasis his). Transcript, "In the Matter of the Inquiry into the Case of G – S – ," Golden Rule Brotherhood (Jan. 21, 1915), OFP, MSS64, Box 270, Org. Recs.; W. B. Thompson, "By Way of Explanation," (unpublished manuscript, ca. Oct. 1916), 2, OFP, Box 278, Org. Recs.

[68] James W. White reported on two incidents of gang rape in which the attackers appear to have gone unpunished. White, "Some Facts About Sing Sing," 38.

the other, there was the man whose "passions are cut off from natural relief." The latter, according to Osborne, was simply acting on an "ordinary" sexual impulse that, because of the deprived conditions of incarceration, had been directed toward a man, rather than a woman. As Osborne wrote in *Prisons and Commonsense*, "Here is a group of men – mostly young and by no means deficient in the natural passions of youth – but cut off from the natural means of satisfying them."[69] Osborne refined this rather crude typology a few years later, in a tripartite taxonomy recalling Sigmund Freud's 1909 classification of inverts in *Three Essays on the Theory of Sexuality*: According to Osborne, in prisons one found the "degenerate," whose "dual nature" made him the passive (and therefore feminine) partner of active, masculine men; the "wolves," a popular term that Osborne appropriated to describe aggressive men who consistently preferred men to women; and the "ordinary men," whose incarceration deprived them of their "natural" sex outlet – sex with women – and who consequently made use of other prisoners as "the only outlet" they could get.[70]

Finding ways to channel the natural passions of "ordinary" men and youths turned out to be one of Osborne's key projects at Sing Sing: Indeed it was a recurring theme of his wardenship. Osborne developed several tactics in his fight against the "vile" practice: He emptied the cellblock of the surplus of prisoners (whom he installed in a dormitory), so as to ensure that there was only one man per cell;[71] he attempted to direct the natural passions of the supposedly ordinary men to nonsexual activities; he implored the MWL to police prisoners' sexuality and to "condemn vice and encourage a manly mastery of the passions;"[72] he set about identifying and isolating both the "degenerate" men who offered themselves as passive partners and the "wolves" who actively preferred other men;[73] and he redoubled his efforts

---

[69] Thomas Mott Osborne, *Prisons and Commonsense* (Philadelphia: J. B. Lippincott, 1924), 88.

[70] Note that Osborne writes the term "wolves" in speech marks. As George Chauncey has argued, this was a popular term in New York City in the 1910s and 1920s. Chauncey, *Gay New York*, 58, 88–96.

[71] In his first few months at Sing Sing, Osborne set up an additional dormitory so that no convict would share a cell with another. When this tactic failed (largely because Superintendent Riley prohibited it), Osborne ruled that only blood relatives and in-laws could be cellmates.

[72] Later, Osborne would write that "sodomy" could only be extinguished with the cooperation of the prisoners. He insisted that the Mutual Welfare Leagues punish those convicts known to engage in voluntary sexual relations, and reserved for the warden cases involving assault. Osborne reversed the practice of punishing the victim and began transferring the aggressor to Clinton or Dannemora. In one outstanding case concerning an apparently voluntary sexual encounter (wherein eighteen men admitted to having had sexual relations with one man), Osborne put the eighteen men to work digging a sewer for the prison. Osborne, handwritten notes for speech to the Legal Committee of the NCPPL, ca. Sept. 1915, OFP, MSS64, Box 270, Org. Recs; Osborne, *Prisons and Commonsense*, 88.

[73] It is also worth noting that the "sex problem" was identified in the same period in which reformers began to crack down on the supply of drugs, most notably opium, in prisons: The effects of opium use were termed damaging to convicts' physical well-being and, significantly, to their capacity for manly self-discipline.

to smash the underground economy that James White had identified as a principal stimulant of prisoners' sexual relations. (According to White, the systematic theft and underdelivery of prison provisions led to hunger among the prisoners, who then sold sexual favors for cash, and used the cash to buy the stolen food on the prison's black market).[74] This latter tactic was especially crucial in Osborne's strategy. As Osborne put it, every prison had "some degenerate creatures who are willing to sell themselves, any time, for a few groceries," and the key to the prison sex problem in general was to ensure that prisoners were, on the one hand, well fed (and therefore not in need of procuring cash for extra food), and, on the other, afforded appropriate mental, physical, and spiritual outlets for their natural passions.[75] In theory, the reconstitution of every prisoner as a waged consumer and producer in a simulated economy would ensure that the prisoner was no longer in a position of emasculating dependence. As long as convicts were eating well, engaging in a market economy that rewarded hard work and promoted financial responsibility, and sublimating their life force in educational and recreational activities, Osborne reasoned, the sex market in prisons would lose both its buyers and sellers.[76]

Osborne's conceptualization of the prison sex problem underscored the new penology's central commitment to innovating various disciplinary activities that would absorb and direct prisoners' energies in the face of limited industrial and other forms of labor. As the new penologists saw it, plays, motion pictures, lectures, musical events, and athletics not only addressed the problem of underemployment and initiated prisoners into the personality-building pasttimes of the ideal citizen, they sublimated the libidinal drive of the ordinary convict. Indeed, Osborne established a number of new activities at the prison in the name of vanquishing the "unnatural vice" that the prison investigators had documented in the early 1910s. Prisoners converted a basin in the Hudson River into a large swimming pool in 1915, because, as Osborne put it, swimming was a "practical method of reducing immorality" and an activity in which prisoners would "work off their superfluous energies. . . . and head off unnatural vice." (Four hundred prisoners per day were working off their "superfluous energies" in the pool by 1916).[77] One of Osborne's support committees, The New York State Prison Council, reiterated this point in defending the innovation of moving pictures, lectures, concerts, and other stimulating activities at Sing Sing. "These were established not as Amusements;" the Council explained somewhat defensively, "but as a definite means to an End" (caps in original): That

---

[74] White, "Some Facts About Sing Sing."   [75] Osborne, *Prisons and Commonsense*, 89.

[76] As part of this strategy, the NCPPL commissioned Emily Seaman of Columbia's Teachers College to study the diets of different New York state prisons and work out a nutritious food plan for them. Minutes of a meeting of the Executive Council, National Committee on Prisons and Prison Labor, Mar. 15, 1915, OFP, MSS64, Box 271, Org. Recs.

[77] Osborne, *Prisons and Commonsense*, 92–3. Osborne's friend and biographer, Frank Tannenbaum, wrote that "(T)he general theory was that strenuous exercise and physical health would reduce morbidity and vice." Tannenbaum, *Osborne of Sing Sing*, 173.

end was "keeping the men out of vermin-ridden cells and of stimulating their minds – inured to the gray and sodden monotony of Prison walls."[78]

It was in no small part to combat prison sex that Osborne and the new penologists paved the way for the introduction of psychiatric and psychological testing to Sing Sing in 1916. Osborne and his supporters considered psychomedical study a crucial tool in their efforts to more accurately classify prisoners and to develop a specialized state prison system; to the classificatory system that administrators had established in the 1890s (and which classified and distributed convicts according to sex, age, sanity, physical fitness, and supposed capacity for reform), the new penologists added the distinctly psychological categories of sexuality and personality. In their view, sexual "degenerates" were a distinct category of prisoner and the prison system ought to identify and deal with them separately. Whereas the new recreational activities, better food, and prisoner self-policing were aimed at eradicating the sexual relations of the supposedly ordinary prisoner, the small army of doctors, psychiatrists, and psychologists who descended on Sing Sing in 1915 and 1916 were chiefly concerned with the group of prisoners Osborne had described as degenerate.

The new penologists' effort to conscript psychiatry and psychology into prison reform was complemented by the reformers' enhancement of general medical facilities at Sing Sing in 1915 and 1916. In February 1915, the New York State Department of Health inspected Sing Sing and recommended that a separate ward be set up for patients suffering from sexually transmitted disease (STD). This recommendation was seconded a few months later by two state investigators who suggested that Sing Sing open a new hospital in which "psychopaths," STD patients, and convicts suffering from contagious diseases would be held separately from prisoners in the general wards. Those suffering from infectious diseases other than STDs would be labeled "normal," while "psychopaths" and STD patients should be held in a ward for "special" cases. The investigators further recommended that a psychiatric study of prisoners be undertaken in which all new admissions to the prison would be thoroughly studied according to a case method, with special attention paid to those with mental and nervous disorders, "sexual perversions," suicidal tendencies, and records of multiple convictions. The 1915 plans for a psychomedical facility at Sing Sing proposed a double innovation of the established prison system: The psychic lives of prisoners would be added to the fields of scrutiny, and the past and present sexual practices (and desires) of convicts would be read as signs of a peculiar psychic type (the psychopath), who, in turn, would be incarcerated in separate facilities.[79]

[78] "A Brief Outline of Some of the Activities Connected with Sing Sing Under Mr. Osborne's Wardenship at SS," New York Prison Council (unpublished report, ca. Aug. 1916), 3, OFP, MSS64, Box 272, Org. Recs.

[79] As Estelle Freedman writes, the concept of the psychopath became part of general medical discourse and popular culture in the 1930s; Glueck's original connection between crime and "perverse sexuality" was reworked so that the term, psychopath, came to refer

The following year at Sing Sing, Dr. Thomas W. Salmon, of the National Committee for Mental Hygiene, and Dr. Bernard Glueck, a psychiatrist who had recently instituted nonverbal intelligence testing of immigrants at Ellis Island, set up the country's first penal psychiatric clinic.[80] Funded by a sizable grant from the Rockefeller Foundation, the clinic proceeded under Dr. Glueck's directorship to examine virtually all of the 683 prisoners committed to Sing Sing between August 1916 and April 1917. Glueck's dense, seventy-page report on his findings was published to much acclaim in 1917; it was the first comprehensive psychiatric case study of adult convicts in the United States. Like the Health Department investigators, Glueck conceived of his studies as just one element in the much larger effort to develop "rational administration" in imprisonment. He and his clinicians proceeded to interview every incoming convict about his family background, sexual practices, health, education, and employment history; they then conducted a series of psychological tests for "mental age" and dexterity, and administered psychiatric tests of the prisoner's emotional state. On the basis of this information Glueck divided all the incoming prisoners into three groups: the intellectually defective (those with low "mental ages"); the mentally diseased (those who suffered from hallucinations and delusions); and the psychopathic, whom he described as the most difficult to define and the most baffling. He concluded that almost six out of every ten of the incoming convicts were either intellectually defective, mentally diseased, or psychopathic.

Glueck's study of Sing Sing convicts was one of the first to theorize the existence of "psychopath criminals," and his work became foundational both in studies of criminality and homosexuality. According to Glueck, approximately one in five of the incoming prisoners was a psychopath. It was to this category that those prisoners with a history of homosexual relations were most commonly consigned. As Glueck put it, the classification of psychopathic was a judgment of the prisoner's entire way of life, not just the crime he had committed; sexual habits were one of four determining fields of enquiry (the others were the family's medical history and the convict's employment and education history). From the beginning, then, scrutiny of prisoners' sexual relations – and homosexual relations in particular – was critical in the study of psychopathology among prisoners. He wrote that, "in contemplating the life histories of these (native-born psychopaths), one is struck very forcibly with the unusual lack of all conception of sex morality." A wide range of sexual activities, and not simply sex between men, was read as psychopathological. He described one in three psychopathic prisoners to be "markedly promiscuous," and nine percent as polymorphously perverse: He was perplexed to find that many individuals who had had

specifically to men who committed sex crimes. In psychiatry as well as in everyday parlance in the 1930s, '40s, and '50s, the term continued to have the valence of homosexuality, and by the same notion, homosexuality was increasingly viewed as psychopathological. Freedman, "'Uncontrolled Desires:' the Response to the Sexual Psychopath, 1920–60," *Journal of American History* 74:1 (June 1987), 83–106.

[80] Salmon joined New York City's anti-vice crusade in 1920.

"repeated" sexual relations with other men had been equally sexually active with women, and concluded simply that these convicts were not "biologically sexually inverted." They were, however, as psychopathological as "biological inverts."[81]

As Glueck subjected Sing Sing prisoners to his battery of tests, the prison's physician, Dr. Amos Squire, began systematically testing convicts for syphilis; he found that twenty percent of prisoners tested positive on the Wasserman test. By 1920, all incoming convicts were routinely given urinalysis, Wasserman, and sputum tests. In his report to the physicians section of the American Prison Association, Squire implicitly acknowledged the prevalence of sexual relations in prisons when he wrote that convicts suffering from venereal diseases should ordinarily be isolated from other prisoners. Having "discovered" the incidence of psychopathology and venereal disease among convicts, the doctors made recommendations as to their treatment. Squire recommended that sufferers of STDs eat at separate tables, sleep apart from the others, and work separately. In addition, they should not be permitted to work in any food preparation jobs or in the barbershop.[82] The administration moved to isolate these convicts from others. In his well-publicized study of the psyches of prisoners, Glueck underlined that the psychopath was the most dangerous individual to be found in the prison and that, at the very least, he should be treated separately from the more reformable prison population (the forty-one percent of prisoners with normal mental health) and, preferably, separate from other abnormal convicts.

Glueck's assessment and prognosis of one case of psychopathology, which he later reported to a national audience of penologists at the American Prison Association's annual conference, illustrates his reasoning. He told the audience about the case of a "19 year old Negro boy" who was serving his fifth sentence for crime and who had been convicted on sodomy charges. Glueck determined that the young man, who had insisted to Glueck that his first sexual relations with men had occurred in a reformatory, was recalcitrant about his sexual desires, and that he was consequently a "menace to society."[83] Such offenders, noted Glueck, should not be allowed to simply serve an ordinary prison sentence; they should be properly studied and treated in psychiatric institutions, and released only upon improvement – that is, rejection of homosexual proclivities. Glueck thought the chances of

[81] Bernard Glueck, "A Study of 608 Admissions to Sing Sing," *Mental Hygiene* 1:1 (Jan. 1918), 94–105.

[82] Squire also reported on some of his experimental methods of treating syphilis, which by today's standards would be considered ludicrous and possibly torturous: They included injecting mercury into muscles, rubbing mercury into the prisoners' skin sixty or seventy times, and injecting arsenic into rectal glands.

[83] Chauncey notes the publication of A. A. Brill's "The Concept of Homosexuality" in 1913, in which the author broke down the traditional distinction between active and passive same-sex partners, and described all men engaged in sex with other men as "homosexuals." Chauncey, *Gay New York*, 123. Glueck, however, did not commonly make use of the term, homosexual, as a noun; the term was not in common usage as a noun until after 1930.

successful "reconstruction in the personality of the psychopath" to be low, but argued elsewhere that readjustment was possible in many cases.[84]

In order to detect and segregate psychopathic and other mentally deviant prisoners in New York's carceral system, Glueck, the National Committee for Mental Hygiene, and George Kirchwey (of the NCPPL), drew up detailed plans for the conversion of Sing Sing into a clearing house. They also developed plans for the construction of a new state prison for "defective delinquents." Upon conviction for a felony, every state prisoner would be admitted to Sing Sing Reception Center for close observation and study and intensive vocational training for three or four months, during which time the prison administration would "define clearly the problem which he presents." The convict would then be classified into one of five categories: "the normal young adult capable of learning a useful trade," "the normal prisoner of more advanced age," "the Insane Delinquent," "the Defective Delinquent," or "the Psychopathic Delinquent" (caps in original. Notably, Glueck capitalized the abnormal categories, consonant with the logic that abnormality – and not normality – signals an ontological "type").[85] The plan provided that the "normal" convicts capable of learning a trade be sent to either Clinton or Auburn, and that the older normal prisoners be put to farm labor at Great Meadow. Insane Delinquents would be sent to Dannemora Hospital for the Insane, and Defective Delinquents to an institution yet to be built. They left the question of the Psychopathic Delinquent open: This "most dangerous" of convicts demanded the most intensive attention, they insisted, but the question of where or how they would be treated was left open. Glueck pondered that many of them would eventually break down and end up in the insane prison, while those who made no improvement would be segregated more or less permanently in the institution for Defective Delinquents.

As well as striving to discover, prevent, and punish sexual relations between convicts in the model progressive prison, the new penologists attempted to change relations between black prisoners and white prisoners. Unlike the matter of sex, neither the "race question" nor the prison's small minority of black prisoners were objects of sustained discourse among Sing Sing's reformers at this time.[86] Nonetheless, race ideology deeply influenced

---

[84] Glueck, "A Study of 608 Admissions to Sing Sing," 149.

[85] The point of distinguishing between two categories of supposedly normal prisoners was that the penologists thought that many of the younger convicts had fallen into crime because of economic deprivation (which they attributed to the prisoners' lack of job skills), and that such convicts were still at a "formative" enough age that they could still acquire a skilled trade of some sort. Normal prisoners of advanced age, conversely, were considered too old to acquire such skills and Glueck presumed they would return to unskilled labor upon release.

[86] This is not to say that advocates of the new penology did not explicitly discourse on the question of African American prisoners (the vast majority of whom were incarcerated in the South, during the 1910s). The same penologists who supported Sing Sing-style reform – with its implicit distinction between white and black prisoners – in the North, explicitly promoted a dual penal system in the South: On their view, African Americans, were capable

and was, in turn, influenced by, the new penological program of reform. At Sing Sing (and at Auburn) the new penologists set about classifying and more formally segregating prisoners on the basis of the "one-drop" criterion of American race ideology. The new penologists conceived of their task primarily as one of assimilating prisoners born in Europe and native-born Americans classified as "white" to an ideal, manly citizenship. Programs that were designed to socialize prisoners as citizens were implicitly aimed at white native-born Americans and European immigrants; certainly, no resources were specifically earmarked for the education or postrelease employment of black prisoners. Many of the educational programs were specifically aimed at Italian, Polish, and German immigrants, with the objective of socializing them to be good Americans. Classes were started in English literacy and civics (the one at Auburn was known as the "Americanization" class) for white prisoners, and on at least one occasion, a large business enterprise sent an Italian-speaking agent to Sing Sing to train and recruit Italian convicts for postrelease employment. Besides crafting a prison program that took for granted that white convicts were the proper object of reform, the new penologists took steps to formalize and rigorously enforce the physical separation of white from black prisoners. Black prisoners were concentrated in the unskilled work companies, and white prisoners in the semi- and skilled-labor companies by day. By night, under Osborne's direct orders, black convicts were segregated from white convicts. Early on in his wardenship, Osborne's expressly prohibited white and black convicts to share cells with each other.

Black prisoners did not miss out entirely on the privileges and activities established under the new penologists. As a rule, privileges that were extended to white prisoners (such as membership in the leagues, participation in sports, etc.) were generally extended to black prisoners, too, suggesting that the new penologists considered black prisoners capable of participating in democracy and civil society. But, as had been the case at Auburn, these privileges were always extended in such a way that they would not undermine the segregation of white from black, nor, more critically, raise a black prisoner above a white prisoner. Indeed, new penological reform in general seems to have formalized race segregation and, not incidentally, widened racial inequality, at Sing Sing.

Finally, the new penologists sought to persuade guards to subscribe to their system while making it clear that guards who were disruptive to it,

only of unskilled labor and incapable of participating in a penal society such as Sing Sing's. They ought, therefore, to be sent to county and state chain gangs and state penal farms. White prisoners, on the other hand, were thought likely to do well in cellular prisons devoted to the socialization of the prisoner. Southern advocates of the chain gang and the use of convicts in the "Good Roads Movement" also considered their program a fully progressive alternative to the penal contract and lease labor systems. See Alex Lichtenstein, "Good Roads and Chain Gangs in the Progressive South: The Negro Convict is a Slave," *Journal of Southern History* 59:1 (Feb. 1993), 85–110; Lichtenstein, *Twice the Work of Free Labor: The Political Economy of Convict Labor in the New South* (London: Verso, 1996), 168–9.

or sought to embarrass its architects, would be dismissed. Early on in his wardenship, Osborne tightened surveillance of the guards: Among other things, he cracked down on absenteeism and began demanding doctor's notes from absent keepers.[87] He also (unsuccessfully) pressed Superintendent Riley to set up a guard training school; the Joint Committee on Prisons supported him in this endeavor, insisting that "management is far more vital than improvement in material appliances."[88] Perhaps most critically, Osborne exerted control over the flow of information in and out of the prison. He began disciplining guards who criticized the reforms in the press, as well as those guards known to be opposed to the reforms. In the service of building guard loyalty to the new system, Osborne restructured the shift system so as to give guards at least one day off per week. He also replaced the two-platoon system with a three-platoon system, thereby allowing the guards to work six eight-hour (instead of seven twelve-hour) shifts. Much as he had done at Auburn Prison, Osborne also encouraged the MWL to pursue better relations with guards. Following the escape of a convict in June 1916, in the course of which a keeper was killed, the Outside Branch of the MWL established a Guard's Widow Fund.[89]

By the same token, Osborne did not hesitate to wield a big stick against prison guards. Although a champion of civil service reform, Osborne appears not to have considered himself subject to New York's Civil Service Law. That law provided that certain procedures had to be followed before a warden could dismiss a guard. Osborne acted decisively and often without regard to procedural regulations to dismiss guards who criticized or complained about the reforms. In the fall of 1915, he dismissed keepers John J. Kennedy and George Meserole for having spoken to reporters and nonemployees about the prison. Guard Charles Carstens was dismissed on a similar charge on October 31, 1915.[90] Civilian employees who criticized the new regime suffered a similar fate, often in contravention of Superintendent Riley's position on the matter. In one instance, Osborne dismissed the store keeper, James J. Kelley, on the grounds that Kelley had made an unauthorized offer to trade a calf belonging to the prison, that he had spoken "disrespectfully of the management of Sing Sing Prison and of the warden thereof," and that he had bought food for the warden's table at unnecessarily high prices. (Kelley took his case to court, and in 1917, the Supreme Court of New York reprimanded Osborne and ruled that Kelley had been wrongfully dismissed).[91]

[87] Memo, Osborne to guards, Sing Sing Prison, ca. 1915, OFP, MSS64, Box 277, Org. Recs.; Guard shift sheets, Sing Sing Prison, 1915, OFP, MSS64, Box 277, Org. Recs.
[88] Mission statement, Joint Committee on Prison Reform (hereafter JCPR), 1914, OFP, MSS64, Box 269, Org. Recs.; and Tannenbaum, *Osborne of Sing Sing*, 186–8.
[89] Report, OBMWL, 1916, OFP, MSS64, Box 269, Org. Recs.
[90] Minutes of the Warden's Hearing, Aug. 10, 1915; Minutes of the Warden's Hearing, Oct. 2, 1915, OFP, MSS64, Box 276, Org. Recs.
[91] The Justices found that the first and second charges were trivial and that there was not sufficient evidence to sustain the more serious charge of incompetent purchasing. In

As the new penologists initiated sweeping changes at Sing Sing, they also orchestrated a number of exhibitions, lectures, tours, and press releases designed to capture popular support for their programs. As early as 1914, when Osborne was engaged in the restructuring of Auburn Prison (see Chapter 8), leaders of the new penological coalition had argued that winning the support of the public through the mass press and exhibitions would be critical in their efforts to enact their programs throughout the state and ultimately the nation.[92] In garnering this support, the penologists coordinated a sophisticated marketing campaign, using all the local and mass cultural media available to them, which aimed to convince Americans that the prisons were in a state of moral crisis, and that they, the new penologists, had the solution to that crisis: The answer lay in the kinds of programs they had established at Sing Sing.

Osborne and his new penological coalition ensured that the reforms at Sing Sing in 1915 received a great deal of publicity. They encouraged members of the nation's élites, including social reformers, businessmen, jurists, club women, journalists, and mass cultural celebrities to tour the prison. Given Sing Sing's proximity to New York City, the prison was well placed to receive such visitors. At one point in 1915, up to 250 visitors toured Sing Sing each day. The more prominent visitors included William Jennings Bryan, Billy Sunday, Tim Sullivan, and Governor Hunt of Arizona; on one occasion, a single group of almost 200 women from the League of Political Education toured the prison.[93] Osborne also traveled around the Northeastern states, and across the Atlantic to Britain, as well, addressing gatherings of civic reformers, academics, church congregants, and businessmen about the problems in the prisons and the Sing Sing reforms. Many of these addresses were given at prestigious institutions (such as Yale University, where Osborne gave the annual Dodge Lectures in Citizenship in 1915) as well as small civic and church groups. Retaining a press clipping service, Osborne meticulously followed the reception of his work and addresses in the regional and national press.[94]

The new penologists also put together a number of exhibitions and films to carry the message of the Sing Sing reforms to a mass audience. The JCPR retained a young female filmmaker, by the name of Katherine Russell Bleecker, to shoot a series of documentaries and educational films on

---

reprimanding Osborne for the dismissal, the justices noted wryly that the dismissed store keeper often had to procure extraordinary items such as Roquefort cheese, gold dust, and olive oil at the last minute because of the "unexpected arrival of many dinner quests at the warden's table." The Justices concluded their finding by ridiculing Osborne's practice of presenting his own sworn testimony in the capacity of witness to himself in the capacity of warden and judge; Kelley was to be reinstated immediately. *The People ex rel. James J. Kelley v. George W. Kirchwey*, 177 AD 706; 164 NYS 511 (N.Y. App. Div., 1917) (LEXIS 5762).

[92] Mission statement, Joint Committee on Prison Reform (hereafter JCPR), 1914, OFP, MSS64, Box 269, Org. Recs.

[93] Tannenbaum, *Osborne of Sing Sing*, 143.

[94] Osborne's Yale lectures were later published as *Society and Prisons* (New Haven, Connecticut: Yale University Press, 1916).

the reform effort. In 1915, the twenty-two-year-old Bleecker made at least four films about life in New York's state prisons, in which she contrasted the harsh "old system" with the enlightened, new penological one. In one of these films, shot at Auburn in 1915, Bleecker had the prisoners shave their heads, dress up in the discarded striped uniforms, and perform the old lockstep march for the camera. She also had a keeper and a prisoner simulate a combination of the old tricing and paddling punishments: A volunteer was to be cuffed, and the keeper was to pretend to hoist the prisoner to the tips of his toes, and then "flog" him using a fake cardboard paddle that Bleecker had had specially made for the scene. The simulation went awry, however, when the keeper actually hoisted the prisoner aloft, causing the man almost to pass out from the pain. (All of this, including the prisoner's agony, was caught on film.) Bleecker also staged a dramatic adaptation of Osborne's *Within Prison Walls*, in which the man himself "starred," shot footage of the real MWL in action, and recorded the second annual Tom Brown anniversary dinner at Auburn.[95] In early 1916, Joseph Choate presided over a sold-out premiere screening of some of these films in New York City.[96]

Around the same time, Osborne's coalition ensured that the reforms at Sing Sing and Auburn would be given a prominent place in New York state's entry for the 1915 Panama-Pacific International Exposition in San Francisco. New York's installation, which was set up in the Exposition's Palace of Education–Social Economy, consisted of a life-scale model of the prison's bureaucratic nerve center: An office was fitted out with filing cabinets and other tools of prison information technology, and photographs and diagrams demonstrated the innovations at Auburn and Sing Sing. As well as running live demonstrations of Bertillon and finger-printing technology, the exhibition included photographs, films, dozens of different wares produced by convict laborers, statistics on New York prisons, explanations of the "Good Roads" work of the convicts, and an explanation of the Mutual Welfare League and the new prison order. Thousands of visitors partook in the fingerprinting demonstrations, and the installation was awarded a gold medal. The following year, the office became part of a traveling new penological exhibition.[97]

As the simulation of a modern prison office, complete with filing cabinets and all the accoutrements of bureaucracy, at the Panama-Pacific Exhibition suggests, the new penologists embraced the bureaucratic technologies that had first been forged in the 1890s and early 1900s. Indeed, Superintendent Riley and Governor Whitman had appointed Osborne with the hope that, as well as stabilizing and improving the prison, he would advance the

---

[95] It is not known whether any of the films have survived. However, the *New York Times* published an illustrated feature article on Bleecker in 1915, in which she discussed her prison work in some detail. "Prison Moving Pictures Taken by a Girl," *New York Times*, Nov. 21, 1915, SM19.

[96] *New York Times*, Jan. 9, 1916, 7.

[97] *The State of New York at the Panama Pacific International Exposition, San Francisco, California, Feb. 20–Dec. 4, 1915* (Albany, NY: J. B. Lyon and Co., 1916), 340–6.

objectives of administrative efficiency, insulate Sing Sing from scandal, and rebuild it as the carceral "jewel in the crown" of the Empire State's penal system. In many respects, Osborne and his new penological coalition did not disappoint: They implemented reforms that central administrators had advocated since Lispenard Stewart had first set about rebuilding the prison system in 1896. Under Osborne, sanitation and food were improved; alternative disciplinary forms were forged; the incidence of injury from assault declined dramatically in the prison, and the theft of prison supplies by keepers and convicts was arrested. Osborne and his support committees had also drawn up blueprints for completing the longterm project of turning New York's prisons into a series of specialized institutions in a single, integrated, and centrally controlled penal system.

However, as Osborne's summary dismissal of state employees and the general manner in which the new penologists executed their reforms at Sing Sing suggest, many of these reforms were fraught with contradiction. Osborne ran the institution autocratically, and in a manner that severely disrupted the routines and violated the rules of the fledgling penal bureaucracy. Indeed, the new penologists' general disregard for the procedures of bureaucracy was evident from the first day Osborne took up the wardenship of Sing Sing. Osborne repeatedly failed to file the requisite monthly reports with the Prison Department and avoided consultation with the central authorities whenever possible. Even more critically, he ignored the orders of his bureaucratic superior, Superintendent Riley, regarding transfers of prisoners to other institutions and celling arrangements. In refusing to cooperate fully with Riley in compiling transfer lists, Osborne disrupted the operation of a critical linchpin of the penal state – the routine redistribution of convicts around the system. Osborne also contravened the fundamental principles of centralized, hierarchical management by personally remunerating his civil-servant secretary and supplementing the salary of the prison's Confidential Agent. Likewise, his allies in the NCPPL and JCPL contravened these principles in hiring civilian instructors and directly supplementing certain state employees' wages. These actions, in effect, created a wing of the prison loyal and accountable to the new penological coalition rather than the central authorities.

As Osborne's treatment of "disloyal" guards and civilian staff indicates, in constructing their model prison, the new penologists routinely bypassed the state prison bureaucracy. The overhaul of prison industries, prisoner classification, and industrial training proceeded at Sing Sing only through the fund-raising efforts and intellectual labor of the new penologists, and the donations of capitalists such as Henry Ford. Osborne repeatedly ignored directives from Superintendent Riley and, in particular, interfered with the central authorities' attempts to transfer prisoners out of Sing Sing. Although the new penologists' Sing Sing programs rapidly achieved many of the official goals laid out over the years by the State Prison Department, the manner in which the reformers set about their task was directly counter to the longterm expansion and intensification of the penal bureaucracy that had been underway since the 1890s. Rather than strengthening the administrative state's command of its prisons, and rather than sealing prisons (and prisoners) off from outside influences, the new penologists opened the prison up to the funding and influence of business, elite philanthropists, and a legion of medicopsychological specialists who were neither in the employ nor under the disciplinary supervision of the established, central penal authorities. In effect, the new penological coalition usurped the formal authority of the prison bureaucracy and relocated policy-making from the state bureaucrats to the semi-private coalition of experts and capitalists assembled at Sing Sing.

In these respects, Osborne's wardenship, and the new penological coalition in general, stood in opposition not only to the patronage forces of boss rule and Tammany Hall, but to the forces of bureaucratization. As loudly as Osborne and the new penologists proclaimed that their reforms represented the bold new system that befitted an advanced civilization, their autonomous management of the prisons was increasingly anachronistic in the face of the more general bureaucratization of American political and commercial life. Indeed, rather than ending the conflict over the prisons, the new penologists fueled it. Proceeding as they did, it was not long before the new penologists reignited the enmity of Tammany Hall and lost the support of Superintendent Riley and the penal bureaucracy.[98] Both narrowed their sites on Osborne in the spring of 1915. By the end of that year, they were joined by the New York State Republican Party, the ranking members of which feared that Osborne, an independent Democrat who had pursued electoral office in the past, might use his widely publicized successes at Sing Sing as a springboard from which to capture the governorship of the state of New York.

What subsequently unfolded among Osborne, Superintendent Riley, Tammany Hall, and the Republican party is difficult to document with any degree of accuracy: Few records of their correspondence survive and the published accounts narrate the struggle exclusively from the point of view of Osborne.[99] What is clear is that in the summer of 1915, there followed

---

[98] There are two published accounts of the conflict that developed around Sing Sing at this time (Rudolph W. Chamberlin, *There is no Truce: The Life of Thomas Mott Osborne* [New York: Macmillan, 1935] and Frank Tannenbaum, *Osborne of Sing Sing*). Both narrate the attack on the new penological reforms at Sing Sing primarily as the story of Osborne's rise and fall as a committed and visionary prison reformer. Although they are not scholarly (lacking documentation and written unabashedly from Osborne's point of view), both might be described as "ripping good yarns" about one of the most important of New York's political and legal intrigues of the 1910s. Both also provide a useful chronology of events.

[99] The account that follows draws on material from the files of the attorney general, Osborne's papers, and press reports, as well as from the accounts of Chamberlin and Tannenbaum. My account differs in emphasis from those of Tannenbaum and, especially, Chamberlin, both of whom were explicitly concerned with exonerating Osborne. Opinions and Files of the Attorney General, Interpreting Criminal and Prison laws, 1892–1957, State of New York, NYSA, RDOC, AO429–77 (hereafter cited as Attorney-General of the State of New York, Opinions). According to Frank Tannenbaum, Riley formed an alliance with

a series of clandestine attempts by Superintendent Riley to secure records and information about Osborne's management of Sing Sing and that he resolved to expel the warden and his powerful coalition of supporters from Sing Sing.[100] By August 1915, Riley was being openly critical of Osborne and was seeking legal grounds upon which to dismiss Osborne. He quietly requested a slew of written opinions from the New York state attorney general's office about the legality of the warden's conduct.[101] Following a complaint from Governor Charles Whitman that a convict from the general prison population had broken the prison rule prohibiting communication between regular prisoners and those on death row, Riley asked the attorney general to clarify the law on the matter.[102] A few weeks later, Riley inquired as to the legality of Osborne deputizing his private secretary (Mr. Church) as warden for periods when Osborne was on leave from Sing Sing (and busy on a lecture circuit, promoting the reforms).[103] He also sought clarification of the law pertaining to the warden's power to fire employees following Osborne's dismissal of the three guards he considered uncooperative.[104]

> some of the upper-middle class convicts at Sing Sing who had suffered a loss of power when Osborne reconstructed the Golden Rule Brotherhood along what he considered to be modern electoral lines. These convicts' consequent resentment toward Osborne was fueled by Osborne's opposition to parole legislation that would have halved their sentences. In 1916, an unidentified Sing Sing prisoner claimed that the Riley/Osborne conflict originated in a disagreement over plans for reconstruction of Sing Sing buildings. According to this account, Riley wanted to build a modern cellblock to replace the old one at Sing Sing, whereas Osborne wanted to replace cellular confinement with dormitories and to turn Sing Sing into a receiving prison, "Horror of SS Cells Shown," *Mutual Welfare League Bulletin* 1:16 (Feb. 21, 1916), 5; Tannenbaum, *Osborne of Sing Sing*, 185–92.

[100] Riley's schemes included dispatching his confidential agent to Sing Sing to retrieve Osborne's prison files while Osborne was away from the prison. In his account of the "confidential agent incident," Tannenbaum notes that Osborne intercepted the agent as the latter attempted to board a train out of Ossining, stolen papers in hand. Osborne promptly repossessed his papers and dispatched the hapless agent back to Albany. Tannenbaum, *Osborne of Sing Sing*, 190.

[101] Attorney-General of the State of New York, Opinions, 181 (Aug. 21, 1915); 184 (Sep. 17, 1915); 185 (Sep. 17, 1915); 196 (Jan. 25, 1916).

[102] Attorney-General of the State of New York, Opinions, 181, (Aug. 21, 1915). In the incident, a prisoner gained access to a death row prisoner, the controversial ex-police lieutenant, Charles Becker (whom Charles Whitman, as the district attorney of New York, had successfully prosecuted), by masquerading as a member of the convict choir that serenaded death row prisoners every Sunday. Chamberlin provides an interesting but unsupported account of this typically dramatic Sing Sing incident: The masquerading singer claimed that he had been a prisoner awaiting trial in the Tombs jail in New York City when he overheard chief witnesses in Charles Becker's trial for murder plot to offer false testimony. According to the prisoner, Becker had been framed. When this convict's story came to light, on the eve of Becker's execution, Osborne ordered his deputy warden to escort the convict to Governor Whitman's office in Albany and to request a stay of execution so the claims might be investigated. Whitman, the former district attorney responsible for convicting Becker, refused. Becker was executed the next day (July 30) as scheduled. It was on this night that Riley's agent, MacDonald, attempted to confiscate Osborne's orders and notes. Chamberlin, *There is no Truce*, 306.

[103] Attorney-General of the State of New York, Opinions, 184 (Sep. 17, 1915).

[104] Attorney-General of the State of New York, Opinions, 185 (Sep. 17, 1915).

Finally, he asked the attorney general if allowing a prisoner to travel home to attend the funeral of a family member, as Osborne had done, was illegal.[105]

The attorney general's office replied in the affirmative to all but one of Riley's inquiries: In the attorney general's opinion, Osborne had broken the law by allowing the convict choir into the death house every Sunday; by appointing a person of insufficient rank as acting warden; and by allowing prisoners to attend funerals and other engagements in cities distant from the place of confinement. (On the other hand, the attorney general opined that the warden had "absolute power of removal" under statute law to remove the officers, as long as he followed certain procedures. The question of whether he had followed these procedures was the basis of a wrongful dismissal suit one of the dismissed keepers would bring against Osborne the following year).[106] Taken together, these opinions suggested that Riley had sufficient legal grounds upon which to reprimand Osborne. Yet, as Riley was probably quite well aware, Osborne's alleged violations were almost entirely petty, and they would be light artillery in what would almost certainly be an attritional battle against Osborne and his powerful new penological coalition.

Riley finally found an opportunity to build a more serious case against Osborne when an extraordinary incident of sodomy came to light in September 1915. A convict reportedly informed Osborne that he had had sex with twenty-one convicts. Instead of following New York state law and notifying Riley of the incident, Osborne dealt with the case confidentially and within the prison. He demanded that the named convicts confess to the act; in exchange, he would punish them within Sing Sing instead of transferring them to Clinton (which Superintendent Riley would almost certainly have done). Subsequently, eighteen prisoners confessed, and Osborne punished them by setting them to hard labor digging a sewer.[107] When Riley eventually heard about the incident and Osborne's handling of it, he and his supporters immediately recognized an opportunity to indict, convict, and dismiss Osborne.[108] Riley promptly initiated Grand Jury proceedings against Osborne and the twenty-one convicts alleged to have had sexual relations with the prisoner. At the same time, a member of the New York State Prison Commission, Dr. Rudolph Deidling, undertook his own investigation of Osborne's management of Sing Sing. Deidling, a vociferous critic of Osborne and ally of Riley, set about gathering all manner of incriminating evidence against Osborne. In late October, Deidling presented Riley with a 304-page report in which he roundly condemned Osborne's management of the prison and demanded his immediate resignation. Shortly afterward, the Republican District Attorney of Westchester County announced a Grand

[105] Attorney-General of the State of New York, Opinions, 196 (Jan. 25, 1916).

[106] Attorney-General of the State of New York, Opinions, 184 (Sep. 17, 1915), 185 (Sep. 17, 1915, 196 (Jan. 25, 1916).

[107] Chamberlin, *There is no Truce*, 328–9.

[108] Chamberlin asserts that Osborne mentioned the case to a member of the Parole Board, who passed the information along to Riley. Ibid., 328.

Jury enquiry into Osborne's management of Sing Sing. The Westchester County Grand Jury was sworn in on November 9, 1915.

There followed a tremendous and very public battle between Osborne and the forces of new penology on the one side and the bureaucrats and Republicans on the other. Ostensibly, Osborne was being investigated for malfeasance and failure to discipline convicts engaged in sexual relations with one another. In fact, however, the new penology, in its most independent and developed manifestation, was on trial. (That the new penology's fate hinged on the question of the sexual relations of prisoners and of the warden was deeply ironic given the lengths to which Osborne and the new penologists had gone to police sex in the prison). Despite facing the threat of transfer to Clinton Prison and lengthened sentences, not one of the twenty-one convicts accused of sodomy testified against Osborne before the Westchester County Grand Jury. Nonetheless, the prosecuting attorney, William Fallon, presented other convicts who were prepared to testify against Osborne.[109] After seven weeks of investigation, the Grand Jury charged the twenty-one convicts with sodomy, and Osborne with perjury and neglect of duty. The counts included several of the petty violations documented by Superintendent Riley. The indictment for neglect of duty included counts of permitting unauthorized prisoners into the death house, failure to exercise discipline over the prison, and encouraging crimes. Most critically, it charged Osborne with committing "various unnatural and immoral acts with the convicts of Sing Prison." Although the language of the indictment was vague, its implication was clear: Osborne, the first American prison warden to discourse on the subject of sex between convicts, and the first to systematically seek out and discipline convicts for homosexual relations, was being charged with committing homosexual acts. He now faced the possibility of having to serve a prison sentence that would be quite unlike the one he had "served" in Auburn in 1914 as Tom Brown. Osborne's integrity, and that of the entire new penological experiment at Sing Sing, was now on trial.

Upon hearing of the indictments, Osborne took leave from Sing Sing to fight the battle; this was a battle not only for his reputation and position at Sing Sing, but for the new penology and the vision of social justice it championed, as well. In preparing for the confrontation, George Kirchwey, Osborne's close ally and former Dean of Law at Columbia University, took up the acting wardenship of Sing Sing while the new penological coalition strategized a defense. In the weeks leading up to the trial, Osborne received a great deal of financial and moral support from convicts, guards, and New York's elite reformers. Ninety-nine of Sing Sing's 101 guards signed a petition in his favor; the Kings County Grand Jury investigated Sing Sing and commended Osborne for his work, as did the Grand Jury Association of New

[109] Fallon went on to become one of New York's leading criminal defense attorneys. Osborne's legal team included two leading attorneys, Huntington Merchant and George Gordon Battle. Ibid., 334.

York. The *New York Times* and several other newspapers supported Osborne, and two large rallies were held at Carnegie Hall in January and February of 1916. The first was organized by a committee of 250 prominent New Yorkers, and was addressed by Charles W. Eliot (president of Harvard), Charles Parkhurst, Adolphe Lewisohn, Lillian Wald, Felix Adler, and a number of other distinguished progressives and reformers. These rallies, each of which was attended by upward of 3,000 people, made for a fantastic spectacle of New York class relations: Not only did Osborne's elite supporters rally to his defense in their numbers, but so did hundreds of ex-convicts. The extraordinary nature of the Carnegie Hall rally did not escape the notice of at least one journalist, who observed in the *New York Tribune* that "pickpockets rubbed elbows with women of another stratum, a-glitter with diamonds, while burglars were sleeve-to-sleeve with burghers."[110]

Meanwhile, the JCPR opened a large traveling exhibition through the Russell Sage Foundation in New York City, and invited the public to view new penological reform, free of charge. Consisting of fourteen installations on New York prisons, penitentiaries, and jails, the JCPR's exhibition was the largest of its kind and drew thousands of spectators. At once an explanation and a justification of the changes underway at the "laboratory on the Hudson," the exhibition was aimed at inciting public support for new penology in general and the Sing Sing reform in particular. Osborne featured prominently as a crusading visionary who was doing battle with the evils of the old system. Visitors viewed photographs, electrical devices, scale models of the prisons, the original Panama-Pacific office exhibit, and a special section entitled: "Sing Sing must go!....A most comprehensive portrayal of the medieval Bastille on the Hudson." Perhaps the most remarkable artifact of the exhibition was a mock-up of a Sing Sing cell complete with operative door lever and two wall beds with artificial "ticks" and dirty blankets. According to the *Evening Mail*, the mock-up of a cell captured the attention of the visitors more than anything else: The visitors "came, stood before it, pressed the lever, but generally drew back when it was suggested they go inside." Set up next to the cell was a petition stand, where visitors could sign their names in support of the demolition and replacement of Sing Sing Prison. Visitors to the exhibition also viewed films on the state prisons in which the old system was unfavorably compared with the new penological reforms at Auburn, Sing Sing, and Great Meadow Prisons. In one film, "Within Prison Walls," Osborne re-enacted his decision to enter Auburn as Tom Brown and the work undertaken at Auburn since then. Visitors to the exhibition were then "taken inside" Sing Sing in "A Day in Sing Sing," which documented the decayed state of the mess hall, cellblock, and chapel, and ended with "a plea for the abolition of Sing Sing, and for the establishment of a new prison on wide acreage." After running for ten days in New York City, the Committee took its exhibition on the road around New York state,

---

[110] Tannenbaum, *Osborne of Sing Sing*, 243. Isaac Seligman presided over the rally, replacing Joseph Choate.

stopping in Buffalo, Syracuse, Rochester, Albany, and a number of other up-state towns.[111]

It was amidst this campaign of support for Osborne and the new penology that the first Sing Sing sodomy case went to trial. It was that of Nathan Kaplan, one of the convicts who had confessed his act of sodomy to Osborne, and subsequently refused to testify against Osborne in the Grand Jury proceedings. Kaplan's attorneys (supplied by Osborne) secured an acquittal by providing evidence that the Westchester district attorney, Frederick E. Weeks, had pressured all twenty-one convicts to perjure themselves and testify against Osborne. This pressure had included the threat of transfer to the most hated prison in the state (Clinton) should they not testify, and the incentive of having the sodomy charges dropped should they cooperate. Kaplan's acquittal was a victory for Osborne and the new penologists which radically undermined the district attorney's case against Osborne; moreover, it revealed the illegal tactics in which the district attorney's office had engaged in order to bring about indictments. With Osborne's trial looming, his supporters resolved to gather further evidence of misconduct.[112]

In the days following Kaplan's acquittal, Osborne and his supporters retained the services of one of America's best-known private detectives, Val O'Farrell. According to Chamberlin's account, O'Farrell set about planting microphonic "bugs" in the offices of District Attorney Weeks in order to recover evidence that Osborne had been framed. (At that point in time, there were no laws prohibiting such surveillance.) In February 1916, O'Farrell rented rooms in the same building in which were housed the offices of District Attorney Weeks, and proceeded to record conversations that took place in Weeks's office over the next several weeks. Using a detectaphone, O'Farrell transcribed hours of conversations among Weeks, the witnesses, politicans, and his assistants. He then wrote a fake set of records, in which he embellished the real transcript with stories of high-level corruption, and proceeded to "hide" these in an office a few floors up from the district attorney's. The ingenious detective then anonymously notified District Attorney Weeks that Weeks's conversations had been recorded, and that he would find a full transcript of the conversations in the offices above. Weeks retrieved the inauthentic transcripts and immediately attempted to call off Osborne's trial.[113]

With the authentic transcripts in hand, and perhaps hoping to unveil a high-level political plot involving both the Republican party and Tammany Hall, Osborne went to trial anyway. When Osborne appeared in court on the

[111] *Prison Exhibit*, pamphlet (New York: Joint Committee on Prison Reform, 1916); *Evening Mail*, quoted in "Horror of SS Cells Shown," *Mutual Welfare League Bulletin* 1:16, (Feb. 21, 1916), 5.
[112] Kaplan was better known as Jack the Dropper, an infamous gangster with the New York City gang known as the Five Pointers. He had earned the moniker, Kid Dropper, and later, Jack the Dropper, through his perfection of a wallet-dropping scam. Luc Sante, *Low Life: Lures and Snares of Old New York* (New York: Strauss Farrar Giroux, 1991), 221, 222, 232.
[113] Tannenbaum, *Osborne of Sing Sing*, 249; Chamberlin, *There is no Truce*, 350.

first charge (that of perjury), he was promptly acquitted. With the knowledge that they possessed evidence with which they could discredit Weeks entirely, Osborne and his attorneys then pressed Weeks to proceed with the second charge, neglect of duty. Perhaps sensing that the case had been lost and that proceeding might destroy his career, Weeks delayed trying the case, and eventually Osborne's attorneys moved that the count be stricken. After some months of legal wrangling, the Appellate Division of the Supreme Court of New York unanimously ruled out the count: As they did so, the bench pointedly rebuked district attorney Weeks for the wording and content of the sixth charge in the count, namely that Osborne had committed unnatural and immoral acts: "The sixth count contains no statement of acts constituting a crime. It contains characterizations that are legally meaningless . . . but oppressively injurious by suggestion."[114] Legally, Osborne had been cleared, but as the court acknowledged, the charge's inference that he had engaged in homosexual relations had already stained Osborne's name.

Osborne returned from his legal travails to manage Sing Sing again in late 1916. Although cleared of all charges, and free of Superintendent Riley (whom Governor Whitman had dismissed in the wake of the Grand Jury fiasco), Osborne faced mounting pressure from bureaucrats in Albany. Perhaps more critically, the support of his allies in the NCPPL and JCPR was beginning to waver. The new Superintendent of Prisons, James M. Carter, proceeded to attempt what Riley had failed to do: subordinate Osborne to centralized management.[115] Once more, Osborne flatly refused. But three months after returning to Sing Sing, and after a relentless barrage of criticism from Albany, Osborne abruptly resigned from the wardenship. In a letter to Superintendent Carter, Osborne made his reasoning plain: "No one can occupy successfully such a position as warden of a State Prison unless the control of his institution remains firmly in his own hands; while he is held to a strict accountability for results. Not only does your recent order [prohibiting third-time convicts from working beyond the prison walls] violate the understanding with which I took office, but they [sic] also violate the very first rule of successful business management."[116] In an embittered open letter to Governor Whitman, Osborne wrote: "Thanks to you, sir, the name I inherited from my honored father and from my mother . . . has been linked in people's thoughts and talk with the vilest of crimes; I have had to fight for what is worth far more than life itself against a powerful and

[114] Chamberlin, *There is no Truce*, 356.

[115] According to Chamberlin and Tannenbaum, Superintendent Carter officially ordered Osborne to desist publicizing his work at Sing Sing. A series of escapes in the summer of 1916 led Carter to denounce Sing Sing discipline as lax. Finally, Carter ordered that no long-term convicts be permitted in the administration buildings or anywhere else beyond the prison walls. This effectively meant that MWL officials who happened to be long-term convicts could not execute their work properly; furthermore, Carter's order effectively dispersed the long-term convicts who comprised Osborne's loyal staff.

[116] Osborne to Carter, Oct. 9, 1916, OF Papers, MSS 64, Box 276, Org Recs., Misc., SS Prison, 1839–1916.

remorseless political organization."[117] Osborne was not exaggerating: The charge that he had engaged in "unnatural and immoral acts" stayed with him until his death, ten years later, and was frequently invoked by critics (including Republican President, Warren Harding) as a means of discrediting Osborne, the new penology, and the Democratic party.

Despite his acquittal, Osborne's reputation as a prison reformer had been severely damaged, and he was fast becoming a liability for the new penological movement. Upon Osborne's resignation and the publication of his letter to Whitman, the Republican newspapers launched a barrage of attacks on Osborne and the Mutual Welfare Leagues.[118] George Kirchwey resumed the acting-wardenship of Sing Sing while Governor Whitman and the Prison Department resolved to find a warden who would both submit to bureaucratic oversight and do whatever was necessary to free Sing Sing from the scandals that had so frequently plagued the prison – and state government – in the previous few years.

* * * * *

With Osborne's spectacular fall from grace came the question of whether the remarkable experiment at Sing Sing would outlive the tenure of its most charismatic director. With the aid of the new penological coalition, Osborne had brought about sweeping changes at two of the country's oldest and most infamous prisons. By late 1916, when he exited the prison, the everyday rules and routines of prison life at Auburn and Sing Sing had been fundamentally altered. Although never fully forfeiting the longstanding dream of full productive labor for prisoners, the new penologists had nonetheless substituted at both prisons a new set of practices aimed at simulating the experience of labor, training prisoners as workers, and instilling in them the values of productive labor. They had adopted a whole new range of alternative disciplinary forms, moving well beyond the earlier progressives' modest supplementary programs of military drill and grade school classes. And, for the first time in the history of American imprisonment, the new post-laboring prison regime enjoyed the unqualified support of organized labor and key captains of industry. Yet, as the circumstance of Osborne's departure confirmed, the political grounds upon which the model prison, and the new penology more generally, stood were far from stable. It remained unclear what, if anything, of New York's prison-laboratory of social justice would survive. In the spring of 1917, as the United States entered World War I and the country underwent mass mobilization for war, the answer to that question would be rapidly clarified.

---

[117] Osborne to Whitman, Oct. 23, 1916, OF Papers, MSS 64, Box 276, Org Recs., Misc., SS Prison, 1839–1916.
[118] Tannenbaum, *Osborne of Sing Sing*, 260–1.

10

Punishment Without Labor: Toward the Modern Penal State

Thus ends a condition of practical slavery.
    Julia Jaffray, General Federation of Women's Clubs, 1936

Early on the afternoon of November 7, 1917, a thousand Sing Sing convicts gathered in the prison yard, along with some thirty guests, to hear a series of speeches by New York Governor Charles Whitman, former U.S. attorney general George Wickersham, Warden William Moyer, and a handful of other distinguished officials.[1] As the stars and stripes flapped in the breeze, the thirty convict musicians of Sing Sing's "Aurora Band" marched into the yard in their sparkling white uniforms and delivered a military rendition of the "Star Spangled Banner." The audience raised its collective gaze toward the sixth floor of the famous old cellblock, where a single slab of stone measuring six by seven by three feet had been dislodged and secured by a heavy rope to a derrick boom. After briefly addressing the crowd, the Governor seized the rope and slowly lowered the slab onto a rail cart stationed 100 feet below. As it came to a rest on the cart, Whitman quipped, "It took a long time to come down." Major James C. McGuire, the state's prison engineer, then pried a chip from the great stone slab using a long steel bar and presented both to the Governor with the somber, if somewhat awkward, words: "This is the first stone from the cell block of Sing Sing Prison and the bar which did the work I present to you."[2]

In the course of the afternoon, the convicts and visitors listened as some of the nation's most distinguished jurists and politicians proceeded to frame the demolition of Sing Sing as a historic event for both the Empire State and American penology. They heard from Charles Whitman that, in his capacity as the Governor of New York, he owed a duty not only to those outside of prison walls but those within," and that it was the duty of "Society and the Commonwealth to house men placed under its care amidst sanitary conditions and humane treatment." By the same token, the Governor insisted, convicts must cooperate with the restructured prison regime: "The future of social prison reform and the continuance of the attitude of the citizens of this country towards this great problem lies in the hands of you men here and in the other prisons of the State, in your conduct and in

[1] The following account is drawn from the *Star-Bulletin* 19:7 (Dec. 1917), 1, 4–6, 8–10.
[2] *Star-Bulletin* 19:7 (Dec. 1917), 1, 6.

your work. . . . I want everyone of you to labor within the walls, to put your best efforts in the work which is assigned you, conduct yourselves like men, and by doing so you will build a new Sing Sing prison."[3] Former U.S. attorney general, George Wickersham, opined on the "obligations" of "this great State" toward its prisoners, following which Charles C. Nott, Jr., a judge of the Court of General Sessions, explained that the state owed three duties to its prisoners: sanitary and health-stimulating living conditions; "kindly, intelligent" treatment (rather than the "stupid and brutal discipline of the German army" or the ill-discipline of the recently deposed Czar); and help finding employment upon release from prison.[4] After a prayer for social justice, the ceremony drew to a close and the prisoners returned to their usual routine, with the exception that 200 convicts now hauled picks, drills, and crowbars to the sixth floor of the cellhouse and began the arduous task of demolition. After almost nine decades of fame and infamy, suffering and protest, the "Bastille" was to be torn down. The struggle, meanwhile, to fix the meaning of its demolition, and the future of progressive prison reform more generally, was just beginning.[5]

This carefully choreographed ceremony marked a crucial juncture in imprisonment's trouble-torn history: For the first time in American penal history, the agents of various arms of government – judges, prosecutors, assemblymen, the governor, and warden – insisted *publicly and in the presence of a great mass of prisoners* that the state owed a duty not only to its citizens but to its convicts, as well. For the first time, these agents appealed directly and univocally to the convicts to cooperate with their keepers and to carry forward the work of reform. At a time when free Americans were being called upon to do their patriotic duty and enlist in the war effort at home or abroad, the rhetoric of duty and consent became tightly entwined in official prison discourse. As agents of the penal state reasserted their dominion over the prison (having effectively expelled Thomas Mott Osborne and the new penologists from the direct administration of state prisons just months earlier), they actively sought to produce convicts' consent to, and active participation in, the building of a new penal order. At the very least, the state's administrators, legislators, and the Governor appeared to have finally learned the most fundamental of the prison's unwritten laws: Even within the high walls of a carceral institution, they could not govern by force alone.

The officials' rhetoric of consent and duty, state and ward, cooperation and care had its origins in the early progressive effort, in New York and elsewhere, to forge a new prison order in the wake of the collapse (or otherwise severe curtailment) of the old contract prison labor system. In the high

[3] *Star-Bulletin* 19:7 (Dec. 1917), 5.

[4] The judge commended the "safe, sane, kind, brotherly discipline of the armies of France, England, and the United States" as models of prison discipline. He also declared that the state owed a duty to find the convict gainful employment upon his release from prison: "Why should not the State take this matter in hand and provide employment for all discharged prisoners?" *Star-Bulletin* 19:7 (Dec. 1917), 5, 8–10.

[5] *Star-Bulletin* 19:7 (Dec. 1917), 5, 8–10.

Progressive Era, as we have seen, the new penologists had refined this discourse, reworked the concept of penal labor, and extended its logic, in an endeavor to generate a just, and systematic, solution to the prison problem. Now, as the nation mobilized for war with the Central Powers, that trajectory of thought, and the disciplinary innovations it had prompted, began to undergo a series of subtle but profound changes: Most critically, the new penological mode of prison discipline gradually tore loose from its moorings in the larger, ethical project of social justice to become a vigorously contested instrument of power. Meanwhile, outside the prison walls, the extraordinary circumstance of a war economy presented progressive prison reformers with an unprecedented opportunity to pursue the systematic restructuring of legal punishment at the state, federal, and even international levels. War mobilization revived, within progressive ranks, the dream of full-time, waged, productive labor for all fit and able prisoners; it also prompted the first federal effort to direct the reconstruction of the nation's penal systems as a whole.

This final chapter of the book concludes the long narrative of the "prison labor problem" and of its central, and highly generative, place in the history of American legal punishment. In the pages to follow, I explore the transformation of new penological prison discipline during and after the Great War, the drive to harness federal power in the service of prison labor reform, and the complex relation that unfolded between these two streams of events. As I argue here, it was in the years between Woodrow Wilson's mobilization for war, in 1917, and Franklin D. Roosevelt's mobilization to soften and save American capitalism, in the mid-1930s, that the problem would be more or less settled, and the labor-based penology of the old system, all but discarded. Ironically, this settlement would deal a final, shattering blow to the progressive prison reform movement to which it owed its origins.

Once again, New York's role in the larger, national arena of penal policy in these years was that of vanguard; throughout the period, but especially after 1934, New York offered an important working model upon which other Northern (and some Southern) states drew. There were two principal reasons for this. First, the basic legal and political terrain on which prison administrators around the country would be compelled to operate after 1934 (because of the passage of federal legislation and two ground-breaking decisions by the U.S. Supreme Court), had been operative in New York since 1896. In fits and starts, following the abolition of contracting, New York's prison administrators had initiated, discarded, and refined new disciplinary techniques that seemed better suited to the constraints imposed by state-use penal law and the ever-vigilant labor unions. The new federal laws effectively pushed the states toward state-use, with the consequences that New York's disciplinary innovations acquired fresh relevance. Second, throughout the period in question (1917–37), New York supplied the federal government with a steady stream of lawmakers, policy advisors, and jurists. At a time in which the Empire State was a bountiful source of national leaders, men and women with first-hand experience of the state's response to the prison labor problem took their insights and reform connections with them to Washington, DC. The 1935 federal law that indirectly mandated a New York-style state-use system of labor for all states was shepherded, and eventually secured, by two former Governors of New York – President Franklin D. Roosevelt and U.S. Supreme Court Chief Justice, Charles Evan Hughes, respectively. Although staunch political antagonists, both had been firm allies of progressive prison reform in New York, and both had supported the early efforts of the National Committee on Prisons and Prison Labor (NCPPL) to bring labor, business, philanthropists, and administrators together to hash out a political solution to the prison labor problem.[6]

* * * * *

The loss of direct control over Sing Sing in late 1916 left the new penologists and, especially, the NCPPL, without their principal laboratory of reform and their most important exhibition space: When Osborne had been warden, journalists, filmmakers, governors, philanthropists, and penologists from all over the country had been able to visit, study, and document a working model of the new penology. The loss of that facility thus came as a blow to the NCPPL. However, it by no means stalled the organization's reform drive. In 1917, Whitin and other members of the NCPPL's Executive Committee redoubled their efforts to educate the public about the new penology, stepped up their lobbying of state and federal law-makers around the country, and consulted with those state governments that had decided to implement New York-style reforms.[7]

In New York, the NCPPL had a critical success when Governor Whitman signed the Sage bill into law, and the State Prisons Department embarked on an ambitious project to turn Sing Sing into a classification prison. This legislation effectively ratified the recommendations of the NCPPL/National Committee for Mental Hygiene report, providing for a replacement prison for Sing Sing and the transformation of the old Sing Sing into a clearing-house to which all newly sentenced convicts would be committed for the purposes of psychiatric, medical, psychological, and vocational classification. Just as the new penologists had recommended, the law provided that all incoming state prisoners would spend some weeks at Sing Sing undergoing

---

[6] Roosevelt, as we have seen, was a long-time supporter of Osborne and the National Committee on Prisons Prison Labor (NCPPL). Charles Evans Hughes had pushed forward with plans to modernize the New York penal system and had actively supported the incorporation of the National Committee on Prison Labor (later, NCPPL).

[7] Although Osborne ceased to be the principal spokesperson of the movement, he continued to play an important role within the movement. Within weeks of resigning from Sing Sing, he met with the Executive committee of the NCPPL to organize a national lecture tour as part of that organization's larger nationwide campaign to promote Mutual Welfare Leagues throughout the United States. The committee hired Osborne a professional manager, who proceeded to coordinate his lecture tours, raise money for the NCPPL by selling seats and memberships, and run fund-raising dinners. The committee also organized a lecture series at Columbia University's Institute of Arts and Sciences in November 1916, and established student essay competitions at New York University, Columbia College, and Barnard College.

interviews and tests before being distributed to one of several specialized state prisons. It also provided for the conversion of the empty prison at Wingdale into a working prison farm, to which those convicts classified as normal but incapable of learning a trade would be transferred. Work on these projects commenced in the spring of 1917 (using prison labor), just as the country entered the Great War.[8]

In the wider legislative field, the NCPPL continued to correspond with governors and lawmakers in various states, offering members assistance as experts in the field of penal reform. In 1918–19, officials in a dozen states sought reports from the organization for the purpose of drafting penal reform legislation.[9] In large part thanks to the NCPPL's efforts on this front, a number of convict leagues, modeled more or less on the Mutual Welfare Leagues of Sing Sing and Auburn, were set up in American prisons in 1917 and 1918. The New Jersey State Prison, the Prison in Jefferson City, Missouri, the Chicago House of Correction, and Westchester County Penitentiary set up leagues, complete with Osborne-style disciplinary tribunals, in 1917–18. A number of women's reformatories also adopted various versions of prisoner self-government: The NCPPL reported, for example, that the New Jersey Reformatory for Women had set up a system of self-government in which women were organized into self-governing cottages, held elections, constituted a parliament, and drafted some of the institutional rules.[10] The U.S. Navy also adopted Sing Sing-style reforms in its military prison. Following Osborne's resignation from Sing Sing in 1916, his old comrade from the Tammany battles – Franklin D. Roosevelt, now Woodrow Wilson's Secretary of the Navy – appointed him warden of the Naval Prison at Portsmouth, New Hamsphire. Lieutenant-Colonel Osborne proceeded to remodel the prison along the same lines as Sing Sing, organizing the 6,000 servicemen–prisoners into a self-government league and removing the Marine guards from the prison.[11] According to the National Society of Penal Information, "true" leagues were founded in the prisons of a half-dozen states, and many more "modified" versions were adopted elsewhere.[12]

Although some of the new leagues were directly initiated by prison authorities, and often at the prompting of the NCPPL, the impetus for organizing

---

[8] *New York Times*, Feb 25, 1917, Magazine, 11.

[9] Some of these are discussed in "Report of the Secretary to the President and Board of Trustees of the National Committee on Prisons and Prison Labor," *Journal of the American Institute of Criminal Law and Criminology* 10:2 (Aug. 1919), 288–91.

[10] NCPPL, Prison Labor Leaflet (PLL) No. 58, "The Delinquent Girl and Woman: Proceedings of a Conference of the NCPPL," Feb. 3, 1919, 11.

[11] Osborne met with no success when he asked Governor Al Smith to appoint him to the temporary wardenship of Auburn in 1923 (in order to restore the league as it had originally worked).

[12] NCPPL, unpublished report to William Jennings Bryan, ca. 1914, OF Papers, MSS64, Box 270, Org. Recs., Misc., National Committee on Prisons and Prison Labor, 1913–21. Arkansas adopted the honor system in its state penitentiary: *New York Times*, May 7, 1933, 1. President Gerardo Machado of Cuba also oversaw the adoption of a New York-style honor system in his new national penitentiary. *New York Times*, Oct. 11, 1931, E8.

others originated among convicts who were familiar with the reforms at Sing Sing and Auburn (thanks, in part, to the NCPPL's remarkable publicity drives concerning those reforms). This was the case at Auburn's historic rival, the Eastern Penitentiary in Philadelphia. A large group of Eastern convicts sought and were granted permission to set up a committee to investigate prison conditions. In a letter to Osborne, some of the prisoner organizers explained that they had been able to obtain for all convicts one-half day of exercise in the yard, permission to write a weekly letter, and permission to buy cigarettes and toothpaste from the commissary. Much as the new penologists had done at Sing Sing, Eastern's "Four Horsemen," as the leaders referred to themselves, also attempted to clean up the black market in sex, food, and drugs by putting a stop to the theft of food from the kitchen and improving the quality of meals. They organized a court for trials of in-house larceny and requested of the warden that "convicted" offenders be removed from the general population. The Eastern prisoners also established an Emergency Hospital for cocaine addicts. (Reportedly, many convicts sought out the hospital service).[13]

The loss of Sing Sing as a laboratory and exhibition space was also partially mitigated by America's entry into the Great War. Mobilization for war provided the NCPPL with an unprecedented opportunity to affect penal reform on a national scale. E. Stagg Whitin and the NCPPL Executive ensured that the committee would have a role in the coordinated efforts of organized labor, major industrialists, and the federal government to build a war economy. As Whitin and other members of the Executive grasped, mobilization was likely to stimulate significant demand for prison labor. With more than 400,000 men passing through American prisons every year,[14] and governmental predictions that military conscription and the demand for munitions and other war-related goods would create an acute labor shortage, the new penologists made the case that American convicts were a mass of untapped laborers who, if properly organized, coordinated, and remunerated could meet that shortage. Convicts, they argued, should be put to work *en masse* in industry and agriculture; doing so would not only solve the labor supply problem but defray the costs of incarceration. The NCPPL also sought to work with organized labor and the federal government to find a way of putting prisoners to work in the armed forces.[15]

Building on their ties with organized labor, the NCPPL spearheaded an effort to enact federal legislation that would provide for the full employment of prisoners and in such a way that it would meet with the approval of

[13] NCPPL, unpublished report to William Jennings Bryan, ca. 1914, OF Papers, MSS64, Box 270, Org. Recs., Misc., National Committee on Prisons and Prison Labor, 1913–21.
[14] NCPPL, PLL No. 43, "Work or Fight! The Growth of the Compulsory Work Movement."
[15] "War Activities," NCPPL pamphlet, ca. 1917, OFP, MSS64, Box 271, Org. Recs.; President's Report, NCCPL, 1917, OFP, MSS64, Box 270, Org. Recs.; Report of Activities of the War Prison Labor and National Waste-Reclamation Section (hereafter WPLNWRS), Labor Division, War Industries Board, ca. April 1918, OFP, MSS64, Box 270, Org. Recs.; Lewisohn to *New York Times*, May 27, 1918, 12.

the trade unions. In the spring of 1917, representatives from the NCPPL and the American Federation of Labor (AFL) set about drafting a War Prison Labor bill. The principal obstacle in the way of absorbing convicts and ex-prisoners into prison industries in 1917 was the 1905 executive order prohibiting the federal government from purchasing goods made in state prisons. Although the NCPPL-AFL bill failed to pass, Whitin and Gompers nonetheless prevailed upon President Woodrow Wilson, in the fall of 1918, to issue an executive order superceding the 1905 order and permitting the federal government to make contracts with the state prisons for the purchase of goods. Wilson's new order provided that the federal government could purchase goods directly from the state prisons, so long as it paid market prices for the goods and the prisoners' wages and hours were the same as those of free workers in the vicinity of the prison in question. Shortly after the order was issued, the NCPPL facilitated the signing of the first such contract.[16]

Wilson's executive order constituted an important symbolic victory for the NCPPL: The federal government had formally recognized the principle that prisoners ought to be paid a wage. (Indeed, the NCPPL honored Wilson, on his sickbed, with a medal for distinguished service in the field of prison labor in recognition of his issuance of the order).[17] But the more important advance for the NCPPL during the war was its newfound role in shaping federal policy. The NCPPL's work, with the AFL, on the federal prison labor bill prompted the U.S. Secretary of War, Newton D. Baker, to appoint an investigator to work on the role of prisons in wartime. This culminated in the establishment of the War Prison Labor and National Waste-Reclamation Section (hereafter, "the Section") of the War Industries Board, and a coordinated effort among organized labor, business, penologists, and local, state, and federal government officials to reorganize and plan penal policy on a nationwide basis. Chaired by Hugh Frayne of the AFL, the membership of the Section included the AFL's John J. Manning; the NCPPL's E. Stagg Whitin; Commissioner General of Immigration, Anthony Caminetti; and representatives from the Federal Board of Vocational Education, the Reclamation and Conservation Division of the Office of the Quartermaster Corps, the U.S. Navy, the Department of Agriculture, and the Department of Commerce.[18] The War Industries Board described the Section's work as

---

[16] NCPPL, PLL No. 44, "The Use of Prison Labor on US Government Work" (1918), 6, 7, 9. The first federal contract awarded under this order was awarded to New Jersey: Two hundred prisoners went to work cobbling shoes for the federal government, at the going rate of 40¢ per hour and eight hours per day. *New York Times*, Nov. 9, 1918, 3.

[17] *New York Times*, Nov. 16, 1919, SM6.

[18] Charles H. Winslow, Captain H. L. Baldensperger, Lieutenant Commander Charles Hartigan, Prof. W. J. Spillman, and E. F. Sweet, respectively. Report of Activities of the WPLNWRS, 4, Labor Division, War Industries Board, ca. April 1918, OFP, MSS64, Box 270, Org. Recs. Hugh Frayne was the Chairman of the Section. NCPPL, PLL No. 43, "Work or Fight! The Growth of the Compulsory Work Movement." "War Department Organization," *The American Political Science Review* 12:4 (Nov. 1918), 701.

a critical element of the complex project of harnessing and directing the "man-power of the nation."[19]

The Section proceeded to generate what might be best described as a coordinated, socio-ecological strategy of penal planning. In the official language of the Section, prisoners and the unemployed were "social waste" that the nation, through federally coordinated action, could usefully reclaim for the war effort. That reclamation would, in part, be effected, the Section reported, by putting prisoners to work recycling another form of "waste" – broken and discarded machinery, junk, and garbage. Section members described their objective as "the utilization of the waste manpower as well as the waste material of the country;" "waste man" would salvage "waste commodity." The waste manpower with which the Section was most concerned were those adult men who were not engaged in productive labor: This included prisoners but also "bums, tramps, and vagrants," prisoners of war, conscientious objectors, and disabled U.S. soldiers and sailors. The Section listed its objectives as "securing (the) cooperation of Government Departments and organizations in reclamation of man-power and waste material," putting prisoners (both enemy and civilian) to work, and re-educating disabled military personnel. The Section set about planning the standardization of all the nation's prison industries, surveying the manpower locked up in the prisons of the states, and coordinating their deployment in the service of the war economy; members generated standardized specifications for prisonmade goods, and made provisions for the distribution of these to government departments and agencies. Prisoners were also put to work building a national road system, and paroled convicts (who, in the eyes of the law, remained "prisoners" subject to state authority) went to work in industry and agriculture. The NCPPL's seven-year campaign to get prisoners out of institutions and into "Good Roads" work was now elevated to the status of official federal policy.[20]

The Section also recommended that civilian prisoners and unemployed men without skills be put to work salvaging any industrial and municipal refuse that might be rich in valuable materials, such as copper, rubber, lead, paper, platinum, tungsten, glass, brass, and silver. They took as their model the Chicago House of Correction, the warden of which had put those convicted of misdemeanors to work in 1914 on municipal waste under the moniker of "community waste reclamation scheme."[21] The Section described the program:

> The [House of Correction] has found the real value of waste man and the waste commodity. Employment is found for the idle prisoners, especially those unfit for skilled labor, in gathering and sorting the waste of the municipal departments. . . . Motor trucks driven by a citizen chauffeur transport the

[19] Report of Activities of the WPLNWRS, Labor Division, War Industries Board, ca. April 1918, OFP, MSS64, Box 270, Org. Recs.
[20] Ibid.   [21] Ibid., 6.

prisoners to the job, where they tear apart discarded fire engines, wreck buildings, or tear up old piping or tracks.[22]

As it set about this massive logistical task, the Section embraced the incentive and reward system that the new penologists had championed at Auburn and Sing Sing (and which was, by then, also in place in the Chicago House of Correction): "It is necessary to provide incentives for the prisoner," the Section's policy documents announced, "and he is given better food, more freedom, better recreational facilities, and wages in return for his labor and loyalty."[23] The NCPPL's disciplinary innovations in the New York state prisons were also now elevated to federal policy.

As well as coordinating this remarkable resuscitation of prison labor, the Section carried another reform initiative of the NCPPL (and of the new penology in general): the absorption of ex-prisoners, upon release from prison, into free industry and other forms of gainful employment. The Section began working with the U.S. Department of Labor, private employment bureaus, and the recruitment managers of a diverse array of businesses. Among other things, the Section recommended that a national industrial classification system be set up, which would allow ex-prisoners to be matched to industrial work (much as Osborne, the NCPPL, and the Outside Branch of the Mutual Welfare League had done in conjunction with the Ford Motor Company and other corporations). The U.S. Department of Agriculture had just completed its standardized classification of that sector of the economy, and the Section took this as its model. "Thus the Section is gradually developing a scientific basis for the study and control of the man-power of the nation," the Section reported to the War Industries Board.[24]

The overall program for integrating convicts, the unemployed, and ex-prisoners into the war effort, the NCPPL and the Section members concurred, would not only forge a more productive, efficient war economy, but would save the dispossessed from themselves and enlist all members of the nation in a cooperative venture to maximize production. From the NCPPL's perspective, these programs also revived an old, and almost forgotten, penological dream: fulltime or near-fulltime productive labor for all adult male prisoners. Although it was abundantly clear that full or near-full employment of prisoners was only made possible by the extraordinary circumstance of America's entry into the world war, the NCPPL, and the Section more generally, planned to make their scheme permanent. It had longterm benefits for the United States, the official papers declared: "Out of the waste human being and waste material, in the place of infection, idleness, disease and destruction, we would develop *as a permanent contribution to our democracy* a

[22] Ibid., 6.
[23] Ibid., 7. Finally, the work of the prisoners not only contributed materials for industrial production, but raised enough funds to cover the cost of the scheme and provide for the prisoners' families. Ibid., 7.
[24] Ibid., 8–9.

system of salvage which will ensure a more wholesome community and a richer heritage" (emphasis added).[25]

As part of this federal drive to put every available set of male hands to productive labor, the question of the mass conscription of convicted felons inevitably arose. New penologists at the NCPPL and elsewhere generally favored the conscription of paroled prisoners into the armed forces, on the grounds that it was both more economic for the state (than having to police parolees) and in the interests of "public safety." Drafting parolees into the armed services would directly subject them to discipline during a time in which state parole boards had even more limited resources than usual for post-release surveillance. As the Commissioner of Correction for New York City, Burdette G. Lewis, recommended to the Mayor's Committee on National Defense, "It is cheaper and more serviceable to maintain supervision over the ex-prisoner when you have him in an organized force than it is if he is left to run about in the community and to make an additional burden upon the local police, because of the difficulties of watching him." The question was one of public order, Commissioner Lewis insisted, and given that "the maintenance of order rests upon the military in wartime" the army owed a duty to enlist ex-prisoners, if only in its lowest and most menial grades.[26]

Some new penologists also favored the conscription of prisoners who were still serving time. However, many civilians, most of the officer corps, and a minority of penologists stood firmly opposed to the conscription of prison convicts, mostly on the pragmatic ground that prisoners were likely to "corrupt" or antagonize the "honest men" of the forces, but sometimes also for the moral reason that convicts would taint the honorable name of the U.S. military. One such opponent of prisoner conscription, Edwin M. Abbot (who was the Secretary of the American Institute of Criminal Law and Criminology), opposed conscription on the grounds that convicts could not be trusted because of their supposedly antisocial tendencies. Furthermore, he argued, free men would resent serving alongside convicts, and the morale of the services would fracture. "We cannot descend, any more than did the proud Roman, to entrust to convicts the defense of the State," wrote Abbott; rather, convicts should be set to work as farmers and laborers.[27] To counter this kind of argument, a number of new penologists who were in favor of conscripting at least some of the nation's prisoners suggested that the states and armed forces work together to establish a vetting system: The states would examine all convicts about to be released and certify those who were fit for military service. One outspoken supporter of this idea, New York's Katharine Bement Davis, suggested that special companies be set up, under the regimental leadership of officers who had experience with convicts. Davis suggested, "Give the regiment a fancy name – as the Russian women

[25] Ibid., 13.   [26] *New York Times*, Sep. 30, 1918, 8.
[27] Edwin M. Abbott, "Our Criminals and Germany's," *Evening Eagle*, reprinted in *Star-Bulletin* 19:4, (Sep. 1917), 2.

have done in the 'Command of Death,' like the 'Legion of Redemption' –
prisoners are sentimental creatures. This would appeal to them and they
would volunteer. The well-known French 'Legion' has always been largely
recruited with men 'with a past.'"[28]

Disagreements over the enlistment of convicts and ex-prisoners in the
military dominated the 1917 meeting of the American Prison Association
(APA) in New Orleans. The debate lasted two days and ended with the APA
agreeing to recommend to President Woodrow Wilson only that ex-prisoners
be allowed to serve in the armed forces. In the end, Provost Marshall Crowder decided that any ex-prisoner besides those convicted of treason, felony,
or an infamous crime could enlist: This effectively enabled those who committed misdemeanors to serve but ruled out most men who had served time
in a state prison. (It is worth noting that regardless of the formal rules governing the enlistment of felons, there are fragments of evidence that suggest
a number of ex-prisoners from Sing Sing – and other state prisons – in fact,
enlisted and went to war, despite Crowder's ruling: The combined bureaucratic capacities of the armed forces and the penal state were unable, or
their agents, unwilling, to thoroughly sift convicts out of the armed forces).

In New York, as in most other states, the Prison Department responded
very positively to the War Industry Board's suggestions for developing the
productive capacity of the prisons in the agricultural sector. In 1917, the cost
of food for New York's 6,000-odd convicts was approximately $500,000 per
annum. The Prison Department had been trying to develop prison farms
for some years (at Wingdale and Great Meadow, among other places), with
a view to providing labor for large numbers of idle prisoners and making
the prisons more self-sustaining. The NCPPL had also lobbied hard for the
establishment of such farms. The war-time shortages of vegetables, fruit, and
meat and consequent price inflation in the food market led the New York
State Prison Department to expedite plans for an extensive system of convict
agricultural production.[29] Sing Sing and Auburn prisoners began working
land outside the prisons, planting enough for 6,000 bushels of potatoes and
hundreds of bushels of barley, carrots, turnips, squash, and other vegetables.
In the Adirondacks, Clinton prisoners planted 1,500 acres of potatoes, and
inmates at Great Meadow, Wingdale, the Valatie State Farm for Women, and
Matteawan sowed seeds and raised cattle.

All told, New York's 6,000 state prisoners farmed approximately $100,000
worth of food in 1917; more importantly (at least from the Prison Department's point of view), the case had been made for sustaining convict farming
once the war against Germany was over: as George W. Franklin wrote in the
state's new civil service magazine, *State Service*, in August 1917:

> (T)he big idea to be drawn from this year's experiment is the grand possibility
> of farming with convicts in the future. There are those who hold vigorously
> that not only prisons but all State institutions will be forced to raise what they

---

[28] Katharine Bement Davis, quoted in *Star-Bulletin* 19:3 (Aug. 1917), 5.
[29] Potatoes had risen to about $1 per bushel.

eat, and that it is coming is positively certain. Outside work for the convict and economy for the State are just what it will mean. There is no valid reason, or even an excuse, to explain why it should not be done now. This year plainly sustains the assumption.[30]

Finally, the war offered the NCPPL an opportunity to extend the scope of its lobbying efforts overseas. "Our responsibility," declared the NCPPL, "is to show here and now what is right and translate it into administration, not only in New York State, in the U.S., not only in England, France and Germany, but in far-off Japan, China and the islands of the seas."[31] The executive committee organized relief for American prisoners of war (POW) in Germany and met with the ambassadors of France, Germany, Britain, Japan, Austria-Hungary, and Belgium to discuss the condition of their prisoners of war and instigate an inspection system.[32] Working with the U.S. government, they offered to assist in the reconstruction of other nations' penal systems, and actively lobbied the governments of France, Germany, Britain, Japan, Austria-Hungary, and Belgium, in the early stages of World War One, to establish POW camps that adhered to new penological principles.[33] Following intensive conversations with the German government, an Osborne-style honor system was established in Germany's POW camps. At home in the United States, the committee also assisted in the preparation and planning of internment camps for German "enemy aliens," and made provisions for supplying the camps with translators from Columbia University. Finally, once the war was over, Whitin and four other members of the NCPPL Executive attended the Paris Peace Conference, where they

---

[30] George W. Franklin, "Farming with Convicts," *State Service* (Aug. 1917), reprinted in the *Star-Bulletin* 19:4 (Sep. 1917), 1–2.

[31] NCPPL, PLL (no number), "Testimonial to Adolph Lewisohn On His Seventieth," May 27, 1919.

[32] "War Activities," NCPPL pamphlet, ca. 1917, OFP, MSS64, Box 271, Org. Recs.; President's Report, NCPPL, 1917, OFP, MSS64, Box 270, Org. Recs.; Report of Activities of the WPLNWRS, Labor Division, War Industries Board, ca. April 1918, OFP, MSS64, Box 270, Org. Recs.; Report to William Jennings Bryan, Secretary of State, ca. Sep. 1914.

[33] Minutes of the Meeting of the Executive Council, NCCPL, Mar. 15, 1917; Oct. 31, 1916; July 19, 1917; "Accomplishment," unpublished pamphlet (1920), OFP, MSS64, Box 271, Org. Recs., public relations material, National Committee on Prisons and Prison Labor, 1910–31; unpublished report to William Jennings Bryan, National Committee on Prisons and Prison Labor (ca. 1914), OF Papers, MSS64, Box 270, Org. Recs., Misc., National Committee on Prisons and Prison Labor, 1913–21. The NCPPL was helped in its work to publicize the leagues by a popular prison drama from the William Fox Corporation, "The Honor System," which delivered a glancing indictment of the decaying old system of imprisonment, while affirming the wisdom of the new penology. The film tells the story of a hapless young man who is drawn into committing a crime, and is subsequently thrown into a brutal prison run by a corrupt, machine-backed warden. After the young man escapes from the prison, the state's reformist Governor appoints him as a prison investigator. Upon returning to the prison as an investigator, however, the protagonist is beaten, thrown into a dark cell, and left to die. Eventually, the Governor institutes an honor system, while the corrupt officials are sentenced to prison . . . where they serve out their sentences under the new honor system. *Star-Bulletin* 19:4 (Sep. 1917), 7.

worked in concert with Samuel Gompers to draft a labor charter for the new International Labor Organization. Thanks largely to Whitin's insistence that prison workers everywhere ought to be paid a wage and treated with "justice," the framers of the international labor charter provided that human labor should not be "considered as a commodity or article of commerce."[34]

As the NCPPL strove to carry its agenda forward on the state, national, and international levels, New York's Department of Prisons moved to consolidate its control over Sing Sing and Auburn. After Osborne resigned from Sing Sing, Governor Charles Whitman announced he intended to bring "iron discipline"[35] to the prisons. In that spirit, he appointed William Moyer, a former federal prison warden with the reputation of a strict disciplinarian,[36] to the wardenship of Sing Sing in December 1916. The convicts and Osborne's new penological coalition braced themselves for the loss of the Mutual Welfare League (MWL), and retrenchment of the various entertainment, exercise, and educational reforms. But from Moyer's first day at Sing Sing, it was evident that neither he nor the state's penal bureaucracy had any intention of turning back the clock or outright abandoning the techniques of new penological discipline. Contrary to the fears of many reformers, Moyer left many of the new penological innovations at Sing Sing and Auburn intact.[37] Indeed, under his command, some of the most important disciplinary practices introduced by Osborne and the new penologists not only survived their creators' departure, but were woven more deeply into the fabric of everyday prison life.

On the day he was due to take up his appointment at Sing Sing, William Moyer did not simply slip into the prison and assume his duties; just as the new penologists had done to such great effect before him, he contrived to

[34] NCPPL, PLL (no number), "Testimonial to Adolph Lewisohn On His Seventieth," May 27, 1919.

[35] Governor's message to the legislature, Jan. 4, 1917, 6.

[36] Moyer was warden of the federal penitentiary at Atlanta from 1905 to 1916, during which time he oversaw the construction of the prison. He was recommended for the Sing Sing post by former U.S. Attorney General George Wickersham and the wardens of the APA. Superintendent of Prisons, James Carter, quoted in *New York Times*, Dec. 7, 1916, 5.

[37] David J. Rothman equates the new penology with the Mutual Welfare League, and concludes that "the concept of a Mutual Welfare League made little impact on prison systems throughout this period." Further on, he strengthens his claim that the league was of little lasting importance: "The Mutual Welfare League made no headway at all." More generally, he argues that the reform efforts of the pre-New Deal era "came up against the prison wall." In a similar vein, Lawrence M. Friedman writes: "Osborne was forced out at Sing Sing; and the status quo soon reasserted itself." However, as a close study of the quotidian practices of the prison in this period discloses, institutional life and administration were radically and irreversibly altered in the course of the Osborne years, and many of the key new penological techniques were subsequently refined and institutionalized. The new penologists affected a decisive break with nineteenth-century penal practice and theory. Moreover, their innovations — and prisoners' and employees' response to those innovations — helped lay the practical and ideological foundations of the modern, managerialist penal state. David J. Rothman, *Conscience and Convenience* (Boston: Little Brown, 1980), 132, 145, 158; Lawrence M. Friedman, *Crime and Punishment in American History* (New York: Basic, 1993), 311.

mark his arrival at Sing Sing with a well-orchestrated celebration of a new age in prison reform. New York's new Superintendent of Prisons, James Carter, arranged for the convicts to be gathered together to receive the new warden. Upon his arrival, the heavy iron door of Sing Sing's last dungeon or punishment cell was ceremoniously hoisted off its hinges and thrown on the scrap heap as a token of the new administration's commitment to progressive prison administration. (In fact, the cell had not been used since 1914). Moyer then addressed the convicts directly, and proclaimed a "square deal" for the men of Sing Sing: He would not, he promised, return to the old system. Rather, he would "treat a man as a man and meet him halfway."[38] Convicts were invited to cooperate with the new prison regime. From the moment he set foot in the prison and throughout his wardenship, Moyer seamlessly deployed the new penologicial rhetoric of manliness and lauded its principle of cooperative relations among warden, prisoners, and staff.

Through 1917, Moyer adapted and institutionalized many of the new penologists' primary disciplinary techniques. All convicts were eligible to join the league, just as they had been under Osborne, and all but a very few did so. Although the jurisdiction of the prisoners' Judicial Board was substantially circumscribed, it was not dismantled altogether. Convict jurists heard the more minor cases of rule-breaking, and continued to expel or suspend MWL members for minor breaches of the prison rules. Moyer remained the court of last resort. The league's print shop, which had been the hub of convict publishing and MWL organizing, underwent a similar change. Soon after arriving at Sing Sing, Moyer restructured the print shop, dismissing forty of its sixty convict workers, and merging the *MWL Bulletin* with the *Star of Hope* to create the *Star-Bulletin*. This effectively allowed the prison administration to regulate convict printing much more closely than had previously been the case.[39]

The MWL continued to have biannual elections, and its committees performed most of the services they had undertaken under Osborne. The league's employment committee worked in conjunction with the Outside Branch of the Mutual Welfare League (OBMWL) to secure positions for ex-prisoners, finding work for more than half of all newly released convicts through most of 1917.[40] The membership committee remained an integral part of the commitment process at Sing Sing: Committee members met regularly with incoming convicts, and explained the rules of the league and of the prison more generally. The education committee continued to run a vocational school, staffed by convict instructors. Warden Moyer encouraged

---

[38] Moyer's address to convicts in December 1916, quoted a year after his arrival. *Star-Bulletin* 19:8 (Jan. 1918), 13.

[39] James McGrath Morris, *Jailhouse Journalism: The Fourth Estate Behind Bars* (Jefferson, NC: McFarland Co., Inc, 1998), 103.

[40] The Employment Committee faltered in late 1917; however this was due to wrangles between the new penologists of the NCPPL and the ex-prisoners who were running the OBMWL (which led the NCPPL to take over the work of securing post-release employment).

the committee to run more classes in 1917. The sanitation committee continued to organize convicts into keeping the yard clean and worked out plans with the hall keeper to have cells cleaned out twice a week. Similarly, the reception committee showed visiting officials and dignitaries around the prison. And Sing Sing's "Aurora Band" played just as regularly as before.[41]

Moyer carried forward other projects initiated under the Osborne regime. Dr. Bernard Glueck continued with his psychiatric work until he was enlisted as a senior psychiatrist in the U.S. Army. As under Osborne, the prison celebrated most national and religious holidays: Sing Sing convicts marked the Fourth of July as they had in 1915 and 1916, with baseball games, band music, speeches, and vaudeville acts from New York City. Chef Louis Beaulieu served the convicts special dinners of roast chicken, mashed potato, bread, cheese, and mince pies on the Fourth and other holidays, much as he had done under Osborne. The convicts ate these meals, as well as breakfast and the mid-day meal in the mess hall, around tables the construction of which Osborne had commissioned, but which were completed under Moyer's direction. Instead of sitting at traditional narrow tables in single file, with all men facing the same way, convicts now sat *around* regular dining tables and faced each other. The new tables not only conduced convicts to make mealtimes more sociable, but were a sign and effect of the ascendancy of new penology: The principles of the new penology had been inscribed in the prison's architecture and spatial arrangements. Where narrow tables and patrolling guards had been aimed to enforce an individuating silence through the nineteenth and early twentieth centuries, prisoners now faced each other and were allowed to converse.[42]

Perhaps most critically, warden Moyer, with the consent of the central penal authorities, expanded and routinized the existing programs of entertainment and athletics. Boxing matches were arranged, and weekly convict baseball games continued, as did competitive athletics. Moyer acceded to the MWL's request to arrange baseball games with civilian teams, and through the summer of 1917 and every subsequent summer through the 1920s and 1930s, outside teams competed against the convicts on "Moyer's Field." A number of theatrical and musical groups traveled up the Hudson Valley to perform at Sing Sing in 1917, including the Criterion Quartette, "Comedienne" Miss Norah Bayes, vaudeville acts, the musicians of the National Guard's Fifteenth (African American) Regiment, the Joy Town Band, assorted comedy troupes, a Chinese magician, and a number of leading concert musicians.[43] Evidently pleased with the order of things at Sing Sing, Warden Moyer invited the NCPPL back to Sing Sing for an inspection.

[41] *Star-Bulletin* 19:1 (June 1917), 15; 19:3 (Aug. 1917), 16; 19:7 (Dec. 1917), 7; 19:8 (Jan. 1918), 14–15.
[42] *Star-Bulletin* 19:3 (Aug. 1917), 10.
[43] *Star-Bulletin* 19:1 (June 1917), 10–13; 19:3 (Aug. 1917), 10–11; 19:4 (Sep. 1917), 15–18; 19:7 (Dec. 1917), 12–13.

The committee politely, though not enthusiastically, commented on the "friendly attitude and co-operation of the officials at Sing Sing."[44]

Whereas live performances by free citizens were a weekly fixture, moving pictures and photoplays became part of the everyday routine of the prison; this was especially so once the United States entered World War One (in April 1917) and New York City's entertainers redirected their efforts toward the troops. By mid-1917, convicts were watching a least one motion picture every night (half again as many films as they had watched in 1916).[45] The projection equipment was updated, thanks in part to a philanthropist from New York City,[46] and under the direction of George W. Thomson (the convict who had originally prevailed upon Warden McCormick to institute movies at Sing Sing in 1914), the MWL entertainment committee continued to organize the movie shows. The committee did all the work related to the shows, from arranging to borrow the films, to advertising the shows and writing reviews for the *Star-Bulletin*. Many film companies, including Vitagraph, Fox, Metro, and Paramount, commenced the practice of loaning hundreds of their latest films to Sing Sing, free of charge. A number of these films were shown to the convicts before being released in civilian theaters and, upon occasion, the stars and directors came to their film's premiere at Sing Sing.[47]

The extent to which movie shows became integral to the prison routine was evidenced by Father George J. Hafford, a visiting Catholic missionary, in February 1918. The priest was surprised to learn not only that attendance at religious services was voluntary, but that convicts could attend moving picture and photoplay shows every night of the week. When making arrangements to conduct a weeklong mission of evening services and doctrinal instruction at the prison, he was informed by the administration that the mission's exercises would have to begin after the evening's screening, because "curtailment of (the films) might cause difficulty." The answer to the priest's nervous question, "Who was going to win, the Movies or the Missionary!" was perhaps a foregone conclusion: The vast majority of convicts watched the movies, while fewer than one-third of the Catholic prisoners, and one-fifth of the general prison population, stayed on for Father Hafford's mission. The low attendance rates at religious services were mirrored throughout the state prison system, as a Prison Department agent complained in December 1917.[48] Almost without exception, the convicts proved their preference for

[44] President's Report, National Committee on Prisons and Prison Labor (hereafter NCPPL), 1917, OFP, MSS64, Box 270, Org. Recs.

[45] *Star-Bulletin* 19:7 (Dec. 1917), 7.

[46] Dr. J. Victor Wilson of the Strand Theater in New York City. *Star-Bulletin* 19:7 (Dec. 1917), 16.

[47] The author and the star of "Polly of the Circus" opened the film at Sing Sing in October 1917; Herbert Brenon brought his film, "The Fall of the Romanovs," to Sing Sing in December 1917. Other stars, including Fox Star and Virginia Pearson, visited the prison in these years. *Star-Bulletin* 19:7 (Dec. 1917), 14–15, 19; 19:10 (Mar. 1918), 22.

[48] *Star-Bulletin* 19:9 (Feb. 1918), 4–5. *Star-Bulletin* 19:7 (Dec. 1917), 6.

romances, Italian war movies, crime and punishment dramas, comedies –
and even Pathe newsreels and the Universal Animated Weekly – over ser-
mons and holy communion. At least as far as attendance was concerned,
America's burgeoning culture industry inspired greater religiosity among
the convicts than did pastors, priests, and rabbis.

Although the authorities occasionally bemoaned the failure of most convicts to attend religious services, they were quick to recognize the disciplinary
value of the mass cultural media of the silent movie and the photoplay. As the
missionary and the prison department agent were well aware, movies were
a successful innovation of prison order largely because they gave the convicts pleasure, and this pleasure was of a very particular kind: the illusion of
transcending the confines of the prison. As the convict chairman of MWL's
entertainment committee, George W. Thomson, put it, the motion picture
"transports one, for a time, from the unpromising, dull environment of the
present to a pictured version of things brighter."[49] An anonymous convict
correspondent affirmed this opinion and wrote that moving pictures "bring
to the millions of people who never travel a realization of the wonders and
beauty of America. 'See America First,' could have no better advertising."[50]
The movies delivered the convict to a certain kind of freedom; or, so the
convict-contributors to the *Star-Bulletin* asserted. This ability of the films to
"transport one . . . to . . . things brighter" induced pleasure and a desire to
return to the movies once more. Recognizing the disciplinary potential of
such treasured experiences, Moyer's new prison administration fostered the
formation of an exchange relationship between prisoners and keepers: The
authorities gave prisoners movies in exchange for their good behavior. Here
was the basic form of Moyer's "square deal."

In the moving pictures department, the striking of a square deal was
facilitated with the help of a number of production houses. The apparent
liberatory effect of movies within prison walls differed little from their effect
in civilian theaters. The movie-makers of the 1910s and 1920s appear to
have understood this and the implication that the prison audience might
be usefully deployed as a predictor of the market success of their films:
Prisoners were a palpable "captive audience" and there is some evidence
to suggest that the film companies conducted rudimentary market testing
by playing their motion pictures at Sing Sing before releasing them on the
general market. As convict entertainment organizer Thomson put it in the
Star-Bulletin's monthly movie column, the convicts had "developed a most
critical sense through having viewed so large a number of photoplay dramas.
Their judgment is held to be incredibly good by photoplay [sic] producers
and managers in that their approval of productions has invariably meant, it
has been found, that the outside public were likewise pleased, making the
production a success both from a financial, as well as an artistic, viewpoint."[51]

[49] *Star-Bulletin* 19:3 (Aug. 1917), 7.   [50] *Star-Bulletin* 19:3 (Aug. 1917), 15.
[51] *Star-Bulletin* 19:1 (June 1917), 6.

Although I have found no evidence to suggest that production companies worked out a formalized system of market research in prisons, directors and stars often visited the prison to present a new film and then talk informally with the convicts about the film afterward.[52] Film companies donated films and equipment, and, at Sing Sing, in 1922, one offered to build a movie theatre that could seat 1,500 people. (Some years later, Warner Brothers also built Sing Sing a parquet-floored gymnasium, complete with bleachers and projection box, by way of thanking the state for allowing the company to shoot a run of Jimmy Cagney films there).[53] There is also extensive anecdotal evidence that some films – most notably the crime and punishment dramas – were re-edited following showings at Sing Sing. It appears that certain filmmakers wanted to hear the convicts' "voice of experience," to garner tales of the underworld, and to verify the authenticity of the movies' depictions of thieves, cops, and the justice system. At least one company, the William Fox Film Corporation, changed the ending of one of its films ("The Honor System," a prison reform drama) when the convicts complained that its ending was sad. This is not to argue that movie producers such as William Fox and Harry Warner viewed prisons solely in commercial terms: As the film historian, Neal Gabler, has observed, many of the early Jewish film producers (Fox, Goldwyn, and the Warner brothers among them) brought a heightened social conscience to their movies and strove to portray the plight of the downtrodden and alienated in a sympathetic light. Given that prisons were widely acknowledged to be places of abuse and degradation in the 1910s, and that the new penologists had succeeded in raising the public's interest in the prisons, it is probable that these filmmakers were drawn to Sing Sing both as a source of gripping, popular drama and because it was an arena of groundbreaking social reform.[54]

If the new penologists identified the U.S. entry into the world war as an unprecedented opportunity to advance their program of reform, many convicts also sensed the opening of a new discursive and ideological space within the field of legal punishment. Judging by the prisoner-written newspapers of the period, many incarcerated men perceived that the armed mobilization of a great mass of the male citizenry, and the attendant discourse of manly, patriotic service, offered prisoners an opportunity to prove themselves fit for the freedoms and responsibilities of American citizenship. Most incisively, many of these convicts drew a conceptual connection between what Woodrow Wilson and other American leaders called the "war against autocracy" around the world, and the struggle to abolish the old penal systems at home. What both struggles had in common, prisoners argued, was the spirit of democracy.

[52] Among the stars, producers, and directors who visited Sing Sing for these purposes were Lillian Walker and Mae Marsh. *Star-Bulletin* 19:4 (Sep. 1917), 7–16.
[53] Denis Brian, *Sing Sing: The Inside Story of a Notorious Prison* (New York: Prometheus, 2005), 146.
[54] Neil Gabler, *An Empire of Their Own: How the Jews Invented Hollywood* (New York: Doubleday, 1988).

As the pages of convict newspapers from 1917 and 1918 disclose, many convicts asserted that the war with Germany was inextricably linked with American prison reform by what they viewed as the single, world-crusading spirit of democracy. The *Star-Bulletin*'s Vann Ness wrote,

> ...the dawn of the day of universal brotherly love is at hand – the world war is but the agent of a mighty force.... The present war of the world is nothing more than the voice of democracy.... the Russian peoples' revolution started from a minor bread riot; however, the yeast of public opinion arose and smothered the false rulers of ages.[55]

On this view, the trench warfare in Europe and prison reform at home were but two fronts in the global war between autocracy and democracy: Convict leaders (whose own "bread riot" of 1913 had helped precipitate sweeping reforms in the New York penal system) made it clear that they wanted to serve on both fronts.

Beginning in the fall of 1917, various groups of convicts began to lobby the U.S. government and the state's prison administrators on the matter of convicts and ex-prisoners serving in the armed forces: They requested, among other things, that both felony and misdemeanor prisoners be permitted to enlist. Through the fall of 1917, the *Star-Bulletin* carried news and reprinted articles about the war and the role of convicts, printing a special "Red Cross" issue, and splashing the iconography of American patriotism across its pages. Referring to "The Big Question of the Hour," the *Star-Bulletin*'s editor, A. W. Vann Ness, wrote that the convict "needs and will gladly welcome an opportunity to serve his country and in that service seek redemption, vindication and death if need be to atone for his mistakes of the past. He patiently and hopefully scans the horizon of bars and walls for the opportunity."[56]

Many of the convict correspondents of the *Star-Bulletin* echoed Vann Ness's words. One wrote the editor, "Prussian Kultur is dying hard, but like the old prison system it has got to go and go for good." The resident cartoonist at the *Star-Bulletin*, Mandey, likened the convicts' labor on the demolition of the Sing Sing cellblock to the soldier's labors in the world war: The cartoon depicts a young boy, in the year 1972, asking his wizened grandfather, "What did *you* do during the big war?" The old man, crouching over his walking stick, replies "I helped tear down Sing Sing, m'boy." A Sing Sing "diploma," dated 1917, hangs on the wall behind them. The idea that the work of prison reform was part of the world's struggle against oppression was repeated in letters, photographic captions, and articles: As the convicts began work on the new prison house at Sing Sing, the *Star-Bulletin* published a photograph of the convict laborers, noting that this was "trench work" not unlike the work "over there." Photographs of "Moyer's Battalion" and the prison band were frequently published over captions that conflated prison

---

[55] *Star-Bulletin* 19:4 (Sep. 1917), 4, 8. [56] *Star-Bulletin* 19:4 (Sep. 1917), 4, 8.

reform and the war effort: "The Spirit of 1917 Finds its Way into Grim Old Sing Sing Prison,"[57] read one such line.

As the American war effort gathered momentum, Vann Ness's editorials became increasingly strongly worded, to the point that in January 1918 he asserted that every "true American," whether foreign or native born, had a "*right*" (italics added) to prove loyalty and love of country; to fight and die for one's country was, he continued, the "white man's chance." In deploying the rhetoric of the rights and duties of men, Vann Ness and other convict contributors extended the rhetorical strategy that their predecessors had first developed in the early days of prison reconstruction in the late 1890s: They mirrored the reformers' language of manliness, with its emphasis upon civic and economic responsibility, back on its authors. In the context of American war discourse, which framed enlistment as a manly duty, the new penological concept that convicts should be treated "like men" lent itself to convicts' efforts to improve prison conditions or be released from prison to join the war effort directly. The *Star-Bulletin*'s resident poet, "Duke," put the matter in the following verse:

> Tho' felons – we are men, Sirs,
> Who are willing to requite
> The wrongs we've done Society –
> By helping in the fight.[58]

The *Star-Bulletin*'s writers and cartoonists were not the only convicts to promote the idea of convict conscription. Several groups of Sing Sing convicts wrote directly to high-ranking members of the armed services and state and federal government, offering their services in the war. In June, 1917 the convict staff of the Sing Sing hospital wrote to the Surgeon General of the United States Navy (W. C. Braisted) offering to attend the sick and injured. The Surgeon General replied that "although the offer is greatly appreciated," the Navy could not utilize them at present. Similarly, the leader of Sing Sing's "Aurora Band," Tony De Genoa, offered the Superintendent of Prisons the use of his band for war-related events. Superintendent Carter commended the band leader on his patriotism but said that there was no possibility of using the band in the foreseeable future.[59] Similar events transpired at Auburn, where the league leaders wrote to Governor Whitman, asking if they could organize a battalion that would serve in Europe and then return to prison. As the Auburn convicts were quick to point out, many

---

[57] *Star-Bulletin* 19:4 (Sep. 1917), 9. Vann Ness also began reprinting articles published in other prison papers and in the civilian press that debated the conscription of convicts. One convict, "R.W.B.," of the Massachusetts State Prison, wrote a lengthy reply to Abbot's diatribe against convict-soldiers, which the *Star-Bulletin* and other prison papers reprinted: Mocking Abbot's "turn to ancient precedent (and), Roman history, to clinch (a) 1917 argument," he dismissed the idea that civilian soldiers were morally any better than convicts, and rubbished Abbot's Lombrosian concept of convicts as a corrupt criminal class. Convicts should be allowed to serve.

[58] *Star-Bulletin* 19:3 (Aug. 1917), 4.   [59] *Star-Bulletin* 19:3 (Aug. 1917), 4.

of the convicts already had military experience from serving in the regular Army, the Navy, foreign armed services, the militia, and military schools.[60] Sing Sing convicts also organized themselves to help in the war effort in other ways. Jewish prisoners set up the Jewish War Sufferers Fund, while over 1,000 convicts contributed $1,000 for a liberty bond, which they then presented to the Red Cross.[61] (Sing Sing prisoners were not alone, here. Nationwide, prisoners purchased some $106,350 worth of Liberty Bonds, and just under $35,000 worth of War Savings Stamps).[62] In August 1917, the convicts set up a drill squad, known as "Moyer's Battalion," which underwent standard U.S. Army drill training. The convicts of the clothing company sewed military white uniforms for the battalion and the band, and the *Star-Bulletin*'s editor publicized the Battalion's preparations for war.[63] Reprinting Katharine Bement Davis's article in favor of the conscription of convicts into a special regiment, editor Vann Ness began referring to the members of Moyer's Battalion as the future soldiers of a "Legion of Redemption." The MWL also erected a flag upon which eight gold stars, each representing a keeper who had been drafted, were embroidered. And prisoners, at Sing Sing and around the country, gave thousands of gallons of blood.

The convicts also celebrated the commencement of the demolition work on the "Bastille" as part of the crusading spirit of war-time America: In the pages of the *Star-Bulletin*, correspondents and poets marked the demolition of the Sing Sing cellblock as both a hopeful and a disconcerting event. Some wrote earnestly of the end of the era of oppressive prison conditions. Frank Lawson, a convict hospital attendant, poet, and regular *Star-Bulletin* contributor, wrote "Sing Sing's Requiem" to mark the occasion:

> Thy day hath come
> Accursed, soul-warping pile of uncouth stone
> Abode of Misery – Monument to man's inhuman hate.[64]

The last stanza of the poem marked the cellblock's demolition as the end of the old system, and the hopeful beginning of the new:

> Gray, mantled tomb, thy course is run.
> The saner thought, the broader, wider view

---

[60] Bulletin, Auburn Mutual Welfare League, July 8, 1917. The convicts offered to fight in Europe.

[61] *Star-Bulletin* 19:9 (Feb. 1918), 16; *Star-Bulletin* 19:12 (May 1918), 13.

[62] "Report of the Secretary to the President and Board of Trustees of the National Committee on Prisons and Prison Labor," *Journal of the American Institute of Criminal Law and Criminology* 10:2 (Aug. 1919), 287.

[63] Although many prisoners embraced the war effort (for whatever reason), the pro-conscription lobby among the prisoners should not be understood as representative of all convicts; in fact, there is some evidence to suggest that men arrested for crimes in New York City were pleading guilty to crimes in order to be imprisoned rather than drafted. The *New York Telegraph*, for example, reported that a Judge McIntyre, of the Court of General Sessions, had noted an upswing in number of conscript-age men who "without any hesitation" entered a guilty plea. Reprinted in *Star-Bulletin* 19:3 (Aug. 1917), 5.

[64] Frank Lawson, "Sing Sing's Requiem," *Star-Bulletin* 19:7 (Dec. 1917), 16.

Hast set the world ahead a hundred years.
Farewell, *bon voyage*, we mourn you not at all.[65]

In the poet's eyes, justice was being done, and the cellblock's oppression of generations of prisoners was being avenged: "The 'Law of Compensation' seeks it due,/Thy day hath come." Others cracked sometimes bitter-edged jokes about the demolition: The cartoonist, Mandey, depicted an old-timer throwing himself across his cell door, protesting to a pick-wielding laborer, "In youth it sheltered me an' I'll protect it now!" In another cartoon, an aging man stands before the judge and pleads, "Please judge – *Don't* send me to Sing Sing – it ain't like the old home no-more!"[66]

The demolition and construction work changed Sing Sing's everyday life substantially: The prison population decreased (as men were transferred out), and more than half the remaining convicts were put to the hard labor of flattening the cellblock and grading the rocky terrain behind the prison. The projected loss of 400 cells in the following six months meant that almost one-third of the convicts had to be drafted to Clinton, Auburn, Great Meadow, or the farm colony at Wingdale. Two hundred-odd Sing Sing convicts began the work of digging and grading the rocky hill behind the prison, while another 200 prisoners worked on the cellblock. The work proceeded according to the new penological principle of the honor system. By March, 1918, one-quarter of the cellblock lay in ruins around the prison yard; visitors to the prison wrote of a prison yard awash in a "rainbow" of pictures, crucifixes, and inscriptions that had been carved or painted on the stones by generations of captives. Mandey joked that the rough stone chips might be valuable souvenirs one day.[67]

As the convicts organized themselves for the war effort and promoted the idea of the "white man's chance" to redeem himself and become a citizen, New York's prison bureaucrats and political leaders seamlessly appropriated the new penological rhetoric of manhood and impressed upon the convicts at every possible moment that convicts and their keepers alike were conducting themselves as men. Whenever the warden or the Governor or another official addressed the convicts, they referred to the prisoners as "Men" or "Men of New York, . . . " and proceeded to assure the prisoners that the state would endeavor to treat them as men. Virtually no speech passed without a request to the prisoners to "conduct yourselves like men."[68] That this was often self-conscious and did not come naturally was made evident in some hilariously botched speeches delivered to the prisoners on Christmas Day, 1917. Warden Moyer began by addressing the prisoners as "boys," then hurriedly corrected himself to say "Men . . . ". A few moments later, he reflected, "Boys – this is the second time that I have called you boys – but I believe there is one time in the year that we feel as if we were boys again, and that is the reason I am calling you boys."[69] Awkwardly attempting to salvage his speech,

---

[65] Ibid., 16.
[67] *Star-Bulletin* 19:7 (Dec. 1917), 2.
[69] *Star-Bulletin* 19:9 (Feb. 1918), 6.

[66] *Star-Bulletin* 19:7 (Dec. 1917), 2.
[68] *Star-Bulletin* 19:7 (Dec. 1917), 2.

Moyer proceeded to say that he hoped that today, Christmas Day, the Sing Sing men could be boys again: "by being happy, being joyous, being glad of the thought of the times that we spent at Christmas seasons in our boyhood days, and then when the holiday season is over we can return to our labor, bravely take up our duties and perform them like men . . . ."[70] A subsequent speaker that day, Prison Commissioner Charles Hubbell, then drew further attention to the administrators' conscious deployment of the rhetoric of manliness when he admitted that he was "in a little doubt whether to say boys or men after what the warden has said to you." He continued,

> Three or four days ago, when Mrs. Hubbell asked if I would go down with her to the Christmas tree of my golden-haired grandchildren, I said: 'I am going up to Sing Sing to be with my boys.' Yet I like to think of you as men and if I did not think of you as men I would not have been here at all, because it was the hope that I might possibly bring something into your lives that would bring more sunshine to you at this Christmas time, and I have been made happy that I was allowed to undertake the work that is in operation here, and which brings me into closer relation with you.[71]

Dr. Bernard Glueck, the Sing Sing psychiatrist and a firm supporter of the MWL, then addressed the prisoners as "Men of Sing Sing" and congratulated Warden Moyer on his "sterling honesty and upright manliness" in his administration of the prison: "The strong man and the manly man in Sing Sing have a great responsibility in our new work. It is to them that we look for the creation of a sentiment for fair work, honest purpose, and a determination to be loyal to the trust imposed."[72]

Whatever the convicts (who were not drinking liquor that day, unlike the loquacious officials) made of these and similar speeches that would be made over the next several years, they continued the tactic of pledging their manly allegiance to the warden. Like the prisoners of the late 1890s, who had first learned to mirror the rhetoric of humane reform and the state's advancement back on administrators, and the Auburn prisoners who had later celebrated the anniversary of Thomas Mott Osborne's entry to prison (as Tom Brown) and commended the administrators who had made that possible, the convicts endeavored to hold the agents of the state to their word. The MWL's staging of an award ceremony for Warden Moyer upon the first anniversary of his wardenship is a case in point: With the cooperation of the guards, the convicts arranged for Moyer to go to the chapel, where the convicts and the band awaited him. As the unsuspecting Moyer walked in, the band burst in to "Hail to the Chief." The Secretary of the MWL then addressed Moyer and the convicts: "We all know how well [the warden] has made good on every one of the momentous problems of prison administration that confronted him, and how his handling of those affairs has brought order out of chaos. We have had, everyday, examples of the manly square deal he is giving everyone of us." The league proceeded

---

[70] *Star-Bulletin* 19:9 (Feb. 1918), 7.   [71] *Star-Bulletin* 19:9 (Feb. 1918), 7
[72] *Star-Bulletin* 19:9 (Feb. 1918), 8.

to present the warden with an engrossed resolution praising him for his interest in the welfare of the convicts; more speeches ensued, followed by the inevitable performance of the "Star Spangled Banner." Once more, the convicts mirrored the rituals and rhetoric of the so-called manly square deal back on the authorities, in a bid to affirm the reforms and innovations of the last few years and, perhaps too, to secure recognition as men, and not just prisoners and criminals.

On first blush, it appears that the war had significantly advanced the new penological program of prison reform. Many of the disciplinary initiatives that the new penologists had championed before the war had become routine parts of New York prison life. Recreation, education, athletics, music, the privilege system, and even the leagues remained an important part of prison life and discipline. Beyond New York, moreover, a growing number of prisons and reformatories had adopted the self-government principle. In addition to these intramural developments, the war had transformed the NCPPL into a highly influential shaper of state and federal penal policy, and had stoked its leaders' confidence that the organization had within its grasp a truly systematic solution to the prison labor problem. (One spokesperson went so far, following the armistice, as to claim that the NCPPL was now in a position to influence penal policy on a global scale: Indeed, in the wake of the devastation of Europe, the organization was now "the only real, driving scientific force which the world possesses on the subject").[73] War mobilization had also reinvigorated the NCPPL's drive to abolish penal servitude and establish waged, state-use prison labor systems around the country. It had also propelled the NCPPL into a position of direct influence, both with regard to federal policy (via the War Industries Board) and in relation to the various state governors and lawmakers who sought out the organization's guidance as they moved to put state prisons on a war footing.

On closer inspection, however, the case for the war's positive impact on progressive reform was not so clear-cut. The NCPPL's newfound influence, during the Great War, proved short-lived. The war demobilization process, which flooded the nation's labor markets with returning servicemen, rendered the full employment of prisoners impossible. Penal labor policies that the NCPPL had hoped would be permanent dissolved along with the War Industries Board.[74] Although, in the years before the war, many states had

---

[73] NCPPL, PLL (no number) "Testimonial Meeting to Adolph Lewisohn On His Seventieth," May 27, 1919.

[74] E. Stagg Whitin, "Self-Supporting Prisons," *Annals of the American Academy of Political and Social Science* 113 (May 1924), 132–3. Despite the loss of direct access to federal power, through the 1920s, the NCPPL continued its effort to develop a variation of the state-use system of prison labor, which it called, in the possessive plural, "states' use." The idea was to establish regional prison labor zones, in which the prisons of one state could sell their wares to governmental agencies in a neighboring state. Again working with the AFL, the NCPPL organized a series of "zone conferences," beginning in 1923, at which state governors pledged to establish prison trade zones. Whitin set up a private agency to coordinate the market (Associates for Government Services). However, this work was cut short by the enactment of the federal Hawes-Cooper and Ashurst-Sumners acts (in 1929 and 1935,

adopted New York's state-use system of prison labor, after the war, a number of these states (including Illinois and Massachusetts) reintroduced the public account system – largely in an effort to compensate for sagging sales under the state-use system.[75] The previous consensus, among Northern penologists, that state-use was the best system as a rule, fractured in the 1920s as it became clear that prisoners could not, in fact, be put to fulltime labor under that arrangement.[76] Meanwhile, within the prisons, the progressive reforms that were carried forward into the war years quite quickly became detached from the larger, ethical project of progressive prison reform. Indeed, they became part of quite a different kind of disciplinary order. What had originated, in the cradle of high progressive reform, as an ambitious, moral project of rehabilitation became, in the course of the war, a more mundane, managerial project of institutional administration. Administrators at Sing Sing, Auburn, and elsewhere increasingly placed more emphasis on making good prisoners out of inmates than on making good citizen-workers out of prisoners. This severing of progressive disciplinary techniques from their higher, moral purpose (of reform) began during the war, and only accelerated in the 1920s. In the course of that decade, in the prisons of New York and elsewhere, the goal of social justice would be more or less fully eclipsed by that of institutional stability.

The instrumentalization of progressive reform was hastened in New York by the ongoing demise of prison industries and vocational training under the state-use system. Several large-scale attempts by successive legislatures and Governors in the 1920s to reinvigorate prison industries flatly failed.[77]

respectively), which indirectly closed down the interstate commerce in convict-made goods. On the development of the so-called "states' use" (as distinct from the "state-use") idea, see Whitin, "Self-Supporting Prisons," 132–3; Whitin, "A Plan for the Interstate Sale of Prison Products," *Annals of the American Academy of Political and Social Science* 125 (May 1926), 260–4; and Hugh Frayne, "The States Use System," *Journal of the American Institute of Criminal Law and Criminology* 12:3 (Nov. 1921), 330–8.

[75] "Convict Labor in 1923," *Bulletin of the U.S. Bureau of Labor Statistics* 372 (1923), 169–235; Howard B. Gill, "The Prison Labor Problem," *Annals of the American Academy of Political and Social Science* 157 (Sep. 1931), 94. Only five states did not re-adopt the public-account system in some degree: New Hampshire, New Jersey, New York, Ohio, and Wyoming. Arthur H. Schwartz, "Legal Aspects of Convict Labor," *Journal of the American Institute of Criminal Law and Criminology* 16:2 (Aug. 1925), 273, fn. 10.

[76] In 1925, Henry Calvin Mohler, the author of a long article on the history of prison labor, observed that "there seems to be increasing disagreement once more" among penologists. Many had come to favor public-account industries, whereas those affiliated with the NCPPL were still fully committed to the state-use system. Mohler, "Convict Labor Policies," *Journal of the Institute of Criminal Law and Criminology* 15:4 (Feb. 1925), 530–97.

[77] Governor Alfred Smith, for example, initiated a massive overhaul of the state prison industries in 1924. On the advice of the NCPPL, he undertook to put prison industries on a business basis. His plan included establishing a state board of prison industries, modernizing all the workshops, paying the prisoners a wage, and appointing a marketing manager. Only the first objective was met. A year later, the State Prison Commission also proposed running Sing Sing's industries on business principles: that is, working prisoners eight hours a day and under strict industrial discipline; nothing changed, however. In 1928, a subcommission of the Baumes Crime Commission recommended a sweeping overhaul of prison

Thirty years after the legislature had first mandated the state-use prison labor system, the majority of New York's state prisoners still had no productive labor or vocational training, and those who did were performing considerably less than a full day's work. Sing Sing's figures were typical: At the beginning of the 1920s, just over one in every three prisoners were engaged in productive labor of some sort, if only for a few hours each day; by the end of that decade, that rate had fallen to less than one in three.[78] Moreover, none of the prisoners who worked put in a full eight-hour day, six-day work week. Sing Sing's industrial supervisors lamented that even though the state had announced several elaborate plans for the revival of prison industries, and spent large amounts of money to that end, "little had been accomplished."[79] Under these conditions, the disciplinary powers of productive labor and vocational training were rendered ever more negligible. In the early 1920s, the wardens responded by extending and routinizing the new penological techniques of discipline (such as recreation and athletic programs) to fill the ever-widening disciplinary void.

Although Osborne and the new penologists had never considered the far-flung Clinton prison fit for a league or self-government system (because of that prison's status as a punishment facility for "hardened" and incorrigible offenders), after the war, Clinton's administrators adopted many of the new penological techniques of discipline. "Trusty" convicts organized recreational activities, including movie screenings and athletics. Regular entertainments and recreational activities became routine in the 1920s.[80] In 1919, a new chapel-auditorium, capable of seating the entire prison population, was opened, and convicts began viewing two motion pictures per week.[81] Indeed, Clinton prison seems to have been better adapted to the dawning age of mass culture than was the local town (Dannemora), which lacked a cinema. The prison cinema became a convict theater in the afternoons and a public, admission-charging theater by night. (Proceeds from the movies paid for the cost of summer recreational activities). Like the convicts at Auburn and Sing Sing, Clinton prisoners lacking a primary education now attended school. Convicts received a few hours of physical recreation on Wednesdays, Sundays, and holidays in the warm months. They also played baseball, both among themselves and with outside teams, and put on a variety show every year.[82] None of this was even couched in the language of

industries; again, no progress was made. Alfred Smith, Special Message to the Legislature, Jan. 21, 1924, quoted in *New York Times*, Jan. 22, 1924, 21; *New York Times*, Dec. 6, 1924, 4; *New York Times*, Aug. 7, 1925, 30; *New York Times*, Dec. 14, 1927, 24; *New York Times*, Mar. 4, 1928, 29.

[78] *New York Times*, Oct. 1, 1928, 45.   [79] *New York Times*, Oct. 1, 1928, 45.

[80] These activities notwithstanding, in 1924 investigators reported that transfer to Clinton was still regarded by the prisoners as a severe punishment. Report, National Society for Penal Information, ca. 1924, 5–6 c. (Thomas Mott Osborne established this society in 1922, on the view that the progressive reform movement was in retreat; it later became part of Osborne Association [1932]).

[81] *DOCS Today* (Oct. 1987), 10.

[82] The tuberculosis patients had movies and radio year-round.

reform, let alone the upshot of a new attempt to make good citizens of bad men: They were simply new disciplinary techniques designed to secure the peace of the prison.

At Auburn, warden Edgar S. Jennings maintained the league and allowed it to run elections for representatives, with the proviso that all MWL officers had to be approved by him.[83] Through the 1920s, the MWL Judiciary Board continued to operate, and suspension from the league remained a critical disciplinary technique. Education also continued at Auburn, with a staff that was predominantly made up of convicts who provided primary schooling up to sixth grade and a civics class in "Americanization." The MWL's principal function at Auburn was to organize and fund the prison's entertainment and recreation programs. The league facilitated daily recreation in the yard, laid a baseball diamond (upon which convicts played each other and outside teams), and organized regular movie shows.[84] Vitagraph, Fox Film Corporation, Metro-Goldwyn-Mayer, and Warner Brothers supplied Auburn with free films through the 1920s. The league continued to put on variety shows for the public twice yearly and occasionally the convicts watched outside entertainments (though the distance of Auburn from New York City precluded regular shows and lectures).[85] As well as being the vehicle through which entertainments were organized, the Auburn league was a linchpin of the disciplinary order: The entertainments and recreation the league organized had the double effect of pacifying the convicts and operating as a privilege conferred in return for obedience. More minor transgressions of the rules were heard before the MWL, which punished offenders by suspending or expelling them from the league (and thereby all recreational privileges). In the first six months of 1923, the Auburn league ordered more than 300 suspensions. As at Clinton, the warden conceptualized the activities as aid to administration, rather than the cornerstones of a rehabilitative, progressive prison order.

It was at Sing Sing that the instrumentalization of new penological reform found its fullest expression. More than any other prison warden, Sing Sing's Lewis E. Lawes insisted that the best prison was one in which the prisoners were well-fed, well-exercised, and frequently entertained. Lawes had risen through the ranks of prison administration from the position of prison guard at Clinton, in 1905, to that of Superintendent of the New York Reformatory for Boys, in 1916, and, finally, in 1920, to the wardenship of Sing Sing. He brought with him an unusually acute understanding of the peculiar problems that beset prison administrators in the years after the abolition of prison labor contracting. A first-hand witness to the great disciplinary and political crises that beset New York's penal system in the early Progressive Era, he also had an intuitive grasp of the "unwritten law" of the prison that

---

[83] Frank Tannenbaum, *Osborne of Sing Sing* (Chapel Hill: University of North Carolina Press, 1933), 273–5.
[84] Movies were shown every night in winter and some nights in summer.
[85] *Star-Bulletin* 19:9 (Feb. 1918), 7.

the convicts would forcefully defend what they took to be their fundamental rights.[86] Between 1920 and 1943, Warden Lawes carefully and skillfully constructed a prison order based on the principle of the square deal and the morale-building techniques that Moyer had begun to refine at Sing Sing. Grasping that the stability of the prison also depended upon outside forces, he also worked tirelessly to legitimize his administration in a slew of books, articles, radio shows, and Hollywood films.

When Lawes arrived at Sing Sing in 1920 to take up his wardenship, he gave all the prisoners a clean disciplinary slate and placed them in "A" grade. As "A graders," they were entitled to all entertainment and recreational privileges. Lawes explained that if they broke a rule, they would be demoted to "B" grade, with limited privileges. A further offense would land them in "C" grade, with no privileges. Good behavior would result in promotion to a more privileged grade. As part of this overhaul of the disciplinary system, Lawes reorganized the sale of tobacco and other comforts at the prison, linking the purchase of those "pleasures" to the disciplinary system: He merged the two commissaries to create a single grocery store, and authorized prisoners to purchase a set amount of goods each week, to be determined by the grade they were in. Lawes then set about extending sporting activities at Sing Sing and made the mass media of radio, film, and newspapers part of the fabric of everyday life. He installed a master radio receiving station in the east wing of the prison and appointed a civilian censor, who then relayed selected radio programs to loud speakers and headphone sets around the prison and cellhouse. He also expanded the prisoner baseball program, established a football team, laid down playing fields and handball courts, and gave the prisoners three hours of outdoor exercise time every afternoon in the summer months.[87] Like Moyers and Osborne before him, Lawes continued the practice of having outside teams come to play the prisoners; in 1925, he also organized a memorable ballgame on the prison diamond, between the New York Giants and the New York Yankees (Babe Ruth was reported to have hit the ball over the field wall for a home run; unfortunately, the outcome of the game appears not to have been recorded).[88]

---

[86] For Lawes's account of his early days at Clinton and Elmira, and his analysis of the prison troubles of the pre-war period, see Lawes, *Twenty Thousand Years in Sing Sing* (New York: Ray Long and Richard R. Smith, 1932), 12–64. Although Lawes understood prisoners' conception of their elemental rights, he recognized few of these rights as having any basis in positive law (the two he did explicitly acknowledge as properly legal were the right to attend a religious congregation of the prisoner's choosing and the right to a minimum food allowance [Lawes, *Twenty Thousand Years*, 186]). Nonetheless, Lawes's actual management of the prisoner indicates that he understood the force of custom in the prisons and that he was very attentive to convicts' sense of fairness in all his dealings with them.

[87] LEL (1): Box 8, File 37, "Black Sheep" Scrap Book; File 36, Mutual Welfare League; and LEL (Supp.): Box 3, file 73, C, Inmate Related Files, Correspondence, 1936–46; Box 3, A, Administrative, Files 60–61; Box 3, File 66, Sing Sing Commissary Dep't Reports, 1936, 1938; Box 3, A, File 71, Sing Sing Files, Administrative, Music in Sing Sing.

[88] Denis Brian, *Sing Sing: The Inside Story of a Notorious Prison* (New York: Prometheus Books, 2005), 129.

As at other New York prisons, the new warden retained the MWL, chiefly as an organizing staff by which to provide entertainments, education, and recreation, and as a disciplinary agency, by which convicts who transgressed minor rules would be policed and punished. Lawes also moved to consolidate his administrative powers *viz.* the MWL (which, just like outside reformers and embattled politicians, was a potentially disruptive force from the administrators' point of view). In particular, he took steps to mute the league's voice beyond the prison walls and to curtail the scope of its activities within the prison walls. The administration clamped down on prisoners' correspondence with the outside world, and warden Lawes established a censorship office where all prisoners' outgoing correspondence (whether letters to loved ones or short stories for publication) and incoming mail were scrutinized for subversive content. Lawes also restructured the league's election process and prohibited the prisoner "political parties" that had emerged in the late 1910s, on the grounds that prison-yard electioneering was overly exciting and emotional for the prisoners, and hence damaging to prison morale. From 1920 onwards, the league's primary obligation was to regulate the leisure hours of prisoners, Lawes directed; its other obligations were to maintain discipline at these events and to represent prisoners' grievances and requests to the warden: "The League was to be a Moral force," insisted Lawes; "If it could not sustain itself in that capacity it was futile and should be eliminated."[89]

Lawes also maintained the automobile, barber, cart, and tailoring classes and made reading and writing courses compulsory for all illiterate convicts. By 1934, all convicts were routinely administered educational tests. Those achieving lower than the level of the sixth grade were then enrolled in classes taught by a civilian head teacher, two civilian assistant teachers, and twenty grade school convict teachers. Ten prisoners taught more advanced courses, and several convicts were enrolled in correspondence college courses run by the Massachusetts Department of Education.[90] It was under Lawes that psychomedical therapies became a critical component of the disciplinary regime, not merely as a means of classifying prisoners (as the new penologists had initially envisioned them), but as a means of managing convicts' daily frustrations, depression, and desire to rebel. Like the educational, recreational, and athletic programs, the psychomedical sciences were given over to the therapeutic pacification of convicts. Glueck's psychiatric Classification Clinic was reorganized and funded by the state in 1926 and proceeded to surveil the entire prison population; clinicians also began attending the warden's court to give advice on disciplining rule-breakers. Convicts were encouraged to seek psychological and

---

[89] Lawes, *Twenty Thousand Years in Sing Sing*, 117–21.

[90] In 1932, Sing Sing offered classes in twenty-nine subjects, including economics, newspaper writing, arithmetic, French, "business geography," and personnel management. Lawes, "How a Warden Looks at Education," speech given at Columbia University, 1934; Lawes, *Twenty Thousand Years*, 170–1.

psychiatric advice from Dr. Amos T. Baker and his staff of psychologists and psychiatrists.[91]

Throughout his career, Lawes repeatedly made it clear in press releases, radio interviews, and a series of books and articles that high prisoner morale was the immediate objective of his penology, and the peace and security of the prison were his foremost concerns. As he put it in an interview in 1924, under his system:

> The men are no longer bottled up, constrained to silence, tyrannized and brutalized by unworthy keepers, or exploited and spied upon. They are permitted some chance of self-expression, some freedom for their personalities. They are shown humane and constructive precepts and they are not repressed, screwed down and baffled. The result is that we have almost done away with those emotional explosions so common in the older kinds of prisons. All acts of violence and attempts at escape are the result of these emotional disturbances.[92]

Lawes conceptualized the various reforms initiated by the new penologists as means to the end of higher morale. On the question of education, for example, Lawes justified the expense of running classes for prisoners: "To me, as a warden, prison schools more than justify their continuance and expansion if for no other reason than to foster and maintain the morale of those prisoners who take advantage of the facilities offered them to study and to learn."[93] In a similar vein, Lawes argued for the benefits of commercial radio at Sing Sing: "I am happy to report," he wrote in *Radio Guide* in 1934, "that since this system has been in vogue, the morale and behavior of the prisoners [have] rocketed sky-ward."[94] As Lawes conceptualized it, the proper objective of prison management was to facilitate "decent, normal and satisfying expression of personal interests."[95] This expression was entwined in a system of incentive and privilege that aimed at keeping the convicts more or less happy. Even fire-fighting (for which the convicts were responsible) succumbed to the logic of Lawes's managerialism. As he wrote, "There is a keen rivalry between the different fire companies and positions on the fire department are frequently given as rewards of merit."[96] So, too, the death of a prisoner (by natural or other causes) became an occasion for boosting the morale of other prisoners: "When a fellow dies," Lawes informed an audience at the New School for Social Research in 1931, "whatever his religious belief was, or if he had any, or if he hadn't, whatever his

---

[91] Aims and Methods of the Psychiatric Clinic (State of New York Department of Correction, ca. 1936), Reports of the Classification Clinic, LEL (Supp.), Box 3, File 63.

[92] Lawes, *The World*, c. Sep. 15, 1924, 1 (LEL Papers, II, Scrap books: Correspondence, 1924–25).

[93] Lawes, "How a Warden Looks at Education," 7.

[94] Lawes, "Radio Goes to Jail," *Radio Guide* 3:37 (July 7, 1934), 3.

[95] Lawes, Radio address over WABC, May 7, 1936; 3, LEL (Supp.), Box 1, File 22.

[96] "Sing Sing Prison Has Its Own Fire Department," *Modern Fire Chief* (no number, ca. 1930), 4–5.

belief was, it is respected. I don't know if that helps a fellow that is dead any, *but I think it helps the fellows who are left behind"* (emphasis added).[97]

Notably, Lawes rarely mentioned the new penological objective of restoring convicts to citizenship. Indeed, he frequently argued that crime originated in the structures and pathologies of modern industrial society itself, and would be eliminated only once those structures were themselves changed. As he saw it, "(u)nder our present social order prisons are a necessary evil."[98] For Lawes, unlike Osborne and the new penologists, the chief task of prison administration was not to "cure" criminals or deter crime; it was to maintain the peace and security of the prison, both within the institution's walls and outside, in the large sphere of penal politics.

Although most, if not all, the disciplinary techniques found in Sing Sing and the other New York prisons in the 1920s owed their origins to the progressives, those techniques were being put to different uses and were taking on very different meanings than the ones progressives had intended. At Sing Sing, the enlightened "republic of convicts" became a bargaining table across which prisoners and administrators hashed out a "square deal;" the goal of making good prisoners of convicts usurped that of restoring convicts to manly worker-citizenship. The lament of one new penological investigator, in 1924, was typical:

> The emphasis today is laid on the gaining of privileges as a reward for conduct rather than in stimulating the sense of individual responsibility for the common welfare, which is the basis of good citizenship. In one case the privileges are used as a (sic) end in themselves; in the other, merely as the means to a very different, and far greater end.[99]

The disappointed observer concluded that the warden "uses the League chiefly to serve the prison administration rather than uses both the League and Administration to serve society."[100] The title of an article by the prison psychiatrist, Dr. Bernard Glueck, neatly captured this important change in emphasis: Although rehabilitation remained a formal objective of imprisonment, "morale-making" was the guiding principle of the new system. Although both the new penologists and the administrators of the 1920s aimed to produce a prison order in which the convict turned outwards from his self, his soul, or his morbid unconscious and became absorbed in activities that sublimated his mental and physical energies, the new penologists had subordinated those techniques to the overriding objective of socializing prisoners as self-disciplined worker–citizens. After the war, conversely, New York's prison wardens consistently reiterated that imprisonment's principal task was essentially managerial in nature: The administrator's job was to

97 Lawes, untitled address at the New School, 15. In the 1930s, Catholic, Jewish, Episcopal, Christian Science, and Salvation Army services were available for convicts. "Religious Services in Sing Sing Prison," LEL, 3, 63.
98 "New Deal on the Outside," *New York Times*, Aug. 16, 1931, 67.
99 Report, National Society for Penal Information, ca. 1924, 9–10.
100 Report, National Society for Penal Information, ca. 1924, 9–10.

maintain what Lawes referred to as the "morale of the domain" and he was to achieve this by establishing various activities that sublimated the passions and desires of the prisoners.[101]

The morale of the domain depended upon prisoners and keepers entering a double relationship of exchange. On the one hand, prisoners exchanged their good behavior for "good-time": That is, if they behaved well, they would regain their liberty sooner. In the meantime, they also traded obedience for the gratifying privileges of attending (or playing in) convict baseball matches, watching movies, making use of psychiatric counseling services, and purchasing tobacco and other small pleasures from the prison commissary. Radio, cinema, recreational activities, athletics, access to a well-stocked grocery, and therapy were all part of one pervasively psychological penal order of sublimation. These various activities were comforting commodities to be purchased with the only hard currency a prisoner possessed: obedience. Lawes did not hesitate to plainly state this point: "Naturally the convicts have to pay some price for the possession of such a cherished bounty. The asking price is a matter of obedience."[102] At Sing Sing, in particular, but to a significant degree in Auburn and Clinton as well, prison order came to rest on a more or less tacit agreement between prisoner and keeper that the former could purchase some measure of pleasure from the latter by resisting the urge to cause trouble. Morale-building, as a technique of maintaining peaceful institutions, took the place of moral reform.

Within a few years of arriving at Sing Sing, Lawes had completed the transformation of the original new penological project into a new, managerialist penal order. Although elements of this penal managerialism could be found in other New York prisons (and in a number of other states, including Texas, Minnesota, Illinois, and California),[103] nowhere was it as fully and systematically developed as at Sing Sing. In the few years either side of 1930, three separate, though related, strings of events would propel Lawes's system to national notice and reinforce the relevance and utility of penal managerialism. The first set of events concerned the passage of tough new sentencing laws in New York in 1926. The "Baumes laws" triggered an unprecedented increase in New York's state prison populations, which, in turn, exerted tremendous pressure on prison administrations; all of this came to a head in 1929, in a series of bloody prison uprisings. Around the same time, the

---

[101] Lawes, *Twenty Thousand Years in Sing Sing*, 102, 151. It should be noted that, as a way of making sense of and justifying imprisonment, the administrative ideology of the 1920s was no less self-consciously ethical than the new penology: In the view of the leading prison administrator of the 1920s, making morale was an irreducibly moral venture. See Lawes, *Twenty Thousand Years in Sing Sing*, 374–81, 390.

[102] Lawes, "Radio Goes to Jail," 3.

[103] See Ethan Blue, "Hard Time in the New Deal: Racial Formation and the Cultures of Punishment in Texas and California in the 1930s," (Ph.D. diss., University of Texas at Austin, 2004), espec. Ch. 6, "Athletic Discipline and Prison Celebrations in the Popular Culture of Punishment," 352–413.

country was hit by the deep recession that would eventually become the Great Depression. Like industry everywhere, struggling prison industries around the country slowed, and, in some instances, ground to a halt. Spiraling unemployment and underemployment rates in the outside world generated further pressure on prison industries, as trade unions demanded that free workers be given priority over prisoners; manufacturers joined the fray, lobbying hard at the state and federal levels to close down state-run prison industries that competed with their own. Finally, Congress intervened. It enacted two laws that had the combined effect of prompting the states to severely restrict the scope of prison industries; they also left those states that had resisted adopting an exclusive state-use system of prison labor (such as New York's) with little option but to adopt it.

As Lawes set about building a managerialist order at Sing Sing in the 1920s, popular attitudes toward progressivism, in general, and progressive prison reform, in particular, had been undergoing a sea-change. The bloody riots, red scares, post-war recession, and federal crack-downs of 1919 and 1920 had already dampened popular enthusiasm for the more ambitious progressive reform movements, including the new penology, by 1921. Subsequently, prohibition's stimulant effect on organized crime, and the outbreak of highly localized, but extremely violent, struggles for the domination of the beer, liquor, and related black markets (most prominently, the Chicago "beer wars" of 1923–24), prompted great concern among middle- and upper-middle-class Americans that a tremendous wave of crime and disorder was engulfing the nation. A series of reports, issued by various state and city crime commissions, declared that the nation was, indeed, in the grip of an unprecedented crime wave. Slowly but surely, in the early and mid-1920s, the press, radio, and concerned citizens turned the focus of public discourse about crime and punishment away from the internal workings of prisons and toward the policing, prosecution, and removal from society of those responsible for the alleged wave.

By 1924, progressive prison reformers were openly lamenting the atrophy of public interest in the cause of humanitarian prison reform; two years later, many noted that this inattentiveness had turned to outright hostility toward a number of the foundational principles of progressive penology. That year, under the leadership of Republican Crime Commissioner, state Senator Caleb Baumes, the Republican-dominated New York state legislature breathlessly enacted twenty-two crime bills that, together, had far-reaching implications for offenders and life in the state's prisons. Popularly known as the "Baumes laws," the new legislation created new crimes, retrenched procedural protections for the accused, abolished the good-time system under which good behavior in prison reduced a convict's sentence, reintroduced mandatory sentencing, and drastically raised maximum sentences for a number of serious crimes. (For example, the maximum sentence for first-degree robbery was raised from twenty years to life imprisonment and, for second-degree robbery, from ten to fifteen years). Most infamously, the Baumes laws strengthened the state's 1907 habitual criminal law by providing that any person convicted of a fourth felony "shall be sentenced to life imprisonment without possibility of parole or commutation of sentence."[104]

The passage of these laws had little, if any, appreciable impact upon New York's supposed crime wave (although, according to an outraged Clarence Darrow, they contributed significantly to a national "hate wave" and constituted an egregious assault upon civil liberties).[105] The laws did, however, play a catalytic and, in many ways, deeply ironic role in the history of legal punishment. In effectively abolishing indeterminate sentences and providing that upon a fourth conviction for felony crime a convict would automatically receive a life sentence without possibility of parole or commutation, the Baumes laws threw a large spanner into the disciplinary machinery of the prisons. As noted earlier, the logic of the new disciplinary system held that prisoners would render up obedience in exchange for earlier freedom and, in the meantime, the pleasures and releases afforded by movies, athletics, tobacco, and various other sublimating activities. The Baumes laws, however, challenged three of the principal presuppositions of this penology: namely, that all but a small minority of convicts would eventually leave prison; that no hardened core of embittered, hopeless "lifers" would accumulate in the prison; and that every prisoner, in theory at least, enjoyed the possibility of early discharge through good behavior. These were important structural preconditions for penal managerialism's system of incentive; without them, convicts had much less reason to cooperate with the administration and far more incentive to rebel.

As well as tinkering with the incentive system of managerial penology, the Baumes laws breached a principle of justice dear to the hearts of prisoners: equality of sentencing (wherein the same crime got the same time, regardless of the convict's record). As Warden Lawes understood very well, equality of sentencing, and more especially prisoners' *perception* that the criminal justice system treated convicts more or less equally, was essential to the task of maintaining the good morale of the prisoners – and, hence, the good order of the prison. The "four strikes" law engendered the situation by which a person

---

[104] For the new sentencing laws, see: Laws of New York, 1926, Chs. 436, 457, 469, 705, 707, 736, 737. For a summation of the passage of the Baumes bills into law, see: *New York Times*, Mar. 18, 1926, 1; Mar. 19, 1926, 20, 23; Mar. 22, 1926, 18; Mar. 24, 1926, 1, 3, 4; Mar. 27, 1926, 8; Mar. 30, 1926, 3, 8; Mar. 31, 1926,: 3, 22; Apr. 2, 1926:, 1,2, 5; Apr. 6, 1926, 8; Apr. 7, 1926, 4; Apr. 8, 1926, 2; Apr. 9, 1926, 8; Apr. 11, 1926, sec. IX, 13. The new laws also directed that all prison convicts were to serve two-thirds, rather than half, of the imposed sentence, and that anyone sentenced to time in prison should serve at least one full year behind bars. The Baumes laws also took aim at criminal procedure, repealing various laws designed to protect the accused from unfair trial practices, and made new crimes of manufacturing and selling certain weapons, including brass knuckles and a variety of poison gases developed during the Great War. Finally, the laws provided for the establishment of a Bureau of Criminal Identification in the State Prison Department, the duty of which would be to generate records for use in the sentencing procedures regarding the new four strikes law.

[105] Clarence Darrow denounced the Baumes laws, and others like them, declaring that the country was "in the midst of the most reactionary period since the Civil War." *New York Times*, Feb. 18, 1929, 9.

convicted of four burglaries would be automatically incarcerated for life without possibility of parole or commutation, whereas a person with a conviction for manslaughter (or even two previous convictions for manslaughter) would more likely serve a sentence of twenty years. This assault upon equality of sentencing prompted Lawes to complain to a reporter from the *New York Times* that the Baumes laws quite perversely provided robbers an incentive to kill their victims and plead guilty to what was now the lesser charge of manslaughter.[106] The third problem posed by the Baumes laws was that their provision for longer sentences and mandatory lifetime sentences for fourth-timers threatened to trigger a rapid increase of the prison populations in prisons that were already putting two, and sometimes three, men in cells measuring just six feet by five feet. The Baumes' laws seemed very likely to overfill the prisons; moreover, the surplus of prisoners would consist not in the usual run of convicts, but in an aggrieved and hopeless class of convicts who considered themselves profoundly wronged by the law.[107]

Once the Baumes laws went into effect in July 1926, prison populations began to grow quite steeply and prison conditions began to degenerate. The initial source of the increase was not a rapid upswing in new commitments, but rather a decrease in the release rate, and people entering with longer sentences to serve: Fewer people were committed to New York's state prisons and reformatories in 1927 than in 1926, but New York's state prison population nonetheless increased quite steadily in the following years, as the first to be sentenced to life under the four strikes law began to trickle into the system. Every year after 1927, commitments to the state prisons increased dramatically. In 1928 and 1929, the population of the four main state prisons increased over eleven percent, or just over five percent per annum.[108] Cellblocks that already held a full complement of prisoners overflowed: By 1929, New York's male state prison population exceeded cell capacity by almost 1,000 men – or twenty percent – of the prisons' capacity.[109] Although, in and of itself, the increase in the sheer number of prisoners exerted considerable pressure on the prison order, the particular source of the surplus population was even more significant. Just as Lawes had warned, the prisons began accumulating miserable and volatile lifetime prisoners, and a larger mass of prisoners serving longer sentences for lesser crimes.[110] At Sing Sing,

---

[106] *New York Times*, Apr. 11, 1926, 23.

[107] Lawes criticized the laws again in 1931, pointing out that the state "had taken away hope by outlandish long sentences. There is practically no hope left," and implying that a direct causal link existed between the new sentencing practices and unrest in the prisons. Lawes, untitled address at the New School, 30, LEL.

[108] These figures are taken from the Bureau of the Census, Annual Census of Prisons, 1927; George W. Kirchwey, "The Prison's Place in Penal System," *Annals of the American Academy of Political and Social Science* 157 (Sep. 1931), 13; *New York Times*, July 28, 1929, xx7.

[109] *New York Times*, July 28, 1929, xx7.

[110] By 1930, New York's prisons held 198 lifetime prisoners convicted under the Baumes four strikes laws; a much larger, but undetermined, mass of convicts serving the newly lengthened sentences was also rapidly accumulating. Lawes, "The Change in Society's Attitude Toward the Criminal" (unpublished address, 1930), 8.

an influx of Baumes "lifers" increased the total number of prisoners serving life terms by sixty-five percent in just sixteen months.[111] These were precisely the prisoners whom Lawes warned would have no hope for the future and who, in their mounting desperation, were likely to resist, escape, or even attempt to overthrow prison authorities.

Prisoners at Auburn and Clinton, the prisons to which the majority of repeat and lifetime convicts were committed, became increasingly restive in these years.[112] Audacious escape attempts multiplied: A train-load of men being transferred out of overcrowded Sing Sing to Clinton in late 1927 attempted a mass break in transit (the attempt was foiled). The same year, Clinton authorities intercepted a cache of weapons, ammunition, and maps intended for a group of prisoners, and learned of plans for a large-scale prison break. In another spectacular, if equally unsuccessful, escape attempt, three convicted felons held in Manhattan's "Tombs" police jail used smuggled pistols to shoot their way to freedom; along the way, the warden and head keeper were shot dead, and two of the prisoners turned their weapons on themselves rather than face trial under the new laws. The rate of smaller-scale escape attempts also inclined – both at the state prisons and at police jails, where accused offenders awaited trial under the new sentencing laws or transfer to a state prison.[113]

Under the strain, the critical mechanisms of managerial prison discipline – sublimation and the activation of a convict's desire to be free – threatened to jam. The respective state prison wardens took immediate steps to head off trouble: All scaled-up security and most rolled back privileges. In the midst of the statewide spate of escape attempts, the warden of Great Meadow abolished the honor league and put the convicts to work building a high wall around that previously low-security prison.[114] At Auburn, warden Edgar S. Jennings abandoned the basic managerial approach and began to crack down on various prisoner-organized activities. Anxious to assert his authority, Jennings moved, in 1927, to cancel the established celebrations surrounding various national and ethnic holidays in the prison. Failing to recognize that such affairs could be restructured in such a way as to stabilize rather than undermine the prison order, Jennings insisted they were inherently disruptive, unruly events: "The Irish-Americans wish to celebrate St. Patrick's Day; the colored men, Emancipation Day; the Italians, Columbus Day; the Polish, a Polish Day; and the Hebrews, a special feast day," he exclaimed in an exasperated memo to the Superintendent of Prisons in 1927. "The rivalry between those few different groups to have

---

[111] In November, 1927, 49 of Sing Sing's 126 life prisoners had been sentenced under the Baumes law. *New York Times*, Nov. 18, 1927, 25.

[112] Chandler, Report to the Governor on Auburn Prison, Dec. 19, 1929, 2, (RGO), 13682–82A, Central Subject and Correspondence Files, Roosevelt, 1929–32, NYSA.

[113] *New York Times*, June 10, 1926, 16; Nov. 4, 1926, 1; Nov. 8, 1926, 1; Jan. 1, 1928, 12; July 16, 1928, 1; Aug. 6, 1928, 1; Aug. 13, 1928, 1; Aug. 22, 1928, 4; Mar. 2, 1929, 12; July 23, 1929, 1.

[114] *New York Times*, Feb. 4, 1927, 9.

a more successful performance, bigger acts, and more entertainment has developed a condition that is very unsatisfactory," he went on: The celebrations had to be curtailed.[115] The warden proceeded to abolish half-holidays, lock-down the prisoners in their cells on Saturday nights, cancel special suppers, reinstate the punishment cells, and suspend various privileges. As warden Jennings cracked down, prisoners began defying orders, the warden punished alleged troublemakers with ever longer periods of isolation in the punishment cells, and the keepers turned against both the league and a warden who seemed incapable of reining in the prisoners.[116] Clinton's warden rolled back privileges and segregated suspected troublemakers in the punishment cells.

At Sing Sing, Lewis E. Lawes took a different tack. Like his colleagues up-state, he quietly tightened security at the prison (chiefly, by suspending visiting, reinforcing the prison wall, and mounting machineguns on the watchtowers).[117] But, at the same time, he stepped up his program of morale-building. Lawes redoubled his efforts to demonstrate his responsiveness to the prisoners and their needs. As well as maintaining established programs, he gave the entire prison a special chicken dinner, motion pictures, and live music on Thanksgiving; likewise, on Christmas day, he and his wife provided the men with movies, a special meal, and small "favors" and gifts. At the request of one "lifer" he ordered the stars and stripes hoisted within sight of the cellblock, in honor of the 300-odd Great War veterans who resided there.[118] He also extended the new psychiatric program at the prison, describing the program as a great asset to prison administration.[119] Finally, he made a number of public statements in which he made it clear, not only to the general public but to the prisoners, that he was unequivocally opposed to the Baumes laws and that he felt considerable empathy for the convicts. All men, including prisoners, had their breaking point, Lawes declared in a 1928 radio address on *Collier's* hour (which was broadcasted live to the men of Sing Sing): All were subject to temptation.[120]

The deteriorating situation in the prisons came to a head in the summer of 1929. At Clinton prison, on July 22, 1929 (almost exactly three years after the Baumes laws had gone into effect), 1,300 prisoners attempted to storm the walls and burn down the buildings. Before a hastily convened force of keepers and volunteers restored order, three prisoners were shot dead and dozens more, peppered with buckshot. Governor Franklin D. Roosevelt

[115] Jennings to Long, Jan. 4. 1927, Seymour Collection, Letters and Organizations, Mutual Welfare League.
[116] Jennings to Long, Jan. 4. 1927, Seymour Collection, Letters and Organizations, Mutual Welfare League. Investigators reported in 1930 that the guards were unanimously opposed to the Mutual Welfare League, and that, in particular, they resented the warden's referral of serious rule-breakers to the league's disciplinary court. George Fletcher Chandler, Report to the Governor on Auburn Prison, Dec. 19, 1929, 2, NYSA, (RGO), 13682–82A, Central Subject and Correspondence Files, Roosevelt, 1929–32.
[117] *New York Times*, June 24, 1927, 3; Aug 20, 1927, 16; Aug. 20, 1928, 16.
[118] *New York Times*, Nov. 26, 1926, 4; Dec. 26, 1926, 18; May 31, 1927, 34.
[119] *New York Times*, Jan. 29, 1928, 19.   [120] *New York Times*, Dec. 3, 1928, 22.

454   *The Crisis of Imprisonment*

indicated, following the Clinton rebellion, that no executive action was needed.[121] However, within days of the Clinton rebellion, the escalating power tussles at Auburn erupted into open conflict. A full-scale uprising broke out. Auburn prisoners rioted for several days, razing the wood and furniture shops, foundry, dye house, store house, and commissary and seriously damaging five other prison buildings. Order was restored only after the National Guard was called out.[122]

Realizing that these riots were probably not isolated incidents, after all, Roosevelt called for an immediate and wide-ranging investigation of the prisons, and for a review of the Baumes laws (which he strongly inferred were responsible for the recent unrest in the prisons).[123] Using a technique he would later put to use as President of the United States, Roosevelt convened a series of "parleys" at his Manhattan residence, calling together a wide array of experts, including prison wardens, members of the NCPPL, and criminologists, to discuss the prison situation.[124] As the investigation got underway in earnest, Auburn prisoners acted a second time to register their frustration and anger at the Baumes laws. In December 1929, a handful of Auburn prisoners rebelled once again, this time taking warden Jennings hostage and calling for the release of their comrades from the punishment cells. When the authorities refused to cooperate, the prisoners put that marvelous technology of penal managerialism – the radio system – to work, broadcasting a general call to riot, and successfully precipitating a second, full-fledged prison uprising. The National Guard was called out once more. By the time order was restored, the principal keeper and eight convicts were dead, four guards and two convicts were seriously wounded, and dozens of convicts and guards had been gassed. (Warden Jennings survived).[125]

Auburn and Clinton were not the only prisons to experience large-scale rebellions in 1929. Following New York's lead, a number of states had legislated Baumes-like four strikes laws. Several other large-scale uprisings and prison breaks broke out across the United States that year, almost always in states in which the prisons had become very overcrowded. Six hundred prisoners in Philadelphia's county prison rebelled and were put down by force. Four days after the July riot at Auburn, almost 4,000 prisoners mounted a full-scale riot at the federal penitentiary in Leavenworth, Kansas, setting fire to the prison and taking possession of the prison arsenal. A lethal, full-scale uprising took place at Colorado Territorial Correctional Facility at Canyon City in October 1929, in the course of which eight guards and five prisoners

---

[121] *New York Times*, July 23, 1929, 3.
[122] Memo (Commander, of New York State Troopers) to Franklin D. Roosevelt, ca. Dec, 1929, (RGO), 13682–82A, Central Subject and Correspondence Files, Roosevelt, 1929–32, NYSA.
[123] *New York Times*, July 30, 1929, 1.
[124] These were held in September and October of 1929. *New York Times*, Sep. 13, 1929; Oct. 24, 1929, 27.
[125] Raymond Kieb to Franklin D. Roosevelt, Albany, Dec. 12, 1929, (RGO), 13682–82A, Central Subject and Correspondence Files, Roosevelt, 1929–32, NYSA. The National Guard at Peekskill, Yonkers, White Plains, Comstock, Dannemora, and Elmira were put on alert.

were killed. Ohio, like New York, had enacted strict sentencing laws in the late 1920s. In 1930, the state prison in Columbus, Ohio, burnt to the ground under suspicious circumstances, killing 322 prisoners and sparking a full-scale uprising (in the course of which 1,000 prisoners took possession of the cellblock).[126]

Notably, convicts at the most infamous of American prisons – Sing Sing – did not riot. Although it was the case that Sing Sing had not borne the full brunt of the four strikes laws (largely because it received mostly shorter-term first and second-time offenders) it was, nonetheless, more overcrowded than at any other point in its history, and it did have a small, but rapidly growing, population of Baumes "lifers."[127] Like his colleagues, Lawes had tightened security as unrest among the prisoners had mounted after 1926. But, unlike the others, Lawes had extended and reinforced the morale-building disciplinary system and sought, at every turn, to shore up the "square deal" between prisoners and keepers.

Upon hearing rumors that Sing Sing prisoners might follow Auburn's example and riot, Lawes deftly deployed a combination of force and empathy to maintain control of Sing Sing. He immediately talked with the Sing Sing convicts and solicited their grievances. While consulting with his wards, he also made it clear that any collective action or protest on the convicts' part would be met with swift and certain repression. An overwhelming show of force punctuated this threat: Within hours of the December uprising at Auburn, three companies of the National Guard went on alert at Sing Sing, a small U.S. naval vessel sailed up the Hudson from New York City, and three more Gattling machine guns appeared on the high wall of the prison.[128] As convicts witnessed this show of force, Lawes quietly suspended the MWL's annual Christmas show on the grounds that a large gathering of convicts might be volatile. As Lawes later told the story, when the league's leaders voted to resign in protest and rumors began circulating to the effect that a riot was imminent, he accepted their resignations and then promptly informed the prison population that the former organizers had resigned and were on their way to Clinton prison. But even at this point, Lawes did not abolish the league or institute a prisonwide crack-down, as Jennings had done at Auburn. Rather, he worked with the league's new leaders (who quietly "agreed" with Lawes that the show, indeed, ought to be cancelled, after all) to calm the prison. Rumors of imminent riot subsided.[129] Some sixteen years after the scandalous rebellion of 1913, and as prisons around the state and in other parts of the country erupted in protest, Lawes had enforced the good order of Sing Sing. Even more critically, he had been seen to have done so.

<hr>

[126] *New York Times*, July 29, 1929, 1; Oct. 4, 1929, 1; Apr. 30, 1930, 1; May 1, 1930, 1.
[127] *New York Times*, Nov. 18, 1927, 25.
[128] Memo (Commander of New York State Troopers) to Franklin D. Roosevelt, ca. December 1929, (RGO), 13682–82A, Central Subject and Correspondence Files, Roosevelt, 1929–32, NYSA.
[129] Lawes, *Twenty Thousand Years*, 45. See also Tannenbaum, *Osborne of Sing Sing*, 267.

Rather than undermining the penal managerial model of imprisonment, the riots of 1929 indirectly facilitated its consolidation and extension throughout New York's state prison system. That the Baumes laws had very likely precipitated the Auburn and Clinton prison riots was not lost on Governor Franklin D. Roosevelt; nor did Roosevelt fail to notice Sing Sing's relative calm and Lawes's apparently adept handling of the unrest there. In a confidential memorandum to Lawes, Roosevelt sought his advice and, in particular, his views on the Baumes laws' impact on prison order. A series of official investigations further called into question both the efficacy and the justice of the Baumes laws and cast a very positive light on Lawes and his well-worked-up model of prison administration. Following the December riot at Auburn, a hastily convened commission headed by Colonel George F. Chandler (former Superintendent of the New York State Police) scrutinized not only the actions of prisoners, but prison conditions and the conduct of the warden, guards, police, and troopers.[130] In his report, Chandler condemned Auburn as an overcrowded prison full of ill-disciplined, underfed convicts and declared that a small group of "desperate" longterm convicts (of the sort generated by the Baumes laws) had taken over the MWL and were more or less running the prison. His objection, critically, was not that the convicts were attending entertainments but that the warden had suffered the MWL to become a thuggish gang under the tutelage of the longterm men.[131] He concluded by recommending that the overcrowding of the prison be relieved and the Auburn MWL, abolished.[132]

In a separate investigation, Joseph M. Proskauer, an associate justice of the Supreme Court of New York, affirmed these findings but was far more explicit in placing the blame for the riots squarely on the shoulders of the Baumes laws. Proskauer urgently recommended that Governor Roosevelt undertake "fundamental and drastic reform" of the state's penal system.[133] The Superintendent of Prisons, Raymond Kieb, also criticized the Baumes laws, and recommended the restoration of compensation time. He publicly

[130] Franklin D. Roosevelt to George F. Chandler, Albany, Dec. 14, 1929; and Roosevelt to James J. Hosmer, Albany, Dec. 14, 1929, (RGO), 13682–82A, Central Subject and Correspondence Files, Roosevelt, 1929–32, NYSA. Roosevelt insisted that the Grand Jury investigate not only prisoners but "any violations on the part of guards, keepers, employees" and others.

[131] Chandler wrote: "These League officers have police powers, administer punishments, order privilege taken away or granted, run entertainment once or twice a year for which they collect money from the general public who attend, and run a baseball club where male outsiders may attend." Moreover, the convicts ran the telephone switchboard, assisted in mail handling and the cleaning of the offices, guard rooms, and hallways, which, Chandler objected, compromised security. Chandler, Report to the Governor on Auburn Prison, Dec. 19, 1929, 2, NYSA, (RGO), 13682–82A, Central Subject and Correspondence Files, Roosevelt, 1929–32.

[132] Chandler also recommended segregating the "incorrigible" convicts from the general population; that the state hire and train at least fifty new guards; reduce the guards' work week to six days (as was the case at Sing Sing); and appoint civilians to the manage the prison's communication and finances. Ibid., 5.

[133] Joseph M. Proskauer to Roosevelt, Dec. 13, 1929, NYSA, (RGO), 13682–82A, Central Subject and Correspondence Files, Roosevelt, 1929–32.

declared: "(i)t was the strongest instrument the office had for the preservation of law and order in the prisons, as each [convict] knew that behavioristic [sic] deviation led to time forfeiture and delayed the date the prisoners might be granted the privilege of again being free."[134] Finally, the National Society of Penal Information (whose membership was composed of veteran progressive reformers) issued a report laying the blame for the first two New York rebellions on the new sentencing laws, the curtailment of the good-conduct system of early release, and the retrenchment of parole.[135]

In 1930, Roosevelt proceeded to act on these recommendations. He and the Superintendent of Prisons consulted with the wardens about how best to rebuild discipline at Auburn and in the system more generally: Warden Lawes's Sing Sing was to serve as the basic model of reform. Notably, prison industries – which, just a few years earlier, had been the object of intensive discussion – were given very little emphasis. In announcing the appointment of two prison planning committees (one on the "segregation" of various classes of prisoners and one on prison industries), Roosevelt indicated that putting prisoners to productive labor would most likely not be part of the solution: Noting that "an idle prisoner becomes a brooder and only too often eventually a plotter" he suggested that "trade schools rather than . . . factories" might be established in the prisons.[136] Instead, New York's prison reforms concentrated on segregating various classes of prisoners, repealing the Baumes sentencing laws, and, slowly but surely, applying the principles of Lawes' managerial penology across the entire state prison system. Roosevelt announced a $30 million program for the improvement of prison conditions, athletics and exercise programs, education, manual training, and the systematic segregation of various classes of prisoners. Notably, when Roosevelt discussed the program he remained silent on the topic of prison industries.[137]

Over the next few years, the principles of the sublimation of prisoners' emotions through a variety of mostly nonlaboring activities, the privilege system, and the occasional show of uncompromising force, were generalized to the entire state prison system. Although, at Auburn, the MWL was abolished (as per Roosevelt's request), the recreational and educational activities its members had organized were eventually reinstituted under the auspices of the state, much as Chandler had recommended. On Lawes's insistence that good food was an important "aide to morale," the quality of prison rations was improved all round.[138] Psychiatrists were hired for each prison and proceeded to play an important role in the assessment of those

[134] *New York Times*, Dec. 22, 1929, xx5.

[135] *Handbook of American Prisons and Reformatories*, 1929. Notably, the Society stiffly criticized Lawes's peaceable Sing Sing for its lack of industries and vocational training.

[136] Roosevelt, quoted in *New York Times*, Mar. 14, 1930.

[137] *New York Times*, Oct. 30, 1930, 20.

[138] Both Lawes and Roosevelt insisted that poor food played an important role in demoralizing the prisoners, and that good food was a precondition for a peaceable prison. *New York Times*, Aug. 3, 1929, 32.

convicts thought to pose a risk to the prison's security. Sing Sing psychiatrist, Bernard Glueck's, taxonomy of mental health was adapted to these ends; in all the prisons, the psychiatrists' primary task was that of adapting petulant, troublesome, or depressed convicts to prison discipline and identifying for segregation (or exile to Clinton) those deemed to be security threats.[139] Penal managerialism's need for guards who would resort to psychological, rather than corporeal, means of managing prisoners, was implicitly recognized in the planning and execution of the state's first guard training programs and the New York State Training School for Guards at Wallkill prison (opened in 1936).[140] Finally, in 1931, at the recommendation of the State Commission of Correction, and with the vocal support of Lawes and Roosevelt, the New York legislature repealed several of the Baumes laws: Most critically, lawmakers reinstituted one of the cornerstones of managerial penology – the good-time compensation plan, under which good behavior was to be rewarded by early release.[141] A year later, Roosevelt signed into law a bill that repealed the mandatory life sentence that another Baumes law imposed on fourth-time offenders: Persons convicted of a fourth felony were now subject to a minimum sentence of fifteen years in prison rather than the mandatory sentence of life.[142]

As part of this general overhaul of the state prison system, Roosevelt also established a State Commission on Prison Administration and Construction, charging it with the task of planning and building six new prisons. The state's second great wave of prison building soon followed, and in four years, five new state prisons were opened (Attica, Bedford Hills, Coxsackie, Wallkill, and Woodbourne). All were to be administered according to much the same managerial principles prescribed for the other prisons of the state. Critically,

---

[139] The trend toward the systematic incorporation of psycho-medical experts into the prison was already underway in the late 1920s (supra, p. 299), but accelerated after the 1929 riots. Its principal objective was the pacification of convicts and the identification and treatment of potential rebels. All the prisons developed segregation wings in which convicts thought likely to disrupt prison order were held. The psychiatrist at the New York state reformatory at Elmira described the function of his department as one of isolating the "underworld of the institution" in one of three sub-units. From time to time, tensions developed between the Wardens and the psychiatrists, as they did at Clinton and Sing Sing in 1935, when the psychiatrists recommended abolishing the prison commissaries on the grounds that they advertised disparities of wealth among convicts: Lawes refused the advice and countered that the convicts' ability to purchase a few groceries went further toward keeping the peace at the prison than did the expensive team of psychiatrists. He quipped to Clinton's Warden Wilson: "We are in the driver's seat. Let's drive and pay no attention to the small boys throwing snowballs." Lawes to Joseph H. Wilson, Ossining, Jan. 31, 1935, LEL (Supp.), Box 3, File 70.

[140] Walter Mark Wallack, *The Training of Prison Guards in the State of New York* (New York: Bureau of Publications, Teachers' College, Columbia University, 1938).

[141] State Commission of Correction, Report on Sing Sing, Jan. 1931, quoted in *New York Times*, Jan. 5, 1931, 48; New York (State) Commission on Prison Administration and Construction, *Progress Report and Proposals* (Albany: J. B. Lyon and Co., 1932); *New York Times*, Feb. 1, 1930, 36; Feb. 20, 1930, 13; Mar. 2, 1930, 6xx, Mar. 20, 1930, 4; Dec. 4, 1930, 27; Jan. 5, 1931, 48; Feb. 17, 1931, 17; Feb. 20, 1931, 13; Mar. 10, 1931, 2; Apr, 11, 1931, 10.

[142] *New York Times*, Apr. 6, 1932, 4.

prison labor was not to be used in the construction of these new facilities: William Green, the President of the AFL, successfully lobbied New York state, and the federal government, to restrict the use of penal labor in public works on the grounds that convicts were provided with "food, clothing, and shelter" while, as the Great Depression wore on, free labor was going without. Prisons were "public works" and as such, it was agreed that free labor, rather than convict labor, should build them.[143]

As the Roosevelt administration moved, in the few years following the riots of 1929, to put its prison system on a firmer, managerial footing, the legal and political terrain of imprisonment around the nation at large had begun to change dramatically. In the 1920s, as noted earlier, all but five states operated public-account penal industries: That is, they put prisoners to work under and for the state making goods for sale on the open market. A significant minority of states (seventeen) still also ran some or most of their prison industries on the old contract system. Both kinds of industries tended to concentrate on a handful of lines of manufacturing: textiles, garment, shoes, and cordage. Moreover, their markets were regional, and sometimes even national, in scope. Although a number of states, including New York, had prohibited the sale of their own prisons' product on the open market, under the interstate commerce clause of the U.S. Constitution they were powerless to prevent the importation and sale of other states' prisonmade goods. Clothing made under sweated contract labor in Maryland's state prison flowed into New York, Ohio, and New Jersey, as did coal and steel from the leased prison industries of Alabama.

Beginning in 1924, free manufacturers in the textile, garment, shoe, and cordage industries mobilized to put an end to competition from prison labor contractors. Meeting with the Secretary of Commerce, Herbert Hoover, industry representatives requested that the Department of Commerce undertake an impartial study of the prison industries in question. Hoover obliged, appointing an advisory committee made up of representatives from both prison and free industry. The committee was bitterly divided on the question and took three years to present its findings. (Even then, the report failed to gain the unanimous endorsement of committee members). Essentially, manufacturers recommended that Congress act to close down competing prison industries by enacting legislation that would allow the states to prohibit the importation and sale of goods produced by prisoners in other states. Repeatedly, since 1890, the legislatures of the industrial states had passed laws aimed at staunching the inflow of convict-made goods from other states, and, repeatedly, the courts had struck these laws down on the grounds that they amounted to state regulation of interstate commerce (a right that the U.S. Constitution reserved to the federal government). In 1928, the manufacturers asked Congress to divest prisonmade goods of their interstate character and thereby free the states to ban the sale of such goods on their markets. Representatives from the prisons in which public-account and contracting were in use understood that such a law would deal a devastating blow to their prison industries, and so strenuously voiced their opposition. They were joined by the APA, the warden-heavy membership of which feared such legislation would force them to abandon prison industries altogether.[144]

Heading into the 1928 elections, the Garment Manufacturers' Association spearheaded a free manufacturers' campaign for federal legislation that would divest prisonmade goods of their interstate character. Sensing that Hoover's business-friendly government might finally act to eliminate the handful of contract industries still at work in American prisons, and thereby lay the groundwork for adoption of a New York style, state-use system of labor, the NCPPL lent its support to the bill. AFL leaders, who had all but given up on the hope of harnessing federal power to eliminate contracting, followed suit (if somewhat skeptically).[145] This broad-based coalition of supporters proved far more influential than the prison administrators who were desperate to hold onto even their failing industries: In 1928 the Republican party added a plank to its platform supporting the prohibition of interstate commerce of convict-made goods, and the Democratic platform promised to make convict-made goods subject to the laws of the state into which they were imported.[146] Six months after the elections, and with Herbert Hoover installed in the White House, Congress enacted the Hawes-Cooper Act. That law provided that after January 19, 1934, "all goods, wares, and merchandise manufactured, produced, or mined, wholly or in part, by convicts or prisoners,"[147] and transported into another state or territory, were to be subject to the laws of that state or territory as though the items had been produced within its jurisdiction. (The two exceptions were goods made by convicts on parole or probation, and goods made in federal prisons for use by federal departments and agencies). Hawes-Cooper was modeled on the Wilson Act of 1890, the groundbreaking federal law that divested alcoholic beverages of their interstate character, thereby enabling the states to regulate their importation and sale.

Mildly stunned by the unexpected passage of precisely the sort of bill for which they had unsuccessfully lobbied since 1890, the AFL quickly moved to draft model legislation for the states, banning the importation of prison-made goods for purposes of sale within the state, whether on the open or

[144] Howard B. Gill, "The Prison Labor Problem," *Annals of the American Academy of Political and Social Science* 157 (Sep. 1931), 83–101; "Prison Labor," (ed.), *New York Times*, Feb. 3, 1929, 54.

[145] In 1928, the AFL called on the political parties to declare their support for a federal law divesting prison-made goods of their interstate character. Linking the interests of manufacturers and workers, President William Green declared: "The manufacture and sale of commodities produced by convict labor in competition with free labor is a menace to working men and women and the manufacturers and industry." *New York Times*, June 11, 1928, 4.

[146] *New York Times*, June 12, 1928, 5; June 29, 1928, 5.

[147] Hawes-Cooper Act, Ch. 79, 45 Stat. 1084 (1929) §1.

governmental market. Four states immediately enacted laws to that effect; another nineteen followed suit in the following five years. By 1938, thirty-three states had enacted bans on the importation of prison-made goods, and only ten states (most of them Southern, and together constituting too small a market to absorb anything more than a fraction of the nation's prison product) allowed the unregulated importation of convict-made goods.[148]

Following the enactment of these laws, the last remaining prison labor contractors were all but forced to ratchet down their operations. Contract industries were not the only ones affected, however: Although largely motivated by the joint opposition of manufacturers, organized labor, and the NCPPL to contracting, the new laws did not target contract prison labor *per se*: Rather, they took aim at the interstate commerce in prisonmade goods, regardless of the system under which those goods were produced. Those public-account industries whose markets were interstate in character also collapsed. In addition, it became very difficult, if not impossible, for the NCCPL's own preferred system of prison labor – a regional version of state-use – to operate: The handful of state governments that sold their prisonmade goods to the departments and agencies of other state governments lost their markets to the new importation bans as well. Finally, Hawes-Cooper had something of a domino effect: As a number of contemporary observers pointed out, the states rushed to close their markets to others. Although not all states prohibited the importation of prisonmade goods, enough of the large ones proscribed the importation and sale of convict-made goods that the nation's prison industries as a whole were dramatically affected. Under these conditions, the interstate market in prison-made goods disappeared in a matter of a few years; the country's remaining prison industries went into rapid decline, and, in most states, the number of prisoners engaged in productive labor fell to levels comparable to those of New York.[149]

The onset of the Great Depression and the federal government's response to the Depression both hastened the collapse of prison industries and further limited the fields of labor in which prisoners could work. State-use industries, which had never delivered on their promise, anyway, went into further decline. Despite a last great burst of organizing activity in the service of the state-use system,[150] the NCPPL was unable to prevent their carefully targeted campaign against contract and public-account prison labor from proliferating into an onslaught against prison industries in general.

---

[148] J. A. C. Grant, "Interstate Traffic in Convict-Made Goods," *Journal of Criminal Law and Criminology* 28:6 (Mar.–Apr. 1938), 855. The ten states permitting unregulated importation of prison-made goods as of 1938 were: Alabama, Delaware, Florida, Missouri, Nevada, North Dakota, South Carolina, Vermont, West Virginia, and Wyoming. Grant, "Interstate Traffic," 857.

[149] Grant, "Interstate Traffic," 855.

[150] The NCPPL convened a broad-based Prison Labor Campaign (composed of thirty-five representatives from business, labor, and the retail sector) for the purpose of helping states legislate the state-use system. *New York Times*, Nov. 29, 1932, 37.

As unemployment rates began to rise and wages dropped, after 1929, trade unions and manufacturers' associations brought considerable pressure to bear on the use of prisoners on state and federal works and projects. Whereas prior to the Depression, organized labor had tended not to contest the use of prisoners in road building, the unions now insisted that such work should go to free labor, rather than prisoners.[151] Likewise, state-use industries that had been relatively uncontested before the depression now became subject to protest, from both manufacturers' associations and organized labor. The American Brush Manufacturers' Association objected that the highly automated brush-making factories at the federal prison at Leavenworth were making it impossible for free manufacturers to compete for lucrative government contracts and were causing "employees of legitimate brush manufacturers [to be] thrown out of work." If prisoners were to be put to work making brushes, they ought to work by hand.[152] Similar cases were made in other industries (including, most notably, the Cotton Duck Association).[153]

Key federal legislation, from Hoover's Reconstruction Finance Corporation (RFC) Act to Roosevelt's National Industrial Recovery Act (NIRA), stipulated that no convict labor was to be used on projects receiving federal loans and aid provided for under the particular act. In the case of the RFC, this applied not only to private borrowers but to the states, municipalities, and all public commissions and "instrumentalities."[154] New Deal legislation extended the exclusion of prisoners from federally funded projects, and brought additional pressures to bear on prison industries. Roosevelt's NIRA allotted $400 million to the states and territories for road construction but grants were made subject to a regulation that "No convict labor shall be employed."[155] The Federal Emergency Administration of Public Works also provided that no convict labor was to be employed on public works (ex-servicemen were to have priority, followed by citizens and naturalizing "aliens" who lived in the area of the proposed project, followed by residents of the state).[156] The U.S. attorney general construed these laws and regulations to prohibit the use of convict-crushed stone on public works; even that old standby of prison wardens desperate to occupy their men in some vaguely remunerative manner now faced extinction.[157] In 1936, the Walsh-Healy Act gave that opinion legislative reinforcement by providing that, in federal contracts for materials worth an excess of $10,000, "no convict labor will be employed by the contractor in the manufacture or production or furnishing of any of the materials, supplies, articles, or equipment included in such contract."[158] Around the same time,

[151] *New York Times*, July 11, 1931, 2.
[152] H. R. Rinehart, assistant secretary of the American Brush Makers Association, quoted in *New York Times*, Sep. 14, 1932, 5.
[153] *New York Times*, Feb. 2. 1933, 20.   [154] *New York Times*, Aug. 30, 1932, 30.
[155] Donald Sawyer, Public Works Administrator, quoted in *New York Times*, June 24, 1933, 1.
[156] *New York Times*, July 2, 1933, xx3.   [157] *Wall Street Journal*, Nov. 24, 1933, 2.
[158] Walsh-Healy Act, U.S. Code 41, Ch. 1, Sec. 35 (1936).

Secretary of Labor, Frances Perkins, and the chief Industrial Administrator, General Hugh Johnson, declared their intention to get the governors and state lawmakers to agree to remove prisonmade goods from the market – altogether.[159]

Under the National Reconstruction Administration (NRA), a slew of industry-wide production codes (agreed upon by unions and employers, and governing wages, hours, and work conditions in a given industry) banned the use of convict labor. In 1934, efforts by both the NCPPL and the APA to submit prison industry codes to the NRA, to establish a Prison Labor Authority, and to use the NRA's Blue Eagle stamp of approval, prompted more than thirty garment manufacturers to pull out of the Cotton Garment Code. Acutely aware that this withdrawal could trigger a collapse of the entire code system, the NRA moved to suspend the sale of prisonmade garments on the open market. Prison administrators themselves appear to have aggravated the situation by failing to adhere to their own compact: Some worked prisoners longer than the prison compact provided and drastically underpriced their goods. Here, free industry had little recourse: The prison compact, like free industry's NRA codes, was voluntary and there was no legal way to enforce it. Moreover, all the codes lost whatever disciplinary power they might have had when the U.S. Supreme Court ruled the NRA unconstitutional in May 1935. (Following that decision, hours of work began creeping back up, minimum wages declined, and "runaway" sweatshops set up in competition with those that still adhered to the code).[160] A critical deficiency in the Hawes-Cooper Act also became evident in 1935: Whereas the statute made prisonmade goods subject to state law, it did not penalize those who did, in fact, import convict-made goods into a state that prohibited such imports.

The AFL, the General Federation of Women's Clubs, and the Garment Manufacturers Association resolved to meet these challenges by pressing for additional federal legislation. The result was the passage of a law that gave the Hawes-Cooper Act teeth. The Ashurst-Sumners Act of 1935 made it a federal offense to knowingly import goods manufactured, produced, or mined by prisoners, for commercial purposes, into any state in violation of that state's laws. The penalty for doing so was a fine and up to one year in federal prison. (The law also provided that all packages containing prisonmade goods and transported in interstate commerce be plainly and clearly marked with the name of the penal institution in which the goods were produced).[161] In the same year, in *Whitfield v. Ohio*, the U.S. Supreme Court was asked to rule on the constitutionality of a state law prohibiting the sale of imported prisonmade goods and the Hawes-Cooper Act:[162] The appellant had been convicted under Ohio law of selling, in Cleveland, some

---

[159] *Wall Street Journal,* July 27, 1933, 2; *New York Times,* July 26, 1933, 5; *New York Times,* July 26, 1933, 17.

[160] *New York Times,* Nov. 15, 1936, E6.

[161] Ashurst-Sumners Act, Ch. 412, 49 Stat. 494 (1935).

[162] *Whitfield v. Ohio* 297 U. S. 431 (1936).

seven dozen chambray men's work shirts that had been made by prisoners at the Wetumpka prison in Alabama. New York and Minnesota filed briefs of *amici curiae* in support of Ohio. The court ruled that both the Ohio statute and Hawes-Cooper were constitutional: Hawes-Cooper, ruled Justice Sutherland, was "in substance the same as the Wilson Act," which divested alcohol of its interstate character and which the court had upheld in *Rhodes v. Iowa* and *In re Rahrer*.[163] Both Wilson and Hawes-Cooper regulated an "evil," wrote Sutherland: The Wilson Act regulated alcoholic beverages, and Hawes-Cooper, "the sale of convict-made goods in competition with the products of free labor."[164] That the latter was indeed an evil "finds ample support in fact and . . . legislation," Sutherland continued, and the state of Ohio had the right and the power to preserve its policy of protecting "free labor . . . [from] the enforced and unpaid or underpaid convict labor of the prison."[165]

With this ruling, the U.S. Supreme Court lent both moral authority and the full force of law to the century-old argument of American workers (joined somewhat belatedly by manufacturers) that placing prison labor in competition with free workers was socially deleterious and immoral. If there were any doubt that the Court considered such competition an evil, this was clarified a year later, in a second prison labor case to come before the court. The aptly named Kentucky Whip and Collar Company, a manufacturing concern that engaged prison labor to make horse collars and strap goods, challenged the constitutionality of the Ashurst-Sumners Act (which made it illegal to knowingly transport convict-made goods into states and territories in which such goods were prohibited, and provided that all packages containing prison made goods be clearly marked with the name and location of the prison in which they were made).[166] The Kentucky company had contracted with the Illinois Railroad Company to transport twenty-five shipments of convict-made bridlery: Ten were to be freighted to states that banned the sale of prisonmade goods, five to states that permitted sales but mandated clear labeling of the goods as convict-made, and ten to states that did not restrict the sale or possession of convict-made goods. The railroad company refused to accept the shipments because, in contravention of the Ashurst-Sumners Act, the Kentucky company had not properly labeled the packages. The company subsequently sued for an injunction to compel the railroad to transport the goods; company attorneys argued before the Supreme Court that Congress lacked constitutional authority to prohibit the movement of "useful and harmless articles of commerce made by convict labor" and possessed no power to proscribe the interstate traffic in unlabeled convict-made goods.[167]

---

[163] *Rhodes v. Iowa* 170 U.S. 412 (1898); *In re Rahrer* 140 US 545 (1891).
[164] *Whitfield v. Ohio* 297 U. S. 431 (1936), 439.
[165] Ibid.
[166] *Kentucky Whip and Collar Co. v. Illinois Central Railroad* 299 U.S. 334 (1937).
[167] *Kentucky Whip and Collar Co. v. Illinois Central Railroad* 299 U.S. 334 (1937), 344–5.

The Kentucky attorneys appear to have believed that the case would turn on their claim that the goods in question were "useful and harmless." As they recognized, the Court had previously upheld Congress's power to regulate the interstate transportation of a variety of goods and persons, including diseased livestock, lottery tickets, misbranded and adulterated foodstuffs, "women, for immoral purposes," liquor, diseased plants, stolen motor vehicles, and kidnap victims. The petitioner sought to distinguish the convict-made bridlery in question from these other objects of interstate commerce. Writing for the Court, Chief Justice Hughes rejected this argument: The material question was not whether the goods in question were useful and harmless (after all, motor vehicles and kidnap victims might be said to be useful and harmless); that, in any case, the Court had recently ruled (in *Whitfield v. Ohio*) that the sale of convict-made goods in competition with those of free labor was an "evil." Moreover, Congress was entitled to regulate interstate commerce where the states could constitutionally restrict or prohibit a harmful form of commerce. The Ashurst-Sumners Act was merely an exercise of Congress's constitutional authority to regulate interstate commerce in such a way as to aid the enforcement of valid state laws.[168] "Congress," concluded Hughes, "is as free as the States to recognize the fundamental interests of free labor."[169]

Together, the *Whitfield* shirts and *Kentucky* bridlery cases sealed the fate of profit-driven prison industries in the United States. Although some legal commentators observed that the rulings broke new constitutional ground because they recognized that an economic evil (and not just a moral or physiological evil) might be the object of Congress's regulation of interstate commerce; for the workingmen and women who had, for many years, decried the use of forced prison labor, the harm had also always been a deeply moral one. The AFL and the General Federation of Women's Clubs greeted both rulings as tremendous, and long overdue, victories for workers: With its heavy dependence on interstate commerce, the fate of prison labor contracting had been all but sealed, declared long-time advocate of women garment workers and cofounder of the NCPPL, Julia Jaffray; the court had effectively ended "a condition of practical slavery."[170] A critical battle in the sixty-year struggle to civilize the market, and discipline the state, had finally been won.[171] The vice president of the AFL, Matthew Woll, jubilantly declared the rulings a model upon which to base a "method for economic planning" in the field of labor rights more generally.[172] Organized labor

---

[168] Ibid, 352.   [169] Ibid., 352.

[170] Jaffray went on to infer a link between prison labor contracting and the recent prison riots. In fact, as we have seen, the large-scale rebellions of 1929 and 1930 had broken out in *postcontractual* prisons. Jaffray in *New York Times*, Mar. 22, 1936, N6.

[171] That victory was entrenched, three years later, when Congress extended Ashurst-Sumners to proscribe the interstate transportation and sale of convict-made goods regardless of the laws of the state into which the goods were transported. Act of Oct. 14, 1940, Ch. 872, 54 Stat. 1132

[172] *New York Times*, Apr. 13, 1937, 52.

now set about extending what its leadership viewed as a critical precedent for federal child-labor and minimum wage laws.[173]

* * * * *

Between 1929 and 1936, both the legal foundation of most states' prison labor systems and the place of productive labor in everyday prison life had come to closely resemble New York's. Before the Great Depression and the New Deal, the prison industries of most states had long since ceased to be as productive as they had been under the ubiquitous contract systems of the Gilded Age; equally, in a good majority of the states, the activity of labor was no longer the sole foundation of prison discipline. However, profit-oriented prison industries of various kinds had clung on, as had administrators' dream of a revival of prison labor. Although they disagreed on how prison industries ought to organize, prison administrators and veterans of progressive prison reform nonetheless still aspired to bring about the fulltime productive labor for every able-bodied prisoner in the country. The Depression and New Deal swept away both the surviving state prison industries and administrators' aspirations. Although many of the Southern states continued to put their prisoners to long, hard hours of labor on penal farms and plantations, prisoners in other states all but laid down their tools and prison production (in anything other than mailbags for the U.S. Postal Service and automobile license plates) all but ground to a halt. The American prison had become post-industrial.

By 1935, the managerial system of imprisonment was primed to become the rule rather than the exception in American legal punishment. Warden Lawes of Sing Sing had become the most prominent penologist in the nation, and the penal managerialism he championed had acquired new relevance as a possible model for prison reform across the country. Whether or not Lawes had a direct and "profound influence in the solution of [the] vexing social problem" of imprisonment (as President Roosevelt asserted, in 1935), the system he fleshed out at Sing Sing anticipated and distilled the basic dynamics of the post-industrial prison order.[174] Although, in the late 1930s, many different configurations of managerial penology would take root in Northern prisons, almost all Northern prison administrations would seek to replicate the subliminatory disciplinary forms that Lawes had refined at Sing Sing (athletics, radio, entertainment, etc.); almost all would cast these as privileges to be gained and lost through good or poor conduct; and, everywhere, the greatest privilege of all – early freedom – would be held out as the ultimate motivator for compliance.

As at Sing Sing, this system of sublimation and incentive was underwritten by new technologies of physical force. After the rebellions of 1929 and 1930, prison authorities around the country began adopting anti-riot technologies that would enable them to quickly restore the peace while avoiding spilling

---

[173] New York Times, Jan. 5, 1937, 10.
[174] Roosevelt to Lawes, Washington D.C., Mar. 13, 1935, LEL, I, Box 2, File 14.

the blood of their convicts and guards. As recent events had proven, bloody prison riots quickly became political problems. In New York, in the 1930s, the Prison Department equipped every men's prison with tear gas dispenser systems, gas guns, and gas grenade launchers, custom-built by Federal Laboratories, Inc. (These piped systems had been in use in banks and pay offices since 1924). At the 1931 meeting of the APA in Baltimore, Maryland, the president of Federal Laboratories explained to an unusually attentive audience of wardens and penologists the advantages of such systems: Tear gas technology would allow prison administrations to "avoid the necessity of calling in outside armed forces, which is expensive to the state, disrupts your organization, and brings considerable undesirable publicity." Concluding his sales pitch with a banal, if unconsciously ironic, reference to one of the most prominent allies of the now-defunct new penology, he mused: "I think it was Theodore Roosevelt who said 'Speak softly and carry a big stick.' You might modernize that today by saying 'Speak kindly, but carry a gas stick.'"[175] Whether he knew it or not, the tear gas salesman had distilled the logic and spirit of America's new, post-industrial mode of legal punishment.

[175] *Proceedings of the Annual Congress of the American Prison Association*, 1931, 294.

CONCLUSION

On the Crises of Imprisonment

The foregoing pages relate the story of the great crisis of legitimacy that struck the American system of legal punishment in the Gilded Age and flesh out an account of the diverse, and often contradictory, reform efforts that this crisis precipitated. As we have seen, America's prison-based system of legal punishment, with which the early Republicans first tentatively experimented, and which the Jacksonians subsequently transformed and institutionalized (in the form of contractual penal servitude), was episodically shaken to its foundations by acute disciplinary, political, and ideological crises. At all times anchored in overlapping fields of power (the plane on which contractors encountered prison keepers and convict laborers, for example, and the fraught arena in which free workingmen grappled with employers and responded to the often violent, dislocating effects of industrialization), the prison proved both a site and an instrument in an ongoing negotiation between distinct segments of American society over the profound moral and political questions thrown up by the rise of industrial capitalism. Although only intermittently aflame in riot and rebellion or under siege from an outraged citizenry, the American prison existed (and arguably, still exists) in a permanent state of crisis. Rather than interpret the various crises of imprisonment as so many signs of the failure or defeat of well-intended penal reformers, I have tried to convey the ways in which the penal system's emergencies were at once destructive and creative. The great legitimation crisis of contractual prison labor, which climaxed in the 1880s and 1890s, ultimately ended in the abolition of the controversial American system of imprisonment, but it also precipitated and conditioned the formation not only of the progressive prison reform movement but, ultimately, the modern penal state itself.

The stakes in the various confrontations in and about prison-based modes of punishment varied over time and space; a potent symbol of state power everywhere, the meanings with which different classes and communities of Americans imbued that symbol were not always the same. Southern farmers and miners articulated their opposition to contractual prison labor in terms different from industrial workers protesting unfair competition with convict labor north of the Mason and Dixon line; the convict–laborers who powered the prison foundries, smelted iron, and punched leather in the prison boot and shoe factories of the Gilded Age demanded something quite different from the state than would the convict–wards of the Progressive Era. At root,

469

however, these struggles sprang from, and directly engaged, what might be called the irreducible fact of the carceral mode of punishment: that is, its unfreedom.

Although it may well be the case, as philosophers from Plato to Hegel have insisted, that involuntary, bonded, unfree relations are *intrinsically* unstable in nature, what we can be sure of is that, *historically*, America's unfree institutions (most conspicuously, chattel slavery) have been the source of some of the most sweeping, and violent, upheavals to have assailed the country in the 230 years since the Revolution. In societies characterized by varying degrees and relations of unfreedom (such as the colonies of the late seventeenth and eighteenth centuries), the condition of unfreedom was a relatively uncontroversial fact of social life; Benjamin Franklin may have threatened to ship rattlesnakes to Britain in retribution for the mother country's dumping of thousands of convicts on American shores, but he did not seek the abolition of convict servitude. (Indeed, to the extent that he supported and promoted Benjamin Rush's work, Franklin was instrumental in advancing the institution of penal servitude). However, in a society in which freedom, in its many permutations, was raised to the status of official religion and inscribed in the highest laws of the land, and in which the dominant social relation was fast becoming that between employer and the free, waged laborer, residual institutions of unfreedom were cast into high relief as exceptions to the norm. In the case of penal servitude, this had two important, and contradictory, consequences: On the one hand, lawmakers, the citizenry, penal officials, and the courts found ways of justifying, to themselves as much as to others, the stripping away of offenders' rights and liberties. In the 1820s and 1830s, the dominant discourse of punishment held that offenders, by their offense, had proven themselves unfit for freedom and a danger to others' freedom (typically, the supposed "natural right" in private property): Incarceration at hard labor was here justified as a means by which the negators of freedom might be fitted for liberty. Rights otherwise held to be "natural and unalienable" could, on this view, be suspended or even terminated altogether. In the 1830s and 1840s, these fictions, in turn, served to build and buttress the moral (and eventually, legal) wall that, down through the twentieth century, and for many years after the death of hard labor penology, separated the unfree convict from the free citizen.

The second consequence of the prison's exceptional status, paradoxically, was the critical attention that institution attracted as the source of a kind of power that was, in Tocqueville's phrase, "despotic" in relation to its prisoner subjects. Much as British parliamentarians had voiced the concern, in the 1750s, that the proposed punishment of public hard labor in His Majesty's dockyards would sow the seeds of a tyrannical, and potentially voracious, form of power on English soil, many nineteenth-century Americans worried that contractual penal servitude constituted a beachhead for a resurgence of unfreedom in society at large. In the grips of the pains of industrialization, and the unexpected revitalization of chattel slavery in the South, workingmen's considerable empathy (before 1840) with their imprisoned brethren gave way to alienation and hostility. As contractors set up shop in the prisons, and the states made only vague gestures at regulating their conduct, workingmen came to see the prisons – and convict laborers – as a potent weapon of state and monopoly power that could be wielded against free worker and republic alike. As we have seen, the mobilization, first of workingmen, then of farmers, miners, and industrial wage laborers, against contract prison labor ultimately brought about the abolition of the practice at the heart of penal servitude.

The political crisis unleashed by the campaign against prison labor contracting was penultimately resolved through its formal abolition (and, ultimately, its actual abolition). But the crisis of imprisonment did not end when the contractors packed up their machinery and exited the prison factories: It metastasized. Having been built on the foundation of productive labor, the material and ideological structures of imprisonment were severely undermined by the collapse of industries. Subsequent efforts, by a first wave of progressives (ca. 1895–1913), to salvage productive labor were effectively defeated, in the political and economic spheres, by much the same force that had brought about the abolition of contracting. The second wave of progressive prison reformers (ca. 1913–17) adjusted to the new political reality by revising old views about productive labor as the font of morality and order, and experimenting with new, nonlaboring forms of discipline; as they did so, they wrought new conceptions of human subjectivity and forged novel means of governance. Some years ahead of the technicians of consumer culture, experimenters at Sing Sing and elsewhere put the still relatively novel principles of sublimation and the human capacity for desire to work in a new penal order. By 1938, with the final abolition of almost all outstanding prison labor contracts and the collapse of most prison industries, the foundations of the new paradigm of managerial penology had been all but laid.

Although no longer directly competing with free workers in the marketplace (at least, in most states), the prisoner's status as a contentious and controversial figure in American society and politics soon revived. In the 1920s, the immediate objects of the new controversies were the kinds of recreational, psychomedical, and educational activities in which the least free members of American society (prisoners) now participated – the very same activities that served as the cornerstones of the new, managerialist penology. Here, once again, the prison became wedged between countervailing, and deeply destabilizing, pressures. On the outside, Caleb Baumes's law-and-order campaign, and his fellow conservatives' attacks upon the progressives' probation system, revealed the formation of a new and potent political constraint upon legal punishment: The activities, resources, and "pleasures" extended to prisoners could not exceed those of the poorest, free, working American. By no means should the state suffer prisoners to participate in, or benefit from, the nascent consumers' republic.[1] On the inside, meanwhile, prisoners mobilized the rhetoric and ideological commitments

---

[1] The term is Lizabeth Cohen's. Lizabeth Cohen, *A Consumers' Republic: The Politics of Consumption in Postwar America* (New York, Alfred Knopf, 2003).

of official managerialism in service of improving their lot. Prisoners made it perfectly clear, both in body and the written word, that they grasped the unspoken agreement under which the authorities traded resources and various sublimating privileges and recreational activities for obedience. As the riots of 1929 (at Auburn and Clinton prisons) confirmed, whenever the authorities acted, under the political and legal pressures brought to bear by Caleb Baumes and other conservatives, to retrench the rather limited pleasures and opportunities afforded convicts, the prisoners considered their "square deal" null and void. In its place, they offered mass escapes and bloody rebellion. Quite early on in its career, then, the modern penal state's fault-lines became visible and made themselves felt; the contractor and his sweatshops were long gone, and with them, the preeminent source of instability in the nineteenth century's distinctive mode of legal punishment. But in their place stood a new and, in time, no less crisis-prone, institution of unfreedom.

Select Bibliography

Archival Collections

Lawes, Lewis Edward. Papers. Series I and II. John Jay School of Criminal Justice, New York, New York.

Lawes, Lewis Edward. Papers. Supplemental Series. John Jay School of Criminal Justice, New York, New York.

New York (State). Records of the Legislature. New York State Archives, Cultural Education Center, Albany, New York.

New York (State). Records of the Department of Correction. New York State Archives, Cultural Education Center, Albany, New York.

New York (State). Records of the Governor's Office. New York State Archives, Cultural Education Center, Albany, New York.

Osborne Family Papers. George Arents Research Library, Syracuse University, Syracuse, New York.

Thomas Jefferson, Public Papers. 1775–1825. Oxford Text Archive: 1993.

Imprints, Newspapers, and Periodicals

American Periodicals Series, Online, 1740–1900.

Early American Imprints, Series I: Evans, 1639–1800 (Archive of Americana).

Early American Imprints, Series II: Shaw-Shoemaker, 1801–1819 (Archive of Americana).

Early American Newspapers, Series I, 1690–1876 (Archive of Americana).

Historical *New York Times* (Proquest).

Historical *Wall Street Journal* (Proquest).

National Committee on Prisons and Prison Labor. Prison Labor Leaflets, 1–58. c.1916 – 1919.

Star of Hope (Sing Sing Prison). 1899–1902; 1905–06.

Star-Bulletin (Sing Sing Prison). 1917–1919.

Annual Reports and Proceedings

American Prison Association. *Proceedings of the Annual Congress of the American Prison Association. 1908–1941.*

Boston Prison Discipline Society. Annual Report. 1825–1850.

473

National Prison Association. *Transactions.* 1873–74.

National Prison Association. *Proceedings of the Annual Congress of the National Prison Association of the United States. 1883–1907.*

New York (State). Prison Department. Annual Report of the Superintendent of State Prisons. 1890/91–1925/26.

New York (State). Department of Correction. Annual Report of the Commissioner of Correction. 1926/27–1934/35.

New York (State). State Commission of Prisons. Annual Report of the State Commission of Prisons. 1895–1925/26.

New York (State). State Commission of Correction. Annual Report of the State Commission of Correction. 1926/27–1934/35.

New York (State). State Commission on New Prisons. Annual Report. 1907–11.

New York Prison Association. *Annual Report.* 1844–1941.

Proceedings of the National Conference of Charities and Correction. 1883–1903.

Legislation and Law Reports

Constitution of the United States of America.

Constitution of the State of New York. 1821.

Laws N. Y. 1822, Ch. 250.

Laws N. Y. 1842, Ch. 130.

Laws N. Y. 1889, Ch. 382.

Laws N. Y. 1892, Ch. 662.

Laws N. Y. 1896, Ch. 430.

Laws N. Y. 1896, Ch. 553.

Laws N. Y. 1896, Ch. 909.

Laws N. Y. 1906, Ch. 670.

Laws N. Y. 1907, Ch. 467.

Laws N. Y. 1909, Ch. 15.

Laws N. Y. 1910, Ch. 365.

Slaughter-House Cases, 83 U.S. 36 (1873).

Ruffin v. Commonwealth, 62 Va (21 Gratt) (1871).

Cunningham v. Bay State Shoe and Leather Co., New York Supreme Court, 1881, reported in *The American Law Review* 2 (Dec. 1881) 811.

Civil Rights Cases, 109 U.S. 3 (1883).

Warren E. Lewis, Appellant, v. The State of New York, Respondent [No number in original] Court of Appeals of New York, 96 N.Y. 71; 1884 N.Y. LEXIS 469 (1884).

Bronk v. Barckley, 7, Sup. Ct. N.Y., 13 A.D. 72; 43 NYS 400; 1897 N.Y. App. Div. LEXIS 25.

United States v. Reynolds 235 U.S. 133 (1914).

People ex rel. Alphonse J. Stephani, Relator, v. Charles H. North, Medical Superintendent of Dannemora State Hospital, Defendant 91 Misc. 616; 155 NYS. 595; 1915 NY. Misc. (LEXIS 1174).

William E. Anderson v. Gabriel Salant, et al [No number in original] Supreme Court of Rhode Island, 38 R.I. 463; 96 A. 425; 1916 R.I. LEXIS 8 (1916).

The People ex rel. James J. Kelley v. George W. Kirchwey 177 AD 706; 164 NYS 511 (NY App. Div., 1917) (LEXIS 5762).

Books, Articles, Reports, Dissertations

Adamson, Christopher. "Toward a Marxist Penology: Captive Criminal Populations as Economic Threats and Resource." *Social Problems* 31:4 (Apr. 1984): 435–58.

Alper, Benedict Solomon and Jerry F. Boren. *Crime: International Agenda; Concern in the Prevention of Crime and Treatment of Offenders, 1846–1972.* Toronto and Lexington, Massachusetts: Lexington Books, 1972.

American Correctional Association. *The American Prison: from the Beginning; a Pictorial History.* College Park, Maryland: American Correctional Association, 1983.

Anthony, E. and H. T. *Beauties of the Hudson.* New York: E. and H. T. Anthony, c.1860–1875.

Appleby, Joyce. "The American Heritage: The Heirs and the Disinherited." *Journal of American History* 74:3 (Dec. 1987): 798–813.

Atkinson, Alan. "The Free-born Englishman Transported." *Past and Present* 144 (Aug. 1994): 88–115.

Atkinson, Paul. *The Ethnographic Imagination: Textual Construction of Reality.* London and New York: Routledge, 1992.

Ayers, Edward L. *Vengeance and Justice: Crime and Punishment in the Nineteenth Century American South.* New York: Oxford University Press, 1984.

Baker, Amos T. "The Psychiatric Clinic of Sing Sing." *Psychiatric Quarterly* 2:4 (Dec. 1928): 464–5.

———. "Clinical Study of Inmates Sentenced to Sing Sing for Murder—First Degree." *American Journal of Psychiatry* 91 (1935): 783–90.

Barnes, Harry Elmer. *The Evolution of Penology in Pennsylvania: A Study in American Social History.* Indianapolis: Bobbs Merrill, 1929.

Beattie, J. M. *Crime and Courts in England, 1600–1800.* Princeton, NJ: Princeton University Press, 1986.

Beaumont, Gustave de and Alexis de Tocqueville. *On the Penitentiary System in the United States and Its Application in France.* Carbondale: Southern Illinois University Press, 1964.

Beccaría, Cesare (trans. Henry Paolucci). *On Crimes and Punishments.* Indianapolis: Bobbs Merrill, 1963.

———. (trans unknown). *An Essay On Crimes and Punishments.* Brookline, Massachusetts: Branden Press, 1983.

Bech, Henning (trans. Teresa Mesquit and Tim Davies). *When Men Meet: Homosexuality and Modernity.* Chicago: University of Chicago Press, 1997.

Bentham, Jeremy. *Principles of Morals and Legislation.* Buffalo, New York: Prometheus Books, 1988.

———. *Panopticon Writings,* ed. Miran Bozovic. London: Verso, 1995.

Bernstein, Iver. *The New York City Draft Riots: Their Significance for American Society and Politics in the Age of the Civil War.* New York: Oxford University Press, 1990.

Blackstone's Commentaries: with Notes of Reference, to the Constitution and Laws of the Federal Government of the United States; and of the Commonwealth of Virginia, vol. IV. Oxford: Clarendon Press, 1765–9.

Blake, George W., ed. *Sulzer's Short Speeches.* New York: J. S. Oglivie Publishing Co., 1912.

Blue, Ethan Van. "Hard Time in the New Deal: Racial Formation and the Cultures of Punishment in Texas and California in the 1930s." Ph.D. diss., University of Texas at Austin, 2004.

Bodenhamer, David J. and James W. Ely, Jr., eds. *Ambivalent Legacy: A Legal History of the South.* Jackson: University Press of Mississippi, 1984.

Boesche, Roger. "The Prison: Tocqueville's Model for Despotism." *Western Political Quarterly* 33: 4, 550–63.

Boies, Henry. *Prisoners and Paupers: a Study in the Increase of Criminals and the Public Burden of Pauperism in the United States; the Causes and the Remedies.* New York: Putnam, 1893.

———. *The Science of Penology: the Defense of Society Against Crime.* London and New York: G. P. Putnam, 1901.

Boyne, Roy. *Foucault and Derrida: The Other Side of Reason.* London and Boston: Unwin Hyman, 1990.

Browning, Frank and John Gerassi. *The American Way of Crime.* New York: G. P. Putnam and Sons, 1980.

Butler, Anne M. *Gendered Justice in the American West: Women Prisoners in Men's Penitentiaries.* Urbana: University of Illinois Press, 1997.

Cahalan, Margaret Werner. *Historical Corrections Statistics in the United States, 1850–1984.* Washington, DC: U.S. Department of Justice, Bureau of Justice Statistics, 1986.

Cantor, Nathaniel F. "The Prisoner and the Law." *Annals of the American Academy of Political and Social Science* 157 (Sep. 1931): 25–32.

Chamberlin, Rudolph W. *There is no Truce: The Life of Thomas Mott Osborne.* New York: MacMillan, 1935.

Chandler, Alfred. *The Visible Hand.* Cambridge, Massachusetts: Belknap Press, 1977.

Chapin, Bradley. *Criminal Justice in Colonial America, 1606–1660.* Athens, Georgia: University of Georgia Press, 1983.

Chapin, Charles E. *Charles Chapin's Story, Written in Sing Sing Prison.* New York: Putnam, 1920.

Chauncey, George. *Gay New York: Gender, Urban Culture, and the Making of the Gay Male World, 1890–1940.* New York: Basic, 1994.

Colvin, Mark. *Penitentiaries, Reformatories, and Chain Gangs: Social Theory and the History of Punishment in Nineteenth-Century America.* New York: St. Martin's Press, 1997.

Comas, Joan. *Who's Who: The Old Testament.* Oxford: Oxford University Press, 1993.

Conley, John A. "Prisons, Production, and Profit: Reconsidering the Importance of Prison Industries." *Journal of Social History* 14:2 (Winter 1980): 257–275.

Cooper, Robert Alan. "Jeremy Bentham, Elizabeth Fry, and English Prison Reform." *Journal of the History of Ideas* 42:4 (Oct–Dec. 1981): 675–90.

Crites, Laura, ed. *The Female Offender.* Lexington, Massachusetts: Lexington Books, 1976.

Curtin, Mary Ellen. *Black Prisoners and Their World, Alabama 1865–1900.* Charlottesville and London: University Press of Virginia, 2000.

Czitrom, Daniel. "Underworlds and Underdogs: Big Tim Sullivan and Metropolitan Politics in New York, 1889–1913." *Journal of American History* 78:2 (Sep. 1991): 536–58.

Davis, Katherine Bement, and Clara Jean Weidensall. *The Mentality of the Criminal Woman; A Comparative Study of the Criminal Woman, the Working Girl, and the Efficient Working Woman in a Series of Mental and Physical Tests.* Baltimore, Maryland: Warwick and York, 1916.

Dawley, Alan. *Struggles for Justice: Social Responsibility and the Liberal State.* Cambridge, Massachusetts: Belknap/Harvard University Press, 1991.

————. *Changing the World American Progressives in War and Revolution.* Princeton, NJ: Princeton University Press, 2003.

D'Emilio, John and Estelle B. Freedman. *Intimate Matters: A History of Sexuality in America.* New York: Harper and Row, 1989.

Devereaux, Simon. The Making of the Penitentiary Act, 1775–1779. *The Historical Journal* 42:2 (June 1999): 405–33.

Dickens, Charles. *American Notes.* New York: Modern Library, 1996.

Dix, Dorothea. *Remarks on Prisons and Prison Discipline in the United States.* Montclair, NJ: Patterson Smith, 1967 (1845).

D.O.C.s Today. Selected articles, 1987–1988.

Doty, Madeline Z. *Society's Misfits.* New York: Century Co., 1916.

Dougherty, J. Hampden. *Constitutional History of the State of New York*, 2nd ed. New York: The Neale Publishing Company, 1915.

Dumm, Thomas. "Friendly Persuasion: Quakers, Liberal Toleration, and the Birth of the Prison." *Political Theory* 13:3 (Aug. 1985): 387–407.

"Edited by Convicts." *The Journalist* 8:4 (Oct. 13, 1888).

Ekirch, A. Robert. *Bound for America: The Transportation of British Convicts to the Colonies, 1718–1775.* Oxford: Oxford University Press, 1987.

Evans, Robin. *The Fabrication of Virtue: English Prison Architecture, 1750–1840.* New York: Cambridge University Press, 1982.

Fickle, James E. and Donald W. Ellis. "P.O.W.s in the Piney Woods: German Prisoners of War in the Southern Lumber Industry, 1943–45." *Journal of Southern History* 56 (November 1990): 695–724.

Field, Anne Porter Lynes. *The Story of Canada Blackie.* New York: E. P. Dutton and Co., 1915.

Fields, Barbara J. "Slavery, Race, and Ideology in the United States of America." *New Left Review* 181 (May/June 1990): 95–118.

Fishman, Joseph F. *Crucibles of Crime: The Shocking Story of the American Jail.* New York: Cosmopolis Press, 1923.

————. Sex in Prison: *Revealing Sex Conditions in American Prisons.* New York: National Library Press, 1934.

Foner, Eric. *The Story of American Freedom.* New York: Norton, 1999.

————. *Reconstruction: America's Unfinished Revolution.* New York: Harper and Row, 1988.

Foner, Philip S. *History of the Labor Movement in the United States*, vol. 1 (New York: International, 1972).

Foucault, Michel. *Discipline and Punish: The Birth of the Prison.* New York: Pantheon, 1977.

————. *Power/Knowledge: Selected Interviews and Other Writings, 1972–77.* New York: Pantheon, 1980.

————. *History of Sexuality, vol. I: An Introduction.* New York: Vintage, 1981.

————. *Ethics: Subjectivity and Truth.* New York: New Press, 1997.

Freedman, Estelle B. *Their Sisters' Keepers: Women's Prison Reform in America, 1830–1930.* Ann Arbor: University of Michigan Press, 1981.

————. "Sentiment of Discipline: Women's Prison Experiences in 19th Century America." *Prologue* 16 (Dec. 1984): 249–59.

————. "'Uncontrolled Desires:' the Response to the Sexual Psychopath, 1920–60." *Journal of American History* 74:1 (June 1987): 83–106.

Friedman, Lawrence. *Crime and Punishment in American History.* New York: Basic, 1993.

————. *A History of American Law.* New York: Simon and Schuster, 1974.

Garland, David. *Punishment and Modern Society: A Study in Social Theory.* New York: Oxford University Press, 1990.

———. *Punishment and Welfare: A History of Penal Strategies.* London: Ashgate, 1987.

Genovese, Eugene. *Roll, Jordan, Roll: The World the Slaves Made.* New York: Vintage, 1972.

Gibson, Helen E. "Women's Prisons: Laboratories for Penal Reforms." In *The Female Offender,* ed Laura Crites. Lexington, Massachusetts: Lexington Books, 1976.

Gildemeister, Glen A. *Prison Labor and Convict Competition with Free Workers in Industrializing America, 1840–1890.* Ph.D diss., Northern Illinois Press, 1977/New York: Garland, 1987.

Gilfoyle, Timothy. *A Pickpocket's Tale: The Underworld of Nineteenth-Century New York.* New York: Norton, 2006.

Glassman, Michael. *New York State, Its History and Its Government. New York: Barron's Educational Series,* 1949.

Glenn, Myra. *Campaigns Against Corporal Punishment: Prisoners, Sailors, Women, and Children in Ante-bellum America.* Albany: State University of New York Press, 1984.

Glueck, Bernard. "A Study of 608 Admissions to Sing Sing." *Mental Hygiene* 1:1 (Jan. 1918): 94–105.

———. *Concerning Prisoners.* New York: National Committee for Mental Hygiene, 1917.

Glueck, Sheldon and Eleanor Glueck. *Five Hundred Criminal Careers.* New York, Kraus Reprint Corporation, 1965 (1930).

Golay, Frank Hindman. *The Face of Empire: United States-Philipinne Relations, 1898–1946.* Madison: University of Wisconsin, 1998.

Godwin, John. *Alcatraz: 1868–1963.* Garden City, NY: 1963.

Goldsmith, Larry. "History from the Inside Out: Prison Life in Nineteenth-century Massachusetts." *Journal of Social History* 31 (Fall 1997): 109–25.

———. "Penal Reform, Convict Labor, and Prison Culture in Massachusetts, 1800–1880." Ph.D. diss., University of Pennsylvania, 1987.

Greenberg, David, ed. *Crime and Capitalism: Readings in Marxist Criminology.* Philadelphia: Temple University Press, 1993.

Haber, Samuel. *Efficiency and Uplift: Scientific Management in the Progressive Era, 1890–1920.* Chicago: University of Chicago Press, 1964.

Hall, David D. *Worlds of Wonder, Days of Judgement: Popular Religious Belief in Early New England.* Cambridge, Massachusetts: Harvard University Press, 1990.

Hall, Kermit L., ed. *Police, Prison, and Punishment: Major Historical Interpretations.* New York: Garland, 1987.

Hart, Hastings Hornell. *Penology an Educational Problem.* New York: Russell Sage Foundation, 1923.

———. *Plans and Illustrations of Prisons and Reformatories.* New York: Russell Sage Foundation, 1922.

———. *Training Schools for Prison Officers: Plans and Syllabi for the United States Training School for Prison Officers, the New York City Keepers' Training School, and the British Training School for Prison Officers.* New York: Russell Sage Foundation, 1930.

Higginbotham, A. Leon, Jr. *In the Matter of Color: Race and the American Legal Process: The Colonial Period.* New York: Oxford University Press, 1978.

Hindus, Michael S. *Prison and Plantation: Crime, Justice and Authority in Massachusetts and South Carolina, 1767–1878.* Chapel Hill: The University of North Carolina Press, 1980.

Hirsch, Adam Jay. *The Rise of the Penitentiary: Prisons and Punishment in Early America.* New Haven, Connecticut: Yale University Press, 1992.

Hobbes, Thomas. *Leviathan: With Selected Variants from the Latin Edition of 1668.* Indianapolis: Hackett, 1994.

The Holy Bible, Standard Revised Edition. New York: Penguin, 1974.

Ignatieff, Michael. *A Just Measure of Pain: The Penitentiary in the Industrial Revolution.* New York: Pantheon, 1978.

Inciardi, James A., Alan A. Block, and Lyle A. Hallowell, *Historical Approaches to Crime: Research Strategies and Issues.* Beverly Hills: Sage Publications, 1977.

Inciardi, James A. and Charles E. Faupel. *History and Crime: Implications for Criminal Justice Policy.* Beverly Hills: Sage Publications, 1980.

Jacobs, James B. *Stateville: The Penitentiary in Mass Society.* Chicago: University of Chicago Press, 1977.

John Keane. *Reflections on Violence.* London: Verso, 1996.

Johnston, Norman Bruce. *The Human Cage: A Brief History of Prison Architecture.* New York: Walker, 1973.

Johnston, Robert D. *The Radical Middle Class: Populist Democracy and the Question of Capitalism in Progressive Era Portland, Oregon.* Princeton, NJ: Princeton University Press, 2003.

Jones, David A. *History of Criminology: A Philosophical Perspective.* New York: Greenwood Press, 1986.

Kealey, Linda. "Patterns of Punishment: Massachusetts in the Eighteenth Century." *The American Journal of Legal History* 30:2 (Apr., 1986): 163–86.

Keve, Paul W. *Prisons and the American Conscience: A History of U.S. Federal Corrections.* Carbondale: Southern Illinois University Press, 1991.

Keyssar, Alexander. *The Right to Vote: The Contested History of Democracy in the United States.* New York: Basic, 2000.

Killinger, George Glenn, ed. *Penology: the Evolution of Corrections in America.* St. Paul, Minnesota: 1973.

Koch, Adrienne, and William Peden, eds. *The Life and Selected Writings of Thomas Jefferson.* New York: Modern Library, 1998.

Lawes, Lewis Edward. *Man's Judgement of Death: An Analysis of the Operation and Effect of Capital Punishment, Based on Facts, not Sentiment.* New York and London: G. P. Putnam and Sons, 1924.

_____. *Meet the Murderer!* New York and London: Harper and Bros., 1926.

_____. *Life and Death in Sing Sing.* Garden City, NY: Doubleday, Doran, and Co., 1928.

_____. *Twenty Thousand Years in Sing Sing.* New York: Arno, 1932.

_____.*Cell 202, Sing Sing.* New York: Farrar and Reinhart, 1935.

_____. *Invisible Stripes.* New York: Farrar and Reinhart, 1938.

_____. *Stone and Steel: The Way of Life in a Penitentiary.* Evanston, Illinois: Row, Peterson and Co., 1941.

Lewis, Orlando F. *The Development of American Prisons and Prison Customs, 1776–1845: With Special Reference to Early Institutions in the State of New York.* Montclair, NJ: P. Smith, 1967.

Lewis, W. David. *From Newgate to Dannemora: The Rise of the Penitentiary in New York, 1796–1848.* Ithaca, NY: Cornell University Press, 1965.

Lichtenstein, Alex. *Twice the Work of Labor: The Political Economy of Convict Labor in the New South.* London: Verso, 1996.

Litwack, Leon F. *Been in the Storm So Long: The Aftermath of Slavery.* New York: Vintage, 1980,

Locke, John. *Second Treatise of Government.* Indianapolis, Indiana: Hackett, 1990.

Lombroso, Cesare. *L'homme Criminel; Étude Anthropologique et Médico-legale.* Paris: F. Alcan, 1887

———. *Crime, Its Causes, and Remedies.* Boston, Massachusetts: Little, Brown, and Company, 1911.

Lombroso, Cesare and William Ferrero, *The Female Offender.* Littleton, Colorado: 1980 (1895).

Mancini, Matthew. *One dies, Get Another: Convict Leasing in the American South, 1866–1928.* Columbia, SC: University of South Carolina Press, 1996.

Mann, Michael. *The Rise of Classes and Nation-states, 1760–1914.* Cambridge and New York: Cambridge University Press, 1993.

Martin, Steve J. and Sheldon Ekland-Olson. *Texas Prisons: And the Walls Came Tumbling Down.* Austin: Texas Monthly Press, 1987.

Martineau, Harriet. *Retrospect of Western Travel,* vol 1. New York: Greenwood Press, 1838.

Massey, Dennis and Thomas Myers. *Doing Time in American Prisons: A Study of Modern Novels.* New York: Greenwood Press, 1989.

Masur, Louis P. *Rites of Execution: Capital Punishment and the Transformation of American Culture, 1776–1865.* New York: Oxford University Press, 1989.

McGerr, Michael. *A Fierce Discontent: The Rise And Fall of the Progressive Movement in America, 1870–1920.* New York: Free Press, 2003.

McKelvey, Blake. *American Prisoners; a Study in American Social History Prior to 1936.* Chicago: University of Chicago Press, 1932.

———. "Penal Slavery and Southern Reconstruction." *Journal of Negro History* 20:2 (Apr. 1935): 153–79.

McLynn, Frank. *Crime and Punishment in Eighteenth Century England.* Oxford: Oxford University Press, 1989.

Meranze, Michael. *Laboratories of Virtue: Punishment, Revolution, and Authority in Philadelphia, 1760–1835.* Chapel Hill: The University of North Carolina Press, 1996.

Meyer, Stephen. *The Five Dollar Day: Labor, Management, and Social Control in the Ford Motor Company, 1908–1921.* Albany: State University of New York Press, 1981.

Mohler, Henry Calvin. "Convict Labor Policies." MA thes., University of Wisconsin, 1923. Publ. in the *Journal of the American Institute of Criminal Law and Criminology* 15:4 (Feb. 1925): 530–97.

Monkkonen, Eric, ed. *Crime and Justice in American History: The Colonies and Early Republic.* Westport, Connecticut: Meckler, 1991.

———. ed. *Walking to Work: Tramps in America, 1790–1935.* Lincoln: University of Nebraska Press, 1984.

Montgomery, David. *The Fall of the House of Labor.* New York: Cambridge University Press, 1987.

———. *Workers' Control in America.* New York: Cambridge University Press, 1979.

———. *Citizen Worker, The Experience of Workers in the United States with Democracy and the Free Market During the Nineteenth Century.* New York: Cambridge University Press, 1993.

Moran, Tom. *Stone Upon Stone; A Sing Sing Anthology.* Chicago: Indigo Press, 1954.

Morgan, Edmund S. *American Slavery, American Freedom.* New York: Norton, 1975.

Morgan, Kenneth. "The Organization of the Convict Trade to Maryland: Stevenson, Randolph and Cheston, 1768–1775." *The William and Mary Quarterly,* 3rd Ser., 42:2 (Apr., 1985): 201–27.

Morris, James McGrath. *Jailhouse Journalism: The Fourth Estate Behind Bars.* Jefferson, North Carolina: McFarland and Co., 1998.

Morris, Richard B. "The Measure of Bondage in the Slave States." *The Mississippi Valley Historical Review* 41:2 (Sep., 1954): 219–40.

Morris, Thomas. *Southern Slavery and the Law, 1619–1860.* Chapel Hill: University of North Carolina Press, 1996.

Nash, Gary. *The Urban Crucible: Social Change, Political Consciousness, and the Origins of the American Revolution.* Cambridge, Massachusetts: Harvard University Press, 1979.

————. *The Unknown American Revolution: The Unruly Birth of Democracy and the Struggle to Create America.* New York: Viking, 2005.

Nieman, Donald G., ed. *Black Southerners and the Law, 1865–1900.* New York: Garland, 1994.

Nietzsche, Friedrich. *Genealogy of Morals.* New York: Anchor, 1990.

Nordau, Max. *Degeneration.* Lincoln: University of Nebraska Press, 1993 (1895).

Nye, Robert A. *Crime, Madness, and Politics in Modern France: the Medical Concept of National Decline.* Princeton, NJ: Princeton University Press, 1984.

O'Brien, Patricia. *The Promise of Punishment: Prisons in Nineteenth-Century France.* Princeton, NJ: Princeton University Press, 1982.

Oestreicher, Richard. "Urban Working Class Political Behavior and Theories of American Electoral Politics, 1870–1940." *Journal of American History* 74:4 (Mar. 1988): 1257–86.

Osborne, Thomas Mott. *Within Prison Walls: Being A Narrative of Personal Experience During a Week of Voluntary Confinement in the State Prison at Auburn, New York.* New York and London: D. Appleton and Co., 1914.

————. *Society and Prisons.* New Haven, Connecticut: Yale University Press, 1916.

————. *The Prison of the Future.* New York: New York State Prison Council, 1916.

————. *Prisons and Commonsense.* Philadelphia: J. B. Lippincott, 1924.

Oshinsky, David M. *Worse Than Slavery: Parchman Farm and the Ordeal of Jim Crow Justice.* New York: Free Press, 1996.

Oxford Companion to the Bible. New York: Oxford University Press, 1993.

Panetta, Roger. "Up the River: A History of Sing Sing in the Nineteenth Century." Ph.D. diss, The City University of New York, 1999.

Patterson, Orlando. *Feast of Blood: Consequences of Slavery in Two Centuries.* New York: Basic, 1998, 177.

Perkinson, Robert. "The Birth of the Texas Prison Empire, 1865–1915." Ph.D. diss, Yale University, 2001.

Petchesky, Rosalind P. "At Hard Labor: Penal Confinement and Production in Nineteenth-Century America." In *Crime and Capitalism: Readings in Marxist Criminology,* ed. David F. Greenberg.

Peterson, Mark A. "The Selling of Joseph: Bostonians, Antislavery, and the Protestant International, 1689–1733." *Massachusetts Historical Review* 4 (2002): 1–22.

Petit, Jacques. *La Prison, Le Gagne, et l'Histoire.* Paris: Libraire des Meridiens, 1984.

Philip, Cynthia Owen. *Imprisoned in America; Prison Communications, 1776 to Attica.* New York: Harper and Row, 1973.

Pick, Daniel M. *Faces of Degeneration: a European Disorder, c.1848–c.1918.* Cambridge and New York: Cambridge University Press, 1989.

Pickett, Robert S. *House of Refuge: Origins of Juvenile Reform in New York State, 1815–57.* Syracuse, NY: Syracuse University Press, 1967.

Preyer, Kathryn. "Crime, the Criminal Law, and Reform in Post-Revolutionary Virginia." *Law and History Review* 1:1 (Spring 1983): 53–85.

Pugmire, Donald Ross. *The Administration of Personnel in Correctional Institutions in New York State*. New York: Columbia University Teachers College, 1937.

Radzinowicz, Leon. *A History of English Criminal Law and Its Administration from 1750*, vol. 5. London: Stevens, 1948.

Rafter, Nicole Hahn. "Gender, Prisons, and Prison History." *Social Science History* 9:3 (1985).

――――. *Partial Justice: Women in State Prisons, 1800–1935*. Boston, Massachusetts: Northeastern University Press, 1985.

Report of the Secretary of the Interior, vol. 5, U.S. Commissioner of Labor, Convict Labor in the United States. Washington, DC: Government Printing Office, 1887.

Rice, Jim. "'This Province, so Meanly and Thinly Inhabited': Punishing Maryland's Criminals, 1681–1850." *Journal of the Early Republic* 19:1 (Spring, 1999): 15–42.

Richardson, Heath Cox. *The Death of Reconstruction: Race, Labor, and Politics in the Post-Civil War North, 1865–1901*. Cambridge, Massachusetts: Harvard University Press, 2001.

Robinson, Louis. *Penology in the United States*. Philadelphia: John C. Winston, 1921.

――――. *Should Prisoners Work? A Study of the Prison Labor Problem in the United States*. Philadelphia and Chicago: John C. Winston, 1931.

Rodgers, Daniel T. *Atlantic Crossing: Social Politics in a Progressive Age*. Cambridge, Massachusetts: Belknap/Harvard, 1998.

Rothman, David J. *Discovery of the Asylum: Social Order and Disorder in the New Republic*. Boston: Little, Brown and Co., 1971.

――――. *Conscience and Convenience: the Asylum and its Alternatives in Progressive America*. Boston and Toronto: Little, Brown and Co., 1980.

――――. "Social Control: The Uses and Abuses of the Concept in the History of Incarceration." *Rice University Studies* 67:1 (Winter 1981): 9–20.

――――. "For the Good of All: The Progressive Tradition in Prison Reform." In *History and Crime: Implications for Criminal Justice Policy*, ed. James Inciardi and Charles E. Faupel. Beverly Hills: Sage Publications, 1980.

Rousseau, Jean Jacques. *The Basic Political Writings*. Indianapolis: Hackett, 1983.

Rush, Benjamin. "An Enquiry into the Effects of Public Punishments upon Criminals, and Upon Society, Read in the Society for Promoting Political Enquiries." Convened at the House of His Excellency Benjamin Franklin, Esquire . . . in Philadelphia, March 9th 1787. Philadelphia, 1787.

Rusche, Georg and Otto Kirchheimer. *Punishment and Social Structure*. New York: Columbia University Press, 1939.

Said, Edward W. *Orientalism*. New York: Vintage Books, 1979.

Salvatore, Ricardo and Carlos Aguirre, eds. *Birth of the Penitentiary in Latin America: Essays on Criminology, Prison Reform, and Social Control, 1830–1940*. Austin: University of Texas Press, 1996.

Sante, Luc. *Low Life: Lures and Snares of Old New York*. New York: Strauss Farrar Giroux, 1991.

Santiago-Valles, Kelvin A. *"Subject People" and Colonial Discourse: Economic Transformation and Social Disorder in Puerto Rico, 1898–1947*. Albany: State University of New York Press, 1994.

Schwartz, Bernard. *Main Currents in American Legal Thought*. Durham, North Carolina: Carolina Academic Press, 1993.

Secondat, Charles de, Baron de Montesquieu. *The Spirit of the Laws, 1752* (trans. Thomas Nugent). London: G. Bell & Sons, Ltd., 1914.

Sekula, Allan. "The Body and the Archive: the Use and Classification of Portrait Photography by the Police and Social Scientists in the Late 19th and 20th Centuries." *October* 39 (Dec. 1986): 3–64.

Sellers, Martin P. *The History and Politics of Private Prisons: A Comparative Analysis.* Rutherford, NJ: Fairleigh Dickinson University Press/London: Associated University Press, 1993.

Sellin, J. Thorsten. *Slavery and the Penal System.* New York: Elsevier, 1976.

Severo, Richard, and Lewis Milford. *Wages of War: When America's Soldiers Came Home: From Valley Forge to Vietnam.* New York: Simon and Schuster, 1989.

Shapiro, Karin. *A New South Rebellion: The Battle Against Convict Labor in the Tennessee Coalfields 1871–1896.* Chapel Hill: University of North Carolina Press, 1998.

Shugg, Wallace. *A Monument to Good Intentions: The Story of the Maryland Penitentiary, 1804–1995.* Baltimore: Maryland Historical Society, 2000.

Simkhovitch, Mary Kingsbury. "Friendship and Politics." *Political Science Quarterly* 17:2 (June 1902): 189–205.

Sklar, Martin. *The Corporate Reconstruction of American Capitalism, 1890–1916.* Cambridge and New York: Cambridge University Press, 1988.

Smith, Joan and William Fried. *The Uses of the American Prison: Political Theory and Penal Practice.* Lexington, Kentucky: Lexington Books, 1974.

Smith, Abbot Emerson. *Colonists in Bondage: White Servitude and Convict Labor in America, 1607 – 1776.* Chapel Hill: University of North Carolina Press, 1947.

Smith, Rogers M. *Civic Ideals: Conflicting Vision of Citizenship in U.S. History.* New Haven, Connecticut: Yale University Press, 1997.

Squire, Amos. *Sing Sing Doctor.* Garden City, NY: Garden City Publishers, 1937.

Stansell, Christine. *City of Women: Sex and Class in New York, 1789–1860.* New York: Knopf, 1986.

Steinberg, Allen. *The Transformation of Criminal Justice, Philadelphia, 1800–80.* Chapel Hill: The University of North Carolina Press, 1989.

Sullivan, Larry E. *The Prison Reform Movement: Forlorn Hope.* Boston: Twayne Publishers, 1990.

Sutherland, Edwin and Thorsten Sellin, eds. *Prisons of Tomorrow: Annals of the American Academy of Political and Social Science* 157 (Sep. 1931).

Tannenbaum, Frank. *Osborne of Sing Sing.* Chapel Hill: The University of North Carolina Press, 1933.

———. *Wall Shadows: A Study of American Prisons.* New York and London: G. P. Putnam and Sons, 1922.

Taylor, Frederick Winslow. *Principles of Scientific Management.* Easton, Pennsylvania: Hive Publishing Company, 1986.

Teeters, Negley King. *The Cradle of the Penitentiary; the Walnut Street Jail at Philadelphia, 1773–1835.* Philadelphia: Pennsylvania Prison Society, 1955.

———. *Deliberations of the International Penal and Penitentiary Congresses: Questions and Answers, 1872–1935.* Philadelphia: Temple University Book Store, 1949.

Temin, Peter, ed. *Inside the Business Enterprise: Historical Perspectives on the Use of Information.* Chicago: Chicago University Press, 1991.

Thomson, Winfred Lee. *The Introduction of American Law in the Philippines and Puerto Rico, 1898–1905.* Fayetteville: University of Arkansas Press, 1989.

"Vita and Bibliography of Bernard Glueck." *Journal of Criminal Pathology* 2:1 (July 1940).

Vorenberg, Michael. *Final Freedom: The Civil War, the Abolition of Slavery, and the Thirteenth Amendment.* New York: Cambridge University Press, 2001.

Walker, Donald R. *Penology for Profit: A History of the Texas Prison System 1867–1912.* College Station, Texas: Texas A & M University Press, 1988.

Walker, Samuel. *Popular Justice: A History of American Criminal Justice.* New York: Oxford University Press, 1980.

Walkowitz, Daniel. "Artisans and Builders of 19th Century New York: The Case of the 1834 Stone-cutters." In *Greenwich Village: Culture and Counterculture.* New Brunswick, NJ: Published for the Museum of the City of New York by Rutgers University Press, 1993.

Wallack, Walter Mark. *Education Within Prison Walls.* New York: Teachers College, 1939.

———. *The Training of Prison Guards in the State of New York.* New York: Teachers College, 1938.

Wesser, Robert F. *A Response to Progressivism: The Democratic Party and New York Politics, 1902–1918.* New York: New York University Press, 1986.

Whitin, E. Stagg. *Prisoners' Work.* Boston: American Unitarian Association, 1915.

Whitman, James Q. *Harsh Justice: Criminal Punishment and the Widening Divide between American and Europe.* New York: Oxford University Press: 2003.

Wilentz, Sean. *Chants Democratic: New York City and the Rise of the American Working Class, 1788–1850.* New York: Oxford University Press, 1986.

Wilf, Steven Robert. "Anatomy and Punishment in Late Eighteenth Century New York." *Journal of Social History* 22:3 (March 1989): 507–30.

Williams, Raymond. *Keywords: A Vocabulary of Culture and Society.* New York: Oxford University Press, 1985.

Wilson, Walter. *Forced Labor in the United States.* New York: International Publishers, 1933.

Wines, Enoch and Dwight, Theodore. *Report on the Prisons and Reformatories of the United States and Canada.* Albany, NY: Van Benthuysen and Sons, 1867.

Woodward, C. Vann. *Origins of the New South, 1877–1913.* Baton Rouge: Louisiana State University Press, 1951.

Yates, JoAnne. "Investing in Information: Supply and Demand Forces in the Use of Information in American Firms, 1815–1920." In *Inside the Business Enterprise: Historical Perspectives on the Use of Information,* ed. Peter Temin. Chicago: Chicago University Press, 1991.

Index

Abbot, Edwin M., 426
Adams, John, 21
Adler, Felix, 413
Ahearn, John Francis, 265
Alabama
  and contract prison labor
    abolition of, 157
    as unrepublican, 164
    opposition to, 79
  and convict-lease, 66, 95, 102, 110,
    146
  and integration of free and convict labor,
    114
  and interstate sale of convict-made goods,
    459
  revival of Ku Klux Klan in, 377
Albany Molders' Union, 113
Allied Printing Trades, 265
Amalgamated Association of Iron and Steel
  Workers, 157
American Academy of Political and Social
  Science, 326
American Brush Manufacturers' Association,
  462
American Federation of Labor (AFL), 459
  and contract prison labor
    as slavery, 162
    federal legislation against, 185
  and state-use system, 204, 232, 388, 389,
    393
  and support for William Sulzer,
    296
  and War Prison Labor bill, 423
  on inter-state transport of convict-made
    goods, 233
  organizing efforts of, 377
American Federationist, 233

American Prison Association (APA), See also
  National Prison Association
  on military enlistment of convicts and
    ex-prisoners, 427
  on urgency of prison labor problem,
    326
  opposition to abolition of contract prison
    labor, 204
  report on treatment of criminal
    psychopaths, 402
  report on veneral disease, 402
American system, See modes of legal
  punishment
Anderson v. Salant, 327
Anderson, William, 327
Annan, Robert, 39
Arizona
  and voluntary incarceration of governor,
    328
Ashurst-Sumners Act of 1935, 463
Atkinson, Alan, 29
Attica Prison
  construction of, 458
Auburn Citizen, The, 329, 334
Auburn Picture Company, 373
Auburn plan, 12, 72
  and fiscal self-sufficiency, 67
  as "congregate system" of imprisonment,
    57, 100
  as national model, 54, 63, 85
  criticism of, 81
  development of, 54, 60
  disciplinary system of, 58, 59, 68
  effective abolition of, 173
  labor ideology of, 58
  opposition by organized labor, 72
  support for, 68

Auburn Prison, 332, 376, 403. *See also* the
    following listings: National
    Committee on Prisons and Prison
    Labor; new penology; Thomas Mott
    Osborne, 17
  agricultural production of, 427
  Americanization class, 404
  and construction of Sing Sing Prison, 64
  and contract prison labor
    contractors, 58, 71
    establishment of, 57, 60
    prisoner idleness, 208
  and investigation of state prisons, 298
  and state-use system
    classification of prisoners, 215
    diversity of manufactures, 210
  conditions at, 82, 274, 289, 456
  construction and operation of, 55,
      63
    proposal for replacement of, 288
  disciplinary practices at, 58, 129, 272
    cellular incarceration by night, 56
    perpetual isolation, 56
  employment of ex-convicts from, 391
  leasing of, 55
  Mutual Welfare League, 378
    and "Honor Camp," 371
    and disciplinary reform, 369
    and recreational activities, 359, 372
    and relationship with administration,
        351, 366, 443
    as national model, 421
    Constitution and By-Laws of, 350
    disciplinary tribunal of, 345
    establishment of, 339, 340, 342, 356
    Executive Committee of, 351, 357
    grievance committees of, 349, 360,
        362
    investigations by, 374
    policing power of, 343, 362, 369
    privileges of, 342, 343, 347, 352
    public attitudes toward, 364, 371, 373,
        378
  penal bureaucratic control of, 429
    and managerialism, 441
  reform efforts
    cooperative model, 355
  riots at, 44, 70, 82, 454
  The Bulletin, 372, 373
  transfer to, 280
  transfers from Sing Sing Prison, 312
Auburn system. *See* Auburn plan
August Priesmeyer and Co., 143
Ayers, Edward, 146

Baker, Amos T., 446
Baker, Isaac V., 298
Baker, Newton D., 423
Baldwin, Stephen O., 384
Barrows, Samuel J., 288
Battle, George Gordon, 327
Baumes laws
  and affect on prison discipline, 448
  investigation of, 456
  overcrowding caused by, 448
  repeal of, 457, 458
Baumes, Caleb, 449, 471, 472
Bay State Shoe and Leather Company
  and contract prison labor, 103, 108, 113,
      173
  integration of convict and free labor by,
      114
Beardsley, William J., 289, 290, 291
Beattie, J.M., 27
Beaumont, Gustave de, 64, 313
  and American system, 8, 16
  and Eastern system, 62
  on Sing Sing Prison, 60, 284
Beccaría, Cesare, 19, 21, 24, 33
Bedford Hills State Prison, 458
Bentham, Jeremy, 25, 107, 298
Bertillon, Alphonse, 217
Bigelow, Charles D., 107, 108
Blackstone, William, 25, 38
Blair, George, 164, 165, 205
Blair, Henry, 171
Blake, George, 296, 297, 298, 300, 301, 303,
    304, 306, 316, 317, 327
Bleecker, Katherine Russell, 406
Blumenthal, Charles, 388
Boies, Henry, 244
Bookbinders' Union, 265
Boot and Shoe Workers International
    Union, 388
Boston Prison Discipline Society (BPDS), 8,
    45
  and opposition to contract prison labor, 60
  and opposition to Pennsylvania plan, 81
  and support for Auburn plan, 54, 61, 67,
      68
  labor ideology of, 81
Boston Transcript, 338
Bradley, Joseph P., 14
Brian, Denis, 252
Brinkerhoff, Roeliff, 230
Brittin, William, 55
Brockway, Zebulon R., 88, 90, 123, 177, 188,
    225
Broome, John Lloyd, 121, 125

Brown, Tom., *See* Osborne, Thomas Mott
Bryan, William Jennings, 406
Buckmaster, Samuel A., 68
Bulletin, The, See Auburn Prison
Burroughs Adding Machine, 390

Cable, George Washington, 170
California
    and contract prison labor
        abolition of, 5, 152
        investigation of, 151
    and penal managerialism, 448
    and reform efforts
        disciplinary practices, 93
    and state-use system, 236, 321
    San Quentin Prison
        and piece-price contracts, 104
        strike at, 146
Caminetti, Anthony, 423
Campbell, Elihu, 120
Cantor, Jacob, 265
capital punishment, *See* modes of legal
    punishment
Carnegie Steel, 390
Carter, James M., 415, 430, 436
Central Labor Union, 265
Century Illustrated Magazine, 170
Chamberlin, Rudolph, 337, 414
Chandler, George F., 456
Chapin, Charles, 247
Chauncey, George, 396
Chesapeake and Ohio Railroad, 117
Chicago House of Correction, 199,
    425
    and convict league, 421
    as model program, 424
Chicago Trades Assembly, 163
Choate, Joseph H., 190, 407
Christian Science Monitor, 338
Christian, J., 117
Civil Rights Act of 1866, 15
Clancy, James M.
    and bread riot of 1913, 308, 312, 315, 316,
        317
    and honor company, 317, 379
    as warden of Sing Sing Prison, 314, 316,
        380
    resignation of, 381
Cleveland, Grover, 173, 184, 329
Clinton Prison, 299, 443
    agricultural production at, 427
    and contract prison labor
        consolidation of prison industry, 100
        diversity of manufactures, 210

iron industry in, 82
and new penology
    disciplinary techniques of, 442
and public-account system, 84
and state-use classification system, 211,
    212, 213, 216, 271
and written contributions to *Star of Hope*,
    246
conditions at, 263, 274, 276
construction of, 80
disciplinary practices at, 128, 254, 453
escape attempts at, 82, 452
investigations of, 256, 299
nonmanufactory labor at, 172, 222
penal bureaucracy of, 261
political patronage at, 260
relationship between keepers and
    prisoners, 448
reputation of, 414, 442
riots at, 453, 454, 472
transfer to, 251, 273, 277, 280, 308, 310,
    312, 397, 403, 411, 412, 438, 455
Clinton, DeWitt, 52, 54, 61
Collins, Cornelius V.
    and creation of penal bureaucracy, 294,
        316
    and disciplinary practices, 339
    and *Star of Hope*, 228
    and state-use system, 229, 264
    indictment of, 294
    replacement of Sing Sing and Auburn
        Prisons, 286, 288
    resignation of, 292
colonial mode of punishment
    "Great Law" of 1682, 24
    and convict transportation system, 25, 26,
        27, 28, 86
    and corporal punishment, 23
    and property crimes, 30
    Great Britain
        "royal," 3
        Bloody Code, 18, 23
        Dock Yards bill, 26, 33
        Penitentiary Act of 1779, 25
        hard labor, 26
        involuntary servitude, 23, 27
        rejection of, 19, 21
        severity of, 23
    Colorado
        and Good Roads Program, 268, 379
        and investigation of contract prison labor,
            152, 153
        and riot at Territorial Correctional Facility,
            454

Columbia University, 391, 428
Connecticut
    and contract prison labor, 101, 154
        Auburn plan, 63
        investigation of, 151
        opposition to, 79, 156
        retention of, 236
    and hard labor, 32
    and prohibition on convict labor, 183
    Wethersfield Prison
        and contract prison labor, 65
        and fiscal self-sufficiency, 67
contractual penal servitude, 155, 156. *See also*
    the following listings: Auburn plan;
    farmers and farm workers; individual
    prisons; individual states; miners
    and attempts to preserve, 12
    and benefits to contractors, 109
    contract prison labor, 6
        abolition of, 4, 6, 10, 11, 79, 92, 132,
            137, 151, 155, 172, 182, 197, 262, 293,
            318, 323, 325, 418, 443
        and Civil War, 83
        and idleness, 132, 133, 134, 165, 172,
            174, 176, 180, 199, 206, 207, 208, 214
        and large-scale contracting, 87, 101, 102,
            105
        and machinery, 119, 188, 199, 200
        and training in mechanical trades, 78
        and use against unions, 83, 112, 113
        as anti-democratic symbol, 164
        as cause of prison over-crowding, 165
        Ashurst-Sumners Act of 1935, 463
        attempts to revive, 322
        consolidation of industrial contracts,
            84, 87, 88, 99, 100, 105, 137
        criticism of, 4, 60
        decline of, 236
        diversification of industries, 77, 93, 95,
            98
        dominance of, 11, 66, 88, 90, 105, 134
        establishment of, 4, 7, 8, 11, 17, 53, 54,
            58, 64, 81, 105
        Hawes-Cooper Act, 460, 463
        investigations of, 88, 92, 93, 121, 151,
            165, 166, 233, 235
        opposition by organized labor, 10, 11,
            12, 69, 72, 91, 150
        Pilsbury system, 100, 120
        profitability of, 4, 8, 10, 58, 67, 84, 85,
            88, 90, 105, 107, 108, 165, 184
        public attitudes toward, 149
        regulatory efforts, 11, 78, 80, 82, 171
    contracting systems, 57
        cancellation of contracts, 97

convict lease, 4, 65, 66, 95, 104, 170,
    184, 237
    factory system, 64, 89, 103, 105, 121, 200
    piece-price, 90, 101, 103, 105, 145, 180,
        188,
        200
    regulatory efforts, 78
    relations of dependency, 10
    studies on, 6
contractors
    and illegal incentives, 71, 95
    and subversion of discipline by, 60
    initial reluctance of, 58
    power of, 8, 11, 66, 90, 93, 106, 115, 119,
        134, 139, 147
    subversion of discipline by, 70
    subversion of legal system by, 164
    market relations, 4, 8, 11, 13, 90, 99, 134
        and convict-made goods, 151, 155, 156,
            157, 175, 182, 188, 189, 197, 199, 200,
            202, 229, 235, 264
        and dependence on market, 98
        and state-use system, 204
        and Tariff Act of 1890, 184
        end of relationship, 10
        financial crisis of 1873, 97
        perception as system of slavery, 162, 194,
            336
    profit imperative, 87, 107, 116
        and prison administration, 91
        and public account system, 104
        and state-use system, 325
        influence of, 8, 11, 84, 88, 90, 95
        removal of, 229
    property crimes and, 30
convicts, 194
    legal status of, *See also* prisoners, 17, 29, 30,
        116, 135
        and "civil death," 117, 118
        and Thirteenth Amendment, 16
        as defined by Constitution, 15
        disfranchisement, 55, 70, 85, 86, 186
        self-education about, 244
        under contractual penal servitude, 60
Cornell, E.L., 150
corporal punishment, *See* disciplinary
    practices
Cotton Duck Association, 462
Coxsackie Prison, 458
Crawford, William, 69
Cray, John D., 59
crisis-prone character of prison system, 1,
    469
Cunningham v. Bay State Shoe and Leather Co.,
    474

Current Opinion, 338
Curtin, Mary Ellen, 102

Dannemora Hospital for the Insane, 211,
    212, 273, 403
Darrow, Clarence, 450
Davis, Charles Henry, 268
Davis, Joseph, 103
Davis, Katharine Bement, 426, 437
Dawley, Alan, 377
Deidling, Rudolph, 411
Delaware
    and retention of contract prison labor, 236
Democracy in America (Tocqueville), 81
Democratic Party
    and abolition of contract prison labor,
        185, 187
    and bureaucratic democracy, 241
Democratic Party of New York State, 281
    and contract prison labor, 171
    and investigation of Sing Sing Prison, 166
    Independent Democrats, 282, 294, 328
        and administrative control of Auburn
            Prison, 382
        and administrative control of Sing Sing
            Prison, 384
    Tammany Hall, 281, 282, 291, 329, 380
        and administrative control of Sing Sing
            Prison, 382
        and campaign against managerial
            reformers, 259, 283, 292, 303
        and campaign against Osborne, 409
        and charges of penal mismanagement,
            281
        and New York Prisons Department, 327
        and Sing Sing Prison, 167
Dick, Frank M., 390
Dickens, Charles, 62, 66, 70, 72
disciplinary practices, 61, 213. *See also* the
    following listings: Eastern
    Penitentiary; state-use system,
    classification program
    "Americanization" programs, 195, 224,
        404, 443
    and anti-riot technologies, 466
    as barrier to rehabilitation, 335
    cellular isolation, 55, 56, 57, 60, 61, 66,
        274, 275, 285, 293, 301, 310, 312, 314,
        337, 344, 369, 379
    conduct marks, 71
    corporal punishment, 17, 46, 59, 60, 119,
        125, 135, 137, 142, 144, 146, 169, 254,
        256, 257, 284, 287
        abolition of, 37, 54, 276, 277
        legality of, 61

public acceptance of, 228
deprivation, 37, 54, 56, 82, 130, 139, 144,
    162, 241, 250, 251, 254, 272, 274,
    298, 301, 303, 312, 317, 334, 335, 336,
    337, 363, 367, 368, 383, 430, 453
    and perpetual isolation, 56, 57, 61, 63,
        69, 81
    honor system, 379, 438
    incentive-based, 214, 221, 325, 337
        parole, 214, 218
    industrial, 100, 111, 112, 120, 207, 226
        and contractor overseers, 125
        as foundation of prison order, 58, 126
        influence of contractors on, 71
        resistance to, 140, 147
        rewards for overwork, 119
    labor punishments, 127, 128
    lock-down, 208, 286, 308, 310, 317
    lockstep march, 59, 207, 270
        abolition of, 194, 226, 276
        military models of, 59, 60, 61, 189, 226,
            337
    privilege system, 95, 227, 317, 334, 383,
        399
        freedom-of-the-yard, 343, 360, 374
        letter-writing, 71, 244
        recreational activities, 372, 374, 443
        restrictions on, 249
        supplementary activities, 209, 326, 416
    reform of, 93, 241, 337
    shock-oriented, 126, 128, 129, 144, 272
        abolition of, 194
    silence rule, 58, 59, 61, 67, 70, 207, 208,
        250, 337, 383
        abolition of, 194, 226, 229, 276
        evasion of, 69
    transfer, 216, 271, 273, 308, 310, 311
*Discovery of the Asylum (The), Social Order and
    Disorder in the New Republic*
    (Rothman), 7
District of Columbia
    and Auburn plan, 63
Dix, Dorothea, 284, 286
Dix, John A.
    and Harlem Prison, 292, 294
    and investigation of prison system, 292,
        294
    and reelection defeat, 295, 330
    and rollback of civil service reform, 291,
        294, 295
    election of, 291, 294, 329
DuBois, W.E.B.
    and convict lease system, 87
Dwight, Louis, 61, 62, 67, 84, 109, 136
Dwight, Theodore, 84, 92, 95

Early Republic
    competition between free and convict
        labor, 6
    hard labor, 6, 21
    wheelbarrow law, 34, 47
    wheelbarrowmen, 17, 33
    house of repentance (penitentiary-house),
        3, 4, 45, 70, 137
    and distrust of freemen, 41
    and involuntary servitude, 9, 10
    as Christian institution, 11
    as model, 38
    criticisms of, 38, 39
    establishment of, 17, 37, 48
    failure of, 50
    moral legitimacy of, 3
    replacement by contractual prison
        labor, 54
    sequestration of prisoners, 37, 40, 47
    stability of, 43, 82
    labor ideology of, 6
    revision of penal code, 32
East New York Shoe Company, 113
Eddy, Thomas, 37, 239
Eden, William, 25, 28
Edmonds, John W., 80
Eliot, Charles, 413
Elmira Reformatory for Boys, 88, 177
    and contract prison labor, 179, 180
    and hard labor, 123
    and Pilsbury system, 179
    disciplinary practices at, 188, 215
    self-policing of, 348
    strike at, 145
Emerson Drug, 390
*Enquiry into the Effects of Public Punishments
    Upon Criminals, and Upon Society*
    (Rush), 36, 39
Evening Mail, 413

Fallon, William, 412
farmers and farm workers
    and opposition to contract prison labor,
        137, 158, 160, 164, 186, 469
    Farmers Alliances, 186
Federal Emergency Administration of Public
    Works
    and ban on convict labor, 462
Federal Laboratories, Inc., 467
Federation of the Organized Trades and
    Labor Unions (FOTLU), 151, 156,
    157, 162, 184. *See also* American
    Federation of Labor (AFL)
Federation of Trade Unions, 163
Felton, Charles E., 199

Fencer, Thomas, 93
Fielding, Henry, 26
fiscal politics of punishment, 5, 81, 262
    and Auburn plan, 63, 67, 68
    and contract prison labor, 10, 54, 70,
        93
    dependence on large-scale industrial
        contracts, 131
    profit imperative of, 90
    profitability for state, 154
    and funding self-sufficiency, 54, 55, 57, 58,
        75, 99, 102, 132, 234
    and state-use system, 201, 210
    penitentiary system, 51
Florida
    and sanguinary punishment, 67
Foner, Eric, 15, 75
Ford Motor Company
    and post-release employment, 389, 390,
        393, 425
    and training programs at Sing Sing Prison,
        389
    Sociology Department
        and screening of convicts, 390
Ford, Henry, 389, 390, 392, 408
Fortune, T, Thomas, 170
Foucault, Michel, 8, 135
Fox Film Corporation, 443
Franklin, Benjamin, 19, 31, 470
Franklin, George W., 427
Frawley, James J., 304
Frayne, Hugh, 388, 389, 393, 423

Gabler, Neal, 434
Garment Manufacturers' Association, 460
General Trades Union, 77
George Junior Republic, 330
    and Thomas Mott Osborne, 330, 394
    as model for prisoner self-government,
        340
George, William R., 330, 331, 376
Georgia
    and contract prison labor, 63
        opposition to, 79
    and convict lease, 66, 95, 157, 186
    and Good Roads Program, 268
Gilded Age, 3. *See also* Progressive Era
    and contract prison labor, 105
        abolition of, 4, 5
        as competitive edge in business, 115
        disciplinary practices, 127, 131
        expansion of contractor power, 119
        large-scale prison contracts, 11, 100,
            134
        piece-price system, 103

prison factories, 103, 121
profit imperative, 87, 88, 90
resistance and rebellion, 139, 142
use against unions, 113
and creation of managerial class, 161
and integration of convict and free labor, 114
and reformatory penology, 225
and revival of organized labor, 112
organizing principle of, 88
popular protest movements during, 10
Gildemeister, Glen A., 6, 134, 151
Glueck, Bernard, 431, 439, 447, 458
and psychiatric study of convicts, 401, 402
and Sing Sing Prison as clearinghouse, 403
Glynn, Martin, 384, 385
Goetz, Frederick, 389
Goldsmith, Larry, 6
Gompers, Samuel, 232, 233, 296, 423, 429
Good Roads Program, *See* individual states
Good Words, 338, 353
Graves, Ezra, 98
Great Meadows Prison, 272, 297, 298, 403, 413
and agricultural production, 427
and construction costs, 306
and transfers from Sing Sing Prison, 312
as low-security facility, 452
Green, William, 459
Grover, La Fayette, 93

Hafford, George J., 432
Hall, Earl, 391
Hall, George W., 176
Hamilton, Alexander, 34
hard labor, 4, 35. *See also* the following listings: contractual penal servitude; Early Republic; labor ideology, 4
alternatives to, 374
and state-use system, 276
as alternative to capital punishment, 21
as contract prison labor, 64, 85, 89
as deterrent, 32, 33
as foundation of system, 53, 54
concept of, 70
colonial development, 26
in British system, 89
legal requirement for, 197, 202, 232, 266, 323
regulation of, 95
Hardin, Charles Henry, 143
Harding, Warren, 416
Harlem Prison, 294
Harriman, Mary W., 291

Hart, Hastings Hornell, 253
Haskell, J., 74, 75, 76, 81
Hatters' Association of the United States, 149
Hayden, Peter, 103
Hayes, Patrick J., 208, 224
Haynes, Gideon, 68, 84
Hearst, William Randolph, 329
Hennessy, John A., 381
high Progressive Era, 378. *See* the following listings; Thomas Mott Osborne; new penology, 378
reform efforts, 12
Hirsch, Adam Jay, 9
Hockaday, John A., 143
Hoffman, John T., 93
Hoover, Herbert
and investigation of prison industries, 459, 460
house of repentance, *See* Early Republic
Hubbell, Charles, 439
Hughes, Charles Evans, 329, 420
Hunter, Wallace B., 306

Idaho
and state-use system, 203
Illinois
and contract prison labor
amendment against, 182
and Auburn plan, 63
federal use in Peoria, 165
investigation of, 151
large-scale contracting, 101
lease of Alton State Prison, 65
prison factories, 103
profitability of, 68, 90
and penal managerialism, 448
and public account system, 84, 441
State Prison at Joliet
integration of convict and free labor, 114
Illinois Railroad Company, 464
Independent, The, 338
Indiana
and contract prison labor
financial crisis of 1873, 98
idleness, 98
large-scale contracting, 101
sale of convict-made goods, 183
and convict-lease system, 65
Industrial Workers of the World, 244, 377
International Harvester, 390
International Labor Organization (ILO), 429

involuntary servitude, 32, 85. *See also* the
following listings: colonial mode of
punishment; contractual penal
servitude, 5, 28
and Fourteenth Amendment, 86
and National Committee on Prison Labor,
325
and Northwest Ordinance, 31, 85
and Rhode Island Constitution of 1847,
327
and Thirteenth Amendment, 14, 85, 198
collapse of contractual penal servitude,
325, 326, 336
convict servants, 29, 41, 42, 86
establishment of, 8
indentured servants, 42
legality of, 14
penitentiary system, 41
Iowa
and investigation of contract prison labor,
151

J.S, Hamilton and Associates, 102
Jacksonian Era
and establishment of contract prison
labor, 54, 138
Jaeckel, John P., 287
Jarrett, John, 157
Jefferson, Thomas, 19, 21, 22
Jenkins, George, 312, 381
Jenkins, John F., 311
Jennings, Edgar S., 443, 452, 454
John Pratt's Coal and Coke Company, 102,
114
Johnson, Hiram, 236
Johnson, Hugh, 463
Johnson, I.G., 83, 112
Johnston, Robert, 240
Joint Committee on Prison Reform (JCPR)
and educational programs at Sing Sing
Prison, 391
and public education efforts, 386, 406,
413
and relationship with Thomas Mott
Osborne, 415
objectives of, 386

Kansas
and contract prison labor
investigation of, 152, 153
and public account system, 133
riot at Leavenworth Prison, 454
State Prison, 130
Kansas Pacific Railway, 133
Kansas Wagon Company, 133

Kaplan, Nathan, 414
Kelley, James J., 405
Kellogg, G.C., 294
Kennedy, John S.
activities during bread riot of 1913, 314
dismissal of, 308, 312
indictment of, 303
investigation of Sing Sing Prison, 300
wardenship of Sing Sing Prison, 299, 301,
303, 308, 379, 380, 397
Kentucky
and contract prison labor, 63, 66
opposition to, 79, 164
profitability of, 108
prohibition of, 171
use against unions, 159
Kentucky Whip and Collar Company, 464
Kirchheimer, Otto, 482
Kirchwey, George W., 403
and *Anderson v. Salant*, 327
as acting warden of Sing Sing, 412, 416
national efforts of, 328
Knights of Labor, 164, 165
and state-use system, 204, 232
boycott against convict-made goods, 156
Declaration of Principles, 151
impact of contract prison labor on wages,
184
national campaign against contract prison
labor, 159
proposal for establishment of penal
colony, 157
support for third political party by, 186
Knights of the Ku Klux Klan
revival of, 377

labor ideology, *See also* fiscal politics of
punishment
and attempts to preserve, 11, 12
and funding of prisons, 99
and George Junior Republic, 331
and Progressive Era, 197, 235
as foundational concept, 5, 6, 53, 174, 180
persistence of, 10, 322, 419, 425
labor market, 77. *See also* contractual penal
servitude
and convict labor
proximity to free labor, 47
and integration of convict and free labor,
114
convict labor and, 6, 10, 107, 108, 235
competition with free labor, 149, 160,
164
depression of wages, 160, 184
equal compensation, 92

insulation from free labor, 200
public-account system, 201
restrictions on competition, 79
Labor, U.S, Commissioner of
study of convict labor systems (1887), 105,
109
Lathrop, Austin
and creation of penal bureaucracy, 316
and creation of state-use system, 205, 209,
229
self-sufficiency of, 210, 262
and supplementary disciplinary activities,
222
labor ideology of, 198
Lawes, Lewis E., *See also* penal managerialism
and Baumes laws, 451, 453
and Sing Sing as reform model, 457
and wardenship of Sing Sing Prison, 252,
443, 455, 457
managerialist approach, 448, 466
Leeds, Henry, 306
legitimation crisis of prison systems. *See*
crisis-prone character of prison
systems
Lewis, Burdette G., 426
Lewis, W, David, 55, 82
Lewis, Warren E., 123
Lewisohn, Adolphe, 413
Lichtenstein, Alex, 113
Lombroso, Cesare, 244
Loomis, C.W., 95, 96
Los Angeles Times, 375
Louisiana
and contract prison labor
Auburn plan, 63
contractor control of prison, 66
petition against, 158
profitability of, 108
and convict lease, 95, 187
Lovely, Collis, 233, 388, 389
Lowrie, Donald, 330
Lynds, Elam
and Auburn plan, 69
and creation of contract prison labor
system, 61
recruitment of contractors, 57, 58
and disciplinary practices, 59, 71, 82
as critic of contract prison labor system, 60
Lyon, F, Emory, 321

M.D. Wells and Company, 114
Madison, James, 22
Maine
and Auburn plan, 63
and perpetual isolation system, 57

and public-account system, 84
Man, The
and competition between free and convict
labor, 77
opposition to contract prison labor, 73,
74, 75
managerialism, *See* penal managerialism
Manning, John J., 423
Maryland
and Auburn plan, 63, 64
and contract prison labor
large-scale contracts, 103
opposition to, 79
retention of, 236
and convict transportation system, 28, 29
registration of transported convicts, 29
and penal colonization, 54
and penitentiary-house, 38, 44
failure of, 51
and property crimes, 30
Mason and Goach, 117
Massachusetts, 65
1879 study on labor practices, 153
and capital punishment, 32
and contract prison labor
abolition of, 5
attempts to revive, 197
Auburn plan, 63
Democratic Party on, 171
factory system, 200
financial crisis of 1873, 98
idleness, 98
investigation of, 151
large-scale contracting, 101
motivational tools, 71
opposition to, 79, 156
piece-price system, 200
profitability of, 68
and hard labor
at Castle Island, 32
and penal colonization, 54
and property crimes, 30
and public-account system, 441
and state-use system, 231, 234, 236, 321
Charlestown rebellion, 43, 44
Department of Education, 445
Early Republic and sanguinary
punishments, 32
involuntary servitude in, 32
reform efforts, 11
disciplinary practices, 93
hybrid system, 199, 200, 231
revision of penal code, 32
State Prison, 6, 67, 140, 144, 231
workhouse, 23

Massachusetts Institute of Technology, 392
Massie, Joseph, 26
Mather, Cotton, 24
McCann, Henry J., 357
McCormick, Thomas
　and "Golden Rule Brotherhood," 383
　and disciplinary reform, 383
　and films at Sing Sing Prison, 432
　and wardenship of Sing Sing Prison, 382,
　　384
McDonough Amendment, 194, 198, 262
　debate on, 190
　enforcement of, 264
　opposition to, 202, 223, 230
　ratification of, 200, 206, 232
McDonough, John T., 189, 190, 194
McDowell, John G., 296, 297
McEnnis, John T., 162
McGuire, James C., 417
McLogan, P.H., 163
Meranze, Michael, 32, 45
Metro-Goldwyn-Mayer, 443
Michigan
　and contract prison labor
　　Auburn plan, 64
　　investigation of, 151
　　prison factories, 103
　Detroit House of Correction, 179
miners
　and opposition to contract prison labor,
　　157, 159, 164, 187, 469
Minnesota
　and contract prison labor
　　ban on competition with free industry,
　　　182
　and penal managerialism, 448
　and public account system, 182
　and state-account system, 200
　Stillwater State Prison, 144, 248
Mississippi
　and contract prison labor
　　as unrepublican, 164
　　consolidation of contracts, 102
　and convict lease, 66, 102, 186
　restrictions on franchise by, 186
Missouri
　and contract prison labor, 66
　　Auburn plan, 63
　　consolidation of contracts, 102
　　criticism of, 95
　and state-use system, 236
　Jefferson City Prison, 145, 421
　State Prison, 102, 142
modes of legal punishment, 5, 81, 385, 420,
　　466. *See also* the following listings:

colonial mode of punishment;
　contractual penal servitude; Early
　Republic; National Committee on
　Prisons and Prison Labor; penal
　managerialism; state-use system, 3, 5
American system, 16, 53, 54
capital punishment
　and colonial practice, 23
　and property crimes, 30
　attitudes toward, 19
　biblical requirement for, 40
　Early Republic use of, 32
　life-long servitude as alternative to,
　　24
　limitations on use, 18, 20
conflicts over, 238
cooperative, 430
deterrence system, 34, 81
development of, 17
enforced idleness, 56
non-laboring, 416
penal colonization, 54
　advocacy of, 52, 157
principle of proportionality, 21
reformatory approach, 92, 93, 95, 126,
　　142, 177, 331
　abandonment of, 134, 142
rehabilitation, 214, 221, 244, 325, 376
　abandonment of, 441, 447
　and disciplinary practices, 335
　and prison conditions, 245
workhouse, 23, 24
Montana
　adoption of state-use system, 203
Montesquieu, Charles de Secondat, Baron
　de la Brède et de, 19, 25
Montgomery, David, 162
moral politics of punishment, 36. *See also*
　Early Republic, house of repentance
　abolition of contract prison labor, 10
　alternative disciplinary activities, 225
　American Revolution and, 18
　and advocacy of workhouse system,
　　24
　and high Progressive Era, 322
　and Thomas Mott Osborne, 336
　as Christian institution, 11
　contract prison labor
　　opposition to, 73
　contractual penal servitude
　　as unrepublican institution, 73
　　debate on, 10, 293
　Early Republic and, 3, 7
　Gilded Age
　　large scale industrial contracts, 107

opposition to contract prison labor, 160
hard labor as mandate, 198
house of repentance, 17
Sing Sing Prison as symbol of barbarity,
287
Morris, Benjamin W., 290
Morton, Levi P., 202, 204
Moyer, William, 417, 429, 438
Murphy, Charles F., 295, 304, 318, 330, 378,
380, 381
Murphy, Jack, 337, 340, 363
My Life in Prison (Lowrie), 330

National Bank of Auburn, 374
National Committee for Mental Hygiene,
401, 403, 420
National Committee on Prison Labor
and 1913 convention, 326
and abolition of involuntary penal
servitude, 328, 337
and prison labor system as slavery, 336
and reform efforts, 323, 326
and Sing Sing Prison, 322
influence of, 322, 328, 329
legal challenge to contract prison labor by,
327
use of publicity by, 328, 333, 334
National Committee on Prisons and Prison
Labor (NCPPL), 359, 378, 397. *See
also* the following listings: National
Committee on Prison Labor; Thomas
Mott Osborne
and coalitional efforts, 420
and consultation with Roosevelt, 454
and contract prison labor
effective end of, 465
and contravention of penal bureaucracy,
408
and convict leagues, 421
and creation of prison farms, 427
and employment bureau, 388, 394
and funding of activities, 392, 396
and Good Roads Program, 384, 424
and Hawes-Cooper Act, 460
and innovations adopted as federal policy,
425
and international efforts, 428
and labor reform in prisons, 389
and relationship with Thomas Mott
Osborne, 415
and Sage bill, 420
and Sing Sing Prison
as laboratory of social justice, 379
as showpiece for new penology, 385
educational programs at, 385, 391

inspection tour of, 431
restructuring of prison industries, 388
and state-use system, 12
and wartime levels of prison employment,
422, 425
influence of, 440
National Conference of Charities and
Corrections, 174, 176
National Federation of Women's Clubs, 324
National Industrial Recovery Act (NIRA)
and federal prohibition on use of convict
labor, 462
National Labor Union, 92
National Prison Association, 98, 234
and Declaration of Principles, 92, 178
and Gilded Age, 134
and identification techniques, 217
and post-abolition convict labor question,
174
and reformatory approach, 93
and Thomas Mott Osborne, 331
as national political coalition, 188
revival of, 174
National Reconstruction Administration
(NRA), 463
National Society of Penal Information, 421,
457
Nebraska
and convict lease, 104
Nevada
and partial state-use system, 202
New Deal, *See also* the following listings: penal
managerialism; Lewis E, Lawes, 5
and end of state prison industries, 466
and exclusion of prisoners from
federally-funded projects, 462
formation of penal state, 3, 12
legislation of, 5, 13
New Hampshire, 26
and Auburn plan, 63
and contract prison labor, 65
and penitentiary system, 51
New Jersey
and contract prison labor
abolition of, 182
damage to free labor wages, 152, 154
financial crisis of 1873, 98
investigation of, 151
and convict-made goods, 459
and Eastern plan, 63
and Good Roads Program, 268
and prison strike, 145
and state-use system, 236
construction of penitentiary, 37
State Prison, 67, 421

New Jersey Reformatory for Women
   and self-government, 421
New Mexico
   and convict-lease, 101, 104
   and Good Roads Program, 268
new penology, 347, 371, 379, 385, 412, 419.
   See also the following listings: Auburn
   Prison, Mutual Welfare League;
   National Committee on Prisons and
   Prison Labor; Thomas Mott Osborne,
   195, 221, 323
   abandonment of, 467
   and disciplinary regime, 221, 399, 442
   and importance of cooperation, 368
   and Sing Sing Prison, 385, 443
   ascendancy of, 431
   public attitudes toward, 386, 413, 420, 449
New York (state), 269. *See also* the following
   listings: contractual penal servitude;
   individual prisons; state-use system,
   54, 63
   "Americanization" program in, 195, 443
   Albany County Penitentiary, 100, 113, 120,
      121, 179
   and contract prison labor
      abolition of, 5, 13, 171, 172, 183, 187,
         281, 293, 294, 318
      and financial crisis of 1873, 98
      attempts to revive, 197
      Auburn plan, 57
      constitutional amendment against, 190,
         191
      investigations of, 93, 151, 153, 165
      motivational tools, 71
      opposition to, 169
      piece-price system, 188
      profitability of, 90
   and corporal punishment
      abolition of, 37
   and development of prison farms, 427
   and Fassett Law, 188
   and Gilded Age
      strikes and riots in prison system, 145
   and Good Roads Program, 268, 371, 383,
      407
   and public account system, 187, 209
   and Yates Law, 188
   Assembly Committee on State Prisons, 98
   Asylum for Juvenile Delinquents, 108
   Bear Mountain
      as site for Sing Sing Prison replacement,
         289, 290, 292, 298
   Board of Classification, 205, 209
   Brooklyn County Penitentiary, 113
   Buffalo mechanics, 73

Central Labor Union, 151
Civil Service Commission
   and penal employees, 219
Commission on New Prisons, 289
   and Sing Sing Prison replacement, 291
   request for resignation of
      commissioners, 292
Commission on Prison Administration
   and Construction, 458
Commission on Prison Improvement, 288
   and design for new prison, 289
   calls for termination of, 290
   charges of cronyism, 290
Committee of Manufacturing, 76
Committee of Mechanics, 72, 76
contractual penal servitude
   establishment of, 53
*Cunningham v. Bay State Shoe and Leather
   Co.*, 474
disfranchisement of convicts by, 55, 70
Frawley Committee, 304
Grand Jury Association of
   commendation of Thomas Mott
      Osborne, 412
Harlem Prison, 292, 294
Joint Committee on Prisons, 100, 405
Kings County Grand Jury
   commendation of Osborne, 412
Kings County Penitentiary, 114, 145, 208
Legislature
   and contract prison labor, 77, 78, 79, 82
Monroe County Penitentiary, 179
Northern New York Institution for
   Deaf-Mutes, 264
penitentiary system, 50, 51, 53, 54
Prison Reform Commission, 307, 317, 320,
   332
   and creation of penal bureaucracy, 259
   and reform of penal system, 328
   classification law of 1897, 213
   formation of, 187, 327
   investigation of prison system, 317
reform efforts by, 5, 11, 12, 75, 194, 229,
   322, 328, 385
   alternative disciplinary activities, 221,
      223, 227
   alternatives to hard manufactory labor,
      374
   as national model, 12, 419
   disciplinary practices, 93
   Moreland Act of 1907, 283, 296
   penal bureaucracy, 209, 241, 281, 282
   piece-price system, 181
   reformatory practices, 225
   state-use system, 200, 209

Select Committee on State Prisons, 76
State Assembly
  investigation of Sing Sing Prison, 166
State Assembly Committee on Prisons, 100
State Prison Commission, 242, 287, 411
  and 1896 Prison Labor Law, 214
  and consultation with organized labor,
    266
  and creation of parole board, 214
  and creation of penal bureaucracy, 202,
    209, 219, 229
  and legal protection of prisoners, 228
  establishment of, 241
  investigation of prison labor systems,
    201
  removal of out-of-state prisoners, 212
Training School for Guards at Wallkill
  Prison, 458
Valatie State Farm for Women, 427
Westchester County Grand Jury
  and investigation of bread riot of 1913,
    312, 317
  and investigation of Sing Sing Prison,
    300, 301, 307
  and investigation of Thomas Mott
    Osborne, 411
Westchester County Penitentiary, 421
  women prisoners in, 70, 211
Workingman's Assembly, 205
New York City
  stonecutters
    opposition to contract prison labor, 72,
      76
New York Clothing Company, 173
New York Garden Magazine, 387
New York Giants, 444
New York Herald, 166
New York Journal, 320
New York Prison Association (NYPA), 80,
  288, 293
  and opposition to abolition of contract
    prison labor, 204
  and prisoner trades education, 230
  and support for Auburn plan, 81
New York Star, 166, 168
New York State Mechanic, 78, 81
New York State Prison Council, 399
New York Times
  and American Federation of Labor, 393
  and Baumes laws, 451
  and conditions at Auburn Prison, 149, 153
  and convict labor problem, 321
  and Ford Motor Company, 391
  and Frawley Committee, 304
  and idleness in state-use system, 204

  and James M, Clancy, 382
  and Sing Sing Prison, 167, 311, 315
  bread riot of 1913, 1, 2, 309
  and Thomas Mott Osborne, 320, 338, 385,
    413
  and William Sulzer, 305, 306, 307
  on contract labor referendum, 172
New York Tribune
  and Thomas Mott Osborne, 338
  on Carnegie Rally, 413
New York Yankees, 444
Newgate Prison, 70
  as penitentiary, 37, 38
  rebellion, 44, 45, 52
Nordau, Max, 244
North Carolina
  and contract prison labor, 95, 182
  and reform efforts, 96
North Western Manufacturing and Car
  Company, 144
Nott, Charles C, Jr., 418

O'Farrell, Val, 414
O'Neill, J.J., 185
Ohio, 70
  and contract prison labor
    abolition of, 5, 174, 182
    Auburn plan, 63
    investigation of, 151, 165
    opposition to, 79
    profitability of, 90
  and reform efforts
    disciplinary practices, 93
  and restrictions on convict-made goods,
    183
  and state-use system, 236
  Democratic Party
    and contract prison labor, 171
Oregon
  and contract prison labor, 183
  and disciplinary practices, 93
  and Good Roads Program, 268, 379
organized labor, 12
  and contract prison labor
    abolition of, 156
    abolition of in New York, 173
    as industrial slavery, 162
    easing of opposition to, 80
    national campaign against, 150, 155. *See
      also* individual states
    opposition to, 69, 150, 159, 161
    use against unions, 113
  and contract prison labor in France, 89
  and federal legislation, 150
  and post-Civil War revival of unions, 91

498

false*Index*

organized labor (*cont.*)
  and post-laboring prison system, 416
  and revival of unions, 112, 149
  and state-use system
    constriction of scope, 12
    opposition to, 263, 265, 278
    support for, 232, 236
    use of prisoners in road building, 462
  and Tariff Act of 1890, 184
  and union organizing at Sing Sing Prison, 389, 393
Osborne, D.M., 329
Osborne, Thomas Mott, 387, 388, 418. *See also* the following listings: Auburn Prison, Mutual Welfare League; National Committee on Prisons and Prison Labor; Sing Sing Prison, Mutual Welfare League
  and Auburn Prison, 322
  and damage to reputation, 416
  and disregard for penal bureaucracy, 408, 415
  and Empire State Democracy, 330
  and eradication of sexual relations at Sing Sing Prison, 396
  and George Junior Republic, 330
  and leadership role, 321
  and penal reform, 195
    cooperative model of, 355
    managerial, 307
    role of guards, 253, 404
  and prison labor problem, 323
  and Prison Reform Commission, 300, 327, 332
  and prisoner self-government, 331, 336, 337
    as Mutual Welfare League, 339
  and *Prisons and Commonsense*, 398
  and psychiatric testing at Sing Sing Prison, 400
  and Sing Sing Prison, 12, 322
    appointment as warden, 375, 384
  and socialization of prisoners, 376, 378
  and support of business leaders, 389, 392
  and Tammany Hall, 295
  and use of publicity, 337, 350, 353, 371, 375, 386, 406
  and voluntary incarceration at Auburn Prison, 319, 328, 332, 334, 375
  and wardenship of Naval Prison, 421
  and *Within Prison Walls*, 334, 336, 337, 407
  background of, 329
  campaign of support for, 412
  cooperation with organized labor, 388
  dismissal of charges against, 414
  indictment of, 412

influences on, 330, 331
investigation of, 409
resignation of, 415
Outlook
  and Thomas Mott Osborne, 337
Outside Branch of the Mutual Welfare League (OBMWL), 396
  and post-release employment, 393, 425, 430
Guard's Widow Fund, 405

Packard Motor Car Co., 390
Paine, Thomas, 19
Parkhurst, Charles, 413
Parkman, Francis, 282
Peck, Charles F., 173
penal managerialism, *See also* Lewis E, Lawes, 447, 457
  and facilitation of consolidation, 456
  and use of psychology, 458
  as national model, 466
Penal Servitude (Whitin), 325
penal state
  clerical workers
    and resistance to reform, 260, 278
  creation of bureaucracy, 209, 215, 229, 242, 276, 277, 293, 316, 408, 409
  and expulsion of patronage system, 219
  and Moreland Act of 1907, 255
  Civil Service Laws, 219
  guards and keepers, 254
    and Civil Service Laws, 219, 257, 260, 381
    and contraband smuggling, 71
    and relationship to contractors, 125
    fraternization with prisoners, 60
    resistance to reform, 48, 253, 278, 404
    status of, 254
  patronage system of, 259, 281
  performance of accountability, 250
  prisoner records, 216, 251
    Bertillonage, 217
  purging of Republicans in, 292
  wardenship, 258
    and resistance to reform, 278
    limitation of authority, 257, 276, 277, 381
penitentiary, *See also* Early Republic
penitentiary system, 67
  Eastern Penitentiary, 61
  reinvention of, 61
Penn, William, 24
Pennsylvania
  "Great Law" of 1682, 24
  abolition of capital crimes, 17

and contract prison labor
  attempts to revive, 197
  discrediting of, 176
  rejection of, 67
and convict transportation system, 28
and proportionality, 22
and state-use system, 231, 236
and workhouse, 24
Democratic Party
  and contract prison labor, 171
Eastern Penitentiary, 61, 63
  and disciplinary reform, 422
  and piece-price system, 101, 104
  and voluntary labor, 62
  isolation system at, 54, 61, 69, 81
  post-Civil War, 140
penitentiary system, 51
  health crisis in, 50
  reinvention of, 61
public account system, 104
  abandonment of, 231
  as alternative to contract prison labor,
    199
  reform efforts, 11
  restriction on sanguinary and capital
    punishment, 20
  revision of penal code, 32
  State Prison Commission, 231
  Walnut Street Jail, 37
    as penitentiary, 38, 48, 63, 70
    rebellion at, 43, 44
  Western Penitentiary, 101, 104
Pennsylvania plan, 68. *See also* Pennsylvania,
  Eastern Penitentiary, 63
  and fiscal self-sufficiency, 67, 68
  cost of construction, 63
Pennsylvania Railroad Company, 390
Perkins, Francis, 463
Perry and Co., 173
Perry, John Sherwood, 111, 135
  and contract prison labor
    and Pilsbury system, 121
    and Sing Sing Prison, 100, 145, 166,
      284
    defense of, 154
    disciplinary practices, 144
    industrial discipline, 112
    large-scale contracting, 160, 191
    profit imperative of, 107
    use against unions, 156
  and integration of convict and free labor,
    114
Philadelphia Prison Society, 176
Philadelphia Society for Alleviating the
  Miseries of Public Prisons, 37,
  39

Pilsbury system, 120
  and contractor-administration
    relationship, 131
  and disciplinary practices, 127
  as national model, 101
  defense of, 154
  effective abolition of, 173
Pilsbury, Amos, 100, 179
Pilsbury, Louis, 98, 101, 135, 153, 160, 166,
  173, 191
Pilsbury, Moses, 100
Pisciotta, Alexander, 177, 178
Pittsburgh Coal Co., 390
Platt, Thomas C.
  and Republican Party, 259
politics of punishment, 12. *See also* the
  following listings: fiscal politics of
  punishment; moral politics of
  punishment
  legal punishment and, 5, 7, 10
  political power struggles, 5, 12
popular protest movements, 4. *See also* the
  following listings: farmers and farm
  workers; miners
  against contract prison labor, 4, 5, 10, 11,
    171
Pound, M.W.F., 204
Powderly, Terence, 157, 165
Powers, Gershom, 60
Pratt, Charles R., 190
Priesmeyer, August, 102
prison factories, *See* contractual penal
  servitude, contracting systems
prison labor problem, *See also* National
  Committee on Prison Labor, 235, 325
  and abolition of contract prison labor, 5
  and central place in legal punishment,
    419
  and federal legislation, 419
  and new penology, 321, 322, 323, 326, 440
  and New York, 12
  and organized labor, 13, 233
  and productive labor, 11, 196, 213, 226,
    288, 325
  and Progressive Era, 11
  and state efforts, 199, 236
  and state-use system, 234, 237, 321
  as basis for reform efforts, 5, 196, 322
  discourse on, 294, 321
  investigation of, 324
prisoners, 336. *See also* the following listings:
  Auburn Prison, Mutual Welfare
  League; convicts; individual prisons;
  National Committee on Prisons and
  Prison Labor, 3
  and idleness, 206, 220, 221

and literacy, 243, 249, 416, 442
prisoners (*cont.*)
prison libraries, 243, 248
and living conditions, 66, 274
convict lease camps, 87
efforts to alter, 71
and race relations, 349, 373, 403
and religious worship, 243, 269
and self-government, 336
good-conduct leagues, 337
self-censoring recordkeeping, 342
and sexual activity, 302, 380, 396, 400, 402
and skills training, 249
classification of, 55, 56, 260
composition of
post-Civil War, 140
legal status of
and master-servant relationship, 123, 124, 125
as wards of the state, 196, 229, 243, 314, 417, 418, 455, 469
perception of rights, 43, 45, 61, 67, 70, 71, 111, 314, 434, 444
public sympathy for, 44, 47, 80, 314
riots, strikes and rebellions, 6, 43, 70, 249, 280, 309, 369, 435, 449, 454, 455, 456, 459, 466, 469, 472
and contract prison labor, 139
and Gilded Age, 142
and house of repentance, 10, 43
and industrial discipline, 137
bread riot at Missouri State Prison, 142
decline of, 60
Sing Sing Prison, 1, 5, 82, 98
use of media during, 2, 149, 280, 309
use of militia to control, 1, 44, 311, 315, 454, 455
women, 211
Prisons and Commonsense (Osborne), 398
Progressive Era, 12, 192, 325, 418. *See also* the following listings: new penology; state-use system
and creation of penal bureaucracy, 209
and labor ideology, 198, 235
and new penology, 195, 221
and prison labor problem, 11
and reinvention of prison labor, 215
focus on stable prison labor force, 212
Good Roads Program, 268
high Progressive Era, 322, 325, 418
and socialization of prisoners, 376
idealism of, 378
scope of reform, 322
paternalism of, 469
reform ideology of, 3, 5, 11, 195, 293

Progressive Party
and abolition of contract prison labor, 237
Proskauer, Joseph M., 456
public account system, 66, 133
and Minnesota, 182
and Pennsylvania, 101
and principle industries, 104
as alternative to contract prison labor, 176, 199
conversion from, 84
nature of, 104
profitability of, 88, 90
rejection of, 201
use by states, 84
public attitudes, *See also* National Committee on Prison Labor
shaping of, 325, 326, 333, 371, 406
toward Mutual Welfare League, 359
Pullman, 390
Punishment and Social Structure (Rusche, Kirchheimer), 482

Ransom, J.B., 276
Rattigan, Charles F., 390
and communication with prisoners, 372
and ex-convict employment, 390
and Mutual Welfare League, 354, 357
and prisoner self-government, 339
and prohibition on political organizing, 369
and Thomas Mott Osborne, 334, 335
as warden of Auburn Prison, 296, 332
Reconstruction Finance Corporation (RFC), 462
reform efforts, *See also* Progressive Era
and abolition of contract prison labor, 93
and attitudes toward hard labor, 198
and bureaucratic democracy, 241
and financial crisis of 1873, 97
and hard labor, 7
and labor ideology, 81
demise of, 11
and public-account, 181
and reformatory approach, 92
and state-use system
recreation of convict identities, 218
and support for involuntary servitude, 9
and the "new penology," 321
Auburn and Eastern systems
as rival models, 62
Early Republic, 32
establishment of state prison systems, 7
federal penal labor reform, 419

Gilded Age
    and contract prison labor, 134
    post-Civil War, 90
    post-independence, 22
    progressive
        legacy of, 12
    Reconstruction Era, 90
    reformatory methods, 95, 102
    support for Auburn system, 59, 67, 68
Report on the Prisons and Reformatories of the
    United States and Canada (Wines,
    Dwight), 92
Republican Party
    1928 platform plank on convict-made
        goods, 460
    and bureaucratic democracy, 241
    and regulation of convict labor, 189,
        190
    and state opposition to contract prison
        labor, 158
    and tariff reform, 190
Republican Party of New York State
    and "machine boss" politics, 282
    and "Platt machine," 259, 282
    and campaign against Thomas Mott
        Osborne, 409
    and charges of penal mismanagement,
        281
    and contract prison labor, 189
    and Independent Republicans, 294
    and resistance to managerial
        restructuring, 259
    and support of tariffs, 189
    attempts to preserve contract prison labor
        by, 173
    attempts to restore public-account system
        by, 202
    Independent Republicans, 282
Reynolds, John B., 130
Rhode Island, *See also Anderson v, Salant*
    and constitutional prohibition on slavery,
        327
    and contract prison labor
        large-scale contracting, 101, 113
    and Eastern plan, 63
    and perpetual isolation system, 63
Riis, Jacob, 230
Riley, John B., 329
    and communication with prisoners,
        372
    and disciplinary reform, 374
    and guards training school, 405
    and Prison Reform Commission, 300
    and prisoner self-government, 339,
        340

and resignation of James M, Clancy, 382
    and Sing Sing Prison, 317, 375
    and Thomas Mott Osborne, 384, 407, 408,
        409
    and transfer of prisoners to Clinton
        Prison, 397
    as Superintendent of Prisons, 296, 299
    dismissal of, 415
Rising Fawn Mines, 146
Rochester Union, 338
Rockefeller Foundation, 401
Rockfeller, John D., 389
Rodgers, Daniel T., 240
Roosevelt, Franklin D., 419, 421, 453, 456,
        457
    and Empire State Democracy, 330
    and federal legislation, 420
    and reform efforts, 13
    and Tammany Hall, 295
Roosevelt, Theodore, 291, 467
    and convict labor problem, 267, 321
    and new penology, 326
    and reform efforts, 195, 319
    and support for state-use system, 237
    defeat of, 296
Root, Elihu
    and convict-made goods, 190
Rothman, David J., 7, 8, 62, 278
Ruffin v, Virginia, 116
Ruffin, Woody, 116
Ruggles-Brice, Evelyn, 331
Rules and Regulations for Inmates of the New
    York State Prisons, 319
Rusche, Georg, 482
Rush, Benjamin, 19, 35, 36, 37, 49, 62, 107,
        239, 470
Russell Sage Foundation, 413
Russell, James, 392

Sage, Omer
    and prisoner idleness, 208, 223
    and *Star of Hope*, 228, 244
Salmon, Thomas W., 401
Saturday Evening Post, 338
Scott, Joseph, 306
    and conditions at Auburn Prison, 298
    and Harlem Prison, 292
    and Tammany Hall, 297
    dismissal of, 296, 297
Sears Roebuck and Co., 390
Selz, Schwab, and Company, 114
Servan, Joseph, 25
Seward, W.H., 77
Shapiro, Karen, 112, 159, 164
Sigerson, Michael H., 167

Sing Sing Prison. *See also* the following
    listings: contractual penal servitude,
    contract prison labor; Lewis E, Lawes;
    National Committee on Prisons and
    Prison Labor; new penology;
    prisoners; Thomas Mott Osborne;
    state-use system
"Bastille on the Hudson," 1, 2, 12, 275,
    280, 283, 378, 413
and alternatives to manufactory labor,
    227
and contract prison labor
    abolition of, 208, 209
    and disciplinary practices, 120, 126, 129
    consolidation of industries, 100
    contractor-keeper relationship, 125
    large-scale contract prison labor, 101,
        113
    Pilsbury system, 120, 129
    voiding of contracts at, 79
and escape attempts, 98
and industrial training programs at, 389
and John Sherwood Perry, 110, 112, 113
and movie industry, 432
and new penology
    recreational activities, 431
    socialization of convicts, 394
and Panama-Pacific International
    Exposition of 1915, 407
and Paris Exposition of 1900, 193, 237
and penal psychiatric clinic, 400
and post-release employment, 390
and prevalence of veneral disease, 400,
    402
and race relations, 403
and religious services, 269
and *Star of Hope*, 243, 277, 286, 372
    as administrative communications tool,
        244, 250
    censorship of, 247
    contributions from other prisons, 246
    establishment of, 227
    merger with *MLW Bulletin*, 430
and state-use system
    classification of prisoners, 215
    diversity of manufactures, 210
and women prisoners, 70
as clearinghouse, 403, 420
as laboratory of social justice, 12, 13, 322,
    376, 378, 385, 416
as model of reform, 457
Aurora Band of, 392, 393, 417, 431, 436
bread riot of 1913, 1, 5, 280, 307, 308, 320,
    328, 379
and media attention to, 313, 317

conditions at, 66, 82, 122, 168, 274, 276,
    280, 285, 289, 293, 299, 301, 307, 311,
    313, 315, 317, 379, 383, 398, 400, 401,
    408, 431, 445
construction of, 48, 64, 65
demolition of, 418, 437
educational programs at, 391, 392
Golden Rule Brotherhood
    comparison with Mutual Welfare
        League, 383
    transformation of, 387
investigation of, 2, 168, 380
Mutual Welfare League, 342
    and training in personal financial
        responsibility, 394
    as national model, 421
    attitude of penal state toward, 429
    establishment of, 387
    establishment of employment bureau,
        388
penal state, 427, 429
    and managerialism, 441
printing industry at, 265
proposal for replacement of, 288, 293,
    307
recreational activities at, 387
reform efforts
    fields of action, 386
    fundraising for, 386
    progressive, 284
    reputation of, 283, 287
Sing Sing Bulletin, 247
Star-Bulletin, 432, 433, 435, 436, 437
strikes and riots at, 82, 98, 144, 145,
    167
training programs at, 392
slavery, 233. *See* the following; South; Sellin,
    Slavery and the Penal System
Sloss Coal Company, 114
Smith, Eugene, 230
Smith, Larry, 43
Smoot-Hawley Tariff Act of 1930,
    184
Sohmer, William A., 300
Some Ethical Phases of the Labor Question
    (Wright), 234
South, *See also* contractual penal servitude,
    contracting systems
and contract prison labor
    abolition of, 138
    attempts to regulate, 93, 94
    diversification of contracts, 95
    integration of convict and free labor,
        114
    opposition to as unrepublican, 164

regulation of, 95
strikes and riots, 146
and lynchings, 377
antebellum prison, 7, 15, 16, 65
chattel slavery
law and ideology of, 9, 14, 29, 94, 470
revival of, 74
convict lease, 87, 93, 94, 95, 102, 104, 116,
138, 170
extraction of federal prisoners, 184
New South
and profit imperative, 87
rate of prisoner mortality, 118
Redeemer Democrats
and contract prison labor, 101
and convict lease, 87
state penal farm systems, 196
South Carolina
and proportionality, 22
and sanguinary punishment, 20, 67
convict lease, 95
South Dakota
and state-use system, 203
Squire, Amos, 402
St. Paul Trades and Labor Association,
182
Star of Hope. See Sing Sing Prison
State Service, 427
state-use system, *See also* the following listings:
individual states; Lewis E, Lawes, 55,
194, 205, 209, 210, 212, 216, 221, 226,
229, 243, 263, 269, 275, 276, 317
alternatives to manufactory labor, 267
Good Roads Program, 317
and constriction of scope, 12
and expulsion of out-of-state prisoners,
276
and federal legislation, 235, 419
and idleness, 206
and organized labor, 232, 236, 263, 265
and state needs, 205, 206, 262, 263
as national model, 12, 13, 204, 230, 233,
237, 242, 440, 460
British model of, 175
classification of prisoners in, 251, 252,
276
and Bertillonage, 252
criticism of, 204
establishment of, 5, 172, 188, 191, 200,
209, 237, 239, 241, 249, 276
failure of, 277, 321, 323, 441
health conditions in, 275, 276
industries of, 209, 264, 441, 449, 459
reorganization of, 325
self-sufficiency of, 210, 262, 267

Stewart, Lispenard, 201, 254. *See also* New
York State Prison Commission
and consultation with organized labor,
232, 266
and non-manufactory labor, 267
and penal bureaucracy, 219, 294
and state-use system, 408
Stillwell, Stephen, 381
Stimson, Henry L., 291
Sullivan, David A., 384
Sullivan, James A., 32
Sulzer, William, 2, 280, 297, 299, 304
and charges of mismanagement, 281
and Frawley Committee, 305
and investigation of state prison system,
317
and penal bureaucracy, 296
and Prison Reform Commission, 300,
327
and Sing Sing Prison, 307, 316
and Thomas Mott Osborne, 329
election of, 295, 332
impeachment of, 317, 328, 380, 381
Swats, Lewis F., 117

Taft, William Howard, 296, 338
Tannenbaum, Frank, 283
Tennessee
and Auburn plan, 63
and contract prison labor
abolition of, 160
as unrepublican, 164
diversification of contracts, 95
opposition to, 79
and convict lease, 102, 186, 187
and investigation of prison system
and voluntary incarceration of
governor, 328
city contracts
and convict labor, 187
free mine workers
and opposition to contract prison labor,
159
Tennessee Coal, Iron, and Railroad
Company (TCIRC), 102, 103, 112,
159, 259
Texas
and contract prison labor
diversification of contracts, 95
investigation of, 152, 153
opposition to, 158
regulatory efforts, 171
and penal managerialism, 448
convict lease, 158
Huntsville Prison, 66

Thomson, George W., 432, 433
Three Essays on the Theory of Sexuality (Freud),
    398
Tilden, Samuel, 282, 295, 306
Tocqueville, Alexis de, 64, 313, 470
    and American system, 4, 8, 16
    and Eastern system, 62
    Democracy in America, 81
    on Sing Sing Prison, 60, 284
Tompkins, Daniel D., 51
Trachtenberg, Alan, 240
Tweed, William "Boss," 282
Typographical Union, 265

U.S. Congress
    and abolition of contract prison labor,
        174, 183
    and ban on convict labor, 267
    and construction of federal prisons, 184
    and convict-made goods, 423
    and federal prisoners, 121, 184, 185
    and legislation concerning use of hard
        labor, 37, 38
    and national convict labor study, 184
    and report on prison labor practices, 88
    and restriction on scope of state-use
        industries, 449
    Civil Rights Act of 1866
        and involuntary servitude, 15
    Tariff Act of 1890, 184
U.S. Constitution
    Fourteenth Amendment, 15, 16
    Thirteenth Amendment, 9, 14, 16, 84,
        198
U.S. Government. *See also* War Industries
    Board
    and use of contract prison labor
        Peoria, Illinois, 164
    prohibition on convict labor, 279
U.S. Industrial Commission, 197, 235
U.S. Industrial Relations Committee, 389
U.S. Navy
    and new penology reforms, 421
U.S. Senate
    Committee on Relations Between Capital
        and Labor, 157, 158, 170
U.S. Supreme Court
    and involuntary servitude, 9, 14
    *Kentucky Whip and Collar Co, v, Illinois
        Central Railroad*, 464
    Whitfield v, Ohio, 463
Union of Iron Molders, Local 00011
    lock-out of, 83, 112
United Mine Workers of America, 159

Van Ness, A.W., 435, 436
Vaux, Richard, 176
Vermont
    and Auburn plan, 63
    and contract prison labor, 65
        large-scale contracting, 101
        retention of, 236
    hard labor
        as alternative to capital punishment, 21
        restriction on sanguinary and capital
            punishment, 20
Virginia
    and Auburn plan, 63
    and capital punishment, 20, 22
    and convict transportation system, 28,
        29
    and legal status of convict servants, 29
    and penitentiary-house, 38
    and perpetual isolation system, 57
    and proportionality, 21
    and *Ruffin v, Virginia*, 116
    State Penitentiary at Richmond, 117
Virginia Colored Farmers' Alliance, 158
Vitagraph, 443

Wald, Lillian, 413
Wallkill Prison, 458
Walsh, Michael J., 310
Walsh-Healy Act, 462
War Industries Board, 440
    War Prison Labor and National
        Waste-Reclamation Section, 423, 424,
            425, 427
Ware, Franklin B., 291, 298
Warner Brothers, 434, 443
Washington, 101, 104
Weeks, Frederick E., 414
West Virginia
    and abolition of contract prison labor, 157
West, Stephen, 40
Western and Atlantic Railroad, 66
Western Union Telegraph Co., 390, 393
wheelbarrowmen. *See* Early Republic
White, James, 380, 397, 399
Whitfield v, Ohio, 465
Whitin, E, Stagg, 324, 359, 423
    and appointment to Prison Reform
        Commission, 327
    and concept of penal servitude, 327
    and legislative efforts, 326
    and National Committee on Prison Labor,
        324
    and *Penal Servitude*, 325
    and prison labor reform, 389

and prison labor system as slavery, 336
and public educational efforts, 420
and Sing Sing Prison, 385
and support of business leaders, 389
and war economy, 422
Whitman, Charles S., 410, 416, 429, 436
and demolition of Sing Sing Prison, 417
and duty to prisoners, 417
and Sage bill, 420
and Thomas Mott Osborne, 407, 415
election of, 384
Whitman, James Q., 9
Whitman, Walt, 66
Wickersham, George, 417, 418
William Fox Film Corporation, 434
Wilson, Margaret, 300
Wilson, Woodrow, 419, 434
and adoption of state-use system, 236
and executive order on convict-made
goods, 423
election of, 296
on convict labor problem, 321
Wiltse, Robert, 64
Winchester Repeating Arms Co., 390
Wines, Enoch O., 84, 92, 93, 95, 109
and labor ideology, 178
and National Prison Association, 92
and power of contractors, 136
Wingdale
as site for Sing Sing Prison replacement,
291, 293, 298
Wingdale Prison
and agricultural production, 427
fate of, 291
scandal surrounding, 292
Wisconsin
and contract prison labor

consolidation of industrial contracts,
101
financial crisis of 01873, 98
large-scale contracting, 101
and Good Roads Program, 268
public-account system, 84
State Prison at Waupun
integration of convict and free labor,
114
Within Prison Walls (Osborne), 322, 334
Women's Department of the National Civic
Federation, 386
Woodburne Prison, 458
Workingman's Advocate, 72, 78
Workingman's Union, 93
World War I, *See* War Industries Board
and agricultural production by prison
labor, 427
and conscription of prisoners, 426
and integration of convicts into war effort,
425
and investigation on wartime role of
prisons, 423
and penal policy planning on a
nationwide basis, 423
and penological reform, 440
Wright, Carroll D., 233
and contract prison labor, 88, 90, 200
investigation of, 109, 153, 184
and federal legislation, 185
and fiscal politics of punishment, 171
and state-use system, 203, 205, 233
opposition to public account system, 177
Wyoming
and state-use system, 236

Yates, Robert, 57